A HISTORY OF THE PROTESTANT EPISCOPAL CHURCH

BY THE SAME AUTHOR

Focus on Infinity: A Life of Phillips Brooks

A HISTORY OF THE PROTESTANT EPISCOPAL CHURCH

RAYMOND W. ALBRIGHT

THE MACMILLAN COMPANY, NEW YORK
COLLIER-MACMILLAN LIMITED, LONDON

First Printing

The Macmillan Company, New York
Collier-Macmillan Canada, Ltd., Toronto, Ontario

Library of Congress catalog card number 64–21168

Printed in the United States of America

JOSEPHO CULLEN AYER

A.M., Ph.D., S.T.D., D.D., D.C.L.

sacerdoti fideli

magistro patientissimo

patri indulgenti

R. I. P.

Contents

Foreword

This history will help commemorate the one hundred and seventy-fifth anniversary of the formation of the Protestant Episcopal Church by the adoption of its constitution at the general convention at Philadelphia in 1789. It suffers the limitation of all single-volume histories; even though it cannot be exhaustive, the author has attempted to retain a constant focus of his lens so that the men and movements during these years may be seen with a minimum of distortion. He is deeply indebted to all those who have previously studied and described these scenes. Bishop William Stevens Perry's *The History of the American Episcopal Church* in two volumes remains the richest collection of sources to 1883, and the author wishes also to express his deep appreciation for and his dependence upon the subsequent histories by William Wilson Manross, E. Clowes Chorley, James Thayer Addison, and George E. DeMille. Since their valued contributions have brought the large body of information about the Episcopal Church into the common domain, the author has sparingly used footnotes except to indicate unusual sources and those not obvious from the text. The bibliography has been reduced to an essential minimum intentionally to provide only the chief sources that may prove helpful in pursuing further reading at this level. A comprehensive bibliography of all sources relating to the Protestant Episcopal Church would be of infinite value to all students of Christian history. *The Historical Magazine of the Protestant Episcopal Church* and the additional publications of the Historical Society of the church are a vast storehouse of invaluable materials and have been used extensively.

The author desires to express his grateful appreciation to the trustees of the Episcopal Theological School for a sabbatical leave that made possible free time for much of this writing; to Doctor John Pomfret, director, and the trustees of the Henry E. Huntington Library, San Marino, California, for providing the opportunity to be a scholar-in-residence; and to the librarian and staff of that library for their valued assistance in using its rich sources for Anglo-American studies.

While it will be impossible to mention the esteemed contributions of many other individuals to this work, the author wishes to express his gratitude for them and to acknowledge especially the help received from Miss Elizabeth

Hodges, librarian of the John Gordon Wright Library at the Episcopal Theological School; Doctor Niels Sonne, librarian at the General Theological Seminary, New York; and Doctor Nelson Burr of the Library of Congress.

R. W. A.

Ash Wednesday, 1964

I

THE BACKGROUND
IN ENGLAND

The members of the state delegations gathered in the first General Convention at Philadelphia just 175 years ago were men from different regions and of variant opinions but with one dominating conviction that the Protestant Episcopal Church in the United States of America should remain forever a continuing living part of the true Church of Christ. The common purpose to build their constitutional and canonical structure on the foundation of the church as they had known it in England became the stable bond that held them steady through long discussions while they discovered agreements on lesser matters. When the convention closed on October 16, 1789, the growing child, nurtured through almost two centuries by the Church of England, had come of age and was ready to assume the duties of Christian maturity. With its structure firmly rooted and grounded in the life and traditions of the church through the earlier centuries, it was ready to face the challenging demands of the New World and to develop its own genius of life, thought, and work in the name of Christ.

No one is quite certain when Christianity was planted in Britain; it may well have been carried there by Roman soldiers. Three bishops from England attended the Synod of Arles in 314. Long before the missionary Augustine was sent by Gregory the Great to take a more fully developed form of Roman Christianity to Britain at the close of the sixth century, an indigenous English Christianity had been widely scattered from the eastern shores through Wales into Ireland and northward through the regions of Northumbria. Celtic Christianity, as the religion of western Britain and Ireland was called, took the curious form of a cenobitic and monastic life as the remains of the stone huts of the early monks attest. By the time of the arrival of Augustine and his monks, Celtic Christianity had already planted its missions on Iona and the east and west coasts of Britain from which missionaries would soon go to Germany and Switzerland.

Although the Roman type of Christianity became the accepted form of religion in Britain after the Synod of Whitby in the seventh century, many early indigenous customs persisted among the English Christians for centuries; and, especially in the north and west, local loyalties prevailed, and their spirit often

1

provided the ground for dissident movements like that of the Lollards, follow-ers of John Wycliffe in the fourteenth century. The nonconformist Puritans several centuries later developed their radical religious ideas along the Great North Road, and the jail in Boston isolated many erring Puritans before they sailed for New England.

Despite its conformity to Rome, the life and government of the church in Britain always preserved something of an independent spirit. Early monarchs reserved the right of approval of church appointments in England and, by two Statutes of Praemunire, forbade the removal of cases from English courts for final adjudication in Rome under penalty for treason. In violation of the law John Wycliffe translated the major portion of the Bible into English in the fourteenth century and openly taught heretical doctrines at Oxford. Coura-geously he challenged the divine right of kingship and papacy and defined both as dependent on conformity to God's will, which could only be deter-mined in the last analysis by the judgment of the people.

In its nonconformity England also shared the life on the continent. Many of Wycliffe's political ideas were borrowed from Marsilius of Padua, and the spirit of Lollardy was similar to that of the Brethren of the Common Life and the Friends of God. It was therefore quite natural that this close tie of English churchmen with those of the continent should continue even after the out-break of the religious revolts there and, perhaps even more significantly, after King and Parliament had established the Church of England in 1534.

After centuries of internal political struggle and domestic strife, England under Henry VII had come to be recognized as a strong national power. When Henry VIII inherited this throne, he was immediately recognized as a peer of European rulers, and, especially since his national treasury was well filled, he was free to carry out his strong convictions at home and abroad. England had shared in the rising power of nationalism, which caused no little concern in Rome when, with increasing frequency, it challenged the undis-puted authority of the church in European affairs. The reform councils of the early fifteenth century were a clear evidence of desire, rising within the church itself, for a correction of polity, practice, and even theology. Failure to achieve these ends in an orderly conciliar way in the normal channels of church struc-ture only postponed the day of judgment and altered the type of correction from orderly revision to explosive revolution.

Before Henry VIII had completed his first decade on the throne of Eng-land, Luther and Zwingli had openly defied the authority of Rome and laid the groundwork for two magisterial forms of the Reformation. There were also those more radical groups who followed most of the ideas of reform to their logical, though often extreme, conclusions and who were called "the radicals" or the Anabaptists. Protesting for their legally acquired rights at the Diet of Speyer in 1529, the Lutheran princes were called Protestants, a name that soon became attached to the entire movement.

Two decades after Luther and Zwingli had openly broken with Rome John Calvin became the leader of Reformed Protestantism in Geneva. By the time

John Knox, who had studied in Geneva, established Presbyterianism in Scotland in 1560, Calvin's capital had become the center of Reformed Protestants, including the Huguenots in France, the Dutch Reformed in Holland, the Presbyterians in Scotland, as well as most of the German-speaking Swiss, who had begun their reform under Zwingli. Calvinistic theology would soon influence a much wider circle, modifying Lutheran theology as interpreted by Melanchthon and providing the major basis for England's Thirty-nine Articles. Meanwhile, Lutheranism was largely confined to central Germany and the Scandinavian countries.

Lutheranism, however, also strongly influenced the religious life and thought in England. Henry VIII, prepared for the priesthood since it was thought his elder brother would rule England, carried on a correspondence with Luther on theological topics and on several occasions attempted political alliances with the Lutheran princes looking toward a united Protestantism. His disagreements with Luther and his answer to Luther's "heresies" earned for him and all succeeding British monarchs the title of Defender of the Faith bestowed by the Pope.

The English Reformation, however, differed in many respects from those on the continent. Coming a generation later, it profited by their earlier errors. While it was also based on a desire for reforms in polity and administration, it was in its earliest stages primarily a political movement supported by a high nationalistic spirit.

There were also genuine and deep religious issues involved. The influences of Wycliffe in the universities and of Colet in preaching and parish administration were still widely felt. The major writings of the continental reformers were read in the universities and sold "under the table" in public shops. Humanists and reformers came to visit their friends in England; among these were Erasmus and Bucer, who made England his permanent home. English scholars also traveled to the continent, not only to Rome and Geneva, but to the major German theological centers as well. So Tyndale studied under Luther at Wittenberg, and Cranmer visited Nuremberg where he fell in love with and married the niece of Osiander, the Reformation leader in that city. Meanwhile, the indigenous English Christianity, long sheltered in the north and west of Britain, continued to make itself felt as a support for English nationalism and primitive Christianity, from which it had developed, in contrast to the later medieval Christianity, which had now been judged by the events of the early sixteenth century and found wanting.

The Defender of the Faith was greatly disturbed by his failure to have a male heir, which he attributed to a curse upon his marriage to Catherine of Aragon, his deceased brother's widow, even though she swore that her earlier marriage had never been consummated. Because of his failure to obtain papal approval for an annulment, which might have been easily accomplished but for the fact that Catherine was the aunt of Charles V, Henry removed Cardinal Wolsey from his dual post as chancellor of the realm and Archbishop of York. Wolsey, whose living in his Hampton Court residence had come to rival the splendor of his monarch, fortunately fell ill and died on his way from York to his trial, and was spared further suffering. The king promptly appropriated Hampton Court.

Under the guidance of his new archbishop, Thomas Cranmer, who developed the new approach to the powerful universities as a proper authority to decide Henry's domestic problem, the king's marriage to Catherine was annulled and his marriage to Anne Boleyn validated in good time to legitimize the birth of Elizabeth. With this pattern of matrimony at the king's whim or necessity established, his future domestic alliances followed quite naturally and ultimately permitted the establishment of the royal succession through Edward VI, Mary, and then Elizabeth.

Open defiance of papal authority in due time had brought excommunication for the intransigent monarch, and Henry decided to continue to press on toward religious independence. Without disturbing the nature or structure of the church, the king, between 1531 and 1534, had wrested submission from the clergy, who ascribed to him the title "Supreme Head of the Church" and who proffered their docile agreement to pass no legal action without royal permission. In this manner evolved the completely autocephalous Church of England, continuing its identity but now completely separate from Rome.

In due time these actions were formalized when Parliament, in 1534, reenacted the laws of submission of the clergy, declared the king "Supreme Head of the Church," and forbade further financial support to the papacy from England. In contrast to the more radical reforms on the continent, where both political and religious disruption had followed their more drastic separations, the Church of England had been careful to preserve its unbroken continuation as a part of the Catholic Church. Constitutionally it had denied the Roman supremacy and, indeed, had severed relations with the Roman Catholic Church, which had been duly reciprocated by Rome. Yet essentially its catholicity had been preserved. The canonical structure of the church, apart from its obedience to Rome; the doctrine of the church, corrected and revised largely through association with the continental theologians; the ordinal for preserving the historic succession in the episcopacy, without a declaration of obedience to Rome; and even the liturgy, simplified, yet keeping the essential elements of catholic worship, were all continuously preserved in the life and structure of the Church of England.

To assure the preservation of catholic orders, liturgy, and doctrine, Henry, who always remained fully catholic in his heart, led Parliament in 1539 to pass an "Act Abolishing Diversity of Opinion" with a death penalty for violation. Throughout Henry's reign, then, Roman Catholics were constantly fearful of death for treason and the Protestants of punishment for heresy if they objected to the doctrine of transubstantiation, or communion by bread alone, or clerical celibacy, in deference to which Archbishop Cranmer temporarily sent back his wife to Germany. Because the population was widely scattered and communication was slow, few Englishmen understood such complicated procedure, and most of them adopted a "wait and see" attitude.

For six years following Henry's death in 1547 the protectors of the youthful Edward VI led the English church far toward the ideas of the continental reformers. Cranmer brought back his wife, and other clergy married. The Bible was now widely read in English, and newly appointed bishops were largely of the Protestant persuasion. The Forty-two (later to be Thirty-nine) Articles, based principally on the Reformed theology of John Calvin, were authorized by Edward. By no means the least of the achievements of this brief reign was the appearance, largely from the hands of Cranmer, of the Book of Common Prayer, first in a largely Catholic version in 1549 and then, under the constructive criticism of Martin Bucer and scholars of Protestant persuasion, in a more Protestant revision in 1552. A liberal religious spirit developed everywhere throughout England during these years, the universities enjoyed greater academic freedom, humanistic learning flourished by the side of theological inquiry, and even the elementary beginnings of Puritanism appeared on the horizon.

Consternation filled the land when Edward died prematurely in 1553 and his elder sister, Mary, the Roman Catholic daughter of her orthodox mother, Catherine of Aragon, came to the throne. Her own religious loyalty and her marriage to Philip of Spain the next year assured the rigorous restoration of Roman Catholicism, which began immediately upon her accession. For five years inquisitorial methods for the suppression of heresy ultimately led to the death of almost three hundred prominent Protestants including the inimitable Cranmer.

The long and fruitful reign of Elizabeth, from 1558 to 1603, proved to be the period during which the Church of England fully developed its structure and stabilized its life and worship. Child of her father's own spirit and a keen observer of recent events, which clearly indicated that the hope for England's future lay with the Protestant cause, Elizabeth, with strong catholic feelings, carefully guided her nation into a blending of the best of both elements in the "Elizabethan Settlement," which was to become a pattern for the Anglican Way.

All this was accomplished by regular legislative channels over more than a decade. Her new Prayer Book was very similar to the Second Edwardian Book, with the Holy Communion offered in both kinds, and became mandatory for public worship under the Act of Uniformity of 1559. The Bible and the canons of the General Councils to Chalcedon in 451, both having been authorities in the early church, became standards of orthodoxy. Only as late as 1571 did Elizabeth approve the Thirty-nine Articles, clearly reflecting the theology of Calvin and to which all English clergy were required to subscribe by Act of Parliament.

But all this achievement was not without a struggle, especially on the part of entrenched Romanism. Although Elizabeth constantly sought moderation, she was willing, when necessary to accomplish her dream of the Church of England, to deprive all but one of her fourteen bishops, who refused to take the Oath of Supremacy, and about two hundred other clergy who failed to conform. Although Rome has challenged the validity of Matthew Parker's consecration, on the grounds of erroneous intention and an irregular ordinal, Elizabeth had guarded precisely against just such an interpretation in carefully preserving the historic episcopacy as a proper claim for the catholicity of her church. Her new bench of bishops included many thoroughly trained at the law, who proved invaluable in guiding their monarch toward that constitutional stability which preserved her church at once from the expanded political ambitions of Rome and the Catholic monarchs of the continent and at the same time from the invasion of the dissident spirit and the eroding and diluting effects of rising Puritanism and nonconformity.

Sympathetically inclined toward the best elements of catholic religion, Elizabeth dealt gently with her Roman Catholic subjects until 1570 when Pope Pius V excommunicated and deposed her. Increased hostility toward their monarch was fostered by the Jesuits, which soon developed into political attempts to overthrow both the English church and state, a plot on the queen's life, and, ultimately, open war with Spain. Not until the Spanish Armada was defeated in 1588 was England free once again to set her own religious household in order.

Having disposed of the right-wing attack on her religious settlement, Elizabeth now faced the increasing pressures of the rising Puritan element within the church. These leaders felt that the Reformation in England had not gone far enough to dispose of the "popish" Prayer Book and the unbiblical Prayer Book ceremonials, or in its demands for more and better preaching and a more rigorous moral life among the clergy and the laity. Only the strong character and will of the Queen probably prevented the now more socially mixed Parliament from irreparably deforming the delicately balanced *via media*.

By no means all of the Puritan demands were valueless. The Church of England might well have been spared future disruption and become stronger to meet future crises had it been possible under Elizabeth to achieve greater simplification of liturgy and ceremonial and more effective preaching and instruction for high moral living, without in any way destroying or even diluting its catholicity. Yet these two issues were always linked together in the Puritan struggle. After 1583, Elizabeth and her Archbishop Whitgift invariably defended the historic Church of England by its Catholic tradition and heritage against the Puritans, for whom the final authority lay in God's revelation in the Bible. Subscription to royal supremacy and conformity to the Thirty-nine Articles and the Prayer Book were required of all who would perform any religious function whatsoever. Under the protection of external conformity, many who were Puritan in spirit carried on secret sessions of "prophesying" (preaching and biblical exhortation), "lectures," and other defiant deviations. More radical leaders like Robert Browne openly broke with the established church and promoted the small groups of Independents, some of whom later became Baptists and Congregationalists. Within a generation Independents and Puritans would send many of their best leaders and thousands of supporters to New England and other American colonies.

While her bishops and legal advisers helped Elizabeth stabilize her church, now threatened with disruption by religious and political forces from the right and the left, she was most fortunate in having two able theologians who demonstrated clearly for all time that the Church of England was both genuinely Catholic and fully Protestant. John Jewell, in his *Apologia Ecclesiae Anglicanae,* clearly defined the traditional nature of the Church of England, showing that it was in every point as fully Catholic as Rome itself. Richard Hooker, on the other hand, in his first five books of his *Ecclesiastical Polity,* gently and reasonably but firmly demonstrated that the Church of England was fully Protestant. To this end he often agreed in part with the Puritans, only to go beyond them by showing their position to be incomplete. So he pointed out that, in addition to the Bible, tradition and reason are also proper sources of authority and that reason may illuminate both the Bible and tradition. He distinguished clearly between faith or doctrine on the one hand and government or polity on the other. Forms of government may be subject to expediencies, he agreed, and, although the church has always been at its best where it has had bishops, it is possible that the true church could exist without bishops if episcopal orders could not be obtained, a situation that would soon arise in the American colonies. Yet he defended the broadest conception of the visible church to include all those who had been baptized and were loyal to Christ and the Christian faith. Again he went beyond the most liberal Presbyterians in showing that it was faith, and not the form of government, which was the true essence of the Christian religion. So he considered that Roman Catholics and Presbyterians, as well as Anglicans, were part of the universal church. Elizabeth's *via media* could never have become a hope for Christian unity without the complete blending of both these Catholic and Protestant elements in essential Anglicanism.

The death of Elizabeth in 1603 brought the Stuart line of Scotland to the throne of England. Although James I is remembered as having authorized the Bible translation that bears his name and Charles I was famed, especially after he was beheaded, for his life of intense devotion, these Stuarts accomplished little for the Church of England except perhaps to draw the lines more clearly between the Anglicans and the Presbyterians. Many of the Nonconformists had gone to Holland under the pressure of James's demands for submission. The Church of England was well divided between the Puritans, who preserved their convictions even though they conformed externally, and the more catholic churchmen who supported all churchly tradition. The latter, with the background of an authoritative church, quite naturally supported the Stuart presumptions to divine right kingship and developed a party alliance that would soon be popularly called Tory. This sharpened their distinction from the more democratic Puritans who followed their position to its logical conclusion in the support of Parliament. Both parties and the church itself would soon suffer from these unfortunate political alliances.

Early in James's reign, in 1604, the Puritans, hoping for toleration because of his Scottish background, presented the king with a petition for less episcopal supervision, more Calvinism, and freedom from the use of the surplice, which he received less than graciously at Hampton Court before the representatives of the eight hundred signers and of his own party. With typical autocratic authority James demanded a new precise conformity to the royal supremacy, the Prayer Book, and the Thirty-nine Articles, with the result that no less than three hundred Puritan clergy lost their livings.

Charles I was no more successful than his father, whom he succeeded in 1625. The unholy alliance between Charles and his archbishop, William Laud —an alliance of absolute authority in state and in church—made it impossible for the Puritans, now logically but also unfortunately allied with Parliament against the king, to expect any redress of their grievances or development of their hopes. These religious and political struggles were now inextricably woven together, and their conjunction increased the magnitude and intensity of the really separate struggles between right- and left-wing statesmen and high and low churchmen. The result was chaos when the Civil War broke out in October, 1642, after the royal failure to control the "Long Parliament" and to prevent its reforming measures.

Although the church situation remained confused during all of the Commonwealth period, sufficient violence was accomplished to leave the church in disorder; many parishes were filled by Presbyterians or Independents, and the common people became either indifferent or openly hostile to religion. Meanwhile Archbishop Laud resorted to forceful measures and threats to abolish traditional English liberties in his persistent effort to preserve the traditional church by a strong defense of episcopacy and apostolic succession and a high emphasis on the sacraments and an ordered liturgy. His way of doing things seemed to many to have become more important than the thing to be done, and his method of defense of that which many held dear made him one of England's most hated men in an age of intense hatreds. His defense of episcopacy became, as it were, a kiss of death; its association with his own personal unpopularity made episcopacy a hated word in England and in the American colonies. Tried as a traitor to the Commonwealth, he was found guilty and executed in January, 1645.

Five years later, in January, 1649, Charles I was beheaded, and, after the Civil War, the reins of government fell into the hands of Cromwell during the Protectorate from 1653 to his death in 1658. He ruled with an uncertain hand in a disunited Presbyterian administration that tolerated most forms of Christianity apart from the Roman Catholic and the Anglican. When his son Richard was unable to rally the forces to support the Commonwealth, even the Presbyterians were glad to unite with Royalists to bring about the election of a new Parliament and the re-establishment of the monarchy in the hope that these measures might once again bring peace to all England. Charles II was recalled by Parliament and inaugurated the Restoration on May 25, 1660, on his arrival from exile on the continent.

Many dreams were rudely shattered when Charles proved himself no devout son of a churchly father but rather a selfish absolutist with strong leanings toward Rome. Puritans suffered under the vengeful hands of the new king and his fully reconstituted Parliament, while the Church of England was re-established, its surviving bishops restored to their respective sees, new bishops chosen for all vacant sees, and previously held church properties restored. Failing in the attempt to reconcile the differences with the Presbyterians at the Savoy conference in 1661, largely because the churchmen found the Presbyterian requests as radical as the earlier demands at Hampton Court in 1604, the leaders of the church directed their efforts toward revision of the liturgy. The new Book of Common Prayer varied little from the Elizabethan book and quickly found universal acceptance in the church in 1661. The following year Parliament authorized this version; the 1662 Prayer Book has remained the only authorized Prayer Book in England and was the Prayer Book used in America until 1790. All attempts at further revisions in England have failed because Parliament has refused to take action, and these delays have proven a major cause for modern appeals for disestablishment.

Supported by a royalist majority, the recently restored House of Lords, and Archbishop Judson, a later incarnation of the Laudian spirit, it is not strange that Parliament, by a new Act of Uniformity in 1662, demanded exclusive use of the Prayer Book in worship and ultimately deprived almost two thousand Puritan ministers.

Although Charles II rigorously regulated the lives of Nonconformists, even forbidding the assembly of more than five persons for worship, he consistently favored Roman Catholics, liberalizing their privileges and allowing Masses to be celebrated in private homes. Meanwhile, Charles had secretly sought military and financial aid from France with the understanding that, when possible, he would restore Romanism in England. If not fully aware of the facts, Parliament must have been suspicious of such intrigues, for it passed a Test Act, in 1673, requiring that all civil and military officers affirm the Oath of Supremacy, take Holy Communion by the Prayer Book rite, and disavow transubstantiation. Whether or not this procedure was more vigorous than the issue required or whether governments are ever justified in using religious prerogatives to enforce purely political ends, it is very difficult to assay at this distance in time and without the details of the setting, in which the fear of returning Nonconformist revolution was exceeded only by the terrifying thought of the possibility of Roman Catholic restoration in England.

Whether or not the intrigue was real, many innocent Roman Catholics were executed for participation in the "Popish Plot" in 1678. The Roman Catholic Church received Charles II by baptism on his death bed, and all England trembled when his brother, James II, succeeded to the throne in February, 1685, for his Romanism was no secret and his resolution to restore papal submission in England was universally understood. When, step by step, James freed the Roman Catholics from the restrictions of English law by his own decrees, respected peers of the realm prepared the ground for the Glorious

Revolution when they invited William of Orange and his wife, Mary, to share the English throne. William and Mary were first cousins, both grandchildren of Charles I; Mary was the daughter of James II, and William was the son of James's sister, Mary. Meanwhile, James II escaped to the continent. William and Mary were crowned on April 11, 1689, using for the first time the royal oath to maintain "the Protestant reformed religion established by law." Never again was England to be without this clear statement about the genuinely Protestant aspect of its established religion, although the Protestant Episcopal Church in the United States of America would discuss the propriety of the use of the word Protestant in its name at many sessions of the general convention in the nineteenth and twentieth centuries.

Since the bishop's oath of allegiance to his monarch at his consecration is perpetual, the Glorious Revolution presented a problem of loyalty for men of keen conscience in the episcopate. Five English bishops refused to declare their allegiance to William and Mary while James II lived, not because of agreement or disagreement with either, but because they believed their previous oaths remained valid. About four hundred clergy shared their view and also shared their fate of deprivation. Believing themselves to be the true church in England, these Nonjurors, as they have been called, consecrated bishops and continued their small body for about one hundred years. Several of these bishops lived in the American colonies but performed no episcopal functions there. The Nonjurors in Scotland became the Anglican Church in Scotland where Presbyterianism was the established religion and never suffered under the stigma of treason, for there their position had no political involvements and was purely a religious matter. By these Scottish Nonjurors, high churchmen in thought and devotion, the church in America would have its first bishop consecrated.

The unhappy divisions and experiences of mutual suffering that led to the Glorious Revolution convinced all England of the futility of such unnecessary anguish. Parliament soon passed the Toleration Act of 1689 under which all save Unitarians and Roman Catholics were granted freedom of worship. The Test Act, however, remained in force so that full political freedom was granted only to churchmen, leaving the Establishment definitely in the hands of Anglicans until the new era after the Napoleonic Wars.

During these years of increasing tension and struggle between the accessions of Charles I and William and Mary, from 1625 to 1689, there was a happy concentration of first-rate theologians whose works were far more influential than their immediate contemporary effects seemed to indicate. Just as Elizabeth had her Jewell and Hooker, so these years produced men like Archbishop Ussher, Stillingfleet, Jeremy Taylor, and the Cambridge Platonists, the so-called "Caroline Divines" of the mid-seventeenth century who left their indelible impressions on the continuing thought and life of the English church.

The more placid state of affairs in England also turned the interests of loyal churchmen to creative social and educational efforts, many of which have had their continuing effects to the present. Thomas Bray, whose fame rests largely on his work as the commissary of the Bishop of London for Maryland, was a successful parish minister in England before and after this brief period of intensive work in America. He was probably more responsible than any other for the founding of the Society for Promoting Christian Knowledge in 1698 and, three years later, the Society for the Propagation of the Gospel in Foreign Parts. The latter he envisioned as providing the men and the means for missionary work in the New World, especially in the weaker colonies and among the Negroes and Indians. The former was designed with a more universal mission in mind, to provide better elementary religious education and good, yet economical, literature for children in England, America, or wherever opportunity provided a means for its distribution. But the real love of Bray's life was his desire to provide adequate libraries, especially for the clergy in America, but also parish and community libraries. In this latter cause more than in any other Bray invested most of his own resources and the energies of his life. Both societies continue to perform their functions to the present.

George I, who understood little of the English language and perhaps less of Anglican Convocation procedure, which had degenerated into endless wrangling, simply suppressed these annual meetings of the bishops and clergy in 1717, and not until 1862 would they be resumed. Lack of power to rule its own house was accompanied by a lack of ministering to the religious needs of the English masses.

In this period of starvation for adequate religious guidance, many Englishmen found an answer to their needs in the Methodist movement begun at Oxford, in 1729, by John Wesley, his brother Charles, and their mutual friend George Whitefield, who would later stir up most of the American colonies with his evangelistic preaching. Although John Wesley always remained a priest of the Church of England and warned his followers of the fatal error of separating themselves from it, his disciples, more notably Thomas Coke and Francis Asbury, led the Methodist movement in America and there established a distinctly new church on Christmas Day, 1784. If only communications had been more rapid and the relations with the mother church not so strained, this branch of the church might have become a power in the new Protestant Episcopal Church in the United States of America, for Samuel Seabury had been consecrated by the Nonjurors of Scotland just six weeks before, on November 14, 1784, and might have provided a line of true succession to this potent movement destined to sweep rapidly from coast to coast in America.

With the outbreak of hostilities between England and the colonies, the church in America was literally orphaned and forced to develop its own leadership and to supply its own resources. Furthermore, the attachment of colonial church leaders to the beloved mother church caused many of them to desert the fields of their labor and return to the homeland rather than face the conflict of divided loyalties. What the church in the New World could and would do becomes the story of the Protestant Episcopal Church in the United States of America.[1]

II

THE CHURCH IN VIRGINIA

Unsettled by religious and political disturbances at home and tempted by the glowing reports from the explorers of the New World, adventurous Englishmen set out to claim new lands for their monarch in competition with settlers from other European nations. Both Anglican and Roman Catholic priests accompanied these earliest English explorers. Sailing under the auspices of Henry VII, John Cabot first discovered and established the English claim to the North American continent on the Feast of St. John the Baptist, 1497. Undoubtedly a priest in his party celebrated Mass on the American shore. The following year a royal bounty of £20 was granted to Lanslot Thirkill, a London priest who was shipping out to Newfoundland, and early in the next century Albert de Prato, a canon of St. Paul's, London, reported to Cardinal Wolsey from St. John's, Newfoundland. "The first reformed fleet which had English prayers and preaching therein," led by Sir Hugh Willoughby in 1533, under the patronage of Edward VI and Sebastian Cabot's company of merchant adventurers, listed a Master Richard Stafford, minister, who was bound by Cabot's code to see to it that daily services were conducted on each of the three ships. Unfortunately the ill-fated fleet never reached American shores but perished in a severe winter in northern Russian waters. During the brief Roman restoration in England under Mary no explorations were made, but with the accession of Elizabeth new voyages and settlements were planned, and in each case there were to be "good order in the dayly service" and prayers unto God for success.

The honor of conducting the first Protestant English service on the shores of North America fell to "Maister Wolfall," who was the "minister and preacher" on Martin Frobisher's voyage to Hudson Bay in 1578. Wolfall preached a "godly" sermon and celebrated Communion on land; the captain of the *Anne Francis* and many other gentlemen, soldiers, mariners, and miners worshiped with him.

While this service was being conducted, Sir Francis Drake was piloting his *Pelican* along the western shores of North America. Sailing northward, he discovered the coasts of California and Oregon and on June 21, 1579, landed for repairs in a "convenient and fit harbor," near San Francisco, which came to be known as Drake's Bay. Here in an extraordinary gathering among the natives, who regarded their visitors as superior beings, Drake's chaplain,

Francis Fletcher, administered the Holy Communion and conducted worship according to the Prayer Book for the first time within the present borders of the United States. This event has been appropriately memorialized by a monument in the form of a large cross erected in Golden Gate Park in San Francisco.

While several other attempts were made to colonize North America during the later Elizabethan years, not one of these would be permanent. Sir Humphrey Gilbert and his half-brother, Sir Walter Raleigh, a close friend of the queen, tried but failed in Newfoundland and Virginia. Raleigh saw the advantages of a colony over a trading post, such as the French had so frequently established, and so attempted such a settlement at Roanoke. It showed every sign of being successful during the years 1585 to 1587, and except for the irregularity of supply ships, a factor which also came near to undoing the Jamestown colony two decades later, it might well have been permanent. For lack of supplies the first contingent returned to England with Sir Francis Drake, who touched their harbor when their spirits were at a low ebb. In 1587 Raleigh sent out a second expedition under the eminent artist John White, whose granddaughter, Virginia Dare, was the first English child born in the New World. Five days earlier, on August 13, 1587, Manteo, a captured Indian, was baptized and became one of the first of his race to be admitted to the church.

White's routine return to England was prolonged, since he arrived there just as the Spanish Armada was approaching. When he finally returned to "The City of Raleigh in Virginia," the new name for the old Roanoke, he discovered that his daughter and grandchild and indeed the entire company had vanished from the location, leaving as the only clue the word CROATOAN carved on a tree. That there was no cross carved on the tree, as had been agreed in case of distress, indicated to White that they might have moved fifty miles inland as they had been prepared to do before he left. Since no one was able to decipher the carving or determine their destination or even the direction they traveled, it has been impossible to be certain whether they fled, were lost, massacred, or absorbed into Indian tribes.

The Gilbert-Raleigh adventures left no settlements, but their permanent contributions to English life in America lay in the details of their charters, which invariably spelled out clearly those guarantees of political rights and privileges by which the future colonists were to be able to pursue their independence. So the charter granted Raleigh on Lady Day, 1584, specified that the settlers should "have all the privileges of free denizens and persons native of England, in such ample manner as if they were born and personally resident in our said realm of England." They were to be governed "according to such statutes as shall be by him or them established; so that the said statutes or laws conform as near as conveniently may be with those of England and do not oppugn the Christian faith or any way withdraw the people of those lands from our allegiance." Through Raleigh's foresight, more than is often realized, these bases for full English prerogatives were to be written into all similar subsequent grants. As late as the opening of Elizabeth's reign in 1558, probably not more than several hundred Englishmen lived beyond the British Isles; a hundred years later, they were widely scattered and well established in America.

Although several attempts at settlement had been made by the English along the Atlantic coast in the early seventeenth century, failure haunted their efforts. So Captain Bartholomew Gosnold with a company of thirty-two lived briefly in the summer of 1602 on Buzzard's Bay of the present Massachusetts coast, and the following year Martin Pring, under the patronage of the merchants of Bristol, spent two months in the harbors of Plymouth and Duxbury. In the spring of 1605 George Waymouth settled near the Kennebec River, a region later to be promoted by Sir Ferdinando Gorges.

England had many trading companies, some of them incorporated as early as the reign of Edward III. Early trading had been carried on largely with the Dutch, but by the accession of James I, there were incorporations like the East India, Guinea, Levant, Morocco, and Muscovy Companies, whose stock was widely held by lords and commoners but frequently with interlocking directorates among the largest holders with controlling interests in many companies. In each case they followed the same pattern by obtaining monopoly rights from the Crown, a system resembling mature capitalism.

The time seemed opportune for expanding English colonization when James I came to the throne, and it took little encouragement to get him to assume a royal leadership and to extend royal patronage to those who would enhance the holdings and interests of the Crown. On April 10, 1606, James I assigned The Great Patent of Virginia with colonization rights between the thirty-fourth and forty-fifth degrees north latitude to two trading companies. The "First Colony," as it was called in the charter (later it became the London Company, and after 1609, the Virginia Company), consisted of knights, gentlemen, merchants, and other adventurers of London. It received the territory between the thirty-fourth and thirty-eighth degrees, or approximately from Cape Fear to the southern border of Maryland.

To the second company, made up of similar persons mostly from Bristol, Exeter, and Plymouth, called the Plymouth Company, was assigned the area between the forty-first and forty-fifth parallels. These colonists were assured of the rights of freeborn Englishmen, and apart from the reservation for the king of one-fifth of the gold and silver and one-fifteenth of the copper mined, few limitations threatened the security of these adventurers. The Plymouth colonists, after a dangerous voyage of more than two months, arrived on the Maine coast on August 7. The following Sunday, August 9, 1607, Chaplain Richard Seymour held an English service on St. George's (Monhegan) Island where they found a cross probably left from an earlier service under Shipmaster Martin Pring in 1603. Just about three months earlier a similar service had been held at Jamestown, Virginia. While some of these settlers found their way back to England in the next few years, it is probable that some of them remained in the permanent, although not officially recognized, settlements in the regions of the present Sagadahoc River and Boothbay Harbor.

The charter of the early Plymouth Company provided specifically for worship and instruction for colonists and "salvages [Indians] according to the doctrine, rights and religion now professed and established within our realme of England, and that they shall not suffer any person or persons to withdrawe any of the subjects or people inhabiting, or which shall inhabit within any of the said several colonies and plantations from the same, or from their due allegiance, unto us, our heirs and successors, as their immediate sovereigne under God." Had this colony been permanent it might have made a vast difference in the history of New England and perhaps of the entire nation. The provisions were no more rigorous than those that would later be imposed upon these very colonists by the Puritan regime of Massachusetts. The Massachusetts colony later acquired the rights to this region and full religious control as well on the ground that their charter provided a northern boundary at the Merrimack River, although the grantor little knew that the river ran from north to south and not from east to west as the last few miles of flow indicated. It remains quite clear, then, that long before Pilgrims or Puritans arrived in Massachusetts the Church of England was by charter established in that colony and its worship regularly practiced.[1]

A convoy of three ships sailed for Virginia from England on December 19, 1606, although they never left the sight of land for six weeks because of unpropitious winds, during which period many lay ill and Chaplain Robert Hunt came close to death. It was May 6 before those 105 passengers arrived in the lower Chesapeake Bay and another week before they chose to settle some thirty miles upland on the north bank of the James River at Jamestown, also named in honor of their king.

It was a mixed lot indeed that Captain John Smith had at his disposal to form the first permanent English settlement in America. The myth that Virginia was settled by Cavaliers has long since been exploded, for only a few, perhaps three, important Virginia families have been traced to the nobility. Desire for an early beginning had caused less than careful screening of these first shiploads of settlers. Among Captain Smith's first 105, there were only twelve laborers, four carpenters, and a few mechanics. Three more vessels laden with fortune hunters and "gentlemen" in name only, because they wished to do no work, finally led Smith to beg his company, "When you send again, I entreat you rather send 30 carpenters, husbandmen, gardeners, fishermen, blacksmiths, masons and diggers up of tree's roots, well provided, than a thousand such as we have." The next ships brought "men of size" but who shared little of the real purposes of the colony. After the overthrow of Charles I, almost a thousand Cavaliers did flee to Virginia but primarily for safety, and on the Restoration most of them returned to England.

Smith's somewhat communistic system of living "out of the common store" failed to produce sufficient incentive for work so that when he developed the more autonomous system of labor he could write, "wee reaped not so much corn from the labors of thirty as now three or four doe provide for themselves," but his colony still did not succeed. The London Company was refinanced and reorganized as the Virginia Company in 1609 and six ships were sent over with eight hundred immigrants, but by 1611 the population was down again to about 150. The area surrounding Jamestown had provided optimum conditions for malaria and dysentery so that most of these first settlers perished in the epidemics.

The government of Virginia had been autocratic from the beginning. Thirteen members of a Council ruled the company in England and selected the names of thirteen settlers who in turn were to rule in Virginia. These names were sealed in a box that was opened on arrival in Virginia, and all those listed save Smith, who had developed an open feud with President Edward-Maria Wingfield, were sworn into office. Through the good offices of Chaplain Hunt, these men, who rarely agreed on anything else but could agree in their mutual admiration for the chaplain, were reconciled in good time to participate in the first service of Holy Communion conducted by Hunt on May 14, 1607. Smith was promptly sworn into the Council.[2]

The Rev. Robert Hunt, M.A., Magdalen College, Oxford, was one of the original petitioners for the London Company charter granted by James I in 1606. In spite of illness and adverse circumstances on the voyage to America, Hunt impressed everyone with his pious life and sincerity of purpose "that the true word and service of God be preached, planted and used . . . according to the rites and doctrines of the Church of England." Already on the long voyage Hunt had demonstrated his pastoral mediating abilities in calming the strains between Smith and Wingfield as well as among other belligerent passengers.

Scarcely had the first church been built in Jamestown when a fire beginning in the storehouse destroyed the town, including the church and Hunt's small but much-needed library. He probably performed the first marriage in the colony in 1608 before he died early in that summer. Despite Hunt's conciliations and his desire "to set forth quietness, peace and love" among his parishioners, personal rivalries and animosities continued so that when a ship arrived with supplies after their first strenuous winter most of the leaders were either in jail or had perished with the majority of the colony.

So, slowly but surely the power in the colony came into the hands of Smith, and, in addition to his domestic problems, his relations with the Indians became ever more strained. Having killed several Indians, Smith was captured and brought before Powhatan, chief of the neighboring Indian confederacy. During the brief period of his "preparation" for execution, Smith befriended two small children, Powhatan's favorite daughter, Pocahontas, and her little brother. On the day set for his execution Pocahontas spared Smith's life by placing her head on his, an act not uncommon in the Indian administration of justice. It meant a special relation and dependence between the two persons. In this case the chief of the confederacy accepted Smith as a son and sent him back to Jamestown to arrange for a treaty between the Indians and colonists. This peace was at best intermittent, and often Pocahontas must have been chided for obstructing justice or arranging so unhappy an alliance. She finally withdrew from her tribe, came to live among the settlers, and soon afterward married one of their leaders.

No longer is it held that American colonies were founded for the sake of religious freedom. Only to Rhode Island did men flee for religious liberty, not from England but from their neighbors in New England. Religious independence was one of many factors in the founding of Connecticut, New Jersey, Pennsylvania, and Georgia, but in the Massachusetts Bay colony, New York, Virginia, and the Carolinas it was unknown. Religious liberty was not a commodity that could be transported from Europe but was a germ that when planted here grew to major proportions. Ironically, most of the values promised by the Reformation were rarely achieved in Europe but had to await the opportunities of the New World to attain their fulfillment.

Actually these ideals were frequently intermingled with religious and economic objectives which grew to be so intertwined that it became difficult to identify clearly what motivations were predominant in a colony. Even though the original expressed motivation was religious or philanthropic, it has been contended that the English colonies, especially Virginia and those in New England, soon became dominated by commercial controls and should be considered mere incidents in the story of English expansion and impelled chiefly by economic necessity.

Such interpretations are not so much in error as incomplete. Most frequently, both religious and economic motivations were blended into something like the Calvinistic conception that spiritual and material prosperity could be mutually beneficial. Already then, and even more through the years, this dilemma presented itself in the moot question of spiritual and temporal authority and sovereignty. In the attempt to delineate the specific roles of the church and state in this new environment, there would be created a complicated national constitution stressing mutual dependence between the states and guaranteeing religious liberty and human rights to all citizens.

With the necessity for a new effort to preserve the colony in Virginia, now reduced to about 150 persons, a new charter was issued incorporating the Virginia Company entirely independent of the Crown. Requests to the parent company for immediate assistance of men, supplies, and "foure honest and learned ministers" brought the needed aid. On May 10, 1611, on the same ship with Sir Thomas Dale, the new governor who brought with him a new code of laws, came also the Rev. William Whitaker, son of the Regius Professor of Divinity at Cambridge, then the seedbed of Puritanism. In the new Henrico Parish, the second in the colony, about seventy miles up the James River, Whitaker farmed his one hundred-acre glebe and ministered to the Indians and scattered settlers. Henrico had a suburb called Hope-in-Faith and was defended by two forts, Charity and Patience, and also became the center for a school for the Indians. In 1613 Whitaker sent to London a pamphlet, "Good Newes from Virginia," pleading for missionaries to the Indians. Of a friend in London he inquired why so few of the English clergy, "so hot against the Surplis and subscription, come hither where neither are spoken of. . . ." The four ministers who came at the request of the colonists were probably Mease, Wickham at Henrico, Bargave, and Stockham.

Shortly before his unfortunate death by drowning in the James River in 1617, Whitaker had converted Pocahontas and baptized her as Rebecca. She was frequently in Jamestown where she met the widower John Rolfe, who would soon be secretary and recorder of the colony and a member of the Governor's Council. He had introduced the extensive cultivation of tobacco for export and so guaranteed the economic stability and future of the colony. He was greatly attracted to Pocahontas and admitted that in her "my hartie and best thoughts are so entangled, and inthralled in so intricate a laborinth, that I was even awearied to unwinde myself thereout." With the consent of the governor and Chief Powhatan they were married about April 1, 1614. With her husband, Pocahontas visited England where she died about March 20, 1617, at Gravesend, just before she was to have sailed back to America. Her visit had aroused much interest in Virginia and its missionary opportunities. King James asked assistance from his archbishops in raising funds for churches and schools for the education of Indians. Through this effort John King, Bishop of London, became involved and was soon named a member of the Council for Virginia. The future spiritual jurisdiction of the Bishop of London over the Anglican Church in America seems to date from this period. Nevertheless, in 1617 Governor Samuel Argall still wrote to the Virginia Company asking Sir Dudley Digges to obtain from the archbishop (and not the Bishop of London) a permit for William Wickham, who was probably only a deacon, to administer the Holy Communion at Henrico as there had been no clergyman there since Whitaker's death.

From the granting of its charter the Virginia Company governed its colony most autocratically. The first code sent from England included several severe measures that read like inquisitorial procedures. The death penalty was attached to blasphemy and derision of the Trinity or the Bible. There were equally unenforceable penalties for absence from church and Sabbath-breaking, and a colonist who refused the religious instruction that his minister decided he needed was to submit to the instruction or be whipped. Under Sir Samuel Argall, a sterner judge and executive than Dale whom he succeeded, the Virginia laws were altered but hardly modified. In 1618 Argall still demanded "that every person should go to church Sundays or holy days, or lye neck and heels that night, and be a slave to the colony the following week; for the second offence, he should be a slave for a month; and for the third, a year and a day."[3]

Under the influence of Sir Edwin Sandys, who assumed the leadership of the disunited and almost bankrupt company in London, a change of government in 1619 brought the gentler Governor Sir George Yeardley to succeed the unpopular Argall. The new governor arrived in April to find in Jamestown only a few buildings—the governor's mansion, and a church, fifty by thirty feet—and comparably little sign of stability in the outlying settlements. Richard Bucke, "a verie good preacher," was the minister in Jamestown, and three other authorized clergymen instructed the colonists. Only about one in twenty of the original settlers had survived. By 1621 the Sandys management had sent over no less than twenty vessels with about 3,500 settlers including "young single women of blameless reputation."

Governor Yeardley brought with him not only authority but specific instructions "for the better establishment of a commonwealth." The first elected body of a representative government in America convened in the parish church in Jamestown on Friday, July 30, 1619. For the election of these representatives all inhabitants over seventeen, even indentured servants, had the right to vote. This form of popular government in America was based on a foundation better than anything in England or the rest of the world before the American Revolution.

Even though there was no open profession of religion, that first House of Burgesses was opened by prayer by the Rev. Richard Bucke, and one of their first acts provided for the proper cultivation of the ministers' glebes and full payment of salaries in the best corn and tobacco. In fact, each plantation had an appointee whose duty it was to collect the ministers' portion out of the best tobacco and corn produced, and if a planter sold any of his tobacco before the ministers' salaries had been paid in full he was subjected to double assessment. The moral life of the colony was still related to the church. To restrain immoderate excess in dress, the rate for public contributions was assessed in church on the dress of men and women. Forced labor was abolished, and the old cruel laws were replaced by others that could be enforced. So instead of being forced "to lye neck and heels all night" for absence from church one Sunday, one might pay a small fine in tobacco. Idleness and gambling were punishable offenses. The first enactment of the assembly provided protection of the Indians from "injury or oppression," and to this end there were restrictions on indiscriminate commingling of the savages and the settlers. Sandys' policy also envisioned hospitals, inns, new churches, schools, and a college at Henrico where ten thousand acres of land were set apart as an endowment.

Indians and whites were to have the benefits of liberal education. Sir Francis Wyat, who succeeded Yeardley in 1621, brought with him authority for a Council of State, probably to assure more royal controls, especially in religious conformity. Governor Wyat was instructed by the company to see "that each town, borough, and hundred procured, by just means, a certain number of their children to be brought up in the first elements of literature, that the most towardly of them should be fitted for college." At the beginning of his term Governor Wyat received instructions, as did his several successors, requiring that Almighty God be duly and daily served according to the form established in the Church of England.

Well pleased with the new turn of events, the company in London observed a day of celebration on April 17, 1622, with a sermon on "Virginia's

God Be Thanked," little realizing that a month earlier, on March 22, the Indians, no longer restrained by Powhatan, had massacred 347 whites in the Henrico region, including the college superintendent, George Thorpe, and had burned the college buildings. Apparently the plot had been long brewing and was a closely guarded secret among the Indians. One Christian Indian, Chanco, informed his master, Edward Pace, of the conspiracy and thus probably spared one-half of the colony from destruction and permanent failure. Pace immediately had traveled overnight to Jamestown and forewarned the governor, and wherever the massacring Indians found resistance, they did not execute the order of their new vengeful chief, Opecancanough. Disease and famine followed the massacre, and of the several thousand but so recently well established, now only about 1,800 survived, and Virginia was once again back to the problem of mere subsistence.

With disaster in Virginia and strife in the leadership of the company in London, the King and Privy Council stepped in and, on the ground that it had failed to propagate the faith and expand trade, abrogated the charter so that Virginia became once more a Crown colony in 1624 and remained so until 1776. The new constitution, however, provided for the continuance of the House of Burgesses, setting a pattern of royal and English colonial government with local participation.

Anglicanism was not established in Virginia until the revocation of the charter in 1624 and the founding of the royal colony. Until this time religious leadership had actually been in the hands of the members of the company, who saw to it that Prayer Book services were provided from the beginning. The King did little but order that "the true word, and service of God and Christian faith be preached, planted and used," thus leaving the church in Virginia to fend for itself. Such freedom resulted in a program of Puritan Anglicanism, reflecting the basic spirit of the settlers in those first two decades of semi-independence. It also revealed the prevailing attitude of the company management and its director, Sir Edwin Sandys, son of an Archbishop of York, who had studied in Calvinistic Geneva and had served in Parliament as a notable leader of the Puritan party. While he was a member of the Church of England and subscribed to the Oath of Supremacy, he also wrote, ". . . if ever God from heaven did constitute and direct a forme of Government it was that of Geneva."[4]

The Virginia burgesses probably knew of Sandys' plan to bring the Pilgrims from Leiden to Virginia, and self-governing "particular plantations" had been set apart for religious dissidents. It may have been from these people that a gentleman bearing letters from Virginia had come to Boston in 1642 asking the New England Puritans to supply them faithful ministers. Although prevented by the Act of 1629 from preaching in public, two Puritan ministers, named Knowlys and Thompson, succeeded in gathering small groups for worship in private homes. The conflict between the Puritans and the established church did not come to a head until Sir William Berkeley became governor in 1642. At his instigation the Virginia Council ordered the Puritan missionaries to return to Massachusetts, and a fine of £100 was set as the penalty for any shipmaster who brought a Puritan minister into the colony. Soon afterward the Assembly passed an act declaring "all ministers whatsoever which reside in this Colony are to be conformable to the orders and constitution of the Church of England and the laws therein established; and not otherwise to be admitted to teach or preach publicly or privately."[5]

Conformity was more easily enforced among the clergy, however, than among the laity, and among the latter great religious diversity persisted for many years. Eventually, when Charles I was imprisoned, Lord Baltimore invited the Puritans to Maryland, and more than three hundred went to that province in 1649. With the establishment of the Protectorate it is possible that not more than several hundred Puritans remained in the colony, and many of these had moved westward into those more distant areas where the arm of the law reached less effectively and where, in the subsequent decades, dissident groups of all varieties, including Anabaptists, Quakers, Methodists, and Baptists, would settle.

Even during the Commonwealth period little change occurred in the religious life of Virginia. When Cromwell's commission arrived in Virginia, the Governor and Council were excused for one year from giving their oath to the Commonwealth, and the Prayer Book was permitted, provided that the prayers for the king were not used in public. This plan worked so effectively that the church in Virginia was permitted to use the Prayer Book until the Restoration, when the accession of Charles II on May 29, 1660, marked also the restoration of the Church of England. In March, 1661, the Virginia Assembly, by the sixth article of its newly adopted code, made it obligatory to use the English Book of Common Prayer in worship.

The Quakers proved most annoying to the colonists so that between 1659 and 1680 four Acts for their regulation and suppression were passed by the Assembly. It is quite possible that the Act of 1662, which required "every person who refuses to have his child baptized by a lawful minister shall be amerced 2,000 pounds of tobacco, half to the parish and half to the informer," may have been aimed as well at negligent Anglicans as at Quakers. The final chapter of the conflict between churchmen and dissidents would come to an end with the passage of the Toleration Act of 1689 under William and Mary, which would guide all future legislation to the end of the colonial period. Eventually in the latter half of the eighteenth century as tensions between the colonies and England increased, less and less heed was given by the colonists to the English government or its provisions.

In the earliest years of the colony farm labor was often done by indentured servants or violators of the colonial laws whose punishment included such service. It seemed only a short step from the status of indentured servant to slavery, and the Virginia planters with no hesitation bought the twenty Negroes offered for sale in 1619 by the Dutch traders, who had, ironically, brought them from Africa on the ship *Jesus*. The birth of the large plantation system through the introduction of slavery and the immigration of hundreds of laborers suited to the demands of farm life was marked by social, economic, and religious transitions. The poorer whites were pushed westward, leaving the good tilled eastern lands to the wealthy planters. The distinction between public and private lands was loosely marked, often greatly to the disadvantage of the poorer farmers on small acreages. By 1653 indentured servants lost their vote, and in 1671 even leaseholders suffered a similar fate. But for his own death, Nathaniel Bacon's Rebellion of 1676 might have succeeded. Berkeley's wrath was demonstrated in a score of executions, confiscation of the property of such victims, and the expulsion of one thousand dissenters from the colony. Although the old English class distinctions were never fully perpetuated in the American colonies, Virginia, perhaps more than most, did develop sharply defined social lines between the wealthy planters and landed gentry on the one hand and the poor laborers on the other.

In this transition the church had been able to do comparatively little to help solve the new problems emerging in this new type of society. Even an oligarchical New England type of theocracy could hardly have done much more, although a staff of clergy cast in the New England mold would most certainly have had much more to say to these conditions. The church at home had been struggling for its very life so that colonial cries for assistance and even requests for bishops and episcopal supervision had gone unheeded in these emergencies. By 1638 Archbishop Laud had completed the arrangements for sending a bishop to America, but the Puritan Revolution ended all this until after the Restoration. It remained in the hearts and minds of English monarchs and churchmen, however, and as late as 1709 Dean Swift wrote to Governor Robert Hunter of New York, "All my hopes now terminate in being made bishop of Virginia."

Meanwhile the church in Virginia languished. The clergy became dependent on the landlord class and often themselves became land- and slaveholders and freely adopted plantation ideals. In 1738 the Rev. Anthony Gavin lamented that he saw "the greatest part of our brethren taken up in farming and buying slaves, which in my humble opinion is unlawful for any Christian and particularly for clergymen." There was little pretense of moral leadership among the clergy. Assembly regulations were required to keep many of the ministers from dice, drunkenness, and other frivolities, which slowly lost them the confidence of their people and led to the growing popularity of the dissident religious leaders who, by 1700, numbered about half the population among their followers.

In many ways the clergy were the victims of the Virginia condition. It was simply impossible to supervise a parish scattered from thirty to one hundred miles along both sides of a river. In 1661 it was suggested that the government construct villages around the parish churches to which the planters might come to spend the weekend and so preserve common worship and the very life of the church.

The Virginia Assembly, by an Act of 1641, provided officially for the English type of parish government by requiring vestries to govern the local

im to England to
he support of the
r Wren to design
and his own ap-
succeeded by the
peared in this list
on, Monroe, and
mes Madison of
ts was conferred
than £3,000 the
fire in 1705. The
inds and skilled
ile William and
lty included six
ght to be repre-

their education,
didates had the
l few wanted to
t abroad for or-
Consequently,
ship upon the

who were less
, wrote to his
n the eleventh
hes in Virginia
n addition, he
esapeake Bay.
many insects
to explore for

confirmation
yal Anglican
ed permitted
er half of the
were built in
hington wor-

ttle approval
att, who was
y the move-
My distress,
s in general,
religion and

lated the church affairs in general,
under the control of the elected
petuating oligarchies favoring the
lergy were supposed to be admitted
g the life of the parish, they were
as 1681, the Rev. Morgan Godwyn
bly handled by these Plebeian Jun-
n Law forbade prolonged vacancies,
appointment except on an annual
y were free to determine and even
ses and at times employed lay read-
ct weekly services. The result was a
and the even greater need for gen-
re only about ten clergymen in Vir-
o attract proper persons to fill the
was granted to those who would risk

to Virginia as governor, his instruc-
es of only those clergymen who had
op of London. This is the first such
f the Bishop of London over colonial
became more conscious of the dire
especially, the Bishop of London de-
represent his authority in the colonial
new hopes. Since these officers could
proved inadequate; but it was a be-
lair for Virginia and Thomas Bray for
church in America.
es in 1685, after some struggles of con-
ed successively in churches at Henrico,
liamsburg. He had been in Virginia but
op of London, appointed him his first
Despite his limitations, Blair was able to
l the number of ministers from twenty-
he time of his death, in 1743, there were
ntly the only person who dared to defy
Andros and was directly responsible for
also tamed other tyrannical governors,
d, demurely wrote that he thought the
ce and tranquillity, under a due obedience
anly conformity to the Church of Eng-

well have been the founding of the Col-
d persuaded the Virginia legislature that
the training of their young men for the

ministry in their own colony. In 1691 the legislators sent
obtain a charter and the necessary funds. Having obtained
Archbishop of Canterbury and the consent of Sir Christoph
the building, Blair came back with the charter, the money
pointment as the president of the college. In this office he wa
later commissaries until 1776. Many distinguished names a
as well as among the alumni, who included Presidents Jeffe
Tyler, and John Marshall, Peyton Randolph, and Bishop
Virginia. The college's first honorary degree of Master of
on Benjamin Franklin on April 2, 1756. At a cost of mor
college building was completed in 1693 only to be gutted b
reconstruction was delayed until 1723 because of lack of
workmen. The new chapel was opened on June 28, 1732. V
Mary began as an English grammar school, by 1729 its fa
graduates of English and Scottish universities who had the
sented in the Assembly.

But with a larger number of candidates and a college fc
the problems of clerical supply were still not solved. Few c
present equivalent of $5,000 to pay for the trip to England,
face the dangers of travel when one out of every five who w
dination died on the journey from disease or shipwreck at s
the Virginia church remained largely dependent for its lea
dwindling supply from England.

Occasionally among these men there seem to have been sc
than genuinely zealous for the church. One, Thomas Fie
friend, Dr. MacKenzie, in England on February 16, 1771, th
week after landing he was chosen rector of one of the best pa
at Kingston, Gloucester County, at a salary of £200 per annu
had his own house and five hundred acres on the river near
The remainder of the long letter provides a description of
and fossils he had found and the rich deposits he hoped so
other specimens that he proposed sending to Dr. MacKenzie

Few prominent Virginia families came into the church. S
involved the same risks of travel as ordination, even mo
families were content to have their children baptized, which
all the benefits of life in the Virginia colonial church. In the
seventeenth century many beautiful, small Anglican churc
Virginia, such as the one in Truro Parish where George
shiped.

By this time the Great Awakening had come to Virginia w
and often open opposition by the Anglicans. Only Devereux
greatly influenced by George Whitefield, seemed to be touc
ment. About his own religious need and experience he wrc
then, did not arise from a painful sense of any particular sin,
but from a full persuasion, that I was a stranger to God and

was not prepared for death and judgment." Not bred in the church, he was led into it by reading the works of James Hervey and hearing of the association of Wesley and Whitefield with the Church of England. After ordination in 1762 he took a small parish where seven or eight older persons communed and by patient teaching built a congregation of nine hundred. Sometimes he had one thousand at a Holy Communion service when many non-Anglicans came to receive. Jarratt was rather shabbily treated by his colleagues but served the church well until his death in 1801.

In 1680 Virginia had forty-eight parishes served by thirty-five ministers. By 1786, when the church was disestablished by the Statute of Virginia for Religious Freedom, there were ninety-five organized parishes and a dozen or more nominal parishes. The rapid rise of the previously restrained Nonconformists after 1786 and the growing spirit of revolt against England proved a severe test for that most agreeably mellow form of Anglicanism in Virginia.

III

BEYOND VIRGINIA
IN THE SOUTH

MARYLAND

Maryland, named for Queen Henrietta Maria, was granted to Sir George Calvert, who died in April, 1632, before the charter and patent could be issued. Within two months the grant was completed to his son Cecil Calvert, Lord Baltimore, who like his father was a Roman Catholic. Although the new colony, which approximated the present boundaries of the state, was a proprietary one, there was the limiting clause in the charter which required conformity to the laws of England and government by the consent of the colonists. Intent on providing a haven in the New World for persecuted Roman Catholics, Lord Baltimore was astute enough to know that to succeed commercially his colony would have to depend largely on Protestant settlers.

Three Jesuit priests arrived on the first ships, which brought about twenty gentlemen and two hundred laborers to Maryland in March, 1634, but no Protestant clergyman came to the mainland of the colony for sixteen years. Soon after their arrival in the first settlement at St. Mary's, however, some devoted laymen built a chapel where they conducted Prayer Book services. Vainly seeking to preserve his charter under the Commonwealth, Lord Baltimore appointed a Protestant governor who, by 1649, had legally guaranteed that any person believing in Jesus Christ would have free exercise of his own religion. When the Rev. William Wilkinson, then fifty years of age, brought his family and servants to this colony in 1650, he still found so little support for the church that it became necessary to resort to business and his plantation to provide an adequate living.

The religious conflicts were not easily resolved in those early years in Maryland. There was no toleration for non-Christians, and the natural hostility between the religious parties, inherited from the homeland, frequently broke down the legal restraints. By an act of October, 1654, Roman Catholics were forbidden to practice their faith and denied protection under the laws. Seldom was violence involved, but name-calling and vituperative language left no doubt about the lack of mutual Christian respect. Many Roman Catholics sent their children abroad for an education. A generation later, on May 25,

1676, one of the three Anglican clergymen in the province wrote Archbishop Sheldon of Canterbury that religion was at a low ebb and that they were unable to minister adequately to the 20,000 souls in the ten or twelve more populous counties. The Roman Catholics by this time had provided for their people, but no attention was given to the development of Protestantism. Even though the Protestants outnumbered the Roman Catholics and the Quakers, each of whom could claim about one-twelfth of the population, a letter written to the Bishop of London on September 12, 1689, reported that "this church, which by charter should be consecrated according to the ecclesiastical laws of England, was converted to the use of popish idolatry."

Taking advantage of the aroused anti-Catholic feeling and other unsettling effects of the Glorious Revolution back home, the more numerous Protestants, under the leadership of John Coode, gathered in a self-styled "convention," seized the government of the province, and appealed to the new king. In June, 1691, William acceded to their request, withdrew the charter, and Maryland became a Crown colony until 1715 when it was restored to the Calverts, who meanwhile had become Protestants. With the arrival of Sir Lionel Copley, the first royal governor, the inviolability of the rights and franchises of the church was established, ten counties were divided into thirty parishes, a constitution for vestries was provided, and a poll tax of forty pounds of tobacco was ordered to provide a fund for the repairing of churches, the support of the clergy, and other pious uses.

Until the arrival of Sir Francis Nicholson, Copley's successor, in July, 1694, there were still but three Church of England clergy, who had "made a hard shift to live" and after marriage were able to "maintain their families out of the plantations [probably the glebes] they had with their cures." Meanwhile, six priests were serving the far fewer Roman Catholics. Governor Nicholson, whose influence for the church might have been greater had his life been more in keeping with her holy teachings, nevertheless brought with him six new ministers and settled them in the new parishes. He began the erection of the only brick church in the colony at Annapolis, the new Maryland capital, and also opened a free school there "to make learning an handmaid to devotion." Even he seemed amazed by the lax standards in his colony where he found "sabbath breaking, cursing, swearing and profane talking: some of the men have two wives and some of the women two husbands; whoring and drinking, especially the last, were too much practised in the country and seldom any were punished for those sins. Few schools and those very mean ones either for number or house." The governor was so much concerned for the welfare of his people that in one epidemic he sent Bibles to the sick and appointed readers to visit them.

Governor Nicholson sought to establish the religion of England in 1694 and 1695, but probably because the Roman Catholics and Quakers opposed it, the King in Council on January 4, 1696, disallowed such articles of establishment, and it would be another six years before the governor's wish could be accomplished. Realizing now more than ever the need for proper supervision of their churches in the colony, the clergy, supported by the governor and the Assembly, sent a petition to the Bishop of London calling attention to "the great and urgent necessity of an ecclesiastical rule here . . . to redress what is amiss, and to supply what is wanting in the church."

A commissary was the logical answer to this request, and in April, 1696, Bishop Compton appointed Dr. Thomas Bray, a successful clergyman and writer, then forty years of age. Delayed for almost four years before he could set foot in Maryland, Bray was able during this period to increase the number of the clergy there to sixteen. When he discovered that these candidates were all poor men who could not acquire adequate libraries for themselves, he immediately set about supplying this need.

In 1698, Bray founded the Society for Promoting Christian Knowledge (hereafter referred to as SPCK) to provide libraries for his own and the other colonies as well as for parishes in England and other parts of the empire. Supported by two archbishops and twelve bishops, Bray and his Society were able to send lending libraries to cities for public use, to parishes for the edification of their members, and to ministers for their private study. Bray felt that each clergyman should have at his disposal no less than £50 worth of books, which in its modern equivalent would have meant an investment of several thousand dollars. The annual report of 1769 shows that by that time about 5,500 books had been given to lending and parochial libraries in English dioceses. In Maryland alone thirty libraries were stocked with approximately 2,500 volumes, and about 1,600 books were sent to the neighboring colonies of Virginia, New York, Pennsylvania, and the Carolinas as well as to Bermuda. The 1795 report indicates that besides these libraries Bray had sent into America about 34,000 additional books and tracts for distribution and had also founded sixty-seven Lending and Catechetical Libraries in England and Wales and sixteen on the Isle of Man.

In the approximately fifty libraries Bray founded in America the gifts ranged from 1,095 books to the library at Annapolis to ten at Albany, New York. Lest these tools which Bray valued so highly be abused or lost, he held the clergy responsible, on pain of personal payment, for all books in the clerical and parochial libraries. The Society once deducted £10 from the salary of the Rev. Mr. Vaughan to pay for the losses of books for which he was responsible. Bray advised that in the case of embezzled books due legal process would bring treble damages and recover the cost of the suit. Nor was he above obtaining warrants from the justices of the peace to search for any lost library books.

Through Bray's interest one gift of £900 from Mr. D'Alone, private secretary to King William, was invested in capital funds from which the income was set aside "for converting the Negroes in the British plantations." Since the work of catechists among adult Negroes proved impractical, the Associates, as those who assisted Bray in the work among the Negroes were called, applied the funds to the instruction of Negro children. The report of the Bray Associates for 1795 includes a full-page diagram describing such a school in Halifax in which forty-one children from five to sixteen years of age were under the instruction of Deborah Clark for six months. Listed are the names of the children and their parents, their age, the books they were using, and the crafts (sewing, knitting, etc.) they pursued.

During the prolonged period before Bray was able to undertake his new post in America, he wrote circular letters to his clergy in Maryland asking them to try to organize their work and improve the churches and the conditions of the parishes before his arrival. He also reassured them, in turn, that he would do all he could on his arrival; he would visit their parishes and help to improve church attendance. In March, 1700, Bray finally appeared in Maryland and immediately set about his inspection and arranging for his annual visitation, which took place in Annapolis on May 23, 1700. The new commissary was hardly prepared for his varied administrative tasks. These involved not only the general supervision of the Maryland churches but even on his first visitation he had to discipline a priest and frankly discuss the morality of his clergy and its effects in the formative early years. With all their own needs so evident Bray nevertheless lent his authority and support to send applicants as missionaries in Pennsylvania and North Carolina and led his colleagues in contributing generously to send an additional missionary among the Quakers in Pennsylvania.

During his first brief visit, Bray had discreetly guided through the Maryland Assembly a law establishing Anglican worship according to the Book of Common Prayer as the standard for the province. Since the visitation had been completed, his clergy urged him to go to England and take the law to the king and speak in its defense. When all conflicts with the 1689 Act of Toleration had been removed, it was approved and Anglicanism was finally established in Maryland in 1702.

Scarcely had Bray returned to England when he wrote another circular letter to his clergy in which he reiterated their decisions when assembled for his recent visitation and especially urged them to supply the deficiency of preaching and to lend and disperse good books. That the church in England might know the status of the churches in the colonies Bray wrote his report, showing seventeen clergymen in sparsely settled parishes with livings of about £25 or £30, although in a few of the better parishes salaries were about three times that amount. By this period the Romanists still remained about one-twelfth of the population, but the Quakers had now grown to be no less than one-tenth. He felt that Maryland alone needed forty mission priests qualified by strength, learning, and youth. Bray had sold his own properties, paid all his expenses to America, and refused reimbursement. Officially his latter years were spent in a parish in England, but much of his time and effort were given to the continuation of the work of his societies.

One of his greatest achievements was the charter granted by the king on June 16, 1701, establishing the Society for the Propagation of the Gospel in Foreign Parts (hereafter referred to as SPG). In part, its aims overlapped those of the SPCK, but the new society was primarily concerned about providing funds to send missionaries to the English settlers in America and also to the Negroes and Indians there. As early as its second year the SPG considered the appointment of a suffragan bishop for America and sought for a promise of his consecration from the Scottish bishops, of whom only six aged men remained, who probably preferred not to have a part in such a new venture.

From 1702 until 1783 the SPG sent 309 ordained missionaries to the thirteen colonies. Assistance was also sent to 202 central mission stations, and some successful work was carried on among the Indians and Negroes, all at a cost of some £227,454, or about one million dollars with a modern equivalent of at least ten times that sum.

After Bray's return to England, Maryland Anglicans had waited patiently until 1716 when two commissaries arrived, one for the eastern and the other for the western shore, but they never proved very effective in times of increasing secularism and sectarianism. Presbyterians and other denominations won an increasing proportion of the population in the east, while the middle and western frontier areas were captured by the German Anabaptists, Lutherans, Reformed, and the Huguenots. Sufficient life and strength remained among the Anglicans, however, to survive the Revolution and to provide active leadership and support at the establishment of the Protestant Episcopal Church in the United States of America in 1789.

THE CAROLINAS

A temporary settlement lasting less than a year was begun at the present Charleston, South Carolina, on Maundy Thursday, April 19, 1660, by a group of colonists from Virginia under the promotion of Governor Berkeley. The Good Friday prayers and the Easter Communion celebrated by Chaplain Morgan Jones were the first Prayer Book services in the Carolinas. Pressed by hunger and the threats of neighboring natives, the colony disbanded and fled to the wilderness where most of them were captured by the Indians; Jones escaped and later served several parishes on Long Island.

The unexplored areas south of Virginia were assigned by royal charter to Edward, Earl of Clarendon, and seven noble associates on March 24, 1663, and a revised charter subsequently limited the grant approximately to the present borders of the Carolinas. In keeping with the pattern of such royal grants, the proprietors were required to obtain the consent of the freedmen of the colony in support of all legislation and were urged to provide religious toleration. The "Fundamental Constitutions," drafted for the proprietors in 1689 by Lord Ashley Cooper, the chief proprietor, and the distinguished philosopher John Locke, were so complex as to be impractical, but they did provide that "the Church of England, which being the only true and orthodox, and the national, church of the king's dominions, is so also of Carolina."

The Charleston community was favored in its growth by its advantageous location at the junction of the Ashley and Cooper Rivers, its good climate and soil, and the fact that its settlers from the beginning were of the substantial sort. Immigrants came from other colonies, from England and the Barbadoes, and among them were Scotch-Irish Presbyterians and French Huguenots who arrived in large numbers after the Revocation of the Edict of Nantes in 1685.

The first church building, erected in 1681–1682 on a prominent high spot designated in the original design drawn by the proprietors, was built of black cypress on a brick foundation. When this church proved to be too small, the Assembly passed an act on March 1, 1711, providing for the erection of a brick structure on the present site of St. Philip's Church on Church Street. Forty years later when the town was divided into two parishes in 1751, all of Charleston south of Broad Street became St. Michael's parish and a new church bearing that name was built on the present site.

Charleston was not most favored by the quality of its earliest clergymen. Although Atkin Williamson was the first Anglican clergyman in the parish and appears to have been there as early as 1680, his character was apparently not above reproach, and he was never accepted as a regular minister. Samuel Marshall arrived in 1696 and two years later was chosen the first rector in Charleston at a salary of £150. The adequate remuneration was worth perhaps £100 sterling but had much lower purchasing power, probably less than half, in comparison to English standards. Generous provision for the clergy, in contrast to the less favorable support in other colonies, guaranteed the church in South Carolina an adequate leadership and helped it to advance and preserve its strength through the century.

On the death of Marshall in an epidemic of yellow fever at the close of 1699 the governor and council asked Henry Compton, Bishop of London, to send another of equal qualifications for

> he by his regular, sober and devout life gave no advantage to the enemies of our Church to speak ill of its ministers; by his sound doctrine the weak sons of our church he confirmed; by his easy, and, as it were, natural use of the ceremonies of our Church, he took away all occasions of scandal at them; by his prudent and obliging way of living, and manner of practice, he had gained the esteem of all persons.

In Edward Marston, Marshall's successor who arrived in 1700, Governor Nathaniel Johnson and those who would keep the dissenters from control found an advocate of exactly the opposite opinions. He was especially violent in his open opposition to a law enacted in 1704 requiring all persons elected to the Assembly to take the Oath of Allegiance and Supremacy. St. Philip's Church, once so well attended, seemed "almost wholly deserted," yet Marston continued, even after the withholding of his salary, until November, 1704. He was finally removed by a board of law commissioners appointed by the legislature in keeping with another law that permitted such a commission to remove ministers on the complaint of their vestries together with any nine aggrieved parishioners. Although he probably never knew it, this law had been enacted to care for his particular case. Despite this humiliation, Marston remained in the colony, pursued his case, and continued to raise a disturbance. In consideration of his family the Assembly voted £150 to his wife, and even this failed to quiet him. In October, 1709, he was prosecuted as a common disturber of the governor and the government, but it was not until 1712 that he finally left the colony.

The troubles in St. Philip's were not over, for Marston's successor, although very affable, proved to be a fugitive clergyman from Maryland with dubious authority. He claimed that his ordination papers had been blown overboard by the wind while he was drying them after a storm. So well intrenched was he within the first year that Gideon Johnson, appointed by the Bishop of London as the first commissary for South Carolina, found it difficult to displace him even after unmasking the culprit. Even after Johnson assumed the rectorship of St. Philip's, it was not easy for him to win the good will of those parishioners who had been hoodwinked by the impostor.

Another able clergyman in this colony, Samuel Thomas, became a missionary among the Yamassee Indians, who had once been converted by Spanish Catholic missionaries and more recently had reverted to heathenism. He also served at the Goose Creek Parish, about eighteen miles from Charleston, where one of the finest examples of a colonial church would soon be erected.

Francis Le Jau continued Thomas's work with only modest success among the Indians, who, having been cheated frequently by whites, had turned warlike. Le Jau worked much more successfully among the Negroes of the colony, and most of the clergy recorded serious efforts to give religious guidance among the colored people. As the number of slaves in the colony increased and became the majority of the population, many masters, being generally of the opinion that a slave grows worse by becoming a Christian, tried to prevent the clergy from instructing them for fear that, in being brought together in such large numbers, they might observe their own strength and so might be tempted to recover their liberty.

The argument so often used by the southern slaveholders that education would make the Negro unruly, dissatisfied with his status, and therefore unwilling to work had arisen earlier in the West Indies and would appear later wherever anyone proposed such helpful steps for Negroes in the colonies.[1] Exactly the same arguments were being used in England in this period to oppose education for the poor whites who would thereby be made presumptuous and unruly.[2]

In 1711, William Fleetwood, Bishop of St. Asaph, preached a remarkable sermon before the SPG at its annual meeting in which he declared that Negroes had potentially the same intellectual powers as whites, that they were in no way inferior, and that they would work for wages. He conceded that baptism did not free a slave but quickly added that slavery was not justified. This sermon was printed in thousands of copies and widely circulated in the colonies, but most English people still believed in the racial inferiority of the Negro mind. Serious Christians asked missionaries whether Negroes could be educated. Even some of the missionaries themselves reported that the Society should realize "that few of them [Negroes] are capable of being instructed." Joseph Ottolenghe, a catechist to Negroes in Georgia, wrote the Society on September 9, 1751, that "in general they [Negroes] are slow of apprehension, of a dull understanding, and soon forgetting what they have learned." In 1741 Abel Alleyne, who admired the good conduct of the Negroes, wrote that it is difficult for many black men to understand the principles of education.[3]

Le Jau complained that his own financial problems, which often required living on Indian corn bread and water with the luxury of milk and fresh meat once a week, were partly related to the fact that he was buying three Negroes on the installment plan and that together they did no more than one English maid would accomplish. The missionaries of the SPG were torn between the purposes of their sponsoring society and the desires of their parishioners. Some clarification was accomplished by June 7, 1712, when an act was passed by the Assembly declaring that any slaves, Negro or Indian, may profess the Christian religion and be baptized but that they shall not thereby be manumitted or set free nor shall their owners thereby lose their civil right, property, and authority over such slaves.

Taking advantage of the confusion during a bloodless revolt led by Colonel Moore against the proprietary government in 1719, the king withdrew the charter and appointed the veteran Sir Francis Nicholson to rule the Crown colony and to care adequately for the affairs of the Church of England. A church school founded by the SPG in 1711 continued to provide for an education in the Latin and Greek languages and the faith of the Church of England.

The year 1719 also marked the arrival of the Rev. Alexander Garden, the new rector of St. Philip's Church, who in 1726 became the last of a line of commissaries. For twenty-three years he served in this dual capacity, ruling amiably but firmly, probably because the new Bishop of London, Edmund Gibson, recently translated from the See of Lincoln, was himself a precise and strict administrator. Reports to the bishop indicated a wide variety in the worship but great regularity in the conduct of services and in attendance throughout the colony. Holy Communion was usually observed four times a year beyond the city, but Garden celebrated in Charleston once a month.

The new commissary was also concerned with the affairs of the church in neighboring provinces and must have helped John Wesley in Georgia, who records his indebtedness to Garden "for many kind and generous offices." Wesley was also impressed with the commissary's annual visitation, which he attended in Charleston in 1737. When George Whitefield first came to Charleston, Garden received him courteously, entertained him in his rectory, and asked him to preach in St. Philip's Church. In the friendship that developed Garden promised Whitefield that if ever he were mistreated as John Wesley had been by the arbitrary actions of the vestry in Savannah he would defend the evangelist "with his life and fortune."

But fate and probably growing diversity of opinions and practice soon compelled Garden to choose between friendship and administrative duties. On Whitefield's second visit to Charleston, Garden was absent, and his curate could not invite Whitefield to preach in St. Philip's. Whitefield accordingly preached at least once in the Huguenot church nearby and three times in dissenting churches. Charleston had become a center of wealth, supplying the popular Whitefield with generous gifts for his Bethesda Orphanage, and large congregations gathered each time he preached. His meetings were now exclusively held in the free churches, even though he occasionally attended worship at St. Philip's. For violating a canon which required conformity to the Book of Common Prayer Garden was finally compelled on April 9, 1742, to suspend Whitefield from the office of the ministry, "being a vagabond clergyman having no Benefice to be suspended from." A flurry of pamphlets from each side did little to clear the issues, which everyone knew involved not merely conformity but the very freedom by which Methodism was soon to become the leading representative of the Christian faith on the expanding western frontiers.

The church in South Carolina had grown to be one of the most favorable situations of the Church of England in America but not without regular opposition from the leaders of other faiths. It was established and guaranteed support by taxation in 1709 but by a majority of only one vote. At no point did the members of the Church of England exceed more than one-half of the population; yet what they lacked in numbers and extension they provided in strength and depth of understanding. The achievements of the church in South Carolina far exceeded those in North Carolina and Georgia because the church people here were deeply interested and were willing to work; they also had the means to support the church and provided for education through the church school and by tutors "that educate their youth à-la-mode."

John Lawson, an Englishman who visited South Carolina in 1700, described the South Carolinians as a "genteel Sort of People" who were "fair frank traders" and had the money and the skill to develop great estates where herds of one thousand to two thousand cattle were not unusual. Thriving settlements grew up near the rich mines and the areas where naval stores were produced. South Carolina's products brought premium prices in Europe and the West Indies because of their quality, neat packing, and careful shipping. This colony had the best militia in America, well mounted and as resplendent in their scarlet uniforms and as well trained as most of the Crown regiments. Although these colonists generally were on the best of terms with the Indians, they defeated the French and the Spanish and once burned St. Augustine and captured the cattle of the Spaniards. Lawson seemed surprised but pleased that all religious groups enjoyed "entire Liberty of Worship" based on the "Constitution of this Government, allowing all Parties of well meaning Christians to enjoy a free Toleration, and possess the same Priviledges, so long as they appear to behave themselves peaceably and well."[4]

Clergy salaries were advanced to £200, and by 1756 this colony no longer needed the support of the SPG. Their church buildings showed considerable variety, ranging from the traditional altar-centered apse to St. Philip's Church with its pulpit prominently set out near the center aisle and the fine old Goose Creek Church with a free-standing raised center pulpit fronted by a communion table on the floor level. Such variety of worship with a strongly social centered concern made its natural appeal to dissenters so that numerous Swiss Reformed and even Presbyterians conformed to the church. The Huguenots requested ministers from the SPG and issued and continued to use their own liturgies with only slight variations from the 1662 Prayer Book.[5]

By the time of the Revolution, South Carolina had a population of about 45,000 whites and 80,000 Negroes concentrated in the eastern tidewater region. Widely scattered large plantations appeared in the middle Piedmont region with its rolling hills, while fewer settlers were scattered in the western mountainous areas. Charleston had become one of the leading cities in America, and most of the religious life and effort was concentrated in the city and tidewater area.

A striking exception was the missionary work of Charles Woodmason, a devoted magistrate who had lived for three years in the Piedmont where he had seen the great need for the church. He was ordained in 1766 by the Bishop of London who sent him into the Carolina back country where he served until the approach of the Revolutionary War.[6] Woodmason was a most unusual type of man to serve as a missionary so far from the stimulation of the English culture he loved so well. When he came to South Carolina to become a planter and a merchant, he left behind him in Gosport a circle of literary friends to whom he wrote descriptive poetry calling the roll of the South Carolina rivers and hills. His poetical epistle of seventy-eight lines written as a tribute to Benjamin Franklin's experiments and discoveries in electricity was written on the Cooper River, South Carolina, in 1753, more than a decade before his ordination, and is now considered to possess genuine literary merit.[7] It is probable that Woodmason's sympathies were with the loyalists, for he left South Carolina in 1770, presumably to return to England where he must have been happy to rejoin his literary circle.

As in all other aspects of its development, the work of the churches in North Carolina lagged far behind that in South Carolina and other neighboring colonies. Even in the functioning of the government the northern Carolina region long remained dependent on the more populous and prosperous southern part of the original province. These colonies existed separately after 1713, and by 1729 North Carolina had come under royal control. The population was largely a migrant one, and many small groups of markedly diverse religious affiliations moved in from adjacent areas. Among these people there was not one clergyman of the Church of England.

When reports of these conditions reached London shortly after 1700, a grant by Lord Weymouth enabled the SPG to send John Blair as their missionary to survey the situation. He found the Quakers and Presbyterians predominating, but those who were zealous for the Church of England were so few that he became discouraged. He baptized about one hundred children, organized vestries, appointed lay readers where he could, and then returned to England hoping to stimulate this work by laying its needs before the Society.

At intervals, beginning in 1708 and through the first quarter of the century, the Society sent out men in pairs, but at best they were able to do little but replace the preceding team amidst the futilities of frontier religious confusion. The Rev. John Urmston came to North Carolina in 1711 and the Rev. Giles Rainsford in the following year. Urmston's letters to the Society vividly depict the hardships the missionary's life involved. He had been promised a house and £100 a year but had received only £30 in five years. While he and his family were "in manifest danger of perishing for want of food," he wrote in July, 1711, "we have lived many a day only on a dry crust and a draught of salt water out of the Sound. . . ." Rainsford, who wrote, "My lodging for the best of my time in this government was in an old tobacco house, and exposed, even in my bed, to the injuries and violence of bad weather," abandoned his mission in 1714.

One notable exception was the record of Clement Hall, who traveled 14,000 miles in eight years, preached 675 sermons, and baptized 6,026 children, 243 of whom were Negroes, and 169 adults, of whom 112 were Negroes. On October 16, 1751, Hall made his report of the previous year and told of traveling 557 miles in thirty-six days during which he preached twenty-five sermons to large congregations, churched 146 well-disposed women, gave the Sacrament to 242 communicants, and baptized 536 whites and twenty Negroes of whom two were adults.[8]

The clergy allowance for these years of the mid-century was £30, and not until the administration of Governor Tryon in 1765 was the Church of England legally established in the colony and a law enacted setting the salaries at £133, with permission to sue for nonpayment. These new contracts required clergy to keep their parsonages and glebes in good repair and left them dependent upon the governor for their appointments and examination of character. Both the laity and the clergy objected to such civil intrusion, and although the clergy roster at one time reached eighteen, it was soon to dwindle again with the approaching Revolution so that Anglicanism remained a minor factor in the ever more diversified religious life of North Carolina.

Writing on August 30, 1775, one missionary said:

> The situation of the clergy in this part of the world is truly critical. . . . Some of them have been suspended, deprived of their salaries, and in the American manner, proscribed by committees, . . . and all this on account of charges against them of opposing the general cause of America. . . . I verily believe that, if the most learned and eloquent divine in England were to endeavor to dissuade the Americans from their present resolution, he would make no impression upon them. . . .[9]

Meanwhile Presbyterians, Lutherans, Methodists, German Reformed, and Moravians became more numerous, multiplied their churches, and laid foundations that soon would make possible the building of church colleges to support their work.

GEORGIA

If ever a philanthropic motivation prompted a settlement in America it was certainly true of Georgia, the thirteenth colony, for here General James E. Oglethorpe and his associates planned to provide a home for English debtors who would otherwise languish in jail indefinitely. The charter obtained from George II in June, 1732, provided religious liberty for all Protestants. That first company, which arrived in early February, 1733, and settled near Savannah, chosen by General Oglethorpe as the center for the colony, was composed of thirty-five carefully selected families including about 125 "sober, industrious and moral persons." Although persons of lesser integrity were soon to appear on these shores, the charitable purposes of the proprietors and the plan for an established church in a pious colony were quite obvious. Georgia's first chaplain, Henry Herbert, brought Bibles, Prayer Books, Psalters, Catechisms, and a religious library, but after a stay of only three months he died on a voyage back to England. The SPG sent his successor, Samuel Quincy, to Savannah in May, 1733. In the process of building a manse, in which a vacant room served as the place of worship, and in beginning his work, he apparently found so much interference from the governor that he also returned to England in October, 1735, having found Georgia "a mere scene of distress."

That the proprietors of Georgia retained their religious motivation is clearly evident in a folio manuscript in the Harvard College Library showing an accounting of all the monies spent by them in the early 1730's. Their concern for the evangelization of the Indians appears in an entry on June, 1735, showing that Sir John Austin had given a Bible in the New England Indian language (John Eliot's translation) that was sent with Robert Hucks to Georgia on board the *Simond* in October that year. To facilitate the work among the numerous German settlers, ten German grammars were sent on the same ship, a 1605 edition of Luther's German translation of the Bible having been sent the previous January. Less conspicuous but probably of much greater usefulness in 1735 was an anonymous gift of one quarto Bible, one quarto Book of Common Prayer, 20 smaller Bibles, 25 New Testaments, 50 smaller Prayer Books, 125 devotional books, 100 hornbooks, 100 primers, and 100 copies of the *A B C with the Church Catechism*.

Despite the early discouraging reports the church was not without competent leadership, for on March 7, 1736, John Wesley had begun his ministry in Savannah. These were the formative years for both Wesley and the colony. Vainly had he sought presentation at Epworth in England to succeed his father, the Rev. Samuel Wesley, who gave the original pewter chalice and paten to the Georgia colony and who died April 15, 1735. On the commendation of Dr. Burton, president of Corpus Christi College, Oxford, and one of the Georgia trustees, Oglethorpe had invited Wesley to his colony. Following the advice of his mother, his brother, Samuel and William Law, the mystic whom he greatly admired, John Wesley and his brother Charles cast their fortunes with the church in the Georgia colony. Charles remained only four months in his parish at Frederica until Oglethorpe lost patience with the young missionary's ill-timed zeal in requiring baptism by immersion and the beatings of the drum four times a day to call to worship.

John Wesley, despite his Holy Club associations at Oxford, was a rigid high churchman who nevertheless used every opportunity which the youthful energy of his thirty-two years permitted to offer his ministry as widely as possible. He occasionally visited his brother's former parish in Frederica and restored daily prayers there, even though these visits required long periods without food and sometimes sleeping outdoors at night. Wesley continued his unquenchable love for learning by studying French and German so that he could conduct services in these languages among the Huguenots and Moravians whom he had learned to admire for their piety. He studied Spanish, he said, "in order to converse with my Jewish parishioners, some of whom were nearer to the mind that was in Christ than many of those who call Him Lord." Occasionally after Evening Prayer he would gather the more thoughtful of his parishioners for prayer and praise and at one such meeting read "an exhortation of Ephraim Syrus, the most awakening writer (I think) of all the ancients."[10]

With all his employment the youthful missionary found it possible to court Sophia Hopkey, the chief magistrate's charming niece, for whom, he admitted in his *Journal* on March 7, 1737, he "should have forgot the work for which I was born, and have set my rest in this world." But on March 8, just exactly one year after John had spoken to "poor Miss Sophy," she was married to William Williamson, who, Wesley said, was not remarkable for greatness, wit, knowledge, sense, and least of all for religion.

Well might Wesley have remembered the words of advice given him by Dr. Burton of Oxford, that he would find in America "abundant room for the exercise of patience and prudence as well as piety." Imprudently he reproved Sophia for improper conduct, probably for gaiety in spirit and dress, and a month later excluded her from the Holy Communion. Accordingly, William Williamson brought suit for defamation of character and damages of £1,000. After indictment by a grand jury on ten of twelve counts the trial was many times postponed and ultimately evaded, but Wesley, both impatiently and imprudently, refused any compromise that might have brought reconciliation. Fewer and fewer persons came to the church services, and the inevitable conclusion became obvious when, on November 23, Wesley placed an announcement in the town square, "Whereas John Wesley designs shortly to set out for England, this is to desire those who have borrowed any books of him, to return them as soon as they conveniently can to John Wesley." After a year and nine months John Wesley sailed from Charleston on December 22, 1737, in the company of Moravians by whom he was to be greatly influenced and in whose meeting in Aldersgate Chapel in London he would soon have "his heart strangely warmed."

As the ship bearing Wesley came into the Downs, it passed another going out and bearing the young George Whitefield, then only a deacon but another missionary of the venerable Society, about to begin his long and influential ministry in America. With his reading of "Publick Prayers in the parsonage-house" at Savannah on Monday, May 8, 1738, at five o'clock in the morning, he began his distinguished career in the New World. By the end of the year Whitefield returned to England where he received priest's orders on January 14, 1739, from Bishop Benson of Gloucester. Many times he would make that voyage across the Atlantic in order to gather funds in England for his projects in Georgia to which he gave his personal attention. In America he divided his time between his Bethesda Orphanage in Georgia, where he clearly expressed his intention to have the religious services in strict conformity with the liturgy of the Church of England, and his evangelistic preaching and participation in the religious awakening that was stirring the churches from Georgia to New England. Although usually associated with the Methodists in the later years, Whitefield, like John Wesley, never left the Church of England and to his death remained a communicant of the church.

After Whitefield's brief incumbency in Christ Church, Savannah, his most distinguished successor was Bartholomew Zouberbühler, whose father was the pastor among the Swiss Reformed in Purrysburg. After a thorough classical English education and exposure to the Church of England in Charleston, young Zouberbühler sought orders in England and was back in Georgia by January 22, 1746. For about twenty years he ministered widely in the province but especially in Savannah where he brought the building of Christ Church to completion ten years after it had been begun on June 11, 1740. While writing about the beauty of his commodious church in 1750, Zouberbühler seemed as much or more impressed that his parishioners were constant in their attendance, and he added, "I have the pleasure to see many Negroes decently join our service." He reported a general increase in religion and that about forty Negroes were under his Christian instruction. On his death he left a bequest to support a schoolmaster for members of the black race.

In 1764 the Rev. Samuel Frink, a recently ordained Harvard graduate, sailed from Boston to Charleston and filled the vacancy in Augusta, Georgia, where he said he found 540 whites, 501 Negro slaves, and about 90 Chickasaw Indians but that they were largely the lower class of people who had little religion and that public worship was kept up principally by a few gentlemen and their families. In 1767 Frink moved to Savannah where, on July 8, 1771, just three months before his death, he wrote the SPG that Savannah had 1,996 inhabitants of whom 1,185 were of the Church of England, 193 Lutherans, 449 Presbyterians and Independents, 49 Jews, 40 Negroes, and 30 infidels. His successor, Edward Ellington, reported that while serving in Augusta he had traveled three thousand miles, baptized 428 persons, and raised the number of communicants from seven to nearly forty.

Until the Revolution, however, Savannah and Augusta remained the only centers where the Church of England had continuous services, and these parishes were 150 miles apart. The former had become a desirable living with a salary of about £500, but the appropriations by the assembly for each of the missionaries among the six thousand or more inhabitants scattered in eight parishes was only £25 a year with here and there a little supplementary income from the SPG.

In a survey of the work of the Church of England in Virginia and the other southern colonies before the Revolution it becomes clear that a lack of an aggressive program allowed much of the religious life and thought in this region to be directed by non-Anglicans. Their strongly evangelical and missionary spirit at times was favorably reflected in the Anglican churches. The prominence of the freemen in the government of all these colonies led also to a significant new place for the laity in the structure of the church. At times, as in Virginia, it brought the danger of oligarchical control by the vestries, and again, as in North Carolina, it left the appointment and supervision of the clergy to the governor.

All attempts to adapt the English system to America failed because of the lack of the authority and tradition which bishops might have supplied. The commissaries sent by the Bishop of London at the turn to the eighteenth century acted for the bishop in holding visitations and supervising the work of the church. While they were empowered to discipline the clergy and even to suspend their orders, they were never able to ordain candidates for orders or even to confirm the faithful. They had all the powers that sufficed to restrain the church but no authority to infuse it with life or to give direction to the new adolescent nation growing toward responsible political maturity.

Equally unsuccessful was the attempt by young idealists, zealous for the declaration and overt practical application of the gospel to colonial life, to adapt the Church of England to the American scene. Men like Wesley and Whitefield in Georgia and Devereux Jarratt in Virginia, without episcopal oversight, tried too quickly and too radically to throw off the restraints of Anglican tradition and customary practices in order to help the hapless colonial people achieve and sustain a practical way of Christian living. Too quickly and too completely they succumbed to the informalities and unrestrained religious excesses of frontier living that were daily temptations to those who sought the good will of their people so that, having won their confidence, they might lead them on into the understanding and appreciation of genuine religious values. For another century this would be the pattern of religious innovations along the frontier, slowly moving westward along the irregular lines of rivers and mountains. During this century, these migrant people would establish their congregations and even their denominations with varying degrees of stability in the beginning and with fluctuating standards of order and worship as the communities grew until the vast majority of the people of America would be found in these free churches.

Because of its English connection and its characteristic innate restraint, the

Church of England was slow in making these necessary adjustments to the needs of frontier life. Had the episcopacy been granted at an earlier date, this church might indeed have become a major factor in sparing this country the extremities that resulted from inadequately directed enthusiasm on the part of many of the early clergy and laity on the one hand and from an inadequately disciplined supervision on the other. The creative fusion of the inherited Christian traditions of more than seventeen centuries with the early American religious zeal and the exciting new lay participation in the life and work of the church after the Revolution would provide a matrix in which Anglicanism could be reborn in America and where the old values would provide the continuing life for the new church in this new land.

IV

THE CHURCH IN
MASSACHUSETTS

Although a score or more attempts had been made to settle on the shores of New England, it remained for the arrival of the Pilgrims in 1620 and the Puritans in 1628 and 1630 to establish the two permanent colonies that would be merged to become a Puritan oligarchy in the New World with more effective and lasting influence than Cromwell's Commonwealth.

Following the Reformation in England, two dissident groups persistently raised their voices in protest against the moderation of these reforms. The Puritans always remained within the church as a loyal opposition party working for the further purification of the church from all Roman Catholic associations. By the seventeenth century they had become a strong and stable party with fixed partisan convictions and were well supported by families of power and means.

When Charles I dissolved Parliament in 1629 and decided to rule by his own authority, the administration of ecclesiastical affairs was entrusted to the very capable but equally autocratic William Laud, Bishop of London, who four years later became the Archbishop of Canterbury. This militant High Church prelate immediately inaugurated a decade of strenuous opposition to and severe punishment for all dissenters so that some of the most able Puritan leaders and thousands of their supporters left England to come to the Massachusetts Bay colony.

Desiring similar ends, the second group of dissidents sought, nevertheless, by separation and the more radical procedures patterned after the continental reformers to correct the errors and to make amends for the default of the church. By the turn to the seventeenth century these Separatists, who commonly followed the ideas of Robert Browne, were themselves divided and sought to perfect their varied ideals in several religious settlements in Holland. At Leiden they were highly respected and are still remembered; their church building has become a part of the university library, and John Robinson, their minister, is memorialized by a prominent plaque in the St. Pieterskerk. Unable to secure a stable livelihood and fearing the dilution of their purposes and the loss of the identity of their families by intermarriage with the Dutch, most of them returned to England with the avowed hope to try another experiment in Virginia.

In England the village of Scrooby, just off the Great North Road, became their chief settlement. Here lived William Brewster, who would become their successful leader and the designer of the Plymouth adventure. Because of the insistence on separation from the Church of England they were called Separatists; because of their wanderings to Holland and then to America they were called Pilgrims; and because they sailed from Plymouth where the company was based their settlement came to be known as the Plymouth colony.

Given largely to simplicity in their social and religious life, these Pilgrims, under the capable leadership of William Bradford, spent most of their first decade in acquiring clear titles to their lands by discharging their contractual obligations to the merchants who had sponsored their voyage. The Compact that they drafted for the government of the new land, which they could see as the *Mayflower* lay in Plymouth harbor, has come to be regarded as a milestone in democratic government. The Separatists placed little emphasis on education and so provided an atmosphere in which feelings and prejudices could easily be fanned to disproportionate importance. For less than sufficient reasons the Anglican Thomas Morton was driven from the colony. While Separatism was rigidly enforced and there was little toleration of any sign of attachment to the Church of England, it was, nevertheless, in this colony that Roger Williams spent some time, and here John Eliot served as a minister while he carried on his missions among the Indians and provided for them a grammar of their Algonquin language and, by 1661, a complete Bible, which he had translated into their tongue.

Minor religious conflicts occurred occasionally when some loyal churchman arrived in the colony. When Robert Gorges came to Massachusetts in 1623 to further one of the colonial adventures of his father, Sir Ferdinando Gorges, he brought with him the English cleric, William Morrell. Although he spent almost a year in the colony and probably found some churchmen, he discreetly refrained from conducting public worship nor did he produce his authorization to enforce conformity until the eve of his departure, because, as Bradford put it, "it would seem he saw it was in vain."

In the following year the London adventurers who sponsored the colony sent over John Lyford, "a preacher though none of the most eminent and rare," as Bradford described him, who at least temporarily laid aside his holy orders to align his sympathies with the colonists. He developed a friendship with John Oldom, with whom he later tried to set up a new congregation in conformity with the Church of England. Within the year both men were forced to leave the colony; Oldom went to Connecticut where he was murdered by the Indians, and Lyford to Virginia where no record of his ministry has been found.

In the summer of 1622 Thomas Morton, an English gentleman with a retinue of thirty servants, established a plantation, Mare Mount (Merry Mount), on Mount Wollaston, a hill near the present site of Quincy. He succeeded well in the fur trade and lived happily and elegantly while in his household he daily read the Book of Common Prayer. In keeping with European custom, Morton erected an eighty-foot pole for the more colorful celebration of May Day only to incur the wrath of Captain Miles Standish. Slowly the evidence was accumulated against him: it was affirmed that his parties were scandalous; that he had cheated the Indians and shot at one of them when he refused to bring his canoe to ferry Morton across a stream; and, perhaps the really decisive factor, that he "was a man that endeavoured to advance the dignity of the Church of England." In 1628 he was arrested and expelled from the colony illegally since Merry Mount was not in the Plymouth colony. Within a year he was back seeking justice, only to be expelled again while his property was burning. As late as 1643 he came back once more and after almost a year in jail sought refuge in Maine where he died a few years later.

The area surrounding Boston harbor was entirely in the hands of churchmen, later to be called the "old planters," before the arrival of the Puritans. About the year 1625, William Blaxton occupied "Shawmut" and claimed the entire central peninsula, which is now the heart of Boston. Blaxton's claim to this valuable property was later recognized by the Puritans when they purchased lands from him, setting apart fifty acres for his own use. This young clergyman had earned a Master's degree at Emmanuel College, Cambridge, in 1621, and had come from England with Robert Gorges two years later to serve as the assistant to William Morrell, the ineffective executive supervisor for the church in Plymouth. Before 1629 "Mishawum," now Charlestown, was occupied by Thomas Walford, a blacksmith, while Samuel Maverick, an uncompromising churchman, was living on Noddle's Island, now East Boston.

When the Puritans established their colony, Blaxton and Maverick were admitted as freemen on October 19, 1630, but about six months later Walford, who was not a freeman, and his wife were banished from Boston for "his contempt of authority and confrontinge officers." Blaxton and Maverick apparently won their status just in time, for the next session of the General Court ordered that "for time to come noe man shal be admitted to the freedome of this body polliticke, but such as are members of some of the churches within the lymitts of the same." Maverick, though "strong for the Lordly prelaticall power," was "a man of a very loving and courteous behavior" and frequently and gratuitously entertained strangers. He may have won his place as a freeman because of his likeable nature and his kindness, especially to the Indians whom he nursed during an epidemic of smallpox.

Blaxton was a man living unto himself, dividing his time between his farm and cattle and his most unusual library of over two hundred books. He never objected to or attended the churches of the Puritans, although he once admitted, as Cotton Mather records it, "I came from England, because I did not like the lord-bishops; but I cannot join with you, because I would not be under the lord-brethren."[1] Yet the Puritans remained suspicious of him and, when they found no more serious charge, criticized the cut of his "canonical coat" which he wore even while farming. By assessing every householder six shillings the Puritans raised £30 to purchase these fifty acres from the lonely Anglican clergyman whose only memorial is the attachment of his name to Blackstone's Point. This transaction was not unlike the bargain purchase of Manhattan Island from the Indians, since the price of the fifty acres would scarcely purchase a one-foot frontage of a tiny lot in an undesirable location today. In 1634 Blackstone, as it was now spelled, forsook his orchard, garden, and spring, which he had enjoyed for nine epoch-making years, and set out southward toward Rhode Island where he settled down to live near Roger Williams but remained far from his opinions. At the age of almost eighty years the Rev. William Blackstone died at Cumberland, Rhode Island, on May 26, 1675. His precious library and his ten "paper books," probably his journal and other original writings, unfortunately were soon destroyed by the Indians.

The settlement of Massachusetts by the more conservative Puritans, who at least in England had remained within the church in their attempts to "purify" it, became a possibility when the Council for New England, in March, 1628, granted a patent for the lands between the Charles and the Merrimack Rivers to the Massachusetts Bay Company formed by John Endicott and five others. Endicott and his party arrived at Salem in 1628 and quickly proceeded to reconstitute the church with complete independence from the church in England. Francis Higginson and Samuel Skelton were chosen to be the ministers at Salem on July 20, 1629. Although they had been ordained in the Church of England, they abandoned these orders previous to their election, saying that a proper ministry was based only on an inward call from God and outwardly from the congregation. This declaration became a pattern for the few Anglican clergymen who became pastors of the churches in New England. George Phillips, who had performed his duties as an Anglican priest on board the *Arbella*, within sixteen days of his arrival in the colony in 1633 repudiated his orders so that it was said of him "if they will have him stand minister, by that calling which he received from the prelates in England, he will leave them."

Yet this was not the spirit of the first settlers at Boston, and even Phillips may have been persuaded to modify his statement to the eminent Dr. Fuller of the Plymouth colony. Roger Williams, an avowed Nonconformist, refused to join the congregation at Boston in 1630–1631 because they would not make a statement in public of their repentance for having communed in the churches of England while they lived there. At the ordination of John Wilson as teacher in 1630 Governor Winthrop recorded in his *Journal*, "We used imposition of hands, but with this protestation by all, that it was only a sign of election and confirmation, not of any intent that Mr. Wilson should renounce his ministry he received in England."[2]

At about the same time a third Anglican priest in Salem, Francis Bright, refused to be intimidated and preferred to return to England. So highly regarded were John Browne, a lawyer, and his brother Samuel Browne, a merchant, that in the first letter from the Governor of the New England Company to Endicott on April 17, 1629, he was ordered to grant each of the brothers two hundred acres of land at the first division. The Brownes were loyal to their church and openly read services from the Prayer Book at their house for any who cared to attend. On the basis of disturbing the peace they were soon afterward summoned before Governor Endicott, who found them "to be of high spirits, and their speeches and practices tending to mutiny and faction" and so ordered them sent back to England. Although they had suffered great losses of property, the Brownes were never able to obtain compensation. The next few years saw more than one hundred loyal churchmen of varying degrees of conformity leave their properties and their hopes for happiness in the New World to return to England. Toleration was short-lived in the Massachusetts colony as when President Oakes of Harvard once told the Massachusetts Assembly in an election sermon that he looked upon toleration "as the first-born of all abominations" and Nathaniel Ward in his *Simple Cobbler of Agawam* called it a "room for hell above ground."

The Puritan fleet that brought John Winthrop and 840 colonists to Boston in 1630 was the beginning of a tide of immigration which within a decade reached at least 20,000 persons. Although no more than one-fifth of them were professed Christians, it was but a brief time until Congregationalism in its fully developed form had become the established religion from the Merrimack to the Cape. Here, what John Cotton, "the un-mitred Pope of a Pope-hating people," preached on Sunday became the law of the church and often, by the next day, the law of the land. So opposed to all forms of democracy was Cotton that he once wrote, "If the people be governors who shall be the governed?"

Puritanism expressed itself in a rigid regulation of daily living for all, with simplicity of speech and dress, austerity in personal conduct, and on every hand the avoidance of the appearance of all forms of evil. Following the same pattern, the affairs of the churches came under similar inelastic regulation. Orthopraxy for the colonists became as essential as orthodoxy for the clergy. Deviations from the simplicity of meeting-house worship were so strictly forbidden that churchmen who much preferred to worship according to the services of the Book of Common Prayer, even if they had to be read by a layman, found the pressures of community conformity so great that for many a return to England was inevitable. In such a climate the Anglican clergy were unwelcome. Equally unwanted were the Quakers and all others who deviated from Puritan life and doctrine. In periods of fanatical fear some radicals associated with heresy became the innocent victims of suspicion and were burned as witches.

The absolute independence of the churches as Governor Winthrop had once defined it, "no church can have power over any other church," was too simple to prevail long in the growing colony. Massachusetts expanded so rapidly that, by the end of the century, it numbered 70,000 inhabitants in seventy towns, more than the population of Maryland, New York, and Pennsylvania taken together, and more than twice the number in the older colony of Virginia.[3]

The formation of a new congregation was sometimes delayed for several years because of the inability to agree on the worthiness of the small number of persons who would become its first covenanted members. The desire for greater efficiency in the calling and placing of ministers and in other matters ultimately led to the formation of associations for mutual counsel and advice. With the diversity provided by the rapidly growing community and the natural dilution of religious intensity in the second and third generations, authoritative pastoral utterances were no longer adequate to accomplish the desired unanimous support of the churches. To prevent such losses, the Half-Way Covenant was adopted to provide that children of nonregenerate members, who had owned the covenant, might be baptized but could not receive the Holy Communion nor vote in church affairs. Such letting down the bars did not solve their problems but rather prepared the group for the creative enthusiasm of the Great Awakening which led by a new route to a religious revival in New England.

From the very start this Massachusetts colony had in it the germ of the new life that was to become America. Here were some of the best English minds with adequate resources at their disposal to carry on the religious and cultural reform, then so recently begun in the persistent conflicts with the Establishment at home, and to direct its momentum. This religious revival soon turned the major thrust of its efforts from negative regulations to a creative, positive program. In 1636, Harvard College was founded, and four years later the newly established Stephen Daye Press published the Bay Psalm Book. Soon John Cotton, Thomas Shepard, and the Mathers were to write so profusely and at such great length that most of their works, especially the larger folios, would be printed in England. The college and the press created a climate for the exchange of ideas which, although under rather rigid supervision for the time being, would soon provide the ground for adventurous living and thinking and would lead to political and religious liberty. That road was not easy and not uninterrupted, but it could not ultimately be denied. Meanwhile, however, Roger Williams and others who fostered a dissident spirit suffered expulsion from the colony, and only those Anglicans were safe who refrained from the public exercise of their faith. Those who opposed the Church of England most violently must have rejoiced and counted it a divine vindication for their cause when it was discovered that mice had attacked John Winthrop's one-volume Book of Common Prayer and the New Testament and had eaten up completely the Prayer Book section leaving the New Testament unharmed.

This prevailing spirit of the colony in its first generation simply made impossible any toleration of the representatives of the Church of England from whose restraints these idealists had fled in open protest. Nothing in all the world could have posed for them so great a threat to their new religious oligarchy as the mere introduction of the Prayer Book, which might become the scandalous seed for the repetition of their recent unhappy experiences. But it was the excessive concern for self-preservation and the overprotection of the few in authority that ultimately led to royal interference and an end to this religious and political absolutism.

Although Charles II failed in his attempt to obtain toleration for Prayer Book usages when he sent commissioners here for that purpose in 1664, he persisted in this effort and in the last year of his reign was busily preparing to vacate the Massachusetts charter to accomplish his desire. James II, who succeeded his brother in February, 1685, finally accomplished this end and sent over Joseph Dudley to be the new "President of Massachusetts, New Hampshire, Maine and the King's Province." When Dudley arrived in Boston on May 14, 1681, he brought with him the Rev. Robert Ratcliffe, promising a new regime for state and church. Failing to obtain permission to use any of the three churches in the town, Ratcliffe settled for a small room in the town house where on May 16, for the first time in New England, he read Morning Prayer in his surplice, which was so great a novelty to the Bostonians that he had a large congregation. Two weeks later a large room and a pulpit were assigned for Morning and Evening Prayer when Ratcliffe preached at the former and Chaplain Buckley of the frigate *Rose*, which had brought Dudley and Ratcliffe to Boston, preached at the latter. Although Ratcliffe's sermons were well received, his own reception was less warm, and not until December, after the arrival of Governor Edmund Andros, was he permitted to conduct services in the Old South Meeting House in the interval between the regular morning and afternoon meetings there. For most of the populace Cotton Mather's pamphlet, "The Unlawfulness of Common Prayer Worship," stated accurately that Prayer Book worship was both papal and idolatrous. There is little wonder, then, that the prolonged services of the morning meeting annoyed the Anglicans and that the long Anglican service and sermon equally annoyed the afternoon Congregational gathering. On Easter the confusion was at its worst when the Congregationalists worshiped from 11 to 2, "because of ye sacrament and Mr. Clark's long sermon." The Anglican service was scheduled at 1:30 and " 'twas a sad sight to see how full the street was with people gazing and moving to and fro."

Over the protests of the civil officers, the court, and the Congregational protagonists, Robert Ratcliffe was able to organize the congregation of King's Chapel within about a month after his arrival. On June 15, 1686, he and ten laymen met for this purpose under the authority given him by the Bishop of London and also elected Dr. Benjamin Bullivant and Richard Banks as church wardens. "Warden" was the designation of an officer in the Church of England from the twelfth century; because of the close relation of state and church, he had both religious and civil duties, such as collecting funds for widows and orphans and the poorhouse. By the seventeenth century wardens were a legal corporation which could sue and be sued and represent the church at law. The people's warden was elected at the annual meeting, and the rector's warden was appointed by the rector, although in 1734 the King's Chapel congregation denied their rector this privilege. The designations senior and junior warden which were common in America probably were borrowed from the terminology of Freemasonry.

Wardens and vestrymen usually shared powers in the parish. Yet occasionally, as in Marblehead, Massachusetts, in 1714, when there was no clergyman to guide them, the church society was organized on a Congregational pattern. They chose a moderator and assistant, standing committees, two surveyors, and five collectors, and then sent a request to the SPG for a missionary to be their rector. In New England, vestries had no civil duties, since they represented the minority, although many such duties were performed by Congregational officers, since they represented the majority and so in effect were the established church. In New England the number of vestrymen varied from six to nine, and there were self-perpetuating vestries as in Virginia. In some of the New England churches, such as King's Chapel, Christ Church, and Trinity Church, the proprietors of pews became the voters and the persons legally responsible for the finances of the church, while in others, especially in the country churches, all the members of the parish were qualified voters. In recent years proprietary pews have almost entirely disappeared from the Episcopal Church.

At the next meeting of the congregation of King's Chapel on July 4, Ratcliffe's salary was fixed at £50 plus whatever the Council might give him, a phrase that was more a gesture than a hope; indeed the Council soon voted that "those that hire him must maintain him." On a Sunday as many as four hundred persons attended the services, and it was not unusual to have seven or eight candidates present themselves for baptism. Others, whose sympathies were with the church, refrained from attendance for fear of a boycott. Early in 1688, subscriptions for building an Anglican chapel brought £256/9s. from about one hundred persons with an additional £30 from Governor Andros and £25 from Sir Francis Nicholson, his deputy in New York. After some difficulty in finding available land, the Council, probably dominated by Andros, freed a corner of the old burying ground where the foundation of the church was laid on October 16, 1688.

As the King's Chapel approached completion on April 18, 1689, the town was filled with people stirred by the news of the Glorious Revolution and the crowning of William III. Hoping for more lenient regulations and for less support of the Anglican Church by the Crown, a band of insurgents led by John Nelson demanded and obtained the surrender of the fort and the governor. Supporters of the government were sent to jail, and the governor was placed under house arrest in the home of his friend John Usher and later sent back to England. In the insurrection the new King's Chapel, then almost completed at a cost of £284/16s., suffered severe damage as stones were hurled through the windows and the doors and walls desecrated with unimaginable filth.

One of the finest tributes to parson Ratcliffe was that through all this disturbance he had remained unscathed, for he had taken pains to win the respect of his Puritan neighbors and had been friendly with those people among whom his lot had been cast. King's Chapel was opened for worship on Sunday, June 30, 1689, when Ratcliffe was assisted by Samuel Myles, Harvard 1684, a son of a Baptist minister at Swansea. Myles had recently returned from England in deacon's orders and would soon become Ratcliffe's successor on his return to England in 1692. By 1706, the SPG offered to pay the expenses for any recommended Harvard graduate who desired to come to England for ordination. Meanwhile, the church was beautifully furnished, and William and Mary gave the communion vessels, a library of theology for the minister, including the magnificent Walton's Polyglot Bible, and an additional £100 to provide for an assistant minister.

The insurgents in New England gained little from their radical appeal to the new rulers. When the new charter of 1691 arrived, it severed the close association between the government and the church which had existed for almost two generations. The Plymouth colony was united with the Massachusetts Bay colony, and the franchise was now based entirely on property rights. The growth and development of the Church of England was hindered by taxation laws which, with slight fluctuation and a few exemptions in Braintree and Newbury, required Anglicans to pay taxes to support the work of the Congregational clergymen until 1735 when all such laws were repealed.

The turn to the eighteenth century marked the beginning of the work of the SPCK and the SPG; one of the first acts of the latter society was to dispatch George Keith and Patrick Gordon to survey the work of the church in America. Here they found probably not more than six clergymen of the Church of England outside of Virginia and Maryland. The church in New England profited greatly from the direct efforts of the SPG missionaries. Among the most important clergy supported by the Society in Massachusetts were Timothy Cutler and Samuel Parker, whose license from the Bishop of London, dated February 20, 1764, has been preserved and who would later be the second Bishop of Massachusetts. All the Anglican clergy in Connecticut in the colonial period were SPG men, and the success of the early work there was due to the quality of these men. Normally a parish would send a request for a clergyman to the Society and hope to obtain a well-qualified one at the salary usually allowed by the Society. In 1742 one congregation in Connecticut elected Henry Caner as their minister without consulting the SPG or the Bishop of London. Samuel Seabury, Sr., father of the future bishop, who served at New London, Connecticut, also established parishes at Hartford, Middletown, and other points in that state.

While the SPG missionaries accomplished much for the church, the commissary system used successfully in the South never functioned well in New England. Roger Price, rector of King's Chapel from 1730–1748, regularly wrote his reports as commissary to the Society but never seemed able to do much supervisory work beyond his own parish, possibly because of the time he spent in extended study and writing. Henry Caner came from Connecticut to succeed Price at King's Chapel in 1748 and served there with distinction until the American Revolution.

In Boston the membership of the church grew so rapidly that Christ Church (the Old North Church) was organized in 1722, and within five years its rolls had increased to eight hundred. A third congregation, Trinity parish, was begun in 1740 with Addington Davenport as the first rector. During this period the growth of the church beyond Boston was equally rapid so that by 1748 there were not only the three parishes in Boston but additional ones in Braintree (1713), Marblehead (1716), Bristol, Scituate (1736), Hopkinton, Taunton, and Salem, where more than a century earlier the brothers Browne had been deported for the introduction and use of the Prayer Book. Although the bequest of land for a church in Dedham was made in 1759, the first church in that suburban community was not erected until 1771. Not all of these centers had full-time missionaries, but the zeal for further expansion was not dampened until the Revolution, for as late as 1770 a missionary was sent into the Great Barrington region who also worked in some of the neighboring New York areas.

Fearing the ill effects of the Nonconformist influences at Harvard College, the SPG selected East Apthorp, a prominent Boston intellectual and vestryman at King's Chapel, to be its missionary in this important post. Upon his ordination he organized Christ Church in Cambridge in 1759 and engaged in many pamphlet discussions with non-Anglicans. He built Apthorp House, once thought to have been intended as the episcopal residence for the Bishop of New England, which is now the Master's residence of Adams House at Harvard.

Apthorp admitted that he was influenced to accept the call to Cambridge because he was a native of the town, by the "agreeableness and healthiness of the place," and "by the friendly and conversible company in it, of both the religious persuasions, and by some favorable opportunities of literary improvement."[4] But his purposes lay much deeper as his pamphlet controversies indicated. Jonathan Mayhew, fearing the introduction of bishops and disturbed at the inroads that Anglicans were making in the New England communities, in 1763 claimed that the SPG in sending missionaries had exceeded the privileges of its charter, which had originally intended, as he said, to limit such missionary work to the Negroes and Indians in America. Apthorp replied that "all the proceedings and the whole history of the society invariably represent it as first intended to benefit the English subjects and then, as an opening should be made, the Africans and Indians."

Mayhew and other opponents of the SPG had probably mistaken the strong emphasis upon missions to the Indians in reports to the Society to stimulate generous gifts for use in America as the only purpose for which the Society had been founded. To set this straight Apthorp quoted from the charter given by William III in 1701 that the primary intention of the society was "to maintain a public religion in the colonies, especially for Britains [*sic*], and to maintain orthodox clergy to instruct our people." Indians were not mentioned, but there was a secondary object appended "to plant Christianity among heathen." Later in his pamphlet Mayhew exposed his real fears, when he accused the

Society of a design to root out Presbyterians and other denominations or to reduce all of them to the Episcopal form.[5] Thomas Secker, looking at the controversy from England, wrote *An Answer to Dr. Mayhew's Observations on the Charter and Conduct of the SPG* in which he wisely warned, "For it is the duty of all men how much soever they differ in Opinion to agree in Good-will and Kind Behaviour."[6]

Perhaps even better understanding of the Congregationalist attack on the motivations of the SPG is seen in Noah Hobart's *A Serious Address to the Members of the Episcopal Separation in New England,* which he published in Boston in 1748 to try to win back the many converts to Anglicanism. He asserted that the reason

> so little is done for those Places that so greatly need the Society's Help, is because so much is thrown away where it is not at all needed, and indeed, where it does rather Hurt than Good. The reason why *North Carolina* is left to sink into Atheism, *Maryland* to become a Prey to Popery, and the *Vast Indian Nations* to perish in grossest Heathenism, is because the large Sums of Money intrusted to the Management of the Society, instead of being employed to propagate the Gospel, are applied to support the Episcopal Separation in *New England,* and other Places, where Christian Churches are already erected, though not in the Episcopal Form.[7]

With the approach of the Revolution, Apthorp returned to England, yet never lost his concern for the colonies. On the occasion of the general fast on Friday, December 13, 1776, Apthorp, then vicar of Croydon, preached a sermon "For the Pardons of Sins, averting judgments, imploring victory and perpetuating peace to the British Empire" in which he suggested that Christianity should have prevented and could terminate the quarrel that had divided the most happy and potent of Christian states. The method he proposed was a magnanimity and moderation by Britain after the victory that he expected Britain to achieve "over seditious and revolted rebels." He believed that if England granted the securities of liberty and a permanent constitution, the colonies on their part would give clear and unequivocal proofs of loyalty and concern for the general interest by their ready subjection.

Less well known than many of his contemporaries, John Checkley proved himself a courageous defender of religious liberty and at the same time an ardent churchman in his defense of the importance of episcopacy. Born in Boston, Checkley studied at Oxford where he was converted to Anglicanism. While living in Europe for fifteen years, he collected many rare books and manuscripts and, on his return in 1717, opened a shop in Boston where he sold such items, medicines, and toys. As he read patristic literature, he became convinced of the apostolic origin of the episcopacy and frequently discussed his opinions in his store. In 1719 he republished in Boston Charles Leslie's *Attack on the Deists* and openly opposed Congregationalism in one of his own pamphlets.[8]

By December of that year he was arrested and fined £6 and costs for refusing to take the oath of allegiance to the king and colony under the provisions of a new law especially designed for his case. When he failed to obtain holy orders after eight months in England, Checkley returned to Boston in 1723 to continue his business and his causes. His next pamphlet contained a lengthy *Discourse Concerning Episcopacy,* which he had compiled from earlier works but to which he added his own opinions that all those are true ministers who stand in the uninterrupted historic succession. He admitted that he was not convinced that this succession must be preserved only in bishops and "whether it may best be deriv'd through the Presbyters, or whether Bishops and Presbyters are not the same, I do not now say." What he contended for was "an uninterrupted succession of Gospel ministers: and he that denyes such a succession of the ministry to be necessary is an enemy to Christianity." Checkley used Leslie's arguments with alterations and additions, applied his attacks on the Quakers to the Presbyterians and Independents, and directed the entire work to New England readers.[9]

After a spirited exchange of pamphlets on episcopacy between Checkley and Edward Wigglesworth, Jonathan Dickinson, a Presbyterian who would later become president of Princeton University, promptly charged Checkley with denying a "coordinate ministry" to the Presbyterians and offered acknowledgment "for your abounding charity in mercifully Damning all the Protestant World but your own Party." "You tell us," Dickinson continued, "that they who have no proper ministers and sacraments never were, nor are they now, any parts of the Catholic Church . . . and thus at one stroke, all the Protestants in the World are cut off from the Catholic Church and the Mystical Body of Christ."[10]

For his controversial publications and his belligerent spirit Checkley was brought before the court once more, fined £50 for publishing seditious libel and compelled to post a bond for £100 for his good behavior for the next six months. The court was careful to preserve the fiction that Checkley was not to be tried for writing anything in defense of the Church of England and the episcopacy or against the Presbyterian or Congregational ministers for they were able to defend themselves. Three clauses were found that betrayed Checkley's Jacobite leanings and reflected on the government, and so he was found "guilty of imagining and contriving by subtility of arguments to traduce the title of His present Majesty." In 1730 Checkley published his defense at his trial and to annoy the Congregationalists he added a final page entitled

By Way of Explication

Question. Why don't the Dissenters in their Public Worship make use of the Creeds?
Answer. Why—Because they are not set down Word for Word in the Bible.
Question. Well—But why don't the Dissenters in their Public Worship make use of the Lord's Prayer?
Answer. Oh—Because that is set down Word for Word in the Bible.

Checkley's opponents also continued their attack with no less bitterness and offensiveness. At one point they republished Samuel Mather's *Testimony from Scripture against Idolatry and Superstition,* originally preached in Dublin in 1660, in which he likened the compulsory use of the Book of Common Prayer to forcing a man to use crutches when he is not lame and asked whether Jesus Christ had worn a surplice. Such vehement attacks and Checkley's controversial exercises probably brought little inspiration to anyone and little help to Anglicanism; many Church of England clergy had been greatly confused by the issues and suffered ill will by association. Yet Checkley did add to the long line of protests against restraint of religious liberty, and he also had a part in founding the Boston Episcopal Charitable Society in 1724.

Although this strong Anglican advocate had failed to secure ordination both in 1722 and 1737, eventually the Bishop of Exeter, with the tacit consent of the Bishop of London, ordained Checkley in 1739. Then almost sixty years of age he became rector of King's Church in Providence, Rhode Island, where he served for more than a dozen years before retirement. In his advanced years Checkley not only attended to his own parish but went sometimes as far as fifty miles to minister to the Indians, whose language he spoke, teaching and baptizing their children as well as some Negroes. Before his death on February 15, 1754, he had learned to follow the advice of the Archbishop of York, who once wrote him, "Arm yourself with the humility and courage of a Christian."[11]

V

BEYOND MASSACHUSETTS
IN NEW ENGLAND

NEW HAMPSHIRE AND MAINE

The region now largely covered by New Hampshire and western Maine was assigned under two grants of the Council of New England. In 1621 Captain John Mason obtained a patent for all the land from the Salem River to the Merrimack and extending up each river to its source and then crossing from the head of the one to the head of the other. The following year a patent was granted to Sir Ferdinando Gorges and Captain Mason for the lands between the Merrimack and Sagadahoc Rivers and extending to the Great Lakes and the St. Lawrence. The former grant came to be known as Mariana and the latter as Laconia. Captain Mason was a loyal churchman and probably saw to it that a minister served his family and approximately fifty employees. On his death in 1658 he left one thousand acres for the maintenance of a clergyman and a like amount to support a grammar school. The name of John Michell appears on the Privy Council Register under June 27, 1638, as having served the church in Laconia. The consistent support of the Church of England by Captain Mason is attested by Governor Winthrop's statement when he heard of Mason's death, "The chief mover in all attempts against us . . . the Lord in mercy taking him away."

At the settlement of Portsmouth, New Hampshire, on May 25, 1640, Governor Francis Williams set apart a grant of fifty acres of land for a glebe to the church wardens, Thomas Walford, the "smith" whom Winthrop had previously banished from Charlestown, and Henry Sherburne. A church building and parsonage were soon erected, and Richard Gibson served here until his loyal churchmanship forced him to return to England in 1642 at about the time the Bay colony was taking over control of these regions.

Sir Ferdinando Gorges set up his first organized government at Winter Harbor on the Saco River in Maine. Richard Gibson had probably come to these regions as early as 1636 and served here until 1640. In that year the twenty-eight-year-old Robert Jordan came and served with good effect at Saco, Scarboro, and Casco, now Portland. An inheritance from his wealthy father-in-law made him an established landowner, and with the additional prestige of his clerical office, Jordan heroically but unsuccessfully resisted the encroachments of the Massachusetts Bay officers. At times he was imprisoned and barbarously treated for performing baptisms and marriages by Prayer Book rites. During King Philip's War, the Indians destroyed his home, forcing Jordan, now aging and infirm, to retire to Great Island (Newcastle) near Portsmouth where he died in 1672 in his sixty-eighth year, the last priest of the Church of England on New England soil at that time.

After many years the parish in Portsmouth was revived in 1734. When the colony was separated from Massachusetts in 1741, Benning Wentworth became its first governor and nobly supported the church during his long incumbency. With practically no help except a few years of service from two assistants, Arthur Browne, having left Providence, Rhode Island, for lack of support, gave his life to the ministry of the church in New Hampshire from 1743 to his death in 1773.[1] Before the Revolution halted the work of the church, the parish in Claremont was established in 1770. In June, 1773, Ranna Cossit became the first rector and served until his return to England in 1785, although because of his loyalty to the Crown he was confined to the limits of the town during the war. Ten years later Daniel Barber assumed the work at Claremont and remained until, in 1818, in his advanced years he was obliged to leave the parish because of his conversion to Romanism, perhaps the first such convert from the Anglican clergy in America. The record of the churches in Maine is very similar, where the work of Jordan was revived and carried on during the century after his death by not more than four scattered missionaries of the church.

RHODE ISLAND

Early Rhode Island history is synonymous with the name of Roger Williams. On being exiled from Massachusetts in 1636, this zealot settled in the region of Providence where he organized Rhode Island and Providence Plantations under a patent granted in 1643 by the Commissioners of the Long Parliament. Moved by his own unhappy experiences, Williams was determined to provide a haven for dissenters; all save Roman Catholics and Quakers were welcome in his colony, and this permitted the free and uninterrupted work of the missionaries of the Church of England.

As early as 1698 the Church of England was established in Newport by Sir Francis Nicholson, and a handsome church was completed in 1709. By 1724 the number of communicants and other attendants had so greatly increased that a new building was planned and completed in 1726. A thirty-foot addition to the fine old Trinity Church in 1762 brought the building to its present proportions. After two brief ministries of David Bethune and John Lockier between the years 1700 and 1704, Lord Cornbury, Governor of New York, at the request of the vestry for a rector, sent them James Honyman, who served there successfully for forty-five years. Frequently he gave of his time to provide religious services for people of other communities, and he soon came to see the need for supervision in the church in America.

In 1709 the foresighted rector wrote the secretary of the SPG, "You can neither well believe, nor I express, what excellent services for the cause of religion a Bishop would do in these parts . . . these infant settlements would become beautiful nurseries which now seem to languish for want of a father to oversee and bless them."[2] Joined with this, one of the first local appeals for the episcopate in America, came the additional request of the minister, church wardens, and the vestry to Queen Anne asking for the establishment of bishops in America and showing what benefits could accrue to the church from such action. Honyman had hoped that he might be able to overcome the disintegrating effects of the many small dissident groups among whom his remnant of true churchmen were set. He even suggested to the governor that a number of competent clergy, set in the various townships under the jurisdiction of a bishop, together with the establishment of schools and a proper encouragement from the government, would certainly improve the work of the church. Yet with visions like these, he found time during two months in 1723 for the painful daily duty of visiting many pirates who were brought to Rhode Island for trial, only to find he had also to prepare them for dying, since they were all convicted and about to be executed.

How much Honyman had to do with the conversion of Samuel Seabury, who had been a Congregational preacher and whose son would become the first bishop of the church in America, is not clear, but he did introduce Seabury to the SPG by correspondence. Seabury was related to and an intimate friend of James McSparran and through him had probably become well acquainted with Dean Berkeley.[3]

In one of his letters to the Society, dated September, 1732, James Honyman asked for a small increase in his stipend to enable him to provide for his family. He apparently did not get it; several years later his stipend was still only £70, which it had been for more than twenty years. Nevertheless he wrote of his happiness in his parish, which he considered better than any between New York and Boston. Not the least of his joys was his sense of achievement, for there remained not a single original member of the parish when he arrived and all he now had did not then belong to it.

Another early congregation was formed in Narragansett County in the lower portion of Rhode Island west of the bay. Although Church of England families had settled here before 1700, the first missionary, Christopher Bridge, did not come until 1706, and only then were plans made to erect the first church. The most distinguished of the rectors of the old Narragansett Church was James McSparran, who was also one of the ablest of all the missionaries sent out by the SPG. He served St. Paul's parish from 1720 to 1757 and frequently took services in neighboring areas. Both he and James Honyman worked faithfully among the slaves; McSparran baptized several Negroes, although he often had difficulty obtaining the consents of their masters.

Honyman had as many as one hundred Negroes attending services, five of whom were communicants.

Despite the fact that Rhode Island had been settled for religious liberty, these missionaries found no help from the government. In 1728, Honyman and McSparran sent a joint memorial to the Society in England describing their difficulties and stated that there was only one baptized Christian in the legislature. McSparran at one point became so concerned about the dangers faced by unwary immigrants that he published in Dublin in 1753 his *America Dissected,* which he called a full and true account of all the American colonies. This pamphlet of about fifty pages contained three letters from McSparran to Colonel Henry Cary, the Rev. Paul Limrick, and William Stevenson in which he described the intemperance of the climates, heat and cold and sudden violent changes of weather, unwholesome air destructive to human bodies, bad money, danger from enemies, "but above all the Danger to the Souls of the Poor People that remove hither from the multifarious wicked and pestilent Heresies that prevail in those parts." To this the title page adds an additional warning, "Published as a Caution to Unsteady People who may be tempted to leave their Native Country."

Yet in the face of such discouragements, the church in Rhode Island flourished through the generous support of the SPG, which expended over £20,000 there, and the able service of well-selected missionaries. In 1720, James Orem was sent to open a mission in New Bristol, where after two years he was succeeded by John Usher, a Harvard convert who gave a long life of about half a century to this work. After only seven years Usher reported that his congregations had already so increased "that there is scarce room in the church to hold them," and therefore he proposed to build a gallery. He was pleased with the 121 baptisms but distressed that he could not comply with the requests of many Negroes for baptism because their masters would not consent. This was a common problem in the region, and Usher tried to correct it by quoting from a recent sermon by the Bishop of St. Asaph's and a letter from the Bishop of London; his report continued, "I have added my own endeavours, both from the pulpit and in private conversation, to persuade them to comply therewith." Apparently he had at least a partial success, for in a letter on April 2, 1746, Usher informed the Society that he had about thirty Negroes and Indians in his congregation and three of them were communicants. Moreover he was pleased that some dissenters had become conformists and that he had been able to receive into the church three who had been Anabaptists.[4]

All during the war years the Society's records reported "the same Missionaries and salaries," although one must wonder how these monies were paid. Apparently the personal ministries of these faithful missionaries were carried on with little interruption, although in 1777, John Graves reported that his churches at Providence and Warwick had been closed. The letters from New England in the 1780's indicate more mild conditions and happier prospects with the churches open for worship where there were missionaries to serve.

Graves alone seems to have been the exception, perhaps the only loyalist who remained behind, for he reported that, although the churches that had been closed were now opened, "he could not be prevailed upon, either by threats or promises, to open his church in the present situation of affairs" and therefore had moved out of the "parsonage-house" and had been formally dismissed by his people.

Dean George Berkeley is inseparably connected with the church and liberal education in early America. In 1725 he published a *Proposal for the better supplying of Churches in our Foreign Plantations and for converting the savage Americans to Christianity* in which he planned the erection of a college in Bermuda for the education of the children of planters and natives as missionaries. Berkeley was so involved in his proposal that he used all his connections to obtain funds for the institution, which he intended to direct at a salary of £100 a year and in which tutors of finest caliber would assist him at a salary of £40. Three promising young Fellows of Trinity College, Dublin, were anxious to be associated with the distinguished philosopher in this American venture where native young people might have an education for £10 per annum. Generous private subscriptions followed when the king designated Berkeley's venture as "so pious an undertaking" and Sir Robert Walpole, the prime minister, promised £20,000. On January 23, 1729, Berkeley landed at Newport, Rhode Island, to be greeted by James Honyman, the wardens, vestrymen, and congregation.

Berkeley, now in the prime of life and career in his mid-forties, had been trained in Trinity College, Dublin, and even before his ordination in 1709 had produced major philosophical works. His major theory, denying the existence of matter apart from spirit, asserted that spirit is the only true substance and that the only true cause is an intelligent will. Revolting against the anti-religious philosophy of his day, he thought atheism followed logically from the dangerous materialism he so vigorously denied. For him the material universe instead of being an end in itself served as a vast system of "symbols" through which God and true knowledge about Him may be known by man. His idea that the world is God's voice and His language a system of symbols and signs is not as remote from modern philosophy as might at first appear.

Berkeley had had a rapid professional advancement. By late 1721, he had returned to Dublin where he was in rapid succession divinity lecturer, lecturer in Greek and Hebrew, senior proctor, and university preacher. In less than a year he was offered the non-resident Deanship of Dromore with a stipend of £1,400, and in 1724 he accepted appointment as Dean of Derry, which Dean Swift described as "the best preferment in Ireland." Meanwhile, he had just inherited a legacy of £4,000. Despite all this good fortune Berkeley turned his hopes toward the New World where he believed that dreams greater than Plato's or Sir Thomas More's might be realized through his ideal university. In *An Essay toward preventing the Ruin of Great Britain* which he published anonymously in London in 1721, Berkeley pronounced his pessimistic judgment on his times, saying that the moral and political diseases of the Old

World, and especially England, had reached the vital organs and were incurable. "Instead of blushing for our crimes," he wrote, "we are ashamed only of piety and virtue. In short, other nations have been wicked, but we are the first who have been wicked upon principle . . . it is to be feared the final period of our state approaches." It must have been in this mood that he wrote

> Westward the course of empire takes its way;
> The first four acts already past,
> A fifth shall close the drama of the day;
> Time's noblest offspring is the last.[5]

Yet the pessimistic dean had not lost hope entirely. He still believed that religion and education together were the panacea by which he would make the New World immune to the ills of the old, and in this venture he was willing to give his life. Doom could still be forestalled, he thought, by a prompt, wise, and efficient organization of religious and intellectual training in America. To these ends he gave much of his energy and fortune in the next few years.

Instead of remaining near Newport for only a few months, while he surveyed the American needs and planned the investment of funds realized as well as those still expected from Walpole, Berkeley's stay was prolonged so that he purchased a farm by the sea several miles from Newport, which he named "Whitehall." Here he continued his studies and wrote his *Alciphron, or The Minute Philosopher*, being seven dialogues designed to answer the freethinkers he had met and to check irreligion and skepticism. Occasionally he would accompany Honyman on his missionary visits to the Narragansett Indians or preach in the church at Newport where he was always welcomed. Berkeley was probably more responsible than any other for the idea that, although each of the sects considered its own the very best form of religion, "they all agree in one point—that the Church of England is the second best."

It soon became clear that Walpole never had intended to send Berkeley the £20,000; in fact, it had already been bestowed as a marriage portion on the Princess Royal. So with limited funds beyond his own resources Berkeley was stranded in America, and his dream of St. Paul's College in Bermuda was dashed. The rather dubious honor belongs to Walpole of having defeated two of the noblest early projects designed for the American church: (1) the creation of four bishoprics in 1715; and (2) the establishment of the missionary college in Bermuda about a decade later.

For the welfare of the church in America Dean Berkeley had given seven years of his life and much of his own fortune. Three years after his return to England he was made Bishop of Cloyne, but he never forgot the needs in America. He felt obligated to return private gifts intended for his American college, but as late as 1747 he transferred to the treasurer of the SPG the £200 whose original donors could not be found, suggesting that £50 be set apart to purchase the most approved writings of the divines of the Church of England "as a proper means to inform their judgment and dispose them to think better of our church."

Before he turned his major benefactions to Yale, Dean Berkeley once thought of establishing a theological seminary for the church in Rhode Island.[6] He may have been dissuaded from this idea and urged to lend his support to Yale instead by Samuel Johnson, who visited him on several occasions during this period. Many were the distinguished visitors who came to Whitehall to sit at the feet of the learned dean, and among them may have been Jonathan Edwards, who later would become one of the major American supporters of Berkeley's anti-materialistic philosophy.

Yale College had been chartered in 1701 and named for Elihu Yale, a churchman and the American-born governor of the East India Company of London, whose benefactions of books and money had brought him this honor. He had had some qualms about supporting an academy of dissenters, for Yale had been founded to perpetuate conservative Congregationalism and as an antidote to the liberal Harvard influences. Despite the fact that its library contained the Book of Common Prayer and such Anglican classics as the works of Hooker, Barrow, Burnet, Hoadly, Pearson, Sherlock, Taylor, Tillotson, and Wake—probably among Yale's gifts—there was little good will for Anglicanism at New Haven. Fines were imposed on Yale students who attended the Church of England services; exceptions were made for communicants who might attend their church only on Christmas and Holy Communion days.[7]

CONNECTICUT

There was a similar anti-Anglican attitude in other parts of the state as well; in Stratford, where George Muirson, a zealous young missionary from Rye, New York, made periodic visits in the fall of 1706 and baptized a number of converts to the Church of England, the town council was so threatened that it forbade any worship apart from the Congregational form. When the missionary next appeared, a member of the council stood in the highway with several other persons "to forbid any persons to go to the assembly of the Church of England and threatened them with a fine of five pounds, as the law directed."

Such fears were well grounded, for the Yale tragedy was soon to follow when its president and tutors would renounce their ordinations to seek Anglican orders. When Dean Berkeley subsequently gave to Yale his ninety-six-acre farm and his library of one thousand books, the trustees feigned gratitude but inwardly feared they had admitted a Trojan horse that might loose new disasters over the now quieted campus. The more would they have been alarmed had they known that President Stiles, not being disposed to allow Samuel Johnson to have full credit for securing so great a benefaction, had persuaded Berkeley himself that "Yale would soon become Episcopal and that they had received his immaterial philosophy."[8]

Berkeley's educational ideas were to influence American education far beyond the Yale campus, for when Johnson became head of King's College in New York, he sought his advice and in turn passed on Berkeley's ideas to Benjamin Franklin when he requested Johnson's aid in planning for the University of Pennsylvania in Philadelphia.[9] Two years after his return to England Berkeley sent a substantial gift of books to Harvard and another larger collection to Yale. Benjamin Coleman, conservative Boston Congregationalist, asked the president of Yale not to accept this gift if it were "clogged with any conditions that directly or indirectly tend to the introduction of Episcopacy."[10] This gift of almost one thousand volumes contained Greek and Latin classics, patristic literature, history, mathematics, medicine, natural history as well as philosophy and divinity, and was described by an early Yale historian as "the best collection of books which had ever been brought at one time to America."

The colonial government in Connecticut, which legally dates from a charter granted by Charles II in 1662, resulted from two earlier Puritan settlements, the first in 1633 on the banks of the Connecticut River at Hartford under the direction of Thomas Hooker and the second, in 1638, under the Rev. John Davenport at New Haven. John Winthrop, the son of the Massachusetts governor, became the governor of Connecticut in 1662 under its colonial charter which was never to be revoked. Although Anglicanism was not legally tolerated in any part of this colony, it was actually less violently opposed than in Massachusetts, partly because of the differences of opinion among the Puritans themselves and partly because there was no official pressure from a royal governor, the only English official in the colony being the collector of customs.

The Connecticut colony had a singularly rapid growth. By 1701, according to a report of Governor Dudley of Massachusetts that was read before the SPG at its meeting on September 19 of that year, Connecticut had within its limits thirty thousand souls in about thirty-three towns, all dissenters being supplied with ministers and schools of their own persuasion. Yet proportionately more churchmen had settled in the Connecticut regions than in any other area of New England. It was therefore to be expected that the first SPG missionaries, George Keith and John Talbot, who visited the region shortly after they had disembarked at Boston on their first exploration for the Society, should have found friendly groups to welcome them. On September 13, 1702, Talbot preached in the morning and Keith in the afternoon in the meeting house at New London.

After a brief period of service for the SPG in Connecticut in 1713, Francis Phillips went on to serve a parish in Philadelphia. He may well have delayed the sending of other missionaries by his exaggerated assertion that the only adherents of the church in Connecticut were men who wished to avoid paying the taxes prescribed by an act of the legislature in 1708 for the support of the Congregational churches. In 1727 this act was revised to permit support of Anglican worship by those who lived near enough—usually within five miles—to the churches to conveniently attend. Taxes paid by such persons were turned over to the support of their minister and gave the SPG missionary equal opportunities. Not until the new Connecticut Constitution in 1819 disestablished Congregationalism were the last religious restrictions removed for all denominations, and the Episcopal Church then also became free to grow more rapidly.

When George Pigot became the rector of the Stratford parish, there were more than one hundred baptized souls with thirty-six regular communicants and frequently two or three hundred persons assembled for public worship. Meanwhile, in the same town the Congregationalists had to replace their minister, Mr. Reed, who was favorably inclined toward the Church of England and was only prevented from going to England for orders by circumstances over which he had no control. To stamp out this Anglican threat in Connecticut, the promising Timothy Cutler, who had graduated from Harvard in 1701, was carefully selected on his ordination on January 11, 1709, to succeed to this vacancy. So highly respected was the young Boston Puritan that, when Yale was permanently settled in New Haven in 1718, Cutler succeeded his father-in-law, Samuel Andrew, as the first president there. Samuel Johnson, Yale 1714, and a tutor from 1716–1719 became the very acceptable Congregational minister at West Haven.

Only a few weeks after his arrival at Stratford Pigot was able to report not only his favorable church statistics but to add that he expected "a glorious revolution of ecclesiastics of this country." Apparently he had quickly won the confidence of Cutler and Johnson and their associates who, being dissatisfied with their ordinations, were ready to seek orders in the Church of England. Although the source of their uncertainty remains obscure, Johnson apparently from his earliest days in the ministry had had some qualms about being a Congregational minister. He admitted that, for his mother's sake and because he was unfamiliar with Anglican procedures at that time, he had accepted Presbyterial ordination so that he could be doing some service to promote the main interest of religion.[11] This early inclination toward Anglicanism was further stimulated when a Mr. Smithson of Guilford gave Johnson a Prayer Book, and he probably spent many hours of study in the rich Anglican collections in the Yale Library before he came to his final decision. Cutler also apparently had had grave doubts since his first ordination. The Yale Library had also played a prominent role for him, and John Checkley is sometimes given credit for Cutler's conversion, but that, curiously enough, was an attribution invariably made by Checkley's enemies. In any event, Johnson and Cutler were not alone in their fears and searchings. Their small circle also included Daniel Brown, a tutor at Yale; Jared Eliot, pastor at Killingworth; James Wetmore, pastor at North Haven; the less convinced but yet concerned John Hart, of East Guilford; and Samuel Whittlesey, of Wallingford, who may not have been as regular in attendance as the others.

During the summer of 1722, these men spent many hours in discussion with George Pigot, the newly arrived missionary of the SPG at Stratford. Rumors of such secret meetings in the Yale Library had reached Boston, but even so conservative a leader as Cotton Mather rather doubted them. On Commencement Day, September 12, 1722, when President Cutler had finished his sermon, he added, "And let all the people say Amen!" Immediately a buzz arose at this obvious sign of Anglicanism; the trustees promptly asked Cutler to meet them the next day and to present in writing some of the disturbing opinions he had privately expressed.

At the special request of President Cutler, George Pigot was present the following day when the seven men asserted that "some of us doubt the validity, and the rest of us are more fully persuaded of the invalidity of the Presbyterian ordination, in opposition to Episcopal." Two others did not sign this document; Buckley of Colchester considered episcopacy to be *jure divino*, and Whiting, of a distant town, declared for moderate episcopacy. After the discussion in the library that day, Hart, Whittlesey, and Eliot were either convinced of their error or dismayed and persuaded by the opposition to return to their former positions.

The confessed converts were anxious to discuss their decision in public, and Governor Gurdon Saltonstall, a former Congregational minister at New London who had read widely in theology, gave them the opportunity in a public meeting in the Yale Library on the day following the opening of the General Assembly in October. Fresh from months of careful study of the sources, the converts easily dispatched the less carefully prepared attacks on their position, and when the discussion reached the haranguing stage, the governor, who had moderated the session with decorum, rose and said that he only designed a friendly argument and so brought the conference to an end. On October 17, the trustees of Yale "excused the Rev. Mr. Cutler from all further service." In contrast to the vituperation and name-calling by their former associates, Cutler and Johnson remained calm. Johnson even wrote a prayer in which he asked God to prevent him from being "a stumbling block or occasion of fall to any soul."

These defections brought consternation to the Congregational leaders. Joseph Webb, of Fairfield, wrote to Cotton Mather in Boston,

> I apprehend the axe is hereby laid to the root of our civil and sacred enjoyments and a doleful gap opened for trouble and confusion in our churches . . . how many more will, by their example, be encouraged to go off from us to them, God only knows. It is a very dark day with us; and we need pity, prayers and counsel.[12]

At a fast observed in the "Old North" Congregational Church in Boston on September 25, 1722, Cotton Mather preached and Increase Mather prayed and "much bewail'd the Connecticut apostacie." The trustees at Yale required all future rectors and tutors to declare their assent to the Saybrook Platform and demonstrate their opposition to "Prelatical Corruptions and Arminianism." Yet year after year some of the finest graduates of Yale sought orders in England until, by 1732, more than one-tenth of Yale's clergy graduates had become Anglican missionaries.[13] Among them was Henry Caner, Yale 1724, who later served as rector of King's Chapel until the Revolution and who was probably more responsible than any other for the first annual convention of the clergy in Massachusetts held in his church in June, 1766.

A week later Cutler, Johnson, and Brown were on their way toward England where they received conditional baptism, confirmation, and ordinations as deacons and priests, the latter by Thomas Green, Bishop of Norwich, in the Church of St. Martin-in-the-Fields on March 31, 1723. The English churchmen vied to present honors to the Americans; Oxford and Cambridge conferred doctorates on Cutler and master's degrees on Johnson. On Easter Eve, April 13, Brown died of smallpox, that plague which took so large a toll among the Americans that some men occasionally specified that they would come over for orders provided these would be completed in the briefest time possible. Whetmore, whose journey was delayed, now joined the group and was ordained before they returned to America late in September.

Johnson succeeded George Pigot as the rector of the church at Stratford and served there for many years. Influenced as he was by Dean Berkeley, he has generally been considered the most effective early opponent of Deism, and his works were used as textbooks in American colleges. In 1742 the clergy asked the Bishop of London to name Johnson as commissary for Connecticut where now there were fourteen churches and seven clergymen and daily calls for more of them. There were apparently more than two thousand adult members of the churches with a constituency of five or six thousand, but the appointment did not follow. In 1754 he became the first president of King's College, now Columbia, where he introduced many of Dean Berkeley's ideas on education. After the death of his first wife, in 1758, and the death of one son and his second wife from smallpox, Johnson had a nervous breakdown and came to Connecticut on February 25, 1763, to spend his later years there until his death in 1772.[14]

Christ Church (Old North) in Boston had already arranged to have Timothy Cutler as its first rector and defrayed the expenses of the trip to England for Cutler, Johnson, and Brown. The cornerstone had been laid in April, 1723, and the church was being built while Cutler was in England and was opened on December 29, 1723. When Cutler came to Boston, the Anglicans numbered about fifteen per cent of a population of twenty thousand which was rapidly increasing. He had immediate success beginning with eighty families and forty communicants; within five years Christ Church had eight hundred members. Here Cutler served for forty-two years, often doing extra missionary work for the SPG in the outlying areas where the foundations he laid have now become strong suburban parishes. At his death on August 17, 1765, in his eighty-second year, Cutler left a valuable library of approximately 1,100 books, many of which are preserved in the Christ Church library.

An unhappy interim ministry of James Greaton, during Cutler's illness and subsequent months, ended late in 1767, and his successor, Dr. Mather Byles, a converted Congregational minister from Connecticut, became rector of Christ Church on Easter Monday, 1768. Being a staunch loyalist, his influence was circumscribed, and on Easter Tuesday, April 18, 1775, his resignation was accepted. It was that very night that Paul Revere's signal lanterns were hung in Christ Church steeple. Not until 1792, when William Walter accepted the rectorship, did Christ Church have a regular minister, although it was used by the French Huguenots in 1778 and occasionally when Samuel Parker of Trinity Church and others conducted services in the church.

It was during these years that the Great Awakening came to New England, centered in the fruitful efforts of Jonathan Edwards and George Whitefield. But these enthusiastic revival movements often led to outbreaks of radical emotionalism that not only confused and disturbed the Anglicans but frequently won converts from and sometimes caused divisions among the other New England churches as well. During these experiences Timothy Cutler became more than ever conscious of the need for the authority of a bishop and wrote that not only "every honest Churchman" but "even many sober dissenters do think a resident Bishop would be a blessing."[15] Cutler found that many Harvard men attended his services and expressed "great affection to the Church of England, and wanting nothing but a resident Bishop to invite them into it."[16]

A second Anglican parish was organized at Fairfield in 1727 and another at New London in 1730, and by 1736 there were no fewer than seven hundred families in Connecticut in communion with the Church of England. By 1742 the colony had seven ministers and fourteen churches built or in process of erection. In 1748, Commissary Price of Boston reported to the SPG that New England then had thirty-six churches of which two were in New Hampshire, five in Rhode Island, twelve in Massachusetts and seventeen in Connecticut. Twenty-five years later there were forty churches in Connecticut served by twenty ministers.

Not least among these missionaries was Samuel Seabury, Sr., Harvard 1724, who, having forsaken his responsibilities as a Congregational minister at North Groton, was introduced to the SPG by a letter of James Honyman of Rhode Island. Subsequent to his ordination early in 1730 he was sent as a missionary to New London. Here he found one hundred members in a community of six hundred inhabitants where his membership soon doubled and where he also found opportunity to establish a mission nearby at Hebron. In 1742 Seabury was appointed to Hempstead, Long Island, where he served until his death on June 15, 1764. In his last report to the Society he declared his membership to be 750 in a population of six thousand and that in his twenty-two years he had baptized 1,071 persons.

In 1748 Seabury wrote the Society that his son Samuel, Jr., who had just graduated from Yale, was reading prayers and sermons under his direction at Huntington, about eighteen miles from Hempstead, and asked that he might be officially appointed by the Society as a catechist. Samuel Seabury, Jr., was soon given this assignment at a salary of £10 a year. After spending the academic year 1752–53 studying medicine at Edinburgh, he was ordained deacon on December 21, 1753, and priest two days later and licensed by the Bishop of London to preach in New Jersey. The Society sent him to serve the mission at New Brunswick where he arrived on May 25, 1754, to begin his ministerial work which, thirty years later, would be climaxed by his election as the first Anglican bishop in America. On December 3, 1766, he was transferred at his own request to Westchester, New York, where, in addition to parish duties, he practiced medicine and conducted a school until the outbreak of the Revolution.[17]

Commencement Day in 1748 brought back to Yale nine Anglicans who, during the course of the day, "consulted the best things they could" for the interests of the church. What they did is not remembered, but the occasion was fraught with significance for the church. That year, with the future Bishop Seabury, the younger son of Samuel Johnson received his A.B. degree; and among the five Anglicans who took the degree of Master of Arts was Thomas B. Chandler, who three years earlier had received his A.B. with Jeremiah Leaming. Chandler, the son of a Connecticut Congregational farmer, would later play a leading role in the attempt to bring bishops to America and in laying the foundation for the constitutional convention of the church. While studying at Yale, he decided not to be a Congregational minister but went instead to England in the spring of 1751 to be ordained on the recommendation of Samuel Johnson. Still without a bishop it is amazing that the Church of England in Connecticut and Massachusetts was able to survive the vicissitudes, banishments, and sufferings of the war years ahead.

VI

THE CHURCH IN
NEW YORK

When Henry Hudson, an Englishman, sailed his *Half Moon* into the river that bears his name and discovered Manhattan Island in 1609, he claimed the lands for the Dutch in whose employ he had sailed. The Dutch fur traders soon made this island a center of trade and, during the four decades the Dutch remained in control of this region, the comparatively few settlers were of varied national origins. Under a charter granted by the States-General of Holland in 1621 the West India Company took over the government of New Netherlands. The generally tolerant spirit of the Dutch permitted the heterogeneous immigration of religious refugees from France, Belgium, Germany, Bohemia, and the Piedmont. The Quakers, however, suffered ill treatment here as in most of the American colonies. By 1647 New Netherlands had only slightly more than two thousand residents, and of these more than half were English. Two years later the Lutherans of no less than seven different nationalities organized a congregation in New Amsterdam with some members living in Albany, New Jersey, and Long Island.

Soon after his restoration, Charles II, remembering the English claim to the American coastline and also being very conscious of the constant trade rivalry with Holland, granted all the region between the Connecticut and Delaware Rivers to his brother James, the Duke of York, on March 12, 1664. When the English fleet under Colonel Richard Nicolls appeared in New York harbor later that year, the Dutch were caught by complete surprise, and Governor Peter Stuyvesant surrendered reluctantly but without resistance. Both the province and the settlement were named New York in honor of its proprietor. Although it provided an unusual situation, Dutch services were continued in the church within the fort, and the English were allowed to use this building, the only church in the colony, for their Prayer Book services after the Dutch had finished their worship. Apparently this amicable arrangement was so mutually agreeable that it was not in the least disturbed when the tables were turned and the Dutch, for about sixteen months, recovered the title to their colony during the war with England in 1673–74. When the English resumed authority, the Dutch were assured of their customary church privileges. For more than thirty years the services in the Dutch church in the fort, in charge of the governor's chaplain, were the only provision for English worship in New York.[1] Charles Wolley was named chaplain in 1678, but it is possible that others may have served previously in this post to which a stipend of more than £120 annually had been attached.

A dually ordained clergyman, Nicolaus van Rensselaer, a younger son of the first patroon of the vast estates held by this family, had received ordination in the Dutch church and also at the hands of the Bishop of Salisbury; he resided in Albany and ministered exclusively according to the rites of the Dutch Reformed Church. His mode of life was such that Governor Andros deposed him in 1677, a rare instance when such a prerogative was exercised by a governor and in this instance probably because of van Rensselaer's Anglican ordination.[2]

The Glorious Revolution that brought William and Mary to the British throne brought momentary national insecurity, which reflected itself in most of the colonies. In New York it provided the occasion for Jacob Leisler to protest against infringed privileges and to give vent to hostile Jacobean and anti-papal feelings in a revolution that accomplished the expulsion of Governor Andros's deputy, Sir Francis Nicholson, but cost Leisler his life.

The government of William and Mary provided for a popular assembly in New York in 1691 but continued its long-time policy of securing the establishment of the church in those colonies not specifically founded by or for dissenters. The popular assembly in New York, which was still controlled by the Dutch, under Governor Benjamin Fletcher in 1693 provided that a "sufficient Protestant minister" be settled in New York. Actually such provision was made for less than half of the counties in the colony and still left in doubt the exact meaning of the word "sufficient." The failure to secure effective establishment in the New York colony had been at least partly due to the scarcity of churchmen. Colonel Dongan wrote as early as 1687 that "here be not many of the Church of England" and added later that in the last seven years not "twenty English, Scotch or Irish families" had come into the colony.[3]

In February, 1694, John Miller, chaplain to the troops in the fort, claimed the generous living provided by the Act of September 22, 1693. Although the governor was inclined to favor him, the council refused, and Miller failed to become the first rector in New York. On his subsequent return to England Miller published his recollections, dedicated to the Lord Bishop of London, in which he suggested as the best possible solution for the settlement and improvement of religion and unity, the conversion of the Indians, the conquest of Canada, and "that his Majesty will graciously please to send over a Bishop to the Province of New York" who would be a suffragan to the Bishop of London. The bishop should have his seat on the King's Farm, "which, though at present a very ordinary thing, yet will it admit of considerable improvement."

Until the founding of Trinity Church in 1697 the only Anglican priest in the colony was the garrison chaplain who conducted worship in the Dutch church in Fort James. When this building fell into bad repair, the Dutch built a new church on Garden Street, and the English obtained permission from the assembly to reconstruct the old one outside the fort. As the church building approached completion, the assembly granted a charter of incorporation for a rector and control by churchmen. The vestry promptly called William Vesey, Harvard 1693, then serving at Hampstead, Queen's County, without orders, and who had been widely commended to them by Samuel Myles, rector of King's Chapel, Boston. Vesey received ordination from the Bishop of London in August, 1697, and on his return was named "assistant" to the bishop, who, by charter, had been named titular rector of Trinity Church. For a short time Vesey officiated in the Dutch church, and when Trinity Church was completed, two of the Dutch ministers took part in his installation service on Christmas Day, 1697. Here Vesey was to spend almost fifty years in a successful ministry due in part at least to his amiable character, his absolute integrity, and his ability to keep the good will even of dissenters, save those irreconcilably anti-prelatical.

Not the least reason for the effective ministry of Trinity Church then and in succeeding years was the grant of the old farm that once belonged to Dominie Bogardus and his wife, of the Dutch church, but which by a grant from Queen Anne had been assigned to Trinity Church in 1705. It was called variously the "Duke's Farm," the "King's Farm," and the "Queen's Farm." Save for a few lots which have been sold at intervals, the tract has been preserved and now covers a large section of downtown New York.

From time to time, beginning about two generations after her death, the heirs of the Widow Bogardus pressed claim to this property in long and expensive law suits that were finally settled in favor of Trinity Church late in the last century. This farm may well have been "an ordinary thing," as John Miller called it in the seventeenth century, but it has "admitted of considerable improvement," as he predicted it would, and today its ground rents provide substantially for the work of Trinity Church.

With the organization of the SPG William Vesey immediately requested missionaries for New York, and between 1702 and 1775 the Society maintained fifty-eight missionaries there. Among the reports of these men, one may read a recapitulation of the total missionary record in the American colonies: there were great good men who established enviable records; lesser men with personal weaknesses; and others who became victims of local circumstances and sometimes even found difficulty in surviving. Samuel Seabury, Sr., came to be so highly regarded in Hempstead, Long Island, that at his death the parish erected a house for his widow. Until his transfer to Westchester in 1766, Samuel Seabury, Jr., ministered effectively at Jamaica. In this period missions were widely established in small communities later destined to become the strong parishes of the present suburban New York area.

These years marked a growth in friendly relations with the French Huguenots, who had always been kindly received in Anglican colonies because of their similarity of worship and who were now welcomed into communion with the Church of England. William Vesey reported that the governor gave the Huguenots some assistance in the erection of their church building in New York City, and, when their minister died, the governor used his influence to bring in a French minister with Anglican orders. In this way L'Église du Saint Esprit in New York City became an Anglican parish. In similar fashion Daniel Bondet, an episcopally ordained French minister in Boston, was brought into the disturbed parish in New Rochelle and won leading citizens to become affiliated with this French Protestant church which conformed to the Church of England.

On Vesey's death in 1746 Henry Barclay, until then a missionary among the Indians west of Albany, came to Trinity Church to serve until 1752. During this period St. George's, now a separate parish, was built as the first chapel of Trinity Church. Samuel Auchmuty, his assistant, followed Barclay and continued his building program in 1766 by erecting St. Paul's, which is still a chapel of Trinity Church and the oldest original church building in New York City. In 1775 Auchmuty was succeeded by his assistant, Charles Inglis, a happy combination of strong Anglican tradition and a warm evangelical spirit, who unhappily was also an ardent loyalist. He left New York with the British evacuation and soon was consecrated Bishop of Nova Scotia where he ministered to thousands of loyalists in exile.

When Governor Robert Hunter invested in land along the Mohawk, he invited Germans from the Palatinate who were willing to leave these fertile areas of the middle Rhineland because of religious uncertainties and the threat of wars. Of the hundreds who came to the Mohawk region most of them retained their Lutheran and Reformed faiths and only a few conformed to the Church of England. Having paid the Indians for their lands, they objected to the governor's attempt to extract additional payment. When they heard of the far happier condition of their fellow emigrants in Pennsylvania, these Germans organized one of the earliest and largest overland treks in colonial history. They took their families, goods, and cattle by a portage from the Mohawk to the headwaters of the Susquehanna River and proceeded to the vicinity of Harrisburg where they settled on the lands adjacent to their fellow countrymen with whom they came to be known as the Pennsylvania Germans.

One of the most valued contributions made by the church in New York was the establishment of King's College, eventually Columbia, which received its royal charter on October 31, 1754, and was supported in part by grants of land from the King's Farm. Trinity Church had offered this generous provision to assure continuous religious instruction and on the condition that Prayer Book services should always be used in the chapel and that the president of the college should always be a communicant of the Church of England. A few months earlier the trustees had already named Samuel Johnson as president, and he immediately introduced Dean Berkeley's ideas of a balanced non-materialistic education. Johnson was also named one of the ministers of Trinity Church where a large vestry room provided the first quarters for the school until the first building could be erected "on the skirts of the city" on the lands given by the church. The cornerstone of this building was laid August 23, 1756. At the first commencement about a score of degrees were awarded; among the seven who received the Bachelor of Arts degree was Samuel Provoost, soon to be the first Bishop of New York.

The attitudes of the colony and the church toward the Indians and the Negroes in New York were typical of most such colonial efforts. The former were usually considered by tribes rather than as individuals, and their religious life was generally the major concern of the SPG rather than the primary concern of any parish. Except for a few cases of integration, the Indians remained in tribes as the wards of the government or the church in any one colony.

The Negroes, on the other hand, were foreigners imported to help the white man complete his conquest of the vast areas of his new world. They were destined to live in small groups in a community where parish and planter shared the responsibility for their welfare and religion. The key to understanding the later slavery controversies and subsequent civil rights struggles was already present in the missionary program of the church, as Professor Frank J. Klingberg recently stated,

> The economic and political implications of the Negro's gain of religious rights before he secured freedom and civil rights, inherent in the program of the SPG . . . had to do with the basic assumption . . . that the Negro would, when civilized, work for his own economic survival and security for exactly the same reasons that actuated the white man.[4]

The particular interpretations of these missionary opportunities in New York and the other colonies are to be found in the reports of the missionaries, in the specific records of their achievements, and in the sermons preached by distinguished English clergymen at the annual meetings of the Society, which at times resemble statements of policy and program.

One of the earliest reports on the American Indians came to the Society from missionary George Muirson just a few months before his death in 1708. In the same letter in which he described the new church building at Rye, New York, paid by the subscriptions of the inhabitants and "a stately structure indeed," he went on to say,

> As to the Indians, the natives of the country, they are a decaying people. We have not now in all this parish twenty families, whereas not many years ago there were several hundreds. I have frequently conversed with some of them, and been at their great meetings of "pawaeing" as they call it. I have taken some pains to teach some of them, but to no purpose, for they seem regardless of instruction; and when I have told them of the evil consequences of their hard drinking, etc., they replied that Englishmen do the same, and that it is not so great a sin in an Indian as in an Englishman, because the Englishman's religion forbids it, but an Indian's does not. They further say they will not be Christians, nor do they see the necessity for so being, because we do not live according to the precepts of our holy religion.[5]

Beyond the early and apparently universal impediment, hypocrisy, missionary Muirson could not understand that his was a provincial answer to a problem far beyond the Rye community and which would involve the later migration under pressure of thousands of native Americans and the transplanting of their culture and means of livelihood.

Governor Richard Coote of New York, the Earl of Bellamont, addressed the Lords of Trade and Plantations in 1700 and suggested that as a matter of state policy some members of the Church of England should be sent to instruct the Indians of the Six Nations to prevent their falling entirely under the influence of the Jesuits and the French. Queen Anne agreed and devised a plan with the Archbishop of Canterbury to send two clergymen. The SPG, however, had no missionaries trained in the Indian languages and so tried to have this work done by the local Dutch minister, Godfridus Dellius, in Albany and the Reformed minister, Bernardus Freeman, in Schenectady, who had already translated some parts of the Bible into the Iroquois language. The Iroquois, as the Six Nations were called collectively, were very important for the security of the English colonies since they occupied the lands along their western frontiers as far south as Maryland. The hopes of the SPG were never fulfilled since both Dellius and Freeman became involved in disciplinary measures by their Classis. Although William Vesey cherished no illusions about his character, he offered public prayers for Dellius in Trinity Church in New York.[6] When this plan failed, the Society sent out Thoroughgood Moor, specifically trained as a missionary to the Indians, who took up his residence in Albany where many of the Indians came to trade. Although Moor visited the Mohawks' Castle, the control of the French made it impossible for him to reside among the Indians, and after about a year he returned to New York and later accepted another appointment in Burlington, New Jersey.

Missionary William Andrews was the next to arrive in Albany in 1712, accompanied by a schoolmaster, Oliver, and an interpreter, Lawrence Clausen. This mission followed the visit of four Indian sachems to the Queen when they came to England to confirm a peace treaty. Although many questioned their sincerity, they presented a request for ministers and teachers to instruct them. Anne was so moved that she ordered a fort with a chapel and residence for the missionary built near the Mohawks' Castle. For several years Andrews found a cooperative spirit that permitted instruction of Indian children in English and in their own language. The Reformed minister, Freeman, had shown his interest in the Anglican mission which he had once been asked to serve by translating the services of Morning and Evening Prayer from the Prayer Book, together with the Gospel of Matthew and other parts of the Bible. These translations were revised by Lawrence Claesse (Clausen) and printed by William Bradford in New York in 1715. It is now one of the rarest American prayer books. As his work stabilized, Andrews moved on about one hundred miles westward to begin a mission among the Oneidas. Although he was still listed at the 1718 meeting of the SPG as "among the Indians" at a salary of £150 and Clausen was still with him at £40 a year, he became discouraged and soon afterward gave up this mission. While he had found congregations of 150 and had received forty Indians as communicants, yet sadly he wrote,

> Their lives are generally such as leave little or no room for hope of ever making them any better than they are—heathens. Heathens they are, and heathens they will still be. There are a few, and but a few, perhaps about fourteen or fifteen, whose lives are more regular than the rest.[7]

The 1720's brought Henry Barclay as the SPG missionary and catechist to Albany where he not only served his people well but, during the absence of a Dutch minister, preached to the Dutch in their own language and admitted many to his membership. After seven years his work had prospered so that his congregation was able to erect a fine stone church building. In 1729 he was succeeded by John Miln who carried on this work by protracted quarterly visits of five days each among the Mohawks. He observed that "many of the Indians have become very orderly and observe the Sabbath," and the commanding officer reported that the Indians "were very much civilized of late."

At the recommendation of Miln, Henry Barclay, Jr., a son of the former missionary, was appointed Indian catechist at Fort Hunter in 1735. After his ordination two years later he returned to take charge of the work among the Indians and the English. In *Notitia Parochialis*, a report on a printed form submitted to the SPG on November 10, 1738, Barclay indicated that there were 10,610 whites in his city and county, 1,110 slaves or blacks, and five hundred Indians under his care among whom fifty were communicants.[8] In addition to the services on Sundays he catechized the Indians in the evenings in groups of thirty to fifty and by 1743 was able to report that only two or three out of the entire tribe remained unbaptized. Intemperance had been rooted out, and he had two Indian schoolmasters assisting him in two towns. Then came the French and Indian War which temporarily halted the work of the mission, and Barclay accepted a call to Trinity Church, New York.

The directors of the SPG had been conscious from the beginning of threats to their program from the competing Roman Catholic missionaries and rival French settlements. In an annual sermon to the Society as early as 1706 Bishop Williams of Chichester asserted that the Anglican missionaries, enthusiastically supported by England, would be able to overcome the reputed advantages of the Roman Catholic priests in performing miracles and using the great funds of the Roman Catholic orders. His hope for the Society lay in that these missionaries "shall teach over again in their lives what they have before taught in their principles."[9]

The English people were very conscious of the political value of friendship with the Indians, and the leaders of the SPG were not afraid to admit that loyalty to England was a proper by-product of their missionary program. Bishop Thomas Secker, in 1741, preaching before the annual gathering of the SPG, said that since the Indians had yielded their lands to the English, the English should teach them a way of living in the remaining lands. Since the colonists had introduced diseases and vices, they should now give the Indians

Christian living in return. And he added, "Every single Indian, whom we make a Christian, we make a friend and ally at the same time."[10]

Three years earlier the Bishop of Bangor put it similarly before the Society, "For every convert to Christianity . . . is a friend to our Country and Government, as well as to our Religion." This same idea was stated negatively in 1748 when Bishop Lisle of St. Asaph warned the Society that if efforts were not increased, Negroes and Indians might be won away and the result would be an assault upon English settlements. He declared, "Our own safety, therefore, should spur us on to list these people in the Service of Christ."

In seeking to win the Indians, the missionaries were by no means alone. The authorities of the British government sought them as fighters and defenders of their outer bastions, colonists craved the Indians' lands, and the traders looked upon them as both a source of their supplies of furs and a consumer of their alcohol, firearms, baubles, and other merchandise. Had it not been for the mellowing influence of the missionary's program of religious and social education, the secularized though noble savage might easily have suffered even more severely as the commercial and military advances overran his lands and culture.

John Ogilvie, a recent Yale graduate, accepted the assignment to succeed Barclay as the missionary to the New York Indians and reported that the Mohawks seemed to possess a serious and habitual sense of religion. Many Mohawks accompanied Braddock on his disastrous expedition, and of the twelve principal men of their tribe who fell in battle, six had been communicants. While on this campaign, their catechist Abraham, who was also one of their sachems, read Morning and Evening Prayer each day. When the troops marched to Niagara, Ogilvie accompanied them and, on February 1, 1760, reported the fine work he had seen being done by the Roman Catholic missionaries among the Indians of the Six Nations confederacy. He had special words of praise for the Franciscan in charge of the chapel at Fort Niagara, who showed special hospitality to the Indians who came to trade, for which he had a special allowance, and then instructed them in the faith. Once converted, the Indians often became staunch defenders of their faith, Catholic or Anglican. General Amherst was much impressed with the decency with which an Indian sachem on one occasion conducted Prayer Book worship at Oneida.[11]

Similar fears and concerns about the Indians were shared in the other colonies as well. East Apthorp told his parishioners at Christ Church in Cambridge, Massachusetts, in 1763 that the frontiers must be secured from further Indian disturbances "by obliging the Indians to recede from our frontiers, or by preventing their communication with the French, or . . . by a firm treaty of peace with them." He preferred the latter and said that it could provide for "civilizing" as well as "saving" the Indians, which processes "are joined in one consistent design; and act uniformly in concert to support each other. Civility will prepare them to admit Religion; and Religion will prevent them from falling back into barbarism." Despite his curious allusion to "our" frontiers, as though they had not first belonged to the Indians, Apthorp was certain that the wars had awakened England and might "retrieve our expiring Virtue" through the propagation of true religion.[12]

Contrary to the apathy that missionaries often found among the leading men in the colony, Sir William Johnson, at first in charge of large land holdings of his family in upper New York and soon to become the distinguished Superintendent of Indian Affairs for the Northern Colonies, gave the generous support of his interest and means to the work of the church; he also used his good will and influence among the Indians whose languages he spoke. Johnson sponsored a new edition of the Prayer Book in 1762 and asked the assistance of Henry Barclay, now rector of Trinity Church, New York, who had not lost his facility in the native tongues, and the young Mohawk leader, Joseph Brant. The work was begun the following year but was delayed because of Barclay's death. Ogilvie agreed to assume this responsibility, and when printer Weyman died after completing only nine sheets, another delay occurred until Hugh Gaine completed the printing of the book early in 1769. In 1767 Johnson supervised a school for Indian boys on the Mohawk River for which the SPG sent over £150. It was also through Johnson's contribution of time and effort that the church's missionary work among the Indians of the northern and southern colonies was coordinated. Like so many others, he was convinced that the church could only be well established in America by providing for the episcopate, toward the support of which he gave twenty thousand acres of land near Schenectady. On December 10, 1768, he wrote the Society, "We cannot have a Clergy here without an episcopate." He told of seeing many churchmen embracing other persuasions, partly because, in the church's dilemma, dissenters, by enlarging on the fears of episcopal power, were winning them as converts.[13]

John Stuart, variously called "the first bishop of Toronto" and "the father of the Church in Upper Canada," took over the Mohawk mission on December 2, 1770. With Johnson's support and assisted by Joseph Brant, the brilliant Mohawk who may have been Johnson's son, he prepared a Mohawk translation of the Gospel of Mark, a large history of the Bible, and an exposition of the Catechism. Charles Inglis, of the Trinity Church staff, also spent some time assisting Stuart before the outbreak of the Revolutionary War.

The missionary efforts among the Negroes were usually carried out by local parish ministers, and only on rare occasions did the Society supply this program. It had indeed provided plans and even printed instructions as to how this work should be carried out in the local situations. Many of the missionary reports indicate careful attention to the evangelization of the Negroes and sometimes of the Indians as well. The SPG sent catechists into New York and Philadelphia with apparently very good results among the Negroes as early as the beginning of the eighteenth century. In the southern colonies the plantation system and the greater dependence of the whites on slavery kept alive the old issues of the relation of baptism and church membership for the Negro with his status as a slave.

One of the most successful ventures in educating the Negroes was carried out in New York City by Elias Neau. Originally a French Huguenot, he had become devoted to the Church of England after memorizing the liturgy while imprisoned for his faith and was appointed a catechist by the Society on April 12, 1705. Although William Vesey was slow to approve Neau's work, largely because he thought it should have been done by an ordained missionary, he nevertheless read announcements in Trinity Church exhorting masters and mistresses to send Neau their slaves on Wednesday, Friday, and Sunday at five o'clock. It was not unusual on a Sunday to find thirty slaves in attendance, while on weekdays only eight or ten came for such instruction. Neau's records show the names of masters or mistresses who sent their slaves and the number but not the names of the men and women they sent.[14] In 1705 he reported twenty-eight women and eighteen men (of whom three were Indians) had received forty-six catechisms and books. When an act assuring masters of their proprietary rights over the slaves after their baptism was passed in November, 1706, Neau immediately found his attendance increasing. Soon he had more than one hundred slaves in his classes which required larger quarters for instruction. In contrast to the reserved habits of the Indians, the Negroes were eager to learn to express themselves, not only in a new language, but also in music for which they were naturally gifted.

Yet even under the legal protection of the Act of 1706, many masters refused to send their slaves to the church and threatened to sell them into Virginia if they went.[15] The Negro uprising in New York in April, 1712, impeded the progress of Neau's educational efforts. The conspirators, who had bound themselves to secrecy by sucking the blood of each other's hands and assured themselves of success by rubbing a sorcerer's powder on their clothes, set fire to a house on Sunday night, April 1. In the ensuing excitement they shot down and stabbed as many white men as they could, hoping to wipe out the whites and thus attain their freedom. When the great gun at the fort called all available men to arms, the revolt was soon quelled, and the surviving conspirators were captured save those who, fearing arrest, cut their own throats or shot themselves and their families. Most Negroes were entirely innocent in this revolt. Although only two of the Negroes apprehended had been even marginally associated with the Trinity Church school—one of them had been trying for two years to get his master's consent for baptism—Neau's work was almost destroyed.[16]

When Neau had established his work once more by 1719, he found in his school not only slaves but free Negroes and also some Indians, slave and free. So highly had Neau's instruction been appreciated that at his death "swarms of Negroes" came to William Huddleston, who had been catechizing slaves and apprentices on Sunday afternoons, asking him to continue Neau's work with them. Similar work was actually continued in New York City and, on a smaller scale, in most of the towns in the colony with good success throughout the eighteenth century. Samuel Auchmuty, an assistant at Trinity Church, reported in 1764 that "not one black that has been admitted by me to Holy

Communion, has turned out bad; or been in any shape, a disgrace to our holy profession."[17]

Auchmuty's success among the Negroes so favorably impressed the vestry that, on the death of Henry Barclay, he was named rector of Trinity Church. He lived on into the War of Independence and prudently said little about his political feelings, but, in 1774, he ventured to say that had an American bishopric been established even twenty years earlier the Revolution might never have taken place.[18] Others have since then raised the same question with the added query whether the momentum of the British anti-slavery movement in the 1830's might have brought to an unseparated America the benefits of emancipation without the loss of one million lives a generation later.[19] Fascinating as such speculations may be, they are difficult to equate by the side of the new birth of freedom and the restatement of the best of the British heritage in the new American nation and of the Church of England in the Protestant Episcopal Church in the United States of America. Both in state and church, these revised statements of long cherished values made provision for unencumbered steps of achievement from the restraints of tradition toward the emancipation of the human spirit. Whether the constitutional provisions for these freedoms in the democratic state and church, with ever larger places for lay participation and leadership, have brought an accompanying commensurate sense of responsibility to guarantee their perpetuity remains to be decided by those who have been set free.

VII

THE CHURCH
IN PENNSYLVANIA
AND NEW JERSEY

PENNSYLVANIA

When Charles II in 1681 gave William Penn title to Pennsylvania, named for his father, Admiral Sir William Penn, to whom the king owed a large debt, the charter contained a provision that services of the Church of England would be permitted there "without any denial or molestation whatsoever." William Penn had become a Quaker and had widely advertised his colony and even distributed his "Frame of Government" in the German language in the Rhineland; it was considered wise therefore to include this provision in the charter of a colony primarily designed to provide a haven for all faiths and even religious dissidents. Philadelphia remained for many years under the control of the Quakers, while the back country was largely populated by German Anabaptists, Moravians, Lutherans, Reformed, and some Scotch-Irish Presbyterians. Within fifty years, approximately fifty thousand Germans came into Pennsylvania so that many persons feared they might become the dominant element in the colony. On the recommendation of Governor Patrick Gordon, the Provincial Council in 1727 inaugurated legislation that required all immigrants from the continent arriving in Philadelphia to take an oath of allegiance to the Crown. While Pennsylvania was one of the most flourishing colonies, churchmen numbered probably not more than two per cent among the quarter of a million inhabitants before the Revolution.

It is possible that there were some members of the Church of England on the west bank of the Delaware River from the time the Dutch surrendered their claims to New York and the British took Newcastle in October, 1664. John Yeo, a missionary in Maryland, did visit these settlements in 1677 and spent several months here in 1678. But more than a decade elapsed after the founding of Philadelphia before the few Anglicans there could have their own church, and so most of them drifted into other denominations. Ironically, it may have been the influence of the learned Quaker, George Keith, that stimulated the English to plan for Prayer Book services.

Keith had studied at the University of Aberdeen as a fellow student with Gilbert Burnet, who would become the erudite historian and Bishop of Salisbury. Keith was soon converted from Presbyterianism to the Society of Friends, whose inner convictions and external valor he admired. When he first came to America in 1682, he settled in Monmouth, New Jersey, where five years later he became the surveyor-general, charged with drawing the boundary line between East and West Jersey. By 1689 he was in Philadelphia where he took charge of the newly established Friends' School. Having heard of the persecution of the Quakers in Boston, he tried to engage leading ministers there in a public debate in April, 1688, and, failing in this, he published severe attacks on their long-established ways of intolerance.

Back in Philadelphia, Keith turned his criticism upon the Friends for their laxity in discipline and heretical beliefs which he insisted bordered on Deism. Expelled from his teaching position, he was brought to trial and given a suspended fine, perhaps in the hope of reclaiming so valuable a person through leniency. His defense of purity in Christian faith and life soon brought against him "A Declaration or Testimony of Denial" at a public meeting of the Friends on April 20, 1692. It was confirmed in Burlington a few months later and in London in 1694. Meawhile, Keith had begun a separate Meeting of Friends and among his followers were "men of rank, character and reputation in these provinces," who soon came to be called "Christian Quakers." In an attempt to vindicate himself before the Friends in England whom he visited in 1694, Keith read widely and became convinced that he really owed his loyalty to the Church of England, which he found to be both Catholic and Protestant and the best answer to the dilemma of the Quakers.

While in England he was received into the church and ordained to the priesthood. At the suggestion of Thomas Bray, Keith prepared for the SPG a description of the state of religion in America which he knew so well and designated specific localities of greatest promise for the church. He also described the divisions among the Friends and stated that he had left about five hundred followers in fifteen Meetings in the colonies.

The Society was so impressed with the recent convert's knowledge of America and its people that in its first important act that body named him their first traveling missionary with authority to explore it for the church. With Patrick Gordon, his associate, he sailed from England on April 24, 1702, and arrived in Boston in June. Gordon died within six weeks of their arrival, but John Talbot, chaplain of the *Centurion* on which they had sailed, was so impressed by the opportunities in this work that he accepted Gordon's assignment. In Boston Keith preached in what was then called "the Queen's Chapel" on "The Doctrine of the Holy Apostles and Prophets, the Foundation of the Church of Christ," which was printed there soon afterward by Samuel Phillips. In it Keith set out six rules "which if put into practice would bring all to the Church of England who dissented from her." Increase Mather boldly opposed these arguments, and the answer that Keith subsequently gave to Mather had to be printed in New York, for no Boston printer would dare print anything that might offend the established clergy there. Induced by Colonel Morris to stay in Boston for the Harvard commencement, Keith became involved in a dispute with President Willard about his commencement address defending rigid predestination. Keith's reply, in splendid Latin, when translated also had to be printed in New York, but his arguments and manner had "a good effect in quieting the minds of many people in these parts and bringing them over to the Church."

Early in 1703, Keith and Talbot traveled from New York through New Jersey to Pennsylvania. On that journey they met numerous "Christian Quakers" or "Keithian Separatists," and many of them "came over with good zeal, and according to good knowledge, to the Church." One opposing Quaker wrote that Keith had been coldly received, bested in an argument by William Davis, a Seventh Day Baptist, and forced to leave Philadelphia with dishonor. The fact is that Keith debated with the unlettered Davis for about five hours, each taking thirty-minute periods, on the morning and afternoon of March 10, 1703, at a public meeting before several hundred people in the "Keithian" Meeting House. Though Keith pressed Davis to explain his division of the Trinity into three Gods and other heresies, Davis continued to rant against Keith and refused to be held to the argument. Finding it futile to continue, the next day Keith refused to appear, but Davis, to the great delight of his "crew" and the crowd in the street, went on for three hours from a public platform to denounce the highly respected Anglican missionary.[1]

During his stay of about two years, Keith not only traveled widely but also supervised the early arrivals among the SPG missionaries. On his return to England he published his report to the Society in 1706 under the title, *A Journal of Travels from New Hampshire to Caratuck, on the Continent of North America.* Subsequently he received the living at Edburton in Sussex where he served the church until his death on March 29, 1716.

It is difficult to think of even the comparatively few members of the Church of England in Philadelphia in the first decade after its settlement without assuming that someone in that colony, which provided complete religious liberty, had assembled the faithful in his home for Prayer Book services. In 1695, twelve years after the laying out of the city and when the population of Philadelphia was still less than five thousand, a simple church building was begun on a lot 140 by 132 feet on the west side of Second Street above High, and a bell was hung in a crotch of a nearby tree.

Among the earliest Prayer Book services in the city were those conducted by a schoolmaster, I. Arrowsmith, who was probably in deacon's orders as such teachers usually were. On March 26, 1698, he wrote Governor Francis Nicholson of Virginia, "We have a full congregation and some very desirous to receive the Sacrament at Easter." In response to this request Richard Sewell, a missionary in Maryland, came to minister to these people in Philadelphia and so became the first Anglican priest to administer Holy Communion in Pennsylvania. Governor Nicholson was widely known as a member of the SPG and a generous patron of the church. On the visit of the SPG missionaries in New York City in November, 1702, he brought five ministers together at his own expense, in the first clerical convocation in that city, to meet with Keith and Talbot and to discuss the welfare and opportunity of the church.

Toward the middle of 1698, Thomas Clayton became the regular missionary here and soon began to win converts from the Quakers and other groups. Under the date of July 12, 1700, just shortly before his death, Clayton wrote the Archbishop of Canterbury that in the four years since Christ Church had been built the parish had grown to more than five hundred sober and devout souls in and about the city. Few congregations in the colonial period grew so rapidly. By 1711 the church was enlarged, and on April 27, 1727, the cornerstone of the present brick church was laid by Governor Patrick Gordon. In its present form Christ Church was completed in 1744, and its chime of bells placed in the tower in 1754. Thirty-five years later, the Protestant Episcopal Church in the United States of America would be born there.

One of the most successful colonial clergymen was Evan Evans, who came to Christ Church in 1700 and immediately continued the expansion of its growth and program. He introduced services at Chichester, Chester, Concord, Montgomery, Radnor, Perkiomen and sent John Thomas, who was his assistant and schoolmaster and in deacon's orders, to take the services at Trinity Church, Oxford. In addition to covering this area of several hundred square miles and taking his own regular services, Evans lectured on the last Sunday evening of each month in preparation for the Holy Communion, and every Sunday evening after Evening Prayer he addressed the young men of the parish. Here he soon found not only his own young men but Quakers and others who dared not be seen by day in the Anglican church but at night were willing to stand outside the church windows to hear his lectures. Before Keith and Talbot arrived in Philadelphia, Evans had already baptized more than five hundred Quakers in Pennsylvania and West Jersey. After Keith's visit the number rose to above eight hundred, clear evidence that many of the members of Christ Church had come from the "Christian Quakers" and as a result of the strong convictions and high principles of George Keith. Many of his associates, who had once earnestly sought to live the disciplined Christian life with minimal support beyond their own inner guiding light, now came to enjoy with him the more structured influence of the tradition and guidance of the historic church. In this happy combination of strengths—the devout life supported by ordered forms of worship—Christ Church went on to hold its position of leadership in the church and community.

When Evan Evans returned to England in 1707, his place in Christ Church was filled by Andrew Rudman, a Swedish Lutheran clergyman, who served there until his death on September 17, 1708. This was one of the many evidences of the cordial relations between the Swedes and Anglicans. That this friendship was based on the common possession of the historic episcopate is clearly implied by Henry M. Muhlenberg in his *Journal*, where he stated his regret that the lack of episcopal consecration among the German Lutherans prevented them from enjoying the privileges of the English church along with their Swedish brethren.[2] However, at this point he was primarily referring to Lutheran pastors in New York. The fine relationship between Anglicans and Swedes on the Delaware was also due to the fact that both were of national churches with Erastian tendencies and both were latitudinarian on church order. The similarity in church liturgy must also have been a contributing factor.[3] There were many exchanges of pulpits between English and Swedish clergymen, and when political changes and depreciation of money resulted in a dwindling supply of English-speaking Swedish pastors, many of these Lutheran congregations accepted the Prayer Book and ministers ordained in England. Old Swedes' (Gloria Dei) Church in Philadelphia is but one example of this tradition.

Evans gave the Society a report of his work as a missionary, and, as so many others had previously done, he stressed the need for a bishop in America so that the work might be stabilized by the discipline as well as the doctrine of the church, "for the one is a fortress and a bulwark of defence to the other." During Evans's several visits to England, Christ Church lost some of its vigor under unfortunate interim pastors, although it continued to send petitions, usually prepared by John Talbot during his supply there, to the Society requesting an American bishop.

In order to restore their congregation to its former strength and position the vestry of Christ Church asked the Bishop of London for "such a gentleman as may be a credit to our communion, an ornament to the profession, and a true propagator of the gospel."[4] When they received no assistance, the vestry finally settled on Richard Welton, a Nonjuror lately arrived from London, who served the parish about two years with but little success. Both he and John Talbot had been consecrated as bishops by the Nonjuror bishops in England. Although their orders were valid, the Nonjurors often failed to have the required three bishops to preserve the regularity of their orders. Whether Talbot and Welton actually attempted to exercise their episcopal powers in America remains a moot question, but many believed that they at least administered confirmation and wore the vestments of a bishop.[5]

While Christ Church was being completed, George Whitefield frequently visited Philadelphia, preached to large congregations in that church, and on November 4, 1739, read prayers and assisted at the service of Holy Communion in the morning. A month later he was back in Philadelphia and compelled to take his service outdoors, for not more than a quarter of his congregation could be accommodated in Christ Church. On his third visit to the city after Easter, 1740, Whitefield attended Christ Church in the morning and heard Commissary Archibald Cummings explain the importance of Christian works from the text James 2:18. In his sermon to about fifteen hundred people that evening he attacked Cummings' sermon, causing much confusion. Many were beginning to suspect Whitefield of fighting "against the church under her colours" and within a short time the commissary of South Carolina would suspend Whitefield from the ministry. The good judgment and conservatism of Commissary Cummings and the other clergy held steady most of the members of the church, and many of the more sober-minded of the dissenters, who were repelled by the excesses of Whitefield, were led to seek refuge in the Church of England. In 1763 Whitefield was again in Philadelphia and then, being much more moderate in his manner, was invited by Commissary Richard Peters and preached in both Christ Church and St. Peter's.

For about twenty years the church in Philadelphia prospered under the constructive ministries of Robert Jenney, until his death in 1762, and his assistant William Sturgeon, whose successful work among the Negroes won public commendation by the SPG. In this period St. Peter's Church was erected, and at its opening on September 4, 1761, the sermon was preached by William Smith, then provost at the college and later a leader of the church in Maryland.

During the ministry of Richard Peters from 1762 to 1775, Christ Church and St. Peter's were incorporated by a special charter granted by Thomas and Richard Penn on June 28, 1765. Two sons of Christ Church became active in its leadership in the last years before the war; William White was named an assistant in 1772, and Jacob Duché, who had been on the staff for more than a decade, was named rector to succeed Richard Peters in 1775. Two years later Duché went to England, and White began his long and distinguished service as rector of Christ Church. Three signers of the Declaration of Independence were members of this church: Robert Morris, the financier of the Revolution, was a brother-in-law of William White; Francis Hopkinson was the rector's warden and organist; and Benjamin Franklin was a vestryman.

In the eighteenth century the churches in Pennsylvania, West Jersey, and Delaware were interrelated, and even parts of Maryland were touched by the missionaries who moved about freely in these wider areas. So John Yeo, coming from Maryland, was accepted as a minister by the court in Newcastle and permitted to conduct services in Delaware. The status of the church here may be seen in the record of the first convention of the clergy held at Philadelphia from Wednesday, April 30, through Monday, May 5, 1760. The Philadelphia clergy who attended included Commissary Robert Jenney, Provost William Smith, William Sturgeon, catechist to the Negroes, the controversial William MacClennachan, and Jacob Duché; Richard Peters was absent. Several Delaware churches sent representatives: Charles Inglis, later to serve with distinction in New York City, represented three churches on Dover Mission, which included the entire county of Kent, and Philip Reading at Apoquinimy reported seventy communicants. Two churches at Lewes served by Matthias Harris, although not represented, sought union with the convention, and Mr. Ross, the minister at Newcastle where the church was "thin of people," found it impossible to attend, as did several other missionaries.

William Thompson, who had just arrived from England, and Samuel Cook and Robert McKean of New Jersey attended the meetings. George Craig of Chester, where the church had once included more than half the town in its membership, reported recent improvement in his work, and Hugh Neill at Oxford said his parish was "in a very flourishing way." The newly arrived Thompson was sent to the vast York and Cumberland Mission, which had three congregations scattered as widely as York, Carlisle, and Huntington. Northampton and Berks were considered frontier counties with no missions; Mr. Morton, an itinerant missionary in New Jersey, occasionally conducted services in Easton, and there was a movement among the people in Reading to obtain a missionary for that town in Berks. Stone church buildings had already been erected in Pequea and in Bangor Parish in Caernarvon.

Those attending the clergy conference in Philadelphia sent a letter, as was usually done at such gatherings, to the proprietors of the province commending Thomas and Richard Penn and telling of their convention. The meeting, which concluded at the commencement exercises of the college, provided good fellowship among the clergy and also publicized the work of the church as Charles Inglis wrote in 1761, "so many black gowns made no inconsiderable appearance, I can tell you, in these parts."

In Lancaster, where Thomas Barton was now the missionary, there was a small church building, and the parish gave promise of growth, probably because of the careful educational efforts of its missionary. Shortly after his attendance at the convention in Philadelphia, Barton must have begun his preparation for *The Family Prayer Book*, which he had printed in 1767 at the famous press of the Ephrata Cloister of the Seventh Day Baptists. In his introduction, signed on May 25, 1767, he said that this was to be used as a supplement to the Book of Common Prayer, especially to promote "Family Worship, a Duty too little attended to." After forty pages of varied prayers for numerous occasions, grace before and after meat, and an evening hymn, he added a section of twenty-seven pages giving directions for guidance in public worship and the use of the Prayer Book. He also included his own practical suggestions for deriving the greatest profit in each part of the service and topical indexes to the collects and Psalms; the final eight pages reproduced the church Catechism. This book is one of the rarest of all American prayer books and is the first to reproduce parts of the Book of Common Prayer in English in this country.

From the beginning of his ministry Barton had tried to Christianize the Indians with only modest success, and although he stayed in the colony until 1778, he was never able to do more than befriend their tribes and help to stabilize the frontier. William Smith later praised very highly the work of Barton who, with two Presbyterian ministers, kept the region united so that it was not lost in the French and Indian War. The church in Lancaster had been begun by Richard Locke, an Anglican missionary to Bermuda who, after eight months there, came to Philadelphia in 1744 and soon afterward became an itinerant missionary in Pennsylvania and West Jersey. While in Lancaster, he organized St. James Parish on October 3, 1744, and also served at Pequea and the Welsh congregation of Bangor Church in Caernarvon. George Craig succeeded him in this large mission, which he invariably called "the waste places of Pennsylvania."[6]

One of the most significant institutions begun in colonial Pennsylvania was the College and Academy which would become the University of Pennsylvania after the war. Although Benjamin Franklin had sketched a plan for the school as early as 1744, it was not until 1749, after he issued his pamphlet, "Proposals Relative to the Education of Youth in Pennsylvania," that the school began with David Martin as its first provost. Franklin and his associates had originally invited Samuel Johnson, who later accepted the presidency of King's College, hoping that he would head their school and institute Dean Berkeley's ideas about higher education.

Seeking to keep learning in its place of central importance, these first trustees set the terms for degrees by the standards of Oxford and Cambridge. The buildings were to be simple, with private rooms ten feet square for each student, and wisely they agreed that the principal expense should be in making a handsome provision for the provost and Fellows. The first tutors were Charles Thompson and David James Dove, an Englishman with sixteen years' experience as a teacher. Thompson was later the Secretary of the Continental Congress and made the first American translation of the Septuagint, which was published in four volumes in Philadelphia in 1808. When Provost Martin, who had also taught Greek and Latin, died two years later, Francis Alison, a leading Presbyterian clergyman in Philadelphia, succeeded him and taught logic and ethics. The really formative leadership for the new college fell to William Smith, born in Scotland near Aberdeen, where he took his degree.

On May 24, 1754, when only twenty-seven and only recently admitted to holy orders in the Church of England, Smith was inducted as provost of the College and Academy of Philadelphia and became its professor of natural philosophy. Alison, in turn, became the vice-provost. Within two years Smith had prepared his "Plan of Education" in which he suggested that proper learning is based on "a general foundation in all branches of literature which may enable the youth to perfect themselves in those particular parts to which their business or genius may afterwards lead them." To this broad cultural yet practical design he added for good measure "scarce anything has more obstructed the advancement of sound learning than a vain imagination that a few years spent at a college can render youth such absolute masters of science as to absolve them from all future study."

While this school was never a church institution, even though men like Commissary Jenney regretted that it was not so, churchmen outnumbered other trustees two to one when Provost Smith wrote the SPG that the church was using its influence there "by soft and easy means." On the first commencement on May 17, 1757, the first name on the list of students to receive the Bachelor of Arts degree was Jacob Duché, later to be rector of Christ Church. When Provost Smith openly supported England's struggle with France in 1758, he was arrested for libel against the pacific policy of a Quaker dominated Assembly and because he had supported Judge William Moore whom the Assembly had impeached. The trustees enthusiastically supported Smith and ordered his classes to hear his lectures at the jail.

Although Smith and Franklin, both men of conviction, occasionally disagreed, Franklin supported Smith at the college and in his wider educational interests. In order to provide for the educational needs of the thousands of Germans in Pennsylvania, Smith led Franklin, Peters, and others to organize in 1754 the Society for Propagating Knowledge among the Germans of Pennsylvania, which was dependent on English resources and so soon failed. It is very probable that it was this project that prompted Franklin's permanent interest in education for the Germans and led to his participation in the establishment of Franklin College (now Franklin and Marshall) at Lancaster.

Smith's popularity now gave him access to sources of larger gifts, and when several successive unbalanced budgets threatened the stability of the institution, he was sent to England in 1762 to raise further funds there. By cooperation with James Jay, who was on a similar mission for King's College, each institution netted £5,937.

The good work of the church in Delaware was badly disrupted during the war, and not until 1841, with the election of its first bishop, Alfred Lee, was there to be a revival of Anglicanism there. But for the devoted loyalty to his people and the magnificent leadership of William White in Christ Church, Philadelphia, all of the strength of the church in Pennsylvania might also have suffered a similar debilitation.

NEW JERSEY

The year 1702 marks the beginning of New Jersey as a Crown-controlled colony and also the beginning of the organized missionary work of the Church of England. New Jersey was named in honor of Sir George Carteret who had been governor of the Isle of Jersey; the lands between the Hudson and Delaware Rivers were granted to him and Lord John Berkeley by the Duke of York in 1664. The proprietors guaranteed religious liberty and government by popular assembly. Three years later the region was divided into East Jersey, where Carteret controlled the northeastern part of the state, and West Jersey, owned by Penn and other Quakers in the southwest areas along the lower Delaware and the Bay. By 1682 Penn and his associates had purchased East Jersey, and twenty years later the two areas were united as New Jersey with all jurisdictional rights once again in the hands of the Crown but with all property rights in the hands of the proprietors, a less than ideal situation.

When the SPG began its work in New Jersey in 1702, Anglicanism was already widely diffused throughout the province, "but as a friendly tendency rather than an organized body." In the northeastern areas the Puritans, who had come in from New England and Long Island, and some Scotch Presbyterians were the most numerous, while southeastern New Jersey remained for a long time a stronghold of the Quakers. Under Keith's influence many of these would later become churchmen.

While there were only twelve communicants in East Jersey in 1700, there were hundreds of baptized members and friends of the church. At least ten communities had unorganized congregations where the missionaries on their later arrival planted parishes which flourished immediately.

Colonel Lewis Morris, a staunch supporter of colonial church work, described the New Jersey situation for the Anglican authorities and made some striking suggestions. He called the approximately eight thousand West Jersey settlers "a hotch-potch of all religions" with the exception of the Quakers, whom he styled "men of the best rank and estates." To win converts to the church from these people, distracted by almost every variety of dissent but with little appearance of real religion among them, Morris suggested that only "a pious Churchman" should ever be governor and, if possible, the membership of the council and magistracy should also be so limited. He felt that Parliament might grant some special privilege to Anglican settlers but suggested that missionaries should preach gratis until their parishes had grown sufficiently to support them. So strong was his feeling about such service that he even suggested that no one should be appointed to the great benefices in England who had not spent at least three years in preaching in America without salary. His plan was never tried, of course, and Morris was the first to welcome the SPG men when they came on voluntary missionary service.

Toward the close of the seventeenth century, chaplains in New York occasionally made visits to the North Jersey shore to conduct services and administer the sacraments. Alexander Innes, arrived from Scotland about 1685, lived for a while in New York and later in Monmouth County, New Jersey, where he was the only priest in the region. By 1695 the desire of the leading residents in Perth Amboy for regular services of the church prompted the request that the Bishop of London send them a priest. By the fall of 1698 Edward Portlock arrived as their pastor, and before the end of the year the old courthouse had been reconstructed as a church. Governor Jeremiah Basse, once an Anabaptist preacher and now under oath to the proprietors not to consent to any act to raise a maintenance for any minister, became a supporting friend of the church. He often took Portlock with him on official visits as his chaplain and arranged to have Portlock preach before the General Assembly on February 22, 1699. About 1701 Portlock moved to Virginia where he served four years more until his anti-feminist fame undermined his influence. He had a favorite cat, Alice, of which his wife became so insanely jealous that she hanged it. So enraged was her husband that he preached a sermon against women in general and his wife very much in particular.

George Keith and John Talbot visited New Jersey on their survey for the SPG; the former had his largest influence in West Jersey among the Quakers, while Talbot worked in the central areas. Impressed with the needs and opportunities there, he settled in Burlington in 1703 and from that point traveled extensively and frequently to serve other points until his death near the end of 1727. His Jacobite leanings and his Nonjuror episcopal consecration were constant sources of embarrassment. For some years he was the lone priest in the entire colony until Edward Vaughan and Thomas Haliday arrived in 1709 under SPG appointment. The former became a great asset to the church for many years, while the latter, a victim of over self-indulgence, was obliged to leave after about nine years of scattered services. Vaughan's great success came in Old St. John's Church in Elizabeth, where from 1709 he gave thirty-eight years of remarkably fruitful service and often ministered in nearby missions as well. He had married a widow of means and vaunted a kind of harmless pomp, but his Welsh humor won him many friends among the dissenters. Vaughan enjoyed a close friendship with the leading Presbyterian pastor, Jonathan Dickinson, and during his ministry had many converts from the Baptists, Quakers, and Presbyterians. His assistant and successor was Thomas Bradbury Chandler, who had served as a lay reader before he became a catechist and missionary. He was destined not only to have a successful ministry in Elizabeth but also to be the leading champion of an American episcopate and a theology of the church and sacraments that would become more widespread under the influence of his son-in-law, Bishop John Henry Hobart, in the next century. In his time Chandler proved himself a typical traveling missionary. In addition to his regular work in Elizabeth, by 1762 he had preached nearly two hundred sermons and ridden more than three thousand miles to minister to the church at Woodbridge and yet had not received more than five guineas from these people.

Many clergymen found it difficult to remain free of debt. Robert Walker reported that a suit of clothing cost him £8 and he paid a surgeon £3 to treat his infected hand. Many turned to other vocations: some taught school and several practiced medicine. Churchmen generally did not approve of having clergy engage in other professional activities and especially disliked paying them fees for professional medical service. Jonathan Odell gave up his salary for four years to help pay for his church building and meanwhile tried to support his family by the practice of medicine. Robert McKean was educated as a physician and ordained to the ministry in 1757; before his death in 1767 at the age of thirty-five he became the first president of the New Jersey Medical Society.[7]

Thomas Haliday, whom Talbot called a glutton, drunkard, and railer, was an example of what the rough frontier influences could do even to the clergy. On one occasion he hit his host on the nose with a decanter and on another threw a cup of hot coffee and a tankard of cold cider at two ladies. Despite such crudity and temper, he seemed to have some success in later years when he served a church in Delaware. Nathaniel Horwood had an unhappy and lonely ministry in Burlington from 1726 to 1730 and also embarrassed his parishioners, who said, "He makes boate men, Sotts and the very Dreggs of human Society his Chief and Valiant Pot Companions." William Lindsay, who served numerous missions in West Jersey, Pennsylvania, and Delaware for a decade until the Society was forced to dismiss him in 1745, had a recor of business irregularities, misappropriation of church funds, and being an habitual drunkard and rake.

But for every such minister in this or any other colony there were many like the comparatively unknown John Holbrooke, who served at Salem, New Jersey, for about four years and later in Virginia after 1729. His ministry was productive, and he was known by everyone as a man of unblemished character, one of the least known but better missionaries of the Society. Few of the New Jersey missionaries were dismissed for negligence or misconduct, and nine of those who served before 1776 are included in the *Dictionary of American Biography*.

Actually the needs were so great and the applicants for foreign missionary service so few that at times the Society and even the Bishop of London took chances on the qualifications of applicants. So Bishop Terrick of London ordained and licensed George Spencer, whom he described as "grave" and "well disposed," because his ship was about to sail, even though his examiner found his qualifications were only "moderate." His ministry was brief and less than spectacular in New York and New Jersey, and his departure for the church in North Carolina was the last heard of him.

Uzal Ogden, Jr., spent the last few years before the Revolution as a missionary in the Delaware Water Gap region and soon came to be recognized as one of the best of the church's tract writers. His philosophical writings included the *Antidote to Deism* and his refutation of Tom Paine's *Age of Reason*. Although he had been trained by Thomas B. Chandler, who commended him as "not enthusiastic," Ogden soon wrote tracts on "Brotherly Love," "A Letter to the Unconverted," and "Family Worship," and was accused of deviating from the Prayer Book services and ultimately ignoring the Prayer Book entirely. Yet he was greatly in demand and served in New York City, Elizabeth, and, after 1788, in Trinity Church, Newark. Ogden openly cooperated with and praised the Methodists and declared he would not cease to be friendly with them, "as I am persuaded they are instrumental in advancing the divine glory, and the salvation of mankind." Ogden was a personal friend of Francis Asbury, whom he entertained in his home. He assured Asbury that "the clergy of our Church in this state are disposed to be friendly to the Methodists; and with cheerfulness, if called on, will administer to them the Divine ordinance." Actually this happened frequently since Methodist ministers lacking episcopal ordination usually refrained from administering Holy Communion. Asbury himself communed in St. Mary's Church, Burlington, in June, 1773. It is not too surprising, then, that twice the General Convention refused to confirm Ogden's election as Bishop of New Jersey primarily because he was suspected of "Methodistical" inclinations and lack of loyalty to the church. In October, 1805, he became a Presbyterian.[8]

The missionary spirit of the church in New Jersey was stimulated in part by a serious concern on the part of men like Colonel Lewis Morris who, as early as 1704, wished the Society to send a Dutch-speaking missionary to the three or four Dutch towns in northern New Jersey. About eight years later with the approval of the Archbishop of Canterbury, the Society printed a Prayer Book with English and Dutch versions in parallel columns. Some of the Dutch, greatly disturbed by the division in their church over the training of their ministers, the question of the use of the Dutch or English language, and the issues of the Great Awakening, sought refuge in the order of the Church of England.

The Great Awakening revivalists, including the Dutch pastors, William Bertholf and Theodore Frelinghuysen, and Presbyterian Gilbert Tennent, not only stirred up enthusiasm in their own churches by their insistence on personal religious experience and conversion but also won some disciples among the Anglicans. In opposition to these revivals and sudden conversions, church missionaries usually stressed the superiority of rational piety, sacramentalism, and Christian nurture. But the revivalists still found a ripe harvest among Anglicans for whom little adjustment to the American scene had been made in their services of worship. Preaching was often long and dull and, as one Scot put it, "a cauld clatter of morality." There were few hymns and fewer tunes; a few canticles and Psalms were deemed sufficient. By the fall of 1705 the pastors of New York and New Jersey tried to promote better knowledge and use of the Psalms and asked the Society to pay the printer, William Bradford, to print a sufficient supply for the missions before next Easter. Scarcely ever were there enough Prayer Books; a clerk often read the responses from a desk, and if the people took a slight part in the service, it was in behaving devoutly and decently. William Skinner, who gave about thirty-five years as pastor in Perth Amboy and founded Christ Church, New Brunswick, once wrote the Society that if they would furnish laborers in proportion to the harvest, schisms would soon disappear and the church would be universally established in New Jersey and "the very Crown would thereby be better secur'd in the Allegiance of the Subjects." But this was not to happen. All over the colonies, emotionally starved churchmen, tired of lifeless formalities, were following the Methodists, who succeeded so well that at times Wesleyan Societies were formed in the Anglican churches. As the confusion of the approaching Revolution brought further disorganization to the church, literally thousands of undernurtured Anglicans fell away to other American churches.

In spite of the church's limitations, the laity often made great efforts to worship, sometimes driving ten to sixteen miles; except in the spring and fall when it would have been an additional strain on their hard-worked horses, there were often two hundred persons in attendance, for example, in Freehold. During the illness of pastors or vacancies, lay readers, many of whom were schoolmasters, read Morning Prayer and a sermon. Some of these were men of real promise and, like Thomas B. Chandler, later became missionaries in the church.

Through the influence of George Keith, the Society, in 1704, decided to open parochial schools where well-trained teachers would drill the children in the Catechism and Christian manners. Negroes and Indians also received instruction, and frequently an evening school was conducted for servants. Sometimes as many as one-third of the children came from homes of dissenters.

In the colonial era New Jersey Anglicans built more than a score of church buildings, of wood and stone, some large and others small. Occasionally churchmen resorted to lotteries which provided as much as £1,000 for building purposes, rationalizing their procedure, no doubt, on the ground that a church is a public building and so, like bridges, could be supported in this fashion. Among the larger structures were Trinity Church, Newark, "built according to the rules of Architecture, So that it will be the best and most compacted Building in the province," and St. John's, Elizabeth, which Chandler considered the finest in the colony. The old church in Shrewsbury, completed in 1774 and then described as "one of the most compleat and best finished Churches in the Province," is the only one of these colonial churches preserved, probably because the community has not grown rapidly. Some parishes patiently took years to build their modest buildings unassisted, and other congregations long remained content to use courthouses or to "creep into the corner of some Country house."

Many church people avoided regular communion either because of "a deep tincture of Quakerism," where sacraments were considered "popish," or because they were frightened by dissenting ministers, who stressed that communicants must be fit persons before they present themselves for Holy Communion. Among the Dutch even Frelinghuysen's deacons would not venture to communion. The SPG's William Skinner cynically wrote of the revivalists that they were "so nicely acquainted with the Almightie's Counsels and Decrees, that at first Sight they can distinguish 'tween Saint and Sinner."

Missionary Robert Blackwell found his people at Waterford "too much tinctured with Methodism," and at nearby Greenwich (now Clarksboro) they were well meaning but "somewhat enthusiastic" and had to be reclaimed "rather by conviction than reproof." And well he might build strong conviction in his people, for he was competing with William Watters on the Trenton Circuit of the Methodist Church, who wrote, "I felt freedom of spirit, and preached as if every sermon was my last. I felt myself on the Lord's business, and forgot all other concerns."

It was just such building of faith and conviction that helped many dissenters, who disagreed with the more radical revivalists, to find their religious needs satisfied in the more ordered ways of the Church of England. Many old established families trace their church connections to this period. Frequently it was the good students, children of the sober and devout dissenters, who declared for the church, and many of them went on to seek ordination. A surprising number of the SPG missionaries in New Jersey were converts from Roman Catholicism or from Protestant denominations, and converts from Judaism were not unknown. Roman Catholics were never numerous in New Jersey and were mostly to be found among the German glassworkers near Glassboro, the miners in Morris County, or the scattered Irish servants. So few were they, however, that Thomas Chandler reported as late as 1762 that there were no "Papists" in New Jersey.

For almost one hundred years before the Revolution the Anglicans frequently had friendly or at least tolerable relations with the leaders of other churches. As chaplain of the fort in New York City, Alexander Innes visited New Jersey in the 1680's and later settled there, where he was respected by the people of all faiths among whom he ministered seemingly without concern for denominational lines. Until the arrival of the SPG's Keith and Talbot, Innes usually was the lone representative of the Church of England in all New Jersey. With the continued mellowing influence of a common life under similar pressures of their common environment, friendliness among religious groups in New Jersey improved in the eighteenth century and dissenters and churchmen cooperated in founding the New Jersey Medical Society.

In founding the Corporation for the Relief of Widows and Children of Clergymen, New Jersey churchmen consulted the English dissenter, Richard Price, and were also greatly helped by Francis Alison, vice-provost at the University of Pennsylvania and president of the Presbyterian Ministers' Fund. In Hunterdon County, Presbyterians and Baptists joined with Anglicans in union summer services. Thomas Chandler was more cautious about such "moderation," which he thought was becoming dangerously prevalent and the cause of apathy among his parishioners.

Ordinarily churchmen cooperated freely with others in planning and conducting schools for community advancement. Yet Governor Lewis Morris, opposed to all dissenters and enthusiasts, refused to grant a charter to the evangelical Presbyterians for their College of New Jersey, later Princeton. When the charter was granted by his successor, Governor John Hamilton, William Skinner expressed a common Anglican attitude of concern that dissenters "trusted with the education of our youth will endeavour to warp them from all their principles and form them according to their own."[9]

Relations with the Huguenots were usually very friendly here, as in New York, and often led to assignments of SPG missionaries to French congregations, whose liturgy was similar to that of the Book of Common Prayer. William Harrison, once a missionary in New Jersey, served such a parish on Long Island for ten years without salary until eventually he had converted most of its members. Huguenot pastors also occasionally served Anglican parishes. Michael Houdin, converted from Romanism to Anglicanism in 1744, was ordained and sent as a missionary to Trenton. He traveled widely in the regions of the Delaware and Lehigh Rivers and eventually spent the years of the French and Indian War as a chaplain in the royal troops and as an intelligence officer under Generals Amherst and Wolfe. Recently found sources indicate that Houdin may have given the English the information about the winding path from the Anse du Foulon to the Plains of Abraham where Wolfe died as his troops won the battle at Quebec. The unidentified clergyman standing in prayer on the extreme right in Benjamin West's "The Death of Wolfe" is probably Houdin. Before his conversion from Rome,

Houdin had been assigned as Superior of a Canadian monastery and may at that time have learned about the environs of Quebec. He spent his last years as a missionary among the French at New Rochelle, New York.[10]

While itself the object of missionary support, the church in New Jersey showed early and constant concern for its own missionary obligations. Although the Indian population of the colony had been greatly depleted by disease and migration, the church did make some efforts to Christianize the remnant of the Delawares, and here and there the names of Indians appear on the baptismal records. Thomas Wood served as a missionary in New Jersey until 1752 and then went to Nova Scotia, where he used his bilingual capacity effectively for the church and also sought to help the Micmac Indians. By 1766 he had not only mastered that language but also prepared a Micmac grammar, together with a translation of the Creed, the Lord's Prayer, and other parts of the Prayer Book which he sent to the publisher that year.

Much more impressive is the New Jersey record of more than 350 baptisms among the Negroes; Abraham Beach had singular success in his work among the Negroes in the New Brunswick area. Frequently slaves, who made the most of this one open door to their improvement, showed excellent achievement in their public examination in doctrine before the congregations.

Thomas Thompson, who took charge of the widely extended Shrewsbury Mission in New Jersey in September, 1745, soon succeeded in ministering far beyond his parish boundaries among the unchurched, illiterates, and Negroes. He became so fascinated by the opportunities among the Negroes that he obtained the Society's permission to open a mission on the Guinea Coast of West Africa, where he worked successfully from 1751 to 1756. Later he published two books, *Two Missionary Voyages*, telling of his life in America and Africa, and *The African Trade for Negro Slaves*, in which he stated his somewhat naive conviction that slavery might be the means of bringing the Negroes to Christianity.

The Church of England was not uniformly distributed or developed as the strained relations between England and the colonies approached the breaking point. In the South where ministers of varying qualifications had come in fairly large numbers, the direction of the church had been left to commissaries of the Bishop of London. In the colonies where Anglicanism was established and where taxes could be imposed on all for the support of the church, the laity came to have a large and sometimes controlling interest, a fact which would later be reflected in the structure of the new church in America.

The most important single instrument in the progress and development of the church was the SPG, not even an official organ of the Church of England, through which £227,000 or about $1,125,000, with a modern money equivalent of more than ten times that sum, was poured into the colonies to support more than three hundred missionaries sent here in the two generations before the war. Actually, from 1607, nearly two thousand Church of England clergymen had served in America for longer or shorter periods. Among these men there were giants, whose foresight and leadership were the determining factors in planting and nourishing the church in America in the late eighteenth century. The settled strength of the church was still in the South, where more than half of the 250 clergy in America resided in Virginia and Maryland. Slightly less than three hundred parishes dotted the vast country soon to be the United States of America.

Swept violently by the Revolution because of ecclesiastical connections and clerical ordination vows of loyalty to the king, it is something of a miracle that a scattered and leaderless church should have been preserved at all. All religious bodies suffered in the war, but Anglicanism came very close to expiration. Other churches had been slowly adapting themselves to the new situation and building their structures and polities in keeping with the new way of American life. For these churches, unaccustomed to and unhindered by the absence of bishops, the adjustments here became so many steps of advance and progress in their work. But for the Anglicans, for whom authority and direction are centered in the episcopate, the colonial era and the new union of the Thirteen Colonies provided almost insurmountable problems. Had the English church found a way to send bishops here at any point up to the middle of the eighteenth century the church might well have been solidly established, distinctly American in its orientation, and prepared to assume a role of leadership in the early constructive years of the new national life. That bishops had not been supplied for an episcopally oriented church was a tragedy that must be appraised.

VIII

THE STRUGGLE FOR
THE EPISCOPATE

The consecration of Samuel Seabury as the first American bishop in the line of the Anglican episcopate in 1784 is approximately the mid-point in the history of the church in America. For 177 years after the settlement of Jamestown, the Church of England, deprived of episcopal leadership, managed to survive the threats in the New World for which she was so ill-prepared; in the last 180 years under episcopal supervision the Episcopal Church's expansion and development have fully justified the efforts of the colonial churchmen in attempting to obtain and preserve the historic episcopate. From the earliest years there were those farsighted leaders who saw the inconsistency of trying to provide the benefits of the Church of England without its order and direction, and in the eighteenth century the cry became increasingly persistent that Anglicanism would be lost without provision for Anglican structure and polity. It is an oversimplification to say that the calls for bishops can be classified by periods because the stream of petitions was constant and varied; yet it is true that the missionaries themselves began the appeals soon after their arrival, the activity of the bishops and others in England followed about mid-century, and the acrimonious pamphlet and newspaper controversies filled the last decades before the war.

As early as 1638, two generations before the SPG was born, Archbishop Laud had planned to send a bishop to New England, but disturbances in Scotland and the subsequent Civil War blocked his proposal. He actually did send William Morrell as a commissary to Plymouth, but he was not gladly received by the Pilgrims and never fully pressed his business. Soon after the Restoration the Lord Chancellor Edward Clarendon presented a similar plan to the king, and a patent was signed in 1673 making Alexander Murray, who had frequently been a companion of Charles II in his travels, the Bishop of Virginia.[1] The fall of Clarendon and the accession of the Cabal Ministry may

have contributed to the failure of this plan, although Archbishop Thomas Secker thought that its failure was the result of lack of financial provision since the necessary endowment was made payable out of the customs, which was an uncertain item. In 1695 Chaplain John Miller in New York naively proposed that a suffragan to the Bishop of London should be named governor of the province and care for both civil and ecclesiastical government. This was exactly what the Puritans feared might happen. Soon after Thomas Bray became the commissary in Maryland, he was convinced of the need for a bishop in the colonies and at once proposed to raise funds privately to purchase a farm in Maryland from which the bishop could derive his living. Through friendship with Robert Hunter, once named Governor of Virginia where he never served and later Governor of New York, Dean Jonathan Swift, best known as the author of *Gulliver's Travels*, was proposed as Bishop of Virginia and later as Bishop of New York. Hunter wrote, "I have purchased a seat for a bishop, and by orders from the society have given orders to prepare for his reception. You once upon a day gave me hopes of seeing you there. It would be no small relief to have so good a friend to complain to."[2] All these plans failed and perhaps fortunately so, for until this point the religious and secular duties of a bishop had not been clearly set out and the introduction of the typical English bishop might have done more harm than good at this time.

The first missionaries of the SPG soon joined the increasingly larger number of American clergy calling for a bishop in the colonies. George Keith and John Talbot emphatically stated the case in the report of their survey of the church in America. Talbot became so ardent in the cause of American episcopacy that when he saw no hope of its immediate accomplishment, he returned to England and in 1722 received consecration from the Nonjuror bishops, only to be temporarily suspended by the SPG when they discovered his episcopal power, which he probably never exercised.

Evan Evans, the successful incumbent at Christ Church, Philadelphia, summarized for the Society in 1707 the needs for a bishop in America, which many had previously written about in scattered reports. In addition to providing for the succession of ministers by proper selection, training, and ordination, Evans wrote that a bishop could lead his clergy under discipline in cooperative effort and support them also in exercising discipline among the laity. To these functions some missionaries meeting in Burlington, New Jersey, in 1705 added: to ordain Presbyterian and Congregational ministers, to confirm, and to protect the church from its enemies. At about the same time Bishop Henry Compton suggested to the Society that a suffragan bishop, acting as an assistant to an English bishop, would fit the situation perfectly so that the needed benefits of confirmation, ordination, and consecration of churches would thereby be added to the already accepted functions of the commissaries.

The Society was so committed to having a suffragan for America that it presented a series of petitions to the Archbishop of Canterbury in 1704, and to Queen Anne herself in 1709 and again four years later, hoping "to compleat the face of decency and order" under a colonial episcopate as Bishop White Kennett put it in supporting the Society's plea. While these appeals were made primarily to the religious interest and devotion of Queen Anne, it must be admitted that at one point in the 1709 document the Society said, "We humbly beg leave to add, that we are informed that the French have received several great advantages from their establishing a Bishop at Quebec."[3] A later petition to King George I added equally objectionable reasons for the introduction of bishops, such as tithes of grants and escheats and a portion of the tax revenue. Such arguments alarmed the Nonconformists, who all along suspected the Anglicans of trying to unite ecclesiastical and civil powers in the transmission of episcopal authority. Apparently one of the early clergy at New Kent on the York River in Virginia had just such an idea in mind when he wrote to the Bishop of London, "If ministers here were as they ought to be we should have no dissenters. An eminent Bishop being sent over here would make Hell tremble, and settle the Church of England here forever."

Whatever her motivation, Queen Anne was quickly inclined to grant the favor and ordered a bill prepared for Parliament. On the eve of the realization of their dream, the proponents for the American episcopate were to be disappointed again when the Queen died in 1715 before the Act could be considered, and so all the work had to be begun anew. So keenly was the arrival of the new bishop expected in New Jersey that Governor Robert Hunter, prompted by Talbot and others, had purchased a "palace" for £600 sterling, which apart from a brief occupancy stood vacant and often in disrepair until 1747 when a fire left the episcopal palace, like the hope for the episcopate in America, in ashes. Thomas B. Chandler discovered in 1785 that this land was the only property in New Jersey owned by the Society. Since it had never been intended for parochial use and consequently no congregation could claim it, it was sold, and ironically the proceeds were placed in a fund for the support of an American episcopate.[4]

The new Hanoverian line brought to the English throne a succession of German rulers whose primary concern was a stable government that would permit no disturbing circumstances in state or church to wean away the tenuous loyalty of their new subjects. A plan submitted to George I provided for four bishops in America: two in the West Indies and one in Burlington, New Jersey, to have jurisdiction from the east side of the Delaware to Newfoundland; and the other with a seat in Williamsburg, Virginia, from the west side of that river "to the utmost bounds of your Majesty's dominions westward." These bishops were to be largely locally supported, but when the governors discovered that fees previously payable to them would now be diverted to the new ordinaries, little support could be expected from this source. Moreover, George I and his Whig administration under Sir Robert Walpole distrusted the clergy, whom they suspected of favoring the Stuart Pretender in the revolt of 1715, and showed no sign of interest in an American bishop.

The Society itself was disappointed but soon came to know the new rulers so well that it made no more attempts to win royal support for its cause. Not so easily discouraged was Archbishop Tenison, who, in 1715, bequeathed £1,000 toward the settlement of bishops in America. Until such time when bishops could be obtained, its income was to be used as a pension to the oldest missionary in colonial service, who was John Talbot, now in need of just such aid. In 1720 this fund was doubled by grants of £500 by Dugald Campbell and Lady Elizabeth Hastings.

When the Church of England failed to provide a plan to supply bishops for America, the successive Bishops of London took great pains to do what they could to provide for the lack. So Bishop Compton, after 1675, ordained candidates and granted certificates to ministers going to the colonies and who might then legally be inducted into parishes by a colonial governor. Such responsibility had been traditionally exercised by the Bishop of London from the founding of the London Company of which he was a member. When Edmund Gibson assumed that office in 1723, he must have seen little hope for an American episcopate under the Hanoverians, and he therefore sought and received a patent setting out clearly his responsibility to supervise the American churches, to provide for and exercise discipline over its clergy, and to appoint commissaries his representatives—a custom begun earlier but unofficially by Henry Compton. Thomas Sherlock, who succeeded Gibson in 1748, once more became hopeful that an American bishopric might be established, and worked toward that end.

The widespread feeling in the American churches is clearly discernible in a letter of June 2, 1718, sent to the archbishops and bishops of the Church of England by the vestries of Christ Church, Philadelphia, and St. Ann's, Burlington, and also signed by the clergy and many of the laity in Maryland, saying in part,

> . . . whereas, for want of episcopacy being installed amongst us, and that there has never been any Bishop sent to visit us, our churches remain unconsecrated, our children are grown up and cannot be confirmed, their sureties [god-fathers and god-mothers] are under solemn obligations but cannot be absolved, and our Clergy, sometimes, under doubts cannot be resolved;
>
> But whereas, more especially for the want of that sacred power which is inherent to your apostolick, the vacancies which daily happen in our ministry cannot be supplied for a considerable time from England, whereby many congregations are not only become desolate, and the light of the Gospel therein extinguished, but great encouragement is thereby given to sectaries of all sorts which abound and increase amongst us, and, some of them pretending to what they call the power of ordination, the country is filled with fanatic teachers, debauching the good inclinations of many poor souls who are left destitute of any instruction or ministry;
>
> May it therefore please your lordships, in your great piety and regard for the government of the Church by Bishops, to think of some means whereby these sorrowful complaints and most grievous misfortunes may be heard and redressed, and that Almighty God may, of his infinite mercy, inspire your thoughts, and assist your pious endeavours to accomplish this evidently necessary work, is the most earnest and daily prayer of. . . .[5]

From other regions now came similar and even stronger appeals. In 1724 Samuel Johnson, the newly ordained missionary at Stratford, Connecticut, wrote the new Bishop of London, Edmund Gibson, who was trying to carry on the sensitively helpful colonial church administration of his predecessor, Henry Compton, that there were

> . . . a considerable number of very promising young gentlemen . . . and those the best that are educated among us, who . . . for want of episcopal ordination decline the ministry, and go into secular business, . . . So that the fountain of all our misery is the want of a Bishop, for whom there are many thousands of souls in this country do impatiently long and pray, and for want do extremely suffer.

The next year six New England clergy, including Timothy Cutler and Samuel Johnson, wrote the Society very specifically that if a bishop were sent, many well-wishers would immediately appear and form new congregations at once.

Such moving petitions from such important men and congregations simply could not be buried in the back of a file. Undoubtedly Bishop Gibson read them often and waited for the "inspiration of his thoughts" for which these petitioners prayed. He did make one very serious attempt to help their cause in 1727 when he invited the clergy of Maryland to nominate one of their own body who was worthy to become his suffragan. They chose Joseph Colebatch, a graduate of Oriel College in 1694, who spent his ministry in All Hallow's Parish, Arundel County, Maryland. When the Maryland authorities learned of his election and his intention to accept the invitation of the bishop to come to England for consecration, a writ of *ne exeat* was applied for and granted by the courts of Maryland confining Colebatch to his colony.

Toward the middle of the century leading English churchmen joined the ranks of the proponents of the American episcopate. At the annual meeting of the Society in 1741 Bishop Thomas Secker of Oxford preached a sermon supporting an American episcopate, in answer to which Andrew Eliot, a Congregational minister in New England, published a pamphlet, *Remarks upon the Bishop of Oxford's Sermon.* This was the first of a flood of pamphlets that would follow in attack and defense of this question in the next generation. Eliot anticipated most of the fears of the dissenters, some of them indeed grounded in previously published intentions of churchmen: that bishops would be supported by colonial taxation and that a complete establishment would inevitably follow with dire consequences for the free churches. Almost thirty years later Eliot, who had been elected to and declined the presidency of Harvard College, wrote Thomas Hollis in England, "The people of New England are greatly alarmed; the arrival of a bishop would raise them as much as any one thing."[6] Occasionally a direct personal appeal was made to independent clergymen in America. So White Kennett, Dean and later Bishop of Peterborough, wrote to Benjamin Coleman of Boston, "I hope your Churches would not be jealous of it, they being out of our line, and therefore beyond the cognizance of any overseers to be sent from hence."[7]

An independent and somewhat varied plan for American bishops was suggested in 1764 by an anonymous writer in England, as may be inferred from the text and from his naive opinion that at that time "the heats too of the most respectable part of the Dissenters are so abated, that in the eye of the most timid Policy apprehension of any considerable uneasiness in that Quarter seems groundless." From the most recently available statistics he reported that the American colonies had 2,104,000 inhabitants, of whom 844,000 were black and 1,260,000 white. Of the whites about one-third, or 401,000, were Anglicans; 391,000 Presbyterians, Independents, and Anabaptists; and the remaining 468,000 included German sectaries, Quakers, Papists, Jews, and unbelievers. He went on to say that

> . . . The Church of England . . . is the only one in those parts distinguished by the want of the Compleat Exercise of Religion according to its Rites and Ceremonies, whilst it desires that all its fellow Protestants may enjoy the full exercise of their religion without any obstruction, according to their forms in every part of his Majesty's dominions.

He then pleaded for completing the Church of England in America and even suggested having four bishops with seats in Burlington, New Jersey, or New York; in Williamsburg, Virginia; at Charlestown, South Carolina; and at Coddrington College in the Barbadoes. Most of their support was to come from England, and he added that it might be "of more assistance to the Governors and useful to the State" if the bishop sat as a member of every Council in his Diocese as the Surveyor General in his Department."

He was overly optimistic in his prediction that

> . . . no objections against supplying it will be made by anyone who has a just value for the doctrine of Toleration, and is a sincere well wisher to Piety, Virtue and good Government; provided the Regulations in settling Bishops are calculated not to offend or disturb those who enjoy their Liberty of Conscience to its fullest extent.

Despite the explanations of the appeals for a bishop and the sympathetic support of the writer of this plan of 1764 and of men like Dean Kennett and the English bishops, leaders in the colonial governments in America remained suspicious. Especially in New England, where the Church of England had rapidly grown after the conversion of Timothy Cutler and his associates at Yale, valiant efforts were made through every possible channel to prevent the authorization of bishops for America. The fact is that the SPG concentrated its efforts in New England, where thirty of its seventy-two missionaries in America were at work in 1764, largely because the work in the South was well established, with forty-two churches in Maryland alone.

The instructions to provincial agents in London frequently indicated that they used their powers to thwart any such plans afoot at the English Court. Samuel Adams, as the voice of the Massachusetts House of Representatives, in 1768 wrote their agent in London,

> The establishment of a Protestant Episcopate in America is also very zealously contended for; . . . We hope in God such an establishment will never take place in America, and we desire you would strenuously oppose it.[8]

Similar sentiments are found in the correspondence between independent clergymen in the two countries. Yet no one put it more frankly than Cotton Mather,

> It was not to be endured that episcopacy should, unmolested, rear its mitred head among the children of men who had said to the world: "Let all mankind know that we came into the wilderness, because we would worship God without that Episcopacy, that Common Prayer, and those unwarrantable ceremonies with which the land of our forefathers' sepulchres has been defiled; we came hither because we would have our posterity settled under the full and pure dispensations of the gospel; defended by rulers that should be of ourselves."[9]

Such lobbying and open opposition was not without its effects in the Hanoverian government still set to preserve its own stability. When Thomas Sherlock, Bishop of London, presented the claims of the colonial churchmen to the Crown once more in 1750, the time was probably inopportune, for the king was about to leave on an extended visit to Hanover. Sherlock was also less adept than his predecessors, Compton and Gibson, but Thomas Chandler explained to Samuel Johnson that the real reason for the failure of this petition was that the Duke of Newcastle and his followers were assured of the entire Puritan vote in Parliament on the condition "of their befriending them."

Bishop Secker clearly saw the significance of such political pressures when he wrote Samuel Johnson in 1754, "We have done all we can here in vain, and must wait for more favourable times. . . . So long as they [dissenters] are uneasy, and remonstrate, regard will be paid to them and their friends here by our ministers of state." Meanwhile, he answered a pamphlet by Jonathan Mayhew of Boston asserting the undeniable right of the church to her own apostolical government and calling the American dilemma without parallel in the Christian world.[10] As late as 1764, even after the type of American episcopacy desired had been defined beyond any point of possible misinterpretation, Secker quietly advised Johnson that party spirit was running high and therefore promotions should continue in "a quiet private manner," and so avoid "the risk of increasing the outcry against the Society."[11] As a last gesture Archbishop Secker bequeathed £1,000 toward the establishment of a bishop or bishops, in the king's dominions in America.[12]

On April 23, 1760, Ezra Stiles, then probably the most learned man in New England and the pastor of Second Congregational Church, Newport, Rhode Island, where he had a major part in founding Brown University, preached a sermon entitled "A Discourse on the Christian Union," which was published in September, 1761, and thereafter widely circulated and discussed here and in England. Based on a history of the churches in New England from 1630 to 1760, it presented a systematic account of American theory and progress toward religious freedom and a demand for continued advance. Stiles, who later served as professor of ecclesiastical history when he became president of

Yale, was aiming toward a "universal Protestant liberty" to be achieved by a union of Congregationalists and Presbyterians in the colonies. In theory he attempted to fuse English Nonconformist ideas about religious and civil liberties with similar American ideas from a vastly different historical background and experience.

Stiles really feared that in the confusion of the divided American churches the Anglicans might overwhelm all other religious bodies, and so he based his call for a solid American unity on his own statistical predictions that the memberships of the respective religious bodies would double every twenty-five years. So he estimated that the Anglicans, who numbered 11,600 in 1760, would grow to 23,200 by 1785, 46,400 by 1810, 92,800 by 1835, and 185,600 by 1860. By the same time the Friends would number 256,000, the Baptists 352,000 and the Congregationalists about seven million. He insisted that this unity must be accomplished in time to win the west or else the Anglicans would not only win there but would throttle religious and civil liberties even in New England. The only guarantee of freedom and security against such a fate he saw in the Congregational-Presbyterian union.

By 1763 the Primate of All England had heard of the threat posed by Stiles as an "intention to invite all parties and sects in the country to unite against the Church of England," and Henry Caner, of King's Chapel in Boston, was certain that it was aimed at the suppression of the church. It is possible that many persons believed that neither religious nor civil liberties were safe in British hands and must therefore be defended. Although this was not the only cause, it probably contributed to the achievement of civil and religious liberty in the United States.[13]

Soon after Thomas Sherlock became Bishop of London in 1748, the bishops deemed it advisable to reassure the church and all concerned of the nature of the episcopate desired for the colonies and thereby to allay the fears of all opponents. While many persons contributed to the discussion, the summary statement was prepared by Bishop Joseph Butler of Durham, best remembered for his famous *Analogy of Religion*. His manuscript was sent to East Apthorp, then rector of Christ Church, Cambridge, who first published this description of the proposed episcopate which should regulate only the Anglican clergy, have no powers of temporal government, be supported entirely without colonial expense, and should not have a seat in places where the government was left in the hands of dissenters, as in New England.

It had been thought that this plan might be universally accepted because it specifically separated the spiritual functions from the civil responsibilities as practiced in England, but it was blocked in Parliament for political reasons and equally opposed by the dissenters in the colonies. Such opposition could hardly be blamed on a lack of clarity of definition or of the reasonableness of the plan proposed. It must be assumed that at least some leaders in the American church groups were afraid that, with their division and internal structural problems, they might fare badly in competition with an efficiently organized and episcopally governed church, especially in New England where about one-third of the SPG missionaries were now at work. This opinion seems justified by the fact that from 1766 to 1775 the Presbyterian Synod of New York and Philadelphia met annually with the Congregational Associations of Connecticut to form a plan of union, not only for promoting common work in the expanding West, but also specifically to prevent the establishment of an American episcopate, and toward this end to cooperate with a dissenting committee in London.[14]

In their convention at Elizabethtown in 1768 the American dissenters declared that

> . . . it is very evident it is not that harmless and inoffensive Bishop which is designed for us, or the missionaries among us request; and therefore we cannot but be apprehensive of danger from the proposed Episcopate, however plausible the scheme may be represented.

Very astutely these religious leaders saw the political involvement in permitting bishops in America, for they added,

> . . . nothing seems to have such a direct tendency to weaken the dependence of the colonies upon Great Britain, and to separate them from her; an event which would be ruinous and destructive to both, and, which we, therefor, pray God long to avert.[15]

These delegates were able to influence their state governments so that Connecticut and Massachusetts instructed their agents in London to oppose an American bishop. Even though Parliament should limit the episcopacy here to purely spiritual functions, the American dissenters asserted that they would still oppose the proposal. To this the London Committee replied that they would do all they could to cooperate in their objective.

As late as 1815 President John Adams would say,

> . . . the apprehension of Episcopacy contributed as much as any other cause to arouse the attention, not only of the inquiring mind, but of the common people, and to urge them to close thinking on the constitutional authority of Parliament over the colonies.[16]

The learned churchman Jonathan Boucher, a minister in Maryland, also discerned the political involvements when he wrote in 1797, "This controversy was clearly one great cause that led to the revolution."[17]

The 1770 Convention of Presbyterians and Congregationalists at Norwalk, Connecticut, recorded a strange procedure in the appointment of committees "to obtain all the instances of Episcopal oppression they can" and "the instances of the lenity of the Connecticut Government with regard to the Episcopal dissenters therein," hoping perhaps to show that the current conditions were more favorable than the Anglicans reported. Yet it must be believed that many of the Presbyterian and Congregational clergymen actually feared that the worst of prelacy must of necessity accompany the introduction of bishops in America, as their minutes recorded: "No act of Parliament can have any security against being obliged, in time, to support their dignity, and to pay taxes to relieve the society in paying their missionaries." And again they confessed, most likely in the words of Francis Alison of Philadelphia,

> . . . great anxiety, not that we are of intolerant principles; nor do we envy the Episcopal churches the privileges of a bishop for the purposes of ordination, confirmation, and inspecting the morals of their Clergy, provided they have no kind of superiority over, nor power any way to affect the civil or religious interests of other denominations. Let this be but settled by an Act of Parliament, and such bishops divested of the powers annexed to that office by the common laws of England, and then we shall be more easy. Without this the introduction of a diocesan into the colonies would throw us into the utmost confusion and distraction.

These fears were unquestionably genuine and none may impugn the integrity of such eminent leaders of the American churches who, when the smoke of battle had been cleared away and the American colonies had achieved their freedom, no longer raised their united voices in objections but rather supported with good will the establishment of the American line of bishops in the Protestant Episcopal Church.

Not the least rancorous part of the conflict about the episcopate ensued in a barrage of pamphlets, newspaper articles, and broadsides in the last decades before the war. In 1763 Jonathan Mayhew challenged the Society's right to forego its primary purposes to Christianize Indians and Negroes in order to proselytize dissenting churches and thus build up the Church of England in the colonies.[18] Immediate answers to the charges against the Society came from Henry Caner of King's Chapel; Arthur Browne of Portsmouth denied any intention to interfere with other denominations but admitted a desire to establish the episcopate which, if and when the majority of the colonists became Anglicans, might indeed be supported by taxation.[19]

Perhaps the most significant reply to Mayhew was the anonymous *Answer* of Thomas Secker who pleaded for tolerance and bishops, on such terms as described by Joseph Butler, without any temporal authority. Mayhew's reply to Secker was restated effectively in 1765 by East Apthorp of Cambridge in his *Review of Dr. Mayhew's Remarks* in which he published in full Butler's description of the desired American bishop as one who would have no coercive power over laity but only over the clergy in episcopal orders, no civil or temporal authority, no colonial maintenance, and no seat in the colonies controlled by dissenters. After calling attention to the similarity between Secker's reply to Mayhew and Butler's four points, Apthorp added, ". . . they are the same and it is the only one [plan] intended to be put into execution."[20]

The most profound argumentation appeared in the extended exchange of ten pamphlets between Thomas Bradbury Chandler of Elizabeth and Charles Chauncy, the leading minister at First Church, Boston. Young Chandler had scarcely settled into his parish in New Jersey in 1746 when he zealously reported to the secretary of the Society on a sermon by Noah Hobart, a Congregational minister at Stratford, Connecticut. Hobart had attacked the Church of England's prerogatives in America and said that a

10 p. exchange.

bishop would not solve the disciplinary problems here but would rather bring harmful religious dependence. Despite the passing of twenty years and many moments of anguish for the welfare of the church, Chandler was still championing the episcopate in 1766 in his letters to his superiors in London as a means of binding the empire together. Had the government wisely supported the church's interests in America he was confident that loyalty and submission to the mother country could have been assured.[21]

In 1767 Bishop John Ewer of Llandaff, in preaching before the annual meeting of the Society, asserted that the religious conditions in America were deplorable and largely to be blamed on the lack of bishops. Charles Chauncy replied in a pamphlet that conditions here were not at all as Ewer described them and that the bishop's classic plea for American bishops was ill-founded.[22] Chandler was now ready to do battle, and his associates in New York and New Jersey, knowing his polemical abilities, urged him to reply. The more serious-minded clergy saw the wisdom of lifting the communication from acrimony to a loftier plateau, and Samuel Johnson, early in 1767, proposed to Thomas Chandler that he make an appeal in a calm and temperate manner. Later that year the young rector produced the first of that famous series of pamphlets under the title, *An Appeal to the Public on Behalf of the Church of England in America*. Chandler claimed that the Church of England was the only religious body not fully tolerated in the colonies and argued sincerely, although somewhat naively, that it was not the fear of bishops but purely political issues such as the Stamp Act that bred discontent in America.

While the *Appeal* was for a purely spiritual episcopate, in an accompanying letter Chandler told the Bishop of London that some other facts and reasons could not be included prudently lest they rouse opposition in America, even though, were they known, they might win support among those who were moved by political motives to support the Church of England in America. When this thinly veiled hope of subsequent establishment for bishops is coupled with his statement of the previous year and the fact that during the war Chandler remained an ardent loyalist, it is difficult to exonerate him by saying he was merely stating discreetly a disparity in loyalty between the northern and southern churchmen.

For the good of the church, which had now twenty-one parishes in New Jersey but only ten priests, Chandler should obviously have avoided all political references and complications. To the *Appeal* Charles Chauncy promptly replied in *An Appeal Answered*, and Chandler, delayed by the virulent newspaper war already afoot and the necessity to raise funds for printing, responded a year later with *An Appeal Defended*. Here he reasserted his confidence that a bishop without temporal powers should arouse no objection, and especially since there was no plan to support him by taxation. The controversial spirit had risen to a high pitch, and Chandler feared that vituperation would hurt his cause. He admitted that his task had been difficult and "that I find it no easy thing to keep myself within the Compass of Decency." Yet friends thought his reply had been "full soft enough," and there is no doubt that through these years Chandler showed great courtesy and in his restraint was a vivid contrast to his opponents. In 1770 Chauncy responded to Chandler with *A Reply to an Appeal Defended* in which he discussed the nature and origin of the episcopal office and reasserted that the real purpose of bishops would be "to episcopize" the colonies. Perhaps facetiously he argued here that Roman Catholic and Moravian bishops might function for Anglicans in spiritual matters. Chandler now decided to do one final answer but thought it best "to put off so hot a Piece of work to a cooler Season of the Year." Even though his New England friends had urged him to be severe, Chandler's *Appeal Further Defended*, which appeared in 1771, was a model of closely reasoned objection to ordinations by Roman Catholics and Moravians and perhaps an oversimplification in the summary of arguments favoring episcopacy. The final blow in this pamphlet battle came from Chauncy in 1771 when, in his *A Compleat View of Episcopacy*, he traced the historical development of episcopacy in the patristic literature to the close of the second century, still insisting that no one had ever anywhere seen bishops like those the Church of England proposed to introduce in America.

But Chandler's pen was by no means to remain idle. When a letter written in 1750 by Archbishop Secker to Horatio Walpole was posthumously published in 1769 in defense of American bishops, Francis Blackburne attacked it in *A Critical Commentary*. Blackburne, an English archdeacon, displayed sympathy with the dissenters, showing clearly why English dissenters had joined their support with those in the colonies. Seeing religious freedom in America, he warned against the introduction of any kind of bishops lest it might be another case like that of the Moravians, who had surreptitiously obtained permission to have bishops in the colonies and went on to make converts.[23] To the support of Secker rose none other than Thomas Chandler, who issued his *A Free Examination of the Critical Commentary* in 1774, appending Bishop Sherlock's memorial of 1750. Much of his argument covered old ground, but he did amass an impressive array of statements by church leaders, largely from the sermons preached before the annual meetings of the SPG, asserting that there was no political motivation in the long quest for American bishops.

The most violent and unpleasant controversy of all, however, appeared in anonymous articles in the leading newspapers of New York and Philadelphia after 1768. The initiative for the word squabbles probably came from the Presbyterians in New York, who had unsuccessfully sought a charter of incorporation and, on being refused, had placed the blame on the Bishop of London. This experience, at the time when Chandler's first pamphlet *An Appeal to the Public* was being read and discussed with excitement, prompted the controversial articles. For many weeks in 1768 and 1769 weekly columns by numerous authors appeared in Parker's and Gaine's papers, each called the *New York Gazette*, and in the *Pennsylvania Journal* and the *Pennsylvania Gazette* in Philadelphia. The articles in New York were signed "The American Whig" and were usually written by William Livingstone; those in Philadelphia bore the signature "Centinel" and were done by Francis Alison, then vice-provost at the College of Philadelphia. Alison was assisted occasionally by Jonathan Dickinson, who had attained fame in 1767–68 in connection with *The Farmer's Letters* opposing the new British imperial policy. The "Whig" articles were reprinted in Philadelphia and those of the "Centinel" in New York; both were widely reprinted and read in other leading cities so that many more persons learned of these politico-ecclesiastical discussions by means of the press than from the larger original pamphlets of Chandler and Chauncy.

Each writer also provoked an answer. Provost William Smith in Philadelphia appropriately enough became the chief respondent to "Centinel," his vice-provost, and usually used the pseudonym "The Anatomist," although some of these answers bore the name "Anti-Centinel." "Timothy Tickle" answered the "American Whig" with "A Whip for the American Whig" who, he claimed,

> . . . has promised not to quit the stage until he has demolished every argument that has been or can be produced in Behalf of American Bishops— and has shown that the most harmless Episcopate in this country, unless Negroes be the Bishops [probably harmless because of their dissociation with the Establishment] would have more fatal tendency, even than the late obnoxious Stamp Act.[24]

Tickle's accusation prompted "A Kick for the Whipper" by "Sir Isaac Foot."

While the opponents of the Church of England charged that bringing bishops to America was simply part of the British imperial scheme, the churchmen replied that no temporal authority was in any way involved. In his very first appearance the "American Whig" had concluded his column by asserting that ". . . it is not the *primitive Christian* bishop they want" and that it would prove absolute desolation and ruin to this new country if they could introduce "the modern, splendid, opulent, court favoured, law-dignified, superb, magnificent, powerful prelate, on which their hearts are so intent."[25] A week after this first "Whig" article appeared in Parker's *New York Gazette*, Thomas Chandler placed "An Advertisement to the Public" in the *New York Gazette* on March 21, 1768, giving his own detailed answer in about two thousand words. The very next week in Gaine's *New York Gazette* Samuel Seabury published his briefer reply under the same title, declaring the assertions of the "American Whig" to be "absolutely, utterly, and intirely false and groundless." So for about a quarter of a million words the battle of assertions and denials continued for almost two years, and the general effect was something short of constructive for either side. Yet the Independents had been able to shift the argument from a confused theological level to the more practical, even political, issues involved, and the whole had a tendency to contribute to the rapidly rising tide of anti-imperialism that would soon ignite a war and sear even the most modest and noble Anglican hopes.

Men on both sides of the controversy must have felt the inappropriateness of their squabbling among themselves when a greater common danger was looming up abroad. William Smith sensed this and gave up in the middle of his arguments in the last appearances of his column to write:

> But, in truth, from the gloomy prospect that seems gathering against us on the other side of the Atlantic, it might be better for you and for me to cultivate *domestic harmony* for the present, and to suspend the settlement of our remaining differences to a more convenient season.

The low level to which the controversy sagged may be seen in a broadside entitled "An Attempt to Land a Bishop in America," which appeared at the height of the disputes, showing a bishop in his wind-swept vestments climbing the rigging of *The Hilsborough*, which flies the Union Jack, and saying, "Lord, now lettest Thou Thy Servant depart in Peace." On board are his staff and disassembled coach, bearing the insignia of episcopacy, and he is hoping to escape from the wrath of men armed with clubs and staves pushing the vessel away from the dock and from a rock about to be hurled by a monkey. A Quaker is there holding a copy of Barclay's *Apology*, others are hurling copies of Locke's works, Sydney's *On Government*, and Calvin's *Works* are about to strike the bishop's head. One of the mob is shouting, "No Lords Spiritual or Temporal in New England," and a legend in the lower left corner reads, "Shall they be obliged to maintain Bishops that cannot maintain themselves?"

But perhaps the saddest blow to the hopes of the ardent supporters of the episcopate for America came from within the church itself, from open opposition in Virginia and the indifference and lack of enthusiasm in Pennsylvania. It had become the custom periodically, when the time was opportune, for clerical associations to send a petition to the SPG, the bishops, and the king requesting a bishop for America. As the tense feelings of the late 1760's brought division of opinions even among the clergy in America, the New York and New Jersey Convention in 1771 decided not only to send a petition but also to send Myles Cooper, president of King's College, to deliver it.

When Cooper and Robert McKean, appointed in 1767 as a missionary in New Jersey, sought the cooperation of the southern churchmen, a convocation of the Virginia clergy was called for May 4, 1771. Although the purpose of meeting was well known and it was already a second attempt to gain a representative showing of the clergy, only twelve ministers appeared in a colony where there were more than one hundred parishes and most of them supplied. After once defeating the measure and then trying to hold it for consideration at a future gathering, the convocation finally reversed its earlier action and gave a not overwhelming approval to the plan. Forcing the issue proved to be unfortunate; Thomas Gwatkin and Samuel Henley, two clergymen who were also professors at the College of William and Mary, protested against the action and in turn were commended, with two others who had opposed the action, by the Virginia House of Burgesses for

. . . . the wise and well-timed opposition they have made to the pernicious project of a few mistaken clergymen for introducing an American bishop: a measure by which much disturbance, great anxiety and apprehension would certainly take place among his Majesty's faithful American subjects. . . .

The lethargy of the Virginia clergy has led some to surmise that the need for a bishop here became among them a good reason to prevent his coming. Such episcopal supervision would also have circumscribed, if not curtailed, the power of Virginia vestries and the large place wealthy and influential laymen held in this church. Too late their errors became clear when, after the war, the easygoing ways of the previous somnolent period no longer carried the church along but, in fact, almost allowed it to die.

In Maryland an attempt to persuade the governor to give the episcopate his support in England was not upheld, and the usual memorial to the archbishop, Bishop of London, and Lord Baltimore was defeated. Even in Pennsylvania the clergy, some of whom supported the early patriots, declined the 1771 proposal to send a personally borne petition to the king. They argued that in the light of the Virginia dissent the churchmen in America were themselves not united and that it might aggravate the intermediary superior officers in England, whose favor they already enjoyed, by impugning their motives and competence.

The proposed memorial and Cooper's trip were therefore cancelled. The convention of New York and New Jersey now turned its attention to the church in Virginia and prepared *An Address from the Clergy of New York and New Jersey to the Episcopalians in Virginia, Occasioned by Some Later Transactions in that Colony Relative to an American Episcopate*, which was printed by Hugh Gaine in New York in 1771. It was signed by eight clergymen, including Samuel Seabury, Thomas B. Chandler, and Myles Cooper, who probably wrote the long document of fifty-eight printed pages. The northern churchmen said they "were surprised and concerned" about the action in Virginia, especially since it was defended on grounds which showed that the Virginia churchmen "have little, if any, Reverence for the episcopal Order." All this was true, but the New York and New Jersey leaders, despite the paucity of means of communication, should have known that Virginia was hardly famed for its loyalty to the Crown and that ecclesiastical jurisdiction had been so localized that even the commissary found supervision impossible.

The efforts to bring a bishop or bishops to America to supervise and direct the life and work of the Church of England were begun in the seventeenth century and carried on much more intensively in the eighteenth, especially in the last generation before the war. Never was there complete common agreement even in the church about the way in which this dream should be accomplished nor how it would operate when completed. As political differences between England and the colonies became more and more obvious, all British policies became suspect and the mere mention of episcopal supervision, to say nothing of episcopal succession, invariably provoked opposition to any constructive plans for the work of this church in the colonies.

Of the various plans that had been suggested none was so naive as the proposal of George Craig of Connecticut, whose geographical perspective was hardly adequate. On September 14, 1764, he wrote the Society that three bishops would hardly suffice and that one should be assigned to Canada, one to Florida and the Carolinas, and one for all the area between these points. Henry Caner made the only suggestion that archdeacons be appointed to fill the needs in America. He must have intended that this office should assume the prerogatives of the commissaries and be strengthened with additional local authority in the regions assigned. When the office of commissary became obsolete in the northern colonies, it was suggested that this office might be revived with new powers, even including the power to ordain and confirm, but this was canonically irregular and was never taken seriously. Never before had the lesson become so clear that a church with episcopal structure is a helpless, headless creature without a bishop.

No one struggled harder to effect the American episcopate than Thomas B. Chandler; he wrote to the Society on May 29, 1775, at the very beginning of hostilities and on the eve of his discreet retirement to England,

> If it shall please God that these unhappy tumults be quieted and peace and order restored (which event I am sanguine enough to think is not far distant) we may reasonably hope that our governors will be taught, by experience, to have some regard to the Church of England in America.[26]

Here is his thinly veiled hope for a British victory and yet, and more significant, a hope that his superiors should see the importance of the church and its work. Quite honestly Chandler had tried to present before his fellow colonists the utter hopelessness of open revolt against Britain. About a year before his departure for England he wrote in *The Friendly Address to All Reasonable Americans on the Subject of our Political Confusions* that America should be the happiest English colony with peace, health, and never failing plenty, and added a warning,

> But a far different prospect, at this time, presents itself to view. The darkness of a rising tempest is beginning to overspread our land. The thunder roars in the distance and appears to be swiftly approaching. It is high time therefore to awaken the thoughtless to a sense of their danger and to think of providing for our common safety.

He was careful to point out that the colonies did not have a chance,

> for they are open and accessible on every quarter and have not a single fortress to cover them, nor one regiment of regular troops to defend them; and they are without military stores, without magazines and without the skills that are necessary for supporting an army.

Statistically, of course, he was correct, but when he went on with his gloomy predictions to chide the patriots in the Church of England, he was dealing, beyond his depth of perception, with those intangibles that were to turn the fates of war against the holders of the resources and in favor of those possessed of a noble idea whose hour had now come. Here the areas of the new freedom would include religion and give all men the opportunity to worship God as they chose and to construct their church orders on inherited or modified plans as they wished. Although it was once believed that, when the battle had turned against the colonists and they seemed to be losing the war, Chandler had stooped to write the pamphlet, *What Think Ye of Congress Now?* it has now been established that this was really the work of Myles Cooper. For ten years Chandler remained in England where he was honored and sustained while his family remained in New Jersey; in June, 1785, suffering with facial cancer, he returned to resume his duties at Elizabeth on a part-time basis until his death on June 17, 1790.

With bishops in the church in America men would not have needed to run the risks of a trip abroad to seek ordination, and the actual normal clergy supply might have proved entirely adequate to its needs. The episcopal selection, direction, and discipline of the clergy would have provided for higher clerical standards and controlled the disputes within the church and in its relation with the colonial governments. By such supervision even the religious life of the laity could have been stimulated, and the work of the church in all the colonies could have been carefully planned on a national basis in vivid contrast to the usual parochial or regional planning which so hindered its efforts. When so much good could be anticipated through the introduction of bishops and so little harm could have come to anyone save in so far as the progress of the Church of England might have been a competitive stimulus to other churches, why were bishops not established in the colonies?

That bishops were needed to complete the structure and to provide the effectiveness of the Church of England in America few serious-minded persons could have denied. The connotation of the word "bishop" and the associations with the idea of episcopal supervision caused many to fear the political and social consequences of their otherwise benign functions. Perhaps Thomas Bradbury Chandler held within himself the real reason why this desirable end was never achieved. He loved both the English church and England and was never able to separate his desire of the success for the former from the accompanying control of the latter. The Church of England had no bishops to send who were acquainted with the American scene and spirit, and the church leaders in the colonies had never devised an adequate way to support a bishop properly from local resources alone. Had it not been for these congenital weaknesses within the church itself and the avowed opposition of the Whig politicians and the dissenters in England and the colonies, the church might well have had a bishop in America. No one can guess what might have been his fate and that of his church. As it was, the time would soon be ripe for the orphaned church to demonstrate its own resilience and, reflecting the spirit of the nation in which it stood, to devise ways and means to make the worship and work of God in the Anglican manner effective in the new country.

IX

THE CHURCH AND THE AMERICAN REVOLUTION

With the firing of the shots on Lexington Green the relation between England and her colonies was ruptured, and the discontinuance of the supporting role of the SPG and the Bishop of London left the clergy and laity in both an orphaned and an impoverished condition. Surprisingly enough, these deprivations made practically no difference in the response of the clergy and churches to the completely new political and social situation. Those whose earlier convictions had led them to live and think in terms of the New World and its opportunity cast their lots with the colonial government and sought to make a significant place for the church. Those whose orientation had never been cut loose from its English moorings at first somewhat patronizingly bided their time and awaited what they believed must be the inevitable collapse of the overly zealous scheme of the patriots; but before the end of the war they sought refuge in Canada or the homeland. Some of them rose to distinction, like Charles Inglis of New York, who became the Bishop of Nova Scotia; others of equal capacity, like Jacob Duché, found minor roles in the Church of England or waited out the war years in England, as did Thomas Chandler, to return in a subdued role to the church in America.

Members of the Church of England stood on opposite sides in the conflict, frequently divided on a geographical basis. Many in New England, New York, and New Jersey were Tories. Often the congregations were made up of those favored by birth and fortune or who served in the professions or British civil or military service. Lieutenant Governor Colden of New Jersey informed the colonial secretary, Lord Hillsborough, that the Episcopalians, Lutherans, and Dutch Reformed were friends of the government while the opponents of the government were mostly dissenters. These loyalists supplied about forty thousand men for the British armed forces, and many more fled from the country before the issue was decided.

Yet three-fourths of the signers of the Declaration of Independence were churchmen. Most of the Anglican patriots were concentrated in the lower middle and southern colonies. In Virginia most of the ninety-five clergy supported the Revolution and only a very few of them failed to receive the notation "loyal and exemplary" in Purdie and Dixon's list of 1774.[1] In South

113

Carolina only five out of twenty-three priests were loyalists, while most of the patriotic leaders in Charleston were members of St. Philip's Church.[2]

On the other hand, in New Jersey Nathaniel Pettit agitated against the payment of taxes levied by Congress, and with Robert Ellison was brought before the committee of safety, fined £8, and compelled to give a £50 bond for future good behavior. Governor William Franklin, son of Benjamin Franklin, was regarded as the "king of Tory Churchmen." When armed men surrounded his home and declared that he could not leave without permission of the Continental Congress, Frederick Smyth, Chief Justice of New Jersey, persuaded him to submit. Thereafter Franklin remained but a figurehead governor and lived in Perth Amboy, which had become a royalist center populated almost exclusively by Anglicans.

Without making a conscious effort to do so, Anglican clergy had drawn families of means and privilege into their colonial churches during the years of expanding opportunity and rising culture in the eighteenth century. Occasionally converts to Anglicanism were even accused of seeking only greater personal freedom of conduct.[3] In many ways this social stratification proved a great disadvantage and resulted in the association of the church with the cause of the loyalists to which most of these people adhered. The loyalists, nevertheless, came from all social ranks; some represented old colonial families, while others were more recent immigrants, and it was not unusual to find that more than half the names on the lists of Tories were of persons born in America. Yet this situation was changing radically in the last half of the eighteenth century so that at the close of the war the church represented much more of a cross-section of American society, which would soon be reflected in the democratic emphasis in the formation of the new church.

The regular meetings of the clergy conventions in the individual colonies, where everything from procedures to conclusions depended on personal and group initiative, also proved a profitable experience in preparation for the new organization. With the end of the war both clergy and laity turned to the only means they knew, the voluntary conventions, to make possible the initial overtures that ultimately led to the formation of the Protestant Episcopal Church. These early colonial clergy conventions became the pattern for the new diocesan conventions in the several states, and their standing committees became an important part of the functioning of the new dioceses.

Almost a decade before the outbreak of hostilities, the New Jersey Clerical Convention meeting in Perth Amboy in October, 1765, reported to the SPG that the British government's "best Security in the Colonies does, and must always arise, from the Principles of Submission and Loyalty taught by the Church. The Clergy in General are constantly instilling these great Principles into the People." This document was signed by seven clergymen including Thomas B. Chandler, whose sentiments had long been well known.[4]

Samuel Seabury, Jr., destined to prominence in the church after the war, was a confirmed loyalist throughout the conflict and frequently defended his position in pamphlets and newspapers. While he was serving the church in

Westchester, New York, he published under the name of "A. W. Farmer" two attacks on the provisional government in his *Friendly Address to all Reasonable Americans, on the Subject of our Political Confusion* and *Free Thoughts on the Proceedings of the Continental Congress,* in which he held up to scorn its economic and political policies. Within a month *A Full Vindication of the Measures of Congress from the Calumnies of their Enemies,* an anonymous answer skillfully prepared in thought and style, almost magically began to turn the popular feeling toward the patriots and their Congress. Although "A Westchester Farmer," as Seabury sometimes signed himself, challenged his anonymous opponent to a prompt reply in another pamphlet addressed to the Merchants of New York at the end of 1774, it was not until February, 1775, that *The Farmer Refuted* appeared, and thereafter the Farmer remained silent. No one was quite certain at that time that the "Farmer" was Seabury, but it came as a much greater surprise—President Myles Cooper of King's College never accepted it—that the most competent and brilliant defenses of the Continental Congress had been written by Alexander Hamilton, then an eighteen-year-old student in King's College.

Soon after Seabury discontinued this debate, he entered into a compact with Thomas B. Chandler and Charles Inglis "to watch all publications, either in newspapers or pamphlets, and so to obviate the evil influence of such as appear to have a bad tendency by the speediest answers." It was probably Seabury's "Alarm to the Legislature of New York" and his personal influence with at least one-third of its members which led that colonial assembly, in session from January to April, 1775, to refuse to recognize the authority of Congress or to confirm its action and instead to memorialize the King and Parliament.

Seabury showed a sincere and pure devotion to the Church of England and, since it was part of the Establishment, to the Crown as well. As the violence increased before the war, Seabury reported to the Society,

> I think that even these disturbances will be attended with some advantage to the interest of the Church. The usefulness and truth of her doctrines, with regard to civil government, appear more evident from those disorders. . . .
>
> . . . the more candid and reasonable people . . . seem heartily tired with the late clamours for liberty, etc., as it appears evident that unbounded licentiousness in manners, and insecurity to private property, must be the unavoidable consequence of some late measures. . . .[5]

Although they found it difficult to trap Seabury among his loyalist friends, a party of Connecticut militia finally found and arrested him in November, 1775. On his release he took refuge behind the British lines, ministering to scattered churchmen on Long Island and practicing medicine to support himself and his family. For his loyalty Oxford University conferred on him the degree of Doctor of Divinity on December 15, 1777. By appointment of Sir Henry Clinton in 1778 he served as chaplain to the King's American Regiment, a refugee unit under the command of Colonel Edmund Fanning, and after the war received a lifetime pension from the British government, which led some American churchmen to be less than happy about his election as Bishop of Connecticut in 1783.

Of similar intensity was the loyalty of Thomas B. Chandler and Myles Cooper, president of King's College, who returned to England on the same ship in 1775 after they had been charged with plotting with the SPG and the British ministry to enslave America. It was about this time that Myles Cooper issued his pamphlet, *What Think Ye of Congress Now?* raising the question how far Americans were bound to abide by and execute its decisions. Cooper expressed the desire that all Americans "may enjoy as much liberty, of every kind as is consistent with good order and safety." He admitted that some of England's acts had been unjust but contended that the processes in Congress had been invalid and that in deciding to support the revolt in Massachusetts it especially endangered the security of all because domination by Massachusetts could be worse than that of Parliament. He gave assurance that the loyalists in New York were twenty to one against the dissenters and that New York would welcome and support the British. That his motives were the preservation of law and national integrity rather than subversive seems clear from a sermon he preached in Oxford more than a year later in which he said,

> When men's Principles are wrong their Practices will seldom be right. When they suppose those powers to be derived solely from the People, which are ordained of God . . . When once they conceive the governed to be superior to the Governors and that they may set up their pretended Natural Rights in Opposition to the positive laws of the state; they will naturally proceed to despise dominion and speak evil of dignities and to open a door for Anarchy, confusion and every evil work to enter.[6]

Samuel Seabury assured the SPG that none of the accusers of Chandler and Cooper "who raised this calumny believe one syllable of it, but only intend it as an engine to turn the popular fury upon the church," which he feared might "fall a sacrifice to the persecuting spirit of independency." This concern was shared by patriots as well, who feared that conflagration once begun might consume them all. Dr. Joseph Warren, who was not a member of the Church of England, wrote the editors of the *Boston Gazette* that, however injudicious some individuals may have been,

> the gentlemen of the established Church of England are men of the most just and liberal sentiments, and are high in the esteem of the most sensible and resolute defenders of the rights of the people of this Continent; and I earnestly request my countrymen to avoid everything which our enemies may make use of to prejudice our Episcopal brethren against us, by representing us as disposed to disturb them in the free exercise of their religious privileges; to which we know they have the most undoubted claim; and which, from a real regard to the honor and interest of my country, and the rights of mankind, I hope they will enjoy as long as the name of America is known to the world.[7]

Apparently Warren had been prompted to this expression by a note from Samuel Adams in Philadelphia; in it he described the opening of the Continental Congress by Jacob Duché, of Christ Church, Philadelphia, who was noted for his superb voice and as a good preacher. Duché read Psalm 35 and the appointed lessons for September 7, 1774, and in all that gathering George Washington alone knelt with the rector during the prayers. In describing the occasion, Adams had written to Warren,

> As many of our warmest friends are members of the Church of England, I thought it prudent . . . that the service should be performed by a member clergyman of that denomination . . . who afterwards made a most excellent extemporary prayer, by which he discovered himself to be a gentleman of sense and piety, and a warm advocate for the religious and civil rights of America.[8]

Although immortalized by being portrayed in his full vestments in a contemporary painting of that important event, Duché, ironically, turned loyalist when the British troops occupied Philadelphia in 1777 and returned to England when these troops evacuated the city. Perhaps with some anguish of indecision he remained in England to serve in the church there. His associate, William White, accepted the rectorship of Christ Church only with the understanding that he would resign if Duché should return. White also became chaplain of the Continental Congress in its darkest hour and at one time was the only Church of England minister in all of Pennsylvania.

One of the most effective loyalist representatives of the Church of England was Charles Inglis, rector of Trinity Church in New York. In sharp focus he described the hardships resulting from imprisonments and the brutal violence inflicted by mobs of misguided patriots on many Anglican clergy and laity. When large numbers of the Dutch also opposed the rebellion but were ignored by the patriots, Inglis concluded that the crime of the churchmen was their loyalty to England. On one occasion a colonial officer told Inglis that General Washington would attend his services and would appreciate the omission of the prayers for the king and the royal family. When Inglis later remonstrated to Washington about the unreasonableness of his request, the general made an awkward apology, leaving the impression that he had never made it.

At another time while Inglis was reading the service, a company of armed patriots led by fife and drums marched into the church and stood for fifteen minutes. The terrified congregation feared an outbreak of violence if the controversial prayers were read, but the rector went on without any omissions and completed the service with no show of force from the armed company. Eventually Trinity Church was closed until General Howe's forces brought the city under British rule for the balance of the war. Inglis has left a vivid description of the destruction of New York including his own losses of about £200. The bells of the city were carried off to be converted into cannon, and in the fire set by the colonial troops about one-fourth of the city was destroyed, including one thousand houses, the rectory, the Charity School, St. Paul's Church, and King's College. The loss of the Church of England alone was more than £25,000, well over a million dollars in its modern equivalent.

Inglis had a unique way of estimating values. In one of his little-known letters to John Jay he tried to persuade him of the folly of continuing the Revolution. Inglis argued that by 1778 the war had already cost the colonies no less than £66,728,960, to which must be added at least £22,500,000 more, as the *Loyal American* asserted, bringing the total American losses to almost £90,000,000, including destruction, loss of revenues, war costs, and seventy thousand men valued by an arbitrary English standard at £70 per man.[9]

Yet before the close of his lengthy letter to England on October 31, 1776, Inglis added hopefully,

> Upon the whole the Church of England has lost none of its members by rebellion, as yet—none, I mean, whose departure from it can be deemed a loss; on the contrary, its own members are more firmly attached to it than ever. . . . I have no doubt but, with the blessing of Providence, his Majesty's arms will be successful, and finally crush this natural rebellion.

He was also ready with a constructive program to follow such a victory, "In that case, if the steps be taken which reason, prudence and common sense dictate, the Church will indubitably increase, and these confusions will terminate in a large accession to its members." That the accompaniments of war are universally and almost impartially destructive is shown by numerous reports that the loyalists suffered as much and more from the rapacity of the king's troops than from the violence of the insurgents.[10]

Charles Inglis was also an inveterate pamphleteer. In 1776 he issued his answer to Thomas Paine, calling his *Common Sense* "one of the most artful, insidious and pernicious pamphlets." Since Inglis attempted to answer Paine point by point, his own ideas were never systematically organized. Arguing that monarchy is the simplest and most stable form of government and best designed for large empires, he reminded Paine that democracy had never been tried and in its complexity must prove most liable to disorders. Admitting that the past relations had been less than perfect, Inglis suggested that the solution lay in reconciliation and constitutional union with Britain. "But the remedy proposed by our author," Inglis declared, "would resemble the conduct of a rash, forward stripling, who should call his mother a d-mn-d b--ch, swear he had no relation to her, and attempt to knock her down."[11] Eventually Inglis, with many remaining loyalist clergy, found his way to Nova Scotia where he became its first bishop after the war.

Among the less well-known loyalists was John Stuart, a missionary among the Mohawk Indians at Fort Hunter in New York. Stuart had a large congregation of faithful Indians about him in the areas west of Albany; he thought "their whole deportment is such as is but rarely seen in religious assemblies that have been better instructed." For their loyalty to the church these Indians were forced to seek a haven in upper Canada. After being held prisoner at

Schenectady for three years, he was exchanged for an American colonel being held by the British in Canada. On arriving at St. John's, Newfoundland, he found many of his Mohawk Indians and continued his work among them with John F. Doty, the former missionary at Schenectady.

While loyalist sympathies must have led some of the missionaries to aid the king's forces, it remained for Jonathan Odell to achieve the dubious distinction of complicity in a spy plot. His father came of an old New England family, and his mother was a daughter of the eminent Jonathan Dickinson, first president of Princeton. Before preparing for orders, he studied medicine and served as a British Army surgeon in the West Indies. Ordained in 1766, he ministered successively at Burlington, Bristol, and Mt. Holly, New Jersey, until 1771 when he resumed the practice of medicine. Odell was a clever satirist and also freely wrote his loyalist opinions in letters to friends; when several of these were intercepted, Congress agreed that he opposed the patriots' cause but felt they must not "violate the right of private sentiment." They continued to keep him under observation, however, and in July, 1776, placed him on parole as "a person suspected of being inimical to American liberty" and ordered him to remain on the east side of the Delaware River within eight miles of the courthouse in Burlington. Using the code name "James Osborne," he became deeply involved in the Major André—Benedict Arnold plot; his trusted messenger, John Rattoon, used the code name "Mercury." In the summer of 1780 Odell deciphered the Arnold letters offering to sell West Point and informing André when Washington might be captured crossing the Hudson. Apparently neither Odell nor Rattoon was ever identified with the plot. After a brief term as an assistant secretary to Governor Sir Guy Carleton of New York and a trip to England, Odell settled in Fredericton, New Brunswick, Canada, in 1784 where he became the secretary of the province, councillor, registrar, and clerk of the Council.[12]

Scores of loyalists of minor stature suffered continual harassments by the patriots and property destruction by both sides, and were forced to discontinue their public worship. Missionary John Sayre from Flushing, Long Island, described just such an experience in his letter to the secretary of the Society on November 8, 1779, telling of the situation in the Fairfield Mission, which had held good promise until the previous July when General Tryon set fire to the town, destroying his church and house, all the church records, and even the valued SPG library. With becoming modesty he wrote, "My own loss includes my little all" and then, showing the superb concern of the true missionary, he added, "But what I most regret is my absence from my flock, to which my heart was, and still is, most tenderly attached."[13] E. Avery of Rye, New York, was murdered by the colonials because he refused to pray for Congress. His body was shot through, his throat cut, and his corpse thrown on the highway.[14]

Also imprisoned as a loyalist was Jeremiah Leaming, missionary at Newport, Rhode Island, and later at Norwalk and Stratford, Connecticut. In July, 1779, his church and all his own property were destroyed by the British under the command of General Tryon. His own personal losses totaled more than £1,200 sterling, but worst of all was the severe maltreatment which crippled him for the remainder of his life, a factor that may have influenced him later in his decision not to accept the bishopric of Connecticut when it was proffered.

Following the treaty of 1783, many clergymen who had remained loyal to England during the war were appointed to chaplaincies in the king's armed forces, while others sought refuge in Nova Scotia, New Brunswick, the missions of Canada, or even in England. The bitter sufferings of these "refugee" clergymen won deep sympathy from the people of England. Preaching before the SPG at its 1784 meeting, John Butler, Bishop of Oxford, spoke of their faithfulness. "Their firm perseverance in their duty, amidst temptations, menaces, and in some cases cruelty, would have distinguished them as meritorious men in better times."

During these trying years there were also some vacillations among the clergy. Jacob Duché, who had been honored by being invited to offer the opening prayer for the Continental Congress, soon afterward returned to England; on the other hand William Smith, who at first was loyal to the Crown and sought to prevent an open rupture with England, ultimately decided to cast his lot with the patriots. With Duché, William White, and the other English clergy in Philadelphia, Smith signed a letter on June 30, 1775, probably written to the Bishop of London, declaring their anxiety: "Would to God we could become mediators for the Settlement of the unnatural Controversy that now distracts a once happy Empire." They then went on to state their hope and prayer

> . . . that the hearts of good and benevolent men in both Countries may be directed towards a Plan of Reconciliation worthy of being offered by a great Nation that have long been the Patrons of Freedom throughout the world, and not unworthy of being accepted by a People sprung from them, and by birth claiming a participation of their Rights.

Just a week earlier on June 23 Smith preached one of his most famous sermons in Christ Church "On the present Situation of American Affairs." In his large congregation that day sat the members of Congress and a battalion of Philadelphia militia. Many editions of the sermon were demanded in America, ten thousand copies were ordered in London, and foreign language translations were issued later. Smith had already explained his moderation and hope for a peaceful but honorable settlement. Now he attempted to show that complete independence from the parent country, or at least licentious opposition to its just interests, was utterly foreign to the patriot's thoughts; that they contended only for the sanctity of charters and laws, together with the right of granting their own money; "and that our rightful Sovereign had nowhere more loyal subjects, or more zealously attached to those principles of government, under which his family inherits the throne."

By August 28 Smith was still working and praying "that a suspension of hostilities and a negotiation could take place, before either side have proceeded too far in measures ruinous to both." Yet he saw clearly that the colonies were forever united now that Georgia had joined the other twelve, and soon afterward he stated that he could not "betray the cause of universal liberty, nor suffer our Church or Clergy to labour under the imputation of departing from those principles which distinguished some of her brightest luminaries near a century past." Such, he reported, were the views of the clergy in the province, with the possible exception of Duché who, after preaching effectively for reconciliation, hesitated to go further toward an open breach with England. Smith insisted that they could not permit "the notion to prevail that the Church Clergy are tools of power, slavish in their tenets, and secret enemies to the principles of the revolution," for to do so "would give a deadly wound to the Church in America." So the die was cast, and everyone now knew where the sentiments of the Pennsylvania clergy lay.

Vainly had Smith hoped that the clergy in the other colonies would not desert their people, lest "we should not have the appearance of a Church or people left." He felt that the clergy should contend for the just rights of America so that people might know that "the Clergy of our Church are as true friends to liberty, and as much devoted to the constitutional and just rights of their country, as any other man in America." After such a clear declaration it was natural that the SPG reluctantly withdrew a small stipend that it had been paying Smith for his occasional services at the mission at Oxford.

Although Smith had opposed the British colonial policy, he came under suspicion when, as "Cato," he published several pamphlets opposing the adoption of the Declaration of Independence, which he accepted quickly, however, after July 4, 1776. When the British approached Philadelphia, Congress placed a watch over Smith as a suspicious character, but he supported the colonials and did not return to that city until they did. For his less than enthusiastic support of the patriots' cause Smith lost his provostry at the College when the original charter was annulled in 1779 and the State Legislature established the University of Pennsylvania in its place. Smith then moved to Chester, Maryland, where he succeeded a loyalist rector and founded Washington College, named for the general. He immediately became a source of strength for the church in Maryland and would soon take a leading part in the organization of the Protestant Episcopal Church.

Peter Muhlenberg, the son of the famous Lutheran patriarch Henry Melchior Muhlenberg, who had been ordained in England, was a patriot of a more impetuous type. While assisting his father in Philadelphia, he received a call on May 4, 1771, to become the minister of the Lutheran church at Woodstock in the Shenandoah Valley in Virginia. Curiously this call was contingent on his being willing to seek Anglican orders, for only so would he be able to enforce the collection of the tithes from his congregation in Virginia where the Church of England was then established. Young Muhlenberg found no conflict here, since his father had always said that there were no doctrinal barriers between the two churches. So without ever feeling that he had ceased to be a fully empowered Lutheran minister, he was ordained in England in April, 1772. When the war broke out he marched off at the head of volunteers from Woodstock to join Washington's troops where he served on the general's staff, ultimately attaining the rank of brigadier general.[15]

Among those many others who supported the colonists and later attained distinction in the church were most of the first bishops. These included James Madison of Virginia; Thomas J. Claggett of Maryland; Samuel Provoost, an assistant at Trinity Church, New York, who served in the patriot forces and later became the first bishop of New York; and the first two bishops of Massachusetts, Edward Bass of Newburyport and Samuel Parker at Trinity Church in Boston. Bass, somewhat reluctantly at first, complied with the requests of his parishioners that he omit the objectionable prayers for the royal family. When the SPG withdrew his support, Bass, now in advanced years, became dependent on assistance from individuals in his congregation, and even though he applied for arrearages after the war, he received no assistance from the Society he had served for so many years. Parker much more openly supported the cause of liberty in Boston, and in 1778 he probably saved the Old North (Christ) Church from being taken over by the Huguenots to whom the Congress wished to give it, since it had stood idle for three years. At the invitation of the vestry Parker preached there every Sunday afternoon and so preserved it for the church. A year later the vestry approved a new form of prayer for Congress and the several states. After the war Parker found himself in a highly respected position in the community and the church, which he was to represent so effectively in its constitutional conventions.

Winwood Serjeant, who became the missionary in Christ Church, in Cambridge, Massachusetts, on September 1, 1767, remained until early in 1775 when, because of his loyalty, he was compelled to flee with his family. Meanwhile, many of his parishioners in the stately houses on Brattle Street, then known as "Tory Row," had also fled, leaving their homes and Christ Church to be turned into quarters for the American soldiers. General Washington came to Cambridge on July 2, 1775, and took command of the army under an elm tree on the Cambridge Common near the church. When Mrs. Washington came to New England later in the year, she requested that a service be held in Christ Church, which she attended with the general on Sunday, December 31, 1775. After that service the fine colonial church lay in disrepair until its restoration in 1790.

Several missionaries in Delaware ingeniously avoided the sharp issues by unique compromises. Samuel Tingley, who disapproved of the brethren in Philadelphia who "made such compliances as are utterly repugnant to the principles, which must necessarily be interwoven in the very heart, soul and mind of a Churchman . . . ," altered his prayer from "O Lord Save the King" to "O Lord, save those, whom Thou has made it our special duty to pray for."[16] Aeneas Ross, another patriot, a brother of George Ross of Lancaster, Pennsylvania, who was a signer of the Declaration of Independence, and of John Ross, husband of Betsy Ross, also omitted the prayers for the royal family. But he permitted a Methodist itinerant preacher to read "a long and full free prayer for the King and a blessing on his Arms, and then delivered an extemporary Oration."[17]

The religious population in America at the outbreak of the Revolutionary War was chiefly distributed among the old established churches, but more and more new groups were being formed in this country who claimed the allegiance of new converts as well as dissidents from the older bodies. There may have been as many as five hundred of these among the more than three thousand congregations that served the three million inhabitants. The 658 Congregational churches were found mostly in New England; the Presbyterians had 543 congregations principally in the middle colonies; the 498 Baptist churches were more widely scattered; and the Church of England had 480 parishes, ranging from a few large and flourishing ones in the larger cities to widely scattered mission stations staffed by the agents of the SPG. The Quakers, who had lost some of their strength to the Anglicans, still numbered 295 meetings, while the Roman Catholics had only about fifty congregations at this time.

Religious freedom had prevailed for about a century in the middle colonies, while in Virginia and the South the establishment of the Church of England served somewhat as a counterbalance for the establishment of Congregationalism in New England. These offsetting influences of the significantly different establishments in the South and North allowed the religious freedom of the middle colonies to become a dominant factor in the American church scene. Perhaps unconsciously, both the lay-dominated, vestry-controlled parish life in Virginia and the New England town meeting joined forces to help produce the Revolution and no one can be certain which was the more influential. No less a man than Thomas Jefferson fought for religious freedom in Virginia and wrote the Statute adopted by its Assembly in December, 1785, that brought religious freedom to Virginia and became the pattern for the First Amendment to the Constitution of the United States.

By the end of the war the situation had markedly changed, and Anglicanism was literally almost destroyed as an ecclesiastical organization as well as a tradition. Opposed to the generally conservative position of the church were the popular philosophy of Thomas Jefferson and the religious liberalism of the Deists. Men now heard of religious freedom coupled with free speech, freedom of the press and economic freedom as an essential part of political liberty. The practical effect of these revolutionary ideas on the conservatively established church was corrosive and disintegrating. Of the five Anglican clergymen remaining in New England outside of Connecticut, four were in Massachusetts and one in New Hampshire. Georgia and North Carolina each had only one minister of the church who supported the Revolution, and one of these had married the daughter of a colonel in the Continental Army. In South Carolina fifteen of the twenty ministers had cast their lot with the colonies, but the religious depression after the war almost negated this apparent position of strength.

In Maryland more than half of the forty resident clergy had fled the colony, and even in Virginia thirty-four parishes were without ministers and twenty-three others had been completely lost. At one low point during the war William White was the only Anglican clergyman in Pennsylvania. Only in Connecticut where seventeen of the twenty clergy remained at their posts, often suffering hardship to do so, was there a sufficient nucleus of the Church of England to preserve the semblance of an organization that would soon take the initiative in the reorganization of the church.

In the more densely populated areas of the country from Connecticut to Maryland the church recovered its strength more quickly than in the rest of New England, where strong prejudices against Anglicanism still prevailed, or in the South, where the churches once established and supported by taxes were now dependent on their own strength. In many instances the strength of the Anglican membership, made up of privileged as well as middle and lower classes, also ebbed with the defection of the latter groups to other denominations where they found the congeniality of social equality, warm fellowship, and moralistic preaching to suit their needs. Even the wealthier landowners remained cool in their support of the church after the war, and it was only when the new Episcopal Church would be markedly influenced by the new Awakening that the church would begin recovering her strength. But the church was not dead, and its weakness must not be exaggerated, for within about six years after the close of the war it had established dioceses in most of the states, obtained its needed bishops, and created a new national church on an original pattern adapted to the new country yet preserving the essentials of historic Christianity.

X

THE CONSTITUTIONAL
CONVENTION

The cessation of hostilities in the war with England immediately suggested to the foresighted leaders of the Anglican churches in America that their decisive hour had arrived and that something must be done to preserve stability and order among them. So far they had not been successful in obtaining bishops, although Roman Catholic bishops were already in America, "exercising their functions over a willing people, without any aid or encouragement from provincial assemblies."[1]

In Maryland the war provided the occasion for the Assembly to pass the "vestry act" in 1779, guaranteeing the rights and property of the formerly established church by identifying it with the Church of England under the name and title of "the Protestant Episcopal Church." Although there was also a proposal to organize the church by legislative enactment and to appoint ordainers to the ministry, this Erastian gesture was avoided through the intervention of Samuel Keene, who opposed the action before the Assembly in Annapolis. After the war the Maryland legislature sought to establish the church and to provide "public support for the Ministers of the Gospel." A copy of this address before the Assembly came to the attention of the Maryland clergy at the commencement at Washington College in May, 1783, and they immediately took steps to see how they might make the necessary alteration to their liturgy, organize their church, and preserve the succession of their ministry.

With the permission of the Assembly the clergy in Maryland gathered at Annapolis on August 13, 1783, and, under the leadership of William Smith, then president of Washington College, adopted a "Declaration of fundamental rights and liberties" and the draft of a charter of incorporation to be presented to the Assembly for approval. The former document is of major importance, for it is an early appearance of the basic principles on which the church would continue: the separate identity of the church with its ancient usages and profession; its full enjoyment and exercise of spiritual powers; the perpetual enjoyment of its property rights; the continuation of the three orders of the ministry for whom its property rights shall be preserved; and the adaptation of her order and worship

125

. . . to the later Revolution, and other local circumstances of America . . . without any other or farther Departure from the Venerable Order and beautiful Forms of worship of the Church from which we sprung, than may be found expedient in the Change of our situation from a Daughter to a Sister Church.

Although the title "the Protestant Episcopal Church" had been used in identifying this now independent church in the Maryland "vestry act" of 1779 and at an earlier convention on November 9, 1780, this name and title was first officially adopted at this convention in the fall of 1783. The question of a proper name for the church arose out of necessity, and varied and curious titles appeared. So in his correspondence with the Scottish bishops in 1782 and 1783 regarding the preservation of episcopacy in America, Dr. George Berkeley, the eldest son of the former Dean Berkeley, referred to the nascent church in America variously as neglected "sons of Protestant Episcopacy" and "the Episcopal Reformed Church in America." As late as December 1784 Jacob Duché called it "ye American Episcopal Church."

As the war drew slowly to a close, William White, fearing that Britain would be very slow to recognize the independence of the colonies and despairing of "our ministry gradually approaching to annihilation," published *The Case of the Episcopal Churches in the United States Considered.* Although a few copies had been distributed to his friends a few days earlier, White's pamphlet was advertised for the first time in *The Pennsylvania Packet* on August 6, 1782, the very day on which Congress received a communication from Sir Guy Carleton and Admiral Digby that prepared the way for eventual peace. Because of the brighter prospects, White attempted to recover his pamphlets and destroyed all save a very few. In a reference to this episode in an episcopal charge as late as 1807 he admitted that if his publication had been delayed a little longer it would never have been issued except with considerable alterations.

Since the episcopal succession could not at that time be obtained from the Church of England, White had proposed that the churches in America should nevertheless form their own independent organization without waiting for the succession but clearly stating their "general approbation of Episcopacy, and a declaration of an intention to procure the succession as soon as conveniently may be." He suggested that one of the clergy be chosen to preside, and, since the term "bishop" seemed so offensive in the colonies, he was even willing to omit it and have the presiding officer called a superintendent or an overseer. Because the chief object of the church was to worship God and to provide the people with instruction and discipline, he argued that to wait further for the succession was to sacrifice the substance to the ceremony. Nor could he conceive that it was necessary to wait perhaps a whole generation to provide "the acknowledged ordinances of Christ's holy religion" because of a disputed point about externals.

Although White declared that the origin "of the order of bishop was from the presbyters choosing one from among themselves to be a stated president in their assemblies, in the second and third centuries," he proposed, nevertheless, that just as soon as the episcopal succession could be secured, the church should provide for a conditional ordination, resembling the form of conditional baptism already provided in the Prayer Book, to validate any inadequacy of ordination by presbyters. Beyond these details he presented a comprehensive plan for the organization of the church on a federal pattern, much as it was ultimately adopted seven years later. White's plan called for an essential unity in an autonomous national body, independent of all foreign, civil, or ecclesiastical jurisdiction and entirely separate from national and state control. Both clergy and laity would be included in its deliberative, legislative, and judicial assemblies structured in a diocesan, provincial, and national order, with an equality of the parishes, and the ministers to be selected by those to whom they minister.

Reflecting on his original plan fifty years later, White told the Pennsylvania Convention in an episcopal charge that in 1782 there seemed to be no canonically regular way to organize the church in time to save it from ruin. At about the same period he wrote to Bishop Hobart on December 31, 1830, supporting his earlier action and publication and declaring that he was still convinced of the primacy of the duty to preach the gospel and to worship God in the best manner that circumstances permit. But he also reasserted his conviction that episcopacy "should be sustained as the government of the Church from the time of the Apostles, but without criminating the ministry of the other churches; as is the course taken by the Church of England."

Apparently one of the first copies of White's pamphlet must have reached Connecticut, for ten of the fourteen clergymen then in that state gathered secretly in the old glebe house at Woodbury on March 25, 1783, to discuss what they called the "Philadelphia Plan" and pointed out its mistakes and dangerous proposals. With the advice and approval of the clergy in New York this Connecticut Convention chose to move in the traditional direction. They voted to ask Jeremiah Leaming or Samuel Seabury to be their bishop, promising their obedience to the one consecrated. Leaming was first named to this office to honor his long, devoted service, but he promptly declined because of age and infirmities sustained during the war. The fifty-three-year-old Seabury accepted and sailed for England, where he arrived on July 7. Following the example of Connecticut, the clergy of Maryland met at Annapolis in August 1783, framed their "Bill of Rights" and elected William Smith, then rector in Chester and president of Washington College, as their bishop. Even though his testimonials were signed by his clergy in Maryland and sent to the Archbishop of Canterbury on August 16, 1783, Smith was never consecrated because of subsequent charges against him.

Right after the close of the Connecticut Convention, eighteen priests from New York, Connecticut, New Hampshire, Rhode Island, Pennsylvania, Maryland, and New Jersey met in New York City on March 26, 1783. They endorsed Seabury's election in Connecticut and petitioned Sir Guy Carleton,

Governor of New York, to request the appointment of Thomas B. Chandler as Bishop of Nova Scotia.[2]

Meanwhile Abraham Beach of New Brunswick, New Jersey, had been in correspondence with William White, hoping "that the members of the Episcopal Church in this country would interest themselves in its behalf, would endeavour to introduce Order and uniformity into it, and provide for a succession in the ministry." On May 11, 1784, the meeting of the Corporation for the Relief of the Widows and Orphans of the Clergy, which brought clergy and lay representatives from New York, New Jersey, and Pennsylvania to New Brunswick, provided the occasion for the appointment of a committee of correspondence to form "a continental representation of the Episcopal Church and for the better management of the concerns of the said Church." By newspaper advertisements in Philadelphia and New York all the clergy of the church as well as "respectable characters of the laity" had been invited to this meeting. This gathering actually consisted of two meetings. After the business of pensions had been accomplished, three delegates were designated to meet with the Connecticut clergy to solicit their concurrence "in such measures as may be deemed conducive to the union and prosperity of the Episcopal Church in the United States of America." There was not yet a sufficient consensus to permit the adoption of basic principles of union, and the southern clergy, among whom episcopacy was less popular, were not even represented at this meeting. Nevertheless two important actions were taken: to call another church-wide meeting for October; and to recognize the laity as a coordinate branch in the church assemblies. Before adjourning, these clerical and lay representatives agreed to try by wide correspondence to stimulate general interest in the next meeting and the proposed union of the church in the states. In this gathering at New Brunswick White heard for the first time that Seabury was in England seeking consecration.

As early as the fall of 1783 William White had advised his vestry of a plan to call the representatives of the Pennsylvania churches to a convention the following spring to organize the church in their state. Under his chairmanship this convention of four clergy and twenty-one laymen met in Christ Church, Philadelphia, on May 24, 1784, and appointed a standing committee to act with representatives of the church in other states in framing a constitution for a national ecclesiastical government. Here, for the first time in Anglican history, the laity officially sat with the clergy in a council of the church; each congregation was allowed one vote. The convention adopted some fundamental principles claiming the independence of the Episcopal Church in the states from all foreign authority and its full and exclusive power to regulate the concerns of its own communion. Stressing its agreement in doctrine and worship with the Church of England and recognizing the three orders of the ministry, the convention declared that the right to enact canons or laws resided in "a representative body of the clergy and laity conjointly" and stipulated that "no powers be delegated to a general ecclesiastical government except such as cannot conveniently be exercised by the clergy and laity in their respective congregations."[3] Here is the evidence of the early intention to preserve local autonomy wherever possible and to give the laity a share in governing the church; for both features William White was largely responsible. This ecclesiastical design of the young Philadelphia rector was preserved in essence by subsequent assemblies and later became the basic outline of the church's constitution.

Abraham Beach also played a leading role in the revival and reorganization of the church. While he agreed in general and cooperated with White, he was more convinced of the necessity for episcopal ordination and disapproved of any unnecessary liturgical changes. Beach participated in the preliminary gatherings and the early General Conventions. His leadership was recognized by his colleagues, who chose him president of the House of Clerical and Lay Deputies in the Conventions of 1801, 1804, and 1808. In 1811 he became the assistant rector at Trinity Church, New York; in that diocese he was a member of the standing committee and repeatedly presided over its conventions in the absence of a bishop, for which office he was considered on several occasions.[4]

Also largely in agreement with White were William Smith of Maryland and Samuel Parker of Massachusetts. These men never questioned the importance of the regular succession, but they could hardly be said to support episcopacy as of divine right. Smith must have had considerable influence in the Maryland Convention of 1784 where he delivered the convention sermon, for the representatives of the churches agreed that

> . . . the duty and office of a bishop differs in nothing from that of other priests except in the Power of Ordination and Confirmation; and in the right of Precedency in ecclesiastical Meetings or Synods; the Duty and Office of Priests and Deacons, to remain as heretofore.[5]

Seabury, however, was greatly disturbed by such conceptions of the episcopacy held in Maryland and other regions of the South. The real problem was not whether to seek and retain a genuine episcopacy but how and when it might be obtained and how it was to be understood and exercised. White clearly asserted subsequently that

> . . . the object kept in view, in all the consultations held, and the determinations formed, was the perpetuating of the episcopal church, on the ground of the general principles which she inherited from the Church of England; and of not departing from them, except so far as local circumstances required, or some very important cause rendered proper. . . .[6]

Although he was only thirty-six, White was generally recognized as the architect and chief guiding spirit in the formation of the Protestant Episcopal Church in the United States of America; yet he was assisted by many others—some of them twice his age—who recognized in the young Philadelphian their natural leader. The scholarly Walter Hook, later Dean of Chichester, who visited the United States in the 1830's, pointed out the similarity of leadership in the English Reformation and in the reconstruction of the church in America. In each case he found "no dominating genius but a balance of good sense and moderate learning contributed to by a collective of variously competent men."[7]

To the "Convention of Clergymen and Lay Deputies of the Protestant Episcopal Church in the United States of America" held in New York City early in October, 1784, came sixteen clergymen and eleven laymen representing Massachusetts, Rhode Island, Connecticut, New York, New Jersey, Pennsylvania, Delaware, Maryland, and Virginia. David Griffith, rector of Fairfax Parish in Virginia, was granted all the privileges of this meeting save voting, since the laws of his state still did not permit the church "to send delegates or consent to any alterations in the Order, Government, Doctrine or Worship of the Church." This convention appointed a committee of four clergymen—William Smith, William White, Samuel Parker, and Samuel Provoost—and four laymen to draft a constitution for the church and to revise the state prayers. No revision was made in the liturgy, and the body voted adherence to the English Prayer Book. To prevent the indiscriminate use of unauthorized persons in the services of the church, especially Methodists or "exhorters," the clergy in the several states were authorized to appoint a committee to examine and appoint lay readers for "the present exigency." The emergency requiring such legislation had arisen from the fact that in most areas the parishes were independent and, in a potentially anarchic situation, could assume all prerogatives without being challenged. White saw the dangerous possibilities when he wrote,

> It was evident that without the creating of some new tie, the churches in the different states, and even those in the same state, might adopt such varying measures as would forever prevent their being combined in one common union.[8]

Although this body was widely representative of the church, it was not a formally organized convention, and its resolutions therefore took the form of recommendations. To its declaration of principles it added a proposal that each state should have a bishop who should have a seat in the General Convention. These actions were reported to all the churches and September 27, 1785, was set for a General Convention in Philadelphia.

Meanwhile, Samuel Seabury had been seeking consecration in England in vain; although his testimonials were in proper order, this request was refused because it would have required taking an oath of allegiance to the Crown. The English bishops also found it difficult to accept the fact that he had applied without an endorsement from the Connecticut legislature. Appealing finally to the Nonjuror bishops of Scotland, Seabury was consecrated on November 14, 1784, by Robert Kilgour, Bishop of Aberdeen and Primus of Scotland, his coadjutor, John Skinner, and Arthur Petrie, Bishop of Ross and Moray, in a chapel at Bishop Skinner's home in Aberdeen. His mission finally accomplished after more than sixteen months in Great Britain, Seabury returned to America the following spring and arrived at Newport at the end of June.

He promptly called the first convocation in Connecticut, which met on

August 3–5, 1785, at Middletown where he ordained four candidates to the diaconate, one of whom was from Maryland, and drafted plans for a revised liturgy. In his first address to his clergy Seabury indicated his awareness of the importance of the ministry in the successful work of the church. Stressing primitive doctrine and practice, he urged great care in preaching and discussing doctrine and in the presentation of candidates for the ministry. Believing that a good clergyman is a useful one, he warned that "a clergyman who does no good always does hurt, there is no medium."[9]

Seabury chose, however, not to attend the General Convention called to meet in Philadelphia the following month, nor was his diocese represented there. He had serious misgivings about White's opinions on episcopacy, feared the autocracy of the laity, and wrote to Bishop John Skinner that the proposed constitution would

> . . . bring the Clergy into abject bondage to the Laity and a Bishop seems to have no more power in the Convention than a Lay member. Doctrine, Disciplines, Liturgies, are all to be under lay control.[10]

When the sixteen clergy and twenty-four laymen assembled in the convention at Philadelphia late in September, 1785, the middle states, Maryland, Virginia, and South Carolina were represented, but no one came from New England. The absence of Connecticut is understandable because the October, 1784, meeting in New York had failed to provide that a bishop should preside, a detail insisted on by Provoost, who despised Seabury as a Tory and Nonjuror. Massachusetts had already professed obedience to Seabury and therefore sent no delegates. White was chosen to preside, and William Smith was named chairman of a committee to draft a constitution, revise the liturgy, and draft a plan for obtaining the episcopate.

The basic work on the constitution had already been done and needed only minor revisions before its adoption four years later. It provided for a triennial General Convention, the first meeting of which was called for June, 1786, to be composed of clergy and lay delegates chosen in their state conventions; these in turn were to be made up of clergy and lay representatives from the respective parishes. In each gathering a majority vote would be considered final. Each state was to have its own bishop, limited in his authority to the churches whose convention elected him; he was to be considered an *ex officio* member of the General Convention. Each clergyman was amenable to the authority of the convention in his state and bound before his ordination by a declaration of loyalty to the Scriptures and to the doctrine and liturgy of the church. The Proposed Prayer Book and the new constitution were to be considered the binding authority in worship and government when ratified by the church in the states.

The revising of the liturgy was so large an undertaking that the committee was continued after the convention, and White and Smith proceeded to do most of the work. In order to obtain the episcopate the convention voted to ask the English bishops to confer consecration on men properly chosen by the state conventions. The conventions were to certify that the laity had concurred in the elections and to obtain a certification from civil authorities that their proceedings were not contrary to the state statutes. Not only in the states were civil officers willing to certify to episcopal elections, but the address to the archbishops and bishops of the Church of England was accompanied by certificates from Richard Henry Lee, President of the Continental Congress, and John Jay, Secretary for Foreign Affairs, and it was presented by John Adams, then the Minister to Great Britain. Meanwhile, the Philadephia body discreetly avoided any action that might impugn Seabury's consecration, although there were several attempts to do so.

In keeping with the request of the convention that the various states choose their bishops, New York, Pennsylvania, and Virginia proceeded at once to do so; Maryland had already elected William Smith two years earlier. In New York the choice fell on Samuel Provoost, rector of Trinity Church and a most zealous patriot, who still saw all the church's problems in political perspective. Pennsylvania chose William White, and Virginia elected David Griffith, who was never consecrated because he could not obtain the necessary funds nor was there a will in Virginia to call a convention to provide him with the needed testimonials.

Following the convention, White and Smith continued their efforts in revising the Prayer Book, being influenced not only by the spirit of the convention but also by the creative opportunity of the moment. Others had also sensed this possibility. Jacob Duché wrote White from England, ". . . a church might now be formed more upon ye Primitive and Apostolical Plan in America than any at present in Christendom. . . ."[11] Charles H. Wharton of Delaware wrote Samuel Parker about the same time, "Perhaps such an opportunity never occurred since the days of the Apostles of settling a rational, unexceptional mode of worship."[12]

While trying to abide by the basic usages in English, the revisers may have taken undue liberties in excising the Athanasian and Nicene Creeds, "He descended into Hell" from the Apostles' Creed, as well as the idea of regeneration from the Office of Baptism. White and Smith were sensitive to suggestions from many sides and conceivably may have gone beyond their own best judgment in including many other changes, such as the optional omission of the sign of the Cross in baptism, in order to please all parties concerned. Both White and Smith later voted to restore the Nicene Creed.

Fifty copies of the Proposed Prayer Book were sent to the English bishops in sheets as they appeared from the printer. This would reconcile the otherwise conflicting dates of their arrival in England. Parts of the book apparently arrived as early as April, 1786, and on June 6 Charles Inglis wrote White from London saying that the whole of the Proposed Book had arrived and the bishops would soon make suggestions. On July 17, 1786, Granville Sharp took the Prayer Book, probably a completely bound copy, to the Archbishop of Canterbury.[13]

As soon as possible after the complete Proposed Prayer Book was received, the archbishops and fifteen of the bishops who were in London and able to attend met to discuss the book and wrote the American leaders expressing several major concerns. They hoped that "He descended into Hell" would be restored to the Apostles' Creed and that both the Nicene and Athanasian Creeds would also be replaced in the book. The bishops could not have been very favorably impressed by "A Form of Prayer and Thanksgiving . . . to be used yearly on the Fourth of July." They desired proper testimonials for each candidate for consecration in England, testifying to his learning, moral character, and faith. And they seemed much concerned about the slighting of episcopal honor and authority by limiting a bishop to *ex officio* membership in the General Convention and hoped that in the future bishops would be guaranteed

> . . . that just and permanent Authority, which is not only necessary for the right Discharge of their Duty and Benefit of the Church; but which is warranted by Holy Scripture and Practice of the Christian Church in every Period of its Existence.

The English bishops nevertheless proceeded at once to ask Parliament for authority to consecrate bishops for countries beyond Great Britain.

Only a few days after the receipt of the first letter another arrived, from the Archbishop of Canterbury and dated July 4, 1786, saying that Parliament had granted the requested authority and enclosing a copy of the enabling act passed on June 26, 1786. The archbishop added that only three such bishops would be consecrated to establish the line in America without requiring oaths of allegiance and supremacy to the king or of obedience to the archbishop. It was also to be understood that none so consecrated, or ordained by a bishop so consecrated, would be permitted to officiate in any part of the British realm. But to indicate their concern about the further revision of the Prayer Book and the direction that the structure of the church organization was taking, the archbishop also added, "But whether we can consecrate any, or not, must depend on the answers we may receive, to what we have written."

That these concerns were widely shared is evident from the unpopularity of the Proposed Prayer Book in the middle and northern states where most of the strength of the church lay. One report indicated that only thirteen copies were sold in New York City. Connecticut accepted only the revision of the state prayers; Bishop Seabury refused to accept the authority of a convention without a bishop to adopt a constitution or make liturgical changes and accused the body of attempting to make the church Episcopal in orders but Presbyterian in government. Against the background of his New England diocese and the prevalence of liberal thinking generally, it is understandable that he should charge that in deleting two major creeds the church might be discarding Christ's divinity with them.

Seabury actually had grave reasons for concern. He had on several occasions refused ordination to James Freeman, the lay reader at King's Chapel, Boston, because of his Unitarian views. The officers of the congregation thereupon ordained him. The congregation at King's Chapel had been depleted when the rector and many members fled to Nova Scotia, and the majority of the new pewholders were Unitarians. On February 20, 1785, this congregation authorized a new Prayer Book, which Freeman completed by March 28 and the congregation adopted on June 19. All references to the Trinity had been stricken from the book, and when a copy reached William White in November, he wrote his disapproval, saying that even though the Revolution had separated the American churches from the Church of England, "we ought to keep in view the characteristics of that church, in adapting our system to our new situation." His advice however fell on deaf ears, and on November 18, 1787, King's Chapel became a Unitarian church when James Freeman was ordained by his senior warden, and the claim of the Unitarian Society to possession of the church property was subsequently sustained by the courts.

In 1786 Seabury proceeded to publish his own Communion Office, a slightly altered version of the 1764 Scottish Communion Office. It was quickly approved by his clergy, and some of them continued its use for almost fifty years.

When the twenty-six deputies met in the General Convention in Philadelphia on June 20, 1786, two major issues claimed their attention. The political obstacles had been overcome with less than anticipated difficulties, but internal problems loomed up forebodingly. The Proposed Prayer Book was not being received with any more approval in the states than by the English bishops now in the process of considering it. The opponents of Bishop Seabury attempted to impugn the validity of his orders; had they succeeded there might easily have been two separate churches in America. With his usual diplomatic skill William White sponsored an action, unanimously supported, that the states should refuse to admit to a charge any clergyman professing canonical obedience to a bishop in any country or state not represented in the convention or to admit into their jurisdiction anyone ordained by an American bishop while the application for consecrations in England was pending. Without directly challenging Seabury's orders, these actions were nevertheless aimed at limiting his jurisdiction to Connecticut. White felt that Seabury's ordination of men for service in other states than his own and his demand of an oath of obedience from them might militate against the favorable reception of the important application now before the English bishops. Fortunately, the crisis involved in an open challenge of Seabury's consecration was postponed with the adjournment until the fall at Wilmington, Delaware, when the replies from England might be known.

On October 10, 1786, the convention reassembled in Wilmington heard the favorable report from Britain and generally acted to comply with the bishops' requests by restoring "He descended into Hell" and the Nicene Creed but refused to add the Athanasian Creed. Consideration of changes in the status of bishops was postponed; before adjournment, however, the convention signed testimonials for the consecration of Bishops-elect White and Provoost but refused a similar approval for William Smith on a charge by the respected John Andrews that Smith had been intoxicated at the previous convention. On

November 2, White and Provoost sailed for England where they were consecrated on February 4, 1787, in Lambeth Palace by the Archbishop of Canterbury, the Bishop of Bath and Wells, and the Bishop of Peterborough. By Easter they were back at work among their clergy.

With three bishops and a constitution and a Prayer Book about ready for final adoption it should have been a comparatively simple step to reorganize the church on a solid ecclesiastical basis and on a national scale, but many problems remained unsolved. Fortunately, these were mainly personal and emotional rather than of an essential nature. Seabury was not popular beyond Connecticut, and his emphasis on episcopal prerogatives and authority and his exclusion of the laity from the church government were violently opposed by his opponents and in the deep South, where clergy and laity alike saw little necessity for bishops. In Connecticut and scattered throughout the North there were others who were equally disturbed by the Presbyterian polity of these southern churchmen. Bishop Seabury took the initiative and wrote to both White and Provoost suggesting that they might meet and move in the direction of a united church. Provoost never answered, and White, claiming an implied obligation to the archbishop not to act with Seabury until three bishops of the English line had been obtained for America, again was able to postpone the confrontation of Provoost and Seabury.

The Constitutional Convention of the church met in Christ Church, Philadelphia, in two sessions from July 28 to August 8 and again from September 30 to October 16, 1789. This marked the beginning of the fully structured Protestant Episcopal Church in the United States of America, for these thirty-eight men—twenty-two clergymen including Bishop Seabury and Bishop White and sixteen laymen—approved and adopted a constitution, a set of canons, and a Prayer Book, which would remain in use with only slight alterations for 103 years. All of this was possible only because the most careful preparation had been made during the preceding quadrennium and probably because the strong sense of national unity had been undergirded recently by the adoption of the federal constitution. Three Episcopalians had actually contributed to the accomplishment of unity in the constitutions of both the nation and the church, although none of the fifty-five members of the Federal Convention was a deputy to this General Convention. However, Charles Pinckney, then only twenty-eight years of age, had represented South Carolina in the General Convention of 1785, and David Brearly of New Jersey and John Rutledge of South Carolina sat in the General Convention of 1786 and the one of the preceding year. It is possible that the church deputies may have sought the advice of members of the Federal Convention, many of whom were Episcopalians; certainly the recent attainment of complete national unity lent both a sense of urgency and hope to the assembly that brought the churchmen to Philadelphia in the summer of 1789.

Bishop White presided at the first brief session, which was given largely to preliminary preparations and discussions of the major canonical and liturgical problems. While most of the states were represented, no representatives came from New England, and the church in North Carolina and Georgia was so weak that no effort was made to have representation at this first session. The absence of the New England representatives is clearly understood from their difference in churchmanship and the fact that both Seabury and Samuel Parker were making every effort to assure a perfect union in the church.

From Boston Samuel Parker wrote the convention,

> The clergy of this State are very desirous of seeing an union of the whole Episcopal Church in the United States take place; and it will remain with our brethren at the Southward to say whether this shall be the case or not— whether we shall be a united or a divided Church. Some little difference in government may exist in different States, without affecting the essential points of union and communion.

From Connecticut Seabury wrote to William Smith on July 23, 1789,

> The wish of my heart, and the wish of the Clergy and of the Church people of this State, would certainly have carried me and some of the Clergy to your General Convention, had we conceived we could have attended with propriety. The necessity of an union of all the Churches, and the disadvantages of our present disunion, we feel and lament equally with you; and I agree with you that there may be a strong and efficacious union between the Churches, where the usages are different. I see not why it may not be so in the present case, as soon as you have removed these obstructions which, while they remain, must prevent any possibility of uniting. . . .

Duly elected representatives came from Delaware, Maryland, Pennsylvania, New Jersey, South Carolina, Virginia, and New York, although Bishop Provoost did not attend. His absence made it possible for the convention to recognize Seabury's fine spirit and to take an emphatic action as early as July 30 unanimously approving Seabury's consecration. It came about through an "Act of the Clergy of Massachusetts and New Hampshire," sent to the convention by Samuel Parker, requesting that the three bishops now in America unite in consecrating Edward Bass, the Bishop-elect in Massachusetts and Rhode Island. The Act was in fact a request for a reconciliation of the three bishops and a union of the church in New England with the church in the other states. This is evident from the fact that no serious protests were raised when Bass's consecration was delayed for more than seven years and from the preamble to the Act, which stated that the request was being made "to encourage and promote . . . a union of the whole Episcopal Church in the United States and to perfect and compact this mystical body of Christ." Parker and his associates were convinced that a further resort to England for bishops was unnecessary, for the church here already had a full complement of bishops competent to do anything necessary to assure its success.

Had it not been for Provoost's obsessive objection to Seabury, the consecration of Bass might actually have brought about the widely desired union.

Bishop Seabury had been enthusiastically in favor of the earlier joint consecration of Bishop-elect Bass; indeed he may have been the moving force behind Parker's letter to the convention, for the Massachusetts clergy had gladly accepted Seabury's supervision. Seabury wrote both White and Smith in similar vein, saying,

> . . . gladly would I contribute to the union and uniformity of all our churches. But while Bishop Provoost disputes the validity of my consecration I can take no step toward the accomplishment of so great and desirable objects. . . . Nothing would tend so much to the unity and uniformity of our churches, as the three Bishops, now in the States, joining in the consecration of a fourth.

It is significant that one of the first acts of the convention, after reading the Act sent by Parker and Seabury's letters to White and Smith, was the unanimous resolution "that it is the opinion of this Convention that the consecration of the Rt. Rev. Dr. Seabury to the Episcopal Office is valid."[14] It was primarily this action that paved the way for the reconciliation of the New England churchmen and their attendance at the later session.

The reading and consideration of the Act provoked some spirit of dissent, but finally the convention adopted five resolutions giving approval to the requests from New England. These proposals were drawn by William Smith after five days of discussion, and on their unanimous adoption the next day, he wrote Seabury:

> . . . I shall ever rejoice in it as the happiest incident of my life, and the best service I have ever been able to render our Church, that the resolves which were offered the next morning were unanimously and almost instantly adopted, as reconciling every sentiment, and removing every difficulty which had before appeared to obstruct a general union.

While the irenic spirit and deft genius of William White as a presiding officer contributed greatly to the peaceful settlement of the divisive issue before the church, credit must also go to William Smith, who drafted the important five proposals, and to Benjamin Moore of New York and to Robert Smith of South Carolina who assisted him. Perhaps second only to White's contribution was the superb effort of Samuel Parker of Boston, who not only maintained an equable spirit among the clergy in New England and with their bishop but also negotiated, first by letter and then in person at Philadelphia, until the reconciliation was accomplished. In his churchmanship his sympathies lay largely with Bishop Seabury, whose inclusion in the church he saw as absolutely necessary to preserve the complete Anglican tradition in the American church; yet in his statesmanship and ecclesiastical polity the Massachusetts churchman more nearly resembled Bishop White. Parker, who was able to blend the practice of the primitive church with expediency, may well have been the least appreciated of the important leaders at the constitutional convention and as responsible as any other for the happy reconciliation of the competing forces and the ultimate union of the church.[15]

Not until three more years had elapsed would the first consecration of a bishop take place in America. On his election by the Diocese of Virginia James Madison had written a letter to Bishop Seabury asking his consent and participation in his consecration; this was little more than a gesture of courtesy, however, for without waiting for a reply from Connecticut, he sailed for England and was consecrated at Lambeth on September 19, 1790. Two years later, after his election by the Diocese of Maryland, James Claggett was consecrated in New York on September 17, 1792, by the four American bishops, three of whom had now been consecrated in England.

Both the Connecticut churchmen and the bishops in England had objected to the deprivation of the bishops of their usual prerogatives in the new constitution. This convention consequently adopted a revision providing that the bishops should constitute a separate House, as soon as there were three or more in union with the convention, with the limitations that this Upper House could not initiate legislation and its veto could be overridden by a three-fifths vote of the Lower House.

Before the deputies recessed they approved a letter to President George Washington, who was serving his fourth month in that office. They commended him as "an animating example of all public and private virtues" and his earlier efforts during the Revolution and in the organization and early administration of the government, adding,

> We devoutly implore the Supreme Ruler of the Universe to preserve you long in health and prosperity, . . . the friend and guardian of a free, enlightened, and grateful people. . . .

Washington was apparently much touched by this gesture and replied gratefully.

Once more the deft hand of White was extended when he wrote Seabury assuring him of his own personal approval of his consecration and inviting him to join the adjourned session of the convention; White even agreed to join in the consecration of Bishop-elect Bass if the English bishops would give their consent and free him from his obligation to them. With alacrity Seabury accepted the invitation to attend the convention and appeared at the next session with two deputies from Connecticut and Samuel Parker to represent Massachusetts and New Hampshire. Bishop Provoost, whose illness had prevented his attendance at the first session, refused to come to Philadelphia in September because too many concessions had been made to Seabury.

In an early action the reassembled convention amended its earlier provision for a House of Bishops by giving the Upper House the right "to originate and propose acts for the concurrence of the House of Deputies" and providing that the veto of the bishops could be overridden only by a four-fifths vote of the deputies, or Lower House. Only in 1808 were the bishops given full veto power. Thereupon Seabury and his deputies and Parker approved and signed the revised constitution and were admitted into full union with the convention. In the absence of Provoost the two bishops withdrew to become a separate house, and Seabury, being the senior bishop, presided. Because Provoost and Madison, by then Bishop of Virginia, objected, this rule was altered at the next convention to permit rotation among the bishops. But in 1795 the senior bishop was once again given the responsibility of presiding in the Upper House, a prerogative that continued until the organization of the National Council and the provision for a full-time presiding bishop in 1919. Since Seabury died in 1796, White occupied the chair in 1798 and at subsequent General Conventions until his death in 1836. White later attested to Seabury's excellent spirit in their efforts as bishops "and especially the Christian temper which he manifested all along."

Most of the time of this convention was given to the revision and the final adoption of the constitution with nine articles, the ratification of seventeen canons, and the revision and final authorization of the first Book of Common Prayer fully approved in the American church. The constitution provided for a triennial convention as the supreme governing body of the church; it included a House of Deputies, consisting of not more than four clerical and four lay deputies from each state, and a House of Bishops. Each bishop was to be elected by a state convention according to its rules and to which his jurisdiction was limited. Dioceses were actually co-extensive with the respective states, but the importance of the states in the federal union, in both the church and the nation, remained so strong that it was not until 1838 that the term diocese was substituted for state in the constitution of the church. Provision was made for expansion of the church by admitting into union with the General Convention any state convention that would accede to the constitution. Bishops and other clergy were to be tried by their respective conventions, but at least one bishop was required at the trial of a bishop, and only a bishop could depose a bishop, presbyter, or deacon. The seventh article of the constitution prescribed that candidates for the ministry should be examined by a bishop and two presbyters and be required to subscribe to a declaration of belief and conformity. The next article made the use of the new Prayer Book mandatory, and the last article made provision for amendments to the constitution by requiring approval in two successive General Conventions. The seventeen canons dealt largely with the clergy; they affirmed the three orders of the ministry and the necessary regulations of preparation for ordination, the performance of parochial duties, the uniform use of the Book of Common Prayer, and the minister's personal conduct.

Because of the opposition to the Proposed Prayer Book, this convention, at the suggestion of Samuel Parker, produced a completely new authorized book by revising line by line the Prayer Book of 1662 still in use in England. Many of the changes had to do with the new state relationship in this country, and hundreds of minor changes were merely omissions of unnecessary words or verbal clarifications or modernizations.[16] The chief purpose here was to make the book useful in the new nation, and the spirit of the General Convention is clear in its Preface:

> . . . far from intending to depart from the Church of England in any essential point of doctrine, discipline or worship, or further than local circumstances require.

The Nicene Creed was restored, and "He descended into Hell" was also put back, but in brackets with a rubric permitting its omission. Similarly the sign of the Cross in the Office of Baptism was restored with permission to omit it. Although Seabury expressed doubt that he could accept the book, he eventually did so, probably because his promises to the Nonjurors who consecrated him were kept; the new Prayer Book included "The Oblation" and "The Invocation" from the Scottish Prayer Book, which in turn had copied them from the First English Prayer Book of 1549.

The Thirty-nine Articles were introduced into the Prayer Book only in 1801 after approval by the General Convention without, however, requiring subscription by either clergy or laity. Three other significant changes were made in the American Prayer Book before the major revision of 1892: "The Ordinal, the Form of Making, Ordaining and Consecrating Bishops, Priests and Deacons" was added in 1792; "The Form of Consecration of a Church or Chapel" was added in 1799; and the "Office of Institution of Ministers" in 1808.

The Protestant Episcopal Church in the United States of America so established represents a remarkable ecclesiastical achievement: an historical church reorganized on new federal principles, with a constitutional episcopate preserved by democratic elections in place of the monarchical episcopate continued by royal appointment, and a constitutional and canonical structure fully preserving the continuity of the historic episcopate and conciliar principle of the Catholic church without sacrificing its rich Protestant heritage and religious freedom.

XI

THE CRITICAL EARLY
YEARS

Both the youthful church and nation found common problems in their growth and adaptation to new and independent responsibility. Both organisms were small; both suffered the untold anguish of awkward adolescence as they moved toward maturity and stability.

From Maine to Georgia in 1790 there were about four million people of whom seven hundred thousand were colored and most of them slaves. Only the six largest cities had a population over eight thousand, in the surprising order, Philadelphia, New York, Boston, Charleston, Baltimore, and Salem. Most Americans were widely scattered over the countryside, and not until 1840 did the urban population approximate one-tenth of the total. This fact alone is one reason for the comparatively slow growth of the Episcopal Church, which was primarily an urban church; it also still suffered from its English associations and lacked a universal appeal because of its generally privileged constituency.

The tempo of life had not been much altered in two thousand years and the speed of traffic on the Appian Way must have far surpassed that on the American roads, which required nine days to travel from New York to Boston and a full month from Charleston to Philadelphia. Communication was equally slow, for it was dependent on carriage and packet. Actually, America might never have become involved in a second war with Great Britain if Congress could have known that the British ministry had already revoked the objectionable Orders in Council before the United States declared war. Further feeling against Britain had been aroused by the Henry-Crillon spy hoax, and many Philadelphia Episcopalians were saddened when Sophia, the daughter of Parson Duché, refused to accept the marriage proposal of John Henry Hobart, then the young deacon in charge of Trinity Church, Oxford, and married instead the very personable Irishman, John Henry, one of the purported spies.[1]

The design of the new American church was complete, and its foundation had been well laid; the raising and completion of the structure remained to be accomplished. Fortunately, its chief designer and most of those who had worked with him in its planning lived on through the next two decades to

141

establish by their common labors a completely stable church compatible with its new environment. In this church there were about two hundred clergymen, fewer than in some of its present dioceses, and its communicants included no more than one in every four hundred inhabitants. Yet the church was now completely reorganized and showed promising signs of recovering from the strains and shock of the Revolution. The new plan of organization gave men hope, and members soon learned to rely on their own resources and to support their clergy voluntarily, in some instances quite comfortably. Even though no major projects were immediately begun, the leaders of the church planned a national program, and many local congregations began to pick up and restore the pieces of their once flourishing parishes.

Now that the church was living under its new constitution with episcopal jurisdiction, it remained for these Americans who had never known bishops to see how well this traditional office could be adapted to the new soil. Misgivings among both clergy and laity existed in all areas, with the possible exception of Connecticut. In 1784 the Maryland Convention had gone so far as to say that "the duty and office of a bishop differs in nothing from that of other priests, except in the power of ordination and confirmation, and the right of presidency in ecclesiastical meetings or synods." For a short time some dioceses denied this latter authority and granted a bishop only an *ex officio* seat in the convention. Bishops and clergy were amenable to their own conventions, and even the bishop in some dioceses might be tried without the presence of another bishop. The exclusive prerogatives of the bishops were few and usually hedged about. In approving candidates for ordination, the bishop was usually required to act with the approval of the convention or the standing committee, a unique American development to provide for interim authority in the conventions. Through the years these standing committees have provided counsel and advice for the bishops, but they have also continued to serve as a check and curb on episcopal authority and are now required to give their approval, in addition to that of the bishops, for the consecration of all bishops.

Now that the church had bishops, the real problem, of course, was what kind of bishops shall it have. In dissociating the new bishops from all the undesired aspects of the English episcopate, Americans were slow to allow the accrual of new, to say nothing of some of the old, prerogatives. Most of these early bishops limited their action largely to confirmation and ordination, until eventually they were consulted in clerical disputes or differences between clergy and congregations. Slowly in a functional manner they came to acquire the historic prerogatives of their office that might readily have been denied them if they had made earlier demands for them.

In Connecticut, where the strong body of some twenty clergy were accustomed to the ways of English episcopacy, Bishop Seabury administered his diocese effectively and with an unlimited authority. He usually began his instructions to his clergy, "I, Samuel, by Divine permission Bishop of Connecticut, issue this injunction," and at least once charged the Presbyterians and Congregationalists to relinquish "those errors which they, through prejudice, had imbibed." In this state, although still hampered by lack of resources and endowments, the bishop was able to exercise episcopal authority in a degree rarely seen in the later church. After the death of Seabury in 1796, Abraham Jarvis, an able and scholarly bishop, led this diocese to become a splendid example of strength and good order.

But in South Carolina a negative reaction had already set in. Fearing the episcopal usurpation of privileges that were considered the rights of the clergy, vestries, and convention, Henry Purcell and two other priests circulated a letter among the rectors and vestries of their diocese urging that one of their number immediately be sent to the bishops in the North to receive authority to ordain and confirm without any additional episcopal prerogatives. They apparently feared that the House of Deputies would soon grant the power of absolute veto to the House of Bishops, as announced in 1792, and asserted that if this occurred South Carolina and Virginia would withdraw from the General Convention. Purcell supported this proposal with his somewhat scurrilous anonymous pamphlet, *Strictures on the Love of Power in the Prelacy*, in which he attacked the American bishops and especially Seabury, whom he accused of instigating the plan.

Meanwhile, the South Carolina Convention had been called into session and unanimously elected Robert Smith, rector of St. Philip's Church, its first bishop. He went to Philadelphia for the General Convention and, after assuring Bishop White that the circular letter had never been approved by the convention, was duly consecrated there on September 13, 1795. Had it not been for the intervention of the very bishops Purcell had slandered, who pleaded for clemency after he publicly recanted, the South Carolina disturber might well have been expelled by his peers in the House of Deputies. When he discovered that the highly respected John Andrews, vice-provost of the University of Pennsylvania, and a deputy from Pennsylvania, had exposed him, Purcell forgot his recantation and openly accused Andrews of slander and challenged him to a duel. Eventually the civil courts placed Purcell under bond to keep the peace. Three years after Smith's death in October, 1801, the South Carolina Convention elected Edward Jenkins as his successor, only to receive his declination because of his age, thus leaving the diocese vacant for a decade. After the General Convention of 1795, South Carolina sent no more representatives to these triennial gatherings until 1814, after the alert and aggressive Theodore Dehon had become the diocesan of the long vacant episcopate on February 12, 1812.

To such opposition and rebellion against authority was added the revolt against dogma. The French Revolution, which influenced the trends of thought in western Europe, was leaving its impression on America as well, but mostly among the intellectuals, who had already been stimulated by German Rationalism and Deism. In some of the leading colleges those willing to be counted Christian could be numbered on the fingers of one hand, while liberals organized themselves into Deistical Clubs. The College of William and Mary was considered the hotbed of French politics and religion. At a literary society meeting there two questions were discussed: "First, whether there be a God? Secondly, whether the Christian Religion had been injurious or beneficial to Mankind?"[2]

Among the Episcopalians, Uzal Ogden of New Jersey became an apologist for orthodoxy in 1795 when he wrote his *Antidote to Deism*, which he described as "an ample refutation of all the objections of Thomas Paine against the Christian religion." In the larger cities Episcopalians found some of their leading laymen, like Benjamin Franklin, tainted by the current philosophies, but Congregationalism, more than any other church, was literally torn by the ensuing controversy, which soon led to its division and the formation of the Unitarian Church. Most of the American churches and the greater part of the population in rural America generally were not disturbed or dissuaded from the satisfaction they found in their warmly emotional, evangelical religion.

The major problems of the Episcopal Church were not yet theological; the pressures of practical issues consumed most of their time and energy. Deprived of parsons, many parishes under most adverse circumstances continued with the services of lay readers. Old church buildings so recently destroyed were slowly brought into respectable repair, but only by great efforts. For the first time in their experience these churchmen were entirely dependent upon their own initiative and resources; there were no revenues from taxes, no grants from the Society for the Propagation of the Gospel, and in Virginia even the glebe lands were sold and the monies appropriated by the state in January, 1802. As early as 1791 the Diocese of Maryland sought more permanent support for the clergy and devised a system for renting instead of selling their pews, "with a preference for choice being given to those who yield up their Pews." This apparently provided a regular annual income and gave rise to the system of charging owners of pews a supplemental annual rental.

Maryland clergy were, however, equally alert to the nonmaterial needs of their parishioners in these days of spiritual lethargy, for among the canons adopted this year, Canon VII provided that ". . . each minister shall . . . explain to his congregation the Liturgy of the Church . . . in Sermons or addresses; laying before them the Beauty, Order, and Fitness of its several parts and urging observance of the rubrics." And lest one become lax in his religious life, Canon VIII provided that "no minister shall admit any persons to the Holy Communion till he shall have conversed with them on the subject; unless he is satisfied that they are regular communicants in his own or some other church."[3]

As the dioceses recovered their stability, many in turn sought approval of their chosen bishops. Thomas Claggett had been consecrated in 1792 for Maryland, where favorable conditions permitted the free exercise of his office. He was limited only by his occasional bouts with the gout and at times by his insistence on wearing a mitre, a custom he shared with Seabury. Claggett, the first bishop consecrated in America, found that the war had left half his parishes vacant and church properties in shocking condition. Fortunately, the Maryland legislature acted favorably for the church, contrary to the action in Virginia, so that vestries retained title to churches, glebes, and all properties that had formerly belonged to the Church of England. Minimal improvements had been made by 1808 so that the General Convention in that year listed conditions in Maryland as still "deplorable."

Among the interesting Maryland clergymen of this period was Mason L. Weems, better known as Parson Weems and remembered as the fabricator of the cherry-tree legend about George Washington. Weems and Edward Gantt, who had been in England about a year and a half seeking ordination, became the first American presbyters ordained under the special Act of Parliament of August 13, 1784, that permitted the ordination of foreign candidates without requiring the oath of allegiance to the Crown. Weems wrote several popular romantic biographies and spent much time as a colporteur, selling books of all kinds from door to door. Such time as remained he devoted to the church; in 1791 he was listed as serving St. Margaret's Parish.[4]

Edward Bass, consecrated Bishop of Massachusetts and Rhode Island in 1797, found few active parishes in these states or in New Hampshire, which also came under his jurisdiction. Before his death in September, 1803, he had been able to accomplish little beyond his own parish in Newburyport. Following Bass's death, an unsuccessful attempt was made to persuade a leading lawyer, Dudley Atkins Tyng of Newburyport, to seek holy orders that he might succeed to the episcopate, but even though he had once seriously considered entering the ministry, Tyng declined the honor. Samuel Parker, who had also previously declined the episcopate, was chosen to succeed Bass and was consecrated in September, 1804. Three months later he died, leaving all New England, apart from Connecticut, without a bishop for seven years.

In New York Bishop Samuel Provoost was elected solely on the ground that he was the only minister in that state who had supported the colonies. Since he did not expect the church to survive beyond his own years, he served with little enthusiasm in the vicinity of New York City until 1801. Then, having failed to block the acceptance of Bishop Seabury, whom he despised because of his British loyalty, Provoost resigned on the ground of ill-health. He retired from the public observance of religion to his farm in the Bowery, where he translated Tasso and excelled as a botanist. In 1811 he suddenly reappeared, probably at the insistence of New York low churchmen, briefly asserting his episcopal prerogative as understood by the House of Bishops, in a vain attempt to prevent the consecration of John Henry Hobart.[5] After the Revolution Benjamin Moore, once a Tory candidate for rector of Trinity Church and an able leader of dignified gentleness, led the New York diocese for the decade and expanded its growth along the Hudson River to Albany, where the church had already been established. He also provided missionaries for the western part of the state, but a partial paralysis forced him to discontinue his active supervision in 1811 when Hobart became his assistant.

Not all bishops-elect were so fortunate as to be consecrated. Charles Pettigrew, elected Bishop of North Carolina in 1794, was apparently unable to reach the General Convention in 1795 because an epidemic of fever interrupted all traffic at Norfolk, Virginia. He returned to his home and died soon afterward. Samuel Peters of Connecticut was denied consecration as Bishop of Vermont because that state had only one clergyman, who left soon after the election, although the technical reason given was that Vermont had not acceded to the constitution of the church. To cover such exigencies a canon was later adopted that at least six resident presbyters were required before a bishop could be consecrated for any diocese. Uzal Ogden was refused consecration for New Jersey, even though elected by more than six presbyters on August 16, 1798, on the technical ground that a majority of the voters were temporarily employed and so not canonically resident. With the American church established, the proposed attempt to secure orders for Ogden in Scotland would certainly have failed. Actually Ogden was an enthusiastic evangelical and considered dangerously "Methodistical." New Jersey had to wait until John Croes, the sixteenth in the American succession, was consecrated in 1815.

The lack of religious interest which has generally been associated with the aftermath of war, and the preoccupation with material things which invariably accompanies a period of rapid reconstruction and expansion, not only affected Episcopalians but all religious bodies in America. The Presbyterians in the General Assembly of 1798 recorded their fear of "a general dereliction of religious principle and practice among our fellow citizens." Yet there were newer areas to the west just opening to settlement where basic principles of integrity necessitated by frontier living were being rediscovered and where the church was beginning to supply the religious support for this life of new adventure. This growth was, to be sure, a slow process, but the church was there, and its influence was being built into that segment of American life to such a degree that it could never be completely lost.

When the Episcopal Church was born, five per cent of the population of this country already lived west of the Alleghenies, many of them along the Ohio River and the adjacent fertile areas in Kentucky and Tennessee. The adoption of the Constitution in 1787 removed the principal objections of the leaders of the separate State of Franklin in the Tennessee Valley and ended 150 years of an unsettled political situation when this area became a part of the "Territory Southwest of the Ohio," to which a governor was appointed in 1790 with residence in Knoxville as the capital. In 1791 the population of this Territory, including both Kentucky and Tennessee, was 36,000 of whom 3,400 were slaves. Kentucky was organized as a state and admitted to the Union in 1792 and eight years later had a population of 221,000. When Tennessee was admitted as a state on June 1, 1796, it alone had 67,000 free white inhabitants and about 12,000 slaves, and these figures had increased by 1800 to about 106,000 whites and 40,000 slaves. By 1810 Kentucky's population had grown to 407,000 with 80,000 additional Negroes, and Tennessee had 262,000 white residents with an additional 45,000 Negroes. Many of these settlers, perhaps 30,000 of them, were Scotch-Irish who had fled from northern Ireland during the Antrim Evictions in the early eighteenth century; from 1730 to 1750 a quarter of a million more arrived on the east coast, and many of them also moved west to Tennessee and Kentucky. Among these people the religious awakenings found candidates for religious renewal, and among these new converts new American churches like the Disciples of Christ were born in about 1830.

The first priest of the Church of England to enter the areas west of the Alleghenies was a Rev. Dr. Allison, chaplain to Colonel Burd and his two hundred men who were given the task of opening a road from Braddock's Trail to the Monongahela River at Brownsville, Pennsylvania, in 1758. After this transitory experience, a whole generation passed before Joseph Doddridge, M.D., came to Washington, Pennsylvania, in 1792 and conducted the first Anglican service in that community.[6] From this point he could survey the large areas and the increasing number of settlers without the ministry of the church. He reported that he was the only Anglican minister in the western part of Virginia where now there should be forty. By 1810 he and several others petitioned the General Convention to establish a new diocese in the area, but, probably because of the death of Bishop Madison, no action was taken. In 1815 Doddridge went as far west as Chillicothe, Ohio, and three years later returned there, but these trips left no permanent effects except as a stimulus to the later missionary enterprise. As late as 1818 Doddridge still disappointedly reported that Roman Catholic missionaries were traversing every part of this country while in Kentucky and Tennessee not one in one hundred churchmen had heard the voice of an Anglican clergyman. St. Luke's Church in Chartier Township, six miles from Pittsburgh, was the first congregation permanently established west of the Alleghenies in 1790. Preaching had begun in Pittsburgh by 1797, but there was no parish there until Trinity Church was organized on September 4, 1805.

Individual Episcopal clergymen accompanied the settlers into the western regions beyond the mountains as early as 1775 when John Lythe participated in the formation of the Transylvania Company at Boonesborough, Kentucky, and opened its first session with a "performance of divine service." Although other missionaries from Virginia and Maryland came to these regions, it would be a long generation before the work of the Protestant Episcopal Church was substantially organized in Kentucky and Tennessee and the areas farther southwest.

Ohio, with a population approaching fifty thousand, became the seventeenth state when it was admitted to the Union. The Great Lakes regions were settled more slowly, hardly because of inaccessibility, but probably because of the greater extremities of climate. This region in fact provided one of the finest interconnections of waterways in the world, as later settlers would discover. Michigan was organized as a Territory in 1806, and Detroit soon came to be recognized as a point that controlled the Lakes and the West. By easy portages between the Fox and the Wisconsin Rivers, and between Big Stone Lake and Lac Traverse des Sioux, the source of the Red River of the North, the traveler had access from Hudson Bay to the Gulf of Mexico and through the Great Lakes to the Atlantic entirely by a water route. At the organization of the Michigan Territory, less than five thousand persons lived in its vast area, and these numbers had barely doubled by the time the first Episcopal missionary, Alanson W. Welton of the Diocese of New York, moved from the western part of that diocese to Detroit in 1821. Unfortunately he lived a very short time in this stern environment, and it was to be several years before the work of the church could be well established here. Before the end of the first triennium, the Episcopal Church became interested in the opportunities in these areas; the General Convention of 1792 appointed a committee to devise "a plan of supporting missionaries to preach the Gospel on the frontiers of the United States." This convention recommended that in each parish the minister should annually preach a missionary sermon and take an offering; these funds were to be collected in each case by the diocesan treasurers and distributed to support missionaries on the frontier.

Although this national effort proved unwieldy at that time and was discontinued within three years, many of the dioceses quickly resumed the effort independently. After the organization of the Society for the Advancement of Christianity in Pennsylvania in 1812, Jackson Kemper made a supervisory trip through its western areas. This first general missionary effort of the church fell under the supervision of the Bishop of Pennsylvania, probably because the opportunities largely lay in his areas; usually an assistant was designated to undertake the detailed work and travel. So physically taxing was this work that Samuel Bowman, an assistant to Bishop Alonzo Potter, died by the roadside in western Pennsylvania. The Diocese of Pittsburgh was organized in 1865, and six years later it reported sixteen parishes, three missions, and twenty-five hundred communicants in Allegheny County.[7]

Meanwhile, many of the American churches, which were more positively influenced by the evangelical motivations of the Great Awakening, were able to organize their own missionary societies. The Congregationalists of Massachusetts, New Hampshire, and Connecticut founded such a society before 1800, and in 1802 the Presbyterian General Assembly placed its missionary work under the supervision of a standing committee. More militant and aggressive were the Baptists, who established the first Baptist association west of the Alleghenies in 1785 and from that base of operation sent out lay and ordained missionaries who penetrated the frontier in every direction. These men, who depended for their support on the labor of their own hands, often maintained farms while using every opportunity to preach the gospel or gather a congregation. In Kentucky alone the Baptists gathered ten thousand members between 1800 and 1803.

Equally successful were the Methodists who, by the time the Episcopal

Church came into being, already had ten circuits in the West; in about twenty years these increased to sixty-nine with more than thirty thousand members. While some Methodist ordained and lay preachers were settlers and largely supported themselves, others called circuit riders remained unmarried. Unencumbered and supported by the offerings of the people to whom they preached, these men were free to spend several months on their long rides from one preaching appointment to the next. Over many years Bishop Francis Asbury, who remained a bachelor, traveled more than quarter of a million miles under all kinds of conditions. Averaging a sermon a day, he preached no less than 16,500 times as he rode over all the settled and frontier areas of this country. Services were not limited to Sunday and frequently took the form of small gatherings at the home of some sympathetic settler, not necessarily a Methodist.

In their attempts to better accomplish their missionary objectives, the Presbyterians and Congregationalists in 1801 agreed to a "Plan of Union" by which their members could worship together in one church and the vote of the majority would determine the ecclesiastical connection of the clergyman to be called. Although these two churches were similar in order and constituency, the denominational consciousness of the Presbyterians was stronger and their migrations more numerous, so that before the union was abrogated a generation later, about two thousand congregations, once Congregationalist, had become Presbyterian, thus accounting for the predominance of the latter over the former in the Midwestern states. These two denominations were also more responsible than any others for carrying educational institutions and opportunities to the West; the Presbyterians alone had founded forty-nine colleges by 1860.

Obviously the Episcopal Church had not yet seen a similar vision of its opportunities or devised an efficient method of administering its missionary responsibilities. Its birth pangs had been a traumatic experience, and many parishes and even some of the dioceses were still primarily engaged in preserving their own existence in the midst of great difficulties. Where such local pressures loomed large, the wider national interests received little attention and won less support. A long extended parochial outlook could not easily be changed into an effective national program, as the more idealistic leaders discovered. The fact is that the church had not yet begun to think nationally, either in assuming its responsibilities or in planning an effective missionary force to carry the gospel to the expanding frontiers of the West.

The importance of the general and diocesan convention was underestimated by most churchmen. The Constitutional Convention of 1789 consisted of two bishops, twenty clergy, and sixteen laymen, and, even though the General Convention of 1808 passed a resolution urging the "propriety, necessity and duty" of sending regular deputations and having all bishops present, the next session in 1811 assembled only two bishops, twenty-five clergy, and twenty laymen. Perhaps the conventions were uninteresting, and their business may easily have seemed less important than the pressing parochial problems. A better explanation might be that the church in America had not yet come to appreciate the central importance of the episcopate nor had proper provision been made for its full support. Even Bishop White served as rector of Christ Church to obtain a living while he administered the Diocese of Pennsylvania with such time as remained.

In Virginia both the religious spirit and public morale were at a low ebb. The wars in Europe had ruined the tobacco market, and the consequently unstable economy, combined with the losses of assets and depletion of the soil, promised little hope of rapid recovery. Deprived of their church properties by legislative action, the Episcopalians in general and the clergy in particular, now comparatively few in numbers and growing fewer, shared the common poverty.

Yet these Virginia churchmen were not without hope; there had been severe reverses but also some signal successes in Virginia. Once in 1775 the sixty-one counties counted ninety-five parishes and about as many clergymen ministering at 164 churches and chapels. By the close of the war many of these buildings had been used for military purposes and were destroyed or irreparably damaged. Twenty-three parishes had been lost entirely, and of the remaining seventy-two only thirty-four had ministerial services. The number of ministers had been reduced to twenty-eight and of these only fifteen held their original posts. In many ways destitute but not despairing, seventy laymen and thirty-six ministers met in convention in Richmond in May, 1785, and resolved to send representatives to the General Convention called to meet in Philadelphia in 1786 and to have a share in facing the problems of the total church. Showing a sense of self-reliance, these churchmen decided to continue the use of the Book of Common Prayer but with needed adaptations; then revealing their antipathy to all things English but with no desire to break the historic continuity of the church, they resolved "that the Canons of the Church of England have no obligation on the Protestant Episcopal Church within this Commonwealth." Their major concern, however, became evident in *An Address*, a moving appeal that they sent throughout the state to their people asking,

> Are the doctrines of our Church less excellent than at any former period? Have you embraced the persuasion of the Church to abandon it in the hour of difficulty? . . . why do you hesitate? We therefore entreat you, by all the ties of religion, to cooperate fervently in the cause of your Church.[8]

Encouraged by this wider perspective, the Virginians also decided to elect a bishop but carefully circumscribed his functions, making him like the other clergy amenable to their own convention. David Griffith, a very able leader, was elected bishop in 1786 but relinquished his office three years later because adequate funds were not available for his trip to England for his consecration. The Virginia Convention of 1790 elected James Madison, the president of the College of William and Mary, its bishop, and on September 19, 1790, he received his consecration from the Archbishop of Canterbury and the Bishops of London and Rochester, making him the third American bishop with orders from the English line. He entered on his new responsibility enthusiastically, pleading with the clergy and laity for more fervent Christian zeal to check unbelief and fanaticism; but the response was negligible, and the bishop made only one visitation of his diocese.

The church recovered more slowly in Virginia than in the North partly because of the difference in the spirit of the clergy. In Virginia, few candidates had been trained at the College of William and Mary; most of the clergy were Englishmen, and many had become indolent or even indifferent. In New England the ministers were usually American-born and -trained, and not a few had become Episcopalians by strong conviction in their maturity.

The Virginia layman could not be excused from sharing in the responsibility for the state of the church. Samuel Davies, the father of organized Presbyterianism in eastern Virginia, reported that educated Presbyterians there, even some trained in Scotland, became indifferent to religion and either tried "to be polite by turning deists, or fashionable by conforming to the Church." He quickly admitted, however, that "had the doctrines of the Gospel been solemnly and faithfully preached in the established Church, . . . there would have been but few Dissenters in these Parts of Virginia." Yet he reported that, even though no dissenting ministers had been settled in Virginia from the beginning, when he came in 1747 it was not long until he was preaching regularly to four or five hundred persons, among whom were eager churchmen and on occasion as many as one hundred Negroes.[9]

In part, at least, the dilemma of the church in Virginia was due to political events and pressure, largely from the competing free churches, which led to the disestablishment of the church. In 1784 the Virginia Assembly had made proper provision for the incorporation of the minister and vestry in each parish, thus protecting its rights and estates, but this act was repealed early in January, 1787. Eventually in January, 1802, the legislature ordered the glebe lands sold for the benefit of the state, leaving the clergy without this necessary support. Many churches fell into disrepair, and even sacred vessels shared the fate of the glebes, and often parishioners despaired as they saw a rapacious purchaser tearing down the old church to salvage its timbers. One marble baptismal font became a watering trough, and Holy Communion vessels were profaned. Bishop Madison was so greatly discouraged in his later years that he gave almost all his attention to the college. After only fifteen ministers and sixteen laymen attended the convention in 1805, seven years were allowed to pass before another diocesan convention was called, and the Virginians failed to send representatives to four consecutive General Conventions. The General Convention of 1808 despaired of this historic diocese and reported that "there is danger of her total ruin," and Chief Justice John Marshall thought the church "too far gone ever to be revived." On May 5, 1814, more than two years after the death of Bishop Madison on March 6, 1812, Richard Channing Moore was elected the second Bishop of Virginia and soon brought new life into the church through his evangelical zeal, coupled with a considerable leaven of high church principles.

Now that the church had begun to reassemble its resources and could see new hope ahead, many leaders like William White marveled that the church had been preserved. In one of his charges the Bishop of Pennsylvania reminded his clergy that in those critical years ". . . we were no more than were sufficient to form a small social circle; in which, whatever related to our communion was discussed, in an unreserved communication of our respective sentiments."[10] With such memories fresh, it was natural that he and others turned their best efforts toward every conceivable constructive step within their reach. During the first years of the nineteenth century individual dioceses organized a dozen or more tract and educational societies designed to promote piety, knowledge, missions, theological education, and even catechetical instruction, although Sunday Schools as such were not begun until 1814. Several states had their own societies "for the Advancement of Christianity" within their dioceses, but Maryland devised the most all-inclusive descriptive title, "The Society for Confirming and Extending the Interests of the Christian Religion in General and of the Protestant Episcopal Church in Particular."

At times their concern led the clergy to apologetic efforts, as in the defense of the recently won and now treasured episcopate. At the consecration of Abraham Jarvis as Bishop of Connecticut on October 18, 1797, William Smith, then rector of St. Paul's Church, Norwalk, preached from Ephesians 4:11–12 and, borrowing from Tertullian, said, "When your captains, that is to say the Deacons, Presbyters and Bishops flee, who shall teach the laity to be constant? Presbyters and Deacons cannot ordain deacons and presbyters much less consecrate a bishop." He concluded that one man or any number of men might as well attempt to create a new world but only a madman would attempt it.[11] As might have been expected, this sermon, when published, aroused a controversy with the neighboring Congregational pastor at Bridgeport, Samuel Blatchford, who published *The Validity of Presbyterian Orders Maintained* to which Smith replied. Every generation to the Civil War would discuss this topic with more or less heat. Most important of all, Smith prepared his "Office of Institution of Ministers" at the request of the clergy in Connecticut where it was first used; with slight revision it was adopted by the General Convention and became a permanent part of the Book of Common Prayer.

Meanwhile, Bishop William White was using every opportunity to show the relevance of the Christian religion to private and public life and to individual and social responsibility. On a Day of General Thanksgiving in Philadelphia on February 19, 1795, he preached in Christ Church on "The Reciprocal Influence of Civil Policy and Religious Duty." Since he believed religion is the very basis of the government's existence, he asserted that society cannot exist without government, which therefore rests on the will of God, who ordained society and qualified men for its enjoyment. Admitting that by example of conduct and by laws government may aid religion, he quickly pointed out that religion may also aid government since religion is the basic principle of all duty.

The bishop was always at his best when speaking of the office of the ministry, as when he said, ". . . the most indispensable qualification . . . is evidently the love of devotion and a temper moulded to the exercise of it." While pleading for a learned clergy, he would quickly add the necessity for obedience to ordination vows. He decried changes of sentiment that disengage men from their promises and called it a profanation that any man "insinuate himself into a church, with sentiments hostile to its order and under vows he has no intention of observing." Speaking with timeless appropriateness he declared, "Our church has prescribed a form of prayer and where men depart from it under guise of a great increase of piety I have been compelled to ascribe it to mere vanity and the exaltation of the self."[12]

At the consecration of Bishop Samuel Parker of Massachusetts at the General Convention in Trinity Church, New York, on September 14, 1804, Bishop White preached on "The Qualifications, the Authorities and the Duties of the Gospel Ministry," using those last two words in juxtaposition as he often did. He stressed the clergy's need for both fidelity and wisdom, the former to be supported by affection, firmness, and diligence, and the latter by knowledge, discretion, and acquaintance with men and manners. In the Scripture, he advised, ministers will find authority to regulate the life and worship of the church and to serve and feed the flock in due season.

On another occasion White asserted that the minister's

> . . . principal field of labor is to proclaim the good news of Grace but also to cherish the Christian state of persons who have been brought to Christ in baptismal regeneration and to recover to grace those who have fallen from it.

Even more difficult than preaching, he said, is "the calling of sinners back, through the pains of repentance, to the mercies from which they have wandered." Despite the clarity of these statements, the bishop was once assailed by John Emory, who claimed that White denied the need of conversion after baptism and that Christians can have "any sensible experience of their conversion."[13]

White always supported the primary place of the authority of the church in relation to the ministry, thinking it too precarious for the minister to depend entirely on his individual judgment. With all of his stress on the qualifications for the ministry, its respect for the authority of the church, and the methods most effective in preaching and pastoral guidance, White was invariably careful to assert the necessity of a genuine personal zeal on the part of the minister. Charging his clergy in 1807 he said,

> Of little effect, however, will be the most powerful arguments and the utmost skill in applying them otherwise than in alliance with a zeal suited to the sacred cause in which it is exerted . . . which is a necessary evidence to the world that we are ourselves satisfied of the truths we proclaim. . . . But truth,

without zeal and diligence, is less likely to be influential than errour, when it makes them the instruments of its propagation.

Then, warning against superstition and enthusiasm, he said,

> These are to be counteracted, not by lifeless profession, but by a rational zeal; not indeed venting itself in any of the little arts, accommodated to the credulity of weak minds; but in words and actions corresponding with the dignity of the subjects, which lift the soul above the world to a communion with its God; and which form the conduct to the practice of whatever is estimable among men.

White well knew the power of the evangelical preachers within and outside of his church and may even have known the famous Devereux Jarratt of Virginia and Joseph Pilmore, a noted Anglican evangelical. It had been on hearing a stirring sermon by George Whitefield, then well advanced in years, in his own parish church in Philadelphia that White had been turned to the ministry. Yet he also knew the severe limitations and even the dangers of fanatical enthusiasm; in warning his clergy against these extremities, he tried to help them conserve the best qualities of a warm and zealous ministry.

Both White and Seabury and probably Provoost were thoroughly familiar with the work of the followers of John Wesley in England and America. When Joseph Pilmore, an itinerant in Wesley's "traveling connection" since 1765, sought ordination twenty years later at the hands of Bishop Seabury, the Bishop of Connecticut before ordaining him to the diaconate on November 27, 1785, accepted, among others, a recommendation from Charles Wesley.[14]

Perhaps nowhere in the structural history of Anglicanism was the lack of rapid communication so disadvantageous as in the late years of the eighteenth century. John Wesley never resigned his orders or left the Church of England. In fact, he insisted that the members of the congregations in his connection should retain their communicant relation with the Church of England and that without such relation the future of Methodism was lost. He always counted his work a movement within the Church of England and never wished it otherwise. Even as late as 1789 Wesley denied the rumor that the Methodists were resolved to separate from the church, saying, "Nothing can be more false." In a widely circulated document Wesley gave specific instructions for the personal conduct of his preachers, such as "N.B. Except in extraordinary cases every Preacher is to go to bed before ten o'clock."[15] A year earlier John Wesley had printed his three-thousand-word pamphlet *Reasons against a Separation from the Church of England*, which was reprinted as late as 1860, to which Charles Wesley added some hymns for Methodist preachers and his own full page testimony supporting his brother's position.

When the Methodist movement began to expand outside of England, notably in Ireland and America, John Wesley prepared for use in these areas a small pamphlet *Order for the Sunday Service*, which was almost identical with the Prayer Book. When favorable reports of the work on the American frontier reached him, Wesley also realized that he must do something to provide the much needed corps of ministers to serve in these parts. Apparently less bound to the traditions at this point than his fellow Anglicans in either England or America, Wesley proceeded with a plan that proved more effective than the long years of pleading for an American bishop.

Between the close of the war and 1789 the Methodist preachers had a phenomenal success in winning not only some dissenters but also many others who were emotionally starved and tired of the lifeless reading of the stated forms of the Prayer Book. Some of these churchmen, notably Joseph Toy, a cousin of William White, became leaders of Methodist "Classes," small cell groups under lay leadership. Ultimately Toy was ordained in 1797 and served as a Methodist preacher until his death in 1826, having given fifty-five years in his church's service and almost paralleling the similarly long service of White, which ended in 1836. Frequently the relations between the Methodists and Anglicans were cordial. Francis Asbury, who by the process of natural selection had become the leader of the American Methodists before 1784, was generally sceptical of the Anglicans but once wrote, ". . . the Episcopal ministers are the most quiet; and some of these are friendly."

The Methodist ministers in America refrained from administering the sacraments of Baptism and Holy Communion and, at their first conference in Philadelphia in 1773, provided by their first two rules for such abstinence, indicating that they counted themselves not as a separated church but as a society or movement within it. "In fact," William Watters wrote in his autobiography, "we considered ourselves at this time [1777] as belonging to the Church of England." The clergy of the Church of England usually were glad to admit the Methodists to the Holy Communion, and many Methodists happily received this ministry, although here and there it was accepted as coming from unworthy hands.[16] Following the war, when the Anglican clergy were widely scattered, some confusion arose among the Methodists because in some areas, as in Virginia after 1780, their ministers insisted on the right to administer the sacraments and even appointed committees of preachers to ordain others. The conservative leaders of the North objected and eventually it was agreed to await Wesley's advice.

Wesley's answer was his plan for establishing the church in America. As early as 1746 John Wesley had confided to his brother, Charles, "I firmly believe that I am a scriptural *episcopos* as much as any man in England or in Europe," thus subscribing to the classic Presbyterian conception that bishops and presbyters are one and the same order. Accordingly, when the time arrived, even though Charles protested, Wesley proceeded to ordain some of his followers for America and later for Scotland and England. If, as Lord Mansfield put it, "ordination is separation," then Wesley's avowed allegiance to the Church of England loses some of its meaning. At Bristol on September 2, 1784, John Wesley ordained Thomas Coke to the priesthood and as superintendent of American Methodists with instructions to ordain Francis Asbury as his associate. With Coke, Wesley sent Richard Whatcoat and Thomas Vasey, whom he had also ordained for the church in America.

On September 10, 1784, just a few days after Coke and his associates had landed in New York, John Wesley posted from Bristol a letter addressed to "Dr. Coke, Mr. Asbury and our Brethren in North America" in which he listed in six paragraphs his instructions for the new church about to be established here. He rationalized that since the English government by deprivation and the American government by choice would exercise no authority over the church in America, he had, on the request of his followers, "drawn up a little sketch." Admitting that many years earlier he had come to accept the equality of bishops and presbyters, after studying Lord King's Account of the Primitive Church, he had, however, refrained from ordaining others, not only for the sake of peace, but because he was determined "as little as possible to violate the established Order of the national Church to which I belonged." He had now brought his scruples to an end because in America there were neither bishops nor parish ministers, and he felt at full liberty to send laborers into the harvest, since in so doing he violated no order and invaded no man's right.

He then set out his plan for organization, with Coke and Asbury as superintendents and Whatcoat and Vasey as elders. He was careful to insist that his ministers use the *Order for the Sunday Service* which he had prepared, "a Liturgy little differing from that of the Church of England," and that they read the Litany on Wednesdays and Fridays, allowing free prayers on the remaining days. The elders [presbyters] were advised to administer the Supper of the Lord every Sunday. Many years earlier Wesley had served in Georgia and knew perhaps most of the problems of the ministers on the frontier, yet he said if anyone would point out a more rational and Scriptural way to feed and guide these poor sheep in the wilderness, he would gladly embrace it.

He concluded with his objections to accepting ordination for his preachers at the hands of an English bishop. He had once asked the Bishop of London to ordain one of his preachers but had been refused. He felt that even if one should now consent to do it, the process would be too slow. He had also come to fear that if they ordained they would wish to govern and said, ". . . how grieviously [sic] this would intangle us. Our American Brethren are now at full liberty to follow the scriptures and the Primitive Church . . . it is best that they should stand fast in that liberty, wherewith God has so strangely made them free."

Charles Wesley was strenuously opposed to his brother's ideas and plan and actually held a strained and cool relation with him in his later years. In the spring of 1785 in a letter to Thomas B. Chandler, who was about to return to America, Charles wrote that he could scarcely believe that his brother would assume the prerogatives of a bishop without having consulted him or even so much as giving him a hint of his intentions. He painfully concluded, "Thus our partnership is dissolved—but not our Friendship."[17]

Had all the lines of communication been open, the separate organization of the Methodist Church late in December that year might have been averted.

Did Wesley know, for example, that while he was ordaining these men, Samuel Seabury was in Great Britain seeking consecration as a bishop for America; and, if he knew, did he perhaps consider it an idle dream? If it could have been known at that now famous Christmas Conference in Baltimore on December 24, 1784, that six weeks earlier Seabury had been consecrated and would soon be back in America as a bishop, would it have made a difference in the action of that body? The answers to these questions must at best be conjectures, but there is at least the possibility that they might have been answered differently than history records them.

Quite obviously Francis Asbury could not have cared less. In fact, he was not at all convinced that Wesley's plan was a good one. He had been caught up in the spirit of independence in America and, on meeting Coke for the first time in Delaware in November, 1784, showed such disapproval of his mission that for a time he refused to consider ordination. Believing that the American Methodists had been about to repudiate their Wesleyan dependence and sharing a quite common feeling in the new nation that American life should be regulated by American authority, he delayed his acceptance as their superintendent until they elected him to this distinction at the conference. Then, on three successive days, Asbury, who had been a very successful circuit rider and lay preacher, was ordained deacon, elder, and general superintendent by Coke, Whatcoat, and Vasey. If a contemporary painting correctly depicts the scene, they were joined by Philip William Otterbein, then minister of the Second Reformed Church in Baltimore, and another clergyman in Anglican vestments, who may have been Devereux Jarratt of Virginia, or, more probably, William West or John Andrews of Maryland. It was Asbury's spirit and power that dominated the conference and the new church, and no one knew it better than Thomas Coke.

Had Thomas Coke, Philip Embury, and Joseph Pilmore, then still in Methodist orders, been able to unite with the northern and more conservative Methodists to control the Baltimore Convention, the story might have had a different ending. Two Anglican priests were alert to the importance of what was going on in Baltimore in 1784 and, in spite of the busy Christmas season, attended the sessions of the Methodist conference. John Andrews, then rector of St. Thomas's Parish in Baltimore County and later to be provost of the University of Pennsylvania, and William West of St. Paul's Church, Baltimore, met with Asbury and Coke. The latter was favorable to a plan that would preserve the unity of the church, but he was simply unable to overcome the influence of Asbury or to sway the conference.

Only when the die had been cast did Pilmore seek ordination from Seabury the following year. The conservative Coke waited for a few years to see how he and Asbury might jointly lead the Wesleyans in America. He soon discovered that the aging Wesley would be able to give little attention to this entirely independent American body, the Methodist Episcopal Church. Coke had been requested to designate Asbury as superintendent, but the minutes of 1787 already show Asbury calling himself a bishop, a term much disliked by Wesley. Asbury's support lay with the large number of enthusiastic circuit riders whose number had multiplied rapidly as the frontier expanded; meanwhile, Coke lost the stature Wesley had intended for him as a colleague and associate of Asbury. Even though he must have seen the difficulties involved in the plan, Coke approached Bishop White and Bishop Seabury with the hope that he and Asbury might be consecrated bishops in the Protestant Episcopal line and so bring the entire Methodist group into the Anglican Communion. Coke's letters to White and Seabury have been preserved and clearly indicate his plan. They also show his absolute sincerity and his concern for the future of Methodism, for which he was willing to make requests he knew to be presumptuous; at no point did he reveal any concern for himself that would justify impugning his motives.

Coke estimated that the Methodists had 80,000 adult members, about 300,000 adherents who worshiped regularly, and a total constituency of 750,000, of whom about one-fifth were Negroes. To serve these people there were 250 itinerants, ministers under annual appointment, and many more local preachers, some of whom were men of considerable ability. Although about half of the itinerants had been ordained, Coke thought that few if any of them would refuse reordination if other hindrances could be removed. His second concern was for the unordained, zealous, pious, and useful men who were "not acquainted with the learned languages"; they might not agree because they feared exclusion if the present or future bishops refused to waive the high educational requirements for ordination. Being realistic, Coke knew that he needed Asbury's acquiescence but doubted that he could obtain it. While he felt that his own influence was increasing in America, "yet Mr. Asbury, whose influence is very capitol, will not easily comply; nay, I know he will be exceedingly averse to it." Fearing that all would be lost if the end were not accomplished before Wesley's death, he urged Bishop White to make haste.[18]

A month later Coke suggested to Bishop Seabury that so high an end would justify great sacrifices. He offered to make the Prayer Book mandatory for Methodist worship and asked that in turn Seabury should show lenience on the matter of ministerial qualifications. More fully than in the letter to Bishop White, he set out what was undoubtedly his more matured thinking. He suggested that he and Asbury be fully consecrated as bishops in the Methodist Church, which, as in England, would remain a Society within the church, regulating its own members.[19] Coke asked the bishops to keep his letters in confidence, lest a premature release of such information might defeat its purpose, little realizing that White's reply to him would be opened by one of his colleagues, possibly by Asbury, with ensuing repercussions as late as 1806. White brought Coke's communication to the General Convention in New York in September, 1792, where the House of Bishops after careful deliberation prepared a well-rounded ecumenical statement without any specific mention of Coke and the Methodists. It stated:

The Protestant Episcopal Church in the United States of America, ever bearing in mind the sacred obligation which attends all the followers of Christ, to avoid divisions among themselves, and anxious to promote that union for which our Lord and Saviour so earnestly prayed, do hereby declare to the Christian world, that, uninfluenced by any other considerations than those of duty as Christians, and an earnest desire for the prosperity of pure Christianity, and the furtherance of our holy religion, they are ready and willing to unite and form one body with any religious society which shall be influenced by the same catholic spirit. And in order that this Christian end may be the more easily effected, they further declare, that all things in which the great essentials of Christianity or the characteristic principles of their Church are not concerned, they are willing to leave to future discussions; being ready to alter or modify those points which, in the opinion of the Protestant Episcopal Church, are subject to human alteration. And it is hereby recommended to the State Conventions, to adopt such measures or propose such conferences with Christians of other denominations, as to themselves may be thought most prudent, and report accordingly to the ensuing General Convention.[20]

The House of Deputies failed to approve the bishops' action on the ground that it might "produce distrust of the stability of the system of the Episcopal Church, without the least prospect of embracing any other religious body." Consequently, the bishops withdrew their resolution which remains, nevertheless, as an admirable early statement, even though an unofficial one, on this important subject. Ably as the idea had been presented before the general and regional bodies of the church, the time was apparently not ripe for a new church still struggling to adapt itself to its new constitution and formularies, to think of further and wider complications of so far-reaching a nature. White apparently saw Coke on several occasions after this but with no practical results of their meeting. Coke, realizing that his position in the Methodist Episcopal Church had been undermined by this open promotion of union, returned to England where, after Wesley's death, he became a major leader among the English Methodists. On his trip to England in 1787 White carried a letter of introduction to John Wesley from Joseph Pilmore but never pressed for an interview when his first overtures were coolly received. Charles Wesley, however, received White warmly since they shared a common loyalty to the church.

Bishop James Madison of Virginia, who had championed the ecumenical resolution in the House of Bishops, was much moved by the possibility of union with the Methodists, who were very numerous in Virginia. He knew them to be quite similar in outlook and religious temperament to the Virginia churchmen or at least to what their bishop wished the southern churchmen were like. Taking literally the bishops' proposal to consider the matter in state conventions, Madison discussed it frankly in his address to his convention in 1793. He said,

There is no one here present but must cordially wish for such a union, provided it did not require a sacrifice of those points which are deemed essentials by our Church; from them we have no power to retreat. But in such matters as are subject to human alteration, if, by a candid discussion, they could be found capable of being so modified as to remove the objections of any sect of Christians who may be actuated by the same catholic spirit, and thereby effect a union, in that case, we should surely have reason to rejoice, not only in the event, but also in being the first to set an example to Christians which it is the duty of all to follow; and, in convincing them that there is infinitely more religion in not contending, than in those things about which they contend.[21]

One more early test of the church's ecumenical spirit came in 1797 when the Lutheran Consistory of the State of New York sought union with the Episcopal Diocese in that state. Although a committee was appointed to consider the proposal and bring it to the General Convention scheduled to meet the following year, the circumstances and perhaps a lack of interest, in a period when religious life and work were at a low ebb, foredoomed the idea to failure. Because of a yellow fever epidemic the General Convention was postponed to 1799, and when the diocesan convention next met in 1801, it was to consider the resignation of Bishop Provoost, which crowded the agenda so that church union had little if any consideration. Had the events fallen in more propitious times the compatibility of these two churches with similar liturgies and little doctrinal variance, as Henry M. Muhlenberg had previously attested, might have made possible long ago a proper relationship now often dreamed of by leaders in both communions. The hope for friendly cooperation in and ultimately for the essential unity of the Church of Christ would remain a constant concern of Episcopalians.

XII

NEW GREAT LEADERS

The War of 1812 compelled Great Britain to fight on two fronts at once, facing a conquering Napoleon on the continent, while she wrestled once again with her former colonies. Both conflicts ended in 1815 when Napoleon met his Waterloo and the Battle of New Orleans was fought unnecessarily after a treaty had been signed in England. For America the postwar years, apart from a few reverses in the early twenties, were years of rapid expansion of area, increase in population, and successes in business. A new era of industrial progress lay just ahead. George Shoemaker and Nicholas Allen had just discovered anthracite coal near Pottsville, Pennsylvania, and the second railroad, although very primitive and only a mile in length, had been completed. A German by the name of König had successfully completed the first steam printing press, and machines soon appeared to facilitate the travel and domestic needs of a rapidly growing population.

Philadelphia was still the largest city in the land with a population of about 100,000, which doubled by 1830. In that year Pennsylvania had a total population of 1,348,233, and the Episcopal Church had 33 clergy, 12 churches, 3,000 communicants, and 12,000 worshipers. New York was rapidly growing, having risen from 60,000 inhabitants in 1800 to 124,000 in 1820; its population of over 200,000 exceeded that of Philadelphia by 1830 when the state of New York numbered almost 2,000,000 inhabitants, largely through migration from New England into central and western New York. In 1812 New York City had 12 Episcopal churches, counting Trinity Church and its chapels, but the people in the teeming city had already become apathetic and indifferent to religion, and were not greatly moved by Bishop Samuel Provoost's "terse, rational and churchy sermons."

By the turn of the century the grip of Deism on America had been loosed by the expanding religious revivals of the Second Great Awakening, which swept the country from the established eastern coasts to the farthest frontier; by the 1820's Deism and atheism were rarely avowed. The transformation of the postwar secular and irreligious spirit into a nationwide religious atmosphere by 1835 was one of the miracles performed by the revivals of one generation. From the colleges, where religious commitments were fostered under such leaders as Timothy Dwight and Lyman Beecher, to the plains, where Peter Cartwright literally conquered the force of evil, men once again professed faith in God. Frequently religious meetings were held in groves where families camped for several days—in later years it was for several weeks—while services were conducted morning, afternoon, and evening. Excesses sometimes led to exaggerated emotional demonstrations, but the result of the revivals was largely wholesome and assured the ultimate triumph of Whitefield over Jefferson and the Deists in the struggle for the American mind. The disparate efforts of revivalists occasionally led to schisms in the major denominations, such as the Cumberland Presbyterian Church organized in 1802, and about 1830 the union of separate evangelistic movements led to formation of the Disciples of Christ under the leadership of Alexander Campbell.

By 1812 the comparatively new Methodist Church already had 158,852 members with an additional 38,505 among the Negroes. The Episcopal Church had also shown some evidence of being alert to the opportunity of these times. In South Carolina A Society for the Advancement of Christianity had been formed, and in 1812, largely under the leadership of the zealous young Jackson Kemper, Pennsylvania had organized a similar body. But generally the close of the first decade of the nineteenth century left the church, as the historian Tiffany described it, in a state of suspended animation.

When the national population had reached about 7,250,000, the General Convention of 1811 reported that the church had seven bishops and 178 clergy; there were probably 220 or more for Virginia, and the southern dioceses had made no report. But the communicant strength of the church hardly exceeded 15,000, and in some areas, notably in the South, clergy and laity alike had become overly interested in secular and political matters; it became necessary to remind the bishops to attend and the diocesan conventions to be represented at the General Conventions. Nevertheless the communicant list continued to grow; from 12,000 in 1800 it mounted to almost 31,000 by 1832, and the number attending church may have been more than three times that figure.

The rapid westward migrations at the beginning of the nineteenth century usually followed three routes: through Virginia across the Blue Ridge Mountains to Kentucky and Tennessee; through Pennsylvania and Maryland to the Ohio and Mississippi valleys; and from New England through the Mohawk Valley. Many of these later emigrants remained in central and western New York and became the nucleus of the Presbyterian Church strongly established there. These regions also became the prime target of the revivalists so that W. R. Cross's volume describing this area in this era has very appropriately been entitled *The Burned-over District*. Here some of the evangelistic innovations, such as the use of the mourner's bench and the protracted meetings for prayer at any and all hours, found their beginning in the 1830's under men like Charles G. Finney.

For many reasons the Episcopal Church was slow to follow the expansion of the American frontier. Its membership rolls were made up of a majority of well-established citizens, many of them of old and well-to-do families often connected officially with the government and the professions. The emigrants were largely farmers, yeomen, and mechanics, and of these this church could claim few. There was still considerable anti-British feeling in America, and a church so recently separated from the Church of England found difficulty in presenting its cause. The new church had hardly begun to operate normally and naturally under its new constitution, completely separated from the Church of England, which until so recently had provided for its support almost exclusively. Bishops were extremely sensitive to the widely prevalent feeling of prejudice against them, even at times in the church itself in the southern regions, and were loath to press their administrative prerogatives too agressively. Then, too, there was a definite lack of well-trained clergy and a severely limited financial support that not only prevented much planning for the frontier but even limited the program of the churches in the established dioceses. It is hardly to be wondered, therefore, that the Episcopal Church did not at once set out on an aggressive missionary program. This would come, and that right soon, but only after a new generation of leaders had been selected.

In the early years of the nineteenth century the Episcopal Church seemed to be halting between a laity waiting to be led and the bishops hesitant or unready to lead. Bishop White in Pennsylvania was now the senior bishop but confined his visitations, an average of six a year for twenty years, to Philadelphia and its environs. Only once in forty-nine years did he cross the Alleghenies and then only in his seventy-ninth year. Madison made only one visitation in Virginia, and from 1805 to 1812 not even a convention was held in that state. Robert Smith, consecrated Bishop of South Carolina in 1795, never administered confirmation or ordained any candidates for the ministry. In New England the venerable Edward Bass, consecrated Bishop of Massachusetts and Rhode Island in 1797, had a minimal clergy staff, and his successor, Samuel Parker, died within three months of his election in 1804 without having performed any episcopal functions. Seven years elapsed before there was another bishop for this region. In all of New England there were but fifteen Episcopal clergymen, apart from Connecticut where there were twenty-two. Here Bishop Jarvis, who succeeded Seabury in 1796, led his diocese in a typically moderate English administration and continued his lackluster preaching, which was "didactic and occasionally metaphysical . . . equally free from fanatical cant and pharasaic formality." Bishop White was no more effective as a preacher; his delivery was monotonous, and his style deficient in point and force. In New York Bishop Provoost retired into secular seclusion in 1801, and his successor Benjamin Moore, a devout and widely respected Christian, served for a decade with less than aggressive leadership.

After the first two decades of slow growth and development, several strong, naturally gifted personalities came to leadership in the Episcopal Church. On May 29, 1811, Alexander Viets Griswold was consecrated Bishop of the Eastern Diocese, an administrative alliance formed to give united episcopal leadership to the weak and widely distributed parishes in New England beyond Connecticut. On the same day John Henry Hobart was consecrated Assistant Bishop of New York to help Bishop Moore, who had suffered a disabling paralysis. In 1814 Richard Channing Moore, until then rector of St. Stephen's Church in New York City, was elected Bishop of Virginia, and four years later Philander Chase was to direct the newly formed Diocese of Ohio. These choices were in many ways to hasten the growth of the Episcopal Church and to determine its destiny in the rapidly growing new nation. Chase became the first to plead for the West and gave aggressive leadership to the work of the church there. Griswold and Moore were typical evangelical leaders who brought the church abreast of its pastoral opportunities, while Hobart, a model old high churchman, developed for the first time a strong churchly definition and an emphasis on the apostolic ministry and the sacraments to combine with the urgency of the gospel as he described it in his self-devised theme, "Evangelical Truth and Apostolic Order."

Not until his consecration to the episcopate did Bishop Griswold come to his full power as a preacher and an effective evangelist. He admitted that in his earlier years he had been far too much employed with sectarian distinctions and controversial topics to the neglect of the essential doctrines of Christ and the duties of Christians, thus contributing to the widely held opinion that churchmen were formalists and bigots, "regarding the Church more than religion and the Prayer Book more than the Bible, . . . destitute of true piety and renovation of heart." But his consecration proved to be the turning point in his life, a genuine religious crisis; he said that it "was the means of the awakening of my own mind to more serious thoughts of duty as a minister of Christ," and consequently his parish in Bristol, Rhode Island, became awakened to religion and "soon began to express a religious concern respecting their spiritual state, and were anxious to know what they should do to be saved."[1]

Griswold had been educated under the tutorship of his uncle Roger Viets, a Presbyterian converted to Anglicanism at Yale in about 1758. From his mother Griswold inherited a deeply religious nature, and from his uncle he received a thorough intellectual training, perhaps the equivalent of the diploma from Yale that he so much desired. The elder Griswold remained loyal to the Crown; for sheltering fugitives his resources were practically confiscated by taxes and fines imposed by the patriots, making it impossible for him to help his son realize his dream. When his uncle fled to Nova Scotia, young Griswold prepared to accompany him, but his early marriage detained him and saved him for usefulness in the American church.

Ordained on June 7, 1795, Griswold began his ministry by serving three small churches in the vicinity of Litchfield, Connecticut, until 1804; he rose quickly to popularity, and after several declinations, he accepted the call to St. Michael's Church in Bristol, Rhode Island. He had left some two hundred communicants to serve about twenty-five families in this well-established parish that had once been a strong congregation. Five years later, after overwork had impaired his failing health and saddened by a death in the family, he was about to accept a call to return to Litchfield and the community he loved when the Eastern Diocese elected him as its bishop, shortly after his forty-sixth birthday. This diocese, newly formed at a convention in Boston on May 29, 1810, was created by the union of the churches in Rhode Island, New Hampshire, Vermont, and Massachusetts, including the district of Maine, none of which was able to support a bishop independently. In all this area there were not more than twenty-four parishes and sixteen clergymen. There was some strength in such parishes as Trinity Church, Boston; St. John's, Providence; and Trinity, Newport; but even in these centers many families had been lost through political loyalties, wealth and personal influence no longer supported the churches, and, especially in Boston, the new Unitarian wave threatened all faiths.

Although the testimonials for Bishops-elect Hobart and Griswold were read and approved at the General Convention at New Haven in 1811, they could not be consecrated there, for only Bishop White and Bishop Jarvis were in attendance. In fact, there was considerable apprehension lest once again the American church would have to call on the Church of England to re-establish the American episcopate. The only other alternative seemed to be to have White and Jarvis, one less than the canonically required number of bishops, consecrate the men. Happily, a few weeks after the close of the convention White and Jarvis were able to persuade Bishop Provoost to leave his retirement and join them in the consecration of Hobart and Griswold on May 29, 1811, in Trinity Church, New York. Griswold seemed perplexed that Hobart, several years younger and elected a year after his own election, should have been consecrated before him and deduced that it was to assure Hobart's precedence in seniority and succession to the office of presiding bishop. Bishop White, however, explained that it was the English custom to give precedence to seniority in academic degrees and so favored Hobart, who had a Doctor of Divinity degree. This custom was soon abandoned in the Episcopal Church, and seniority was henceforth determined by priority of election.

The success of Griswold's episcopate began in his own parish in Bristol where, after meetings for prayer and inquiry and by personal counseling, he prepared for confirmation a hundred candidates, almost half of them adults, and trebled his communicant list. The bishop knew the importance of these personal religious experiences, but he was careful to note that these people had not been "encouraged in ranting or in any enthusiastic raptures; nor did they incline to any extravagance; but gladly hearkened to the words of truth and soberness." This remarkable awakening of the spiritual life in St. Michael's Church, Bristol, in the summer of 1812, which had often crowded the recently enlarged church, not only influenced the religious life of the congregation, but also led to a revival of religious interest in the diocese as a whole. By the time of the diocesan convention on September 30, 1812, Griswold reported that he had visited all the parishes at least once, that on his visitation he had confirmed 1,212 persons, ordained one deacon and two priests, admitted five candidates for orders, and that there were increases "in numbers, piety and attention to the doctrines and discipline of the Church."

Throughout his episcopate Griswold continued to serve a parish at Bristol and later at Salem and yet in a single year, 1833, preached 123 times in other places. Following the death of Bishop Jarvis, he briefly supervised the work of the church in Connecticut. On the death of Bishop White in 1836 he became the presiding bishop of the church and wrote two pastoral letters in 1838 and 1841, the latter delicately balancing the respective places of faith and good works in a definition of the doctrine of justification by faith. As the presiding bishop, he also carried on an extensive correspondence with the Anglican bishops in Great Britain and the colonies and opened the way for full intercommunion between the Episcopal Church and all the churches of Anglicanism. Griswold developed missionary societies throughout the diocese and also cooperated with interdenominational Bible societies and helped to organize Bible, Prayer Book, and Sunday School Societies. He was more responsible than any other for the organization of the Domestic and Foreign Missionary Society by the General Convention in 1820. Griswold's zeal for missions was reflected among his clergy. In 1833 the Massachusetts clergy voted to give two Sundays each year to preaching in the missions of the diocese. They also held monthly missionary meetings and pledged to raise the equivalent of at least one-tenth of their salary for missions in the diocese.

Although many who had helped to plan for the confederation of the Eastern Diocese felt that this arrangement might serve permanently in this area where the work of the church had languished, no one had dared to dream that Griswold would be the only bishop to serve it. Yet so it was, for in less than thirty years the original twenty-four parishes had become almost one hundred and the church in each of the states so well developed that only respect for their aging bishop delayed their separation to form four additional dioceses beyond Vermont, which had organized as early as 1832.

New England was now growing rapidly; in 1833, Boston had a population of 70,000, and Massachusetts had more than 610,000, among whom there were only 1,900 communicants and about 10,000 persons who regularly worshiped in the Protestant Episcopal churches. Among the 100,000 people in Rhode Island, twenty Protestant Episcopal clergy were at work; in Vermont there were eighteen clergy among 300,000 people, in Maine only seven clergymen among 400,000, while New Hampshire had the same number of clergy for a population of 300,000. The real strength of the Protestant Episcopal Church in New England lay in Connecticut where there were now eighty clergy in a population of 300,000. Boston now had thirteen Unitarian churches, nine Congregational, one Roman Catholic, and six Protestant Episcopal parishes. Throughout the state of Massachusetts thirty-five parishes were scattered, but nine of these were vacant at the time of the diocesan convention on June 19, 1833, which was attended by thirty clergymen.

At the age of seventy-three Griswold reflected on the progress in the Eastern Diocese and reported that by 1839 seven of the original thirteen churches in Massachusetts had been rebuilt and twenty-five new ones had been erected; in Rhode Island the original four churches of 1811 had increased to seventeen with another under construction; in New Hampshire the five churches had become nine; and in Maine there were five where once there had been only two. In Vermont, where there were no churches in 1811, twelve buildings had been completed and four more were under construction by the time John Henry Hopkins was elected the first bishop of the new diocese in 1832.

Griswold remained always a modest man, deliberate in his manner, never given to overt demonstration; he was always respected and held in deep affection by those who recognized his quiet charm and simple but complete devotion to his tasks and to his friends. Beginning as a moderate high churchman, Griswold matured during his ministry; he never emphasized the distinctive doctrines of the church and sacraments less but in addition always stressed the indispensability of the gospel and its personal experience and application.

Almost simultaneously with the revival in the Episcopal churches in New England came the rebirth of the church in Virginia, where Richard Channing Moore was elected by a special session of the convention on May 5, 1814, to fill the vacancy left by the death of Bishop Madison on March 6, 1812. For years there had been little episcopal supervision, and that convention had mustered only seven clergymen and eighteen laymen, representing fourteen parishes. The next quarter of a century under the fruitful administrative leadership of Bishop Moore, who had also become the rector of the Monumental Church in Richmond, was to make this faltering diocese one of the leading and most powerful centers in the life of the church.

A New Yorker by birth, Moore was brought up in the godly home of a successful merchant, studied under private tutors, and, after an apprenticeship with a leading physician, had begun the practice of medicine by the time he was twenty-one. He enjoyed a very successful practice in New York City for about six years and developed habits, including profanity, which were hardly in keeping with his family heritage. While waiting his turn in a barbershop, Moore casually picked up a Bible and read, "Saul, Saul, why persecutest thou me?" which led him to reflection and the turning point of his life. He immediately gave up his medical practice and was ordained on July 15, 1787, the first ordination performed by Bishop Provoost.

For two years he served Grace Church in Rye, New York, twenty-one years at St. Andrew's Church on Staten Island, and then came to St. Stephen's Church in New York City, where his next five years brought him wide recognition and tremendous influence. Vast congregations came to St. Stephen's Church where, in addition to the regular services, Moore offered "the social means of grace," including weekday services with free prayers and hymns, to aid his parishioners in their religious efforts. When Bishop Hobart disapproved of such proceedings, Moore refused to give them up on the ground that they were

> . . . neither inconsistent with the principle, nor prohibited by the canons of the Church. And although some condemn them as irregular and Methodistical, I cannot, as a minister of Christ, give them up. For I know that God's blessing is on them. They are the nurseries of my communion.[2]

Something of Moore's power and influence may be seen in the fact that, at the close of one afternoon service, a representative of the congregation rose to say, "Doctor Moore, the people are not disposed to go home; please give us another sermon." He did so, and when they still remained, he preached a third and then added, "My beloved people, you must now disperse—for although I delight to proclaim the glad tidings of salvation, my strength is exhausted, and I can say no more." Sixty communicants were added to his church because of that one service. Moore kept the bars high, demanding strict conformity and almost Puritanical standards of his people; communicants were required to refrain from cardplaying, dancing, and attendance at the theater. Such demands were not immediately popular in Virginia where churchmen lived by rather casual standards, but within a decade he had led the diocesan convention to declare that communicants should refrain from dancing in public, theater attendance, horse racing, and gambling, which "stained the purity of Christian character."

With vigor and enthusiasm Bishop Moore traveled the wide areas of the Virginia diocese, calling the disaffected people to their neglected churches; the clergy and other bishops were amazed at the almost immediate response to his appeals for a sound faith, high Christian standards, and loyalty to the church. After less than two years he was able to report 750 confirmations and twenty vacant parishes now supplied by clergy. He not only gave himself unsparingly to visitations but urged his clergy to visit neighboring vacant parishes to provide services wherever possible. Generally a strict disciplinarian and canonist, Moore ignored a canon of 1804 forbidding preaching by candidates for the ministry, in order that his long neglected people might hear the gospel. He required the full use of Prayer Book services but urged additional gatherings for prayer and fellowship, seeking everywhere not only to develop a high morality but also the rich, personal experience of divine grace. These meetings, some of them resembling revivals, were less emotional and ecstatic than those of the freer churches and in many respects resembled extended preaching missions with emphasis on Bible study. Even the annual conventions became occasions of inspiration as well as legislation.

Within a few years Bishop Moore became convinced that in order to have an adequate supply of ministers, properly trained for work under his direction, some provision must be made in the diocese for such preparation. Although a professor of theology had been added to the staff of the College of William and Mary in 1820, the students failed to register for these courses, and so plans were begun the following year to establish a theological school in Williamsburg. By 1824 the school was opened at a newly chosen site in Alexandria; the first members of its faculty were William H. Wilmer and Ruel Keith, who had taught theology at the College of William and Mary. A few years later the Virginia Theological Seminary was relocated on "The Hill" near Alexandria, where through the years it has trained hundreds of men in the Moore and Meade tradition as evangelical leaders in the church.

After fifteen years of strenuous effort by the bishop, the diocese elected

William Meade, who had been largely responsible for Moore's election and shared his spirit, to assist the aging leader, with the understanding that Meade should not automatically succeed him. In addition to the heavy responsibilities in his own diocese, Moore had acted as Bishop of North Carolina from 1819 to 1823 and assisted in the Diocese of Maryland between 1827 and 1830. Beyond his own church Moore gave much time to interdenominational efforts, serving as president of the Virginia branch of the American Bible Society, and he was always cooperative in community philanthropic efforts. Long before the ecumenical movement became popular, Bishop Moore told one of his conventions, "We stretch forth the right hand of fellowship to all who in sincerity call upon the Lord Jesus Christ."

Bishop Moore lived into his eightieth year and by 1841 was able to see the fine fruit of his labors. The original seven clergy with whom he began his work had now increased to one hundred, and the fourteen parishes represented at the convention that elected him in 1814 had become 170. For twenty years he had continued to work by the side of Bishop Meade; on his death the latter was immediately chosen to succeed him and carried on this important work to the outbreak of the Civil War, laying a substantial foundation which even that catastrophe could not destroy and which has continued to provide a base for the nurture of strong men of evangelical faith for its own churches and the mission fields of the church. Curiously, the evangelical spirit and fervor once represented by the less effective methods and manner of Devereux Jarratt in this same diocese, only a few decades after his death and in the hands of the gifted, charming, gentle but persuasive Richard C. Moore, became the very life and strength of the Episcopal Church in Virginia. Moore's influence lingered long in those parishes and missions where his ministry of fifty-four years had touched and enriched the lives of the people of God.

Frequently the history of the church becomes the history of its bishops, but this follows only because bishops are natural leaders in movements in which other ministers and laymen are also very much engaged. So these evangelical bishops were supported by many very able clergymen who shared both their views and their efforts for the advancement of the church. Since clerical deputies to the General Convention are fairly representative of the ministry of the church, it may be assumed that in 1820 about fifteen per cent, but not more than twenty, could be counted evangelical. A decade later this ratio had risen to fifty per cent, and by 1840 as many as two-thirds of the ministry of the church belonged to the evangelical ranks.

Among the distinguished evangelicals was Gregory Townsend Bedell, for whom St. Andrew's Church, Philadelphia, was built in 1823 after he had agreed to become its rector. Crowds literally surged into every corner of that church to hear the heart of the gospel and the redeeming love of God for all men declared with intense fervor by this frail preacher. Every listener was challenged to consider the dangerous alternative to rejecting God's love, and through Bedell's ministry, Episcopalians and many other Christians were led to new spiritual vigor and power.

Bedell was succeeded in 1835 by John Alonzo Clark, who came from an unusually successful ministry of three years in Grace Church, Providence, Rhode Island. Here he had conducted "parochial visitations," weekday meetings in private homes where, amid prayers and suitable hymns, he made moving appeals for repentance and faith. Rarely has the Episcopal Church seen such phenomenally sudden growth as here where, in about seven months, his communicants increased from 41 to 157.

Even in the Diocese of New York, which was substantially high church under the leadership of Bishop Hobart, James Milnor, who came to St. George's Church in 1816, carried on a strongly evangelical ministry. A man of unusual gifts, Milnor had been a Quaker; trained as a lawyer, he was elected to Congress from Philadelphia as a Federalist in 1805. When he married an Episcopalian, he attended St. Paul's Church and heard Joseph Pilmore, from whom he learned much of his theology and style and in whose spirit he was to lead St. George's to a most successful and diversified ministry.

In St. Ann's Church, Brooklyn, Benjamin C. Cutler had a remarkably successful evangelical ministry, and Alexander H. Vinton served in this same spirit and with great effectiveness in Boston, Philadelphia, and New York. John S. Stone, married to a daughter of Bishop Griswold, emulated the spirit of his father-in-law in his ministries at St. Paul's Church in Boston, where he greatly influenced the parents of Phillips Brooks, and as the first dean of the Philadelphia Divinity School and of the Episcopal Theological School in Cambridge. The long-lived Stephen Tyng, after graduating from Harvard at seventeen, engaged in business until his conversion, which he described as "the turning point of my life. I arose from my knees with a fixed determination, and without a single hesitation or doubt. I was converted."[3] Called to the "divided and contentious" St. Paul's Church, Philadelphia, in 1829, he quickly won the support of the parish and community so that he was obliged to preach at three services every Sunday. In addition he lectured on Wednesday evenings and attended Saturday night prayer meetings; his popularity increased, and soon St. Paul's came to be known as "Tyng's Theatre." He succeeded Milnor at St. George's in New York in 1845 where he continued a similarly successful ministry for thirty-four years.

Samuel H. Turner, a staunch evangelical churchman learned in the Old Testament literature, became the first professor at the General Theological Seminary, but it was at the Virginia Theological Seminary that the majority of the evangelicals were trained. Here, under the teaching of Dean William Sparrow, James May, Joseph Packard, and others of similar spirit, young men were taught the doctrines of the Protestant Reformation and an ecclesiastical polity conforming to the Preface to the Ordinal, as Bishop John Johns reported it. He described the faculty's position thus:

> We have held fast the atoning work of our Lord as a satisfaction to divine justice, as well as a revelation of the divine love; justification only by the righteousness of Christ; regeneration only by the power of the Holy Spirit; the Sacraments as the signs and seals of spiritual grace.[4]

Sparrow, who urged his students to "seek the truth; come whence it may, cost what it will," was considered by Phillips Brooks as one of the ablest men he had ever met. Brooks, who was trained at Virginia Theological Seminary, later also stressed the necessity of personal religious experience supported by Christian doctrine.

William H. Wilmer, president of the College of William and Mary, who also taught theology at Virginia Theological Seminary when it first opened, wrote one of the church's first important theological works, *The Episcopal Manual,* in which he pointed out clearly the compatibility of strict order in the church and evangelical religion, including its animated social worship meetings. Wilmer's book, published in Baltimore in 1815, was an attempt to explain and vindicate the doctrine, discipline, and worship of the Protestant Episcopal Church as taught distinctively in the Book of Common Prayer. It was both theological and devotional, embodying suggestions for family worship and prayers for special occasions. He specifically tried to avoid the dangerous extremities to which the church might succumb: to undervalue her order and institutions or to exhaust her zeal on externals and so permit the spirit and essence of the gospel to evaporate.

Briefly stated, the position of the evangelicals included a stress on man's sinful limited nature and the necessity for atoning grace without which there can be no justification by faith. Although refusing to deny the validity of other ministries, they held to the three orders, including the episcopate, as defined in the Preface to the Ordinal, to confer the essential external commission on the ministry. Episcopacy for them was not really essential to the *esse* of the church but very essential, *bene esse,* to the best and highest development of the church.

Holding to the Holy Scriptures as the sole ground of faith, rather than accepting the tradition of the Fathers as an additional source of authority, the evangelicals accepted the Apostles' and Nicene Creeds primarily because they could be substantiated from the Holy Scriptures. Shunning all semblance of sacerdotalism, they held to the two Dominical sacraments as outward and visible signs of inward and spiritual grace but denied baptismal regeneration. Bishop Thomas M. Clark of Rhode Island said there was no great difference of opinion in the church at that time about the nature and efficacy of the Lord's Supper; all agreed with the Twenty-eighth Article of Faith that the Lord's Supper is taken and received by the faithful only in a spiritual manner. Carefully avoiding the use of the words altar and priest—they preferred presbyter—evangelicals generally supported the slogan "No Priest, No Altar, No Sacrifice." Although these evangelicals dreaded formalism only little less than sin itself, the actual differences between them and the high churchmen in the early years were comparatively few. Phillips Brooks, who had been greatly influenced by Alexander H. Vinton, shared many of the evangelical views even in the later years when many considered him a broad churchman. He said the evangelicals stressed

... an earnest insistence upon doctrine, and upon personal, spiritual experience, of neither of which had the previous generation made very much. Man's fallen state, his utter hopelessness, the vicarious atonement, the supernatural conversion, the work of the Holy Spirit—these were the truths which ... 'Evangelical' men urged with the force of vehement belief upon their hearers. ... They laid hold upon the souls and consciences of men. They created most profound experiences. They made great ministers and noble Christians. It was indeed the work of God.[5]

John Henry Hobart, already a recognized leader of the old high church party, was consecrated with the evangelical Griswold on May 29, 1811, and immediately set about the administration of the Diocese of New York with greater efficiency than any American bishop before him had demonstrated. A descendant of an early Congregational minister, Peter Hobart, who came to Massachusetts in 1635, John Henry was born in Philadelphia in 1775, where his father was well established in business. After preparation at the new Episcopal Academy, he studied at the University of Pennsylvania and went to Princeton for his junior and senior years where he graduated with honors in 1793. Unhappy with the prospect of a life in business, he returned to Princeton in 1795 in the role of a tutor, began his studies for the ministry, and received the degree of A.M. in 1796. Associated here with keen leaders of the Presbyterian Church, he was constantly defending the claims of Anglicanism, nevertheless sharing and at times leading in the informal weekly prayer meetings and at the same time seeking to resolve his own personal problems.

Having lost his father when he was only a year old, Hobart was greatly influenced by the devotion and early instruction of his mother and by Bishop White, who baptized and confirmed him and sought to give him special guidance. Convinced that his should be a life in the church rather than an academic career, he received ordination as a deacon at the hand of his friend Bishop White in 1798, in his twenty-third year. Even in these early years the persistent willfulness that would later impair his creative ministry revealed itself in his relation with his bishop. He not only disagreed with White but, already showing his gift for administrative analysis, rather presumptuously wrote,

> On referring to the canon you mention I find my wishes [to preach in various churches while he was a tutor at Princeton] cannot be gratified. . . . The canon, however, is contrary to this idea. . . . I must be permitted to say that, in my opinion, it imposes a great hardship on candidates for the ministry. . . . The plan I have suggested will, I think, comply in spirit with the requisitions of the canon. . . .

For less than a year after his ordination Hobart served several small churches near Philadelphia and then accepted a call to Christ Church, New Brunswick, where he came under the influence of Thomas Bradbury Chandler, one of the strongest leaders of the pre-Revolutionary church in America and its most ardent defender of the episcopate. Whether he left Philadelphia because the charming daughter of Jacob Duché had refused his proposals of marriage is not certain, but very soon he was attracted by Mary, the daughter of Thomas Chandler, to whom he was married before he moved to Hempstead, Long Island, in May, 1800. Within another six months he was on the staff of Trinity Church in New York City where he was ordained to the priesthood by Bishop Provoost and was destined to spend his remaining years.

During his brief stay in New Brunswick it fell to Hobart's lot to assist in the publication of Doctor Chandler's biography of Samuel Johnson, which acquainted him with the Connecticut churchmanship fathered by Johnson and popularized by Bishop Seabury, who had died just a year before Hobart was ordered a deacon. Never would he lose, however, the influences on his life of his devout mother, the fatherly Bishop White, and his non-Episcopal friends at Princeton with whom he had prayed so freely and regularly. So well balanced in his life were evangelical and high church influences—by some erroneously considered mutually contradictory—that he often declared his own true position to be for "Evangelical Truth and Apostolic Order."

While the duties in Trinity Parish, with its three large congregations, were very heavy, Hobart still found time to become the secretary of the House of Bishops in 1801, possibly at the invitation of his friend Bishop White. In that same year he was named to the Board of Trustees of Columbia College, on which Alexander Hamilton and other distinguished leaders served, and was also named secretary of the diocesan convention. In 1804 he was elected a deputy to the General Convention where, during the next two terms, he served as the secretary of the House of Deputies.

Hobart's ability lay not only in doing well those things others asked or elected him to do but also in sensing a need and providing for it on his own initiative. So when he discovered a lack of missionary interest and proper educational opportunities for training for Christian service, he joined with others in 1802 to establish the Protestant Episcopal Society for the Promotion of Religion and Learning in the State of New York. In 1806 he founded the Protestant Episcopal Theological Society, for which he drew up the constitution and bylaws, to bring the clergy to weekly meetings for prayer and the criticism of sermons and essays. Its object was

> . . . the advancement of its youthful members in theological knowledge, in practical piety, and in all those principles, duties and dispositions, which may fit them for becoming orthodox, Evangelical, and faithful ministers of the Protestant Episcopal Church.[6]

By such means he sought to implement the course of study provided by the Canons of 1804 for ministerial candidates. His own strong conviction he once stated before the diocesan convention: "Without a ministry, the church cannot exist, and destitute of a *learned* as well as a pious ministry, she cannot flourish."

Meanwhile *The Churchman's Magazine,* the only journal being published in the church, seemed to be languishing under the editorship of the aging William Smith of Norwalk. Hobart moved it from New Haven to New York in 1805 and became its editor for the next four years. In 1817 he founded *The Churchman's Journal*, the first diocesan paper in the Episcopal Church; eight years earlier he had taken the lead in founding the Bible and Common Prayer Book Society, which has continued to distribute these books to the present. Some evangelicals disagreed with Hobart's insistence on this joint distribution on the ground that the Bible had not so been distributed in the early Christian centuries. He also organized the Protestant Episcopal Tract Society in 1810, the Sunday School Society, and the Protestant Episcopal Press.

Deeply concerned that his people might make the most of their religious opportunities, Hobart prepared two devotional and educational manuals, which appeared in 1804 and 1805. A *Companion for the Altar*, adapted from a similar English work, was the first American attempt to provide a devotional guide for use before, during, and after the Holy Communion. A *Companion for the Festivals and Fasts of the Church* was also compiled by Hobart with his own additions to an English work of the same title by Robert Nelson that had appeared in 1703. It contained appropriate meditations to be used in connection with the Collects, Gospels, and Epistles provided in the Book of Common Prayer for the Holy Days.

In the preface to this latter work Hobart included his "Preliminary Instructions Concerning the Church," in which he stated that the church was divinely formed and that its bishops, priests, and deacons received their authority from Christ through the Apostles and their successors. Accordingly, all men were obligated to seek their salvation through the church and, failing this, were in schism and sin. Such exclusive claims for the church soon provoked critical responses from leading Presbyterians and further replies from Episcopalians including Moore and White. Hobart, whose articles in the pseudonymous series were usually signed "Vindex" or "Detector," gathered this material, most of which had appeared in *The Albany Centinel*, and published it in 1806 in his *A Collection of Essays on the Subject of Episcopacy*, which only served to renew the controversy. Following further exchanges of essays and letters, Hobart issued his *An Apology for Apostolic Order and Its Advocates*, which added little clarification but did concisely set out the opposition of Episcopalians generally to the Calvinistic doctrine of predestination that was then a delicate subject among many Presbyterians. It was in the closing words of this work that Hobart unfurled his standard, "This banner is 'Evangelical Truth and Apostolic Order.'" These publications were followed by others: *A Companion to the Book of Common Prayer; The Christian's Manual of Faith and Devotion; A Catechism on Confirmation; The Pocket Almanac; The Church Catechism;* and an extensively annotated edition of D'Oyley and Mant's *Family Bible*.

In the light of these achievements there remains little wonder that when Bishop Moore suffered a stroke, the diocesan convention selected as its assistant bishop this thirty-five-year-old junior assistant minister at Trinity Church.

There is no question that his diocese wanted Hobart as their bishop, but there were several unhappy incidents that slightly marred the beginning of his auspicious administration.

With all of his genius Hobart was not without his faults; he was very sensitive and particularly intolerant of all opposition to his plans. At times, he acted impulsively, but he was usually the first to sense his own errors and freely confessed his mistakes and, fortunately, never harbored grudges or hostility over long periods.

Despite his popularity, his election had not been unanimous, and there were several futile attempts to stay his consecration. To Cave Jones and Abraham Beach, the other assistants at Trinity Church, the election of their junior assistant seemed incredible; Jones especially seemed perturbed that one who had shown evidence in their personal relations of characteristics less than commendatory for such high office should have been named to the episcopacy. He accordingly published his grievances in a pamphlet called *A Solemn Appeal to the Church*, attempting to show that Hobart was temperamentally unfitted for the episcopate. Although it should have been ignored, Hobart's sensitive nature was so injured that he replied with *A Statement Addressed to Episcopalians*, only to have Jones issue his stinging retort, *Dr. Hobart's System of Intolerance*. No one was edified and the church was not advanced by the straining of the bounds of courtesy on both sides.

Jones was supported by such distinguished evangelicals as Richard Channing Moore, then rector of St. Stephen's Church, and Henry I. Feltus of St. Ann's Church, Brooklyn, and even a number of laymen led by John Jay. But the will of the diocese was clear, and on May 29, 1811, Hobart was consecrated as the assistant bishop; five years later, on the death of Bishop Benjamin Moore, he succeeded him as diocesan and rector of Trinity Church.

The controversy was, however, not completely dissipated by the consecration. When Jones refused to resign, the Trinity Church vestry appealed to Bishop Moore, who removed him and temporarily suspended him from the ministry. At this juncture, under the influence of the dissidents, Bishop Provoost, on October 6, 1812, wrote a letter to the diocesan convention declaring that he was resuming his episcopal prerogatives which he had temporarily resigned more than a decade earlier. He reminded them that the House of Bishops had not accepted his resignation and that accordingly he was ready "to concur in any regulation which expediency may dictate to the Church; without which concurrence I am, after the resolution of the House of Bishops, bound to consider every episcopal act as unauthorized."

It is possible that at the time of Hobart's consecration Bishop White and Bishop Jarvis may have anticipated that some tension might follow the choice of so young and aggressive a person as Hobart, or they may have feared that conflict might arise in the diocese because of the contrast between the strongly Seaburian high church ideas of young Hobart and those of Bishop Benjamin Moore, whose rule had been benign during the years while Hobart was so rapidly coming to prominence. In their letter to Hobart certifying his consecration they had specifically stated that he had been elected "to assist the Bishops of the Church [in New York] in the duties of the episcopal office and to succeed in case of survivorship." This may have been merely their attempt to remain consistent since they had never recognized Provoost's resignation, but it certainly provided Provoost with a ground for his communication of 1812. The diocese would hear no more about the controversy and drafted a lengthy resolution stating that they acknowledged Benjamin Moore, and no other person, to be their true and lawful Diocesan Bishop.

The Jones case was submitted to five judges of the State Supreme Court who supported Bishop Moore's action in removing him from the staff of Trinity Church but also awarded him a financial settlement. Jones later became a chaplain in the United States Navy; Abraham Beach retired on a pension; Richard C. Moore soon became the Bishop of Virginia; and Henry I. Feltus became a warm admirer and supporter of Hobart.

Another slight flurry was caused when one who signed himself "Hieronymous" issued a pamphlet, *Serious Thoughts on a Late Administration of Episcopal Orders Submitted to the Calm Reflection of the Bishops of the Protestant Episcopal Church*, impugning Hobart's consecration, since Bishop White in laying hands on Hobart had inadvertently omitted the essential words, "In the name of the Father, and of the Son, and of the Holy Ghost." John Bowden published a reply, *The Essentials of Ordination Stated*, defending the validity of Hobart's ordination. Bishop White, a highly respected authority on the early church, had not been conscious of the omission but, when questioned, said that these words had not been a part of the form of the Church of England until the reign of Charles II, were never in that of the primitive church, or even currently in the Roman Pontifical.[7] Interestingly enough no one had called attention to the same omission in the consecration of Bishop Griswold in the same service, so this episode also must be charged to Hobart's opponents, who sought rather to embarrass him than to preserve the integrity of holy orders.

Hobart himself was shamed by all these events, which he called disgraces, but was undaunted by them and promptly went on to recreate the episcopal office as he demonstrated its possibilities in the diocese and the church at large. He remained a man with great strength and some weaknesses. He ruled autocratically, dissolving a clergy association whose powers he feared, rebuked his laity, and usually was most severe with the few evangelicals among his clergy. His sensitivity to opposition and his desire for approval became very evident when, on his return from two years of recuperation in Europe, he refused to accept an address of welcome until it would be amended to include approval of his whole episcopal course. Since not all agreed with his churchmanship or his policies, it required a long debate before his clergy could satisfy the bishop with a mutually agreeable phrase testifying to the soundness of his policy and the correctness of his proceedings.

But Hobart was a great bishop, a great benefactor of the church, and a striking figure. Of below medium stature, he had a large head and a strong and flexible voice. Being very nearsighted, he wore powerful spectacles behind which his weak but bright eyes snapped; of necessity he memorized his sermons for effective preaching. Hobart preached rapidly, with force and sometimes with so much emotion that he was accused of being "Methodistical." His generally warm and imperturbably open manner won him friends everywhere in and beyond the church. Always resourceful, he was an alert leader in the House of Deputies and, as a bishop, always ready with new plans for advance. His administration at times seemed to have the air of military precision, yet his clergy usually knew him only as a warm friend. Of the 178 clergy in the church in the year of his consecration, ninety-three were in regular correspondence with Hobart, and his posthumously published letters required six large quarto volumes.[8]

On his assumption of the episcopate New York City had a population of less than one hundred thousand persons and seven Episcopal parishes, of which Trinity Church was the largest. Hobart served both as rector of Trinity Church and as bishop of a diocese of forty-six thousand square miles, extending from the eastern extremities of Long Island to Canada and west to Lake Erie. In all this area he found two missionaries, Davenport Phelps and "Father" Daniel Nash, and at his death he left fifty busily at work among the Indians, German immigrants, and settlers from New England. Always interested in promoting the church constructively through the Sunday Schools and the frontier missions, he was the first bishop to travel so extensively. In 1811 he had twenty-six clergy; by 1829 there were 133 in 165 congregations well distributed in all the larger communities and with two in Rochester and two in Buffalo.

Supported by the extensive resources of Trinity Church, Hobart immediately plunged into the work upstate along the Hudson and to its western extremities. In his second year as bishop he traveled two thousand miles and confirmed 1,100 members in thirty-three parishes. On another visitation he traveled four thousand miles. Hobart personally visited the Indians in central and western New York, and the Oneida Indian chiefs were among his regular correspondents. He was the first American bishop to travel so widely about the missions of the church at a time when there were no railroads and the steam packet ran only to Albany. Beyond that stage, canal boat and horseback were his only means of travel, and it seems fitting that his end should have come at sunrise on Sunday morning, September 12, 1830, while he was on a westward visitation in Auburn. The New York community, where the bishop had brought the church to be highly respected, honored Hobart in his death as he was carried down Broadway through large crowds and buried beneath the chancel of Trinity Church.

By this time the resources of the Diocese of New York had improved so that when Bishop Benjamin T. Onderdonk was elected to succeed Hobart, the episcopate was separately supported, and William Berrian became the rector of Trinity Church. Eight years later the strength of the church in the western areas of the state had increased sufficiently to permit the organization of the

Diocese of Western New York. William H. DeLancey became the bishop of this first diocese to be separately organized within a state already occupied by another diocese.

Hobart was probably more responsible than any other person for the establishment of the General Theological Seminary. Alert to observe the trend in other communions that had established theological schools, Hobart sensed the need for more adequate formal training of the clergy of the Episcopal Church. Until this time most ministers had attended college and then read theology under the guidance of a mature rector, much as a student read law in the office of a practicing attorney. By 1813 Hobart had proposed to his diocesan convention an institution "the object of which shall be to train up young men for the ministry, not only in literary and theological knowledge, but in evangelical piety, and prudent but fervent zeal for the advancement of the kingdom of Christ." The following year he published a prospectus for a grammar school and theological college on lands he had already purchased in New Jersey for this purpose.

At the General Convention of 1814 Christopher E. Gadsden of South Carolina proposed a general theological seminary, but the resolution was defeated because it was supported only by his delegation and those from Virginia, Massachusetts, Rhode Island, and several delegates from Maryland. Bishop White and Bishop Hobart had not supported the resolution because they favored diocesan seminaries more easily controlled by the bishop. By a resolution originating in the House of Bishops, that convention, however, decided to study the advisability of having a general seminary. Three years later the convention voted to establish such a school and appointed a committee of nine, with an equal representation of bishops, presbyters, and laymen.

Although Bishop White and Bishop Hobart still favored diocesan seminaries and Bishop John Croes of New Jersey was not convinced of the necessity for such schools, the committee named Nathaniel Bowen and William H. Wilmer, soon replaced by Thomas C. Brownell, as fiscal agents to gather funds for the school in the middle and southern states. Subsequently the New England areas were solicited by T. Y. How and Samuel F. Jarvis, son of the Bishop of Connecticut, and a year later in the spring of 1819, when the funds were adequate to pay the salaries of the faculty, the school began its instruction in New York. Jarvis, who soon resigned to accept the rectorship of St. Paul's Church, Boston, and Samuel H. Turner were its first teachers, and among the first six students were two future bishops, Manton Eastburn and George W. Doane. Hobart gave the school no support, not even adequate housing facilities, so that the General Convention in 1820 voted to move the school to New Haven where its former agent, now Bishop Brownell, gave it a kindlier reception. Here the school received some support, especially from South Carolina, and the library of John Pintard became the nucleus of the library destined to become one of the finest theological libraries in the country. The endowments were increased by almost $30,000 and Bird Wilson was added to the faculty.

Meanwhile, Bishop Hobart had been free to pursue his own purposes in establishing a diocesan seminary in New York, with a branch on the college campus at Geneva, under the auspices of his previously established Theological Education Society. In his address to the special convention in October, 1820, Hobart admitted sending a pastoral letter throughout the diocese stressing "the advantages to be gained from this school" and expressing open fears that the controls of a general seminary would rest in a General Convention where a diocese with seventy clergy and 120 congregations (his own) would have the same vote as a small diocese with two clergymen and two congregations. He felt that the direction of a general institution should be proportioned on the basis of benefactions to it, which obviously would leave the major controls in his hands. Soon afterward, Hobart also published a pamphlet in which he heartily commended his school to the patronage of his people, declaring that the policy of the church clearly permitted it and that his plans were not exclusive or in opposition to the General Seminary, but rather aimed at providing a clergy of superior training for the responsibilities of his large and growing diocese. In pleading for his New York school, Hobart announced his intention to invite students and to solicit support from all areas of the church, as well as to keep the school in conformity with the regulations of the General Convention and the courses prescribed by the bishops.

Meanwhile, Jacob Sherred, a wealthy layman of the New York Diocese, on his death left a legacy of almost $60,000 "to a general seminary, if established in New York, or to a seminary established by that diocese." Hobart now held the winning hand, and when a special General Convention was called to decide whether the money should go to the diocesan school already established or to the General Seminary, even if it should return to New York, Hobart agreed to a union of the schools in New York with a merging of faculties and resources. In the compromise Hobart won all his points; all the bishops became trustees, *ex officio*, and the remaining members of the board were to be elected by the dioceses on the basis of the number of their clergy and the total gifts contributed to the school. For many years this proportional representation made for a cumbersome administrative board, but it left the control in the hands of the Bishop of New York, who not only became the head of the institution, but also its Professor of Pastoral Theology and Pulpit Eloquence. Hobart proudly delivered the sermon in Trinity Church that marked the opening of the school in New York City on March 11, 1822. Although the early years were at times precarious because of lack of resources, the first building was completed in 1827 on sixty-two lots on the North River given by Clement C. Moore, son of Bishop Benjamin Moore, and professor of Old Testament but best known for his Christmas poem, " 'Twas the night before Christmas: A Visit from St. Nicholas." The school at Geneva was discontinued in 1824, but the college there, which owed so much to Hobart, later came to bear his name and continues as a thriving institution.

With his own institution firmly established, Hobart seemed to forget his earlier pleas for diocesan prerogatives in theological education and openly criticized as disloyal to the church those who sought such schools. Meanwhile Virginia, within four years from its modest beginnings in 1820, had well established its school in the city of Alexandria, and both Maryland and Massachusetts had made similar but unsuccessful attempts. In Maryland the supporters of the school, authorized by the Diocese in June 1821, and for which the constitution was adopted on June 11, 1822, were thwarted by Bishop James Kemp, who felt that it would compete with the General Seminary. In Massachusetts a committee to found a theological school brought John Henry Hopkins from Pittsburgh, where he had been instructing theological students in addition to doing his parish work, to become an assistant at Trinity Church, Boston, with the agreement that he would also open a theological school in Cambridge. When, after only a few months of instruction, he found inadequate interest and support, Hopkins accepted election as Bishop of Vermont in 1832. Although the supporters of the school in Massachusetts raised additional funds, the continued lack of interest and the panic of 1837 delayed their plans for another generation. It was also during these years that Bishop Philander Chase established his theological school in Ohio.

Much more successful was the Episcopal Church's educational venture in Hartford, Connecticut, where Washington (now Trinity) College was founded in 1824. This city had less than ten thousand inhabitants, but about ten per cent of them were Episcopalians. The first class was graduated in 1827, and by 1835 one-half of the 115 alumni had been admitted to holy orders. Bishop Brownell guided the college through most of this period and saw to it that the school had a fine library of over twelve thousand volumes, a well-trained faculty, and that the annual cost to a student remained modest, ranging from $137 to $184.

By training and by strong conviction Bishop Hobart was a staunch high churchman of the Laudian type with no tendency whatsoever toward Rome or to ritualistic innovations. He was especially influenced by the English theologians Richard Hooker, Launcelot Andrewes, and Edward Stillingfleet. At the General Convention of 1826 he did propose liberalizing the use of the church's liturgy because many worshipers felt the services in the Episcopal Church were entirely too long. He had proposed an alternate preface and prayer in the Confirmation Office and alternate and abbreviated Psalms and Lessons in Morning Prayer but insisted on retaining Ante-Communion, which many clergy omitted without authorization. But the time for this advanced idea had not yet arrived, and he contented himself by emphatically declaring a principle for safeguarding the future against hasty or injudicious changes, that "no alterations shall be made which have not been adopted in one General Convention, made known to the different diocesan conventions, and finally adopted in a subsequent General Convention," which remains essentially the current practice. Very astutely Hobart recognized the dangers of retaining regulations which, by their impracticality, lead to violation, consequent variations, and often long-lasting irregularities. He told the General Convention of 1827 that "law can be enforced with more salutary effect, and with less odium, when it has been accommodated, as far as possible, without departure from essential principles, to those circumstances which are urged as a plea for violating it."

Perhaps nowhere better than in his "charges" to his clergy and diocesan conventions, an English church practice that he introduced effectively in the Episcopal Church, do his doctrinal positions become crystal clear. In 1818 he delivered such an address before his convention on *The Corruptions of Rome Contrasted with Certain Protestant Errors* and the very next year set out in contrast the Anglican position in *The Churchman: The Principles of the Churchman Stated and Explained in Distinction from the Corruptions of the Church of Rome and the Errors of Certain Protestant Sects*. While deprecating the errors in the Roman and sectarian extremities, Hobart never limited salvation to Anglicans but freely granted that God's grace and the benefits of Christ's atonement belonged to the pious and sincere members of all Christian groups. Even in his own church he feared that the word "evangelical" was being misused by being identified with those who laid little stress on the nature of the church and its ordinances or who freely moulded the liturgy according to their own whims, whereas he insisted that every true high churchman must be evangelical. Indeed, he tried to rescue the precious word by saying,

> In the *correct* sense of the term, High Churchmen disclaim the imputation of not being Evangelical. It is only when faithless to their principles that they are not preeminently so. Pardon, Justification, eternal life, as the free gifts of God the Father, through the merits and intercession of his eternal Son, and through the renovating and sanctifying agency of the Holy Ghost—these are the great Evangelical truths which alone render of value or of efficiency the ministrations and ordinances for which the High Churchman contends.[9]

For Hobart the principal difference between the evangelicals and high churchmen was essentially one of method and emphasis, although many of his successors would have disputed this point.

Hobart was always very careful to deny any relation between high churchmanship and formalism and cited as examples the great English divines Thomas Ken, Hartwell Horne, and William Jones. In his interpretations of the sacraments Hobart would hardly satisfy most modern churchmen who cherish his party name. He considered the word "sacrifice" foreign to the thought and liturgy of the church and held that the bread and wine in the Lord's Supper were symbols of the body and blood of Christ. He denied with equal vehemence the doctrines of predestination, invocation of the saints, and especially auricular confession and private absolution, which he considered "an encroachment on the rights of conscience, an invasion of the prerogative of the Searcher of hearts."

Occasionally his opponents called him a bigot, which roused the bishop to write an old instructor, Stanhope Smith, in 1817, "High churchman as I am, I think I am a stranger to bigotry of heart." Rightly he insisted that bigotry had nothing whatsoever to do with opinions but only with "the *spirit* in which they are held, and the *manner* and *means* by which they are avowed and advanced." Only he is a bigot, Hobart wrote,

> . . . who holds any opinions in that *spirit* of blind and inveterate prejudice which, imperfectly acquainted with the evidences of the correctness of those opinions, views with contempt and scorn all opposing claims; . . . who seeks to coerce them to his own sentiments, and thus to advance those sentiments by any other *means* than fair judgment, and an honorable and candid policy.

Despite this broad and liberal spirit, Hobart was ever concerned about too much liberality, which bred indifference. In writing on this point and the ecumenical spirit, the bishop actually became prophetic when he told his diocese in 1819 that it was dangerous to widen "the enclosures of charity, so as to embrace those who believe most, and those who scarcely believe anything." Modern churchmen can testify how foresighted he was when he expressed fears that

> . . . liberality to men would be extended to their *opinions*, and that from admitting the equal sincerity of the former, the acknowledgment would be made of the equal truth, or to speak more properly, of the equal *indifference* of the latter, so that sincerity of intention would be considered as the only standard of truth, and the age of liberality become the *age of indifference*.[10]

Whether his prophecy about ecumenical trends will be as accurate as his prediction of the current indifference resulting from exaggerating liberality only the long future can tell. Describing that period when the errors and heresies that deform the fair face of Christianity shall be corrected, he said,

> At that period when the discordant sects that now divide and distract the Christian family, profess "with one heart the faith delivered to the saints," and "with one mouth glorify God," the principles professed, the feelings cherished, the language uttered, will be the principles, the feelings and the language of the High Churchmen.

That he was here still speaking of the conjunction of his happy phrases Evangelical Truth and Apostolic Order cannot be denied in the light of his constant emphasis on this essential unity. All through his ministry this had been his theme, and even as early as 1815 he had charged his diocese:

> There is often an invidious distinction made between the doctrine and institutions of the Gospel; and yet they both have a divine origin, and they are inseparably connected as means to the same end—the salvation of men. Justification by a living faith in the Lord and Saviour, Jesus Christ, and through the sanctification of the divine Spirit, is a fundamental doctrine of the Gospel. It pervades all the articles, and animates all the offices of our Church; and her ministers should make it the basis of all their instructions and preaching.[11]

That he did exactly that himself is attested by the English Archdeacon John Strachan, who visited in this country the following year and wrote of Hobart's preaching,

> It was impossible to hear him without becoming sensible of the infinite importance of the Gospel. He warned, counselled, entreated, and comforted, with intense and powerful energy. His manner and voice struck you with the deep interest which pervaded his soul for their salvation, and found ready entrance into their hearts. He appeared in the pulpit as a father anxious for the eternal happiness of his children—a man of God preparing them for their Christian warfare—a herald from the other world, standing between the living and the dead, between heaven and earth, entreating perishing sinners, in the most tender accents, not to reject the message of reconciliation which the Son of the living God so graciously offered for their acceptance.[12]

Yet, from his training in the traditions of the church and his wide experience through the years, Hobart knew the dangers of attempting to live the Christian life or to do the work of the church in isolation from those supporting means of grace on which a churchman depended. He feared that the foundations of sound and sober piety in the order, unity, and beauty of the church and the true ministry of the church might be superseded by a secularism with a cold, unfruitful, and comfortless system of heathen morals or a wild enthusiastic sectarianism condemning the divinely constituted government and priesthood of the church. So to his very end he adhered, as he once described his position, "in all essential points to the faith, ministry and worship which distinguished the apostolic and primitive Church, and particularly to the constitution of the Christian ministry under its three orders of Bishops, Priests and Deacons."

When fevers and other illnesses incapacitated Bishop Hobart in 1822, he followed medical advice and spent two years in travel on the continent, but mostly in England where he was very well received and entertained and of which he became very fond. His churchmanship was not unfamiliar to the British, but to see it combined with an ardent democratic spirit seemed peculiar. One clergyman wrote, ". . . it was funny to see honest democracy and sincere episcopacy fast yoked in the man's mind, and perpetually struggling in his heart."[13]

John Henry Newman greatly admired Hobart and may very well have patterned his own style of preaching after the union of doctrinal certainty with a real passion for souls that he found in the American bishop. Canon C. P. S. Clarke suggested that the idea of publishing the *Tracts for the Times,* which a few years later was to give so great an impetus to the Oxford Movement, may have been copied from Hobart's wide use of tracts. This English movement, which would soon affect the American church, could possibly have come under the influence of the old American high churchmanship through its prime representative, the Bishop of New York.

Associated with Hobart in the high church movement, although overshadowed by him, were Theodore Dehon (1776–1817), the second Bishop of

South Carolina, and John S. Ravenscroft (1772–1830), Bishop of North Carolina. The former, trained at Harvard and under the ministry of Samuel Parker, was an able and persuasive preacher and stressed the value of the sacraments and conformity to the Prayer Book and its rubrics. He introduced the observance of the weekday Holy Days and emphasized the observances of Lent and Holy Week. Bishop Ravenscroft, a man of commanding figure, entered the ministry of the church at the age of forty-five and after six years was elected Bishop of North Carolina. A man of wide business and varied religious affiliations, he became an ardent Hobartian churchman and stressed a steadfast and uniform adherence to the liturgy and offices of the church. He was succeeded by Levi Silliman Ives, the most extreme of the early high church bishops, who defected to Rome after a few years of service in North Carolina. Another bishop who idolized Hobart was James Kemp (1764–1827), elected first as Bishop Claggett's assistant in Maryland in 1814 and afterward his successor. These men were always overshadowed, however, by the brilliant performance of Hobart in his more prominent diocese with its consequently greater opportunities.

On his death the leadership of the high church party, however, fell to the hands of Hobart's pupils, who had been well trained under his own guidance. Bishop Benjamin Onderdonk (1791–1861) who succeeded him, excelled as an administrator but tired many of his hearers by the reiteration of Hobart's arguments for apostolic succession and ultimately lost his influence through indiscretions for which he was brought to trial. Much more influential was Bishop George W. Doane (1799–1859) of New Jersey, a poet, who for five years taught at Trinity College and after 1830 served as rector of Trinity Church, Boston, before his consecration.

Still another of Hobart's pupils was the brilliant William R. Whittingham (1805–1879) who was well versed in the sources of the catholic tradition and who edited *The Churchman* for five years before becoming Professor of Ecclesiastical History at the General Seminary in 1836. Elected Bishop of Maryland in 1840, he gave more than thirty years to perpetuating the churchmanship of Bishop Claggett and Bishop Stone. His administration was shorn of some of its potential effectiveness by the increasing inflexibility of his mind. He was never a ceremonialist, abhorring Roman usages, but led his diocese with a rigid demand for obedience to every letter of the Prayer Book.

Although he came to his convictions entirely apart from Hobart's influence, John Henry Hopkins (1792–1868) came to similar churchly opinions by his own study. Trained and very successful in the practice of law, he sought ordination and accepted a call to Trinity Church, Pittsburgh. From there he went to Trinity Church, Boston, in 1830 as an assistant to George W. Doane and also became the first theological professor in the Diocese of Massachusetts, which had just begun its short-lived theological school. Upset by Doane's political maneuverings and the lack of support for the school, Hopkins accepted election as Bishop of Vermont in 1832 and went on to become one of the church's unconventional leaders, always disturbingly guided by his own honest convictions. In addition to being a successful metallurgist and lawyer before he entered the ministry, Hopkins remained a poet, a painter, an architect, and a gifted musician. He designed a church, copied masterpieces, prepared the plates for Alexander Wilson's *Ornithology*, experimented with lithography, composed his own musical setting for the Communion Service, and wrote a treatise on Gothic architecture. He had carefully studied the Christian literature of the first fifteen centuries and on the basis of this independent research came to his conclusions that the Holy Communion should be administered with the mixed chalice and unleavened bread.

Among the other bishops who were high churchmen of the older order mention should be made of Thomas B. Brownell (1779–1865) in Connecticut and his predecessor, Abraham Jarvis (1739–1813); Henry U. Onderdonk (1789–1858), Bishop White's assistant and successor in Pennsylvania; William H. DeLancey (1797–1865), first Bishop of Western New York; George Upfold (1796–1872) of Indiana; Thomas G. Atkinson (1807–1881) of North Carolina; William H. Odenheimer (1817–1879) of New Jersey; John Williams (1817–1899) of Connecticut; and Jackson Kemper (1789–1870) of Wisconsin. Presbyters of influence in the movement were Bird Wilson, a professor at the General Seminary; Francis L. Hawks, rector of St. Thomas' Church, New York City, and the distinguished historian; and Samuel Seabury (1801–1872), grandson of the first American bishop, who edited *The Churchman* and founded the Church of the Annunciation in New York City where, as its rector after 1838, he perpetuated the Hobartian churchmanship.

XIII

THE FRONTIER CHURCH

The differences between the evangelicals and the high churchmen were basically in spirit and emphasis rather than in essentials of doctrine or polity, with some variable exceptions. Both evangelicals and high churchmen stressed the doctrine of corrupt human nature, the moral and religious helplessness of man, and the consequent necessity of atonement and justification; the former sought these graces by faith and the latter through the church, the sacraments, and the apostolic ministry. Neither group seemed to understand the importance of the doctrine of the Incarnation. Both parties agreed on the personal nature of religion; the evangelicals emphasized the necessity of personal acceptance of Christ by faith, commonly called conversion by many Protestants, while the high churchmen, without underestimating the value of such experiences, preferred to find them within the church order where they could be stabilized by the sacraments and ordinances. Evangelicals generally stressed strict morality and a life of devotion and piety, while high churchmen sought the life of penitence and faith in union with the church and by participation in its means of grace administered by the hands of her authorized ministry. Both groups considered the bread and wine in the Lord's Supper as symbols and memorials of the body and blood of Christ, although high churchmen generally spoke of the Eucharist and stressed the necessity of an authorized apostolic ministry. The evangelicals may have emphasized less the relation of the church and its ministry but emphasized more the church as the blessed company of all faithful people. The Hobartians believed that union with the church and its threefold ministry was essential to salvation, although granting rather grudgingly that God might save those "who do not negligently or wilfully continue in separation from it." While evangelicals also held to three orders of the ministry, they never impugned the validity of other ministries or sacraments; they might have considered them irregular but never invalid as many high churchmen insisted they must be. The difference in spirit and emphasis becomes clear in their respective attitudes toward the Prayer Book; Hobart and the high churchmen considered non-liturgical services "nurseries of enthusiasm," while evangelicals with no less regard for and observance of the Prayer Book considered these services as legitimate supplemental means of grace.

While worship in the colonial period had often been comparatively free and varied, after the Constitutional Convention even the evangelicals expressed a high appreciation of the worth of the Prayer Book. Bishop Meade once described it as "the most perfect of all liturgies" and argued that it be "maintained in its purity and integrity," while his neighbor, Bishop Kemp, warned the Maryland clergy not "to mutilate and change the Liturgy." By the 1830's the careless conduct of services, once quite common, had been banned by both parties, and there was not yet any sign of "enrichment" of the liturgy even among the most ardent high churchmen, although some smugness and contentedness with status in the true Catholic Church led some Episcopalians to lose their great opportunities for expansion in those years. Even church architecture reflected the changing times. Churches resembling Greek temples, of which St. Paul's Cathedral in Boston is one, that were once the mark of an evangelical parish appeared less frequently, and modified Gothic began to appear. The old high center pulpits, of which both St. Philip's and St. Michael's in Charleston, South Carolina, still preserve magnificent examples, made way for an elevated chancel with the communion table at the far wall, although evangelicals still "administered," while high churchmen "celebrated" Holy Communion. The offerings were not "presented" or even "received" but usually placed on the floor at the front of the main aisle. In order to provide a clear view of the altar the pulpit and the lectern were moved to the sides of the chancel. Crosses appeared on some altars and also replaced other ornaments on the steeples.

Most churches were in use all day on Sunday; some evangelical parishes began with Sunday School at nine o'clock, followed by Morning Prayer and Sermon at 10:30; the Sunday School reconvened at two, with Evening Prayer at three or four o'clock, and occasionally there was a special Sunday evening service. In those years most rectors preached at both the morning and late afternoon services; usually there were long doctrinal sermons laced with many scriptural references and often wanting in simplicity and directness. Sometimes evangelicals would add an exhortation after the sermon, which occasionally consumed an hour. The morning service usually included Morning Prayer, the Litany, and Ante-Communion. Some evangelicals freely omitted the latter in order to abbreviate the service, which led Hobart, who opposed such liberties, to press for legislation by canonical action in the General Convention to regularize possible changes in the liturgy.

Vestments were also simpler than at present; a minister wore a long surplice without a cassock, tippet, or stole. Before preaching the sermon, he exchanged the surplice for a black preaching gown with bands and wore black silk gloves with the forefinger slit to facilitate turning the pages of the sermon manuscript. At the Holy Communion, with no vestments save the surplice, the minister usually stood at the north or Gospel end of the altar and faced the people in reading the service. The surplice fell into disuse, and as late as 1838 a recommendation of its use in all parishes had to be withdrawn in the General Convention because of strong opposition. The ordinary bread and the chalice with unmixed wine were placed on a plain linen cloth on the altar, which had no flowers or candles and was often without even a cross. Even bishops at times used no vestments at all; on his trips to western New York Bishop Hobart at times omitted not only his episcopal robes but even the black gown. By contrast, George Doane and William R. Whittingham carried with them a supply of surplices so that the clergy who assisted them might be properly vested.

After 1789 the first official hymnal included the metrical Psalms of Tate and Brady with twenty-seven more modern hymns, and only after 1808 were thirty more hymns added. Fear of undue emotionalism led Bishop White and his associates to try to avoid the excesses they had seen among the free churches, which used the more subjective hymns and rhythmic tunes. Where choirs were used, they wore no gowns and usually sat in a gallery at the rear of the church. The General Convention of 1826 issued a new Hymnal with 212 hymns from varied sources, mostly non-Anglican, which served the church for the next generation. The newer hymns were well adapted for use in the week-day services, such as the lectures and prayer meetings that became well established in the evangelical churches during this period.

The prayer meetings grew naturally out of the weekly lectures; on one occasion Gregory T. Bedell invited those in attendance at his Friday evening lectures who desired further counsel to remain after the benediction, and he was amazed that only half of the congregation withdrew. Quickly these special services spread to other parishes until the Saturday night prayer meeting became almost a badge of an evangelical parish, just as an early service of Holy Communion on Sunday marked the high church parish. The evangelicals made much of the observance of Lent and Holy Week, sometimes conducting daily prayer meetings and three services on Friday in addition to the stated services of the church. Confirmation was never regarded as a sacrament but was always taken very seriously by the evangelical rectors, who not uncommonly met the candidates in sections three times a week for personal consultation in addition to the regular weekly meeting of the entire class.

In Virginia, largely under the leadership and influence of Bishop Meade, protracted meetings called Associations, not unlike the popular camp meetings, were widely observed throughout the diocese. Such meetings were held in private homes or in the churches and frequently lasted through three days or more with services three times a day. The ministers alternated in preaching, and frequently persons not associated with the church were won to a religious profession. After several years the Associations became larger Convocations where similar meetings reached more people. The evangelical spirit of the Virginia church reached its finest expression at the annual conventions, where sometimes as many as twelve hundred persons were in attendance; the day began with prayer meetings at six o'clock and ended in a similar meeting with one or more sermons. This was in vivid contrast to those earlier conventions in Richmond when few persons attended the sessions and many clergy and laity had been seen only at the taverns. This new evangelical fervor led to enthusiastic support for the church in Virginia and other dioceses, made for generous offerings and gifts for missions and the seminaries, and frequently resulted in refreshing periods of revival when members were led to new understanding of the religious life and many persons were for the first time won to the church.

The evangelical leaders were not unaware of the dangers in such services, which left so much to the individual discretion of the clergy. Even Bishop White called attention to these dangers as early as 1815. Though he later came to stress the importance of the church and its ministry and sacraments, White never lost his original appreciation of the evangelical spirit. In 1819 he preached in New Haven on "The Gospel as the Power of God unto Salvation," and in his sermon at the consecration of Hobart and Griswold in 1811 he made it very clear that "Gospel morals without Gospel doctrine, is not Christianity."[1] Apparently it was a common charge against the Episcopal clergy in the early nineteenth century that they "are preachers of morality merely and that they frame their discourses to delight the imaginations and to flatter the vanity of their audiences . . . but neglect to enforce the fundamental doctrines of the Gospel." Preaching in Natchez in 1827 before the Mississippi Episcopalians then holding their third annual diocesan convention, James A. Fox denied these and related charges and insisted that a change of heart, or conversion, is necessary to salvation and is clearly taught in the Articles of Religion and the liturgy of the church.[2]

To perpetuate these values for the church the Protestant Episcopal Evangelical Society was organized in Philadelphia in 1813 to promote religious knowledge, invigorate pious affections, and develop Christian fellowship. In addition to founding colleges and seminaries for the training of the clergy, the evangelicals established the Evangelical Knowledge Society, and the Protestant Episcopal Sunday School and Tract Society, mutually supported by evangelical and high churchmen. In reaction to the Oxford Movement and its influence in America, they organized in 1848 the Protestant Episcopal Society for the Promotion of Evangelical Knowledge, often abbreviated to the E.K.S., to publish books, tracts, and Sunday School materials. Its abbreviated service from the Prayer Book, *The Mission Service,* was widely used and more than six hundred books and hundreds of Prayer Books were sold for as little as ten cents. This Society also published two regular monthly journals, *The Parish Visitor,* for parochial distribution, and *The Standard Bearer,* for use in the Sunday Schools. The Evangelical Education Society, organized to provide funds for needy theological students, was less successful, for many students refused to give assent to the rigidly stated conservative theological dogma required of grantees.

This was also the period in which the church periodicals first made their appearance in great profusion, for they were not official publications. Among these useful organs were the *Layman's Magazine,* begun in 1815; *The Church Record* (1822), which became *The Philadelphia Recorder,* and later, when it absorbed *The Washington Theological Repertory* (1819), became *The Episcopal Recorder* (1831); *The Gospel Messenger and Southern Episcopal*

Register (1824); *The Gambier Observer* (1830), later *The Western Episcopalian; The Southern Churchman* (1835); *The Church Advocate* (1835); *The Protestant Episcopal Review;* and *The Evangelical Quarterly.* In addition to performing the editorial duties and supplying articles for these journals, many evangelicals also published books on theology, sermons, reminiscences, and an abundance of excellent biographies.

Two conflicting opinions of contemporary leaders indicate both a rise and decline of evangelical strength in the church by the close of this period. Bishop Thomas Clark of Rhode Island, who had just entered the ministry in 1836, later wrote that the growth of the church was very much in the evangelical direction, for their numbers had doubled in a decade, being strengthened by the influx of clergy from other churches.[3] On the other hand Stephen H. Tyng, a strong evangelical, declared that the majority of the approximately five hundred clergy was about equally divided between the moderate followers of Bishop White and Hobartian high churchmen, while there were probably no more than fifty who would have been willing to stand with Bishop Griswold.[4] It was in fact the period of greatest strength for the evangelicals, for soon, under the influence of the Oxford Tracts, high churchmanship would be further fostered, and because of the liberalizing cultural influence on the leaders of evangelical convictions, the spirit and emphasis of this party would be widened and known as the broad church movement.

Discerning leaders on both sides feared the outbreak of dissension in the church over the differences between evangelicals and the high churchmen that were being more and more clearly drawn through rising party spirit. When Bishop Griswold told his Eastern Diocese in 1825 that "discordant sounds of party distinctions" were being heard "which every friend of the Church should exercise his utmost prudence to oppose," he was obviously referring to the elections of suffragan bishops in Maryland and Pennsylvania. Only after three years of contention was James Kemp elected as Bishop Claggett's assistant in Maryland, where a majority of two-thirds of the clergy and lay votes was required. Smarting under their defeat, the low churchmen sought to block Kemp's consecration in 1814 on the canonical ground that no constitutional provision was made for assistant bishops and, failing in this, even threatened a schism in the church by asking the aged Bishop Provoost to consecrate a bishop for them. The conflict subsided under the wise leadership of Bishop Kemp, who was named provost of the University of Maryland in 1815 but never allowed this office to interfere with his duties as diocesan. However, after his untimely death in a stagecoach accident in 1827, the difficulties flared up once more. Since neither party could muster a majority for two years, it was not until 1830 that, by the wise provision of a nominating committee, the name of William M. Stone was presented and he was elected. After Stone's death eight years later, many leading clergymen declined nomination, and at a subsequent special convention after eleven unsuccessful ballots a serious proposal to cast lots was rejected. Having failed again in eighteen ballots in 1838 to elect a bishop, a nominating committee was appointed which brought in the name of Professor William R. Whittingham of the General Seminary faculty, who was promptly chosen and consecrated on September 17, 1840.

The Diocese of Pennsylvania had similar difficulties, and, because of the large number of persons involved and the intensity of the rivalries generated, the struggle to elect an assistant for Bishop White marks a high point in internal dissension and party strife. Bishop White, who was approaching his eightieth birthday, obviously needed an assistant. At the convention in 1826 William Meade of Virginia, the candidate of the evangelicals, actually received twenty-seven votes, and Bird Wilson, who was the choice of "the friends of the bishop" but did not vote, received twenty-six. When the election was postponed, both parties immediately organized for a spirited contest. In the interest of reconciliation both Meade and Wilson withdrew their candidacies, and the election at the convention held in Harrisburg on May 2, 1827 became a rivalry between John Henry Hopkins, still rector of Trinity Church, Pittsburgh, and Henry U. Onderdonk of Brooklyn, New York. The high church caucus saw victory ahead if Hopkins would vote for himself, a precedent set in the previous elections of White and Chase, but finally had to settle on Onderdonk as their candidate because of the immovable modesty of Hopkins. The evangelicals, with no hope of electing a candidate, chose to support Hopkins as the lesser of the evils. The illness of a high church deputy momentarily threw consternation into the convention, but when he arrived in a carriage the next morning in time to cast his ballot, the issue was decided; Onderdonk received twenty-six of the fifty-one ballots cast. The laity assented by a vote of seventy-two to fifty-eight.

The contest had been a bitter one and ill will lingered long in the diocese. The evangelicals refused to sign Onderdonk's testimonials, and twenty-five clergy and fifty-eight lay delegates signed a Remonstrance in a final attempt to block the consecration. Benjamin Allen, who had led the low church forces, published in Philadelphia an open *Letter* to Bishop Hobart, accusing him of being "the worst enemy of the Liturgy, the greatest opponent to the spread of Episcopacy, and the certain author of entire ruin to our Church, if your policy prevail. . . ." He went on to accuse the bishop of seeking the authority of an archbishop and attempting to control all episcopal elections. He insisted that it had been Hobart's influence that had caused the defeat of William Meade in the very first ballot for an assistant in Pennsylvania by using his friendship with Bishop White to promote the influence of the so-called "friends of the bishop." Before he closed his letter Allen charged Hobart with the worst offense of all in attempting to block Bishop Chase's efforts to provide a theological seminary for the Diocese of Ohio. Oddly enough Hobart distrusted Henry Onderdonk, primarily because he was accustomed to omit the service of Ante-Communion like a low churchman, and had once told delegates from Pennsylvania to "take Meade of Virginia a hundred times rather than H. U. Onderdonk."

Hobart preached the sermon for the consecration of Onderdonk; in this service no low church bishop or presbyter took part, and he unnecessarily excoriated the evangelicals and denounced their principles and methods, especially their non-liturgical services and social means of grace. Bishop White had been busily engaged in arranging the work for his new assistant and, in the year Onderdonk was chosen, made a four-hundred-mile tour of the northeastern areas of his diocese. The venerable Bishop White was humiliated and his later years made heavy by these unfortunate evidences of dangerous division. Fortunately he did not live to see the resignation and suspension of Onderdonk less than two decades later when he confessed to the guilt of intemperance.

After long and careful reflection about all these disturbances, White finally expressed his concern for the stability of the church and his accompanying proposals in a charge to his diocese at its forty-seventh annual convention in Philadelphia in 1831, where he spoke on "Sustaining the Unity of the Church." He discussed the burning issues relating to episcopacy itself; the need for assistant or suffragan bishops now properly provided by a canon adopted by the General Convention in 1829; the possibility of a bishop's resignation of his jurisdiction, prompted no doubt by Bishop Chase's resignation and his own memory of the Provoost case, and then emphatically opposed the consecration of a bishop by one bishop alone. Having disposed of these obviously necessary discussions, the aged bishop expressed the real burden on his heart; amid the party tensions of the recent years, he had become increasingly conscious of the dearly bought heritage of the church, for the preservation of which he now entered his moving case. He pleaded for flexibility in all matters of administration lest "extreme tenaciousness and reluctance to moderate alteration will give vigour to the opposite extreme of ill-digested projects of reform without measure and without end." Remembering how he had seen the Quakers wait patiently until "the sense of the meeting" would determine their action, White suggested that because of the inequality of representation in the General Convention that body should not carry any very important act of legislation by a small majority, especially if a considerable minority thought it infringed materially on their faith or on the worship of the church. Always disturbed by signs of strife and disunity, White concluded his charge with a plea for the preservation of the union so dearly bought and so successfully preserved and cherished for over forty years.[5]

Three years later the octogenarian gave his last charge to his diocese in a still more reflective and reminiscent mood when he and the diocese celebrated their fiftieth anniversaries at the convention in 1834. His address on "The Past and the Future" was based on events connected with the organization of the Protestant Episcopal Church and the lessons they inculcate. He spoke of the period after the Revolution when the authority of the Bishop of London was withdrawn and

> . . . every congregation was independent of all exterior control, either in England or America. There remained, however, the principles inherited by them from the mother church, in doctrine, worship, and in ecclesiastical

constitution. These were the materials giving reason to the hope that there might be raised from them a real communion resembling that from which we are descended, as nearly as local circumstances should permit.[6]

Although the bishop was to have about two more years, never again did he rise to such a height or speak in such large and clear perspective about the church he loved and to which he had given his life. He pointed out her continuity of Christian history and predicted for her a unique place in the continuing church in America that he had promoted from her very beginning.

Beyond the church Bishop White had also wielded a tremendous influence. In Philadelphia he was considered second only to Benjamin Franklin as a leader in the community, where he served as a member of no less than seventeen community organizations, frequently as president and often as founder. For forty-nine years he gave his attention to much needed prison reforms. He was for many years the chaplain of the Congress, where he knew its leaders, many of whom were his parishioners, and where he was able to exert a quiet, but nevertheless significant, influence for good.

In 1820 he had published his *Memoirs of the Protestant Episcopal Church,* one of the best primary sources for this period, and three years earlier completed his largest and most significant scholarly work, the two volume *Comparative Views of the Controversy between the Calvinists and Arminians,* based largely upon a careful study of patristic sources; it was probably the best piece of scholarly work done in the first century of the church's history. Many other works appeared in pamphlet form, and the body of his manuscripts, together with his annotated copy of the English Prayer Book used for a decade before 1786, remain in Christ Church where his body lies buried beneath the chancel. White had helped to consecrate Bishop Claggett and the next twenty-six bishops; he had laid hands on his disciple and friend Jackson Kemper, the first missionary bishop of the church, in his last act of consecration. With Bishop White's death came the end of an era; he had led the church to the firm establishment of its foundation, and it was to be the intrepid Jackson Kemper and many others who would lead the church to future development and wide missionary expansion.

The Episcopal Church was slow to marshal its full strength in support of a missionary program commensurate with its size and its resources. The early decades of the nineteenth century were required to recoup many of the losses suffered during and because of the wars with Great Britain, but this was by no means the sole reason. Before Hobart, most of the bishops of the church were men of moderate abilities as administrators and often were encumbered by parish as well as diocesan duties; of necessity they had to move slowly and carefully to establish in good favor the episcopal office that had been so long opposed by American religious leaders and even some Episcopalians. The Episcopal Church had patterned its canonical structure after the national constitution, making the General Convention an assembly of sovereign dioceses separated by state boundaries. The phrase "the Church in the State of

————," a designation long used instead of diocese, described a regional sovereignty that lived on longer in the church than in the national government; but despite such loyalties, Episcopalians soon developed a strong sense of cohesiveness. Ironically, the exaggerated assertion of states' rights would divide the nation over slavery, while the impregnable solidarity of its federal unity would preserve the Episcopal Church from schism during that crisis.

From the beginning many leaders were sensitive to its missionary obligations but seemed unable to stimulate an adequate enthusiasm, so that the Episcopal Church responded slowly to the missionary opportunities on the frontier. The General Convention of 1792 appointed a joint committee of the two Houses to plan for and support frontier missionaries, but three years later this responsibility was relegated to the state conventions where it was received with varying degrees of indifference. In the pastoral letter in 1808 Bishop White and Bishop Claggett once again reminded the church of this obligation "due to our western brethren," but little was done beyond advising the clergy in the scattered western areas to organize and accede to the general constitution of the church so that bishops might be elected for their regions. When the General Convention convened in 1814, John D. Clifford presented a certificate authorizing him to represent the church in the State of Kentucky, but because that organization was not officially recognized, he was limited to an honorary seat. Fifteen more years passed before Kentucky could meet the constitutional requirements for admission to the convention, and only in 1832 did that state receive its first bishop, Benjamin Bosworth Smith. Such delays in organization were not limited to the frontier areas, for New Jersey, which already had a state organization in 1785, had no bishop until 1815; similar delays brought the first bishops to North Carolina in 1823; to Delaware and Georgia in 1841; and to Maine in 1847.

By contrast with these delays in the better developed eastern areas, the opening of the western dioceses may not seem to have been too long delayed; in fact the delays in the West, which prevented the church from making its full contribution to the expansion of the nation during these years, may have been due to this functional failure at the home base. Before the eastern dioceses were fully organized, Mississippi, where the Episcopal Church had been first established in 1792, elected William Mercer Green its first bishop in 1825; Tennessee, organized in 1828, received the episcopate in 1834; Kentucky, organized in 1829, already had its bishop by 1832; and Michigan, where services had been held before the Revolution, was organized as late as 1832 and obtained its first bishop four years later.

In South Carolina the work of the church was largely concentrated in Charleston, where St. Philip's and St. Michael's were among the strong parishes in the nation. When Theodore Dehon, after a successful pastorate in Newport, Rhode Island, came to St. Michael's in 1809, he quickly won the confidence of the diocese, which had been revived under the leadership of his predecessor, Nathaniel Bowen, who had recently been called to Grace Church in New York. On October 15, 1812, Dehon was consecrated Bishop of South

Carolina and immediately undertook a diversified program that included co-operation in interdenominational programs and plans for a "free church" where the pews would be rented by wealthy parishioners but free for the use of all who wished to worship. In addition to serving his own people faithfully, he found time to supply vacant parishes and to befriend his clergy. On his death five years later he was succeeded by Bowen, who returned to the diocese where he was still widely loved.

The Diocese of South Carolina very early proved its missionary concern when in 1810 it organized the first of many state Societies for the Advancement of Christianity to send missionaries where needed in that state, to aid candidates for the ministry, and to distribute Bibles, Prayer Books, tracts, and other literature. Speaking at its twentieth anniversary celebration, Edward Thomas reported that this Society had supported eighteen missionaries and that five were still active. By this time South Carolina was also supporting the Protestant Episcopal Missionary Society of Charleston, organized in 1819 and composed mostly of young men, and the Protestant Episcopal Female Domestic Missionary Society, organized in 1821. The former supported missionaries in remote parts of the state, and the latter provided public and private Christian instruction for the poorer people of Charleston. Although it might appear that their intensity of interest had bred duplications of effort, there was probably sufficient diversification of function here to justify each of these organizations.[7] After many lean years the Diocese of North Carolina organized a missionary society in 1818 and five years later, under the supervision of Bishop Moore of Virginia, elected John S. Ravenscroft its first bishop.

In New Jersey the church was organized on a state-wide basis as early as 1785 but remained variously under the jurisdiction of Pennsylvania and New York until 1815 when John Croes, of Polish descent and a veteran of the Revolutionary War, was elected bishop. This diocese immediately responded to his effective leadership until 1832 when his successor, George W. Doane, continued a similarly successful administration. Slow to take on strength despite its location in the very midst of strong dioceses, Delaware remained under the jurisdiction of neighboring bishops until 1841 when Alfred Lee, an eminent Biblical scholar, became its first bishop.

In Pennsylvania the Society for the Advancement of Christianity provided the needed stimulus for this strong diocese to undertake its responsibilities in its own western areas. The first published report, which appeared in 1813 and contained the constitution of the society and a list of its members, indicated that its funds were being used to support young men studying for the ministry and to provide necessary books for them. It was also supporting two missionaries: Joseph Pilmore in a missionary congregation near Philadelphia, and Jackson Kemper as Bishop White's traveling agent in the western parts of the state. The report included the bishop's instructions asking Kemper to keep records of his preaching places, all baptisms, visits, and the names of persons desiring confirmation, and their disposition about supporting the church. On his trip lasting three months Kemper went as far west as Pittsburgh and found many places where no less than six or eight missionaries might be used. Kemper reported prophetically,

> I cannot but think that the establishment of our church in the whole western part of the United States will depend in a great measure upon this society. *The Advancement must be gradually from the East.*

Kemper never lost this conviction and soon would become its living embodiment.

From August 15 to December 14, 1814, Kemper made a second trip to western Pennsylvania and even ventured into Ohio. The Episcopalians in these areas immediately responded to these signs of concern and assistance. In Brownsville, Pennsylvania, eight members gave $500, and additions soon brought the amount to $1,200, enough to build a church seating between two and three hundred persons according to the Society's report of 1814. These church people were so anxious to have regular services that they offered a salary of $1,000 for a minister who would serve this church and another in Connellsville. Two years later the reports indicated that the funds had grown so that the church was built of stone at a cost of $3,000 and was adequate to accommodate from four to five hundred persons.

In 1816 the Society for the Advancement of Christianity in Pennsylvania sent Samuel Phinney to the central and western parts of the state; immediately after his ordination to the diaconate on June 9, 1816, Jacob M. Douglass toured western Pennsylvania and inspired the members in Pittsburgh to repair their church building and to call a minister for whose services they also offered the phenomenal salary of $1,000. It required the guidance and leadership of John Henry Hopkins to build their beautiful new church, which Bishop White consecrated in 1826 on his only visit to this city. He also confirmed 135 persons, and two years later the rector had prepared many more candidates for this rite. On this tour Bishop White, then seventy-eight years of age, traveled 830 miles and confirmed a total of 503 persons.

Douglass reported that he had found that the Episcopalians in Somerset had combined their resources and efforts with those of the Lutherans and had jointly built a frame church with galleries and called it St. Peter's Church.[8] This is the first such "union church" established by Episcopalians. Similar union churches ranging from simple log buildings in the colonial era to the later large edifices of stone or brick had been built in eastern Pennsylvania by the Lutheran and Reformed churches. The custom in these union buildings was to have each clergyman conduct services on alternate Sundays, and occasionally they held services each Sunday at different hours.

William A. Muhlenberg visited Huntington, Pennsylvania, as a missionary for the Society for the Advancement of Christianity from August 15 to September 15 and reported that a neat brick church was being erected as a union church to be used jointly by Episcopalians and Lutherans. In his enthusiastic account of the outlook for the church in that town, he predicted that a resident minister could soon have one-third of the town in his parish. He regretted that for lack of a rector many Episcopalians had become Methodists.

The leaders of this movement were conscious of similar work that denominations were carrying on. In his address to the meeting of the Society in 1828, Kemper congratulated it on its achievements but added "our liberality has been exceedingly circumscribed." He went on to commend the Presbyterians for launching a campaign for $40,000 for missions in New Jersey and the American Board of Foreign Missions for its successful campaign to raise $108,000.[9] Since the Society was limited to support the work in Pennsylvania, the diocese, now roused to its missionary responsibility, in 1816 organized the Episcopal Missionary Society of Philadelphia to carry on missions beyond the state. The Episcopal Female Tract Society was also organized in 1816, and some of its tracts were bound and distributed for use on steamboats. The Common Prayer Book Society of Pennsylvania, begun about 1818, published its own stereotype edition of the Prayer Book.

The General Convention of 1814 crystallized the missionary program of the Episcopal Church by commending the Societies for the Advancement of Christianity to all the dioceses and, as one after another adopted this plan, the missionary interest continued to grow throughout the church. Six years later the Domestic and Foreign Missionary Society established by the General Convention drew most of these efforts into one national organization.

Although there were many contributing factors and other interested persons, the formation of this missionary society for the entire church in 1820 was due to Bishop Griswold more than to any other person. As early as 1814 he had delivered a charge to his Eastern Diocese on "The Missionary Duty of the Church" and followed that with a pastoral letter on the subject. During the next year some of the leading members of the church received a circular letter from Josiah Pratt, secretary of the English Church Missionary Society, suggesting the cooperation of the American and English churches in the work of missions. In his reply, Bishop Griswold included his charge and pastoral letter, from which the London *Missionary Register* printed excerpts in 1816. In subsequent correspondence Pratt suggested that the church in America should organize its own missionary society and offered a gift of £200 sterling from the English society if this were done; this accounts for the gift of about $1,000 to the Domestic and Foreign Missionary Society of the Protestant Episcopal Church newly organized by the General Convention in 1820. Membership in this Society was voluntary, and one could choose to become an annual member at $3.00, a life member at $30, or a patron at $50. Although funds for both foreign and domestic missions were available in fairly equal amounts, the foreign efforts were delayed, and the domestic missions received most attention in the early years.

Despite the free use of the words "missions" and "missionary" in these years, the Episcopal Church had not made a sharp distinction between them and the normal and regular work of the church; perhaps it does not deserve credit for anticipating the present widely held position that "missions" is simply the church properly at work performing its full function. It would also be unjust to these early nineteenth-century workers on the frontier if by the designation "missionary" we meant that they were being supported by the church at large, for most of them were living meagerly on the support of their parishes, and many of them were using their own resources. The Domestic and Foreign Missionary Society was slow to formulate a policy, and when it did, it assumed some local support for its missionaries but tried to bring the total salary for a regularly appointed missionary to $500 a year by its supplementary support. Many received less, and others were entirely locally, although modestly, supported.

Even regularly appointed missionaries at times waited long for their salaries; when Richard Cadle, after four and a half years of service, in 1829 left Detroit, where his parish had agreed to pay him $125 a year, he lacked $200, or almost one-third of his salary for that period. Daniel Nash, a pioneer of the pre-Hobartian era, served in western New York for many years, subsisting entirely on the small contributions of the scattered people he served. Others who ventured in the frontier service on their own initiative included Palmer Dyer, who went to Illinois where there was only one other minister of the church in that entire state, and Ezekiel G. Gear, who went to Ohio, Illinois, Wisconsin, and later became the first missionary for the church in Minnesota. Henry Caswall, who came from England in 1828, served in Ohio, Indiana, and in Lexington, Kentucky, where he taught in an early theological seminary founded by Bishop Smith.

The church, faced with a shortage of both men and resources, was able to give more attention to the areas just behind the frontier than to the frontier itself. The very nature of Episcopal Church services was better adapted to conditions in the settled areas, even though they may have been ever so primitive, than to the open frontier where the entirely free services seemed more effective. Facing honestly the limitation of resources in men and means, the church decided to limit its scope rather than lower its standards for its ministry and service.

A primary example of the pioneer missionary of this period is the inimitable Philander Chase, destined to become the first Bishop of Ohio and of Illinois. Chase was born into a Congregational family on a New Hampshire farm where he acquired his love for the soil, which would never leave him. After enrolling at Dartmouth College in 1791, Chase discovered the Book of Common Prayer, became completely devoted to the Episcopal Church, and soon became a lay reader. On completing his work at Dartmouth in 1795, Chase was married to Mary Fay and the following year decided to seek ordination. He persuaded Thomas Ellison, rector of St. Peter's Church in Albany, to accept him as a student to read theology while he taught school to support his wife and first son born in 1797. After two years of typically intense application Chase was ordained by Bishop Provoost on May 10, 1798, and immediately assigned as a missionary in central New York. For a year and a half he worked tirelessly, preaching 213 times on his travels of more than four thousand miles.

He baptized 319 infants and fourteen adults and left small groups of communicants that would become the parishes in Auburn, Batavia, Canandaigua, and Utica.

After serving the churches at Poughkeepsie and Fishkill for two years while teaching school to help him support his family, Chase accepted Bishop Moore's invitation in 1805 to undertake the work among Episcopalians in New Orleans. Here he organized the parish that would become Christ Church and sponsored a school for Protestant children including his own two sons. After almost six years in the South, where his wife's tuberculosis had not improved, Chase sought a proper educational opportunity for his children and accepted a call to Christ Church in Hartford, Connecticut. In this community he spent six years, which he later described as the happiest years of his life, while his boys studied in an academy at nearby Cheshire.

Although he had reached the age of forty-two when many would have considered themselves settled for life, Chase was caught up in the enthusiasm for the West that generated a tremendous wave of migration from New England to western New York and to Ohio, which had become the seventeenth state in the Union in 1803. Always a missionary at heart and with nothing to assure him of support except his own enthusiasm and his confidence in the missionary injunction from his Lord, Chase left his family early in 1817 to explore the possibilities for the church in Ohio. In the region now surrounding Salem, he found several families for whom he preached his first sermon on March 16; three months later he purchased a large farm near Worthington, where he promised to be the minister for some Connecticut families as well as for five small congregations in communities including Columbus, Delaware, and Zanesville.

The congregation in Worthington included many families that had emigrated from Hartford County, Connecticut, and services had been conducted there by visiting ministers and lay readers, one of whom was Captain Charles Griswold, a brother of Bishop Griswold. When Chase first arrived here, he found many persons had been fully prepared by Roger Searle, his predecessor, for admission to the church, and soon he had more than forty communicants. Under his leadership, St. John's Parish was well organized, and many adults were prepared for baptism. When he returned later as their bishop, Chase confirmed seventy-nine persons in this parish on his first visit.[10] When he became the principal of the local academy, he brought his family to Worthington, but his wife, long weakened by tuberculosis, died within the year.

Chase had very quickly become well known throughout the state in Masonic circles as well as in the church. Early in August, 1817, he preached before the Right Worshipful Grand Master and the officers and members of the Grand Lodge of Ohio at Chillicothe, and in the last week of December, he preached in Columbus before the Most Excellent Grand Chapter of Ohio, of which he was a member. In this sermon, preached for both occasions, Chase asserted that Masonry bears testimony to the truth of Christianity and that Masons cannot, consistently with their principles, be infidels since Masonry is nothing more than Christianity in type and allegory.[11] In his attitude toward Masonry, as in many other ways, Chase differed from Bishop Hobart of New York. On the occasion when Hobart went to Detroit for the laying of the cornerstone of St. Paul's Church on August 11, 1827, the Freemasons came to march in the procession. The bishop said, "We have come to lay the cornerstone of a Christian church and not a heathen temple." The Masons disappeared and came back later in a more subdued dress.[12]

Early in 1818 Chase and Roger Searle, the only other clergyman in the state, together with nine laymen organized the Diocese of Ohio. Searle had arrived from Connecticut a month before Chase and had organized twelve congregations in six weeks, baptized 178, and admitted 107 to Holy Communion. Among the leading laymen in Ohio were Ezra and Charles Griswold, brothers of Bishop Griswold, and the most prominent clergy were Searle, Chase, and James Doddridge, a priest and physician who had come occasionally from Virginia to conduct the first services in Ohio before 1800. Another leader in the church in Ohio was James Kilbourne; he was a many-sided man in deacon's orders, who had organized St. John's Church in Worthington in 1804, the earliest parish in the state; in his later years, however, he gave only his marginal time to the church. He was at various times an explorer, company manager, merchant, surveyor, mill builder, newspaper publisher, major in the militia, and had served in the state legislature and as a representative of the young state in the United States Congress. Chase had quickly come to prominence by his missionary journeys from Akron to Cincinnati, and it was quite natural that at the next meeting of the convention on June 3 when five clergymen were present he was unanimously elected Bishop of Ohio. The venerable Dr. Doddridge, who might have been elected to this office if the election had come a year earlier, was given only an honorary seat without a vote in this convention because his home was still in Virginia.[13]

After his consecration by Bishop White and three other bishops in Philadelphia on February 11, 1819, Chase returned to Worthington; that summer Sophia Ingraham, a former parishioner in Poughkeepsie, New York, became his second wife and shared with him the rigorous life on the farm as well as his many other activities. That the church remained his major concern is evident from his record of traveling more than twelve hundred miles and preaching more than 180 times during his second year as the Bishop of Ohio. Unable to attend to the needs of his farm and serve the church as well, he accepted the invitation to become president of the new small College of Cincinnati, where another Episcopal clergyman, Thomas A. Osborne, held a professorship, and moved to that city late in 1821. Even though Chase was able to organize a diocesan missionary society in 1821, his new position simply further divided his time, while the needs of the rapidly increasing population of Ohio multiplied. He seemed powerless to help the church make the most of all these opportunities since there was no provision for assistance from the national church.

At the suggestion of his son Philander, who had read an English reporter's favorable appraisal of the work of the church in Ohio reprinted in the *Philadelphia Recorder* in 1823, Chase decided to seek assistance from the church people of England, not only to support his churches, but also to make possible a theological school in Ohio. Before undertaking such a large venture, Chase solicited the judgment of the other bishops but received encouragement from only two of them. Even Bishop White remained unenthusiastic; he considered such a venture unnecessary and feared that it might be humiliating to seek aid from England. Bishop Hobart was violently opposed to the idea, especially since it might deflect funds and perhaps even students from the General Seminary. Hobart had been authorized to solicit funds in England for the General Seminary, and although he was to sail for Europe at about the same time, primarily for rest and recovery of his health, he refused to sail on the same packet with Chase, lest by so doing he might lend tacit approval to Chase's projects.

Despite all the attempts to discourage him, Chase was indomitable, and his sheer charm and patience won the generous support of several of the wealthy English aristocracy. He carried letters of introduction from Henry Clay to Alexander Baring and Lord Gambier, with whom Clay had been associated in negotiating the Treaty of Ghent in 1815. These associations also prepared the way for Chase's solicitations among many other benefactors. George W. Marriott, an English high church clergyman whom Chase had met casually, introduced him to Lord Kenyon, who in turn introduced him in wider circles. By a strange coincidence Lord Kenyon had heard that when Chase left New Orleans in 1808 to accept a call to Hartford, Connecticut, he had freed a slave, named Jack, for whom he had paid $500; this humanitarian act made a deep impression on Lord Kenyon and other English aristocrats.[14] After more than eight months Chase returned with gifts of over $20,000 and soon afterward received an additional $10,000 from the same sources. Bishop Hobart, whose reports to the trustees at General Seminary indicate he gathered less than $1,000, seemed more discomfited than ever and had the temerity to suggest that Chase should divide his receipts with the General Seminary or perhaps merge the institutions.[15]

On his return to Ohio, Chase reported his good success to his convention on November 3, 1824, and described his plan for the future school; before the end of the year—an almost incredible accomplishment—the Ohio legislature had passed an act incorporating "The Theological School of the Protestant Episcopal Church in the Diocese of Ohio." Early in 1826 this charter was amended to permit the granting of academic degrees by the president and professors of Kenyon College, the name by which these schools were popularly known. These expanded facilities were Chase's plan for the proper cultural as well as theological training of his ministers and, while the theological school did not have a separate faculty and building until 1839, his candidates from the beginning were given a balanced education.

More than two years elapsed after the charter was granted to Kenyon College before the school was able to move from Worthington, where Chase had taught the first thirty students in his own home and adjacent temporary quarters. Among those boys under Chase's instruction in that farmhouse seminary sat a son of Henry Clay, his benefactor, and Salmon P. Chase, his nephew, who was about to go on to Dartmouth and later would become the Chief Justice of the United States Supreme Court.[16] The new campus of about eight thousand acres in Knox County became the center of the new community, named Gambier in honor of a generous benefactor, the Admiral Lord Gambier. The college was named Kenyon in honor of another donor, Lord Kenyon; the seminary, Bexley Hall, for Lord Bexley; and the chapel bore the name of Lady Rosse.

For such a large and independent undertaking Chase won the support of his diocesan convention in June, 1826, although many persons felt that it would have been more practical to accept the promised support of several Ohio towns rather than settle the school in the wilderness. Columbus, with about three thousand inhabitants, might have been a good location, and Chillicothe was even larger, with an Episcopal church established there, although it was not as flourishing as the Methodist and Presbyterian churches. The Moravians were well established with two congregations in Gnaden-hütten, and since they were recognized by Episcopalians as in the apostolic succession, their ministers preached in Episcopal pulpits, occasionally exchanged with Episcopal rectors, and were generally friendly to the church.[17] Chase was adamant on the point, however, because he wanted his young men free from the temptations with which the larger community life threatened them, a point that he argued often but with little convincing effect.

When the school with sixty-five students and the faculty moved to Gambier in June, 1828, it very quickly became clear that Bishop Chase, who had almost singlehandedly brought the institution to that point, intended to retain his full control over it. But unfortunately for him and for the church the bishop was better qualified to build than to govern. The church has known few men of his energy and capacity for work, and without his leadership in Ohio this diocese, and certainly these schools, would have come much later. Leading evangelicals, such as Gregory T. Bedell and Benjamin Allen of Philadelphia and James Milnor of New York, supported Chase in his efforts to secure funds and in the distribution of his pamphlet, *A Plea for the West*, in which he stressed the necessity of bringing to the frontier cultural opportunities similar to those in the East. Both Chase's title and idea were freely borrowed by Lyman Beecher in his later popular publication on this same theme. Since Chase had the full responsibility for the institution and its support, much of which he had to gather in continuous solicitation throughout the church, it was quite natural that his would be the dominant role and that some of his associates would count him domineering. By nature and circumstance Chase was ill-equipped for diplomacy, and even his best friends conceded that he was willful, very sensitive to any criticism, and intolerant of opposition. Yet anyone who was so constructively engaged was naturally open to criticism. One member of his faculty, who wished to be not only his chaplain but also the bishop's assistant, proved to be particularly meddlesome, charging that funds given for one purpose were used for another and that the walls of some of the buildings were too thick. In reply Chase published his "Defence of Kenyon College,"[18] in which he carefully itemized all his expenditures for the college and its equipment. Including the cost of the land, the entire Kenyon enterprise had cost almost $38,000. Chase had personally been very generous to the college; in addition to many unlisted personal expenditures, he had given the college his library, a gift of $1,000, and another sum of $1,000 to build a house for his family, which would become the property of the school two years after his death.

Chase consistently refused to delegate authority and on his many absences left the administration of the college to Mrs. Chase, which bred distrust among his faculty. Many elements conspired to bring about the ultimate crisis in 1831; his paternalistic concern as well as his determination to keep control of the standards of life of his students and even of his faculty roused the ire especially of the latter, who wished to live their own lives. Chase had been particularly strenuous in his discipline of a member of his faculty and students who violated the rules against the use of "ardent spirits." On one occasion when the bishop unexpectedly came on students and faculty who had been drinking, one intoxicated opponent of his policies violently assailed him.[19]

But the school had really outgrown the beneficent episcopal paternalism, and both the faculty and almost two hundred students accused the bishop before the diocesan convention of using "absolute and unlimited" power. When this body failed to support him unconditionally and recommended instead that new rules of government be drafted by a new board of trustees and then asked the bishop not to invoke his episcopal powers in the administration of the school, Chase called their action "evasive, ignorant, malignant and hypocritical" and promptly resigned both the presidency of the college and the Ohio bishopric, which he insisted were inseparably connected. Chase's resignation on September 14, 1830, ended a long period of frustration for him, the leaders of the convention, and the college faculty, but the bishop was persuaded to stay on until a successor could be chosen at the next diocesan convention. The bishop agreed when he was assured that William Sparrow, an able and irenic theologian on his faculty who would later become the well-loved dean at the Virginia Theological Seminary, would assist him through this period. Meanwhile, the trustees also paid Chase the $3,371.22 they still owed him for personal funds he had advanced during the building of the college.[20]

Apparently prepared for such an emergency, which may have been not entirely unanticipated, the Ohio Convention at once elected as its new bishop the thirty-two-year-old Charles P. McIlvaine, who had served as chaplain at West Point, rector at St. Ann's Church, Brooklyn, and was destined to serve Ohio for forty years and become a widely recognized intellectual leader among the evangelical churchmen. That Chase had not alone been to blame became evident when Bishop McIlvaine encountered similar difficulties, which fortunately were ultimately resolved in his favor. Since the resignation of a bishop was still a moot point, the General Convention the following year censured Chase for "dereliction" and gave its consent for the consecration of McIlvaine but adopted a canon requiring the consent of two-thirds of the diocese and of the General Convention for future episcopal resignations.

Broken in spirit temporarily and very unhappy in Ohio, Chase purchased one thousand acres of land in Michigan, where he applied his avocational gifts as a farmer so diligently that in a few years he had established a very successful enterprise with his own lumber mill and more than one hundred cattle. At fifty-six Chase might have been happy to spend the rest of his days in these peaceful agricultural pursuits in his "Valley of Peace," as he called his new home near Gilead, had he not been challenged to consider the resumption of episcopal duties in the church.

The Diocese of Illinois, organized by three ministers and several laymen at its first annual convention on March 9, 1835, elected Chase its bishop without any promise of support apart from thirty-nine communicants in that vast area. Although now almost sixty years of age, Chase accepted and, after a survey of several months, set out for England where he hoped to find more support for his new diocese, and the college it needed, than was available to him anywhere in America. His judgment was vindicated, for by May, 1836, he returned with pledges of about ten thousand dollars. But the Illinois frontier was conquered more slowly and less completely, and Chase himself was soon left without adequate resources. The Domestic and Foreign Missionary Society in 1836 made a grant to the diocese and gave the bishop a salary that year; but since Chase had not been appointed by the Society and was not under its jurisdiction, this allowance was ruled unconstitutional and was not repeated. From his diocese Chase received little financial assistance; even after eight years of service, in 1843 he received only $173 from this source. But there were fruits of his labors more pleasing to the bishop. By 1845 he had twenty-five ministers in twenty-eight parishes with over five hundred members, and three years later his membership had doubled.[21]

While the cornerstone for the first building of Jubilee College was laid in 1839 at Robin's Nest, Peoria County, Illinois, instruction was not begun until 1845.[22] Meanwhile, Chase traveled to the eastern areas of the church soliciting scholarships of $100 each, which were readily subscribed by leading laymen, such as William Appleton and Amos Lawrence in Massachusetts. So heartened by the response was Chase that he wrote from Norwich, Connecticut, asking the Illinois legislature for a charter, which was ready for him on his arrival at Peoria. He encountered some delay in arranging with the State Council of Revision to preserve full church control of the college, but this provision was firmly written in the charter.[23] Although the college finally received its charter in 1847, instruction had begun two years earlier.

Once again Chase had gone to the wilderness and purchased three thousand acres for his new college campus; yet even he was never able to undergird it adequately for the difficult years during and after the Civil War when it closed its doors. Much of the original campus was later acquired by the State of Illinois and has been converted into a State Park.

In Illinois, especially in his later years, Chase seemed to be in less public favor than in his earlier pioneering days. His attempts to be discreet on the slavery question brought him into wordy wars with the abolitionists, and he was repeatedly attacked for hedging on this major issue.[24] To his very end Chase remained obsessed with his responsibility for every detail. One doctor on a vacation to the West made a special trip by coach to see the bishop and his college near Peoria. He arrived on the stage which also carried the mail and reported that he had to wait for some time before Chase would admit him, for the bishop was also the postmaster and had to sort the mail.

Only in his later years did Chase receive any help in his large task, when Henry J. Whitehouse of New York was elected his assistant bishop, and he was well advanced in his seventy-seventh year when he died on September 20, 1852. Bishop Philander Chase was mourned chiefly by the very few who had been able to break through his social reticence and constant employment, but he was highly respected by thousands of clergy and laity in and beyond the church. They had known him as an indefatigable pioneer missionary who had carried the church to the frontier and there made it an effective instrument of the gospel through evangelism and education.

While the missions on the domestic frontier were often begun on individual initiative, the large undertaking of foreign missions required the sponsorship of the Missionary Society. Although such effort was delayed beyond the end of this period, beginnings had been made in establishing short-lived missions in Crete, Greece, and Persia, and later in Africa and China where the future was to prove even more fruitful. The mission in Crete was discontinued soon after its beginning. When Greece wrested its independence from Turkey in 1827, with the assistance of the Allied Powers, John J. Robertson of Maryland offered his services to the Society as a missionary to that country. The Greeks had long had the sympathy of the American people, and, after an inspection trip in 1829, Robertson soon was able to raise funds primarily to make the benefits of education available to the Greek people long deprived of all cultural opportunities. With the support of the Society and instructions for their work, Robertson and his family, the Rev. and Mrs. J. H. Hill, and Solomon Bingham, a printer, sailed from Boston on October 2, 1830. On their arrival they found Greece without schools and with most of its churches in ruins. By 1831 Mrs. Hill had opened a school for girls in Athens, soon to be followed by a similar one for boys; by 1835 a kindergarten and a training school for teachers had been added, and six hundred had been enrolled in these church schools. Meanwhile, by 1833 Robertson and Bingham had established the printing plant at Syra, and for about five years it became the active publishing center from which both religious and secular literature were widely distributed. When the Board reassigned Robertson to Constantinople, the press was discontinued. Although the enrollment in the schools had reached one thousand by 1843, the Board of Missions, with other missionary opportunities at hand,

and under some criticism for operating so large a cultural venture, officially abandoned this mission but continued an annual subsidy of $2,000 to the Hill schools until 1899. Hill, who was the first of a long line of foreign missionaries to go out from the Virginia Theological Seminary, resigned after almost thirty-nine years in the service of the Greek Mission and died in 1882 in his ninety-first year.

A similar attempt was made to establish a mission in the predominantly Mohammedan country of Persia when Horatio Southgate, a twenty-three-year-old priest who very much wished to work among the Moslems, was appointed by the Board in 1835. By 1837 he had explored this field, won much good will, and was able to work effectively in cooperation with other Christian groups, especially the Orthodox leaders, under whose direction most of the Christian work in Persia was carried on. In Constantinople, on his return toward America, he met Robertson, and together they worked among the Moslems there. After his enthusiastic report the General Convention in 1844 consecrated Southgate Bishop of the "Dominions and Dependencies of the Sultan of Turkey." Both in Turkey and Persia the Orthodox leaders felt threatened by a new episcopal authority, and the previous cooperative spirit was strained. Little had been accomplished in this difficult and dangerous invasion of Moslem areas, and when Southgate also came to disagreements with the managers of the Missionary Society, he resigned in 1850 and returned to Boston, where he became the successful rector of the Church of the Advent.

While the Domestic and Foreign Missionary Society and numerous individual heroic missionary pioneers and the several diocesan societies had successfully begun the missionary work of the church in both the domestic and foreign fields, no one was completely satisfied that the church had done her best. The truly great missionary advance lay just ahead and awaited the new realization that the Christian mission is the church at work and that in it each Christian must have a share.

XIV

THE GREAT
MISSIONARY OUTREACH

The Protestant Episcopal Church was now ready to undertake its full missionary responsibility, but these were difficult years for all the churches on the frontier. A once united national spirit slowly gave way to the rise of sectionalism through the increasing tensions over slavery and the differences between the eastern and western ways of life. Even some of the missionary appeals to the churches stressed the barbarism of the West and the threat such a neighboring lack of culture posed for the established East. Deprecating words were spoken about the moral standards tolerated on the frontier, and even the frontier preachers, who earned their livings by farming and had little opportunity for self-improvement, were invidiously compared with the better-trained missionaries being sent out by the home mission boards in the East.

As a result of such strong sectionalism the Baptist Church was divided, and by 1846 there were no less than sixty-eight thousand Anti-mission Baptists. Alexander Campbell, the founder of the Disciples of Christ, won many followers by similar sectional appeals. In the Lutheran Church an Americanizing party supported a liberal interpretation of the Augsburg Confession, and in the Presbyterian Church a similar liberal tendency, including a strong antislavery spirit, led to the disruption of the church when the General Assembly in 1837 expelled four synods with more than five hundred churches and over one hundred thousand members. The division of almost every major denomination in the country over the slavery issue and the rapid rise of many new sects in the frontier areas, where few religious traditions and restraints were observed, were about to lead this country into a fertile period of proliferation of religious groups.

From these influences the Episcopal Church could hardly escape; although slavery could not permanently divide the church and the anti-missionary spirit never became widely prevalent, the rise of strong allegiances to the evangelical and high church parties did disturb the harmony in the church and shear it of some of its power, and theological differences would eventually bring about a schism in the church. Such signs of weakness were doubly unfortunate in this period of rapid expansion, which brought millions of immigrants from northern Europe and multiplied the gross national product many times. Among the immigrants came many Lutherans, who long maintained their national customs and language in their services, and about four million Roman Catholics in one generation before the Civil War. During this same period the Episcopal Church would multiply its communicant strength fivefold, increasing from about thirty-one thousand to one hundred and fifty thousand, but, because of the large immigration and increase in population, it represented only a doubling of proportional strength from one in 416 of the population in 1830 to one in 209 by 1860. Meanwhile, the clergy increased fourfold from 592 to 2,450 in 1865.

After the organization of the Domestic and Foreign Missionary Society in 1820, Amos G. Baldwin, the agent for the Society, explored the possibilities for work in the West and reported that William Wall was serving several parishes in Kentucky in an area that promised to be a fertile missionary field. On May 20, 1824, the Society appointed its first domestic missionaries, sending Melish I. Motte to St. Augustine, Florida, and Henry H. Pfeiffer to Indiana; these first ventures proved to be only temporary.

More successful was Thomas Horrell, who spent several years in Missouri representing the church in the rapidly growing city of St. Louis, which already had more than five thousand inhabitants, where the church remained permanently established. Among those first missionaries, appointed in 1824, were also Richard F. Cadle, assigned to Detroit, and Norman Nash, sent to Green Bay, Wisconsin. Cadle, an alumnus of Columbia College, had been ordained in 1817 and arrived in Detroit on July 12, 1824. In that expanding trading center of two thousand inhabitants he found a Roman Catholic, a Methodist, and a Presbyterian church but only three or four communicants among the attendants at his services. His efforts led to the formation of a Sunday School, a Bible class, and a parish of which he became rector on March 22, 1825; his salary was $125, with some additional assistance from the Missionary Society. During the summer of 1827, Cadle made a missionary trip via the Great Lakes to Green Bay, Wisconsin, and also founded St. Andrew's Parish in Ann Arbor, and St. John's in Troy, Michigan. In Detroit his success was crowned by the erection of St. Paul's Church, a sixty- by forty-foot brick edifice with an eighteen-foot square tower rising to a height of twenty-four feet; its completed cost was $4,500, at a time when the entire scaffolding for the project cost $8.50 and the plastering contract was twenty-eight cents a square yard. The building was consecrated on August 24, 1828, by Bishop Hobart while on his missionary tour to Green Bay. After nearly four and a half years in Detroit, Cadle was inadequately supported, and although he did not complain, he accepted with relief the appointment to succeed Nash at Green Bay early in 1829.

Nash had once worked effectively among the Oneida Indians in New York but had never been successful at Green Bay, which was then a part of Michigan Territory. When the Indians were moved to this community, he had been requested to establish a school on the mission but soon became discouraged by the Society's disapproval of his extravagant plans and the slow arrival of promised government assistance. Nash had an artistic temperament, gave much time to painting, and was hardly the sturdy frontier type needed in this area. Cadle, being a good business manager, promptly cleared all titles on his arrival and went on with building the school, but was frustrated by the slow arrival of government aid. Because of his disappointment and possibly because of an unfortunate reaction to his discipline of an Indian boy on Christmas Eve, 1833, he resigned on February 5, 1834. He later went on to be the Society's first missionary at Prairie du Chien and, in 1838, became post chaplain at Fort Crawford. In his later years Cadle moved back to the East and, after serving parishes in New York and Vermont, ended his ministry in the service of churches in Sussex County, Delaware, where he died on October 26, 1857.[1]

Also associated with the Green Bay Mission during these years was the enigmatic Eleazer Williams, adopted son of an English surgeon, Thomas Williams, and whose mother was part Indian. Trained by the Episcopal Church for missionary work among the Indians, he was ordained by Bishop Hobart in 1826; he had only slight success among the Indians of New York, perhaps because he sought acceptance as the head of the Iroquois even though he was not a full-blooded Indian. While working among the Mohawks, he prepared a translation of parts of the Prayer Book for Bishop Hobart. When the Indians from New York moved to Wisconsin in 1821, he accompanied them to Green Bay where he married and lived until 1850; afterward he returned to New York. His undoing may have been due to his claim to the throne of France because of his resemblance to the lost Dauphin who would have been exactly his age. When the Prince de Joinville was in America, Williams met him at Mackinac where they conferred at length. So impressed were many of the French Royalists that years later on the death of Williams' grandchild the French government asked for and obtained affidavits.[2]

By the summer of 1832 Michigan had at least five organized congregations beyond Detroit, and preparations were made at a convention in September that year which led to their admission in union with the General Convention, which met the following month. For the time being this work was supervised by Bishop McIlvaine of Ohio, but realizing the need for their own bishop, the annual convention of 1835 proceeded to an election that brought Samuel A. McCoskry from St. Paul's Church, Philadelphia, to be the first Bishop of Michigan; his consecration fell on July 7, 1836, just about three weeks after this state was reduced to its present size by an Act of Congress.

During these years, while the church sought to meet its missionary responsibility, the church leaders became increasingly aware of the inadequate supply of men for the ministry. The Church Scholarship Society, by order of its directors, issued a sixteen-page church-wide "Appeal," which appeared in Hartford in 1831, explaining its purpose "to assist all meritorious young men designing to enter the ministry of the Protestant Episcopal Church." From 1817 to 1824 only 150 candidates volunteered for the ministry, and the number remained the same between the years 1824 and 1831; at this time, when the church needed hundreds of young men, there had been less than a five percent increase in candidates. The prospectus declared that the commendable purposes of the Society were "to render just so much assistance as will serve to prevent discouragement at the same time that it leaves the motives to personal exertion in full exercise." The trustees at Washington (Trinity) College offered half tuition for ministerial candidates, and other institutions soon announced similar inducements.[3]

At about the same time Stephen H. Tyng, at the request of the Episcopal Education Society of Pennsylvania, preached a sermon in St. Paul's Church in Philadelphia on the importance of uniting manual labor with intellectual attainments in a preparation for the ministry. He suggested profitable labor instead of mere exercise as a proper companion for the education of ministerial candidates, not only for its own values, but also because the church lacked funds. He recorded that while more men were coming to the three seminaries in New York, Virginia, and Ohio it was only a beginning, and twice as many were needed as were being graduated each year. Pennsylvania did not yet have a seminary, but the Episcopal Education Society had purchased eighty acres on the Delaware River three miles north of Wilmington, Delaware; there it planned to give twenty-five students the opportunity to do manual work four hours a day and spend six or more hours regularly in study. Although the plan was based on the experience of four theological seminaries of other churches, it never proved a feasible plan in the Protestant Episcopal Church.

Although the hour had not yet arrived for the appointment of missionary bishops, the church was becoming conscious of the importance of having bishops on the frontier. In 1828 the Missionary Society sponsored Bishop Hobart's visit to the Indian Mission at Green Bay, Wisconsin, as well as the visits of Bishop Thomas Brownell to the South and Southwest in 1829 and subsequently until 1837. Bishop Brownell's assignment from the Society was

> to visit that portion of our country which lies west and south of the Allegheny Mountains, to perform Episcopal services wherever they may be desired; to examine into the condition of the missions established by the Board; and to take a general survey of the country for the purpose of designating such missionary stations as may hereafter be usefully established.

The bishop spent four months of the winter of 1829–1830 in traveling six thousand miles, consecrating churches, ordaining clergy, organizing dioceses, and holding many confirmations. He subsequently reported that in these areas there were four million people and only twenty Episcopal congregations and twenty-three Episcopal clergymen but that he was hopeful because a very large portion of the wealthy and intelligent planters appeared disposed to support the church.[4]

Mississippi had been a part of the United States for twenty-eight years and a state—although only about half its present size—for only nine years when the four Episcopal congregations and five clergymen were received into union with the General Convention in November, 1826, at Philadelphia. Jackson was little more than an Indian trading post, and the six counties around Natchez, where the four churches and their 150 communicants were located in 1830, reported a population of 61,960, half of whom were Negroes. Since no bishop had previously visited the state, Bishop Brownell conducted the first confirmations in December, 1829. That the leaders in this state were alert to their opportunities is shown by the report of the church's work among the Negroes, which appears in the *Journal* of the second convention held in Natchez in May, 1827. By the next convention they had organized a Society for the Advancement of Christianity and a branch of the Protestant Episcopal Sunday School Union newly formed at the General Convention in 1826. A. A. Miller, the rector of Trinity Church, Natchez, reported that in his Sunday School "not only the children of the members of the church may be brought up in the nurture and admonition of the Lord; but a plan has been devised that colored children may also be rightly instructed in the knowledge of religion" and that he was greatly assisted in this work by the women of his parish.[5]

While the Domestic Committee of the Missionary Society did provide a special fund for work among the Negroes, it was through the efforts of the bishops and their clergy and some diocesan organizations that the most effective program of church work was offered. Concern is always personal, and that the church had genuine concern for its Negro members was demonstrated at a confirmation service conducted by Bishop Charles T. Quintard in Tennessee. The bishop found that a colored man who had been properly prepared did not present himself with the others for the rite. After confirming him alone, the bishop apologized immediately to the congregation for repeating the rite and to the consternation of some went on to say, "This person should have come forward with the other candidates, for, in the bestowal of her spiritual blessings, our mother, the church, hath never had a child to honor before the rest."[6] Where planters cooperated with the local clergy the church worked very successfully in ministering to the Negroes through the sensitive prewar years, and while many preferred the less liturgical churches, there were nevertheless thousands adhering happily to the Protestant Episcopal Church. In New York, Philadelphia, and other large cities separate Negro congregations were organized, and some free Negroes were admitted to the priesthood; between 1866 and 1880, however, only twenty-seven colored men were ordained and only seventeen of these were in the South. In 1884 the trustees of the Virginia Theological Seminary chartered the Bishop Payne Divinity School at Petersburg, Virginia, primarily to train Negroes for the ministry of the church. Instruction was begun in 1887, and after a generation of service, this separate school was discontinued, and since that time the theological schools of the church have never been without Negroes in their student bodies.

The success of the multistate Eastern Diocese led to the adoption of a plan in 1834 to incorporate Alabama, Mississippi, and Louisiana into the Southwestern Diocese, but the following year the church adopted a new policy of electing missionary bishops that superseded this questionable venture in so large an area. In 1844 Francis L. Hawks, until recently of St. Thomas' Church in New York City and now a resident of Mississippi, declined the election as bishop of that state largely because the failure of his boys' school in New

York had involved him in financial embarrassment. Meanwhile, Bishop James Hervey Otey of Tennessee, who had paid an earlier visit to the state with Bishop Brownell in 1835, and Bishop Leonidas Polk gave such time as they had available to guiding the affairs of the church in Mississippi until William Mercer Green was consecrated as the first bishop of this diocese in 1850. The Bishops of Tennessee and Alabama were elected and supported independently by their dioceses; although these men were not missionary bishops in the sense that they were supported by the church-at-large, they were nevertheless among the best examples of the missionary spirit and zeal.

The area that had once been a part of "The Territory Southwest of Ohio" was developed extensively by pioneer farmers in the early years of the nine-teenth century, but the urban centers developed much more slowly. Memphis was still only a prosperous village in 1832 with a population that grew to eighteen hundred by 1840 and to seven thousand by 1850. The phenomenal successes of the revivalists of the Second Great Awakening among these people resulted in their wide distribution among many Protestant denominations and sects. As late as 1890 when Tennessee had a population of one and three-quarter million people, the religious bodies were still very small; there were eighteen thousand Roman Catholics and three thousand Lutherans, but none of the other religious groups including Congregationalists, Dunkers, and Jews had as many as two thousand members.

It was in this region that James Otey devoted his life in service to the church. He stood in the line of two distinguished families: his father was descended from Sir John Pettus, a member of Parliament and one of the founders of the Virginia colony, while his mother was of the family of Tobias Matthews, who at the turn to the seventeenth century was Bishop of Durham and later Archbishop of York. After graduation from the University of North Carolina, Otey taught school until, by careful examination of the Prayer Book he used for the daily opening exercises, he was led to give his life to the church and was ordained by Bishop Ravenscroft in 1825. Physically adapted to the frontier, six feet four inches tall and well built, he soon achieved good success in the regions of Franklin and Nashville. For about eight years he taught school and served as minister of a small church in Franklin. At first there was only one other Episcopal minister in the state, but by 1829 the number increased so that under the guidance of Bishop Ravenscroft they organized the Diocese of Tennessee in 1829. On June 27, 1833, when Otey was almost thirty-four years of age, he was chosen the first Bishop of Tennes-see and the following January 14 was consecrated in Christ Church, Phila-delphia, as the thirtieth bishop in the American line.

Although he had but five priests and three deacons and his communicants numbered only 117, Otey laid his foundations well. While he averaged fifty confirmations annually during his first fifteen years, between 1850 and 1860 this average had risen to 115. In 1844 he had fifteen clergy and about four hundred communicants, but a decade later these figures had risen to seventeen and eight hundred respectively; by 1860 he had twenty-seven clergy and fifteen hundred communicants. In addition to working in his own diocese, Otey served for ten years as the provisional Bishop of Mississippi and Florida and from 1842 to 1844 as Missionary Bishop of Arkansas, Louisiana, and the Indian Territory, where he covered over four thousand miles, traveling usually on horseback. Although a frontiersman, Otey was a conservative who had strongly supported the Union and deplored the war. Yet when the Secession came, he lent his strength to the Confederate cause until the end. Otey died during the war on April 23, 1863, and no conventions were held until September 6, 1865, when Charles T. Quintard was elected bishop and the first steps were taken to divide the large diocese.

In 1842 Otey had preached three significant sermons; in the first one on "The Unity of the Church," which was probably directed toward the followers of Alexander Campbell, he discussed the Apostles' Creed as a concise summary of scriptural truth. The second was "On the Ministry," which he described as deriving proper authority through ordination and the sacraments as witness to the continuity of orders. In the final sermon on "The Apostolic Succession," he ascribed to the three orders of the ministry the authority to teach, baptize, and exercise discipline in the church. These sermons, which were published in 1843, impressed the various church groups in Tennessee and neighboring states by their clear statement of doctrinal position in a time and place where this was infrequently being done. Although some friends feared that these sermons might delay the growth of the church, Otey saw his communicant strength double in a decade and redouble in the next six years.[7] His doctrinal emphasis was strikingly similar to that of Edward Washburn and others in New England, which would eventually find embodiment in the Lambeth Quadrilateral.

When Alabama was admitted as the twenty-second state of the Union in 1819, few white people lived outside of Montgomery; seven years later Tuscaloosa was designated the capital city. Although Samuel Hart of Charleston, South Carolina, spent about a year there as the first Episcopal missionary in Alabama around 1764, more than sixty years elapsed before the Domestic and Foreign Missionary Society sent Robert Davis to plant the church there; by January 7, 1828, he succeeded in organizing Christ Church Parish in Tuscaloosa. Soon afterward, Davis became one of several commission agents to solicit funds for the Missionary Society.

The visit of Bishop Brownell in January, 1830, when he presided over Alabama's primary convention in Mobile, brought little immediate effect, but by the following year the diocesan organization was functioning with two clergymen, one in Montgomery and one at Tuscaloosa, where the University had just been opened. Although Bishop Brownell returned in 1835 and 1837, the work of the church in this region was delayed, probably because of the national financial crisis by which the South was even more gravely affected than the industrial North. While New York had lost $100,000,000 in business failures, New Orleans alone had lost $27,000,000, and following the panic, unprincipled exploiters preyed on the frontier regions of the South. Among these depressed people there were occasional outbreaks of religious revivals and some transient waves of religious enthusiasm. In 1844 when Alabama had fifteen ministers serving in as many parishes with 450 communicants, the diocese elected Nicholas H. Cobbs of St. Paul's Church, Cincinnati, as its first bishop, and his consecration followed on October 20.

Cobbs was a successful and popular minister in Virginia and had recently been nominated as Bishop of Texas in 1841 and soon afterward as an assistant to Bishop Meade in Virginia. When he moved to Ohio, a free state, he emancipated his slaves, who were, however, so attached to him and his household that they accompanied the family to Cincinnati. The bishop ministered sensitively to the Negroes of his diocese, and one of the few sermons he published dealt with the duty of masters to slaves. For many years he also maintained a friendly relation with other religious groups and even the revivalistic sectarians.

Bishop Cobbs lived modestly on his salary of $1,500, which included his expenses for his extended and frequently dangerous travel. On one such visitation he was delayed two weeks as a result of injuries when the stagecoach in which he was riding overturned. By 1849 his clergy had increased to eighteen; six years later four more were added, and there were twenty-six parishes in the diocese. On his travels Bishop Cobbs inquired for Episcopalians in every community and visited them or sent a clergyman to do so. He kept a list of such scattered families of the church, which by 1860 included 103 communicants. In this same year he happily reported that his clergy now numbered thirty-two and that there were 1,650 white and 214 colored communicants in thirty-eight parishes. The bishop was a good business man; in 1846 he established a fund for disabled clergy and their families, and as a result of astute investments in the Memphis and Charleston Railroad, it grew rapidly to the time of the war.

Although Cobbs always preserved a high appreciation for the historical church, he was not a ritualist and genuinely feared the innovations of Rome that were appearing in some of the northern regions. He said he wanted no novelties introduced into his churches and in 1849 published a tract entitled *An Answer to Some Papal Objections*. One of the truly effective bishops of his era, Cobbs was perhaps most widely known as the embodiment of Christian gentleness. His last public service was the sermon he preached at the laying of the cornerstone of the University of the South at Sewanee, Tennessee, in October, 1860, when appropriately he took as his subject "The Sum of the Gospel is Sympathy." He died the following January 11, 1861, one hour before Alabama seceded from the Union.[8]

The University of the South grew out of the proposals of Bishop Otey of Tennessee and the initiative of Bishop Polk of Louisiana who sought the support of nine southern bishops in 1856. Numerous similar institutions had been founded in the South in recent years: the Methodists had established Randolph Macon and Emory; the Baptists, Rector, Richmond, and Wake Forest Colleges; Alexander Campbell had opened his seminary at Bethany,

West Virginia; the Cumberland Presbyterians, a school at Lebanon, Tennessee; and the Roman Catholics were building schools in many areas. The bishop found similar precedents in his own church, for other Episcopalians had also made similar ventures; in 1837 Bishop Doane had begun a school in New Jersey, and a little later Bishop Littlejohn opened one in Maryland. Furthermore, Polk was convinced that too many southern boys were going north for their education and coming home with dangerous abolition ideas. Since he considered slavery "a singularly humane and civilizing arrangement" and worth perpetuating, he believed the time had come for the South to have its own school.[9] Polk's idea was so well timed and the response so generous that within a few years about $500,000 was available to purchase ten thousand acres at Sewanee and to begin the building program. The war, which cost the church the life of Bishop Polk, who served as a Confederate general and was the strongest supporter of the University, also swept away all these funds. The lands remained, however, and soon after the close of the war the planning for the schools at Sewanee was resumed.

For the first time in 1835 the Protestant Episcopal Church realized that it *was* the Missionary Society and began a missionary program that was to become a continuous series of real accomplishments both at home and abroad during the next century and a quarter. To give adequate support to the missions at home, in Europe, and to those recently undertaken in China and Africa, the leaders of the church saw the imperative need for more efficient organization and especially for raising larger sums of money. While many members had been contributing generously to missions in the recent decades, there were no apportionments for missions and no guarantees that specific funds would be available annually for careful budgetary planning. At one point when the missionary treasury seemed insecure, Presiding Bishop Griswold pledged his private credit to make possible the uninterrupted missionary program. With the General Convention about to convene in 1835, the Board of Directors of the Missionary Society at the suggestion of James Milnor appointed a committee to study the problem.

Before this committee could meet, three of its nine members, Bishop Doane, Bishop McIlvaine, and Milnor, happened to be together unofficially when the last asked the bishops what they would think about reporting that the church *is* the Missionary Society and should carry on its work through a board named by the General Convention. Each bishop said that a similar idea had been in his mind; so was born the plan, adopted later that year by the General Convention, which declared "the Society shall be considered as comprehending all persons who are members of this Church." No longer was it necessary to pay a fee to join the Missionary Society, as the custom still prevails in the Church of England. Instead of being relegated to a subsidiary branch of the church, missions was now conceived as the responsibility of the whole church performing its full function. That portion of this task which related specifically to the home and foreign mission fields was to be administered by the General Convention through a Board of Missions consisting of the bishops and thirty members elected by the convention. For almost a century it was this Board, with slight variations in its size, that directed the missionary work of the church until 1919, when the National Council assumed this responsibility. Between the annual sessions of this Board its duties were administered by the Domestic and Foreign Committees, each with a secretary, treasurer, and general agent.

The new organization at once proved its greater efficiency, and more funds became available for the mission fields except during the depression years of the late 1830's. In the three years before 1835 the average income of the Missionary Society was about $26,000, while more than twice this amount was reported by the Board of Missions as the average income for the three years following 1835. This represented an average annual gift of well over one dollar per member, while in a similar triennial period just before the Civil War, when the membership had almost trebled to one hundred and forty thousand in twenty years, the average annual giving for missions had risen to only $136,000. The first attempt at anything like the modern weekly envelope system of financial support for the church was made in New Jersey in 1833 where, at Bishop Doane's suggestion, weekly missionary offerings were appropriately wrapped, received with the offerings, and, after being recorded, were sent on to the Board of Missions. Such systematic giving trebled the missionary gifts in one year. For many years, however, there was no missions quota system, and by the Civil War less than half of the parishes contributed to the Board of Missions.

Of even greater significance for the church was the new canon adopted by the General Convention providing for missionary bishops to serve in areas unorganized by the church at home and abroad. Before 1836 there had indeed been bishops on the mission fields but always as elected by their respective dioceses and not under the control of the Missionary Society. The missionary bishops, supported by and subject to the direction of the Board of Missions, were to be elected by the General Convention or, in the interim of its sessions, might be elected by the House of Bishops upon a request from the Board of Missions and with the approval of a majority of the Standing Committees of the dioceses. These missionary bishops were members of the House of Bishops; for the first time this indicated that the episcopate of the Protestant Episcopal Church was aggressively promotional. The election of bishops did not come after the work on the frontier had been established; they led out into the unorganized areas to lay the foundations properly for the new work of the church. The Protestant Episcopal Church in 1835 had twenty-two dioceses; seventeen bishops, of whom Jackson Kemper was a missionary bishop; 772 clergy; between eight and nine hundred congregations, of which 590 were specifically reported by twelve dioceses; and upwards of forty thousand communicant members of whom 36,416 were reported by nineteen dioceses. By comparison, the Methodist Church then had six bishops, 2,458 ministers, and 638,784 members, with perhaps two million constituents closely allied with the church and its families.[10]

While there appears to have been a tacit agreement from this period that domestic missions would be directed by the high churchmen and foreign missions work would fall to the evangelicals, there were some notable leaders in this latter group who dissented from this division of fields. Bishop Griswold, Stephen H. Tyng, William Sparrow, and Alonzo Potter, later Bishop of Pennsylvania, all felt that it was a grave error, but the election of Jackson Kemper and Francis L. Hawks, both high churchmen, as the first missionary bishops indicates the agreement was in effect. Hawks declined his election as Bishop of Louisiana, Arkansas, and Florida, but Kemper, a superb example of an old high churchman, was consecrated Bishop of Missouri and Indiana on September 25, 1835. The bishops later elected for the foreign fields were largely evangelicals, and most of them as well as most of the missionaries to foreign fields had been trained at the Virginia Theological Seminary, the chief center of evangelical strength.

As a result of the revival of the missionary spirit accompanying the Oxford Movement, a number of seminary graduates with high church theological inclinations volunteered for the western missionary fields. Because of the shortage of missionaries, the Society gladly accepted their services. Within a few years the high church spirit so completely dominated the home mission fields that it became evident at the General Convention of 1847 that most of the western deputies were supporting Anglo-Catholic policies. As such reports reached the church at large evangelical laymen withheld their support, and by 1850 the Society had suffered a marked decline in income.

Several attempts were made by the evangelicals to overcome the ill effects of such party division in the missionary program. When the General Convention created the Northwest and Southwest Missionary Districts in 1835, it was agreed that both high and low churchmen would be represented in the episcopal choices; further ill will was created when both bishoprics fell to high churchmen. In 1851 the Episcopal Missionary Association for the West was organized by a group in Philadelphia and was admitted as an auxiliary society by the Board of Missions, with the understanding that the funds it raised would be expended at its direction through the Domestic Committee of the Society. Although this group was able to obtain money that had never been available for the program controlled by high churchmen and was able to establish churches in new areas in the West, the high churchmen generally were opposed to it, even though they conceded its practicality, since it violated the church's system. When Henry W. Lee was elected Bishop of Iowa with the good will and financial support of the Episcopal Missionary Association, this diocese immediately showed signs of strength and grew from twelve parishes and eight ministers to thirty parishes and twenty-five ministers in about four years, and its endowment of $3,000 multiplied tenfold in the same period.[11]

In 1859 the election procedure was repeated: the moderate bishops threw their support to the high church candidate for the Southwest, and the high church bishops stood together against the evangelical candidate for the Northwest so that he was defeated by one vote. Not unnaturally the low churchmen cried, "When money is needed, evangelical men are one with their high church brethren; when offices are to be filled, they are proscribed." Now more than ever distressed at the influence of the Oxford Movement on the church's missionaries, the evangelicals showed reluctance to support the domestic missions program in which they lacked any sense of control; consequently they tried, though futilely, to lead the Board of Missions to return to the voluntary principle, followed in its program before 1835, in which there were no party distinctions but in which contributions were channeled as far as possible in keeping with the donor's wishes.

Failing in this, the low churchmen carried out their threat that "the money of evangelicals would not go to extend the Laudian theology in the West much longer" and organized the American Church Missionary Society on May 9, 1860, to "advance the mission work agreeably to the views of religious truth and obligation which distinguish our Evangelical Church, and occupy still more extended fields of labor." In addition to supporting domestic missions, this Society became largely responsible for the church's work in Latin America—in Mexico, Brazil, Cuba, and Haiti. Suffering inevitably under the division of resources, the Board of Missions suggested a union with the Episcopal Missionary Association for the West and the American Church Missionary Society, which was effected only in 1877; the latter Society still remains a corporate entity within the parent body.

Although Jackson Kemper was a high churchman, he was essentially and foremost a Christian missionary and was about to set out on what has probably been the most fruitful single ministry in the annals of the church. His admirable and commendable churchly spirit was most clearly expressed before the eighth annual Indiana Convention in St. Stephen's Church, Terre Haute, during the first week of October in 1845. The church was then being challenged by the rapidly increasing growth of the Roman Catholic Church, and Kemper urged his clergy

> to study the subject in all its bearings—to trace its rise and progress and deleterious influence on the Church of God—to make themselves masters of the principles and events of primitive times—and to become well acquainted with those views which led to the Reformation, and which were established in our Mother-Church by the blood of those glorious martyrs, Ridley, Cranmer and Latimer.

Then revealing his truly catholic but not Roman or ritualistic loyalty, he went on to warn,

> And those among us, if there be such, who cherish what may be called Romanizing tendencies, which at times, perhaps, amount to nothing more than a romantic feeling, and undefined admiration for some of the solemn but vain ceremonies of the Church of Rome, are to be entreated with kindness, and won, by scriptural arguments and well known facts, to the old paths in which *we* tread, as did the early confessors, before Popery and its defilements were known.[12]

The Missionary Bishop of Missouri and Indiana and the Protestant Episcopal Church were born in the same year, 1789. Of German background, he was reared near Poughkeepsie, New York, and, after graduating from Columbia, studied theology with Bishop Moore and with John Henry Hobart, who had just joined the staff at Trinity Church in New York. Ordained in 1811 by Bishop White, he immediately joined the bishop's staff and remained his aggressive assistant for twenty years. During this period he was the first missionary agent and the chief sponsor of the activities of the Society for the Advancement of Christianity in Pennsylvania. It was Kemper more than any other who also encouraged Bishop White to visit his scattered rural parishes and to undertake the eight-hundred-mile visitation to the western borders of that state when the bishop was seventy-eight years of age. In the last four years before his election as missionary bishop, Kemper served as rector of St. Paul's Church in Norwalk, Connecticut.

Following his consecration, Kemper immediately set out for the West and took with him Samuel R. Johnson, who became the second Episcopal minister in Indiana and, a decade later, was named a professor of theology at the General Seminary. Kemper continued his journey to St. Louis where he became the church's only minister in Missouri; Peter Minaud was soon called to assist him with his duties as rector of the church. Scarcely settled in his own responsibilities, Kemper set out in the early wintry months of 1836 to supply the Diocese of Illinois, while Bishop Chase made his second visit to England to obtain funds for his diocese and Jubilee College. In May, 1837, Bishop Kemper laid the cornerstone of a new church in St. Louis and then went on to spend the summer in directing the work of the church in Indiana.

Soon after he returned from Illinois in the spring of 1836, he undertook further explorations up the Mississippi and the Missouri Rivers as far as St. Charles and saw the limitless opportunities for the church. Realizing the need for clergy, Kemper determined to establish a college to train them. Assisted by a gift of $20,000 from John P. Stagg, the college became a reality late in 1836 on a beautiful site five miles southwest of St. Louis, and in January, 1837, it was chartered by the legislature. The bishop always seemed to be embarrassed about soliciting further support for the institution because in his absence his friends had named it Kemper College. The eve of the financial Panic of 1837 was an inauspicious moment for such an adventure, and, always in financial difficulty, the college closed its doors in 1845.

Despite his responsibility for the church in two states, Kemper agreed to make an episcopal tour of the South with Bishop Otey, and when the latter fell ill, Kemper went on alone to spend the first four months of 1838 visiting most of the parishes and confirming members in Louisiana, Mississippi, Alabama, Georgia, and Florida. Louisiana and Florida were so well organized that later that year they were received into union with the General Convention.

Even greater must have been Kemper's joy at seeing his missionary district of Indiana organized late in August and received into union with the same

General Convention. Since there were only nine parishes and ten ministers, the Diocese of Indiana requested permission to remain under the jurisdiction of the missionary bishop until its strength increased. When this diocese at its fourth annual convention in Indianapolis late in May, 1841, elected Kemper as its diocesan, he modestly declined but agreed to continue his oversight until a bishop could be selected. This proved to be another eight years with many disappointing declinations before George Upfold of Pennsylvania was finally chosen at the convention in 1849. Meanwhile, Kemper continued his careful supervision and won men of ability, some of them leaders in other churches, to join him in serving the Protestant Episcopal Church in these areas. One notable accession was Andrew Wylie, formerly a Roman Catholic priest and president of the state university, whom Kemper ordained to the diaconate in 1842. Two years later, Wylie preached the annual convention sermon.

Kemper's favorable reports from the West served only to spur the church to extend his supervision. The General Convention in 1838 decided to divide the western areas into two missionary dioceses at the latitude of thirty-six and a half degrees and assigned all areas north and west of this line to Kemper and then proceeded to consecrate Leonidas Polk as the missionary bishop for the southern and southwestern areas. On hearing of his new assignment Kemper is reported to have said, ". . . a bishop spread out over 100,000 square miles of territory will make a very thin bishop indeed." This division brought both Iowa and Wisconsin Territories under Kemper's jurisdiction, and Polk, who was primarily missionary bishop for Arkansas, also received responsibility for Mississippi, Louisiana, and the Republic of Texas.

Polk had been won for the church at West Point where he read a religious pamphlet casually distributed by Charles P. McIlvaine, later Bishop of Ohio, and through his influence was prepared for confirmation. His rigorous military training also prepared him for the arduous travels necessary in his vast district. In 1819 he traveled about five thousand miles covering his southwestern jurisdiction, and it seems only natural that in 1841 he should accept election as the diocesan in Louisiana. Three years later George W. Freeman was chosen missionary bishop to replace him. That these regions were wisely chosen for cultivation becomes evident from the fact that Texas became a diocese as early as 1849 and a decade later elected Alexander Gregg its first bishop; Arkansas became an independent diocese in 1871.

Meanwhile, Bishop Kemper had turned his attention to Wisconsin. Soon after his first visit to this state, where he found the only remaining Indian Mission in the church among the Oneidas at Green Bay, he consecrated the first church building in that place. Bishop Kemper visited the eastern states to obtain men and support for his work, establishing a policy pursued by missionary bishops ever since. After several interviews with students at the General Seminary, he found three men who were willing to undertake a missionary experiment in Wisconsin. These volunteers, James L. Breck, William Adams, and John Henry Hobart, Jr., son of the bishop, had been greatly influenced by the Oxford Movement and sought the opportunity to live and work in a semi-monastic mission under Kemper's supervision. When these three men received the approval of their bishops, Bishop Kemper gladly received them and assigned Richard Cadle as their superior, a role in which he was ill-cast. His young clergy thought Cadle had "need for a further realization of Catholic truth," and he thought them "over-employed about celibacy and habits of dress." Cadle was more interested in the practical religious life and once said, "The imposition of celibacy I candidly do not like, not being in the slightest degree Oxfordized."[13]

These young men had been living on missionary grants while they built St. John's in the Wilderness at Waukesha, Wisconsin, in 1841, but the following year they moved to a five-hundred-acre tract among the Nashotah Lakes that Bishop Kemper had purchased for their experiment in theological education. On Cadle's withdrawal Breck reluctantly assumed the duties of leadership, directed their ministries, and supervised the erection of a small frame building, the first Nashotah House.

Inspired by the Oxford Movement, Breck and his companions had planned a missionary venture that would combine a rigorously disciplined ascetic life with the pursuit of the original apostolic purpose. This multiple program became clearer when they were able to build at Nashotah a monastery, a seminary, and a center for their missionary program. Their ordered monastic life began at five each morning; throughout the day they recited the canonical hours, performed manual labor, and traveled widely in missionary efforts. In the first three months such trips took them nearly two thousand miles on horseback and 736 miles on foot. For their zeal these men suffered extreme poverty, and because of their convictions, at least three novices entered the Roman Catholic Church.

Hobart left the community after two years, but there were now thirty students and more than half of them were intent on a career in the church. By 1847 six graduates of Nashotah had been ordained deacons by Bishop Kemper, and the following year under Breck's leadership, the school, now supported by a board of trustees, obtained a charter. Breck was primarily an ascetic and a missionary; when he left, not unexpectedly, two years later, Azel D. Cole became the successful administrator of Nashotah House for the next thirty-five years. Meanwhile, William Adams, a man of scholarly temperament who had resigned from the mission about the time Hobart left, returned to Nashotah in 1845 with the understanding that he would devote his entire time to teaching. Three years later he married Bishop Kemper's daughter, Elizabeth, and became so strongly convinced of the error of his previous devotion to monasticism that he declared celibacy to be morally wrong. Breck went alone to Minnesota in 1850 to repeat his success there in founding a mission house and a seminary, where soon twelve postulants were preparing for orders. Nashotah House, so firmly established, has made a continuous contribution of leaders to the church.

This was the period of the transplanting of the Indian tribes remaining in the eastern states to the territories beyond the Mississippi. Although the church at the time had little work among the Indians, the Domestic Committee of the Board of Missions in the spring of 1844 directed its secretary and general agent to make a survey of the situation in the West generally, and particularly in the newly formed Indian Territory. Between 1833 and 1840 most of the Indian tribes had been removed from the states east of the Mississippi and Missouri Rivers and from Missouri, Arkansas, and Louisiana; 250,000 of the total 275,349 Indians in the United States were now living in the territories provided for them in the West.

The report published after this survey in 1844 described the situation along the entire route traveled and commended particularly the missions of the Baptists, Presbyterians, and the Methodists, who had expended $170,000 on one school and mission among the Delawares. Although few Episcopalians were found in the West, the report proposed a plan to be submitted to the General Convention in Philadelphia that fall. It included a missionary bishop for the Indian Territory, boarding schools for girls distributed among the tribes, and a central manual training school for boys. It had been discovered that for very little money captured Indian children could be purchased, and it was proposed that such children should be purchased and set free to be trained as missionaries and sent back to their own tribes. They could also be trained to teach Indian women how to improve their own homes without disturbing tribal traditions. The report specifically recommended that at all events care must be exercised that the Indians' natural jealousy of the white man not be increased. This proved to be difficult, especially because the government's payments for lands surrendered by the Indians in the East were often only a fraction of their true value; one such payment of $20,000 was made to the Wyandots for lands in Ohio fairly appraised at $125,937.25. The Society must have been pleased with the report that one Episcopalian on the frontier, who had had his children baptized by a Methodist minister, said that he had done so with the specific understanding that "when a man of 'true grit' came along, he should do it over again."[14] While the General Convention in the fall of 1844 gave most of its time to heated discussions of the Tractarian Movement, it did take action based on this report when it named George W. Freeman as Missionary Bishop of Arkansas, with the definite assignment to exercise jurisdiction over the Indian Territory even though there were no missionaries in that area at that time.

Meanwhile, Jackson Kemper, having once again refused election as a diocesan—this time in Maryland—explored the areas of his new responsibilities in Wisconsin and Iowa; he also led the church in Missouri to become a diocese in 1840 and supervised it until Cicero F. Hawks of Buffalo, New York, became its bishop in 1844. Kemper's work in Iowa was delayed by a lack of men to serve in the rapidly increasing settlements. The earliest work in this state had been begun in 1836 in Dubuque by Richard F. Cadle and carried on subsequently by Ezekiel G. Gear and J. Batchelder. Here again are great names often submerged in the mass of details about conventions, elections, and episcopal visitations. Bishop Kemper, in addressing the first annual convention in Iowa in 1854, paid tribute to Batchelder as the pioneer of the church in Iowa as he had formerly been in Illinois. Cadle had served the mission in Detroit and the Indian Mission in Wisconsin before coming to Iowa. Gear would later become the pioneer of the church in Minnesota. This diocese had a slow beginning; but when it became the special project of the Episcopal Missionary Society for the West, new missionaries arrived, and adequate funds were provided to help the church achieve diocesan status by 1853. The following year Henry W. Lee of the Diocese of Western New York was elected its first bishop.

Although "Father" Gear, as he was endearingly called in his later years in Minnesota, held the first services in that state, it was not until June 24, 1850, that substantial missionary work was begun there when James L. Breck, Timothy Wilcoxson of Connecticut and John A. Merrick of Pennsylvania organized The Associate Mission for Minnesota. Still imbued with much of the monastic and celibate spirit which had inspired their first missionary venture in Wisconsin, Breck soon became resigned to the propensity of his colleagues for married life and eventually succumbed to matrimony himself. This mission, which at one time had twelve workers, served a large part of Minnesota. From its headquarters at Christ Church in St. Paul, Breck went out to establish two missions among the Chippewa Indians, the only Indian missions of the church beyond Duck Creek near Green Bay, Wisconsin. Sensing the need for trained clergy and a theological school, he founded Seabury Seminary at Faribault, which much later would be merged with the Western Theological Seminary to become Seabury-Western in Evanston, Illinois. In 1867 Breck left Minnesota to pursue his missionary purpose all the way to the West Coast where the new work of the church was being established in California. Here he established an associate mission at Benicia and also founded the Missionary College of St. Augustine and St. Mary's School for Girls. Before his death on April 2, 1876, Breck had demonstrated for the church the practical and logical conclusion to true catholic thought in the disciplined Christian life. In his final sermon before leaving for California he said,

> Now that the altar is in its rightful place, and preaching no longer supersedes the Sacraments, . . . it becomes a solemn charge with the Clergy that they rightly instruct the people not only in the significance of these things, but in their practical uses . . . so that, whilst there is a return to Catholic doctrine and primitive worship, we must have, to make these vital, a living personal return to discipline.[15]

In rapid succession Bishop Kemper also saw the fruit of his labors fulfilled in the birth of dioceses in Minnesota, Kansas, and Nebraska. At his call and under his leadership the primary convention met in St. Paul, Minnesota, in September, 1857, and the first annual convention was held the following May in the same city. Henry B. Whipple was elected the first Bishop of Minnesota in July, 1859, and consecrated at the General Convention in Richmond, Virginia, that fall. Bishop Whipple, who had received only one vote on the first episcopal ballot, proved to be one of the church's most successful diocesans.

By an Act of Congress on May 30, 1854, the Territory of Kansas was thrown open to settlement, and so rapid was the immigration that within five years a constitutional convention had been held, and by May 20, 1861, Kansas was admitted to the Union. During the rush of people and religious groups into this area, the Board of Missions appointed John McNamara its first missionary to Kansas. A former missionary in western Missouri and now president of Nebraska College at Nebraska City, Nebraska, McNamara was able to serve only about a year during those troubled times. Late in 1856 Hiram Stone established the first permanent parish in this state at Leavenworth, then a town of about two thousand. Eight new parishes followed in rapid succession, including such important locations as Atchison and Topeka, and Bishop Kemper immediately assumed episcopal supervision. With ten resident clergymen the diocese was organized in 1859 and that fall was received into union with the General Convention. Since this was the year Bishop Kemper resigned as the missionary bishop, Bishop Lee of Iowa assumed episcopal responsibility for Kansas until December 15, 1864, when Thomas H. Vail of Iowa was consecrated the first bishop of that diocese. On assuming his duties, he found three small churches completed and occupied and four others begun. At the close of his twenty years as its bishop this diocese had more than thirty clergymen, thirty-two churches, fifteen rectories, and thirty or more additional missions or preaching stations throughout the state. Each new church in the diocese had been built with assistance from the bishop in amounts varying from $350 to $2,500. Such development was typical of the church's new missionary program where, in the primitive Christian manner, the bishop was sent out to establish and lead the church rather than to wait until the church had been established and able to support a bishop.

Jackson Kemper lived to see the organization of one more diocese in the vast areas he alone had once supervised when Nebraska became a diocese in September, 1868. When the General Convention of 1865 divided the far western areas apart from California into five missionary jurisdictions, Robert H. Clarkson was named a missionary for one of those areas comprising Nebraska and Dakota. Three years later, seventeen of the clergy and twelve lay delegates met in Trinity Church, Omaha, to organize the separate Diocese of Nebraska within the boundaries of that state. Bishop Clarkson served until his death in 1884 when he was succeeded by Bishop George Worthington.

Meanwhile, Bishop Kemper, now aged seventy, resigned his missionary jurisdiction in 1859 and devoted himself entirely to Wisconsin where he had accepted election as diocesan in 1854. There was then no canonical restriction on serving both as diocesan and missionary bishop. Happily he served these last eleven years in his favorite state until his death on May 24, 1870. Twenty-four years before he retired as missionary bishop he had begun with only a vast missionary district and no dioceses and with only two clergymen to assist him. After his years of endless travel and untiring effort in these areas he now left four other bishops, six organized dioceses, and 172 ministers, of whom twenty-seven were in Missouri, twenty-five in Indiana, thirty-one in Iowa, twenty in Minnesota, ten in Kansas, four in Nebraska, and fifty-five serving under him in Wisconsin. On his retirement as a missionary bishop in 1859 the unorganized area of the West was divided into the Northwest and Southwest missionary jurisdictions. Henry C. Lay became the Missionary Bishop of the Southwest, and Joseph C. Talbot, of the Northwest, where he supervised an area of three-quarters of a million square miles extending to the Continental Divide. The church had also asked him to visit New Mexico and Arizona, so that it was no wonder that he often referred to himself as the "Bishop of All Outdoors." Beyond the mountains Thomas F. Scott, formerly a Presbyterian, who was consecrated in January, 1854, held the missionary jurisdiction of Washington and Oregon, which then included the state of Idaho; William I. Kip had recently become the bishop of the Diocese of California. At long last the church had completely encompassed the areas of this large country from the Pacific shores, where Drake's chaplain first conducted a Prayer Book service, to the long Atlantic coast, where loyal churchmen had first read the services of the church in the late years of the sixteenth century.

XV

THE OXFORD MOVEMENT
AND PARTY SPIRIT

This same period, which saw the rise and development of the new missionary program and planning in the Episcopal Church, brought from England an influx of the Oxford Tracts and a significant influence by the Oxford Movement. For several centuries the Church of England had been suffering from centrifugal tendencies, throwing off the dissenters whom it could not assimilate, which had greatly impoverished that body and seriously disturbed its balance and proportion. In the first century after the Reformation the Puritans had been expelled, and in the eighteenth century the Methodists could no longer be contained so that the English church lost that sense of balance that the stabilizing presence of critical reformers and enthusiastic exponents of the evangelical point of view might have preserved. Wesley himself never withdrew from the Church of England, and many of the other evangelicals remained in the church, emphasizing personal religious experience and piety and stimulating generous support for philanthropy. Gradually the evangelicals became associated with non-conformity and seemed to lose a serious interest in theological exploration and religious traditions.

Meanwhile, the main body of the Anglican Church had drifted toward an inactive and often impotent churchmanship that lacked the zeal of the earlier Caroline divines and of the later Anglo-Catholics and became content with its security as part of the British Establishment. When bishops, who were inordinately concerned for the approval of the government, found no time to meet with their clergy in diocesan synods or provincial convocations, it followed naturally that there should be little sense of cohesiveness among the clergy; even the services of the church were performed indifferently and with little concern for uniformity.

With a wider spirit of tolerance, bred largely from the influence of the Industrial Revolution and increasing world trade, Parliament, in 1828 and 1829, revoked the earlier restraining laws and no longer barred Dissenters or Roman Catholics from public office or even the House of Commons. When the church opposed such social and political reforms, culminating in the Reform Bill of 1832, which gave more control to the working classes made up mostly of Dissenters, many loyal Englishmen became despondent about the church.

In such an apathetic atmosphere the Assize Sermon of John Keble, preached in the university pulpit on July 14, 1833, by this highly respected Oxford professor, re-echoed loudly throughout England. Speaking on "National Apostasy," he lamented the impotence of the church, which, by its subservience to the state, had endangered its constitutional prerogatives and its creeds; he urged a renewed appreciation of the valued traditions that belonged to the church in its own right and not merely as a department of the Establishment. Under the stimulation of sympathetic clergymen like Hugh Rose and Hurrell Froude about seven thousand clergymen and nearly two hundred and thirty thousand heads of families sent petitions early in 1834 to the Archbishop of Canterbury declaring their loyalty to the church and her polity and doctrine.

The most potent factor in the dissemination of this new religious interest and vigor, which soon came to be called the Oxford Movement from the point of its origin, was the wide distribution of "The Tracts for the Times." Forty-six of the ninety tracts of various lengths appeared in 1834, and the remainder during the next seven years. While most of these rather technical discussions on the nature of the church and the sacraments, apostolic orders, fasting, etc., were written by John Henry Newman, who soon became the most widely known and most controversial leader of the movement, others were prepared by Keble and the venerated Edward Bouverie Pusey, Regius Professor of Hebrew at Oxford. Because of the importance of these pamphlets, the movement was sometimes known as Tractarianism, and on occasion it was called Puseyism, usually in a derogatory sense.

Two emphases predominated in these tracts. There was the clear and resounding emphasis on the historic Christian doctrines, not only as items of a creed, but also as principles of action. This led to a restudy of the Church Fathers and a rediscovery of the source of Anglicanism's doctrine and polity in the primitive church. Here also was a new sense of the authority of the ministry derived from ordination at the hands of those who stood in the historic apostolic succession, which most appropriately at this period served to assert the authority of the church as completely independent of the state.

A second emphasis pointed to the accumulated traditions of the church through the centuries and appeared in 1841 in its most controversial form in Newman's *Tract Ninety*. Contending that the tradition of the church must have been contained in embryo in the Bible and the early church teachings, Newman pressed this developmental theory to the point where he asserted that the Bible could only be properly understood in the light of this tradition. That Newman in this period was passing through a crisis in his religious experience is clear from his contemporary writings and his exceedingly effective preaching in St. Mary's Church, Oxford, which bore a strong resemblance to the enthusiastic preaching of Bishop Hobart, who had visited him a decade earlier. In his *Tract Thirty-eight* he said, "As I will not consent to be deprived of the records of the Reformation, so neither will I part with those of former times." English churchmen generally, however, were unable to accept any idea that would impinge on the self-sufficiency or authority of the Scriptures.

Much sharper was their reaction to Newman's idea, expressed in *Tract Ninety*, that the doctrines he and the Tractarians held could be reconciled with the Thirty-nine Articles. It was hardly the popularity of these creedal statements that led to this outcry; few persons read or discussed them, and when they did, it was often to propose their revision. The Articles, however, were still regarded as a prime defense against papalism, and all the Church of England clergy and members of the universities were required to subscribe to them. Since the Articles were a part of the English way of life, their association with Roman doctrine, even after Newman's exclusion of certain perversions and abuses in Roman dogma, brought the whole issue to a climax. The Oxford Movement was widely condemned, its leaders were severely criticized, and the *Tracts* were banned from publication. Evangelicals particularly objected that Newman's support of the place of good works in salvation violated the cardinal Reformation doctrine of justification by faith.

The lines and issues were so clearly drawn that retreat seemed impossible, and on that dark and stormy night of October 8, 1845, Newman threw himself at the feet of the Passionist Father Dominic and requested "admission into the One Fold of Christ." W. G. Ward, Frederick W. Faber, and scores of others followed soon afterward. H. E. Manning, formerly Archdeacon of Chichester, rose rapidly to become a Roman Catholic bishop and cardinal; although Newman was also ultimately admitted to the College of Cardinals, his role remained inconspicuous to the end. Perhaps of even greater significance for Christian history is the fact that Pusey and Keble remained in the Church of England.

Although most of the English bishops and leaders in both Oxford and Cambridge openly opposed the Oxford Movement and some of its principal adherents had gone to Rome, its influences have been felt continuously in Anglicanism throughout the world. In its essence this movement was an emphasis on Christian tradition, particularly that before the eleventh century, including the historical episcopate, by which succession it laid claim to catholicity and received the title Anglo-Catholic. The more advanced adherents regarded the more recently developed doctrines, such as the Immaculate Conception of the Virgin Mary and a belief in purgatory, as permissible but not required. Liturgical revisions and enrichment ultimately made externally obvious the new spirit that had been developing internally among Anglo-Catholics. Many pious followers of the Oxford divines sought and found an enrichment of their religious lives in renewed devotion to and understanding of the church and its sacraments; for some, this meant the rediscovery of the church's devotional classics and prayers, while for others, it led to the newly established orders complete with Rules and Breviary. Still others found in this religious revival the ground and support for their own increased practical Christian living and action. In the next generation men like Frederick Denison Maurice would rise from such stimulation to relate Christianity to human needs and go on to correct social injustices and to provide educational opportunities for the humble and the poor.

Meanwhile, the church in America had been moving in a similar direction but under different conditions. Entirely free of the limitation of state control, religion in America had spawned diversities that diluted the inherited Christian faith and tradition so that they were hardly recognizable. The Great Awakenings had engendered a far greater general interest in religion than could be found in England in this period so that the challenge to the Episcopal Church was one of direction as well as promotion.

The churchly direction that its leaders, especially the old high churchmen, were able to give to the entire American Christian enterprise proved to be its greatest opportunity and responsibility. Beyond this, the still largely Protestant America heard little about the great Christian traditions and liturgical worship. The forms of thought and worship produced by the magisterial Reformation had become largely dissipated; there was a generous sprinkling of Calvinistic theology, but even the more recently arrived German Reformed and Lutheran immigrants made rapid compromises with the frontier religion as they moved westward to the Mississippi Valley. On the eastern seaboard the older established Reformed and Lutheran Churches had also allowed the American evangelistic fervor to divide their ranks; those who defended the Heidelberg Catechism and Palatinate Reformed Liturgy and the inherited Lutheran Confession and Liturgy were hard pressed by those who would rather conform to the new American religious pattern. There were some signs of a revival of what may well be called fully Christian, rather than high or low, churchmanship in the newly established Mercersburg (Pennsylvania) Theological School of the Reformed Church. Here John W. Nevin, who admitted that he was much influenced by Tractarianism, and Philip Schaff, who brought with him from Germany an historically oriented appreciation for the church and its formularies, combined their efforts in mid-century to develop the Mercersburg Theology, the most unique American contribution to religious thought strongly centered in the church and its ministry and the sacraments.

Among the Episcopalians, the nature and authority of the church had been ably defined by men like William White, especially in his middle and later years, and John Henry Hobart and their disciples. For them the church was grounded in Biblical authority and ably and continuously administered by an episcopate in uninterrupted historical succession from the Apostles and adaptable to widely variant situations, even those of the American frontier. They held that the true church, founded on the Lord Jesus Christ, was preserved in its essential qualities, even though division and subdivision of structure had occurred at various intervals. So they considered the Protestant Episcopal Church a branch of the continuous church from the beginning, carrying on the historical faith and order under the Canon Law developed by the councils of the church and varying only in those portions no longer applicable in the new situation in America.[1]

Already in 1807 John Henry Hobart had published his *Tract on Episcopacy*, which received the highest commendation of Hugh J. Rose, one of the earliest leaders of the Oxford Movement in England. During his European visit, Hobart spent many months in England and often discussed theological topics with English churchmen, among whom he was widely and kindly received. He dined with Newman at Oxford in March, 1824, and may have influenced this young potential leader far more than has heretofore been admitted. But apart from all mere conjecture, Newman wrote a glowing tribute to Hobart in his "The Church Principles of Bishop Hobart." Had Hobart's influence been merely casual, this controversial churchman would hardly have written about it after fifteen turbulent years and in that period of his life when his own religious allegiance was approaching a crisis.

John Keble is probably better remembered for *The Christian Year* than for his sermon at the opening of the Assize in 1833. This devotional classic, which renewed in England a spirit and temper rarely known since the days of Lancelot Andrewes or even since the mystics of the fourteenth century, first appeared in 1827. Seven years later it was edited and published in America for the first time; its wide and continuous circulation in this country has had a more constructive influence than the more controversial *Tracts*.

So favorable was the reception of the *Tracts* in America, however, that Charles S. Henry, a publisher of the *New York Mirror*, ventured to bring out an American edition in 1839, while the series was rapidly nearing its conclusion in England; he hoped thereby to help check the rising and contrasting threats of Rome and rationalism. In his introduction he suggested that the Anglican doctrines relating to the church and the ministry had been better preserved in America than in the English Establishment.[2]

America also proved a better host to the *Tracts* than did the land of their origin; Bishop Stewart of Quebec once said that he had heard more about the *Tracts* in New York in three days than he had heard in London in a year. After 1835 Samuel Seabury frequently commented favorably on them in his editorials in *The Churchman*, although he was cautious to warn that Newman's devotional practices were needless. The natural perusal of the *Tracts* by the younger men, especially those in the General Theological Seminary, became a stimulus that sent out James Lloyd Breck, William Adams, and John H. Hobart, Jr., to their missionary adventure in the West; at the same time it led other students like Arthur Carey and Edgar Wadhams so far toward Rome that the former suffered long investigation before his ordination and the latter soon defected to Rome. These "angry young men" ran far beyond the older high churchmen who had defended Anglicanism, with its rich catholic traditions once rescued and preserved in the Reformation, counting it central in the Christian stream of history. To these younger zealots the Reformation was a travesty that had *de*formed the church by ignoring the accumulated medieval heritage that they felt must now be recovered by the restoration of Roman usages and dogma to make the church truly catholic. In the exceedingly difficult matter of dealing with these men, the dean and faculty of the seminary came under severe criticism and investigation, for it was assumed, and perhaps with some justification, that the young men had been encouraged by at least some of their teachers.

The controversy between the high and low churchmen had constructively run its course in the American church by the time of the appearance of the *Tracts,* and the question must at least be raised whether the true Anglican traditions might have been better preserved for all time had they been entrusted to the hands of the American theologians rather than to the Tractarians. The major doctrinal differences between the high and low churchmen had been quietly reconciled, so that both sides accepted the historicity of the apostolic succession; they differed only on whether it was essential to the nature of the true church. Even baptismal regeneration had been mutually accepted in the original connotation of that term, and would not become a controversial issue until much later when regeneration, in the revivalistic connotation, came to mean a personal, moral transformation of human nature.

Something of the irenic influence of this reconciled partisanship is found, curiously enough, in a work written in 1836 by Calvin Colton, a Presbyterian clergyman. After deploring the increasing usurpation of clerical prerogatives by the laity in the Presbyterian and Congregational Churches, he went on to show the detrimental effects resulting from "the excessive amount of labour that is demanded of the clergy, . . . attributable almost entirely, to an appetite for certain novelties . . . sermons and meetings without end, and in an almost endless variety . . . enough to kill any man in a short period." Then, in almost ecstatic language, he described what he believed to be the stability of the Protestant Episcopal Church: no inconsiderable difference of opinion among both clergy and laity but with no evident controversies. This he attributed to the use of the common liturgy, the open freedom of discussion even of controversial subjects between clergy and diocesan, and the reticence to promote anything that cannot be carried with a tolerable degree of unanimity.[3]

But there were still obvious differences in practice between the parties; these were more matters of taste than essence and centered largely about the freedom to make liturgical adaptations or to add additional services or join with other bodies in worship. If they had not been stimulated by the *Tracts,* some of these men might never have brought their best work to publication; but there is the other possibility that, unhurried and unfrightened by the ensuing controversies, the able leaders of this generation, one of the best this church has produced, might well have entered more creatively into discussion with the Mercersburg theologians, the Andover liberals, and the Princeton conservatives.

The wide acceptance of the *Tracts* and the accompanying developments in America posed a threat for many conservative churchmen, which Bishop Moore of Virginia described in 1839 as "a revival of the worst evils of the Romish system." He was probably the first bishop to show such concern because, as he wrote a friend, of "the disposition manifested by some of our brethren, both in England and this country, to unsettle the religious opinions of the members of this Church."[4] When William R. Whittingham, the high church history professor at the General Seminary, was elected Bishop of Maryland in 1840 without disavowing the *Tracts*, as had been widely requested in the diocese, it became clear that the Oxford influence had not yet fully penetrated the church and that the conflict had not reached its peak. This slow reaction may possibly be explained by the fact that there was less to become excited about in America, since the old high churchmen had long been emphasizing the central truths discussed in the earliest *Tracts*.

While Bishop Moore feared the movement because of its disturbing nature, the eminent Bishop Brownell of Connecticut, in his episcopal address to the diocese in 1840, said that he saw no real danger here but that he feared more the rise of "individualism" in religion. He had recently come from several visits to the dioceses in the frontier states where revivalism was running rampant, and he now emphatically opposed the idea that conversion alone saves the individual and commended the values of "pious nurture." After describing the effects of the Oxford Movement on the American church, in a later address to his convention in 1847, Brownell expressed the hope that no ill effects would result from Tractarianism. Then, with what seemed like precocious insight, he predicted that

> . . . in our country the great danger to Christianity lies in a wide-spread tendency to Rationalism . . . fifty years more will not elapse before the chief controversies of the church will be not with Sectarianism but with Infidelity.[5]

But Bishop Brownell was not unaware of the Tractarian threats, which were increasing; in his charge to the clergy of Connecticut in 1843 he said:

> It is happy for us, my brethren, that we have, in our Book of Common Prayer, *a standard of faith and worship,* conformable to scripture, and agreeable to the practice of the Church in the earliest and purest ages of Christianity. It will be the object of this present discourse to recommend to you a strict adherence to this standard; shunning, on the one hand, those corruptions and superstitions of the Church of Rome, which it was so carefully framed to avoid, and equally rejecting, on the other hand, the errors connected with ultra-Protestantism, and all the extravagances which recently sprung from it.

The first major theological attack on Tractarianism came in 1840 from Bishop Charles P. McIlvaine of Ohio, the most theologically competent leader of the evangelicals. He preached a sermon on "Justification by Faith" before his convention and later in the year published his major attack in his *Oxford Divinity Compared with that of the Romish and Anglican Churches.* Here he condemned the movement as unscriptural, contradictory to the Anglican doctrines and Articles, and "thoroughly Popish in principle," primarily because it had surrendered the truths of the gospel and the doctrine of justification by faith. Summing up all the possible deviations from Angelicanism that he could foresee in the seminal principle of the Tractarians, he concluded that the only logical thing for them to do was to move in a body into the Roman camp.[6]

When the thunder of *Tract Ninety* fell on American ears, other bishops, notably Manton Eastburn and William Meade, joined the vocal opposition; while they may have exceeded McIlvaine in excessive acerbity, no attack penetrated so deeply to the heart of the issue as that of the Ohio bishop. Pursuing his attack relentlessly at the twenty-sixth annual convention of his diocese in Gambier in September, 1843, McIlvaine warned against this attempt to "unprotestantize" the Church of England and pointed out the dangers of flirting with Roman doctrine in Anglican dress, which he counted little less than deception. He said:

> The whole system, you see, is one of church instead of Christ; priest instead of Gospel; concealment of truth instead of "manifestation of truth"; ignorant superstition instead of enlightened faith; bondage, where we are promised liberty—all tending directly to load us with whatever is odious in the worst meaning of priestcraft, in place of the free, affectionate, enlarging, elevating and cheerful liberty of a child of God.

His greatest fear, the bishop concluded, was not the defections to the Roman Church but the Romanism of the Protestant Episcopal Church.[7] Writing to another bishop in that same year, Bishop Philander Chase expressed similar feelings:

> It is said that approximations to Rome are innocent. Not so. . . . The disposition to *reform the reformation* is as dangerous as it is foolish and should receive a rebuke from every Protestant bishop.[8]

There were, on the other hand, some distinguished leaders of the Episcopal Church who clearly and unqualifiedly defended the *Tracts*. Among them were Bishop George W. Doane of New Jersey, Bishop William DeLancey of Western New York, Bishop Benjamin T. Onderdonk of New York, and Samuel Seabury, editor of *The Churchman*, whose editorials openly attacked the position of Bishop McIlvaine and other evangelicals. In the ensuing controversies open hostility developed between the Bishop of Ohio, who resented these attacks, and the Bishop of New York, who was the sponsor for *The Churchman*, which carried over unhappily into the trial and suspension of Bishop Onderdonk several years later.

In addition to McIlvaine's *Oxford Divinity*, John S. Stone, who had recently moved from Boston to the Diocese of New York and who was shocked by Bishop Onderdonk's Tractarian leanings, wrote two further conservative evangelical defenses: *The Mysteries Opened*, published in 1844, and *The Church Universal*, published in 1846. More in harmony with the *Tracts* were William I. Kip's *The Double Witness of the Church* (1842), a defense of the authority of Scripture and the tradition of the church, and *The Episcopate* (1855) by Hugh D. Evans, an Anglo-Catholic layman from Maryland.

Bishop Doane in 1834 published the first American edition of Keble's *The Christian Year*, annotated and with additional poems of his own and some by William Croswell, soon to be the first rector of the Church of the Advent, Boston. Seven years later Doane consulted with Keble and Pusey in England and came back enthusiastically supporting Anglo-Catholicism. Often known as "the John Keble of the American church," Doane wrote the hymns "Fling Out the Banner," "Softly now the light of day," and "Thou art the Way, to Thee alone." Although he was once described as "strongly, perilously human, having all the faults of an ardent nature," he was probably "as complete a specimen of high church bishop as this world has seen."[9]

Bishop DeLancey expected no injurious effects in the church from the *Tracts*, although he warned of the necessity of sifting the wheat from the chaff and proposed a repudiation of everything inconsistent with the Bible and the Prayer Book. He also carefully stressed the major catholic truths held by the American old high churchmen before Pusey was born.[10]

Bishop Whittingham, who had to contend with Roman tendencies in some areas of the Diocese of Maryland, was generally in agreement with the Oxford Movement but warned of its accompanying dangers. Denying the propriety of universal liberty without a commensurately disciplined responsibility, he deplored the radicals who used the methods of right-wing Roman Catholicism or left-wing sectarianism and commended the Book of Common Prayer and Canons as proper guides.[11] At about the same time he warned his diocese of the dangers of identifying religion with externalities, and, after admitting the difficulties of the times and acknowledging the laxity in the church and criticism from all sides, he asked his clergy to demonstrate personal probity and to preach the reproof of sin and the judgment of God. "Our preaching wants completeness," said Bishop Whittingham, who was generally considered one of the greatest preachers of his time;

> We give the people scraps and shreds of doctrine . . . and exhort too much in general terms. Probably there has never been anywhere a population more generally and at the same time superficially acquainted with the outlines of the Gospel, than that in our country. What is wanting is depth, depth of knowledge; and still more depth of conviction.[12]

Influenced by his observation of the Roman Church abroad, Whittingham was uncompromising in his opposition to the papal system. He thought it was in error in "setting the letter above and instead of the spirit; authority above and instead of conscience; dogmatic formula above and instead of evangelic faith."[13] Since some of his clergy were among the converts to Rome, he felt strongly about the renunciation of baptism and ordination, which he once described as a "sin akin to apostasy." After Newman's conversion to Rome, which Whittingham considered less significant than Pusey's remaining in the Church of England, he frankly wrote Pusey, "If schism be sin, we must treat schismatics as sinners, or be ourselves partakers of their guilt."[14] To one friend who was about to renounce his orders Whittingham wrote without reserve,

You meditate treason to the Church of God. You are about to plunge your-self headlong into a wicked schism. I adjure you by the love you once bore to me not to do this dreadful deed. . . . It is no light thing to take the step you have once taken; but when once in the bosom of the Church of God to lift your heel against it, and forsaking it to embrace an inveterate and deadly schism, is among the most heinous sins that Satan, in the garb of an angel of light, is ever suffered to delude the self-confident, the presumptuous, the headstrong, the unruly to commit.[15]

For forty years this eloquent, brilliant, and scholarly, yet oversensitive and, at times, impulsive bishop jealously defended the prerogatives of the episcopate and devotedly served the church, which next to Christ, its head, was his only love.

Much less dramatically but equally effectively, Nicholas H. Cobbs, the gentle, humble, and guileless first Bishop of Alabama, quietly helped the church to perceive the richness of its catholic heritage. He considered the *Tracts* as more beneficial than harmful, and while supporting apostolic order and holding a high appreciation of the sacraments and ordinances of the church, he was an ardent defender of evangelical truth. Greenough White, who happily described the bishop as "a saint of the southern church," said that the staple of his religious character was evangelical: "That was the warp upon which was woven the sacramental pattern of his life." An episcopal colleague once described Cobbs as "the wisest and best man, the most earnest preacher, the gentlest pastor, the meekest prelate, the soundest churchman of these latter days."[16]

Similarly guarded was Bishop Hopkins's support of the *Tracts*. He also had met the English leaders Pusey and Newman in 1838 and held the *Tracts* "in high estimation" and "of a most useful tendency"; he felt that they produced "clearer notions of Church principles and a far higher estimate of their value" and "a more elevated standard of clerical character." Hopkins declared that "the apostolic ministry is not the *essence*, but of the *order* of the Church" and denied the common Tractarian doctrines that episcopacy is essential to the very being of the church, that the church is infallible in interpreting Scripture, and that the Thirty-nine Articles can be reconciled with Roman dogma. On the contrary he asserted that the Church of England is both Reformed and Protestant, and at the same time insisted that the true catholic position was tenable among Anglicans since the words catholic and Roman were far from synonymous.[17]

In these attitudes of the Episcopal Church leaders there had already become clear a typical Anglican desire for finding and holding the best of all possible positions. This becomes even clearer in the teachings of Bishop Thomas C. Brownell of Connecticut, Bishop Jackson Kemper, and Bishop Alonzo Potter of Pennsylvania, who represented the largest American group of moderate churchmen. Brownell did not expect any material changes in the doctrine, discipline, or usages of the church to result from the Oxford Movement but welcomed it as leading toward the elucidation and establishment of catholic truth. Bishop Kemper asked his Diocese of Wisconsin to hold steady in the troubled times and to let no party spirit divide them and at the same time denounced "the blasphemies of Rome" as "our most formidable evil."[18] Alonzo Potter spoke of the imminent danger of hankering "after the private confessional, and the sacrament of penance, after more power and less responsibility for the clergy, and more responsibility and less liberty for the people."[19]

Bishop Alonzo Potter proposed in 1853 that the church should not try to cure the ill effects of the Tractarian disease by defending the pervert who remains in the church that he has ceased to love and overwhelming him with reproaches the instant he quits it. He urged that the church should guard against "the earliest approaches to an insidious will-worship and a disguised Romanism" and should be constantly on the watch to detect such signs of approaching defection, as

> . . . the Church is more prominent than her Head—sacramental grace more insisted on than holiness of heart and life . . . outward unity before fellowship of the spirit in the bond of peace—the liberty wherewith Christ has made us free repudiated for a bondage to ordinances and prostrations of mind and soul before some imaginary or self-constituted vice-gerent of Heaven.

Bishop Potter's warning may have been prompted by such incidents as the heresy trial of O. S. Prescott, a presbyter in the Diocese of Massachusetts, for holding the heretical doctrine of transubstantiation; teaching that Mary is the proper object of worship, was without sin, and is an intercessor; and for practicing auricular confession and priestly absolution. Since the court gave only an opinion of "no judgment," Prescott was not disciplined and wrote a submissive letter to Bishop Manton Eastburn.[20]

Among the parish clergy new doctrines were often considered as the disturbers of the peace of the church and the cause of its impotence. One rector, Andrew B. Paterson of Trinity Church, Princeton, told his congregation on the Sunday after Christmas in 1845,

> It is perfectly obvious that novel interpretations of the articles which have long had a fixed and definite meaning, by men of acknowledged authority and sanctity, must be attended with injurious results. Whatever shakes and undermines general and settled belief; whatever makes men uncertain, as to the grounds, or meaning of the articles of their creed, does an immediate injury to practical piety. . . .[21]

Although moderate churchmen had expected no overt disturbances, tension was building up in the church, and the occasion which aroused the storm was the ordination of Arthur Carey by Bishop Benjamin T. Onderdonk in 1843. Arthur Carey came to the General Seminary in 1839 where the *Tracts* were already very influential. A brilliant youth with ascetic inclinations, he became a devotee of Newman and fell under suspicion primarily because of his association with B. B. J. McMaster, a radical and contentious extremist who was about to defect to Rome, where he soon quarrelled with his superiors. When

Carey came to Bishop Onderdonk for ordination in 1843, the bishop, sensing the wide suspicions of heresy, brought the controversial candidate before eight assessors for a thorough doctrinal examination. Most of the questioning was done by Hugh Smith and Henry Anthon, rectors of St. Peter's and St. Mark's Churches respectively and leading New York low churchmen who disapproved of Carey. Soon after the examination they tried to prevent Carey's ordination by widely circulating an opposing pamphlet and by rising to protest at the time of the ordination when Bishop Onderdonk asked if there were any impediment.[22]

Samuel Seabury, one of Carey's examiners, in reviewing this pamphlet which claimed that Carey had asserted that there was no doctrinal difference between Rome and the Protestant Episcopal Church in the United States of America, claimed that it was full of omissions and distortions.[23] At the examination Carey had actually said that he did not deny but would not positively affirm the doctrine of the Council of Trent. Subsequently, Carey published a statement of his position that seemed to justify Bishop Onderdonk's ordination.[24] Seabury accepted Carey as his assistant at the Church of the Annunciation, and when the promising young cleric died a few months later, it became clear that his controversial experience, which might have been almost any other provocative incident, had served to incite a thorough investigation of the General Seminary, to occasion the trial of Bishop Onderdonk, and to stir up a feverish discussion of Tractarianism at the General Convention in 1844.

For several years it had been rumored that the General Seminary was a seedbed for Tractarianism. Before his election as Bishop of Maryland, William Whittingham was the very popular professor of ecclesiastical history at the seminary, a brilliant scholar who was the center of the Oxford influence and who grounded his position in Christian antiquity. In many ways Whittingham seemed to be a proper successor of the old high churchmen and a true catholic. After his death, Bishop Arthur C. Coxe said of him, "In him Antiquity was known here, was professed here and lived here; he was the grand apostle of it before we heard of Dr. Pusey."[25] John D. Ogilby, who succeeded him in 1840, held similar convictions and soon became the object of official investigation. Bishop Benjamin T. Onderdonk, who taught ecclesiastical polity at the seminary, was himself accused of having officially and publicly endorsed the *Tracts* without any reservation even after the appearance of *Tract Ninety*.[26]

Henry Onderdonk, Bishop of Pennsylvania, was generally sympathetic with the position of his brother in New York but moved with so much caution, even before the Carey case, that before ordaining him, he subjected James L. Breck to an examination for more than three hours and a further investigation of half that length before an examining presbyter. Actually Breck was involved in the incidents at the seminary but proved to be a good risk and one of the most effective missionaries of the church. Even though their patron, Whittingham, warned against rashness and the taking of all kinds of vows, Breck and several other students had undertaken the monastic life as the basis for their teaching and preaching mission in the West because they held that only in that fashion "can the Romanist be made to feel sensibly the power of the Church Catholic."[27]

As the news of the Carey ordination spread across the church, many leaders, including three bishops, McIlvaine, Chase, and Hopkins, protested, and an investigation of the seminary followed. While this fever was rising, Bishop Hopkins issued four letters under the title, *The Novelties Which Disturb Our Peace*, in which he once and for all declared his conviction about Tractarianism,

> . . . that the fundamental error of this system is one and the same with the theory of Romanism . . . that the visible Church is the reservoir of all spiritual influences; that grace is given by her and *only through her instrumentality*. This view is grand, sublime and imposing; but I believe it to be thoroughly unscriptural in principle, false in fact, and dangerous in operation.[28]

That there was in fact during these months an underground pro-Roman conspiracy at the General Seminary has since become clear. Professor S. H. Turner, writing about it later, said,

> . . . there were students whose views in some points were Romish, and whose intention was, after entering on parochial duties within our Church, to endeavor gradually to lead their congregations along with themselves to the Church of Rome.[29]

The faculty and three bishops later dealt with these men; several Middlers were asked to withdraw, and others were appropriately admonished.

Prompted by a request from the South Carolina Convention, the trustees of the school appointed a committee that attempted to poll opinions of the faculty in writing and in person. On their refusal the committee resigned, and the investigation fell to the bishops as "Visitors" to the Seminary. The report prepared for submission to the General Convention in 1844 concluded, "the Trustees feel assured that the General Theological Seminary has never been in a more healthful condition than it is at the present time." But the trustees were seriously divided. A motion to strike this phrase from the report was defeated by a vote of twenty-six to twenty-five, with such prominent bishop-trustees as Kemper, Hopkins, and Brownell voting with the minority. At the General Convention a minority report was presented, and the House of Bishops, pursuing their duty as Visitors, appointed a committee that prepared forty-two questions to which the faculty were requested to submit answers in writing.

The questions ranged from Puseyism to Calvinism and German Rationalism. The answers indicated that the *Tracts* were not being used as texts but had been commended for student reading by Bishop Onderdonk. Samuel Turner, professor of Old Testament, replied that he considered the whole theory of rationalism as "neither more nor less than disguised infidelity." Bishop Onderdonk was more guarded in his statement that there were

. . . more apparent than real discrepancies between the decrees of Trent, considered as embracing mere *opinions*, and our standards; but that these decrees, considered as setting forth and enjoining the *faith* are incompatible with the doctrines of this church.

He also claimed that he taught the Holy Scriptures, as containing all things necessary to salvation, and primitive catholic tradition, "as a rule for the right understanding of Scripture." Professor Ogilby, who had indiscreetly attacked Doctor Tyng during the convention, was given a thorough oral examination and, in his written replies, was more precise to say that he counted the decrees of Trent "as artfully contrived to deceive and beguile the unwary" and that he thought it would be inconsistent for any minister of the Reformed Church to receive them.[30] After three meetings, the bishops declared that they found no interior evidences that superstitious or Romish practices were allowed or encouraged in the Seminary and ordered the questions and faculty answers printed and distributed as the best antidote to current rumors.

Suspicions of many, however, were not allayed, and controversy almost brought about the closing of the Seminary. Resignations and other disturbances there had required temporary replacements by acting professors. At the meeting of the trustees on June 26, 1846, Bishop William H. DeLancey presided by virtue of his being the oldest bishop present. On his own responsibility he brought before the board a resolution that the next General Convention be requested to consider and decide on the expediency of dissolving the Seminary and that its assets be returned to the contributing dioceses. He grounded his proposal on the presence of distrust, suspicion, and hostility toward the institution and felt that its dissolution might bring peace and prosperity to the church and especially to the Diocese of New York. Although this resolution was not adopted, it was again seriously considered a year later.[31]

Meanwhile, the General Convention met in New York in October, 1844, and was in large part given over to the Tractarian controversy with no less than four full days devoted to its consideration. Some of its more militant opponents proposed an emphatic denunciation of the movement, but even a second, more moderate resolution asking the House of Bishops to promulgate a clear doctrinal statement was lost, probably because no one really wished the bishops to be placed in the position of doctrinal arbiters. Then, too, catholic doctrine had too long been widely held in the church to permit it to be swept away in a torrent of opposition to its more radical proponents. The net result was a standard of tolerance, fraught with all the dangers of indifferentism but with the possibilities of fruitful and constructive theological development as well, a spirit that has characterized Episcopal Church polity since 1844. Almost without opposition the House of Deputies resolved that they

. . . consider the Liturgy, Offices and Articles of the Church sufficient exponents of her sense of the essential doctrines of Holy Scripture; and that the Canons of the Church afford ample means of discipline and correction for all who depart from her standards. And further, that the General Convention is not a suitable tribunal for the trial and censure of, and that the Church is not responsible for the errors of individuals, whether they are members of this church or otherwise.

The convention ended on a comparatively irenic note, having dispatched much important constructive business, including the naming of two bishops for the western areas. The House of Bishops, nevertheless, showed its due concern in the emphatic language of the pastoral letter circulated soon after these sessions. While this letter implied criticism of Tractarianism and roundly condemned "the blasphemous doctrine of Transubstantiation and the abominable idolatries of the Mass," it was primarily a positive declaration emphasizing justification by faith and included an exhortation that seminary professors ground their students in sound doctrine. In no uncertain terms the bishops, mindful of the Carey case, said,

> We feel it our duty to declare, that no person should be ordained who is not well acquainted with the landmarks which separate us from the Church of Rome; and being so, who will not distinctly declare himself a Protestant, heartily abjuring her corruptions, as our reformers did; and it is our solemn counsel to all professors in our theological seminaries, and all others who are concerned in the preparation of candidates for holy orders, to be faithful in their duties, that neither Romanists on the one hand, nor enemies of the Episcopal Church on the other, may have cause to boast that we have departed in the slightest degree from the spirit and principles of the Reformation, as exemplified by the Church of England.[32]

The General Convention of 1844 also found time to define by canon the proper procedures for the resignation and the trial of bishops. Both issues had caused confusion in the church because of lack of canonical regulation and had been under consideration for several trienniums. This new canon made it possible for a bishop to resign directly to the House of Bishops, without the consent of his diocese, and also clarified the procedure for the trial of a bishop, which the Convention of 1841 had determined must be by a court composed entirely of his peers. While these specifications were largely planned by the high churchmen to lend dignity and prestige to the episcopal office and to save bishops from embarrassing attacks by their own dioceses, they were soon to be used to bring to trial several high church bishops who might never have been prosecuted in their own jurisdictions.

Despite the declaration of toleration in 1844 a genuine tragedy occurred in the church when the trial of Bishop Benjamin T. Onderdonk for irregular conduct with women, but with no implications of adultery, gave an opportunity for those who opposed his ardent support of the *Tracts* to press their personal animosities toward the Bishop of New York. Some of his supporters went so far as to blame the entire episode on the polity dispute and thus exonerated their bishop. The uncontroverted evidence leaves little doubt about the facts in the case, and only the high respect for the office undoubtedly led to his suspension on January 3, 1845, rather than to his deposition. Since his suspension remained indefinite, it was not until the General Convention in 1851 provided a canon permitting the election of a provisional bishop that Jonathan M. Wainwright was chosen for that semivacant diocesan post. Onderdonk's suspension was never removed, and he lived in retirement until his death in 1861.[33]

The General Convention of 1844 had adopted changes in trial procedures making it possible for a bishop to avoid trial by confessing his guilt. The resignation of bishops had also been regularized by requiring the consent of the House of Bishops. At least the first of these measures was adopted in the hope that it would facilitate the handling of the case of Bishop Henry U. Onderdonk of Pennsylvania, a brother of the Bishop of New York, who had been charged with intemperance. He confessed his guilt and explained that he had become addicted after he had taken some liquor for a chronic digestive disorder on the advice of a physician. He had, however, given up the use of alcohol and probably should have been more mercifully treated. His support of Tractarianism had also brought him strong opposition even in his own diocese where the evangelicals were in control, and when he resigned his jurisdiction, the diocese refused to accept it. Even though Onderdonk resigned his jurisdiction to the House of Bishops according to the new canon of 1844 and confessed his guilt to them, he was indefinitely suspended from office. This sentence was removed in 1856, but he was never restored to office since Alonzo Potter had been elected his successor; during the remaining two years of his life he lived in retirement.

Bishop George W. Doane of New Jersey was also brought to trial in 1852 and 1853 for mismanagement of funds in connection with St. Mary's Hall in Burlington by which he was forced into bankruptcy. Cleared of criminal intention by his diocese, the House of Bishops in 1852 accepted that decision as their own, until it became clear that this action was uncanonical. The following year, with hardly more canonical propriety, the House of Bishops dropped all proceedings since Doane had been proven inept in business affairs but had not really been guilty of any crime beyond substantial incompetence. Clemency under these circumstances may have been easier than in the cases of drunkenness and social improprieties, but Doane was also a superior parliamentarian, and in a case that ended in an acquittal by a seven to six vote of his peers, Bishop Doane had indeed made "the trial of a bishop hard" as he had once predicted he would. Since the same bishops were usually involved in these prosecutions, it becomes even more difficult to exonerate the Onderdonks on the basis of vengeful partisanship; Bishop Doane was as ardent a Tractarian as the brothers, and it is preposterous to impugn the motives and integrity of the House of Bishops or even an Episcopal court. Bishop William S. Perry once attributed these disciplinary measures to "the desire of presenting before the world a standard of unimpeachable personal purity in a bishop," rather than "any possibility of party triumph or personal revenge."[34]

Occasionally differences of churchmanship between a bishop and his priests also led to the necessity for discipline and even new canonical provisions. In

Maryland Bishop Whittingham insisted upon full episcopal prerogatives during his visitations, including his right to celebrate the Holy Communion and to pronounce the absolution and benediction at Morning and Evening Prayer, as well as appropriating the collections for diocesan use. Joseph Trapnell opposed the bishop and was convicted before a diocesan court from which there was no provision for an appeal. The General Convention in 1850 adopted canons prescribing a bishop's rights and duties on visitations, largely supporting Whittingham's claims and ordering that visitations to each parish shall be made at least once in three years. This latter provision was probably aimed at Massachusetts, where Bishop Manton Eastburn had refused to visit the Church of the Advent in Boston because the first American Anglo-Catholic parish refused to bring its services and internal arrangements, including the placing of flowers on the altar, into conformity with the prevailing usage, as Bishop Eastburn defined his wishes. Eastburn ignored the canon of 1850 since it was only a recommendation. Only after the Church of the Advent petitioned the General Convention did that body in 1856 provide that a parish not visited once in three years shall apply to the Presiding Bishop for a Council of Reconciliation to be composed of the bishops of five neighboring dioceses.

Further tragedy befell the church as men of strong catholic convictions defected to the Roman Catholic Church. This was not an entirely new experience, for each generation had seen some converts to Rome, although no previous period had seen so many. Few of the earlier converts became as prominent as Mrs. Elizabeth Ann Bayley Seton (1774–1821). She was baptized and confirmed by Bishop William White, was converted to Rome in 1805, and subsequently founded the Sisters of Charity in the United States. Because of her good life and work, her cause for beatification was formally introduced before the Curia in Rome in 1940. Mother Seton was declared "Venerable" by Pope John XXIII on December 18, 1959, and her beatification followed on March 17, 1963. She is the first American woman to reach the final step toward sainthood.

Under pressure from the faculty several students, some of them of unusual ability, left the General Seminary and ultimately found their way into the Roman Catholic Church. James Roosevelt Bayley, after a brief service at St. Peter's Church in Harlem, left as early as 1841, subsequently became the first Roman Catholic Bishop of Newark (1853–1872) and for his last five years, the Archbishop of Baltimore. Edward Putnam was converted and left the Seminary in 1844, and soon afterward seven others left including Edgar Wadhams, who later became the first Roman Catholic Bishop of Ogdensburg. Nashotah House lost six men. Nathaniel A. Hewit and Francis Asbury Baker of Maryland, after defecting, united to found the missionary Paulist Fathers. Clarence E. Walworth, a converted Presbyterian, became an effective Roman Catholic mission preacher, while George W. Doane, elder son of Bishop Doane, became rector of the cathedral at Newark, chancellor of the diocese, vicar general, and a monsignor. No men of the stature of Newman and Manning in England left the Episcopal Church, and far fewer converts left the Episcopal Church than the Church of England.

Since 1789 not more than fifty ministers of the Episcopal Church had submitted to Rome, and more than half of these had been converts to this church from the ministries of other Protestant communions in their mature years. This tendency was a logical development in a church that had rapidly expanded the ranks of its clergy from 534 in 1830 to 1,589 in 1850 and for more than a century since then has received more than half of its ministers from such sources. Of the 1,976 clergy ordained between 1822 and 1855, the generation most affected by Tractarianism, twenty-nine or about one and one-half per cent entered the Church of Rome. Nineteen of these had been ordained in the 1840's, the period of greatest controversy. The defections were widely spaced so that not more than two occurred in any year except 1855, when there were four, and 1849 and 1852, when there were five. Four of the twenty-nine eventually returned to the Episcopal Church. Some seminarians and other candidates, never ordained in the Episcopal Church, eventually found their way to Rome.[35]

There were also conversions from Rome during these years. The Rev. Dr. Newell, educated in Roman Catholic schools in England and at the Sorbonne, became a professor at St. Edmund's College in 1825 and served as its president from 1833 until he came to the United States in 1837. He served as a parish priest until the promulgation of the dogma of the Immaculate Conception in 1854, when he left the Roman Catholic Church and sought admission to the Episcopal Church. In 1872 Bishop Quintard of Alabama restored him to the priesthood, and he served the Episcopal parish at Ashwood until his death in 1889 at almost ninety-two years of age.[36]

Of the four who returned to the Episcopal Church, Pierce Connelly and John Murray Forbes had unusual careers. Connelly and his wife were converted to Rome while he was serving Trinity Church in Natchez, Mississippi. Before he could be ordained on July 6, 1845, his wife agreed to take a vow of perpetual chastity, and the following year she founded the Society of the Holy Child Jesus and died in that faith. Connelly, however, returned to the Episcopal Church in 1850, with his three children, and after restoration to the priesthood, served more than thirty years as the rector of the American Episcopal Church in Florence, Italy.

John Murray Forbes served with distinction in both the Episcopal and the Roman Catholic Churches. After graduation from General Seminary in 1834 he became rector of St. Luke's Church in New York. Influenced by his study of the *Tracts,* he left the church fifteen years later in October, 1849, with his curate Thomas S. Preston, and together they entered the Roman Catholic Church. So successful was Forbes's pastorate at St. Ann's Roman Catholic parish in New York City and so highly was he regarded that Pope Pius IX awarded him the degree of Doctor of Sacred Theology and Archbishop Hughes of New York sent him to Rome to organize the now famous American College for Priests there. Ten years later, however, with equal honesty and integrity, he returned to the Episcopal Church where he was gladly received after proper disciplinary waiting. In his letter to Archbishop Hughes, Forbes wrote that he had been converted "with a deep and conscientious conviction that it was necessary to be in communion with the See of Rome," but now that he had found it impossible to endure the Roman yoke, he added,

> . . . but this conviction I have not been able to sustain, in face of the fact that by it the natural rights of man and all individual liberty must be sacrificed —and not only so, but the private conscience often violated, and one forced, by silence at least, to acquiesce in what is opposed to moral truth and justice.

In a later conversation with friends in the Episcopal Church who happily reversed his deposition, he said that he had come back "to retain my regard for the truth." Ten years later his church demonstrated its confidence in him by naming him dean of the General Seminary.[37]

The only churchman in high position to leave the Episcopal Church for Rome was Levi Silliman Ives (1797–1867), Bishop of North Carolina and a former Presbyterian, who on graduation from the General Seminary married the daughter of Bishop Hobart. He rapidly moved from Hobartianism to Tractarianism and by 1849 supported auricular confessions and transubstantiation. He had also introduced many Anglo-Catholic usages and founded a religious order at Valle Crucis. Under pressure from his own diocese, he gave reassurances of his loyalty, which were accepted in 1851. When he asked during the following year for a six months' leave to travel for his health and requested an advance of $1,000, this, too, was granted. On December 22, 1852, he wrote from Rome to his convention telling of his conversion and resigning his diocese. Since the resignation should have been made to the House of Bishops, his act was uncanonical, and he was accordingly deposed. Ives's defection seemed to be the convincing evidence of a basic instability in his nature. Before he sought ordination in the Episcopal Church he had been a promoter of revival measures among the Presbyterians, and after he became Bishop of North Carolina, he had said,

> . . . our branch of the church . . . belongs to that portion of Christ's body which is the most scriptural, primitive and truly catholic in its character; and that no one embraced by holy baptism within its pale can depart from it without the grievous sin of doing despite to the Holy Ghost.[38]

Thomas Atkinson became his successor in the Diocese of North Carolina, and Ives became an American pioneer in Roman Catholic charitable work.

As the defections to Rome continued, the church generally became frightened by the threat from that quarter. While eleven of the fourteen bishops elected between 1830 and 1840 were high churchmen, only five of the fifteen elected in the next controversial decade could be claimed by this party. The fears of the evangelicals became evident in their establishment of distinctly party journals, societies for education, and two independent missionary societies. During the General Convention in New York in 1847 the Protestant

Episcopal Society for the Promotion of Evangelical Knowledge was formed to overcome Tractarian influences. Henry Anthon was typical of the leading evangelicals of this period; he not only shared in each of these new undertakings but also had a part in establishing *The Episcopal Quarterly Review* and founded *The Protestant Churchman,* "racy in style and fearless and decided in statement," to counteract the influence of *The Churchman* then being ably edited by Samuel Seabury.

Ironically, the strongest deterrent to the developed Anglo-Catholic type of Tractarianism appeared in a division in the ranks of the high churchmen, which often caused the differences between them to be felt as keenly as those which separated them from the evangelicals. The old high churchmen emphasized theological principles while the advanced Anglo-Catholics stressed ceremonial usages, yet the conjunction of their influences brought new devotion and zeal to the life and work of the church, making for a vital combination of Christian life and worship not unlike that of Frederick Denison Maurice in the English Church. Bishop Horatio Potter of New York happily described the far-reaching constructive results of these days of struggle thus,

> Coincident with this revival of Catholic truth and the primitive ethos, was a powerful revival of spiritual life and energy. Noble churches went up by hundreds in quarters where before not five had been added in a century. Colonial Bishoprics established all round the globe, and served by Catholic-minded men of the true Apostolic spirit—new life infused into the whole parochial system at home—a spirit of earnest devotion taking possession of the great schools and universities, in which the youth of the land are trained —unwonted devices and efforts to reach and reclaim the children of vice and misery—more abundant prayers and alms—*these* are some of the abundant tokens . . . that the Church as a whole has arisen and shaken herself from the dust.[39]

Perhaps the chief benefit of the Tractarian struggle was the clarification of essential differences between the parties in the church and at the same time the rise of an increased tolerance for a variety of theological opinion within the general limits of the Holy Scripture, the Book of Common Prayer, and the Anglican tradition and polity. Hereafter there would be less concern about enforcing conformity in either doctrine or practice, and only the attempts of minorities to bend the entire church to their points of view would lead to major crises. Between the evangelicals and the high churchmen, the broad churchmen would arise with a primary concern for truth from any source and a great variety of attitudes toward liturgical observance. Such liberties made possible the elimination of sharp distinctions of party allegiance and ultimately led in this century to a cross-fertilization throughout the church that makes accurate party differentiations very difficult and represents a comprehensiveness many non-Anglicans believe must ultimately characterize a more united Christendom.

The effects of the Tractarian Movement slowly but surely also revealed themselves throughout the church in the increased interest in the form of the liturgy, the greater frequency of the celebrations of Holy Communion, the vestments of the clergy, the design of church buildings, the improvement of the music in the churches, and the concern for high standards of Christian living among the laity and clergy. Bishop Whittingham, while rector of St. Luke's Church in New York, had introduced daily services in 1832 and within a decade such observances had spread from Massachusetts to Ohio and were widely observed in New York, Pennsylvania, and New Jersey. The 1840's also saw the celebrations of Holy Communion, often infrequently and irregularly observed until that time, become a weekly observance. Dean E. A. Hoffman of the General Seminary wrote a widely distributed pamphlet, *The Weekly Eucharist*, which stressed the Scriptural authority and the testimony of the Church Fathers and Reformers for this practice.

Many observances later associated with Tractarian developments were introduced as early as 1827 by William A. Muhlenberg at his boys' school at Flushing, Long Island. Here he used candles and flowers on the altar, Christmas carols and Christmas greens, acolytes and a vested choir of men and boys. An accomplished musician, poet and hymn-writer and a man of general artistic temperament, Muhlenberg had come to appreciate good music and colorful worship in his early days in the Lutheran Church and from his study of Roman Catholicism. He admitted that his innovations were prompted by purely aesthetic motives, but they made a lasting impression on many who studied with him.

One of Muhlenberg's most influential students was the similarly gifted John Ireland Tucker; in 1844 he founded the Church of the Holy Cross at Troy, New York, which was built according to early English design and had a stone altar. His influence on American church music grew out of his *Tucker Service Book* with chants and prefaces, which, even though they were not of the highest musical worth, set a trend in the church. The observance of Saints' and Holy Days, the use of flowers in the sanctuary, the wearing of surplices and colored stoles, and the custom of facing the altar for the *Gloria* and the Creed may have been first introduced by Tucker in the Church of the Holy Cross. Here full choral services, with canticles and psalms sung to Gregorian tones, were begun in 1844, and these choral celebrations of the Holy Communion antedated any such observances in the English cathedrals.

Soon after Bishop Whittingham came to the Diocese of Maryland in 1840, on his first visit to the western shore, six of his clergy "agreed" to wear cassocks, but for a long time everyone knew that a cassock was not only the mark of a clergyman but of one who was particularly concerned "to please his bishop."[40] On the other hand, the Bishop of Maryland was rigid in his opposition to any attempts at enriching the ceremonial and at times warned his more susceptible priests. The New York Ecclesiological Society, of which John M. Forbes, then rector of St. Luke's Church, was the president, provided the first serious attempt in the church to study liturgics.

For many years Episcopalians had avoided the use of hymns as "provocative of enthusiasm" and chanting only slowly took the place of metric psalmody, partly because it was difficult and also because of its association with the Roman service. Even laymen objected to changes in this direction; when a New York choir sang the *Gloria* at the conclusion of the Psalm, a lay delegation petitioned the bishop to stop "this abominable Popish innovation." The widespread use of choirs also multiplied parish problems. In Richmond, Virginia, St. James' Church apparently sought to improve the quality of its choir in 1840 but discovered that while the elimination of certain voices might improve the music, it certainly could also disturb the peace. So on June 2, 1840, the vestry ruled that their previous legislation had never intended to remove from the choir anyone who had been a member of the choir on February 21, 1840, and that all members of that date "are hereby considered a member of the choir and entitled to their seats therein."[41]

The Gothic Trinity Church in New York, designed by Richard Upjohn, was dedicated on Ascension Day, 1846, and soon became the ideal after which many church buildings were patterned. In New England serious objections arose following the renovation of Trinity Church, Nantucket, where Frederick Pollard, the young priest who had recently been graduated from the General Seminary in 1843, removed the old three-level pulpit, and erected a reredos in the chancel, where he set up a credence and an altar on which he placed two candlesticks. The Epistle and the Gospel were read from their now customary sides of the altar, and the Offices from a fald-stool facing the altar. He used wafer bread for Holy Communion and was assisted by an unvested server.[42]

More belligerent was the response of Bishop Eastburn when he discovered what he considered ceremonial irregularities and Roman ornaments at the Church of the Advent in Boston, where he had already found sufficient deviation in parish customs to detain him from regular visitations. The congregation knelt facing the altar and chanted the Psalter; the rector preached in a surplice; the altar was covered with a crimson cloth with four candles on a retable behind it; and a window was ornamented with "the popish symbol," the cross. When the bishop asked William Croswell to agree to read the prayers while facing the congregation, the rector refused on the ground that he would not add to the promises made at his ordination. For years Eastburn refused to visit the parish, and the confirmands were regularly brought to some other church to receive the imposition of the bishop's hands.[43]

When the Gothic St. Paul's Church was completed in Columbus, Ohio, in 1846, Bishop McIlvaine refused to consecrate it until the stone altar had been replaced by "an honest table with legs." Bishop Otey accompanied Bishop Polk to Riverside, Tennessee, to consecrate the church there, and was shocked to find what he called the unmistakable signs of ritualism that was already rampant in the East—a cross over every gate, three crosses on the roof, one on the belfry, and five crosses inside, as well as the large moveable cross on the altar. Since he feared these Romeward tendencies, he refused to consecrate the church until the number of crosses had been reduced.[44]

Many other bishops were, of course, in sympathy with these trends, and gradually observances that a century ago were counted radical and Romish became generally accepted; it was only after 1900 that advanced ceremonialists began to introduce vestiary embellishments and liturgical enrichments. Before 1837 there were hardly six surplices in all Ohio, and before the Civil War most churchmen considered free pews, daily matins and vespers, a weekly Holy Communion, the observance of Saints' Days, stone altars and colored frontals, candles and crosses, surplices and stoles as the obvious signs of ritualism and usually blamed them on the influence of the *Tracts*.

Beyond these externalities, much as in the Christian Socialist Movement sponsored by Frederick D. Maurice and his associates in England, those parishes with the enriched services and the free pews succeeded in interpreting religion effectively for the common working man who had been unable to appreciate the nuances of theological refinement or the significance of apostolic succession. In this spirit William Muhlenberg was about to present to the General Convention his "Memorial," which would suggest further ways in which the church could break down the inherited alliance of wealth and social position with the Episcopal Church, reach out to the unchurched masses, and even build better relations with other Protestants.

At both the parish and diocesan level this new development in the thought and worship of the church frequently stimulated the promotion of a more consistent Christian life for the members of the church. Under the leadership of their devout and able Bishop Cobbs, the Diocese of Alabama in its convention of 1849 adopted a canon on lay discipline. It provided that every communicant in the diocese shall observe daily family prayers, heads of families shall instruct those under them and send their children to catechetical instruction, notorious transgressors shall be excluded from Holy Communion and sponsorship in baptism, and confirmed persons failing to come to Holy Communion for twelve months shall be dropped from the roll of communicants.[45]

In the mid-nineteenth century the church was plagued not only by a rising party spirit within but at times also by anti-Episcopal attacks from without, but with less frequency and less virulence than in the eighteenth century; these often took the form of local word battles from pulpits and in the press. Sometimes these disputes involved aspects of the domestic party struggles. Such was the case when J. A. Shanklin, rector of Christ Church in Macon, Georgia, replied to an unnamed opponent who had apparently charged that the Episcopal Church did not believe in a "change of heart," was not interested in revivals and missions, was deficient in vital piety, and tended toward Popery. In a pamphlet entitled, *Some Objections to the Episcopal Church Considered and Answered*, which was widely distributed by the Protestant Episcopal Society for the Promotion of Evangelical Knowledge, Shanklin discussed vestments, forms of prayer and the liturgy, and described their history and use. He denied that Episcopalians were proselyting but agreed that many conversions came through those who learned to know and love the church, "as a general rule, the more persons know of the Episcopal Church, the more they love her, and those who know her best love her most."[46]

One argument that ran through several pamphlets printed in the early 1840's involved the validity of Episcopal and Methodist orders in the ministry and seemed to reach a climax in Allen Steele's review of *The Episcopal Church Defended*, in which this Methodist pastor of St. John's Church, Batavia, New York, and a member of the Genesee Conference, traced Methodist authority through John Wesley to the Church of England. Another battle of words resulted when William Potts, a Presbyterian clergyman in St. Louis, preached a sermon before his presbytery on the Scriptural authority for the Presbyterian form of church government. He was challenged by a pamphlet *An Episcopalian's View of a Sermon*, to which he replied in a forty-one-page pamphlet of his own. Although it settled nothing, this pamphlet duel permitted each contestant to reassert the classic answers to the moot question of episcopacy and authority in the church.[47]

Early in this period Samuel Farmer Jarvis (1786-1851), son of the second Bishop of Connecticut and professor of oriental languages at the college in Hartford, preached a sermon before the Board of Missions in St. Thomas's Church, New York, on June 26, 1836, in which he made one of the earliest attempts to describe the real presence of Christ in the sacrament. Jarvis proved himself to be a prophet when he said that Christian unity was necessary to the conversion of the world; tracing unity and disunity in the church through the centuries, he showed that strength invariably followed unity. Pleading for tolerance that no one be banished from the church for varying sacramental ideas, Jarvis claimed that the Church of England and the Episcopal Church should be strong and show missionary zeal because Anglicanism had preserved and striven for unity more than most churches.[48]

This plea was timely, for the denominations in America were multiplying rapidly because of differences of opinion and emphasis and many of them were increasing in strength. Similar internal differences also arose in the Episcopal Church over such matters as the participation in weeknight prayer meetings and other informal religious exercises. Admitting that the object of these "social means of grace" was designed to infuse evangelical piety into lifeless forms, Bishop Hobart roundly opposed the superseding of the liturgy by

> . . . the extemporaneous effusions of unordained men; thus changing the character of our Church, and assimilating it, in a greater or less degree, to religious opinions and practices, which her institutions disallow and condemn.[49]

When the bishop objected to Milnor's free prayers in St. George's Church, the evangelical rector said he was ready to stand trial; and when the bishop ordered the rector to dismiss a prayer meeting in his church, Milnor replied, "Bishop, I *dare* not prevent my parishioners from meeting for prayers; but if you are willing to take the responsibility of dismissing them, you have my permission."[50]

In a similar spirit Bishop Hobart urged his clergy not to cooperate with interdenominational Bible Societies on the ground that in distributing the

Book of Common Prayer with the Bible through their own New York Bible and Common Prayer Book Society they diffused religious truth more effectually than by circulating the Bible alone. The bishop probably had a more important reason, as he once described it,

> A profession of liberality pervades all such associations which renders it unfashionable, unpleasant and unkind for Episcopalians to doubt the equal excellence of Presbytery and Episcopacy, of extempore worship and a liturgy. When Episcopalians are brought into this state of liberal indifference, if they are not prepared to renounce their principles, they are at least deterred from laying peculiar stress upon them, and from advocating and enforcing them.[51]

Despite Hobart's attitude, many bishops served in Bible Societies, and the constitution of the American Bible Society, organized on May 10, 1816, was drafted by a member of his Trinity Parish in New York. Several years later in a convention address in 1822 he repeated even more precisely his position about such societies:

> They inculcate that general liberality which considers the differences among Christians as non-essential; and they thus tend to weaken the zeal of Episcopalians in favor of those distinguishing principles of their Church which eminently entitle her to the appellation of apostolic and primitive.[52]

Although it had been an unpleasant controversy, it marked the end of any such attempts at curtailment of personal liberty and Christian spirit in interdenominational relations.

Since the Episcopal Church had no official periodical, each party supported its own journals on a regional and national scale. The evangelical party sponsored *The Episcopal Recorder* in the East, *The Gambier Observer* in the Midwest, and *The Southern Churchman* in the South. The high church party supported *The Churchman*, which became the vehicle to promote all things Tractarian; it became the medium for Samuel Seabury, then its editor, to launch his critical attacks on low church leaders for many years. With party spirit running high, these journals were hardly impartial news agencies, and no editor lacked enthusiasm in supporting his own party. So vitriolic had the conflicts become that in 1838 the House of Bishops said these journals were too much filled with unprofitable controversy, manifested a spirit of strife and contention, and were inconsistent with brotherly kindness and Christian love.

As the high church party gained control of the major church institutions, largely as a result of Bishop Hobart's influence in the earlier years, the low churchmen organized their own educational and promotional agencies, such as the Protestant Episcopal Evangelical Society, the Episcopal Education Society, and the Protestant Episcopal Society for the Promotion of Evangelical Knowledge, incorporated in Pennsylvania in 1848. This last Society issued hundreds of books and tracts, two monthly periodicals for use in the parish and church schools, and generally became the promotional agency for the evangelicals during the heat of the controversies.

With the increase of interdenominational agencies to carry on the cooperative religious efforts of the American churches, there arose a difference of opinion on this subject in the Episcopal Church. The evangelical clergy for years had freely taken part in interdenominational meetings and often participated in services in other churches and occasionally invited ministers of other denominations to take their pulpits. The high churchmen generally disapproved of these actions, assuming that an Episcopal clergyman was bound by his vows to use the Prayer Book liturgy even when conducting a service in a non-Episcopal church.

Men in high places such as H. van D. Johns of Baltimore and John Cotton Smith, rector of the Church of the Ascension in New York, were sharply censured, and Bishop Horatio Potter issued a pastoral letter in the Diocese of New York in which he asserted that the church makes a fundamental distinction between ministers episcopally ordained and those not episcopally ordained, and he threatened admonition, suspension or degradation for further violations. Stephen H. Tyng challenged the bishop, reminding him that Bishop Griswold preached in other churches and invited other ministers to preach in his church and that Bishop White had told him to "preach for all who invite you. . . . Employ the Prayer Book as much as you can usefully and consistently with their habits." He concluded his letter to Bishop Potter: "And while we love you as our bishop, we cannot concede, even to your wish, that which is to us a dear and valued principle of the doctrine of Christ."[53] J. C. Smith, W. A. Muhlenberg, and E. H. Canfield wrote similar letters, and Bishop Potter proposed no discipline. When Stephen H. Tyng, Jr., preached in a Methodist church in New Brunswick, New Jersey, three years later, he was brought to trial for the canonical violation that he had officiated in another's cure without his permission; he was publicly admonished by the bishop. In a similar instance when a minister in the Diocese of Ohio was presented to the standing committee for preaching in a Congregational church without using the Prayer Book or vestments, the case was not considered a proper ground of presentment.

By 1868 the General Convention saw the need for clarifying this church law and, after various revisions, adopted a canon that remains substantially the current position of the church and provides that, with the consent of the bishop, Christian men who are not ministers of the Episcopal Church may make addresses in the church on special occasions. The rigidity or liberality with which this canon has been interpreted has varied through the years with the attitudes of the diocesans, but more and more freely the Episcopal clergy have participated with other clergy in services, especially those of an ecumenical character. From the earliest years of their associations in this country, the relations between the Episcopalians and Moravians had been a friendly one since they shared an apostolic ministry. This feeling became very evident in 1838 when Bishop Doane accepted a deserted Moravian church building, Zion Chapel, at Moravia near Swedesboro, New Jersey, and dedicated it as an Episcopal church on April 26 of that year. The exchange of letters with Bishop van Vleck of the Moravian Church was most cordial.[54]

XVI

THE CIVIL WAR
AND MISSIONS

The outbreak of the Civil War and the formation of the Confederate States of America found the bishops of the Episcopal Church in these states still fully in authority in their dioceses but no longer in the United States of America. Under the necessity of reorganizing the general structure of the church, which some bishops welcomed and others accepted reluctantly, delegates from Alabama, Florida, Georgia, Mississippi, South Carolina, Louisiana, and Tennessee assembled at Montgomery early in July, 1861, to draft plans for the permanent organization. These churchmen still considered themselves a part of the continuing church and responsible for its obligations; at this preliminary meeting they appointed a missionary committee to receive funds for the domestic missions in Texas, Arkansas, and the Southwest as well as for foreign missions. Before the war ended they had assumed responsibility for the support of Bishop William Boone in China and Bishop John Payne in Liberia, both of them from southern dioceses.

In the fall of 1861 at an adjourned meeting in Columbia, South Carolina, representatives from eleven dioceses adopted a provisional constitution for the new church, largely under the leadership of Bishop Stephen Elliott who had been Bishop of Georgia since 1841. Most of the southern bishops were aged or infirm; Leonidas Polk, since 1841 Bishop of Louisiana and for three years before that the Missionary Bishop of the Southwest, would have been another able leader, but since he had been trained at West Point, he was soon commissioned a general in the Confederate Army. When the provisional constitution had been adopted by the required seven dioceses, the first General Council (the term deliberately chosen because of its use in the ancient church) of the Protestant Episcopal Church in the Confederate States of America convened in St. Paul's Church, Augusta, Georgia, from November 12 to 22, 1862.

At no time was the church in the Confederacy completely united. The bishops and deputies of the seven dioceses gathered at Augusta, including Virginia, North Carolina, South Carolina, Georgia, Alabama, Mississippi, and Texas, received the Diocese of Arkansas into union with the Council, an act that was later recognized by the General Convention as a valid organization of that diocese. Officially the church now comprised eight bishops and 375 clergy, but there were also three bishops and seventy-three clergy in Florida, Louisiana, and Tennessee where hostilities prevented ratification of the constitution. Florida eventually added its approval in December, 1863. Long distances separated the major centers of church life, and military campaigns frequently separated large areas of the church; and with the waning of hopes for a Confederate victory the southern dioceses of necessity often acted independently. Several editions of the Book of Common Prayer of the Protestant Episcopal Church in the Confederate States of America were issued after the first General Council; at least two different editions bore a Richmond imprint of 1863, although some of these were probably printed in England. It is probable that another complete edition was lost at sea.[1] The Diocesan Missionary Society of the Protestant Episcopal Church in Virginia published at least one edition of *The Army and Navy Prayer Book* in Richmond in 1864. It contained a service of Morning Prayer and two shorter services, plus twelve pages of occasional prayers, an order for Confirmation, four pages of Psalms and four additional pages of Psalms and Collects to be substituted in Morning Prayer for the *Venite, Te Deum* and *Jubilate* to create an office for Evening Prayer. Although bishops and rectors ministered to the military as they were able, the Confederate church also supplied chaplains. One of them, James B. Aviett, on September 27, 1862, requested a supply of tracts and added that the army was resting below Winchester on the Martinsburg Pike. He wrote, "Rumors are afloat that the enemy are in force . . . about Leesburg. . . . Surely we have great cause to be supremely thankful to God for his many blessings to us as a people."[2]

The church in the South also continued its ministry to the Negroes throughout the war years. In the pastoral letter issued after the General Council in 1862 the bishops clearly stated their intention to continue the historic church and to continue the doctrine, discipline, and worship they had once shared with the church in the North. All the essential structure of the church was carefully preserved, but the southern leaders were equally careful to embody in the pastoral letter a clear and significant statement about their responsibility to the Negroes. They said:

> Slaves of the South are not merely so much property, but are a sacred trust
> committed to us, as a people, to be prepared for the work which God may
> have for them to do, in the future. . . .[3]

By 1865 the church in South Carolina consisted of 3,404 white and 2,142 Negro adult members, and during the preceding three years twice as many Negroes as white people had been baptized there.

At the close of hostilities the churches shared in the common national tragedy. Many of the denominations were permanently divided, and others only in the recent decades have been able to reunite. Although it suffered like all the rest, the Episcopal Church in the North and South had never declared a separation. The church in the Confederacy always asserted its lineal connection, and at the General Conventions in the North in 1862 and 1865 the complete roll of the dioceses beginning with Alabama was always called. The dioceses in Louisiana and Tennessee had been prevented by the military operations from meeting in convention to approve the proposed constitution and so had never broken their union with the northern body. Believing that the collapse of the Confederacy spelled the end of the church separation, the Dioceses of Texas, Arkansas, and North Carolina sent deputies to the General Convention in Philadelphia in 1865. Bishop Henry Lay of Arkansas and Bishop Thomas Atkinson of North Carolina also attended and quietly responded to the roll call as they took their seats in the House of Bishops. Bishop Arthur Cleveland Coxe of Western New York, who was sitting for the first time in the House of Bishops, described this moving scene:

> So then, the first work, which was immediately and happily accomplished, was the recognition of the Southern Dioceses as still a constitutional portion of the Church. The Southern Bishops and brethren who appeared and took their seats gave voluntary assurances of loyalty to the Government, of their acceptance of the new condition of things as regards the Negro, and of their resolve to perform all their duties as men and as citizens, and as Christians, under the National authority as established in the land . . . never was a Convention more free from the ignoble influences of passion and prejudice. . . . In spite of questions, on which the whole Nation had been so terribly convulsed, and on which men still feel so deeply, I repeat it, the Convention was wonderfully harmonious.[4]

The bishops and leaders of the church in Georgia, South Carolina, Alabama, Virginia, and Mississippi met in Augusta, Georgia, in the Second General Council of the Protestant Episcopal Church in the Confederate States on November 8–10, 1865. After professing the consecration of Bishop Richard Hooker Wilmer of Alabama and the admission of Arkansas as a diocese as valid acts, this council quietly dissolved itself and the church it represented. Diocese by diocese southern churchmen in the early months of 1866 voted to renew their relation with the Protestant Episcopal Church in the United States of America.[5] Bishop Wilmer, who had been consecrated by the Confederate bishops, was received into full standing on January 31, 1866, in New York City, when he declared his conformity to the Protestant Episcopal Church in the United States of America, just as any other bishop in proper orders from a foreign country would have been received.

An understandable sensitivity on the part of some southern churchmen remained after the war; Bishop Wilmer asked his clergy not to pray "for the President and all in civil authority," on the ground that only military authority existed in Alabama. Whereupon General George H. Thomas, who was in command there, suspended him and all his clergy from their functions. On the protest of the bishop and an appeal to President Andrew Johnson the order was revoked, the southern churchmen mollified, and an essential principle of American constitutional rights vindicated.[6]

A purely local incident in Richmond in 1868 is indicative of many similarly delicate situations that arose from the freeing of the Negroes. T. G. Dashiell, rector of St. Mark's Church, asked city officials to close one of their offices across the street from his church an hour earlier on Mondays. Many Negroes passed through the narrow street near the church to visit this office which would normally close at 4 P.M. The rector reported, however, that Negroes often continued to mass there as late as 5 o'clock so that it was difficult for his congregation, made up largely of ladies, to reach the church door. He concluded that refusal of this request would be tantamount to prohibiting worship.[7]

So also the destruction of church property presented Episcopalians with a staggering situation in many southern states. A Committee on the Destruction of the Churches in the Diocese of South Carolina during the War presented to the convention meeting in Charleston in May, 1868, a report that simply said, "On the return of peace the church had disappeared. The mode of its destruction is not known." Several shells had hit St. Michael's Church, Charleston, but the tower still stood. Fearing the loss of the bells, which had been sold in England during the Revolution and returned intact after the war, the vestrymen had hidden them under a shed in Columbia, only to have them badly cracked when the Federal soldiers burned the shed. After this war these bells were returned to England and recast and now again hang in the historic church tower. In this old southern city St. Philip's Church suffered most, although its spire also was spared. So deep was the poverty in the South that in this former prosperous city the once wealthy Charlestonians were unable to raise $8,000 to restore St. Philip's, until finally a private loan was negotiated for this purpose. The burning of Christ Church in Columbia by Sherman's army in February, 1865, was a loss of at least $30,000, probably the greatest single church loss in the state. In South Carolina alone, ten churches and eleven rectories were burned, three churches simply disappeared, twenty-two parishes were suspended, and every church building from the Savannah River to Charleston had been damaged. The clergy were forced to seek jobs and to fish, hardly as a recreation, to make a living, and church endowments and investments of at least $184,000 were lost.

When the next General Convention met in New York on October 7–29, 1868, all the southern dioceses were represented again, and Bishop Thomas H. Vail of Kansas could have spoken for all in attendance when he said:

> The one pleasant matter, which, amid all the differences on subjects discussed, could not cease to be pleasant, was the reunion of the brethren, who had, for a time, during the late war been separated. All were in their places again—bishops, presbyters, and laymen—with the same interest in our common work as ever, each taking his place as though it had never been vacant, in the one brotherhood, and without one word or thought on the part of any in reference to the sad past, which is gone, we trust, forever.[8]

Such trust and confidence was bred not by official legislation but rather by mutual love and respect and strong personal ties of friendship which would not break no matter how great the social or political strains. Within a month after the war had ended, Phillips Brooks, like many others, began and continued to send money, much of it his own, to his former associates at the Virginia Theological Seminary, now struggling to re-establish their churches. Years later Bishop Alfred M. Randolph of Virginia, then a rector in Baltimore, told how Brooks had come to see him almost directly on his return from Europe and how they had talked until long after midnight. Bishop Randolph wrote:

> I shall never forget his gentleness and sweet reasonableness and sympathy throughout the conversation. I try to imagine the change and the elevation that would come into human life in all its relations if a spirit like his could ever gain the ascendancy over the prejudices, the self-assertions, the narrowness, and the ignorance of the matter of men.[9]

The wounds in the church were healed more quickly than those in other groups, primarily because of such difference in spirit and temperament. Recognizing this, the church very quickly tried to improve the situation. Thomas March Clark, Bishop of Rhode Island, spoke before the city authorities and citizens of Providence on July 4, 1871, on "Our National Crisis" and, after a brief review of the ninety-five years of our national history, quickly came to face the current issues. He decried the spoils system and pleaded for strong, good men in government, saying that scoundrels, whose last refuge is patriotism, and incompetent men in government are this country's greatest dangers. Many persons, he declared, had lost confidence in all existing parties and in their doubts longed to see "a higher and better class of men, throughout the land, in stations of power and influence." Clark, like so many others, had implicit confidence in the judgment of Lincoln. He told of one meeting with the president on the eve of a special session of Congress during an effort to raise money for the war, when Lincoln said:

> This war is a question of money; that side will beat whose resources prove to be the greatest and hold out longest, and if the war should continue until we have spent five hundred million dollars, the pecuniary ability of the country is such that the credit of the government after the war is over will be better than it was after the close of the Revolutionary struggle.

Lincoln's judgment indeed was vindicated; five hundred million dollars were expended and then thousands of millions more and the nation, again reunited, stood.[10]

At the close of the Civil War there were only 160,000 Episcopal communicants in the country, and most of these were in the North. Those who lived in the towns and cities in the South were more easily gathered once more into parishes. In Alabama in 1862 one-half of the communicants lived in the larger towns, and by 1892 this proportion had risen to two-thirds, in conformity with the population trend at that time. During these thirty years the communicants in the cities increased four hundred per cent from eight hundred to thirty-two hundred, while those in the country areas of Alabama grew only fifty per cent from eight hundred to twelve hundred. So in the generation after the war the church in the cities of Alabama grew eight times as rapidly as in the country areas, a phenomenon not at all peculiar to the South. In the North, with cities growing even more rapidly, the Protestant Episcopal Church multiplied fourfold, doubled its clergy strength in this generation, and became very largely a city oriented church. Whereas in 1860 the ratio of population to communicants was 209 to one, before the end of the century it had become 102 to one.

Following the Civil War all sections of the reunited country were struggling for the placidity that they had known before 1861 and were never again to see. The North was already in the grip of the accelerated Industrial Revolution, developed to a greater efficiency by the stimulus of war-time demands. Slowly and inexorably the machine moved westward during the next decades, replacing thousands of workers on the farms and at the same time drawing thousands into new employment in the rapidly growing cities. While some industrialization reached into the former Confederate states, it would remain for the next century to bring intensive industrialization to revolutionize this area. Meanwhile the South had its own problems of readjustment. Crushed by indescribable destruction everywhere, the people of the South were in dire need but sensitive about accepting any assistance or guidance, to say nothing of military and governmental direction.

The white man, largely without means, and the Negro, freed but with no experience in freedom, often struggled independently in search of a new life. The usual postwar corruption with its accompanying apathy to social responsibility opened the way for the rise of industrial empires built on monopoly and for the amassing of great personal fortunes in the South and wherever resources and need combined to create opportunity. Aggressive entrepreneurs took advantage of the limitless natural resources and the social and economic needs of the expanding population long before adequate agencies of regulation could approximate a balance between rewards and responsibilities in such inevitable stages of rapid development and improvement.

Although errors of judgment and misguided and sometimes actually criminal exploitation of labor and natural resources would lead to periods of depression in 1873 and 1893, the lines on the business and industrial charts were sharply upward during this long period of development in our national life. So successful were these years that the reports of opportunity in America drew additional millions of immigrants from Europe to provide sufficient hands to operate the new and increasingly complex industrial machine. Most of these immigrants were Roman Catholics from the Mediterranean countries and Ireland, and they sought only economic opportunity and not religious or political liberty. Before the Civil War the Roman Catholic Church had only four and a half million members, most of whom were of German and Irish background. The growth of this church had been rapid; its membership rose from six hundred thousand in 1830 to three and a half million by 1850. Each successive decade added at least a million members to its rolls, and by 1880 the Roman Catholics numbered about ten million.

The same wave of business advance that swept the comparatively few to the heights of wealth and affluence dashed others into poverty and slums. Rapidly acquired wealth was unable to produce as quickly an accompanying sense of the appropriate and beautiful, so that frequently the homes of the *nouveaux riches* were monstrosities of bad taste. Less visible at first, but nevertheless equally real, were the social forces at work that from economic suppression would soon breed labor unrest and ultimately violence. Challenged by industrial achievements, even the natural scientists began to probe new frontiers and in the observation of wider perspectives came to new and often disturbing conclusions, such as those found in Charles Darwin's *Origin of Species* in 1859.

In all these areas of a dislocated and confused society the church was to find its greatest opportunity; how successfully it had done its work remained to be determined. Here were regional wounds to be healed, complicated ethical and moral issues to be clarified, emerging social stratifications to be held in cohesion, cultural and educational challenges to be met; and even the church's own order and structure, together with its systems of thought, had to be brought into practicable adjustment for the times.

While the church was about to give much of its attention to missions in the West, the opportunities among the Negroes in the East were not overlooked. What had previously depended upon the independent initiative of local clergy in the South now became a more sustained effort on the part of the general church. To the original concern about the Negro's religious life was now added provision for his education and adjustment to his new social status. Even during the war years Phillips Brooks, who was then rector of Holy Trinity Church in Philadelphia, like many other leading clergymen, gave weeks of his time and tireless effort to the national movement known as the Freedmen's Relief Association, which was also interested in the education and rehabilitation of Negroes. Brooks preached to the Negro troops, opened a Sunday School for Negro children, and also became an ardent supporter of Negro suffrage.[11] One rector baptized twenty-seven Negro children at a single service during the war, and in 1864 Bishop Wilmer confirmed twenty-one Negro adults in Tuscaloosa, Alabama.

Since many of the southern churches were in need of assistance the general church quickly realized that the postwar social problems must be faced by the church at large. The General Convention of 1865 established the Freedman's Commission, with J. Brinton Smith as secretary and general agent; it surveyed the needs, raised funds—more than $26,000 in its first year—and opened ten schools for the colored throughout the South, and also contributed to the support of an orphanage in Memphis. This well-organized agency expended almost $100,000 in its first three years and increased its staff of teachers from twenty-six in 1866 to sixty-five two years later. Similarly, the number of pupils, working at first at the most elementary levels, increased from sixteen hundred to about five thousand. By 1870 this organization became the permanent Commission on Home Missions to Colored People and five years later had increased its schools to thirty-one. Within a few years specifically religious work was added to the educational effort, and by 1890 it was supporting 62 white and 44 Negro clergy, 117 Sunday Schools, 65 parochial and 12 industrial schools. St. Augustine's Normal School and Collegiate Institute was chartered on July 19, 1867, through the joint efforts of the Freedman's Commission of the church and a group of clergy and laymen of the Diocese of North Carolina. This co-educational institution at Raleigh has become St. Augustine's College and is affiliated with the American Church Institute for Negroes, approved by the Board of Missions and organized in 1906 to set standards of instruction and to solicit support for the church's larger schools for Negroes.

The expansion of the church before the Civil War had carried missionaries and well-established congregations as far as the Mississippi, but only after the war was the "Wild West," from the prairies to the Pacific, brought within the influence of the church to any comprehensive degree. That this territory still deserved the term "Wild West" is seen in a letter the young Bishop Daniel Sylvester Tuttle wrote to his wife in July, 1867, on his way to his new assignment as Missionary Bishop of Montana with jurisdiction in Idaho and Utah. Since there were no railroads beyond Nebraska, he was traveling in a stagecoach operated by Wells Fargo and Company. So many horses had been stolen and men murdered that for two weeks the company refused to operate its stages to Salt Lake City. On his safe arrival there several weeks later, he wrote to describe how they were escorted by three cavalrymen as they rode day and night for more than 150 miles through most hostile country.

Now that the Episcopal Church had observed the effectiveness of using bishops to establish and direct its missionary work, the General Convention of 1865 divided the West, apart from California, into five missionary jurisdictions and named a bishop for each. Oregon and Washington were under the direction of Bishop Thomas F. Scott, who had actually begun his supervision there in 1853 when a large part of Idaho was also under his care. Arkansas and Indian Territory had been supervised by Bishop Henry C. Lay from 1859, and Bishop George M. Randall was chosen in 1865 to direct the work of the church in Colorado, Montana, Idaho, and Wyoming. In one of his episcopal reports he told of his searching diligently but not being able to find any territory like Wyoming, which was not officially set apart by the government until 1868. The coming of the Union Pacific Railroad transformed the Wyoming wilderness, and Cheyenne soon became an important center for the state and the church. In 1866 the House of Bishops added New Mexico to Randall's jurisdiction. More than a decade later Bishop Ethelbert Talbot, his successor, described the primitive conditions in New Mexico and told of his observing General Lew Wallace as he sat quietly writing *Ben Hur*, apparently oblivious to the threat of the noted desperado, "Billy, the Kid," to shoot him on sight.

For the fourth region in the West comprising Nevada, Utah, Arizona, and, for one year, New Mexico, the House of Bishops selected Mark Antony DeWolfe Howe; on his declination they named Ozi William Whitaker its first bishop. Utah was also detached in 1866 and joined with Montana and Idaho to form the jurisdiction for which Daniel Sylvester Tuttle was chosen bishop in October of that year. Tuttle, destined for fifty-six years in the episcopate, was given this difficult assignment while he was serving Zion Church in Morris, New York. Since he was under thirty years of age, he was not consecrated until May, 1867, whereupon he set out immediately for his district of 340,000 square miles and about 155,000 inhabitants.

For about two years Tuttle lived in Virginia City under the most primitive conditions and with little success. On the arrival of his wife and baby in 1869 they moved to Salt Lake City, Utah, which had been organized as a territory in 1850. So largely was this territory under the influence of the Mormons that by 1896, when it became a State, nine-tenths of the one hundred thousand inhabitants belonged to the church. By his friendly attitude to the Mormons and by his positive preaching and program Tuttle firmly established the Episcopal Church there. He founded St. Mark's Hospital and Rowland Hall, a school for girls, both of which were patronized by the Mormons and continue in present use.

By 1880 the work in Montana was sufficiently established to become a separate missionary jurisdiction with Daniel Sylvester Tuttle as its bishop. Six years later after a second election as Bishop of Missouri he accepted that diocesan post. He had found it was difficult to leave Montana for he had nurtured these churches from their beginning and now there were two parishes, thirteen organized missions, twelve clergy, and almost one thousand communicants. For thirty-seven years he served in Missouri, the last twenty also as the Presiding Bishop of the church by virtue of his seniority among the bishops.

When W. F. Adams, Missionary Bishop of New Mexico and Arizona, reached Santa Fe with H. Forrester on February 6, 1875, he found one parochial organization but no other in his whole jurisdiction. Adams soon became ill and resigned, having been unable to cope with an area of over 235,000 square miles with 120,000 people, including many Mexicans, in New Mexico and 65,000 in Arizona. He was succeeded by George K. Dunlop who served this missionary district for about eight years.[12] Soon afterward, New Mexico and Arizona became a new missionary district, and its primary convocation was held on May 4, 1880. A decade later Bishop J. Mills Kendrick, who succeeded Bishop Dunlop, happily reported that, after all the neglect of these regions, "we have today more strength than any religious body in Tucson, except, of course, the Romanists who have been here for three hundred years." Clergy supply was still a problem, for he had with him in the district only five clergymen, and two of these were deacons.[13] The fifth missionary district consisting of Nebraska and Dakota was assigned to Bishop Robert H. Clarkson; his successor in 1873 was William Hobart Hare, one of the most distinguished leaders in the westward expansion of the church.

The work of the church in the far West made slow progress because of the size of these areas, the comparatively few missionaries available, and the lack of adequate resources to support the efforts of those who volunteered for these difficult assignments. During a period of five years Bishop Randall received only slightly more than $100,000, for which, however, he was able to show real property valued at more than that amount. For all his missionaries in three areas he was receiving only $3,500 a year, while one Presbyterian missionary in Wyoming was being paid $1,500. To supply the needed clergy Bishop Clarkson founded Nebraska College and Divinity School and the Omaha Collegiate Institute, but they did not prove to be the answer and were later discontinued.

To such internal difficulties must be added the uncertainties and irregularities of the social and particularly the economic conditions of the frontier states, where gold brought thousands of immigrants to California in the mid-century and left it thirty years later with the good times gone forever, as Bishop Wingfield reported in 1880. The decline in the production of silver left Nevada with a smaller population than that of Salt Lake City, which had grown rapidly with the coming of many Mormons. Despite these conditions the three churches in Nevada became ten in the decade before 1880, and the ministers increased from one to seven; even in the more depressed years that followed the church continued to grow in the cities. In these eight states and territories in 1880 the church was represented by sixty-seven ministers and 3,800 communicants. So well had these foundations been laid that eighteen years later the clergy numbered 174 and the communicant strength approximated seventeen thousand.

On the West coast John H. D. Wingfield, selected at the General Convention of 1874 for the new Jurisdiction of Northern California, was consecrated on December 2 that year to supervise the church in this large area separated from the Diocese of California. He began with 14 clergy, 1,923 members, 709 communicants, and 887 attending the church schools. By 1885 he had confirmed 1,219 persons but still had only 713 communicants, a gain of only four in more than ten years due largely to the migrant nature of the population.[14]

Further evidence of the growing strength of the church was becoming clear in its diocesan expansion and subdivision. While the western missionary jurisdictions were often regrouped for the purpose of greater effectiveness, the older established dioceses were frequently subdivided, avowedly for the same reason but not always with the same effect. New York became the first state-wide diocese to be so divided when Western New York was separated in 1839, and Albany, Central New York, and Long Island became independent jurisdictions in 1869. The new Diocese of Fond du Lac was carved from Wisconsin in 1875, Springfield and Quincy from Illinois in 1877, and East Carolina from North Carolina in 1883. With many more problems than those usually involved in a subdivision, the Diocese of Maryland, after very careful study of membership concentration and natural boundaries, voted in 1867 that Washington, D. C., should become a separate diocese as soon as this prescribed area had fifteen parishes; at the same time it made similar provision for a diocese (now Easton) on the Eastern Shore.[15]

Before the Civil War the Episcopal Church work among the Indians was limited to missions among the Oneidas in Wisconsin and the Chippewas in Minnesota, where James Breck had planted two stations. Bishop Henry B. Whipple, who had a phenomenally successful episcopate in Minnesota, became so much concerned about these Indians that in 1868 he pleaded with the Board of Missions to demonstrate the genuine interest of the church in the welfare of these and all other Indians. Following this appeal and another from President U. S. Grant, the General Convention of 1871 ordered and the Board of Missions created a Commission on Indian Affairs to defend the rights of the Indians. The Board of Missions promptly sent a secretary to investigate the conditions in Minnesota and Wisconsin and along the Missouri River as far as Cheyenne, the region for which the Episcopal Church had received educational jurisdiction from the United States government. The report published in 1872 stressed the need for more education for Indian children, better school houses and educational equipment, new churches, many Christmas gifts for children, and clothing and food for the aged and the poor. But probably the greatest need of all was to convince the Indians of the white man's sincerity, for almost universally the Indians distrusted the whites "who make promises but fail to keep them."

The church now created a separate missionary jurisdiction, including Indian reservations in the present South Dakota and western Nebraska; it was called Niobrara, after the river dividing these states, and was placed under the direction of Robert H. Clarkson, the bishop of these areas. By 1871 five white missionaries and three Indian clergymen with five women helpers were at work here. It remained, however, for William Hobart Hare, who in 1873 at the age of thirty-four was consecrated Bishop of Niobrara and the one-hundredth in the American Episcopate, to accomplish an almost miraculous missionary feat in ministering successfully among these Indians and the officers and men of the government military agencies. The missionary work among the Dakotas progressed so extensively that S. D. Himan, a missionary, and Thomas H. Robertson, the interpreter to the mission, prepared and published in Faribault as early as 1862 a *Dakota Church Service for the Mission of St. John.*

So rapidly and so successfully did the work grow in Niobrara that the Indians themselves offered to help in its development. By 1878 a *Form For Making Catechists in the Missionary Jurisdiction of Niobrara* was printed in English with its Dakota equivalent on facing pages. Three years later the Indian Commission of the Protestant Episcopal Church published an English-Dakota Service Book of 139 pages, consisting of parts of the Book of Common Prayer, for use in this jurisdiction.[16]

Bishop Hare considered his work more that of a superintendent than a settled pastor, yet everywhere he made friends and ministered to all whom he met. His splendid training and cultural background in Philadelphia, where his father was dean of the Philadelphia Divinity School, and his gentle and affable manner made him an ideal choice for this difficult and dangerous but rewarding work. Hare was in Europe when the Sioux or Dakota Indians massacred General Custer and his men in June, 1876. Rarely in over thirty years of service was Bishop Hare absent from his field, but on this occasion he had agreed to a proposal of the House of Bishops and was traveling for the recovery of his health in England, France, and Italy from December, 1875, to September, 1876.

By 1883 Bishop Hare's jurisdiction had been limited to the area which six years later became the State of South Dakota; his responsibilities here included all the work both among the white men and Indians as he thought there should be no segregation. The following year Hare reported he had five native clergy, five native candidates for the ministry, twelve native catechists, seventeen white clergy, four white catechists, and twelve women helpers. By the end of the century the missionary work on ten Indian missions was grouped into the Niobrara Deanery, including ninety congregations, fifty-seven church buildings, thirty-two communicants, six white and fifteen Indian ministers, and fifteen catechists and lay helpers. One of the ironies of history occurred here in 1891, when the daughter of Chief Gall, leader of the Indians in the Custer massacre, presented an offering of $800 from the Niobrara branch of the Woman's Auxiliary and on July 4, 1892, Chief Gall himself was baptized in the Episcopal Church. In an Indian population of twenty-five thousand, about ten thousand persons were baptized and took part in the work of the mission. Although it was a strain on the limited staff, regular Sunday services were conducted at about eighty locations.

In the earlier years the annual convocation of the Deanery brought together several hundred Indians, but by the end of the century these gatherings often numbered three thousand or more Indian men and women from all parts of South Dakota. Some of them had traveled for days to meet at a selected mission station and set up hundreds of tepees and tents. There was genuine triumph for the church militant as these great processions with decorated banners marched to the open air services of thank offering, preaching, and the Holy Communion.

Bishop Hare had also established four industrial boarding schools for Indians, which were supported increasingly by the Missionary Society and the Woman's Auxiliary and correspondingly less by governmental grants. The church was favored by similar although hardly as extensive successes in its Indian work in Oklahoma and Minnesota. Just before Bishop Hare died late in 1909, the mayor and aldermen of Sioux Falls, speaking for the people of South Dakota, told him, "The civilization of our western Indians is due more largely to you than to any other man."[17]

Conditions in the Orient and a lack of material support from the American church limited its foreign missionary work in Liberia, China, and Japan in the generation following the Civil War. The Church in Liberia, the oldest of the surviving foreign missions of the Protestant Episcopal Church, had been planted there in 1835 after fourteen years of planning and almost twenty years after the American Colonization Society had established that country in 1817 to promote the return of free Negroes to Africa. While never officially associated with the Episcopal Church, the American Colonization Society was strongly supported by the evangelical churchmen, who helped to purchase lands in western Africa and to resettle these "free persons of color willing to emigrate to the land of their fathers." This project was approved by the Diocese of Virginia and by such leaders as Thomas Jefferson and Henry Clay. Two years after its beginning William Meade, later Bishop of Virginia, became a special agent for the Society and once negotiated with the Governor of Georgia to purchase a number of captured African slaves, confiscated by that state for illegal entry and advertised to be sold publicly on May 4, 1819.[18]

The first Episcopal missionary to Liberia was a Negro layman, James M. Thompson, a resident of Monrovia, who served as a teacher in the congregation begun by Episcopal residents in Monrovia in 1834.

The following year he was joined by the first ordained missionary, Thomas S. Savage, who was also trained in medicine, and a little later by John Payne and Lancelot B. Minor. By 1850 Payne, a Negro, had been designated by the General Convention as Bishop of Cape Palmas and Parts Adjacent, and five years later his diocese included all of Liberia. Although he had faced serious problems of administration and the difficult climate had impaired his health, Bishop Payne came to his retirement in 1871 with a report that the mission now had nine organized churches, twenty-two additional missionary stations, and two boys' schools. John G. Auer, the only remaining white missionary, succeeded Payne but survived his consecration by only a few months, and many of the previous gains were lost during the next six years. It was not until February, 1877, that Bishop Charles C. Penick arrived from America and, despite the difficult climate, gave five years to the reorganization and expansion of the mission and left the church on his retirement with eleven clergy and over five hundred communicants. After another interval of three years Samuel D. Ferguson began his phenomenal episcopate of thirty-one years, during which he became not only the most highly regarded Negro religious leader in Liberia but also was able to build Cuttington College and establish the work of the Episcopal Church in Africa on a permanent basis.

The first Episcopal missionaries in China were Henry Lockwood and Francis R. Hanson, who sailed from New York in June, 1835, after six months' study of medicine. Although Christianity had been known in China since the early seventh century and there were about a quarter of a million Christians in the empire, the time was not yet ripe for rapid missionary expansion. In fact, China was hardly ready for the infiltration of any foreign influences and restricted foreigners to living in a single narrow area in the port city of Canton. Lockwood and Hanson went directly to Canton but soon discovered that it would be advisable to proceed to Batavia in Java for a better opportunity for language study in the Chinese colony there. Gravely ill from exposure to the tropical climate in Java, Hanson returned to America in 1838, and Lockwood came back a year later. This left the mission in charge of William J. Boone, a graduate of a medical school and of the Virginia Theological Seminary, who, with his wife, had been appointed to the mission in 1837. When he felt completely trained in the Amoy Chinese dialect, Boone moved the mission back to China in 1842, settled on the island of Amoy off the Chinese coast, and became the real founder of Anglican missions in China.

These were years of upheaval in China, punctuated by two wars with Great Britain in 1840 and again from 1856 to 1858. In settling the first peace by the Treaty of Nanking in 1842, China ceded Hong Kong to Great Britain, opened five ports to foreigners for residence as well as trade, and granted all foreigners "extra-territoriality" so that they might live and be governed by their own customs and laws. After the second war ten more ports were opened, and foreigners were granted the right to travel in the interior, thus opening the vast areas of this ancient land of culture to missionaries. The Protestant churches were quick to make the most of this opportunity, and by 1864 about two hundred missionaries representing twenty-four denominations had begun their efforts to Christianize this land where religion and culture had so long been blended in an ancient way of life. In 1849 the Church Missionary Society sent out an English bishop for Hong Kong and after about thirty years another bishop came to China under the auspices of the Society for the Propagation of the Gospel. These missions of the Church of England and the Episcopal Church remained entirely independent and often competitive until the twentieth century, when they were brought into a single enterprise.

When William J. Boone saw the large opportunity in China, he came back to arouse the church in America to the possibility of a great missionary undertaking and to find helpers who would join him in such an adventure. In 1844 he became the first bishop of the Anglican Communion for purely foreign missionary service. At his consecration at the General Convention that year he and his fellow missionaries were admonished by Bishop William Meade to show full appreciation for the ancient Chinese culture and, since the task was far greater than any foreign missionaries could hope to care for adequately, to seek at once to develop a body of native Christian missionaries, including priests, teachers, and translators. Similar ideas had been expressed by Bishop William White, and apparently the Board of Missions had already wisely adopted them as its method and basic philosophy.

With eight new fellow missionaries, all from the Virginia Seminary, Boone arrived in Shanghai in June, 1845, to open the mission in that metropolis. The Virginia Seminary supplied almost all the missionaries for both the China and Japan missions until the end of the century. Boone was soon joined by other clergy: Cleveland Keith in 1851, Robert Nelson in 1852, Channing Moore Williams and John Liggins in 1856, and S. I. J. Schereschewsky in 1859. In the latter years Williams and Liggins transferred their efforts to Japan. While Liggins soon was forced to return to America because of ill health, Williams stayed on and became the first Episcopal Bishop of Japan in 1866. When Bishop Boone died in 1864, the church, probably ill-advisedly, also placed this growing work, with its demands for exacting administrative attention, under the hand of Williams, who for twelve years of overloaded responsibility served as "Missionary Bishop in China, with jurisdiction over all the missionary operations of this Church in China and Japan." Within three years after moving from Japan to take charge of the missions in China Williams laid the foundation for a hospital, and by 1871 his missionary staff consisted of nine presbyters, including two natives, two native laymen, and six foreign women missionaries. During this brief period the mission prospered so well that the number of confirmations well exceeded those of the previous twenty years.

In Japan, where Christianity had been established three centuries earlier by Francis Xavier and the Jesuit missionaries, openly professed Christians were often severely persecuted; in the middle of the eighteenth century, when Japan erected the sea wall that isolated her almost entirely from the rest of the world, Christians were driven underground. When Commodore Perry arranged for the treaty in 1835 that provided for foreign residence and commerce, the first steps had been taken which by 1859 brought the first missionaries, including Williams and Liggins, to Japan. Limited at first by the strict edicts against Christianity still in force, these missionaries were permitted only to teach English. However, the Japanese were very eager to learn this language, and the missionaries quickly discovered what has since proved to be a most efficient modern technique: by exerting Christian influence in such an indirect way they were very effectively performing their missionary responsibility. Such methods of indirect teaching often resulted in more loyal converts to Christianity than the purely evangelistic methods had produced.

At the end of the Shogunate in Japan and just after the revolution had restored the emperor to power, Bishop Williams came once more to Japan in 1868; although he had not yet been relieved of his responsibilities in China, he came this time to give his major attention to the rapidly expanding opportunities in this country, where the new openness to the ways of the rest of the world was soon to make the Japanese people able competitors of other nations. Just as the old Japanese restrictions against Christianity were relaxed, in 1874 Williams was relieved of his responsibilities in China, where Samuel Schereschewsky was named his successor, and became Bishop of Yedo (now Tokyo). At first his efforts bore little fruit; the first convert was baptized by Williams in 1868 and there were no more until 1872. Two years later, however, twenty-one persons were baptized, and then, by an unprecedented series of missionary successes to 1890, there were 865 communicants, more than the church could report on any other foreign field. This achievement was largely the result of Williams's ministry among the great middle class, between the nobles and the common people, who desired an opportunity for education. Soon after he arrived in Tokyo, he had established a divinity school that grew into St. Paul's University, now a flourishing accredited institution. He also established St. Luke's Hospital in Tokyo by whose services and evidence of Christian concern hundreds more were soon won to the church.

While Christianity spread so rapidly and widely in Japan that many leaders were predicting it would soon join the ranks of Christian nations, the British missions seemed to grow less and by 1882 reported only two hundred communicants among Japan's thirty-eight thousand Christians. Five years later they joined with the American mission to form a synod, the beginning of the autonomous national church now known as the Nippon Seikokwai, the Holy Catholic Church of Japan, in which Japanese and foreigners shared equal membership. Its constitution was based upon the four basic Anglican assumptions, which would come to formal recognition as the Lambeth Quadrilateral the following year: The Holy Scriptures, The Nicene Creed, the two Sacraments, and the three orders of the ministry. The new church also used the Anglican Prayer Book and the Thirty-nine Articles. Since it was at first dependent upon foreign bishops and resources, it was slow to move toward practical autonomy, but it was the beginning of the church that is now the strongest branch of the Anglican Communion in the Orient. At a second synod in 1894 the church was divided into six dioceses, two of which remained connected with the Protestant Episcopal Church. John McKim became Bishop of the Missionary District of Tokyo in 1893, and S. C. Partridge, of the Missionary District of Kyoto, where he was succeeded in 1912 by Henry St. George Tucker, who was destined to a remarkable career in the church. Although many missionary enterprises in Japan suffered reverses during the rise of the nationalistic spirit during these years, the Anglican churches were only slightly checked, probably because of the autonomy in the Holy Catholic Church of Japan.

After Williams became the Bishop of Tokyo in 1874, the China mission fell into the relatively weak administrative hands of the brilliant linguist and scholar, Samuel Isaac Joseph Schereschewsky, a converted Polish Jew, who translated the Bible into Chinese.[19] His consecration as Bishop of Shanghai was delayed until 1877, and four years later he was forced to resign after suffering a paralysis. Always interested in raising the standards of education and committed from the beginning to the necessity for a native-trained ministry, Bishop Schereschewsky bought a large property outside of Shanghai and at once set about planting the St. John's School, which afterward became the strong St. John's University under the able F. L. Hawks Pott. Other promising institutions of the church at this time included St. Mary's School, near St. John's, the Boone Memorial School, which later became Boone University at Wuchang, and St. Luke's Hospital in Shanghai.

On the retirement of the ailing bishop, William Jones Boone, son of the first Bishop Boone, was chosen for this important missionary jurisdiction, but he lived only seven years more. In 1893 he was succeeded by Frederick Rogers Graves, who gave this missionary jurisdiction almost half a century of wise and capable, although at times rigid, administration. Meanwhile, the work of the China mission had been extended well inland, with some stations as far as six hundred miles up the Yangtze River at strategic centers like Wu-chang and the educational and industrial center of Hankow. Here J. Addison Ingle became the bishop when this area was subdivided from Graves's jurisdiction in Shanghai in 1901. Ingle was succeeded only three years later by Logan H. Roots, and, in 1910, the still larger Hankow District was again divided, and the new area, the Missionary District of Wuhu (later Anking), became the jurisdiction of David Trumbull Huntington. As early as 1897 Bishop Graves convened the first meeting of all the bishops of the Anglican Communion in China, which, by 1915, resulted in the semi-independent national church called the *Chung Hua Sheng King Hui,* or Chinese Holy Catholic Church.

Little is known of recent developments in the church in China, but it must obviously have suffered as it shared the tragic national experiences of the last two generations. Humbled by the defeat at the hands of Japan in 1894 and 1895 and by its futile attempts to bring about internal reform and to expel foreign influences in the Boxer Rebellion, the world's most populous nation has sought solace and new hope in the Communist illusion. It may be hoped that a church which grew from about five hundred communicants in 1890 to almost thirty-five hundred in 1915 and until the last decade was known to have at least twelve bishops shall have proved sufficiently stable to bear its true witness. After the Second World War two new dioceses were created out of the Diocese of Victoria, Hong Kong, to continue the church in China: the Diocese of Yun-Kwei includes Yunnan and Kweichow provinces, and the Diocese of South China is composed largely of Kwantung province. The Diocese of Kong-O, the official name of the Diocese of Victoria, Hong Kong, covers Hong Kong and Macao and, operating by the Chinese Canons and Constitution under the guidance of the Archbishop of Canterbury, remains the most substantial evidence of the Chinese Holy Catholic Church.

To carry on these global missionary enterprises the Domestic and Foreign Missionary Society structure was simplified for greater efficiency. In 1877 the General Convention constituted itself as the Board of Missions, leaving the operational details to the monthly meetings of the Board of Managers, a group of forty-six members absorbing the duties of the former Domestic and Foreign Committees. As a more irenic spirit came to prevail between the formerly opposing church parties, the American Church Missionary Society, once the agency of the strong evangelical party, became an auxiliary member of the Board of Missions and was soon entirely absorbed by it. With the formation of the National Council in 1919 the direction of the missionary work of the church became a function of this general administrative agency.

For many years, and especially after the Civil War, the women of the church sought ways in which they might help promote the work of missions in the church, sometimes working independently in parishes and again in diocesan organizations. These sporadic and scattered efforts were drawn together into the Ladies Domestic Missionary Relief Association mainly through the efforts of Mary A. Emery and Julia C. Emery of Massachusetts. In 1868 this Association became the Woman's Auxiliary to the Board of Missions, and three years later the Board of Missions formally organized this agency. This Auxiliary, once primarily occupied with the gathering of boxes of clothing and raising funds to supplement the salaries of missionaries, by 1874 had become a department of the Board of Missions and as such had a constructive long range program aimed to help all other departments of this Board through a systematic organization of the women of the church in parish, city, and diocesan bodies. By 1910 every diocese and missionary district in the church had its own branch of the Woman's Auxiliary. *The Spirit of Missions,* for many years a promotional organ for missions generally, also promoted the work of the Auxiliary, which is now known as Episcopal Churchwomen.

Miss Julia C. Emery, long the executive of the Woman's Auxiliary, organized a Junior Auxiliary in 1889 to enlist the interest of girls in the church's missions. This period also saw the organizing of the Girls' Friendly Society by Miss E. M. Edson in 1877 and the Daughters of the King in 1885, to promote prayer and Christian service among women; the Junior Division of the Daughters of the King was begun in 1896 with the same objectives for young women.

A major achievement of the women of the church was the establishing in 1889 of the United Thank Offering of prayers and gifts through the concern of Mrs. Richard H. Soule of Boston and Miss Julia Emery. Through this Offering the women of the church support the mission of the Episcopal Church in ways above and beyond the general church budget for domestic and foreign missions, as well as intercommunion projects at home and abroad. From the first modest offering of $2,188 in 1889 these gifts grew to an offering of $107,000 in 1901, and the offering presented in the triennium ending at the General Convention in 1961 totaled $4,339,190. Now that the Episcopal Church had become world-wide in its interests, its scope of thinking, and its actual involvements, greater and greater personal and material resources were constantly being required.

XVII

DIVISION AND UNITY

Ironically the latter half of the nineteenth century produced both unitive and divisive movements in the Episcopal Church. As early as 1835, when the church first embarked on its modern missionary program which involved all members, William A. Muhlenberg published his *Hints on Catholic Union.* He suggested a confederation among the leading American Protestant churches and presented a plan for such a confederacy through (1) the expanded use of the Apostles' Creed, (2) an ordination sufficient and not repugnant to the Word of God, (3) the use of common hymns, prayers, and lessons from the Bible, and (4) a council on common affairs. Muhlenberg's hope was that these "Articles of Union" might lead to a church in which all who participated would be parts of the Holy Catholic Church. His basis for such a union came very close to the four essential points of the Lambeth Quadrilateral that modern Anglicans usually support in ecumenical conversations. He urged that some system be devised by which Episcopal bishops could ordain candidates, who could show evidence of due qualification and sound faith, for the ministries of other churches. He even dared to hope that non-Episcopalians might agree to Episcopal ordination as an accepted standard, and in his time this hope was not as far from realization as it may now appear.

Although frustrated at many turns, Muhlenberg won supporters who were willing to sign his memorial to the General Convention of 1853. Alerted by the fissiparous nature of Protestantism and the consolidation of forces among American Roman Catholics, the signers of this memorial led that General Convention to ask whether the Episcopal Church, with its fixed worship and canonical structure, was adequate to meet the challenges of their time. Although the immediate results were small, the memorial aroused a new critical approach and gave a new direction to the life of the Episcopal Church. As a result, liturgy, canons, and Christian unity have been considered by every succeeding General Convention. Muhlenberg's stimulation led eventually to the Prayer Books of 1892 and 1928 and to the present canonical structure undergirding Episcopal Church polity.

Muhlenberg was not alone in supporting such advanced ideas, although few of his contemporaries supported so many of them so effectively. Trained with Jackson Kemper under Bishop William White, Muhlenberg spent seventeen years in education as founder and head of Flushing Institute and St. Paul's College on Long Island. When he became rector of the Church of the Holy Communion in New York in 1846, he quickly developed a unique parish life that provided educational and social service opportunities in the community. He founded St. Luke's Hospital, the Sisterhood of the Holy Communion, and in his later years attempted a communal Christian experiment at St. Johnsland on Long Island. Widely recognized as one of the greatest Episcopal Church leaders of the nineteenth century, Muhlenberg is best remembered for his memorial and the impetus he gave to liturgical renewal and the church's ecumenical outlook. In 1841 the young and perhaps over-zealous Thomas Vail, who would later be the first Bishop of Kansas, published *The Comprehensive Church*, in which he went further than any of his contemporaries to invite all other Christians to unite with the Episcopal Church. He even anticipated that the Episcopalians might be outnumbered and lose control of their parishes, conventions, and laws, and he added sincerely, "We are willing to be melted down with you, in our own crucible, into one mass of Christian love and fellowship." In 1858 William H. Lewis, with a less irenic spirit toward the Roman Catholics, defended the ecumenical posture in his *Christian Union, and the Protestant Episcopal Church in its Relations to Church Unity*.

Of far greater importance was the contribution of Edward A. Washburn, rector of St. John's Church, Hartford, Connecticut, who published A *Catholic Work of the Protestant Episcopal Church in the United States of America* in 1855, asserting that this church manifested the changeless unity of the catholic church in the great institutions of the Sacraments, the ministry, the Holy Scriptures, and the Creeds. Washburn profoundly influenced his friends Phillips Brooks and William Reed Huntington. Brooks both preached and represented these ecumenical ideals and a broad spirit of tolerance; yet he wisely cautioned that to be tolerant one has to have something to be tolerant about.

Preaching in All Saints' Church, Worcester, Massachusetts, on January 30, 1870, Huntington told his parishioners that the only hope of Christian unity lay in the Anglican principle. He concluded that its essential points, which cannot be surrendered without self-destruction, are: (1) The Holy Scriptures as the Word of God; (2) The Primitive Creeds (the Apostles' and Nicene Creeds) as the Rule of Faith; (3) The Two Sacraments Ordained by Christ Himself; and (4) The Episcopate as the Keystone of Governmental Unity.[1]

Through the influence of Bishop A. N. Littlejohn, Huntington's four points appeared in the report on Christian unity presented to the General Convention meeting in Chicago in 1886 and after adoption came to be known as the Chicago Quadrilateral. At the opening of the Third Lambeth Conference in London in July, 1888, Bishop Henry B. Whipple of Minnesota preached the opening sermon before 145 bishops, of whom twenty-nine were from the United States, in which he presented these same four points, which, with but a few clarifying emendations, were adopted officially as the statement of the bishops of all Anglicanism and are known as the Lambeth Quadrilateral.

When the turbulence of the Civil War had subsided, the divergent trends in the internal development of the Episcopal Church, which had been interrupted by the slavery crisis, came to the fore again and with increasing and demanding force. Before the war the earlier followers of the Oxford Movement, like their contemporaries in England, had deprecated all innovations in forms of worship or revival of disused vestments. But in the 1850's the Anglo-Catholics in England sought the revival of many Roman Catholic practices, including eucharistic vestments and colored stoles and paraments. So sharply was the Church of England divided that the Church Association, a conservative organization, expended almost £40,000 in attacking the English Church Union, a high church body, and in attempting to stay the advance of Anglo-Catholicism.

A similar situation soon developed in America, where party lines were clearly drawn, and although bitterness and formal trials were largely avoided, endless arguments consumed the time of hundreds of persons in conventions, and ultimately the church suffered its only schism because of it. Differing sharply from the early high churchmen of the Hobartian type, the Anglo-Catholics of the next generation sought to demonstrate their particular doctrines of the Eucharist and the priesthood by traditional ceremonies and vestments. The committed high churchmen usually defended their ritualism theologically and canonically since the Prayer Book offered few directions about ceremony. They argued that the Prayer Book was not originally intended to do away with the accustomed practices of the sixteenth century and, since no rules forbade the revival of these earlier practices, it was quite proper to do so.

Opposed to both the Oxford theology and ritualistic excursions that supported it were the evangelicals and even some of the older Tractarians, who saw here a dangerous threat to the unity of the church. Generally siding with the conservative and traditionally Protestant element in the church were the laymen, who shared the grave concern about the introduction of such Roman Catholic ceremonial. Both sides also had many adherents whose concerns were largely aesthetic or sentimental, seeking advance in ceremony because of its beauty, as William Muhlenberg had done, or seeking to stem it for emotional reasons.

The case for the evangelicals was considerably weakened because they were seeking relief from canons for themselves at the same time that they sought to bind the ritualists by new canons. They wanted alternate forms or the right to omit the objectionable "regeneration" passages in the Baptismal Office. These low churchmen also objected to the recently enacted canon, which practically put an end to preaching in other than Episcopal pulpits by forbidding any priest of the church to officiate within another's parish without his consent.

During these years some parishes in New York, Philadelphia, Baltimore, Providence, and Boston introduced free pews and more ritualistic services with candles, crosses, and colored stoles; they usually observed daily matins and vespers and celebrated the Eucharist every Sunday and on Saints' Days. When the influence of Nashotah House became more widely felt, the really "advanced" churches stressed sacramental confession and absolution, fasting communion, and non-communicating attendance at Mass.

Disturbed by the potential dangers from any further extension of the ritualism conflict, some of the old high churchmen sought the advice of Presiding Bishop John Henry Hopkins, who published *The Law of Ritualism* in September, 1866. He argued that the liturgical practices of the second year of Edward VI were by statute the legal ceremonies for use in the Church of England and so the practices of the ritualists were not only permitted here but required by canon law. He reasoned that all English canon law not specifically repealed was in force in the Episcopal Church, but he failed to add that some of the practices of the ritualists were forbidden by the English Canons of 1603, which had not been repealed. Hopkins approved of variety in ritual usages and prophesied with amazing accuracy that most of the contested practices would eventually become the custom of the Episcopal Church.

On January 10, 1867, the House of Bishops issued a declaration signed by twenty-four of them, a clear majority, denying that any of the Prayer Books or the canon law of the Church of England was applicable in the Episcopal Church with "the force of law . . . such as can be justly cited in defence of any departure from the express law of this Church, its Liturgy, its discipline, rites and usages." Asserting that the Episcopal Church had the right to prescribe its own ritual, the bishops condemned the Anglo-Catholic use of candles, incense, and genuflection as expressing the Roman Catholic doctrine of the Mass, and called "the adoption of clerical habits hitherto unknown, or material alterations of those which have been in use since the establishment of our Episcopate, . . . an innovation which violates the discipline of the Church."

These bishops were very careful to reserve "each for himself his rights as ordinary of his own diocese, and also his rights as a member of the House of Bishops sitting in general convention." Many resolutions on ritualism from many sources came to the General Convention at its next session in New York in 1868 and much of its time was given to their discussion.

While it appears never to have been discussed as a separate item in the convention, a petition that had been circulated among the bishops late that summer proved a sobering factor in that House and probably helped to keep a moderate tone and something of a conciliatory spirit in the following sessions. The petition was signed by at least thirty leading presbyters in the church, including such men as William H. Cooper who drafted it, F. B. Nash, John Crocker White, W. Preston, George Slattery, William Sparrow, J. Cotton Smith, C. W. Andrews, Richard Newton, William Newton, C. W. Quick, and Phillips Brooks, the last two having appended "qualified" to their signatures, implying their general approval but not of all the specific points mentioned. The petition stated the case of the evangelicals in the Baptismal controversy very clearly and is one of the best examples of the creative and constructive ability of William H. Cooper. It said:

> . . . it is now with us a positive conscientious conviction that we can-not, and we ought not, longer to use in our ministrations the terms in question—particularly those parts of the Baptismal office which assert the invariable spiritual regeneration of the baptized: an assertion, we respectfully submit, in no wise necessary to the validity of the Sacrament . . . others of us ask no concessions for themselves; but they ask them on behalf of brethren-beloved whose consciences are aggrieved, and whom they do not wish to see driven from the Church.

Declaring their absolute sincerity, these men indicated that they also wished that the Catechism might be revised and that all phrases might be eliminated from the Prayer Book which by some have been intrepeted to sanction "the doctrine of the Real Presence in the Eucharist," and that "the ministry is a sacrificing and absolving priesthood." The plan of the evangelicals had been carefully devised: the appeal was made to the bishops during the summer so that they might after consideration express an opinion which even though it would "have no force in law . . . would have great weight with us, and with the church at large" and might bring relief by action of the General Convention. Apparently more deeply grieved than most of the leaders of the church knew and yet also earnestly seeking to preserve the unity of the church, they concluded:

> We are persuaded that in this way the dangers which now threaten the peace of our communion may be happily, in great measure averted. On the other hand, we cannot but fear, that should no pacificatory action be taken, the consequences may be incalculably disastrous.[2]

Although a majority of bishops had signed the specific document of January, 1867, the attempt to make it the official declaration of the House of Bishops at the General Convention of 1868 failed. The lengthy discussions at this convention resulted in a majority and a minority report from the Committee on Canons to whom the numerous resolutions had been referred. But in the end, the only action taken was the appointment by the Bishops, at the request of the Deputies, of a committee "to consider whether any additional provision of uniformity, by canon or otherwise, is practical and expedient." The able members of that committee to make the proposed three-year study were Bishop Alfred Lee of Delaware, a veteran administrator and a Biblical scholar who would serve on the American committee to prepare the revised version of the New Testament; Bishop John Williams of Connecticut; Bishop William H. Odenheimer of New Jersey; Bishop Thomas M. Clark of Rhode Island; and Bishop John B. Kerfoot of Pittsburgh, who was attending his first convention as a bishop.

Following the convention, the bishops issued their pastoral letter, in which they avoided any pronouncement about ritualism but attacked "the unscriptural and uncatholic pretensions of the Bishop of Rome" and added a strong defense of the Anglican Reformation. In what was probably a reply to a point made on the floor of the convention by Milo Mahan, professor of ecclesiastical history at the General Seminary and one of the church's ablest priests and scholars, that the liturgical practices of the high churchmen were not mere trimmings but symptoms of a world-wide return to a greater catholicity in doctrine and devotion, the bishops roundly condemned

> any doctrine of the Holy Eucharist which implies that, after consecration, the proper elements of bread and wine do not remain; which localizes in them the bodily presence of our Lord; which allows any adoration other than of our Blessed Lord Himself: . . . which, in any way, asserts that his sacrifice upon the cross was not a full, perfect, and sufficient sacrifice, oblation and satisfaction for the sins of the whole world; and which would add to our Liturgy ceremonies and rites designed to teach all or any of these things.[3]

While this letter did not carry canonical authority, it nevertheless set out clearly the opinion and judgment of the House of Bishops as then constituted. It also set the stage for an exciting convention three years later.

While the church was moving in the direction of generosity in the interpretation of externals such as ceremonial observances, it was showing less elasticity in the interpretation of doctrine, especially that of baptismal regeneration as derived from the words used in the Baptismal Office. This doctrine had been a moot point in the Episcopal Church since its very beginning, and at times it was vigorously opposed by the low churchmen who invariably, but unfortunately, thought the words literally meant an instantaneous moral change in the recipient at the time of baptism. Historically, the word "regeneration" had been used in connection with baptism from the first century but during the Great Awakenings had taken on a new specific meaning akin to conversion. With such a narrower conception in mind many of these low churchmen not infrequently omitted the words "regenerate" and "regeneration," and such deviations, like those of the high churchmen, were almost invariably overlooked.

As the influence of the Tractarian Movement became more widespread in America, the extended theological discussion of both Sacraments brought this divergence in the Episcopal Church into a new focus. In August, 1868, Franklin S. Rising, clerical secretary of the American Church Missionary Society, anonymously published a significant pamphlet entitled *Are there Romanizing Germs in the Prayer Book?* in which he described the germs as "certain seminal doctrines which in due time spring up and bear Romanism as their fruit." Unfortunately for the church, this capable evangelical leader was killed four months later in a steamboat explosion on the Ohio River while he was travelling as an agent of the Society. In the years before the General Convention of 1868 it had often been explained that "regeneration" was used in the Baptismal Office hypothetically and not absolutely, which did not really clarify the issue. C. W. Andrews had published a pamphlet *Seven Senses of the Term Regeneration,* and there were also the Prayer Book churchmen who defended the literal meaning of the term. Rising's pamphlet had dispelled the subterfuges of which the low churchmen were tiring, since evasions avoided rather than solved the basic problem growing constantly more acute. Believing that the danger lay in the Prayer Book terms themselves, these leaders sought to have the terms changed, alternate readings provided, or rubrical permission granted to omit the objectionable words. Ominously, Rising echoed the judgment of William Cooper and his co-signers that the unity of the church was being threatened and that "if they are denied this relief, it will be necessary for them to seek it wherever they can find it."

Already in September, 1868, William H. Cooper, who had come from the Church of England and served several parishes in this country, had become an ardent evangelical advocate. He had once served as a missionary in Spain, where he married a Spanish woman, and more recently had worked for the American Church Missionary Society in the Church of Jesus in Mexico where he saw Roman Catholic life and religious practices at first hand. Cooper wrote a series of articles in the *Protestant Churchman* calling for a conference of evangelicals and a committee for the revision of the liturgy and canons to push toward a pure Reformed Church, evangelical in doctrine, fraternal in aim, and catholic in spirit. His radical conclusion that in the event of failure they must recognize that truth is above order and separate from the church if necessary may well have frightened the moderate churchmen and contributed to the ultimate failure to find a peaceful solution to this problem. A committee, including such distinguished names as Richard Newton, chairman; Thomas Jaggar, secretary; William A. Muhlenberg; William R. Nicholson; J. Cotton Smith; William H. Cooper; Heman Dyer; A. H. Vinton; L. W. Bancroft; and Franklin S. Rising, met in New York to consider proposed revisions of the Prayer Book and prepared a proposed memorial to the General Convention. This was then presented to the evangelical churchmen, who held party meetings between the sessions of the convention. Such meetings were not uncommon, and there was no impropriety involved, for ten bishops were present. Bishop McIlvaine promised to present the memorial to the General Convention, but when the caucusing group could not agree on the form of presentation, the plan failed. The dissidents were unable to agree on the degree of change desired; some wanted reforms; some, interpretations; others called for immediate separation; and many wished nothing done at that time. Great advantage always accrues to those defending the status quo, and in the confusion among the others nothing was done. Numerous impassioned pleas were delivered, and George David Cummins, the relatively new Assistant Bishop of Kentucky, was reported to have been at his best here but not ready or willing to lead a radical action. At a similar meeting of evangelicals held earlier in Philadelphia the leadership of the party was in the hands of Charles E. Cheney of Chicago, who stressed the need for greater liberty for the clergy, and of Stephen Tyng, Jr., then under fire in New York for having preached in a non-Episcopal church, who spoke for absolute secession from the sacramental system of the church. Only the positive position of the three evangelical bishops present, McIlvaine, Lee, and Eastburn, saved the meeting from radical legislation.

Cummins had come into the Episcopal Church from the Methodist Church where he had once served in his early twenties as a circuit rider on the Baltimore district. At nineteen he was graduated at the head of his class from Dickinson College. Because of his strong conviction Cummins sought confirmation and in 1845 was ordained a deacon by Bishop Lee of Delaware. He soon came to be widely known as a great preacher and a popular leader, and after serving several parishes he was consecrated a bishop in 1866. Many of the clergy later agreed that had Bishop Cummins decided to assert his gifts by leading a schismatic movement in 1868 he might easily have had the concurrence of most of the other bishops present. Perhaps as many as four or five hundred of the clergy, some of them prominent in the church, would have given him their support, and they would invariably have been followed by thousands of leading laymen. The hesitance of Cummins, the poise of the conservative evangelicals, and perhaps the tinge of radicalism on the fringes of the movement may have spared the Episcopal Church an even greater tragedy. From this time on there was a slow but very definite disintegration in the leadership and influence of the once very powerful and aggressive evangelical party, for which Bishop Hopkins four years later wrote a biographical epitaph, *The Rise and Fall of the Low-Church Party*.

But the enthusiasm of the moment unfortunately refused to be quenched. A memorial signed by twenty-two presbyters reached the General Convention of 1868 asking, in addition to liturgical freedom in the Baptismal Office, the right to preach in any church, subject only to consent of that church, and the freedom to recognize ministers of other churches as ministers. The House of Bishops denied the desired liturgical latitude on the ground that it was incompatible with the uniformity of the services of the church and that it "would expose the convictions and rights of a Congregation to be sacrificed to the scruples or peculiar views of the minister."[4] Shortly afterward, however, eleven evangelical bishops addressed a letter to the other thirty-nine bishops, hoping to preserve "the harmony of our beloved Church" by pleading for "affectionate consideration" for the conscientious scruples of the reformers. It was a minority opinion, and Bishop Horatio Potter of New York spoke for the majority when he expressed amazement that responsible churchmen and bishops "had countenanced such propositions which could only end in a 'mortifying discomfiture'."

After the close of the convention, William H. Cooper suggested that as a unified procedure all the clergy who shared these convictions agree immediately to exchange pulpits with other orthodox Protestant ministers, to omit the objectionable words in the Baptismal Office, to omit the word "oblation" in the Office of Holy Communion, and, if any one of them should be brought to trial and disciplined, to invite him at once into their pulpits and suffer the consequence. But even Cooper was no longer very hopeful after the General Convention of 1868, for he wrote, "The once great evangelical party lies prostrate before Baal, beaten, disorganized, humiliated." Discouraged but not yet defeated, the liberals formed an organization in Chicago on December 9, 1868, and almost a week later adopted the awesome title, "The Protestant Episcopal Society for the Propagation of Evangelical Religion in the Northwest." Within three months this Society raised more money for missions than the Missionary Board of the Diocese had received in twice that time.

Early in 1869 the evangelical movement took a new turn when its leaders, for the moment laying aside the pressure for their own requests, opened an attack on Bishop H. J. Whitehouse of Illinois. In mid-February a two-page finely printed "Protest" appeared, warning of the impending dangers to the church from such heretical teachings as regenerative baptism, the eucharistic concurrences of Eastern, Western, and Anglican doctrines, and also the substantial agreement in Orders, Creed, and Sacraments in these churches. All of this had been based on the address of Bishop Whitehouse before the Illinois Convention in 1868, Morgan Dix's *Manual of Instruction for Confirmation Classes*, or James DeKoven's *Catechism for Confirmation*. Following the offending passages, the protesters concluded:

> We solemnly declare that, in our judgment, the preceding extracts *are not in harmony* with the doctrines and principles of the Protestant Episcopal Church, but directly the reverse, in many particulars, of the teachings of her Articles, Liturgy and Homilies—the very reverse of the principles in defence of which many of the Bishops and other dignitaries of our Mother Church endured the fires of martyrdom.
>
> And we furthermore declare it our fixed purpose and intention under God, to do what in us lies towards the freeing of this, our beloved Church, from the domination and perpetuation of such sentiments and doctrines. And, for the integrity of our present action, we appeal to the Great Searcher of Hearts, and, for our vindication, to the candid judgment of all earnest, thinking, Christian men, and more especially to that of the members of our own Protestant Episcopal communion.[5]

This document was signed in Chicago on February 18, 1869, by six clergymen, including William H. Cooper and Charles E. Cheney, and seventeen laymen.

An additional step was taken by the increasingly dissatisfied low churchmen when they called a Council of Evangelical Episcopalians to meet in Chicago later in 1869. Controversial articles in the secular and religious press soon indicated the inflammable nature of the situation, and many evangelicals, including Bishop George David Cummins, tried to deter the more vigorous protagonists. In this spirit Cummins censured Cooper for his premature statement about the possibility of schism, which antedated a similar suggestion by Mason Gallagher. Cummins, who moved much more slowly toward such an eventuality, insisted that such haste had "inflicted irreparable injury upon the Evangelical cause and has served most sadly to divide and scatter our ranks."[6] At this point the bishop was certain that error could be checked, and he tried to combat all influence toward separation, saying, ". . . to go out of her communion because there is treachery within is to lower the flag and surrender the citadel to her enemies."⁷ He declared his own position at that time very clearly:

> And as to the Bishops of the Evangelical School I shall never believe until convinced by stubborn facts that any of them is prepared to follow your leading. . . . I make no claim of any right to give advice except as coming from one who loves the Evangelical cause and whose heart is most deeply pained to see it wounded in the house of its friends. . . . You can never induce the great body of Evangelical men to leave the Protestant Episcopal Church until one of two things occurs—either until the church itself in her standards becomes unEvangelical or until Evangelical men are denied the liberty of preaching the Gospel, and of developing and extending their principles through their own agencies. . . . If you "Radicals," as you call yourselves I believe—would only be patient and await God's Providence, I believe Evangelical men would be found acting within the next five years as a unit, a solid mass, ready to do what God devolved upon us.

Cummins waited just about that length of time, but unfortunately the result was not the one he predicted but the tragedy Cooper foresaw. In a letter to Bishop Whitehouse on February 3, 1869, Cummins stressed the unity of the church and decried all attempts to split it. He testified:

> For myself, I love the Protestant Episcopal Church more fervently as life advances. To me she is the fair and pure bride of Christ, "the glory of the Reformed Churches" as Bishop Hobart called her in 1814, in the General Convention that year: loyal to Christ and His truth in her articles, offices and homilies, and probably as free from imperfections as a church can be, composed of fallible men, in whom the work of God's grace is always incomplete.⁸

The Chicago Conference of Evangelical Episcopalians opened its sessions on June 16, 1869, with fifty-seven clergymen and laymen in attendance. By no means all of them were in sympathy with the movement, as president Felix R. Brunot discovered when the meeting became hopelessly snarled by the filibustering of the obstructionists who had come to Chicago only to prevent positive action by the group. It was even impossible to adopt the prepared agenda, which included discussions on the constitution of the episcopate as an office or order, the purpose and use of a revised liturgy, and relations to other, and especially non-Episcopal, orthodox churches. Only after long argument was it possible to hold a catholic service of Holy Communion to which non-Episcopalians were invited.

For most of the evangelicals the Chicago meeting lost its significance when the chief emphasis turned out to be a plea for "tender revision of the Prayer Book to conciliate dissidents" but only by slow and deliberate action. One attempt to pave the way to bring recusants to trial and to sustain bishops who attempted to discipline recalcitrants, which might have been interpreted as aimed at ritualists as well as at evangelical radicals but was obviously intending the latter, failed to win support. While most of the effect of this conference was negative, it did reaffirm the "Protest" and passed three positive resolutions: (1) to promote fraternal and Christian relations with ministers of other churches, especially in such institutions as the American Bible Society; (2) to make a careful revision of the Book of Common Prayer, needful for the best interests of the church, and (3) "that all words or phrases seeming to teach that the Christian ministry is a priesthood, the Lord's Supper a sacrifice, or that Regeneration is inseparable from Baptism should be removed from the Prayer Book." This third resolution became substantially Article IV of the later Declaration of Principles of the Reformed Episcopal Church.

On sober reflection the leaders of the radical party admitted that the conference was too far in advance of the people to accomplish its primary aims. Yet one attendant thought that had they been able to prepare the way to change twenty words in the Prayer Book all parties in the church could have been satisfied. The leadership of the older evangelicals was waning, and the younger men were hesitant to display aggressiveness. When asked his opinion, Bishop McIlvaine had replied that whatever he might think he did not feel called upon to declare it from the housetops. George Cummins still waited hopefully. Also present in that gathering was Colonel Benjamin Ayering, Ph.D. who would later write *Memoirs of the Reformed Episcopal Church*. J. Crocker White was the only representative of a large number of New England evangelicals who were absent, not for want of sympathy with the movement, but because of the distance. The meeting in Chicago was not ignored by the church at large; even those who had no sympathy with its purposes could not bring themselves to regard it with contempt. The editorial pages of the church press were filled with concern for the impending struggle. The editor of *The Episcopalian* called the gathering a serious conference where progress had been made but "the Evangelicals may find the path onward tortuous and not so direct as they could desire."

Meanwhile, on July 20, 1869, Charles Edward Cheney, the successful rector of Christ Church, Chicago, was arraigned for trial by Bishop Whitehouse for omitting the objectionable phrases from the Baptismal Office. He had been innocently exposed by an evangelical colleague who was leaving the Episcopal Church to become a Baptist minister and who cited him to the bishop as an example of many who were thus altering this Office. Feeling obligated by his canonical duty, Bishop Whitehouse brought Cheney to trial before a court devoid of any of his friends or sympathizers. He never denied his guilt but tried to explain that such omissions were customary in the church and overlooked in other dioceses. Whitehouse was inflexible in the performance of his duties, and Cheney, proving to be an intractable low churchman, was suspended from office on February 17, 1871.

When he disregarded the sentence, the bishop, after a second trial, deposed Cheney for contumacy the following June 2, only to have the decision reversed by a civil court. Cheney had been a highly successful and influential leader, and his loss was seriously felt both in his diocese and throughout the church. Many fellow evangelicals, including five seminary professors and other prominent churchmen, communicated their sympathy to Cheney and assured him that he was in the right and had done what many others in the church were doing. The next General Convention would declare for the comprehensiveness of the Episcopal Church position, but these words brought little solace to the disturbed evangelicals. Likewise, the House of Bishops, although without authority to make formal doctrinal pronouncements and unwilling to make the matter an official action of their House or the convention, did nevertheless make a statement, while acting in Council, in 1871, that the word "regenerate" in the Baptismal Office "is not there used as to determine that a moral change in the subject of the Baptism is wrought in the Sacrament." Unfortunately in the emotional tension that ensued, this statement was considered only as a further verbal subterfuge by the more radical evangelicals who were now making their influence felt.

Shortly after Cheney's deposition it was rumored that William Cooper, who was then still serving as rector at St. John's Church, Lockport, Illinois, and was thus amenable to Bishop Whitehouse, was also marked for trial. Since no one would accuse him and the bishop had no direct evidence compelling him to action, the issue never arose, but Cooper was disturbed. Late in September, Bishop Cummins urged Cooper to remain calm, assuring him that many bishops were coming to favor changes in the Prayer Book, but no action in this direction was taken at their meeting the following month. Then suddenly, as though by previous arrangement, the evangelical bishops began to publish statements in the church press, supporting the Scriptural nature of the Prayer Book but only rarely suggesting any measures of freedom through omissions or alternate phrases. Cummins still seemed hopeful of removing all difficulties and retaining all dissident parties in the church. Fearful, however, about his future under the jurisdiction of Bishop Whitehouse, Cooper withdrew from the Diocese of Illinois in the winter of 1870 and was installed in St. Michael's Church, Mount Pleasant, Iowa, where Bishop Henry W. Lee happily received him. Rejoicing in his new freedom, Cooper continued to assert his convictions and to practice the broad catholic principles to which he was so thoroughly committed. On one occasion he arranged to have Joseph Dugdale, a distinguished member of the Society of Friends, speak in St. Michael's Church.[9]

Here and there across the country clergy were leaving the Episcopal Church to serve in other communions. Hopeful to the end that he might be able to help accomplish the reforms he and his evangelical colleagues desired for their church, Cooper at last gave up in despair and wrote Bishop Lee on March 31, 1871, resigning his ministry in the Protestant Episcopal Church and asking for letters dismissory to the Church of England from which he had come eighteen years earlier. When his request was denied and Bishop Lee about six months later deposed him instead, Cooper believed that he had been denied his right, decided to take the canonical consequences, and renounced the ministry of the Protestant Episcopal Church on canonical and doctrinal grounds.

This was a tragic end to a stormy career in the church for one whose ideas and ideals for it were shared by a great many bishops and hundreds of the clergy. His aggressive zeal, shared by fewer of his colleagues, led him to be at the center of every controversial issue of the previous years, and without his persistent, although at times widely annoying, leadership, the church might have moved much more slowly toward reforms. On April 16, 1871, *The Protestant Churchman* published much of his letter of withdrawal and said, ". . . he was one whom our church can ill afford to lose . . . there ought to be a place in our church for such a man. . . . To afford such a place it is only necessary that liberties which until recently have been recognized should continue to be recognized. . . ."

Meanwhile, Cooper immediately set about founding Immanuel Church as an independent congregation in Chicago. A new church was dedicated on September 10, 1871, which he considered the first Reformed Protestant Episcopal Church of Chicago to which the Free Church of England gave full recognition. The congregation quickly adopted the newly created Union Prayer Book, which embodied the changes Cooper had sought for the Book of Common Prayer. Within a month the new church and the personal resources of Cooper and many of his lay friends, who had helped him underwrite the cost of the new building, were consumed in the great Chicago fire which struck on October 9, 1871. Discouraged and disappointed, Cooper finally decided to accept an invitation to become a missionary in Mexico, which he knew so well, where he spent the next years working for the American Foreign Christian Union.[10]

Among the other clergy, many of them Cooper's former associates, who withdrew from the Episcopal Church about this time were Mason Gallagher, Marshall B. Smith in New Jersey, Salmon H. Weldon of Ohio, and B. B. Leacock, who had been rector of the Church of the Epiphany in New York. Such withdrawals freed the church of many of its less patient and more radically left-wing leaders, but, as always in such radical actions, it also meant the loss of men of quality and strength. Two decades earlier the defections had been from the right wing of the church, when men like Levi S. Ives, Bishop of North Carolina; George Hobart Doane, eldest son of Bishop Doane of New Jersey and brother of William C. Doane of Albany; and James Kent Stone, son of Dean John S. Stone, moved into the Roman Catholic Church. Significantly the Reformed Episcopalians, unable to find a traditional catholic haven when they defected a few years later, chose to move neither left nor right but to continue both the episcopate and the Prayer Book of the Episcopal Church, which should provide both a hope and a basis for reunion with this small church of less than one hundred parishes.

The next session of the General Convention met in Baltimore in the fall of 1871. The long-awaited report of the committee, of which Bishop Alfred Lee was the chairman, was presented, proposing a regulatory canon which would have forbidden eleven specific practices common to the usages in most Anglo-Catholic parishes:

1) The use of incense,
2) Placing or retaining a crucifix in any part of the church,
3) Carrying a cross in procession in the church,
4) The use of lights in or about the holy table except when necessary,
5) The elevation of the elements in the Holy Communion in such manner as to expose them to the view of the people as objects of adoration, in or after the prayer of consecration, or in the act of administering them, or in conveying them to or from the communicants,
6) The mixing of water with the wine as part of the service, or in the presence of the congregation,
7) The washing of the priest's hands, or the ablution of the vessels in the presence of the congregation,
8) Bowings, crossings, genuflections, prostrations, reverences, bowing down upon or kissing the holy table, and kneeling, except as allowed, provided for, or directed, by rubric or canon,
9) The celebration or receiving of the Holy Communion by any Bishop or priest, when no person receives with him,
10) Employing or permitting any person or persons not in Holy Orders to assist the minister in any part of the order for the administration of the Holy Communion,
11) Using, at any administration of the Holy Communion, any prayers, collects, gospels, or epistles other than those provided in the Book of Common Prayer by canon.

Having thus limited the ceremonies, the committee also recommended canonical provision (1) to prevent a rector from introducing the Choral Service or (2) from employing a surpliced choir without the consent of the vestry or contrary to the prohibition of the bishop, (3) to forbid any chancel arrangement that would prevent the minister from officiating at the right end of the holy table, and (4) to establish the present episcopal robes as appropriate dress for bishops but limiting all other ministers to a white surplice, a black or white stole, bands, a black gown or a black cassock not reaching below the ankles. To be sure that every possible point would be covered by their proposed legislation they added, ". . . in all matters doubtful, reference shall be made to the ordinary, and no changes shall be made against the godly counsel and judgment of the Bishop."

Days of discussion followed this report, and motions, substitutions, and amendments taxed parliamentary skill and patience in the stormiest session since 1844. As the days wore on, it became quite clear that there was too much diversity of opinion and breadth of interpretation in the church to permit the adoption of such specific legislation. Only two leaders of the 1844 Convention survived: Bishop McIlvaine of Ohio remained one of the staunchest of the low churchmen; and Bishop Whittingham of Maryland, once considered the most objectionable of the high churchmen, now quite logically in keeping with his old high church position had become an arch-opponent of ritualism. Bishop Alfred Lee and Bishop Manton Eastburn ably stood by Bishop McIlvaine, while among the deputies William Mead, M. A. DeWolfe Howe, and Daniel

C. Goodwin became the low church leaders. The ritualists could not yet claim a single bishop, but in the lower house their number included distinguished deputies like James Breck, John Tucker, Henry Waterman, and James De-Koven, destined to be one of the ablest men of the party. As the discussions continued and the partisan lines and issues became more clearly drawn, the decorous and conciliatory spirit that had characterized the debates in earlier conventions and notably in 1868, broke down, and one could hear mutterings of "trumpery of Rome" and "Zwinglian." At the height of the debate and from a quarter where an answer was probably least expected came the solution to the dilemma. James DeKoven, Warden of Racine College in Wisconsin, a charming gentleman of impeccable character, one of the truly great orators and debaters of the generation, and the emerging leader of the ritualists, rose to declare his own position. Often while he spoke the gavel fell, but men of all parties cried, "Let him go on," anxious to hear his amazingly frank testimony:

> . . . I believe in the Real, Actual Presence of Our Lord under the form of bread and wine upon the altars of our churches. I myself adore and would, if it were necessary or my duty, teach my people to adore, Christ present in the elements under the form of bread and wine.
>
> And I use these words because they are a bold statement of the doctrine of the Real Presence, but I use them for another reason: they are adjudicated words; they are words which, used by a divine of the Church of England, have been tried in the highest ecclesiastical court of England, and have been decided by that ecclesiastical court to come within the limits of the truth held in the Church of England.[11]

Although he must have known that such frankness could forever limit his possibilities for preferment and the episcopate, DeKoven spoke openly and honestly. By so doing he also defeated the committee's proposal, which had already been approved by the majority of the deputies but failed to obtain the concurrence of the bishops. His hearers apparently agreed that to control doctrine by legislation about ceremony is not a clear or fair index of orthodox doctrine or that ceremonial. DeKoven argued cogently that in Anglicanism questions of doctrine had always been regulated by canons dealing directly with doctrine, so that "if people teach false doctrine they should be tried and suspended, or punished in accordance with that canon." Although the phrase "Living Liturgy" was not yet in common use, this convention acted wisely by enacting legislation that emphasized the essential comprehensiveness of historic Anglicanism and that permitted the development of significant liturgical and ceremonial improvements. These changes provided for greater flexibility in worship and more orderly and richer devotional opportunity without doing violence to the genius and tradition of the Episcopal Church. Actually most of the ceremonies under discussion have since become standard practice in many high church parishes and are at least sympathetically understood elsewhere.

The official action taken by this convention as a result of the committee's work of three years and the prolonged debates appeared in two brief resolutions, one negative and the other positive. The former condemned "all ceremonies, observances, and practices which are fitted to express a doctrine foreign to that set forth in the authorized standards of this Church." The positive action declared that

> . . . the paternal counsel and advice of the Right Reverend Fathers, the Bishops of the Church, is deemed sufficient at this time to secure the suppression of all that is irregular and unseemly, and to promote greater uniformity in conducting the public worship of the Church, and in administration of the Holy Sacraments.

Despite their refusal to concur in the restricting legislation during the convention, the House of Bishops spoke emphatically in the ensuing pastoral letter condemning auricular confession, veneration and invocation of the saints, and Eucharistic adoration. But the hour was late, and these cumulative and internal disruptive forces were about to rend the church in a way that the slavery question and even four years of Civil War had not been able to do.

The individual withdrawal of ministers, which began three years earlier, and the trial and deposition of Charles Cheney in 1871 followed fairly closely the pattern that some foresighted evangelical leaders had predicted. They had once declared that, unless they organized their strength and acted together, their cause would fail by attrition, so that each would face individual discipline or be forced from the church. In the interim between 1871 and 1874 the leadership of the more militant of the evangelicals fell from the hands of the presbyters and was at last accepted by George D. Cummins, Assistant Bishop of Kentucky. He had been displeased with the disciplining of Cheney, and since his consecration in 1868, had increasingly disagreed with his diocesan, Benjamin Bosworth Smith, who from 1868 was also the Presiding Bishop of the church, about the increase of ritualism permitted in the Diocese of Kentucky. He became restive because he observed that throughout the church the liberties of the Anglo-Catholics went unchecked, while those of the evangelicals became more circumscribed. Cummins himself suffered from such circumscription in October, 1873, while the Evangelical Alliance, an international body, was meeting in New York. The bishop preached the sermon and received the Holy Communion in an interdenominational celebration of the Lord's Supper in a Presbyterian church and was greatly criticized for both acts. The English Bishop of Zanzibar, who was then in New York, protested formally to Bishop Horatio Potter of that diocese, but no act of discipline followed. Cummins, who was a brilliant preacher, also became involved in several disputes with Bishop Whitehouse of Illinois, who had tried to prevent him from preaching in that diocese. When ill health overtook Bishop Smith in 1872, he went to live in Hoboken, New Jersey, and Cummins naturally expected that the administration of the diocese would fall to his hands. However, the diocese, acting without a precedent, asked Bishop Smith to continue his jurisdiction *in absentia,* in part perhaps to prevent any question about his continuance as the Presiding Bishop of the Church.

Probably no one of the recent annoyances would have been sufficient to arouse Bishop Cummins to think of separation, which had actually been suggested to him by William H. Cooper as early as 1868 and the following year by Mason Gallagher. He had become exceedingly worried about the future of the church in which ceremonial advances continued unchecked and about which he seemed to be able to do nothing even in his own diocese. Current doctrinal interpretations, especially of the Sacraments, also seemed to him to point in the direction of de-Protestantizing the Episcopal Church. It is possible that the unpleasant episode connected with the meeting of the Evangelical Alliance in New York City may have been the determining factor in prompting the precipitate action he was about to take. The church was still a generation removed from an executive full-time Presiding Bishop, to whom a disturbed bishop might have had recourse, and there was no National Council to direct church affairs in the interim of the sessions of the General Convention. Then, too, the titular Presiding Bishop was his diocesan, and apparently there were sufficient grounds of difference between them that Cummins felt little desire to discuss or negotiate his personal difficulties by such personal confrontation.

Accordingly, on November 10, 1873, Cummins wrote Bishop Smith that he was transferring his work and office "to another sphere." The Presiding Bishop immediately instituted proceedings against Cummins for abandoning the communion, suspended him from the exercise of his ministry, and on June 24, 1874, pronounced his deposition. The House of Bishops in session at the General Convention unanimously sustained the deposition on October 17, 1874. While nothing was done officially about the schism, it weighed heavily on every mind, was often discussed privately, and actually had a mellowing influence on the convention. Many staunch evangelicals and others of more moderate persuasions deplored the open break and felt that although it was an almost inevitable conclusion to the events of the preceding years, it was nevertheless most unfortunate. Low churchmen like Stephen Tyng and broad churchmen like Phillips Brooks believed it would accomplish little good; the latter once lightly referred to the embarrassment of the high churchmen:

> What a panic it must make among the bishops to know that a stray parson is around with a true bit of their genuine succession, perfectly and indisputably the thing, which he can give to anybody he pleases! Nothing like it since the pow-wow among the gods when Prometheus stole the fire.[12]

Cummins and his associates, eight ministers and nineteen laymen, met in New York City on December 2, 1873, and organized the Reformed Episcopal Church. Charles Edward Cheney was elected a bishop and consecrated by Cummins on December 7. Cheney, in turn, after the death of Cummins on June 26, 1876, consecrated Bishop J. H. Reinkins. Although there was ground for calling this episcopate irregular, since on two occasions at least it had been perpetuated through consecration by a single bishop, there was never any question about the validity of the orders of this church.

The new church quickly adopted the Proposed Book of Common Prayer, prepared by Bishop William White and William Smith and presented to the General Convention in 1785. The Declaration of Principles adopted at this first meeting stated the Reformed Episcopal position on episcopacy, in terms reminiscent of Richard Hooker, that it was recognized "not as of divine right but as a very ancient and desirable form of church polity." In true sixteenth-century style the Declaration denied doctrines considered erroneous, such as (1) the existence of the Church of Christ in one order or form of ecclesiastical polity; (2) that Christian ministers are priests in another sense than that in which all believers are "a royal priesthood"; (3) that the Lord's Table is an altar on which the oblation of the Body and Blood of Christ is offered anew to the Father; (4) that the presence of Christ in the Lord's Supper is a presence in the elements of Bread and Wine; and (5) that Regeneration is inseparably connected with Baptism.

The very fact that so large a negative element was present in the Declaration could indicate that these men withdrew from the Episcopal Church, not only because the doctrines that they held in common with many low and even some high churchmen were challenged at times, but also because the General Convention refused to require complete doctrinal uniformity by denouncing the doctrines they opposed. In this demand for rigid monolithic uniformity to guarantee the orthodoxy of the true church these men failed to understand the real genius of Anglicanism, which, through creative tension between varying shades of mellowed reasonableness, produces the comprehensiveness within which millions of Christians discover their faith and experience religious satisfaction.

A further look at the disrupted situation in the church led the bishops and deputies to the next General Convention in the fall of 1874 to reopen the question and to attempt in a more politically astute way to control the ceremonial advances by revising Canon 20, "Of the Use of the Book of Common Prayer." In the achievement of this solution the evangelicals received the support of many conservative high churchmen and even some of the older Tractarians, like Bishop Coxe of Western New York and William Dexter Wilson of Cornell University, who had popularly presented Tractarianism in *The Church Identified* to express his own personal convictions but also in an attempt to stay further disruption.

By his plea for Anglican comprehensiveness no less a high churchman than James DeKoven, in what was probably his greatest speech before any of the four conventions he attended, did much to bring about the solution. To avoid lengthy discussions the convention had agreed to a limitation of thirty minutes on all speeches but gladly waived this rule to permit the eloquent deputy from Wisconsin to deliver a carefully prepared address by which he was able to change the convention's entire approach to the ritualistic controversy.

Heretofore parties had each sought to gain advantage for their own group and to limit their opponents as much as possible by regulatory legislation. DeKoven changed the very basis of the argument to one of comprehensiveness in Anglicanism with greater freedom for all. He even pleaded for a broader interpretation of Baptismal regeneration and the Zwinglian doctrine of the Eucharist as proper in such historical Anglican comprehensiveness. This generous conception of doctrinal diversity within the limits of Anglican orthodoxy was not really new in DeKoven, although he did much to publicize it. Professor Samuel F. Jarvis, an eminent canonist of the General Seminary faculty, had supported it as DeKoven indicated in his address, and John Cotton Smith also had recently propounded it independently in a paper at the first meeting of the American Church Congress in New York shortly before the opening of this session of the General Convention. Quoting Jarvis's sermon before the Board of Missions, DeKoven said both those who believed in a real change in the Eucharist "by which the very elements themselves, though they retain their original properties are corporeally united with and transformed into Christ" and those who held a purely spiritual presence in the Sacrament must be tolerated in the church. In his concluding pleas DeKoven urged the church to give its major attention to the current challenging opportunities rather than to dissipate its energies and resources by quarreling about debatable issues that gave no promise of easy solution.

When the high churchmen saw that this proposal was about the best which they could expect to achieve in this convention, the canonical revision was adopted with little opposition:

> If any bishop have reason to believe, or if complaint be made to him in writing by two or more of his presbyters, that within his jurisdiction ceremonies or practices not ordained or authorized in the Book of Common Prayer, and setting forth or symbolizing erroneous or doubtful doctrines, have been introduced by any Minister during the celebration of the Holy Communion, such as
>
> a. The elevation of the Elements in the Holy Communion in such manner as to expose them to the view of the people as objects toward which adoration is to be made,
>
> b. Any act of adoration of or toward the Elements in the Holy Communion, such as bowings, prostrations, or genuflections; and
>
> c. All other like acts not authorized by the rubrics of the Book of Common Prayer:
>
> It shall be the duty of such Bishop to summon the Standing Committee as his Council of Advice and with them to investigate the matter.[13]

The canon further provided for the admonition of the offender and, in the refusal to heed the admonition, for the bringing of the offending priest to trial for breach of his ordination vow. Only one trial is known to have resulted from this canon. Oliver S. Prescott was admonished for introducing ritualistic practices in St. Clement's Church, Philadelphia, but no punishment beyond admonition was administered, and St. Clement's continued in its ways despite episcopal disapproval.[14] The experience of another generation proved the obsolescence of this canon, and in 1904 it was unanimously repealed.

Before the adjournment of the convention in 1874, the House of Deputies indicated its opposition to Anglo-Catholicism in still another way, when it refused to confirm the election of George F. Seymour, Dean of the General Theological Seminary, as Bishop of Illinois because his name had been widely associated with Charles C. Grafton and the dissemination of the doctrine of the corporeal Presence among the Seminary students. During the following triennium the standing committees of the dioceses similarly refused to confirm the election of James DeKoven for the same diocese. DeKoven's worth and personal integrity were above the suspicions of his most hostile critics, so that his rejection must have been on the ground that a high churchman should not be a bishop.

Despite his advanced position in which he once described Mary as "the bringer-forth of God, the ever Virgin,"[15] DeKoven probably came nearer being a bishop, without ever becoming one, than any other man in the Episcopal Church who would have accepted the office. As early as 1866 he had been nominated as coadjutor to Bishop Kemper of Wisconsin but failed to be elected because of the opposing old high churchmen. The universal appeal of his charm and ability may be seen in that, six years later in the spring of 1873, he barely missed election as Bishop of Massachusetts.[16] On the death of Bishop William Armitage of Wisconsin in 1873, DeKoven was among the nominees to succeed him and on the fourth ballot was elected by the clergy, but the laity did not concur. When the lay deputies to the General Convention failed the following year to confirm George F. Seymour as Bishop of Illinois, that diocese chose DeKoven, only to find another rejection, this time by the standing committees of the dioceses, whose approval was necessary beyond election by both Houses of the diocesan convention. Probably because DeKoven had spoken in defense of his own doctrinal position during the Wisconsin election, the rumor circulated that he wanted to be a bishop, which was very likely unfounded but certainly did not help him in future considerations.

On August 31, 1875, DeKoven withdrew his acceptance of election in Illinois, when it became clear that the standing committees would not confirm his election, and clearly defined his sacramental views which had come into question. His own words now seemed to indicate a modification of his classic utterance before the General Convention four years earlier; he wrote that "Whenever and wherever I have asserted that Christ is present '*in the elements,*' *under the form or species of bread and wine,* I mean that He is present sacramentally and spiritually, and thus really and truly." Apparently, and probably significantly, it was now the laymen into whose hands had fallen the leadership of the opposition to Anglo-Catholic doctrine and the accompanying ritualism, for in this same year the lay order in the Diocese of Fond du Lac failed to approve DeKoven's election by the clergy as their bishop. While the high churchmen occasionally tried in a similar way to block the election of other bishops, as Seymour led a violent attack almost twenty years later against Phillips Brooks, the bishop-elect in Massachusetts, time and growth made such differences an inadequate ground for such dramatic and far-reaching expression. In fact within four years Seymour became the Bishop of Springfield and in another ten years Charles C. Grafton, a most ardent Anglo-Catholic, became Bishop of Fond du Lac. About the only remaining topic that could divide the General Convention along party lines in the last two generations has been the term "Protestant" in the name of the church; the high churchmen invariably wished to drop it, and the rapidly growing center group of moderate churchmen, who consistently refuse to be identified with any party, have been able to defend it.

The year 1874 may serve to indicate the close of three distinct periods of growth in the high church movement in the Episcopal Church. During the first fifty years the old high churchmen had asserted the catholicity of this church, then new in America, stressing especially the necessity of her orders and the validity of her Sacraments. In the latter part of this period they showed some antagonism toward the multiplying American sects, an attitude soon to be shared by men like John W. Nevin and other leaders of the Mercersburg Movement in the Reformed Church, who had also been influenced by the Oxford Movement.

During the second period, which included the twenty years before the outbreak of the Civil War, many of the high churchmen turned their attention to the external evidences for these doctrines, now well established, to reemphasize the nature and importance of worship and to introduce appropriate vestments and ornaments for the greater effectiveness of worship. More frequent celebrations of the Holy Communion emphasized the centrality of the Eucharist, and the observance of the Church Year provided a well-balanced lectionary and also proved to be a great help for the emerging church schools and the teaching ministry of the church. In supporting these innovations, the high churchmen were joined by many whose churchmanship was much more moderate. The most effective single provocation of these advances was the Muhlenberg Memorial of 1853, largely the creation of William A. Muhlenberg, who shared much of the spirit but not the doctrinal or ceremonial novelties of the younger high churchmen and so quite appropriately called himself an Evangelical Catholic and published two large volumes of *Evangelical Catholic Papers*. Some of the younger high churchmen of the period, such as James DeKoven, stressed acts of adoration of the Real Presence in the Sacrament and considered the Sacrament not only a means of communion but stressed its sacrificial nature and spoke of Masses and even Requiem Masses. These men generally were inclined to seek authority for their embellishments and practices in the lost treasures of the Middle Ages and so differed markedly from the old high churchmen who had stressed the primitive church and highly regarded the corrections of the Reformation.

In the third period of development following the Civil War, some high churchmen left a major portion of their party behind as they sought the still fuller catholic spirit by introducing specifically Roman Catholic forms, vestments, and portions of the liturgy, as well as ornaments and ceremonies, which they felt Anglicanism had lost at the too strenuous Reformation in the sixteenth century. In this group were to be found the so-called Romanizers, who were willing and even desirous to accept everything Roman save papal infallibility. They were colorful and vocal and gained a disproportionately large influence so as often to discredit genuine high churchmanship and frequently to misrepresent the Episcopal Church. Such men "have been confined to obscure, not to say sentimental cliques," said Ferdinand C. Ewer, one of the most learned high churchmen and one of the clearest writers of his time. He compared them to "butterflies flitting about a rock . . . utterly without influence . . . and of brief career" and declared that they were rejected and ignored by the catholic party.[17]

Only a few years earlier he had revealed his own feelings when he compared Protestantism and Romanism and said, "Protestantism is diversity without unity; Romanism is unity without diversity; Catholicity [is] diversity in unity. . . ."[18] Ewer had run the gamut from a childhood in a high church parish through Unitarianism to agnosticism and ultimately to Catholic orthodoxy and so combined an unusually fine qualification with a great concern to show an inclusive catholic viewpoint. He presented his most systematic statement in a series of sermons in his own parish, Christ Church, New York, in 1868 under the title *The Failure of Protestantism*, which cost him his popularity and ultimately his prominent, fashionable parish. With the consent of Bishop Horatio Potter he organized St. Ignatius Parish, where he freely developed the altar arrangements and ceremonial to suit his theology. In the last years of his life he defined "What is the Anglican Church," saying, "She is not a *via media* between Rome and Protestantism, but embraces all that is good in both. She is Catholic." To Ewer, then, more than to any other, Episcopalians owe the clarification of the commonly used phrase "bridge-church." Anglicanism then is not a bridge at all nor even a compromise but rather a golden mean in the Greek sense, a moderate way between extremes. The taut but not disruptive tension between the extremities produces a creative religious and theological synthesis in which a rational and critical Protestant judgment, making for constant correction and purification, is tempered and kept from the limits of error by the stability of the historical, Biblical, sacramental, and truly catholic tradition.

Impressed by Ewer's clarity and good judgment, Bishop Frederic Dan Huntington of Central New York asked that he provide a definition of the *terminus ad quem* of the Catholic movement which might be helpful to thousands in the church who were perplexed by party slogans. To this request Ewer replied in his last publication that this *terminus* was "the Anglican Reformation; the Anglican Church reformed as in Edward's [VI] day . . . there is not a particle of yearning . . . to go one fraction of an inch beyond the principles of the real Anglican Reformation as set down in Edward's First Prayer Book."

Although party lines have grown dim and often indistinguishable in the last fifty years and most of the appointments, vestments, and ceremonies contested in the earlier periods have become common practice across the church, there is still a difference of theological presupposition and especially a difference of feeling and spirit within the comprehensiveness of Anglicanism in America. By 1875 even church architecture was reflecting the changing spirit; the high or three-deck pulpit had gone, and the shallow recess for the communion table had become an apse in which altars of carved wood or stone with a cross and colored frontals had become the norm. Among the laymen this may have reflected itself in the religious journal of his choice or the high or low parish he chose to attend or even whether he preferred the eight o'clock Holy Communion service celebrated in eucharistic vestments or the eleven o'clock Holy Communion with surplice and stole. The old preaching gown was rarely used, and a surplice with tippet or stole became the customary practice. In more recent years some ministers, reasoning that preaching of the Word and administration of the Sacraments are given equal emphasis in Article XIX and that the Bible is more important than the Prayer Book, wear stoles for all services. Shades of churchmanship also reflect themselves in the clergy's preference of bishops; some clergymen prefer to work in a high and others in a low diocese. Types of churchmanship established in the several dioceses shortly after the Civil War have often perpetuated themselves; so the churchmanship of new bishops usually reflects the predominant churchmanship in the diocese, and the bishop in turn will probably favor those of kindred spirit in admitting clergy to his diocese. High churchmen generally were not widely selected for the episcopate before the Civil War, but since that time certain dioceses have invariably selected their diocesans from this group.

As the membership increased, the larger dioceses were first subdivided, in part at least through the influence of the high churchmen who rightly contended for the more direct personal supervision of the bishop among his people. The provincial system, a logical consequence of this trend by which dioceses were grouped into areas, after considerable promotion by John Henry Hopkins, Jr., was nominally introduced in 1907 but never became as effective as its sponsors anticipated.

Far more significant was the introduction of cathedrals in the last half of the nineteenth century, a movement that Hopkins also supported enthusiastically. In 1861 the Church of the Atonement, Chicago, was presented to Bishop Whitehouse as the first American pro-cathedral. The cornerstone for the cathedral in Davenport, Iowa, was laid in 1867, and others were soon begun in Nebraska, Utah, Maine, Springfield, Colorado, and Minnesota, where the first cathedral in the Episcopal Church was regularly organized by Bishop Whipple. Only by the end of the century were resources adequate to begin cathedrals on the major European scale. In 1884 work was begun on such a cathedral in Albany, New York, and soon thereafter similar beginnings were made in Philadelphia, New York in 1892, and Washington in 1907. Only the last two have made substantial progress, and the Cathedral of St.

John the Divine in New York is now nearing completion. At first the cathedrals were little more than renamed parish churches but eventually, especially the cathedrals built on nobler scale, came to be looked upon as a house of prayer for all people and freed of parochial obligations. In the more recent years some chapters and deans have sought to make even some of the more representative cathedrals centers of parish life again.

The Anglo-Catholic movement developed other characteristics of a more structured order. *The Living Church,* founded in 1878, while not an official journal, promoted its ideas. "The Clerical Union for the Maintenance and Defense of Catholic Principles," more briefly and popularly known as "The Catholic Club," was begun in 1887 and sought to bring increasing emphasis on Eucharistic worship and to defend the Episcopal Church from rationalism and latitudinarianism, on the one hand, and from Roman denials of Anglicanism's catholic claims, on the other.

It was natural that during the years in which so much attention was given to vestments and ceremonies there would be evidence of concern about music in the church. In the middle of the last century the House of Bishops, already reckoning with a perennial problem for Episcopalians, considered it "a most grievous and dangerous inconsistency when the house of prayer is desecrated by a choice of music and a style of performance which are rather suited to the Opera than to the church." Hoping to bring some kind of order out of the apparent disparity and great variety of practice throughout the church, the House of Bishops in 1859 resolved that rectors should control the music in their parishes, seek to involve their congregations in a devotional spirit, and promote congregational singing.

To assist in the program for better congregational response and participation in worship the church also improved its Hymnal. In 1865 a supplement of sixty hymns was added, and six years later the General Convention authorized the exclusive use of the church's first official Hymnal. This new and much larger book of 496 hymns was the result of competent critical revision that introduced 241 entirely new hymns while keeping many of the original 212 and the supplement. Since no hymn tunes were included, it was not long until various musical editions appeared with some resulting confusion, which was at least partially rectified by the revision of 1892.[19]

In 1874 the General Convention, which was still trying to bring order into the widely disparate liturgical practices in the church, sought to do a similar service by adopting a Canon "Of the Music of the Church," which remains the general rule of the church. Earlier attempts to place responsibilities upon the clergy had made the unwarranted assumption that ministers were competent to exercise authority in the field of music. Well-established congregations frequently engaged professionally trained soloists, choir directors, and organists with the not unusual result of conflicting opinions and not a little tension within the choirs and sometimes the music committees, which often embarrassingly involved the rector as well. Although it was not until some years later that the theological seminaries introduced professional musical training for the clergy, the bishops in 1874 clearly placed final authority in the hands of the rectors when they ruled that:

> It shall be the duty of every Minister of this Church, with such assistance as he may see fit to employ from persons skilled in music, to give order concerning the tunes to be sung at any time in his Church, and especially it shall be his duty to suppress all light and unseemly music, and all indecency and irreverence in the performance. . . .

The results were not by any means uniform throughout the church, but it was a beginning in the ordering of public worship that would soon lead also to a revision of the liturgy and the Book of Common Prayer during the next decade.

XVIII

THE CHURCH AND
MODERN THOUGHT

The early 1880's marked a backward and a forward look for the Protestant Episcopal Church. The General Convention of 1883, meeting in historic Christ Church, Philadelphia, provided the opportunity to survey the achievements of the century since the earliest clergy conventions had prepared the way for the constitutional organization of the church in 1789. With such a large perspective the comparatively recent clashes of party spirit melted into insignificance and the amazing sense of unity of purpose made this assembly of churchmen a most creative one. Significantly, Bishop Thomas M. Clark of Rhode Island preached the opening sermon on the theme "The Mission of the Episcopal Church." He recalled that this church was essentially a conservative body built upon an ancient pattern and reminded his colleagues that additional valued traditions were about to be recovered in the revision of the Prayer Book. Then, in his conclusion he turned the minds of the bishops and deputies from their proud heritage to the immediate opportunities before them, saying,

> There is other work for us to do beside fortifying and defending our citadel. Constitutions and canons are of value, so far as they aid in discharging the mission intrusted to us, and no farther. Rubrics are only the regulating power of the machine, indispensable parts of the mechanism, but without any inspiring force. And while we coninue to walk in the old paths, let it be with an accelerated pace, and with our eyes looking forward and not backward.

The rich heritage of the church was visibly demonstrated in the colorful consecration of Henry C. Potter as the Assistant Bishop of New York in his own parish church; the service following the procession of about forty bishops and three hundred clergy seemed singularly appropriate in the beautiful Gothic Grace Church on lower Broadway. This year saw the consecration of four other bishops, for Indiana, Virginia, North Dakota, and East Carolina, bringing the total number of bishops for the century since Bishop Seabury's consecration to one hundred and thirty-three.

A careful review of the progress of the church indicated that in the fifty-one years since 1832 the number of dioceses had increased from 18 to 48; the parishes, from approximately 500 to about 3,000; the clergy, from 592 to 3,572, about a sixfold growth with an additional 401 candidates for holy orders in training. During the same period the communicant strength of the church grew from about 31,000 to 407,481, a thirteenfold increase, while the national population was only quadrupled. While this represented an average increase of twenty per cent in every triennium of the century, the growth during the preceding thirty-three years was almost five hundred per cent, reflecting a rapidly rising trend that began after the Civil War. Between 1880 and 1883 alone, 62,692 communicants were added to the church rolls.

The church now had 3,732 church and chapel buildings, 1,307 mission stations, 45 hospitals, 48 orphanages, 32 homes for the aged and others, 99 academies, 17 colleges, 16 theological schools, and 56 other institutions. To support such large undertakings, the church's receipts increased in even greater proportion than its membership. In 1835 the total offerings for the Domestic and Foreign Missionary Society were $11,750; forty-five years later the total gifts for missions alone were $1,296,962, and the total offerings that year exceeded $20,250,000. During the last triennium before 1883 these gifts for all purposes increased more than forty per cent to almost $29,000,000.

No more significant action was achieved by this session than the preliminary adoption—it required approval by another session of the General Convention for final authorization—of the report of the Committee on the Revision of the Prayer Book providing additions for the enrichment of the services and flexibility in their use. More responsible for these revisions than any other individual was William Reed Huntington who moved from All Saints' Church, Worcester, Massachusetts, to succeed Bishop Potter at Grace Church, New York. Well trained in the broad New England cultural background, Huntington had developed a progressive spirit that at once aligned him with the broad churchmen theologically and with the ritualists liturgically.

Few changes had been made in the Prayer Book since 1789, with the exception that the Office of Institution for Ministers was added in 1804. The Muhlenberg Memorial of 1853 did contemplate some radical changes in the direction of abbreviation and flexibility, but the differences in spirit were still too great and the conservative attitude that the Prayer Book should never be changed remained too strong to permit immediate results. Among its remote effects, however, was a lingering desire for liturgical improvement, and by the deft leadership of William R. Huntington, the General Convention of 1880, after a previous rejection three years earlier, authorized a joint committee of both Houses to consider a Prayer Book revision "in the direction of liturgical enrichment and increased flexibility."

The committee was well balanced between the high and low churchmen, and Huntington, whose instinct for liturgical expression was widely recognized, was named its secretary. The convention was assured that no radical attempts would be made to Americanize the Prayer Book, and from the outset it was agreed that no changes would be made in doctrine, thus preventing the reopening of the earlier baptismal controversy, or in the Communion Service, thus preventing any controversial ritualistic innovations. Huntington had traveled widely and studied all the background sources necessary to move toward a purer liturgical refinement. In this work he had been aided by members of the committee and generously supported by J. Pierpont Morgan, who occasionally sent him important studies and rare volumes of Roman Catholic and Huguenot liturgies.

The committee recommended 196 changes in text, which were printed in a volume called *The Book Annexed,* being the Prayer Book as it would appear if the committee's proposals were incorporated. Most of *The Book Annexed* was approved in 1883 with little opposition except from the extreme low churchmen, who feared that revision meant more ritualism and moving away from Protestantism, and some extreme high churchmen, led by Arthur Ritchie, who preferred no revision at all to one which would not satisfy them fully.

When this report was presented to the General Convention three years later, immediate opposition, which had been building up in influential quarters during the triennium, brought severe and unjust criticism that the changes which had been so well received and approved in 1883 were liturgically, historically, and doctrinally unsatisfactory. William Reed Huntington, who had done the historical research and was the prime mover in these liturgical reforms, was crushed and withdrew from the committee, and the revision was remitted to a new committee for review and report. So delicate had the subject become by 1889 that a minority report to end Prayer Book revision almost carried both houses at that convention.

Three years later the General Convention materially reduced the alterations and produced a revised version of the Prayer Book that remained the standard for thirty-six years. The touch of Huntington's skilled hand was reflected in this book and especially in his superb new collect for the Feast of the Transfiguration, an observance newly introduced among the Holy Days. Fortunately, the report of the earlier committee was preserved in printed form, and most of its valued proposals, which had been rejected in 1892, were reconsidered later, and many of them became a part of the present Book of Common Prayer as revised in 1928.[1]

To meet the urgent contemporary problems and to provide for its own adequately trained leaders the Episcopal Church followed the rapidly developing trend and enlarged and improved its educational facilities at all levels from preparatory schools through colleges and theological seminaries. In the twenty years after 1878 American high schools increased from eight hundred to fifty-five hundred, while the illiteracy rate fell from seventeen to eleven per cent. Americans everywhere were reading, and before the end of the century at least nine thousand public libraries were reported.

A perennial shortage of clergy had plagued the Episcopal Church from the colonial days, and now it required not only more but better trained ministers. For at least a decade after the Civil War the General Convention thought it was providing adequately by founding more church boarding schools and colleges where young people might continue to receive the Christian nurture begun in the homes of the church. This latter ideal, although often tritely expressed, was singularly important; all too soon the corrosive influence of the rising scientific secularism seared and often depleted the religious life of the family. Under these circumstances fewer young men found religious vocations, and the church, far from reproducing its own ministry, received many of its clergy from other churches. In 1889 the General Convention established the Church University Board of Regents to promote education through the church and to provide funds for this purpose, but this Board was discontinued in 1898, having done little beyond providing for a few scholarships.

Educators in the church responded to the appeal for more schools, and by 1883 there were about one hundred academies and private schools operating under the blessing of the church and providing opportunity for a college preparatory training in a religious environment. About half of these schools still exist, and among them are some of the nation's leading schools of this type. Frequently, the heads of these institutions were clergymen who sought to inculcate academic excellence and high moral character through study in an environment where the church normally had an important role in the life of the community and so to help these young people avoid the sterility of the irreligious life.

In the last twenty years of the nineteenth century the number of American colleges and universities increased from 350 to 500 and enrollments almost doubled, reaching 100,000 students. It was during this period that many of the important technical schools, women's colleges, state and other universities came into existence and the older colleges constantly raised their standards. While most of the early educational institutions in America had been founded by the churches, primarily to train ministers, the financial support now required to keep abreast of the public and heavily endowed private institutions was raising increasing difficulties for the church-related schools and colleges. Kenyon College was reorganized in 1891 and again in 1912, and two new schools, St. Augustine's and St. Paul's, joined the ranks with Hobart, Trinity, and the University of the South as well-established colleges of the church. Racine College was begun at Racine, Wisconsin, in 1852, and St. Stephen's College at Annandale-on-the-Hudson, New York, in 1860. The former soon discontinued its college grade work, and the latter, on the seventy-fifth anniversary of its founding by John Bard, was named Bard College. In 1908 William Smith College for women was established on its own campus adjacent to Hobart College at Geneva, New York. Geneva Academy, begun in 1796, became Geneva College in 1822 through the interest of Bishop John Henry Hobart, and thirty years later the name of the college was changed to honor the bishop. These schools in Geneva share a common faculty, library, and laboratories, and have been incorporated under the name of the Colleges of the Seneca. More recently, Shimer College at Mt. Carroll, Illinois, has become officially related to the Episcopal Church.

These schools retained as one of their primary functions the guidance and training of young men for the seminaries of the church. And lest the young people of the church who were attending educational institutions other than those of the Episcopal Church should be overlooked, the General Convention as early as 1879 proposed that in every collegiate center in the country there should be placed a competently trained pastor to meet and guide these young people. Little was done about this proposal, however, until after World War I.

The church's ministry to college students is now sponsored by the Division of College Work, under the direction of the Home Department of the National Council; its program is carried on through the National Canterbury Association, composed of the Episcopal student organizations in many colleges and universities. To promote and strengthen this work of the church in educational centers the Church Society for College Work assists in the placement of a clergyman who ministers to students, arranges student conferences and retreats, raises funds, and recruits men for the ministry. The National Commission on College Work is an advisory body appointed by the Division of College Work to assist in policy planning and in the allocation of grants and scholarship funds.

The seminaries of the church were also improved by passing through this testing period. Although the General Seminary was the only theological school under the direct sponsorship of the General Convention, it had suffered academic and financial reverses, and it was not until these ties were materially strengthened in 1883, under the leadership of Dean Eugene A. Hoffman, that this school showed marked improvement. With assistance from his family and through his own efficiency and generosity, the dean was able to raise the endowments to one and a quarter million dollars, erect a major portion of the present buildings, acquire an original Gutenberg Bible, and make other adequate provisions for the expansion of the valuable theological library. This seminary's golden days of academic leadership, however, still lay ahead.

When the Civil War made it impossible for Pennsylvania to send its candidates to the Virginia Theological Seminary, Bishop Alonzo Potter opened the Philadelphia Divinity School in 1861 with George E. Hare as its first dean. By a wise selection of its faculty this school very quickly developed a high standard and an enviable academic reputation. With the close of the war the badly damaged properties of the Virginia Seminary at Alexandria were restored, but it remained a long generation before its academic efforts proved to be as fruitful as its missionary training. Most of the foreign missionaries of the church received their academic training and caught their evangelistic spirit at this institution, and without it the entire program of the church would have been seriously impaired. Berkeley Divinity School at Middletown and later at New Haven, Connecticut, and Nashotah House in Wisconsin grew beyond the limits of diocesan influence during these years and sent their graduates into other areas of the church. The former had been founded in 1854 by Bishop John Williams and remained a center of Connecticut churchmanship under his influence for forty-five years; the latter, under the influence of Bishop Charles Grafton and Bishop George Seymour and other high churchmen, soon became the center of Anglo-Catholic training and drew students of this persuasion from many parts of the church. With the opening of missions in the far West the clergy supply became a major problem. In 1871, Bishop Randall, in charge of Colorado, Wyoming, and New Mexico, wrote that his greatest trial had been "to obtain ministers ready to go to this land and stay there long enough to 'possess it.'" To help solve this acute situation he founded a school for boys at Golden, Colorado, and Bishop Clarkson created Noraska College and Divinity School and the Omaha Collegiate Institute, all of which proved to be short-lived. St. John's Theological College, established in Greeley, Colorado, in 1910, graduated more than one hundred men before it closed its doors in 1935.

Four additional seminaries were begun in the continental United States during this generation. After an abortive attempt in 1835 and much concern about it since that time, the Episcopal Theological School was begun at Cambridge, Massachusetts, in 1867 as an immediate result of a gift of $100,000 by Benjamin Tyler Reed. Its charter specifically stipulated that its purpose was to set forth a Protestant, Biblically centered point of view, free from all taint of pre-Reformation tradition, doctrine, or usage. The benign leadership of its first full-time dean, John Seely Stone, a devout and scholarly evangelical, provided the stable environment in which its first faculty, especially Peter Henry Steenstra and Alexander V. G. Allen, introduced critical Biblical scholarship and the resulting newer theological ideas from Europe to the American theological schools.

The long established University of the South opened its theological school in 1878 under the sponsorship of the southern dioceses, for whom it provided a supply of clergymen to supplement those from the Virginia Theological Seminary and Bexley Hall, which had been training clergy at Kenyon College since the days of Philander Chase. Bishop William E. McLaren of Chicago opened the Western Theological Seminary in his city in 1885 and directed it personally for its first twenty years; in 1933 it was merged with the Seabury Seminary to become the Seabury-Western Seminary in Evanston, Illinois. To provide an adequate supply of clergy for the West Coast Bishop William F. Nichols of California organized the Church Divinity School of the Pacific in 1893, which has since then become one of the leading seminaries in the Berkeley center of theological schools. In 1951 the Episcopal Theological Seminary of the Southwest was begun in Austin, Texas, and the church has also established seminaries in Brazil and Puerto Rico. To provide opportunity for theological study in their own dioceses some bishops have opened diocesan seminaries where men prevented from study in the eleven seminaries of the church may prepare for ordination.

The program of religious education in the local parishes of the Episcopal Church hardly kept pace with the growth of its own communicant strength or with the growing Sunday School movement that was rapidly expanding across the nation through the stimulation of county, state, and national Sunday School associations and other interdenominational organizations for young people. Traditionally, the Episcopal Church had less to do with inter-denominational efforts, such as Bible Societies and Sunday School associations; while it was quite possible to dissipate the limited material and personal resources of a parish in diffused interdenominational efforts, the church might well have profited from some cooperation and limited participation in such movements. With little guidance from the general church before 1884, the promotion of these efforts fell largely into the hands of the rectors, resulting in a very uneven development across the church. Amazingly, the same committee on Christian Education which advised the General Convention in 1865 that the Sunday School program should be kept subordinate to the church and under the supervision of the rector proposed to that body the advanced idea that Protestant ministers should cooperate in arranging with the public school authorities to have children released for one or two hours each week for religious instruction by the clergy. Eventually in 1884 the newly formed American Church Sunday School Institute attempted to arouse greater enthusiasm for Christian education and to provide a closer bond between the twenty-two thousand teachers and three hundred and fifty thousand pupils in the church's Sunday Schools. *The American Church Sunday School Magazine* was published to provide materials and guidance for the teachers. By the end of the century the Sunday Schools enrolled about four hundred and thirty thousand pupils, almost three times the one hundred and fifty-eight thousand listed at the close of the Civil War, and the teaching staff had increased from eighteen thousand to about forty-six thousand during the same period.

Well in advance of the American churches was the local adult education program in the Episcopal Church, which began in New York and rapidly spread throughout the entire church. In the 1880's the Diocese of Albany promoted a "Society for the Home Study of Holy Scripture and Church History" with the Bishop of Albany as the president. Its program, which was not unlike many modern university home study courses in its design, provided printed reading outlines with a guidance letter to each subscriber, one of whom lived as far away as Richmond, Virginia. At the end of each study period printed examination questions were forwarded to each student, who soon afterward received not only a printed sheet with the correct answers but also a personal letter from the reader of his examination suggesting ways for further study and improvement.[2]

More specifically designed to improve the Christian instruction in the church schools were the Sunday School Commissions, which spread rapidly across the church about the turn of the century. Bishop Henry C. Potter was aided by Pascal Harrower, a competent educational leader among his clergy, in this innovation to modernize the organizational structure as well as the pedagogical methods of the schools in the Diocese of New York. More than twenty manuals were prepared for the various courses, which included the Bible and the Prayer Book as well as educational methods, child study, and psychology of religion, a subject then coming into popularity through the publications of Edwin D. Starbuck. So successful was this program, which in a few years had given hundreds of teachers a new insight into the meaning of their important work, that more than twenty dioceses inaugurated similar efforts before World War I.

More important than any of the church's internal problems was the revolutionary change in world thinking in the latter half of the nineteenth century. The internal struggles had recently rent the church structure, but this new external intellectual renaissance was forever to change the atmosphere in which the church must live and even the spirit and method of approach to its responsibilities as the church. While learning to live together with a comprehensive tolerance that permitted catholics and evangelicals to pursue their preferences in a broadening process of assimilation, the best leaders of all parties were now called upon to face the corrosive as well as the corrective effects of the new science that appeared to attack the very bulwarks of the church. Effectively preserving its unity in this engagement, the church would emerge genuinely a new creature, shorn of many of its accretions and eccentricities, its faith renewed, its doctrine restated in the new vernacular, yet essentially reasserting and defending its foundation in Christ and its traditional genius in His service.

The Anglican leaders, who most successfully absorbed the shock of this attack and adroitly separated its irrelevancies from its genuine values, have usually been called the broad churchmen. Although Latitudinarianism, with its roots in eighteenth-century England, antedates the Broad Church Movement, as it has been ineptly called, the tolerantly progressive spirit implied in that term is perhaps a better description of these nineteenth-century churchmen than the designation "movement" would imply. Lacking almost completely any form of organization, these zealous thinkers wrestled independently, as all thinkers must, yet cooperatively, to bring the constructive judgment of scientific liberalism, with its accompanying threats of secularism, to illumine and refine the inherited dogmas and traditions of the church.

This broad spirit in the church can be traced to no single source but to many, including the new physical science, German rationalism, and Biblical criticism. An immediate cause is often traced to Charles Darwin and his fellow scientific writers, but this literature was itself a product of an earlier age of inquiry. Long before its appearance there had been born both in England and on the Continent a progressive religious spirit that reflected itself in a critical, honest, and usually reverent approach to theological ideas and the Bible itself. Perhaps the wit's characterization of Thomas Arnold of Rugby "that he woke every morning with the conviction that everything was an open question" described more accurately than many would have liked to admit the temper of the truly broad approach to truth from any source and at any cost.

Back of these liberal movements in England and America lay German rationalism, readily identifiable with Hegel's philosophy and its impingement on theology through the Tübingen School of Biblical critics who tried to force the New Testament into the Hegelian mold. Using approved scientific methods, other critics investigated the church, the Bible, and even the life of Jesus, just as any other subject would be investigated. The results of such applications came to be known as "Lower Criticism," concerned primarily with textual analysis and a pure Biblical text, and "Higher Criticism," a literary criticism designed to investigate the time, place, background, and authorship of Biblical literature. Although both groups sought only scientific accuracy in their investigation, they soon became suspect in such circles where verbal inspiration of the Scriptures was still held. Other conservatives considered these scholars too objectively scientific and therefore inadequately prepared to deal with such materials, which required some sympathetic understanding for their fullest comprehension.

The results of Friedrich Schleiermacher's attempt to utilize the benefits of scientific criticism without destroying the essence of Christianity were probably less successful in Germany than the efforts of similarly minded men in Britain. While Samuel T. Coleridge, Benjamin Jowett, and Frederick D. Maurice were pursuing philosophical and theological investigations, Thomas Henry Arnold, Henry H. Milman, Arthur P. Stanley, and Richard Whatley by their historical writings sought to show that religion and the Bible could be studied scientifically like any other sources and that such studies could be pursued critically but at the same time reverently. Whatley, a leading liberal at Oxford and later Archbishop of Dublin, who shunned all party identifications and counted high and low church as equal bigotries, fathered the broad spirit and by his books as well as his forceful and witty conversations influenced the younger Arnold, Maurice, and their contemporaries. Probably the greatest of all the liberals was Maurice, who not only influenced contemporary English theologians and preachers like Frederick W. Robertson but also English politicians and social reformers for whom the interpretations of Maurice became the ground and support of labor movements and liberal education for the working classes. Although it may have been a moment of enthusiasm that prompted Julius Hare to describe Maurice as "the greatest mind since Plato," his subsequent and especially his recently growing influence gives promise of fulfilling that judgment. More than any other English leader at the time, Maurice influenced American life and thought, especially through Phillips Brooks, who became so ardent a follower of the English reformer that he became a member of the "F.D.M. Club" in Great Britain and wrote an introduction to a volume of his works published in Boston in 1886. Here Brooks described this early Christian Socialist as one "who threw himself with intrepid earnestness into every moral and religious and political question of his day . . . and lived all the time in the profoundest thoughts and truths which belong to all times."[3]

In 1860 progressive English churchmen published an epoch-making and highly controversial book, *Essays and Reviews*, whose aim it was, they said with typical English restraint, "to illustrate the advantage derivable to the cause of religion and moral truth from a free handling, in a becoming spirit, of subjects peculiarly liable to suffer by the repetition of conventional language, and from traditional methods of treatment." A leading spirit in this effort was Frederick Temple, then headmaster at Rugby but later to become Bishop of London and eventually Archbishop of Canterbury. Temple feared the "unwholesome reticence" that he observed among English clergy and hoped that this volume might break through it and, by saying startling things worth saying, might stimulate freer discussion of the obviously important issues before the church. Since each of the seven writers, all but one of them ordained, worked entirely independently, varied views were expressed without attempt at reconciliation and consequently with some confusion. Baden Powell, Professor of Geometry at Oxford, on examining the evidences of Christianity, said that miracles, once considered the chief support of Christianity, "are at present among the main difficulties and hindrances to its acceptance." Benjamin Jowett, in writing on the interpretation of Scripture, denied that the gospel and the love of truth could ever stand in opposition and asserted that "the same fact cannot be true in religion when seen by the light of faith and untrue in science when looked at through the medium of evidence or experiment."

Break through the reticence this book most certainly did, for within a year seven editions of it had been published, and in 1862 E. M. Goulburn published a volume of *Replies to Essays and Reviews.* Two essayists, Rowland Williams and Henry Wilson, were found guilty of heresy in the Court of Arches, and Bishop Samuel Wilberforce, of Oxford, who considered the book "a lurid jet of the great Anti-Christ," suggested that all of the contributors should be forced to withdraw from the ministry. Even though the Judicial Committee of the Privy Council reversed the heresy conviction of Williams and Wilson, twenty-five English bishops publicly denounced the *Essays* as inconsistent "with an honest subscription to the formularies of our church." In the United States the House of Bishops sanctioned the condemnation of the controversial volume in a pastoral letter written by Bishop McIlvaine in which he declared emphatically that rationalism had no place in the church. Individual American bishops like Whitehouse of Illinois and Upfold of Indiana warned their people against the licentious and rationalistic English heretics and, as late as the pastoral letter of 1886, the House of Bishops still almost helplessly spoke of the "flood of infidelity which is sweeping over our land."

The question of Biblical authority was forcibly raised in England with the appearance, between 1862 and 1879, of the multi-volume *The Pentateuch and the Book of Joshua Critically Examined* by John W. Colenso, a brilliant Cambridge Biblical scholar who was then Bishop of Natal, South Africa. While translating the Bible into Zulu, he felt driven to examine the conclusions of the German Old Testament historical critic, G. H. A. von Ewald, with which he came to agree, much to the consternation of his superior, Robert Gray, Metropolitan of South Africa, who deposed him. In 1865 the American bishops approved Gray's action, which was not sustained by the civil authorities, however, when Colenso defied the sentence, on the ground that the Metropolitan lacked jurisdiction in the case. With a similar critical approach Colenso also published a *Commentary on Romans*. The controversial bishop clearly had denied the doctrines of the inerrancy of the Scripture, eternal punishment, the substitutionary atonement, and supernatural knowledge in Jesus; and, what many considered worst of all, he had introduced the methods of Higher Criticism to England.

Dean A. P. Stanley, whom Maurice once called "a bigot for toleration," invariably proved himself a reconciler of the diverse and straying elements among the liberal churchmen in England so that they were able to work together. From his moderate position, *Essays and Reviews* seemed primarily of a negative tendency, yet he, and many others like him, maintained a progressive point of view, which defended the right of free discussion and research in theological as well as other areas and asserted that freedom of speech and thought belonged to the clergy as well as to the laity.

Rationalism and liberalism were hardly innovations in America or in its religious thought. Deism had tested religious orthodoxy before the American Revolution, and by 1844 the bishops investigating the General Seminary were asking its professors whether they considered any portion of the Book of Genesis "in the nature of a myth." The middle of the century also marked the appearance of such new and agnostic scientific writers as Darwin, Huxley, Spencer, and Tyndall, who no longer concluded that new scientific wonders were but new and more wonderful evidences of the Creator, as Sir Isaac Newton and Robert Boyle and their earlier contemporaries had done, but saw in the new scientific discoveries the clear evidence that there was no God and that only matter and being were real.

In part, at least, the answer to the new challenge to traditional creed and dogma also came from England, where men of a broad and liberal posture insisted on sharing the intellectual struggles honestly and clearly asserted their confidence in the blending of a broad yet simple Christianity with an enlightened historical sense that would free them to find a comprehensive catholic truth. Here were men like Maurice, Robertson, Stanley, and Charles Kingsley, often called broad churchmen—a term that they repudiated—who never organized a party but generated a movement that was to affect the American church as much as their own. In America they were joined by Edward A. Washburn, Thomas M. Clark, Alexander H. Vinton, William W. Newton, Henry C. Potter, William R. Huntington, and Phillips Brooks, who, if not the greatest, was certainly the most influential of them all. This theologically progressive spirit soon produced the eminent critical Biblical scholars Brooks F. Westcott, Fenton J. A. Hort, and Joseph B. Lightfoot at Cambridge. Here were men who had broken out of the Anglican paddock, who were not confined to any party, and whose common bond was an open-minded, free inquiry into all possible sources of truth, be it the Bible, patristic literature, the classics, or the sciences. Here were no longer the surpliced ranks of religious men marching in accepted conformity; they were courageous and adventurous thinkers, tempered indeed by training and tradition, and seeking a common end in the free quest for truth. The old struggles by which Protestants sought to curb the advances of Rome and low churchmen sought to fetter the ritualists had now become obsolete. The battle was now between Christ and Man, The Church and Science, Christianity and Atheism, and many there were who trembled at the thought.

In England the "F.D.M. Club" met regularly to discuss the ideas of F. D. Maurice, and in this country Brooks organized the "Clericus" in Philadelphia, where carefully selected progressive ministers met monthly for similar discussions. On his removal to Boston in 1869 he organized a similar club there, and Edward A. Washburn organized another in New York City; soon Episcopal rectors of a like-minded spirit were gathering regularly in similar groups in the major cities of the United States. These American broad churchmen also published a weekly paper, *The Living Church*, which lasted only six weeks, probably from lack of promotion rather than interest.

In the spring of 1874 some twenty of these broad churchmen met in New Haven to organize the American Church Congress, patterned after an English organization of the same name. It was designed to provide a national forum where major issues before the church might be freely discussed by the most thoughtful men of all parties without the necessity of taking definite action as at an official convention. Many of these men were weary of the discussions at recent diocesan and general conventions where, for three trienniums, men had argued about the length of stoles while the world waited without God or hope.

Bishop Thomas M. Clark of Rhode Island, an open-minded and widely trusted leader in the church, was the only bishop present at the first planning meeting at New Haven in May, 1874. Indicative of his unusual breadth of interest and versatility is the little-known fact that just three years earlier he had written one of the very early science fantasy novels about *John Whopper, the Newsboy* who made a killing by selling American newspapers in China at a fantastic profit, shortly after their publication in Boston, because he had found a bottomless cave which became his secret delivery route.[4] In the Church Congress venture Clark was associated with Edward A. Washburn, Phillips Brooks, Henry C. Potter, J. C. Smith, Edwin Harwood, and about a score of others. They felt that the church had come to a decisive moment and that, since the General Convention was not apt to be critical, it was necessary to provide a place where the difficult issues would not be explained away but faced honestly by "going deeper, embracing all nature," as Brooks put it. On the eve of the New Haven planning meeting he wrote, "There is a curious sort of sensitiveness and expectancy everywhere in the Church, a sort of feeling and fear that things cannot remain forever just as they are now. . . ," and with eagerness but serious concern he confessed, "Next week we go to New Haven . . . to see what can be done to keep or make the Church liberal and free."[5] Ten years earlier lack of interest would have made such a meeting impossible, but now men were begging to be invited.

The first session of the American Church Congress was held in New York City just before the General Convention in the fall of 1874, amid threats that it would "destroy the peace of the church" or prove to be just another form of party caucus. Horatio Potter, Bishop of New York, refused to preside and warned that the excited spirits of the Congress might disturb the tranquility of the convention, which might indeed have pleased not a few of its members. Alexander H. Vinton presided at the opening sessions until the arrival of Bishop Henry B. Whipple of Minnesota, highly regarded for his missionary achievements and magnificent spirit, who was greeted with an overwhelming ovation when he asserted that most attendants believed that "to the loyal, all things are loyal."

The invitation list to that first Congress included at least five bishops and represented all the varied points of view in the church. At the very first meeting this inclusive spirit was well stated by John Cotton Smith in a paper on "Limits of Legislation as to Doctrine and Ritual," in which he clearly and independently expounded a plea for comprehensiveness as the genius of Anglicanism. This would be restated more eloquently and with a much wider hearing a few weeks later by James DeKoven before the General Convention. This first Congress also heard papers on the timely topics "The Mutual Obligation of Capital and Labor" and "The Relation of the Church to Other Christian Bodies." The next year William Reed Huntington continued the theme with his classic statement that "truth is truth, however and whencesoever obtained, and we can never have occasion to be either afraid of it or unthankful for it." These Congresses continued well into this century, and their contributions have been well preserved and analyzed in Roland Cotton Smith's *Fifty Years of the Church Congress*. That not everything said and done at these sessions was of major significance is best attested by Phillips Brooks, who was a regular attendant from the beginning and who hated nothing worse than sham, when he wrote his brother that the "speakers tow all great subjects out to sea and then escape in small boats through the fog."[6]

Just as the Congress movement had united all the more open-minded liberals in the church, so the opposition to it brought together all types of conservatives from low churchmen, like Bishop McIlvaine, to the Anglo-Catholic Charles Grafton. In their common cause against the inroads of rationalism and its consequent infidelity, these men of vastly different views united to denounce the "Episcopal Unitarians, who with the Prayer Book in hand teach views directly opposed to it, an invasion far more dangerous than the covert Popery."

Meanwhile, similar controversies were appearing and sometimes raging in other American churches. Five members of the faculty of the Andover Theological Seminary were tried and one was found guilty of heresy in 1886. Charles A. Briggs, a leading Presbyterian and Professor of Biblical Theology on the faculty of Union Theological Seminary in New York, was charged with questioning the Mosaic authorship of the Pentateuch and with teaching "that errors may have existed in the original text of the Holy Scripture as it came from the authors." In his defense before the Presbytery of New York in December 13–16, 1892, he denied that his teaching was contrary to the Bible or the Westminster Confession. Although there was much opposition when Briggs, who had always admired the Episcopal Church, applied for ordination at the hands of Bishop Henry C. Potter, the bishop nevertheless ordained the recalcitrant Presbyterian in 1899, tacitly showing the approval of at least one major segment of the church for Higher Criticism.

The way for the wide approval of such a step had been paved in England by the appearance of *Lux Mundi,* a series of twelve essays edited by Principal Charles Gore of Pusey House at Oxford in 1889, by which most English Anglo-Catholics had been led to a modified approval of the rapprochement of the new Biblical criticism and the accepted theology. Gore declared that the purpose of this book was to restate the claim and meaning of theology in the light of new development so that "the Church, standing firm in her old truths, enters into apprehension of new social and intellectual movements of each age," and so giving proper place to all new knowledge shows "again her power under changed conditions to the catholic capacity of her faith and life." Under this influence many Anglo-Catholics accepted such critical conclusions and stood with men of the broad spirit in holding doctrines like the divine immanence, the divine expression through natural law, the historical Jesus, the importance of His character and teaching, and the social emphasis of the gospel.

Yet in the American church Anglo-Catholics were slower to accept these findings, and some of them raised strong opposition to Bishop Potter's action. By ordaining Briggs, however, the bishop settled an issue that has never been officially raised: that the literal inerrancy of the Scripture is not an official doctrine of the church and that critical studies are not only permitted but are indeed essential for the study of Biblical and historical theology. While several unofficial attempts were made later by small groups of bishops to reassert traditional orthodoxy, the prevailing position of the House of Bishops was clearly stated in 1897 and has never been withdrawn: that the competent, critical, but reverent study of the Bible was essential to a healthy faith in the church; they said:

> A faith which is always or often attended by a secret fear that we dare not inquire lest inquiry should lead us to results inconsistent with what we believe is already infected with a disease which may soon destroy it. But all inquiry is attended with a danger on the other side unless it be protected by the guard of reverence, confidence and patience.

After some extended discussions across the church, wide concurrence appeared for a similar progressive statement in a small book, *Creeds and Loyalty,* written by members of the faculty at the Episcopal Theological School in Cambridge.

Still another attack came from one entirely different source and was probably prompted on personal grounds. William Montgomery Brown, then rector of Grace Church in Galion, Ohio, in 1899 published a sermon on *The Blessing of Unjust Criticism or the Protestant Episcopal Church Defended against Five Unjust Allegations,* in which he accused Henry C. Potter of deprecating the Episcopal Church on the occasion of his sermon at the centennial commemoration of Washington's inauguration in New York. He accused Potter of having asserted that the Protestant Episcopal Church generally "cuts an inconsiderable figure in public affairs" and said that at the recent commemoration he had proved unworthy of the occasion. Believing that Potter had been too modest in his appraisal of the Episcopal Church, Brown asserted on the contrary that the Episcopal Church had contributed two-thirds of the signers of the Declaration of Independence, fourteen of the twenty-three presidents of the United States, an equal number of vice-presidents, a majority of the cabinet members, and all the chief justices save two. He then advised those who are inclined to cast aspersions upon the Episcopal Church to follow the example of Henry Clay who, after careful inquiry and investigation, was baptized, confirmed, and remained a faithful member of the church. Brown stated that

> Henry Clay told the clergyman to whom he applied for holy baptism that among the considerations which induced him to become a member of the Episcopal Church rather than of any other, was the fact that years of observation and study had led him to the conclusion that the stability of our government depends upon the perpetuation of two institutions. 'One of these, and the most important of the two,' said Mr. Clay, 'is the Episcopal Church, and the other is the Supreme Court of the United States.'[7]

Later in his life after elevation to the episcopate, Brown became so enamored of the writings of Darwin and Karl Marx that he published *Communism and Christianity,* which ran through many editions, at least one hundred and fifty thousand copies in England and in many foreign languages. He was also so concerned for labor and the socialist movement that he claimed capitalists were using religion against the socialist movement and that workers must dislodge the capitalist class from power. He asserted:

> No man can be consistently Socialist and Christian. . . . It is therefore a profound truth that socialism is the natural enemy of religion. Through Socialism alone will the relations between men in society and their relations to nature become reasonable, orderly and completely intelligible, leaving no nook or cranny for superstition. The entry of socialism is consequently the exodus of religion.[8]

Brown was a man of promising capacities, and he had once been a special lecturer at Bexley Hall, Kenyon College. He defied his fellow bishops, challenging them to examine him theologically and psychologically. It was a sad day for the church when a man of such powers and position defaulted his trust by a radicalism that simply could not be tolerated. He was deposed for avowedly doctrinal reasons that were obviously involved with radical socialism and later resigned.

Despite such an unfair attack as that of William Montgomery Brown, Henry C. Potter proved himself to be a bishop of singularly good sense and fair judgment in so many instances that he has been considered one of the best representatives of broad churchmanship in the latter part of the nineteenth century. He had once served on the staff at Trinity Church in Boston, and during his fifteen years as the rector of Grace Church in New York City, from 1868 until his election as Assistant Bishop of New York in 1883, he made that parish one of the finest early examples of an institutional church, carrying its influence into many social and community activities. Continuing this practical social concern into his later years, the bishop wrote the Introduction to Edward Judson's *The Institutional Church*, published in 1899. William Reed Huntington continued Potter's program at Grace Church; similar widely varied social and religious activities were also carried on the neighboring St. George's Church under the ministry of W. S. Rainsford, and would become the pattern of the larger inner city parishes in the Episcopal Church and generally throughout Protestantism during the next generation.

His nonpartisan spirit made it possible for Bishop Potter to deal fairly and expertly with problems of deviation to the left and the right among his clergy. In the year before he became the diocesan, R. Heber Newton, rector of All Souls' Church, published a series of sermons *Right and Wrong Uses of the Bible*, based on the new Biblical criticism. The case became one of Bishop Potter's first major disciplinary responsibilities, and wisely he would not allow to be brought to trial an issue no majority vote could ever decide. On the contrary, he asked Newton to desist from such controversial topics for the sake of peace, while at the same time admitting his lack of authority to compel his compliance. Newton reluctantly complied with the bishop's request for the good of the church, and the matter was discreetly dropped. A few years later Newton turned his alert mind in the direction of the defense of the Christian faith and published his *Philistinism: Plain words concerning Certain Forms of Modern Scepticism*, a strong polemic against increasing scepticism.

The following year Bishop Potter approached in a similar spirit the case of the very advanced ritualist, Arthur Ritchie, recently come to New York as rector of St. Ignatius' Church after being censured by the Anglo-Catholic Bishop William E. McLaren, of Chicago, for introducing Roman Catholic practices into the Prayer Book services. When Ritchie continued his violations, which were apparently so radical that they were even denounced by Bishop Grafton and Bishop Seymour, Bishop Potter refused to visit St. Ignatius' Church until he desisted. Pursuing a precedent set in the Newton case, Ritchie also agreed to conform to the bishop's request if Potter would waive his right to compel conformity. While his elasticity in the light of modern toleration in such matters may seem insignificant, there was no question of the bishop's canonical authority in this case, and few bishops in his time would have been as tolerant.

Despite these precedents, the church did suffer the indignity of several trials for heresy but on the ground of the individual conclusions derived and not for pursuing Biblical criticism. By comparison with other denominations these incidents were few and depended largely on the spirit of the bishops involved. In 1890 Howard MacQueary published *The Evolution of Man and Christianity* in which he denied the doctrine of the Virgin Birth; he was suspended by Bishop G. T. Bedell of Ohio and afterward resigned his ministry. When Phillips Brooks was elected Bishop of Massachusetts in 1891, Bishop Seymour and other Anglo-Catholics on doctrinal grounds tried to prevent the confirmation of his election by the bishops and standing committees. They failed in their ill-tempered attempt largely because of the high regard for the irreproachable and Christian character of Brooks.

Perhaps the most celebrated heresy trial to come before the church was that of Algernon Sidney Crapsey, the exceedingly popular rector of St. Andrew's Church in Rochester, New York, who was widely known as a lecturer and a liberal Christian leader in advanced social movements. He had been strongly influenced by his friend and co-worker, Walter Rauschenbusch, once a Christian missionary working in the New York slums and later a member of the faculty at the Baptist Theological Seminary in Rochester. Crapsey not only shared his views but also joined in his efforts to relate Christianity effectively to government and the working classes. Crapsey had published *The Greater Love* (1902) and *Religion and Politics* (1905) and subsequently added *The Rebirth of Religion, The Rise of the Working Classes,* and an autobiography, *The Last of the Heretics,* in 1924. For denying the doctrine of the Virgin Birth and asserting that Jesus was in all things physical as are we, he was brought to trial in 1905 before Bishop Walker of Western New York, convicted of heresy, and when the decision was sustained by a Provincial Court of Review, he resigned his ministry. Greatly and widely beloved as a genuinely Christian character, Crapsey died in poverty.

One of the least controversial theologians in this period was William Porcher DuBose, a Biblical scholar at the University of the South, where the church has long maintained a theological faculty and one subsequently involved in the struggle against segregation. His stature was hardly appreciated by his American contemporaries but abroad he was recognized as one of the foremost Anglican scholars, largely through the merits of his chief work, *The Soteriology of the New Testament.* His evangelical spirit was balanced by Anglican tradition, in no small part because of his early reading of the Mercersburg theologians.

Although considerably disturbed by such matters of integration and discipline, the national body of the church developed new vigor in its confrontation with progressive social and intellectual movements and was about to face its greatest opportunities for growth and expanded influence.

XIX

SOCIAL ACTION AND THE RISE OF THE ORDERS

Contemporary with the religion and science confrontation throughout Protestant Christendom was another involving religion and society, which was more limited to the English-speaking world and especially affected the Episcopal Church. As early as the struggles over the Corn Laws and the Factory Acts in England between 1832 and 1848, the laboring classes had discerned that the landowners were largely churchmen and that most of the mills were owned by dissenters. The distinctions in religious affiliation meant nothing to the workers; they saw only the vast gulf between them and the church. When workingmen in England obtained the right to vote, they quickly legalized trade unions, and by the 1870's strikes were easily begun where laboring conditions were the worst both in England and the United States.

Adam Smith's *Wealth of the Nations,* although published in 1776, was often reread as a preface to Henry George's *Progress and Poverty,* which appeared in 1879, and Karl Marx's *Das Kapital* of 1867 became the guidebook of the socialist movement. The growth of larger cities crowded myriads of people into tenements, so that the once homogeneous parish became a small oasis in the vast downtown desert areas in most large cities in England and especially in America. Despairing of adequate congregations and support, many of the churches moved out of the congested districts to the uptown residential areas, only to find that even there the family solidarity had begun to disintegrate and that the church could no longer depend on the family as the unit of parish structure but was ministering more frequently to isolated and lonely people. By the close of World War I the churches almost everywhere had become separated from the masses, and laborers generally sought their guidance and hope in labor unions and their leaders.

Such dissociation and alienation of interest cannot be blamed solely on selfish economic motivation. The equalities promised in American idealism had not been achieved, and often the church was the first to delay the progress toward such attainment. Alonzo Potter, the father of Henry C. Potter who would soon take an almost diametrically opposite point of view, published his *Political Economy* in 1840, opposing trade unions as harmful to laborers because they were contrary to the laws of nature, which he equated with the laws of God. For almost a generation similar ideas were being expressed defending the doctrine of individualism and the law of supply and demand with open competition in the free market of goods and labor. Episcopalians were by no means alone in supporting the established order; Henry Ward Beecher and many other leading American clergymen opposed shorter work days and denounced labor unions during the strikes of 1877. While the twin encounters between the church and science and the church and social order frequently and almost simultaneously involved the same alert personalities, it was not always the case that the liberals in one movement were similarly liberal in the other; frequently it was the Anglo-Catholics who developed the most advanced liberal ideas and the best progressive programs in Christianizing the social order.

In America this movement to show the relevance of Christianity and the church to the needs of the proletariat in practical social terms they could understand followed almost a generation after similar efforts in England by men like Frederick Maurice and Charles Kingsley. Episcopalians and many other American church people had the highest regard for Maurice, who combined a broad-spirited churchmanship and academic status with an intimate knowledge of and relation with the underprivileged lower classes in England. He and his colleagues sponsored Workingmen's Associations, established a Workingman's College, and published *The Christian Socialist* in their attempts "to reach the unsocial Christians and the un-Christian socialists." For his zeal Maurice lost his professorship in King's College, London.

Maurice founded the Christian Social Movement and published a series of tracts, *Politics for the People,* in which he expounded his creed that politics for the people cannot be separated from religion. He contended that men must either begin with atheism or with a faith in a living and righteous God who rules even the social order. He supported his efforts with a substantially new theological emphasis in his *Theological Essays.* Here he described sin as a condition of humanity, rather than an act of will; baptism as a declaration of sonship rather than a regeneration of a new relation between man and God; atonement as the fulfillment of the law of righteousness by the perfect obedience of Jesus; and revelation as the unveiling of the nature of God to the souls of men. Despite this consistent and substantial theological undergirding, his best attempts never reached beyond the slight correction of inequalities and injustices in the accepted stratification of English society. It remained for his devoted American followers to blend his superb Christian idealism with the social idealism of their still new and less inhibited society to produce a new outlook and program often popularly called the Social Gospel.

The violence displayed in the strikes of 1877 and 1886 proved to be a sufficiently severe shock to awaken the Episcopal Church leaders and many others like Washington Gladden in Columbus, Ohio, and Lyman Abbott in Brooklyn to the necessity to speak at once to this burgeoning question. America, of course, had had its social liberals from the eighteenth century when John Woolman sought prison reforms and the abolition of slavery. More recently, William A. Muhlenberg had created a design for the institutional parish in his Church of the Holy Communion, after which Grace Church and St. George's in New York were patterned in the closing years of the century. Here every conceivable form of social service was offered by a large staff with adequate facilities and supported by powerful and enlightened preaching and interpretation of the gospel.

Muhlenberg once wrote a sermon on *The Woman and Her Accusers*, which he preached in many churches for the benefit of the Midnight Mission organized in January, 1867, for the rescue of fallen women. He described the visit of two men of the mission board to a "notorious house" to rescue two girls being detained against their wishes, and the subsequent freeing of two others. As a result of Muhlenberg's sermon several of the bishops issued pastoral letters in their dioceses in behalf of the work of this mission, and eventually a house of reception was maintained by the church in New York to aid unfortunate girls. Meanwhile the southern churchmen, especially in the Diocese of Virginia, sought to preserve impeccable Puritan morals and as one means to that end in 1872 published a pamphlet on *The Incompatibility of Theatre Going and Dancing with Membership in the Christian Church*. In this appeal to the people of their parishes the clergy of the Convocation of the Valley of Virginia even quoted the church fathers in their attack on dancing as sinful and went on to claim that ". . . the Theatre is a school of vice" and opera only "more subtle and difficult of apprehension."

Not until the last quarter of the century did the church generally become involved in the movement for social justice and improvement. Many Episcopalians, however, clung to their conservative opinion that the church should not invade social, political, and economic areas but concentrate on its mission to develop personal religion and morality. Despite this social conservatism and the normally restrained tone of the life and work of the Episcopal Church, it nevertheless produced some of the most progressive leaders and interpreters of the Social Gospel movement.

In 1884 the American Church Congress invited Henry George, whose *Progress and Poverty* had been widely read among the laity and clergy during the preceding five years, to discuss the question, "Is Our Civilization Just to the Workingman?"; five years later it sponsored a panel discussion of socialism to which Christian socialists were invited. The perennial stormy petrel, R. Heber Newton of New York City, nationally regarded as a leader in the progressive social work of the church, suggested a farsighted development of a cooperative society, and bishops such as Henry C. Potter and Frederick Dan Huntington openly opposed such injustices as child labor, sweatshops, the insufferable conditions of the slums, and fixing wages like commodities, according to the law of supply and demand, which invariably favored the capitalist.

Within the Episcopal Church at least three organizations were formed within four years to activate the ideals of these leaders and to bring together in strength the efforts of enthusiastic proponents. The next few decades proved to be the experimental and formative period in which elementary and highly specialized groups and efforts came to be absorbed into the major church structure and its official agencies. "The Church Association for the Advancement of the Interests of Labor," popularly known as CAIL, was organized in 1887 by interested clergy of New York who, despite wide opposition, were soon joined by many clergy across the church. James O. S. Huntington, founder of the Order of the Holy Cross, was its prime mover; his father, Bishop of Central New York, was its president for seventeen years, and forty-seven bishops of the church lent their names and influence as honorary vice-presidents. Within a few years chapters had been established in other cities, and labor unions came to recognize CAIL as a friend striving with them for alleviation of intolerable living and working conditions and seeking constructively to arbitrate disputes and to achieve just laws regulating labor practices. CAIL continued until 1928, when its work was absorbed by the new Division of Industrial Relations under the National Council.

Less widely known and much less effective were the Society for Christian Socialists, organized in Boston in 1889 by two clergymen, W. D. P. Bliss and Philo W. Sprague, and the Christian Social Union, founded two years later in New York. Both groups were primarily educational and sought the dissemination of the social teachings of Jesus. Leading spirits in the latter organization were Scott Holland and Richard T. Ely, its secretary, who was just completing a decade as Professor of Economics at Johns Hopkins University before moving on to the chair of political economy at the University of Wisconsin. Ely, a highly respected churchman, published some of his strongest convictions in 1899 in his *Social Aspects of Christianity and Other Essays.* Bishop Huntington was the first president of the Union, which, by 1897, was supported by about seven hundred members in chapters distributed in the leading cities. When it was discovered that the work of the Christian Social Union was being duplicated by the new church-sponsored Joint Commission on Social Service, it was dissolved in 1912.

Although only the enlightened minority of the church became involved in Christian social action before World War I, there were progressive pastors like George Hodges in Calvary Church, Pittsburgh, who taught that the church was just as much interested in society and politics as with what is commonly called religion. Early in 1889 when Boyd Vincent was elected Assistant Bishop of Southern Ohio, Hodges assumed the rectorship and quickly demonstrated his deep religious convictions and his tremendous concern for the practical application of the gospel. Although he remained only five years, the record as it appears in *The Parish Advocate* includes new missions in industrial areas, enlarged budgets and benevolences, and membership participation in welfare work. All of this was supported by an emphasis on proper preparation for membership, instruction in the nature and history of the church, and regular worship. Hodges introduced the early service of Holy Communion in Calvary Church and invited Father Huntington, O.H.C., to conduct a Lenten retreat. The theme of parish life is indicated in a regular feature in the *Advocate* entitled "Worship and Work."

In his efforts to make the work of the church effective, Hodges cooperated with other Christian leaders and proved himself an early example of the ecumenical spirit. In one of his last editorials about Calvary Church, Hodges expressed the ideals he had helped it achieve:

> It represents piety rather than partisanship, devotion rather than denomi-
> nationalism. It is a Protestant Episcopal Church, but it pronounces those
> adjectives under its breath, accounting them as sectional and temporary
> characteristics, while it puts a good, round enthusiastic emphasis on the noun
> to be first a church, representing the Lord Jesus Christ, and trying to do His
> work, and having fellowship with all others, Roman Catholic, Unitarian,
> Presbyterian, who are striving for the same good purpose—this we account
> here the chief and best ideal. Creed, controversies and differences come after,
> and a long way after.[1]

Late in 1893 the trustees of the Episcopal Theological School in Cambridge, Massachusetts, selected this young rector to succeed the popular Dean William Lawrence who had just been elected to succeed Phillips Brooks as Bishop of Massachusetts.

Although the Church Socialist League, begun in 1911, lasted less than a decade, the Church League for Industrial Democracy, organized by clergy and laity in New York in May, 1919, has been a vital force in promoting study and action in applying Christian principles in national and international life. At times the active supporting membership of the Episcopal League for Social Action, as this organization was later called, exceeded one thousand persons who sought by public meetings, conferences, and a quarterly journal to keep the conscience of the church alive to industrial and other social issues. The League's original statement of principles declared that "only that social order can properly be called Christian which substitutes fraternal cooperation for mastership in industry and life." Among the leaders of this effective group have been Professor Vida D. Scudder, formerly of Wellesley College, and William B. Spofford, its executive secretary for many years; in addition to being a rector, he had also held a position as labor manager for a leading clothing manufacturer and from 1919 edited the weekly church paper *The Witness*. The Episcopal Church through its Department of Christian Social Relations now maintains Divisions of Health and Welfare Service, Social Education and Community Action, Urban Industrial Church Work, World Relief and Church Cooperation, and the Episcopal Social Work Conference.

After several abortive attempts monastic orders for men and women in the Episcopal Church were begun, largely to supply the need for such persons in the Christian social work of the church and to give expression to the deepening devotional life accompanying the rise of the catholic movement in the eighteen-sixties and eighteen-seventies. As early as 1820 William A. Muhlenberg resolved to remain celibate so that he might better perform his duties in the church.

Under the guidance of E. B. Pusey in 1845 orders for women were established in England for the first time since the Reformation, when a sisterhood was organized in London to work among the poor, and with the same intent the Society of the Sisters of Mercy was begun in Davenport in 1848. These short-lived orders were soon followed by the permanent Community of St. Mary the Virgin at Wantage and the Sisterhood of St. Margaret at East Grinstead.

In 1852 William A. Muhlenberg organized the Sisterhood of the Holy Communion to work at first in the parish infirmary and later in St. Luke's Hospital in New York. Loosely structured with no perpetual vows and with no thought of expanding beyond the parish, the Sisterhood served the local needs effectively until 1863 when the order was suspended. Several of the sisters, however, were committed to the monastic life and two years later, under the leadership of Harriet Starr Cannon, who had entered the original order in 1857, organized the Sisterhood of St. Mary, the first permanent order for women organized with the approval of a bishop in the Anglican Communion since the Reformation. On the Feast of the Purification, 1865, Bishop Horatio Potter received the profession of Sister Harriet and four others to devote themselves to a "quest of a higher life in perfect consecration of body, soul and spirit to the Lord" and to perform "spiritual and corporal acts of mercy." He immediately placed in their care a home for abandoned girls, the House of Mercy, St. Barnabas House, and the Sheltering Arms. In 1870 they opened St. Mary's Hospital and St. Mary's School, and two years later, a convent and novitiate were built at Peekskill, New York, overlooking the Hudson, from which two convents and twelve education and charitable institutions are now directed.

Bishop C. T. Quintard invited the sisters to the Diocese of Tennessee, and five years later, at the invitation of Bishop E. R. Welles, they assumed charge of Kemper Hall, a school for girls in Kenosha, Wisconsin, where St. Mary's Convent was established as a center for the order's work in its western province. The Community of St. Mary, as these sisters soon came to be known, came under severe criticism during the party strife in the church because of its obvious association with the Anglo-Catholics, but it soon proved itself convincingly and won an undisputed place in the church. Heroically seven sisters volunteered for service in the yellow fever epidemic in Memphis, Tennessee, in September, 1878, and four of them died in less than a month. Since then their work has expanded across the church and to the mission fields. Their example soon produced other orders for women, such as the Sisterhood of St. Margaret in Boston in 1873; the Community of St. John the Baptist at Ralston, New Jersey, in 1881; the Sisterhood of the Holy Nativity in Wisconsin in 1882; the Community of the Transfiguration in 1898; and the Order of St. Anne in 1910.

The Sisterhood of the Holy Nativity, organized in Wisconsin by Charles

C. Grafton to promote retreats, assist in parish visitations, organize guilds, and gather candidates for confirmation, has established a free lending library and makes altar bread and ecclesiastical embroidery. The Society of the Transfiguration, the first order to send nuns to the foreign mission field, was begun in Ohio and now maintains missions and homes in three states and in China and Puerto Rico. The Order of St. Anne is unique in that each of the seven convents in five states, England, and the Philippines is autonomous. All sisters take vows of poverty, chastity, and obedience, which are made annually for three years and after that for life; sisters of the First Order are enclosed with the primary object of perpetual intercession and care of children, while sisters of the Second Order are not habited and usually work outside the convent. Of the no less than fifteen separate orders for women in the church at least seven are operating on a national and four on an international scale. So wide an appeal have these orders developed that there are now more professed sisters in the Anglican Communion than there were in England before the Reformation.

Beyond these professed orders the Episcopal Church has also seen development of the work of deaconesses between the years 1871, when William R. Huntington sponsored a motion that led the General Convention to consider the establishment of the primitive order of deaconesses, and 1889 when the canon approving this action was adopted. By subsequent revision the canon now makes provision for unmarried, or widowed, devout and competent women under appointment by the bishop to assist in the work of the parish, mission, or institution under the direction of the rector or priest in charge. The type of work in which a deaconess may serve includes ministering to the sick and the poor, social work, college work for women students, and instruction. They also have authority to baptize infants in the absence of a minister, to carry on the church's work with women and children, and, in the absence of a minister, to read Morning and Evening Prayer and the Litany, and, when licensed by the bishop, to give instruction or deliver addresses at such services. To provide for the adequate training of deaconesses two schools were established in 1891, St. Faith's in New York and the Church Training and Deaconess House in Philadelphia; in 1908 St. Margaret's House, the Deaconess Training School of the Pacific, was organized at Berkeley, California, where some courses are taken in the Church Divinity School of the Pacific. In 1952 this work on the East Coast was united in New York at Windham House, a graduate center where women preparing for full-time work in the Episcopal Church may also study at the General Theological Seminary and other graduate schools. With increased needs these schools have enlarged their programs, and several theological schools of the church have admitted competently prepared women to their regular courses in preparation for wider service in the church. Through such schools hundreds of women have been trained and served in the missionary and parochial work of the church. More than one hundred women remain in the Order of Deaconesses, and no less than five hundred professionally trained women, many of them on a full-time basis, serve the church in similar work. Although orders for women just missed approval by the General Convention in 1880, by 1913 this triennial body approved religious communities for men and women.

During these same years the Episcopal Church received its first permanent monastic order for men. The first of these, the Society of St. John the Evangelist, was introduced when Charles C. Grafton, reared in the Church of the Advent, Boston, went to England in 1865 after six years of parish experience in Baltimore to obtain help in his desire for the more rigorous order of the monastic life. Having tried various experiments in asceticism, Grafton was introduced by E. B. Pusey to Richard M. Benson, an English priest of similar inclinations. These two, with Samuel W. O'Neill, until then a tutor at Eton, in 1886 made their profession as members of the Society of St. John the Evangelist at Cowley, near Oxford, where they established a community and soon came to be popularly known as the Cowley Fathers. Although they followed no medieval monastic model, this new order did combine some of the features of both the Benedictine and the Dominican rules, adopted a simple habit of Anglican pattern and assumed the triple vows of poverty, chastity, and obedience. Both English and American novices, including Oliver Prescott, joined the order during the next few years.

An opportunity arose to bring the new order to America when the Church of the Advent in Boston was without a rector in 1870. The vestry invited the Cowley Fathers to take charge of the parish, and at Easter, 1872, Grafton, assisted by Oliver Prescott, assumed the rectorship of the parish and at the same time became the head of the new American Province of his order. Grafton soon gathered about him several younger men of promise like Arthur C. A. Hall, later Bishop of Vermont, and Edward W. Osborne, later Bishop of Springfield. Although he introduced the full ritualistic service with altar lights, chasuble, and incense, he won the approval of the new Bishop Benjamin Paddock, probably because of his good judgment in submitting all his plans freely and fully to the bishop with his promise of obedience. Very quickly the work of the order spread beyond Boston. Hall became the head of a training house for novices in Connecticut where eight probationers were enrolled. Less happy was the experience of the Cowley Fathers at St. Clement's Church in Philadelphia, which became the center of the order in that city, when Prescott assumed the rectorship of that parish in 1876, and was joined by several associates as his assistants. Prescott soon aroused the disapproval of the bishop for ritualistic violations and was forced to resign, but the parish remained a center for the work of the Society and became especially notable for a succession of great preachers including Father Maturin and Franklin Joiner.

Conflict of authority brought the Cowley Fathers in America into disfavor with their English Superior R. M. Benson, who demanded complete obedience. Grafton and Prescott had been promised the independence of the Society in America when they had twelve members here; disappointed by the continued requirement of obedience to Cowley, both men were released from the order in 1882. After several years more at the Church of the Advent, Grafton was elected Bishop of Fond du Lac in 1889. In 1883 the Society bought the building formerly used by the Church of the Advent and named it the Church of St. John the Evangelist, with Hall and Osborne in charge. Hall, who was now the head of the American Province, won wide favor in the Diocese of Massachusetts and was elected a deputy to the General Convention in 1889, indicating acceptance of the monastic order by a traditionally low church diocese after more than fifty years of disapproval and opposition. Among Hall's friends was Phillips Brooks, who had come to such distinction by the time of Bishop Paddock's death in 1891 that he was quickly nominated as his successor. Hall voted against Brooks but on his election firmly supported him against the opposition of high churchmen led by Bishop George Seymour. For such fairmindedness Hall was applauded by the church in general but incurred the disapproval of his Superior who removed him from his office as Provincial and ordered him to return to England for discipline. So incensed by this episode was the promising young priest-associate Charles H. Brent that he withdrew from the Society. When Brooks died suddenly in January, 1893, Hall was favorably mentioned as his successor and in August of that year was elected Bishop of Vermont. Until his death in 1930 he served with distinction in the House of Bishops and continued to write many books interpreting Anglo-Catholic theology.

Slowly the Cowley Fathers extended their educational and missionary work from coast to coast through the services of priests and lay brothers living under the vows of poverty, chastity, and obedience; in 1914 the American Province at last became autonomous, and in 1921, when the American Congregation was constituted, Frederick C. Powell became its first superior. The monastery of St. Mary and St. John, erected along the Charles River near Harvard University in Cambridge, was completed in 1926 and has become the mother house of the Cowley Fathers in America. The Canadian Congregation of the Society was founded in 1939, and the Province of Nippon, with its work centered about St. Michael's Monastery in Ayama, and St. John's House, Tokyo, Japan, remains under the jurisdiction of the American Congregation.

Another leading monastic order for men of the Episcopal Church is entirely American in origin and grew out of the Holy Cross Mission in New York where James O. S. Huntington and two young priests tried to interpret the gospel by living and working in the slums of the lower East Side. While attending a retreat in 1880, Huntington first felt the impulse to enter the monastic life and soon afterward took over the Holy Cross Mission where he was assisted by Robert S. Dod and James G. Cameron who shared his zeal and point of view. The following year they adopted a simple habit and lived by a common rule while they proved their vocation. Dod and Cameron dropped out, but on November 25, 1884, Huntington made his profession as the first member of the Order of the Holy Cross before Bishop Henry C.

Potter in the presence of his father, of Bishop Charles Quintard, and Bishop Thomas Gailor. Potter, then Assistant Bishop of New York, was severely criticized for sanctioning sacerdotal celibacy within the church and himself became alarmed when a few years later Huntington accepted a gift of a farm at Westminster, Maryland, and withdrew with his associates to seek deeper roots for the order in the contemplative life. This change of direction came only after ten disappointing years during which only Father Allen and Father Sargent had joined him in the order, which seemed doomed to very slow growth.[2]

Huntington, meanwhile, had tried every possible form of social service; he even spent the summer of 1889 living and working *incognito* among farm laborers in order to understand the workingman better and to be better understood. He also continued his studies beyond the religious and devotional life so that he might be on most intimate terms with the advanced thinking of socialist and other progressive writers. In 1911 he became one of the founders of the Church Mission of Help, designed to aid working girls between the ages of sixteen and twenty-five with their difficult personal problems.

With the definite intention of founding a permanent American order, Huntington drafted a rule with its own distinct character and a special emphasis on cleanliness, and in 1900 the monastery at West Park, New York, was begun as the headquarters for the order. In 1905 St. Andrew's School for mountain boys in eastern Tennessee was built, and the following year Kent School was opened in Connecticut, where the name of Father Sill, its founder and headmaster, is still revered. For about seventy-five years after Bishop John Payne became the first Missionary Bishop to Liberia, that assignment proved to be one of the most difficult in the church with an average tenure of about thirteen years for the bishops during that period. The Order of the Holy Cross volunteered to assume responsibility for this mission, and the House of Bishops in 1925 elected Robert H. Campbell, O.H.C., as Missionary Bishop of Liberia, the first monk in the Episcopal Church to become a bishop while still a member of an order. In 1945 the Order of St. Helena was founded for women who observe the rule and constitution of the Order of the Holy Cross and live and work under its direction. The mother house and Convent of St. Helena are located near Newburgh, New York.

Although it was not a monastic order, the Brotherhood of St. Andrew was organized in 1883 in St. James Church, Chicago, and is now international in scope. Based on rules of daily prayer and weekly service, the Brotherhood enables men and boys to understand and perform the duties accepted in Baptism and Confirmation and so to participate more fully in the life and work of the parish. The men of St. Andrew generously support the missions of the church and occasionally undertake specific projects, such as Christian student centers in Japan. Following thirteen years of devoted service as a Church Army missionary in western Pennsylvania, Gouverneur P. Hance founded the St. Andrew's Brotherhood in 1913 to provide a mixed life of prayer and work for laymen under the triple monastic vow. The mother house at Gibsonia, Pennsylvania, is a center for a ministry to convalescent and incurable men and boys.

Near the close of 1927 the Church Army, an evangelistic and missionary society of the laity founded in England in 1883, was introduced in America and became a cooperating agency of the National Council of the Protestant Episcopal Church. Supported by voluntary gifts, the Church Army maintains a training center in Brooklyn, New York, to prepare men and women for a lay ministry in the evangelistic and missionary work of the church at home and abroad.

After two earlier unsuccessful attempts the Order of St. Benedict was introduced in America in 1939 when religious, trained at Nashdom Abbey in England, settled at Valparaiso, Indiana. In 1946 this order moved to St. Gregory's Priory near Three Rivers, Michigan, where prayer, ordered study, and obedience express the vocation of the Benedictine life. The Order of St. Francis and its subsidiary, the Order of Poor Clares, were moved to Mount Sinai on Long Island in 1928 where, in addition to the full monastic life, they offer opportunity to live in the world while sharing in the life of the order as Tertiaries under less rigid vows.

As early as 1889 Bishop Grafton had proposed a canon to approve and regulate monastic orders. It was not until 1913 that the General Convention adopted the canon "Of Religious Communities" by which these orders were placed under the direction of the diocesan bishops and required to recognize the doctrine, discipline, and worship of the Episcopal Church and to agree that "in the administration of the Sacraments the Book of Common Prayer shall be used without alteration save as it may be lawfully permitted by lawful authority." While these orders—eleven for men and fifteen for women —have remained comparatively small, they have served the church most helpfully in educational and missionary work, in conducting missions and retreats, and generally in providing opportunity for individuals and groups under discipline to develop and strengthen the devotional life.[3]

The work of the orders has been closely related to the social, reform, and missionary work of the church of which they continue to be an effective part. Many members of the Episcopal Church have also participated in the work and share in the support of local social settlement centers and of such national movements as the National Prison Association, the American Red Cross, the Young Men's Christian Association, the Young Women's Christian Association, the Salvation Army, and also the Woman's Christian Temperance Union. In undertaking social settlement work, the growing number of institutional churches followed the pattern set by Grace Church and St. George's in New York. During the last fifteen years of the century St. George's played a particularly active role under the direction of its aggressive and energetic rector William S. Rainsford and with the generous and cooperative support of J. Pierpont Morgan. To the rich literature dealing with the church's social responsibility Episcopal Church scholars added such contributions as Professor

Henry S. Nash's *Genesis of the Social Conscience*, in 1897, and a more popular appeal for the social outlook, *A Valid Christianity for Today*, by Bishop Charles D. Williams of Michigan, in 1909.

As early as 1901 the General Convention appointed a Joint Commission on the Relations of Capital and Labor to investigate causes of disturbances and to act as mediators if desired. Although no such service was ever requested, the commission did report to the next triennial convention condemning "the tyranny and turbulence of the Labor Union" but at the same time asking the church not to condemn the movement of organized labor since it is essential to the well-being of working people. By 1910 this commission had become the Joint Commission on Social Service to study social and industrial conditions, to coordinate the various agencies in the church for social service, to cooperate with similar bodies in other communions, to encourage sympathetic relations between capital and labor, and to deal with kindred matters with discretion. This commission of fifteen, composed of equal representation of bishops, presbyters, and laymen, under the direction of field secretary Frank M. Crouch and his assistants, was able to accomplish more in the next nine years than any of its predecessors. Before the end of World War I more than eighty dioceses and missionary districts had developed some similar structure for social service, although only a few of them could afford salaried secretaries. Working closely with the Joint Commission was the Church Mission of Help which, by the end of the war, had formed its own National Council and was formally recognized by the General Convention. Soon its work spread throughout many dioceses where it has functioned effectively as the Episcopal Service for Youth under the National Council's Department of Christian Social Relations. This Service now offers young Episcopalians opportunity for consultation with psychiatrists and other specialists and the advice of trained and experienced caseworkers.

As the social issues pressed upon the church more vigorously, the General Convention spoke for the Episcopal Church with increasing clarity throughout the war period; in 1913 it asserted that

> . . . the Church stands for the ideal of social justice . . . and demands the achievements of a social order in which the social cause of poverty and the gross human waste of the present order shall be eliminated, and in which every worker shall have a just return for that which he produces, a free opportunity for self-development, and a fair share in all the gains of progress.

It then called on the church to act so that mutual understanding, sympathy and just dealings may supplant prejudice and injustice and that "the ideal of a thorough-going democracy may be finally realized in our land."

In phrases suggested to the House of Bishops by the Society of the Companions of the Holy Cross, a society of women promoting intercession, thanksgiving, and simplicity of life, the convention declared three years later "that the service of the community and the welfare of the workers, not primarily private profit, should be the aim of every industry and its justification."

Churchmen were asked to "scrutinize the sources of their income . . . and to give moral support and prayer to every just effort to secure fair conditions and regular employment for wage-earners, and the extension of true democracy to industrial matters."

By 1919 the bishops and deputies sought

> . . . the acceptance of "the principle of partnership as the business aspect of brotherhood," the submission of all industrial differences to competent boards of arbitration and the recognition of service to the community as a whole, rather than individual gain, as the primary motive in every kind of work.

The following year the bishops assembled at the Lambeth Conference asserted that whenever moral issues are directly involved in working out economic or political theory "the Church has a duty to see that the requirements of righteousness are faced and fairly met." This conference, which included most of the Protestant Episcopal bishops, resolved that

> Even in matters of economic and political controversy the Church is bound to give its positive and active corporate witness to the Christian principle of justice, brotherhood, and the equal and infinite value of every human personality.

As the whole social structure manifested signs of disorder, problems of the Christian home, personal morality, and divorce kept asserting themselves with increasing emphasis at the turn of the century. The church had long been conscious of those problems and had tried for years to cope with them. During the previous three decades the number of divorces in the United States had increased almost three hundred per cent, and the situation was still further deteriorating. By the outbreak of World War I the rate had risen to one divorce in every ten marriages and a decade after its close it had soared to one in six.

As early as 1808 the General Convention had resolved that it was contrary to the law of God for a minister to remarry any divorced person except an innocent party in a case of adultery. On the technical ground that resolutions are not legally binding, the convention enacted this traditional principle into a canon in 1868 but still left it without a power of enforcement. By 1877 this weakness was corrected when the canon was restated as a prohibition that no minister shall remarry "any person who has a divorced husband or wife still living, if such husband or wife has been put away for any cause arising after marriage." This new canon not only made enforcement possible but also provided a basis for annulment on the grounds of premarital impediments which would be used with increasing frequency. To safeguard the interpretation of this new canon it was required that each case shall be brought to the bishop for his examination and approval. After a testing of more than twenty-five years the General Convention in 1904 enacted additional requirements that one year must intervene between the divorce and remarriage and that the bishop shall seek legal advice based on court records before giving his consent, and furthermore that no minister is obligated to perform a remarriage for a divorced person. To distribute the responsibilities of this canon equally on the ministers and the members of the church, the convention, eighteen years later, supplemented it by forbidding a member to be party to any marriage which it is unlawful for a minister to perform. This canon has been discussed frequently, but no essential changes have been made; the responsibility for final decision still resides in the bishop. In 1931 the convention did restate the canon more positively and required ministers to provide public and private instruction on marriage and its responsibilities and urged persons who felt their marriage threatened to seek the counsel of a minister.

XX

THE WORLD-WIDE
MISSION-FIELD

During these years the Episcopal Church consolidated its national structure by binding regional dioceses and missionary districts into provinces and by expanding the western dioceses. By canonical action in 1907 the General Convention divided the church into eight provinces to promote the general work of the church more effectively on a regional basis. For this purpose it provided for a Provincial Council and also for a Provincial Court of Review for cases of discipline. In each province a synod consisting of the bishops and deputies from the dioceses and missionary districts met in the interim between the sessions of the General Convention. With the increased efficiency in all areas of the work of the church achieved by the creation of the National Council in 1919, the significance of the provincial program diminished.

While the church in the eastern areas consolidated its growth and the General Convention improved its structure for greater efficiency, the church on the frontiers was still continuing to expand in the western areas and on the mission fields. New dioceses had been begun in Nebraska in 1868, Arkansas in 1871, Colorado in 1887, and in Oregon in 1889. In 1874 the Diocese of Texas was subdivided to form the Missionary Jurisdictions of Northern and Western Texas; the former became the Diocese of Dallas in 1895, and the latter, the Diocese of West Texas in 1904. An additional Missionary District of North Texas was set apart in 1910.

Already in October, 1867, James Lloyd Breck, who had served twenty-five years in developing missions in the Northwest, especially in Minnesota, had led a party of seventeen missionaries, including five clergymen, seven young candidates for the ministry, and five women, to California. They planned for new missions along the three-thousand-mile coast where five hundred thousand persons already lived. He sought the aid of the entire church to pay for lands, to establish missions, schools, a theological seminary, and $3,000 to pay for passage of the party. Breck was much more prophetic than he knew when he wrote of the future, ". . . a no distant future, which will count up its millions, with great cities, and the command of the commercial interests of the world!" Regretfully he wrote of the church's delay:

If the Pacific Coast was as Minnesota, when the Associate Mission entered it, in 1850, and found there but three small hamlets in the entire Territory, I should not be sending forth such an appeal as this. But we are *fifteen* years behindhand in this work, and already whole districts have become agricultural, and numerous villages and even cities have sprung into being, and hence we have much to battle with that would never have existed had the Associate Mission been there, as it ought to have been, in the infancy of the Coast.[1]

At least a small beginning had been made when Trinity Church in San Francisco, the first church on the Pacific coast, was opened on October 28, 1849. An early photograph showing three women standing outside this building indicates that these were very possibly the only women in this parish in a predominantly male community. The Diocese of California developed more slowly in its northern regions than in the San Francisco and Los Angeles areas, where each of these cities would be the seat of a flourishing diocese within about twenty years and a completely new missionary district would be set up across the mountains. Such expansion in part at least resulted from the wise planning of the church in 1874 when it established the principle that the church as a whole should support its larger missionary districts even though they lay within the bounds of a strong diocese. As a result, many missionary districts have since been formed within older dioceses with the usual result that the older dioceses have expanded their growth much more rapidly in the narrower confines of the more compactly controlled areas.

By the time of its fiftieth anniversary at the California Convention in 1900, Bishop William F. Nichols reported 758 confirmations, 5,549 families, 8,558 communicants, 5,991 in the church schools, a total property value of $697,-548.08, and $169,912.22 received in the preceding year. Such success must be attributed to the early efforts of Breck and the first missionaries as well as to their successors who, a generation later, were still alertly asking, "What steps shall be taken to plant the church . . . in those new city centers of vastly increasing population."[2]

Meanwhile, the Missionary Jurisdiction of Northern California had already been separated and held its primary convocation at Sacramento in May 6–7, 1875. By 1898 this district had been enlarged and become the District of Sacramento, with Bishop William H. Moreland in charge, and in 1907 there were eighteen parishes and twenty-seven organized missions with forty-five clergy, 1,493 families, and 2,957 communicants.[3]

The Los Angeles Diocese was separated from California in 1895 and quickly became a center of growth for the church. Fifteen years later the California Diocese still had sufficient strength so that a missionary district called San Joaquin, now a diocese, was established across the mountains. Beginning with twelve priests and one deacon, fourteen church buildings and seven rectories, and 1,687 communicants, less than some larger present day parishes have, Bishop Louis C. Sanford was able in five years to lift his communicant strength to 2,147 in twenty-two parishes and organized missions. This was a period of rapid national expansion and a time to challenge the best of the clergy who moved west with the people. Their courageous service may well be summarized in a letter from John Cornell, first rector of St. Matthew's Church, Laramie, Wyoming, who wrote Bishop E. S. Thomas, ". . . we bought a saloon at Wyoming Station and turned it into a chapel."[4]

In the early years of this century the West still presented many dangers and discouragements for the missionaries of the church. Bishop Franklin S. Spalding wrote from Utah about 1914:

> This is a small and difficult field. I drove a number of miles last Sunday to services in a shack. I was there before anyone else, lighted the fire in the stove, swept out the place. A little group came who thought I ought to thank them for the privilege of speaking to them. I spoke of one's duty to one's neighbor. A drunken woman interrupted and said that one should look out for one's self. I tried to straighten her out. . . . All I can say is that God calls some of us to do this work. As for myself, I love it and would not be anywhere else.

Tragically a few months later the bishop was killed by a speeding motorist in Salt Lake City.[5]

When the total communicant strength of the Episcopal Church reached 484,020 in 1890, 48,569, or about ten per cent, lived in the area west of the Mississippi and in the mountain states and 11,197, or about two and one half per cent were on the Pacific coast. Twenty-five years later the church's communicant strength had risen to 1,010, 874, and the corresponding statistics for these areas had risen to 105,531 and 42,384 respectively. Despite this rapid growth of the church the West still held ten per cent and the Pacific region had reached almost four and two-tenths per cent, both well in advance of the population trends in these areas.

At the close of the Reconstruction period there were six million Negroes in the former slave states; twenty years later they had increased to eight million. By 1890 the Commission on Home Missions to Colored People added specifically religious work to its earlier educational efforts and in that year supported 62 white and 44 colored clergy, 117 Sunday Schools, 65 parochial schools, and 12 industrial schools. By 1898 such aid was reaching 75 colored clergy in 34 dioceses.

The best programs of the church were carried on in its well-established schools for the Negroes, and in 1906 the American Church Institute for Negroes was organized to seek substantial support for St. Augustine's School in Raleigh, North Carolina; St. Paul's School in Lawrenceville, Virginia; St. Athanasius' School; St. Mark's School; and the Vicksburg Industrial School. Many of these institutions had industrial departments for special training in the crafts, but few Negro students sought theological training.

With the rise of strong racial feelings in the South, it was to be expected that the General Convention would receive complaints of discrimination against Negroes in the southern churches. Deputies from this region at times recommended a Negro episcopate or even a separate Negro church, but the General Convention invariably stated that the Episcopal Church recognizes no racial distinctions. Southern churchmen generally supported the revision of the canons to permit the election of suffragan bishops who would not have the right to succession. An earlier canon of 1829 had forbidden such elections, and although enabling legislation was introduced in 1904, it was not until 1910 that it became canonically possible for a diocese to elect a suffragan to assist the bishop without automatically having the right to succeed him. Suffragans were granted seats in the House of Bishops, but without vote, and were eligible for election as bishops, missionary bishops, or coadjutor bishops with the right to succession. In 1946 the suffragan bishops became voting members of the House. While the office of suffragan bishop was primarily created because of the increasing size of many dioceses that desired assistant bishops without the right of succession, this canon did also provide the opportunity for the election of Negro suffragans as many southern churchmen had originally intended.

This period also marked the national territorial expansion beyond the mainland of the United States, adding the Hawaiian Islands, the Panama Canal Zone, the Virgin Islands, Alaska, Puerto Rico, and the Philippine Islands. Alaska, covering almost six hundred thousand square miles, was purchased from Russia in 1867, partly as a reciprocation for Russia's friendliness to the national government during the Civil War, but no less as a sound investment. Twenty years elapsed before John W. Chapman began the church's first mission work at Anvik, three hundred miles inland on the Yukon River. Starting with a sawmill and a boiler engine, he began to build his mission with his own hands and was soon assisted by a sixteen-year-old Eskimo lad who also served as an interpreter and whom he later adopted. With the mission established, Chapman was joined in 1895 by Bertha W. Sabine, who took charge of the school, and Dr. Mary V. Glenton, a medical missionary. Meanwhile, in about 1890, the missionaries E. H. Edson and Dr. John B. Driggs had opened another mission center among the Eskimos at Point Hope, and a third was begun at Tanana in 1891.

Convinced of the stability of these missions and of the genuine interest among the Eskimos and the settlers, the General Convention in 1892 created the Missionary District of Alaska. Peter T. Rowe, who until then had been a successful missionary in northern Michigan, was elected its first missionary bishop the following year. The Klondike Gold Rush soon brought Alaska to the attention of everyone; many adventurers came into this territory, and the imagination of thousands of members of the church made this field one of great popular interest. Before the end of the century Bishop Rowe had seven clergy, and ten white lay readers working on thirteen stations; four hospitals within five years had increased to seven. These missions engaged in a wide variety of programs; beyond the usual schools and health centers they included a cooperative venture in the breeding of reindeer at Tanana. By 1905 about five hundred communicants were distributed among the scattered missions, by 1915 this number reached one thousand, and since then it has redoubled several times.

Associated with Bishop Rowe in this heroic work was Archdeacon Hudson

Stuck, who traveled fifteen thousand miles by dog sled and twice that distance by the mission boat in ministering to these appreciative people, who erected the Hudson Stuck Memorial Hospital at Fort Yukon in 1916. Bishop Rowe gave forty-seven years to the episcopate in Alaska, serving until 1942. When he was seventy-five years of age Bishop John B. Bentley became his suffragan and twelve years later succeeded the venerable bishop. When Bishop Bentley became the vice-president of the National Council in 1948, he was succeeded by William J. Gordon, Jr., who has carried the work to its present excellent state of development.

By the Treaty of Paris on December 10, 1898, at the close of the Spanish-American War, the United States acquired Puerto Rico and the Philippines and assumed a temporary protectorate over Cuba. The Hawaiian Islands had been annexed in August that year and became a Territory in 1900. Although Puerto Rico had been nominally Christian for four centuries, little social progress had been achieved by the Roman Catholic Church. When James H. Van Buren was consecrated the first missionary bishop for this island in 1902, he immediately set about helping the masses overcome illiteracy, poverty, and disease. Charles B. Colmore, his successor in 1913, continued a similar program of attack on these basic impediments to any missionary program by building a hospital and training school for nurses in the capital city of Ponce, a training school for women workers at San Juan, a parochial industrial school at Mayaguez, and an experimental farm at Quebrada Limon.

Just before the war with Spain, Manuel Ferrando, a disaffected Roman Catholic priest, withdrew from that church and took with him many members of his parish whom he organized as the Church of Jesus. In order to perpetuate his expanding work, he received episcopal orders from the Reformed Episcopal Church; when he brought his followers, then numbering four priests, two deacons, and about twenty-five hundred members, into the Episcopal Church in 1922, he was given a supplemental consecration and became Bishop Colmore's suffragan. With this additional strength the church was in a better position to minister to the rapidly increasing population of several million souls in this crowded island of only thirty-six hundred square miles. For a little more than a decade Bishop Albert E. Swift has directed this missionary district; its present communicant membership is almost four thousand, and thirty-two clergy and twenty-four lay readers minister to the baptized membership approaching ten thousand.

In 1917 the United States purchased the Virgin Islands from Denmark, and the Episcopal Church quickly added these islands to the Missionary District of Puerto Rico the following year. The Church of England, which had ministered to the impoverished West Indian Negroes of these islands, assigned its work and properties with three large congregations and almost three thousand communicants to Bishop Colmore's care. By action of the House of Bishops in 1947 the Virgin Islands became a separate missionary district under the care of the presiding bishop who has currently assigned their supervision to Bishop Swift. This mission has grown to more than sixty-five hundred members and shows promise of further growth under the leadership of capably trained priests.

The new Republic of Panama was recognized in 1903 by the United States, which soon afterward acquired the Canal Zone preparatory to building the canal that joined the Atlantic and Pacific Oceans in 1914. Following its previous policy, the Church of England gave over its work in these regions to the Episcopal Church, which in 1919 formed the Missionary District of the Panama Canal Zone including also the region of Panama lying south and east of the canal as well as parts of Colombia. While the canal was in process of construction, a number of temporary mission stations were operated under the jurisdiction of the Bishop of Washington, but these were closed about 1915. Under the administration of Bishop James C. Morris, who was consecrated in 1920, the work took on new life as the church tried to minister more adequately to the West Indian Negroes who had once been affiliated with the Church of England and to the increasing military personnel and associated civilians. Harry Beal served here as missionary bishop from 1937 and was succeeded in 1945 by Reginald H. Gooden. The church membership here is about seventeen thousand of whom more than one-third are communicants.

The Missionary District of Central America, including the Republics of Costa Rica and Nicaragua, was separated from the District of the Panama Canal Zone and organized in 1956; on June 5, 1957, Guatemala, El Salvador, and Honduras were transferred from the Diocese of British Honduras and added to this District of which David E. Richards became the missionary bishop the following October. There are now about twenty clergy and almost fifty lay readers to serve the sixty-five hundred members in the thirty-six parishes and organized missions among the more than ten million Latin Americans in this District.

Lying also in the Caribbean area is the independent Negro republic of Haiti, being one-third of the island of which the Dominican Republic occupies the remaining larger portion. As the Civil War was beginning, a group of Negro emigrants led by an American Negro priest, James T. Holly, settled in Haiti, then populated largely by descendants of French-speaking slaves and a small group of mixed blood who controlled affairs in the cities. With the aid of the American Church Missionary Society and the Board of Missions, Holly founded the Church of the Holy Trinity at Port-au-Prince. By 1874 his work was sufficiently established to win approval of a covenant with and support from the Episcopal Church. Holly came to New York where he was consecrated by Episcopal bishops as the first bishop in the Orthodox Apostolic Church of Haiti, as his church was called. In this capacity he served effectively until his death in 1911. Two years later, on petition from Holly's followers, Haiti was constituted a missionary district of the Episcopal Church, which absorbed the Orthodox Apostolic Church. Administered by neighboring bishops, it made little progress until Harry R. Carson was consecrated its first white bishop on January 10, 1923. He quickly proceeded to a work of rehabilitation in a land where churches were often of mud and thatch and schools were conducted outdoors. He erected a convent, which was occupied in 1927 by the Sisters of St. Margaret, who now maintain the Stewart School for Girls and St. Vincent's School for handicapped children. The bishop also built two other schools, a bishop's house, and by 1928 had completed Holy Trinity Cathedral in Port-au-Prince. Most of his clergy were trained in a seminary he founded in the same city. When Bishop Charles A. Voegli succeeded Carson in 1943, he opened the Episcopal Seminary at Mt. Rouis to train the native ministry of the church. The church has about thirty-three clergy and more than thirty-five thousand baptized members of whom more than one-third are communicants.

Although the House of Bishops anticipated a missionary work in the Dominican Republic by assigning it to the jurisdiction of the Bishop of Puerto Rico in 1923, no work was actually begun there until 1928 when it was reassigned to the Bishop of Haiti. Comparatively little was achieved until the last generation because of limited personnel and resources, and recent political disturbances and uncertainty have further hampered this work. By 1951 there were four priests, more than three thousand baptized persons, and almost two thousand communicants.

In Cuba, for which the United States assumed a protectorate in 1898, the Episcopal Church had long been represented by Edward Kenney, a missionary who held services there as early as 1871, primarily to provide for the needs of the American and English residents. Roman opposition led the Spanish government to forbid this Protestant work, so for some time Kenney officiated on Sundays on an American warship in Havana harbor. The Female Bible Society of Philadelphia distributed Bibles on the island as early as 1882, and the Ladies' Cuban Guild of the same city added its support when one of the Bible Society's agents was ordained and organized congregations there. Later, the American Church Missionary Society added its support to this work, and the Bishop of Florida occasionally visited Cuba for confirmation. There were five clergy, about one hundred and fifty communicants, and at least six congregations had already been formed when the General Convention established the Missionary District of Cuba in 1904 and consecrated Albion W. Knight as its first bishop. Two years later a cathedral designed by Cram, Goodhue, and Ferguson was begun in Havana, and about the same time Esteban Morrell, a converted scholarly Roman priest, began training a native priesthood for this mission. When Hiram R. Hulse succeeded Bishop Knight in 1915, the church in Cuba had thirteen priests, about seventeen hundred communicants, and sixteen hundred pupils in its Sunday Schools. To provide much needed education for the thousands of illiterate islanders, Bishop Hulse opened dozens of parochial schools at widely scattered points and promoted several higher grade schools such as the Cathedral School for Girls at Havana and All Saints' School at Guantánamo. Thirty-five years later these numbers had mounted to twenty-seven priests, most of them native Cubans, almost forty-two thousand baptized persons, and a communicant strength of nearly seven thousand. Alexander H. Blankenship succeeded Hulse in 1939; although the political disturbances and revolutions have severely interfered with further progress of the church in Cuba, the previous decade brought the membership to almost seventy-two thousand of whom about ten thousand are communicants.

The Missionary District of Mexico, organized in 1904 when the House of Bishops elected Henry D. Aves of Houston, Texas, as its first bishop, had an interesting if often disappointing history in its first half century. In the years immediately following the War with Mexico freer communications were established with that country and Episcopal Church leaders learned of the retarded conditions in Latin America where more than one-third of the Roman Catholics of the world lived in comparative ignorance and superstition. A major opportunity for Protestant missionary work appeared in 1857 when the new and more liberal constitution in Mexico provided for freedom of worship. For more than a decade the Episcopal Church carried on its work through agencies beyond its own jurisdiction like the Mexican Missionary Society, the Mexican Catholic Apostolic Society, and the American Church Missionary Society, which supplied some missionaries as well as funds.

Meanwhile, progressive clergy and laymen, seeking to reform the church in Mexico and free it from its obsession with wealth and power as well as from foreign control, founded the independent Church of Jesus and asked the Episcopal Church to consecrate a bishop. When Henry C. Riley, an Englishman reared in Chile and for many years engaged in mission work in Mexico, was consecrated in 1879, he had about seventy organized congregations and about thirty-five hundred communicants. With the waning of the reform spirit in state and church, Protestant missionary work became exceedingly difficult, and Bishop Riley resigned after only four years, leaving the Church of Jesus congregations to face twenty years of hardship and losses.

New hopes for this work arose with the arrival of Bishop Aves, and in 1906 the Church of Jesus voted to become a part of the new missionary district and provided a strong foundation for this serious missionary effort of the Episcopal Church. The Mexican national reforms after 1910 became more secular and nationalistic with increasing difficulties for Protestants and especially those churches with foreign alliances. Frank W. Creighton, who succeeded Bishop Aves in 1926, had been in Mexico approximately five years when the law that permitted only Mexican-born clergy to serve Mexican congregations forced him to withdraw to the United States and to direct this work across the border. Discreetly he resigned in 1933, and Efrain Salinas y Velasco became the Episcopal Church's first national bishop in Mexico in 1934, and for almost twenty-five years he led the church through troubled times. He was succeeded in 1958 by José G. Saucedo, a thirty-three-year-old graduate of the Virginia Theological Seminary, who has led the church progressively to develop and train its own clergy and lay readers, to emphasize religious guidance in educational centers, and to undertake more of its own material support. The Overseas Department of the National Council appropriates about $150,000 annually to assist this missionary district. Now aided by two suffragan bishops to develop the possibilities in many new areas, the young bishop of the Mexican Episcopal Church has under his jurisdiction thirty-two priests and over six thousand members of whom about thirty-five hundred are communicants.

In South America the first mission of the church was established in southern Brazil by James W. Morris and Lucien L. Kinsolving, recent graduates of the Virginia Theological Seminary, who began their study of the Portuguese language at São Paulo in 1889 and a year later moved to Porto Alegre, where they held their first services in rented quarters. Ten years later Kinsolving was consecrated the first bishop of the Brazilian Episcopal Church, which then consisted of five stations and seven clergymen of whom four were Brazilians; in 1900 it was constituted an independent Anglican church. Seven years later when the General Convention received this church as the Missionary District of Southern Brazil, Kinsolving was reassigned as its bishop; he remained in this office until 1928 and in this period opened and developed the Southern Cross School at Porto Alegre, which has grown to a position of great influence in that city. Under his episcopal supervision this mission was markedly strengthened; the communicants increased from 365 to almost 3,400 and his clergy from seven to thirty-two of whom twenty-eight were Brazilian. This pioneering bishop often told of his satisfaction in making extended visitations and of his joy in lying under the stars at night with his head on his saddlebags.[6] William M. M. Thomas succeeded Kinsolving in 1928 and carried forward this work until 1949 when Louis C. Melcher succeeded him.

In that year the House of Bishops divided this district into three: the Missionary Districts of Central, Southern, and Southwestern Brazil; and Melcher became the Bishop of Central Brazil the following January when the subdivision became effective. After eight years he was followed by Edmund K. Sherrill, who has continued to lead this missionary district with more than thirty clergy, twenty-five lay readers and almost three thousand communicants among approximately five thousand baptized members. While this represents only about one-fourth of the communicants and one-sixth of the baptized membership in Brazil, this district exceeds the others in its church school program, where nearly 140 teachers and officers are training about seven thousand pupils, more than twice the number in the other two districts. The current strength of the church in Brazil consists of eighty clergy, more than thirty lay readers, over eleven thousand communicants, and more than thirty-one thousand baptized members. From 1950 Edgmont M. Kriscke served as the Missionary Bishop of Southwestern Brazil until 1955 when he succeeded Althalico T. Pithan in Southern Brazil. Plinio L. Simoes became the Missionary Bishop of the Southwestern District in March, 1956. The church now conducts nine primary and secondary schools in Brazil and maintains its own theological school at Porto Alegre.

These were the years in which the church also moved into the islands of the Pacific. The Hawaiian Islands, often called the crossroads and melting pot of the Pacific, remained a native monarchy from their discovery by Captain James Cook in 1778 until 1894. Then, after four years of revolution, the white settlers successfully set up an island republic, and at their own request were annexed to the United States in August, 1898, and became a territory two years later. The original Polynesians then numbered only about one-quarter of the some one hundred and fifty thousand inhabitants, while English, Americans, Chinese, Japanese, Koreans, and others, attracted by the happy combination of ideal climate and fertile soil, made up the remainder. The next generation saw this population more than treble, and recently it has passed six hundred and fifty thousand. The multiplicity of backgrounds produced an unusual variety of religious faiths, making work among the islanders difficult but challenging.

Shortly after the first Anglican missionary had arrived in 1833, the church was well begun, and when the first English bishop came in 1862, the king and queen of the Islands were among the first to be confirmed. St. Andrew's Cathedral was opened in 1887 and became the center of missionary activity on Oahu. With the annexation to the United States the jurisdiction was transferred to the Episcopal Church, the Missionary District of Honolulu was organized in 1901, and the following year Bishop William Nichols of California took possession for the presiding bishop. The first American bishop, Henry B. Restarick, was elected by the House of Bishops on April 16, 1902, and, having been well prepared for his work by a widely varied experience in the Diocese of Los Angeles, gave vigorous and wise leadership to the mission for eighteen years, so that when he retired because of illness in 1920 the membership of the church had increased four hundred per cent while the island population had increased only forty per cent.

John D. La Mothe was elected Restarick's successor on October 20, 1920, and when he arrived almost a year later, he found the mission in such good order that he continued its established policies. However, he immediately expanded the capacity of the church schools on the island and opened several new parishes. He had found that scores of applicants had been turned away from the Iolani School, which already had fifty boarding students and three hundred day pupils representing eight nationalities. The school was moved to a new site in 1927 where many more boys have been enrolled. Nearby was the boarding and day school of St. Andrew's Priory, mostly attended by Hawaiian girls. At the Cathedral were two congregations, one Hawaiian and the other Anglo-American. St. Luke's Mission served the Koreans; St. Peter's the Chinese; and Trinity, the Japanese; each mission had its own school. Small churches were also established on the islands of Kauai, Maui, and Hawaii.

When Bishop La Mothe died unexpectedly on his way to the General Convention in 1928, the leadership of this missionary district was entrusted to Bishop S. Harrington Littell, who had had rich experience in the China mission. When he arrived in 1930, he immediately used his experience in the Far East to improve the work among the Orientals on the Islands. The bombing of Pearl Harbor on December 7, 1941, delayed his imminent retirement so that he could preserve the stability of the mission during the influx of thousands of servicemen. In 1944, Harry S. Kennedy succeeded to the jurisdiction of the Missionary District of Honolulu and has continued his work aggressively in the westernmost state of the Union from which American secular and religious influence penetrate widely into the Far East.

The strength of the Episcopal Church here is approaching twenty thousand members, almost two-thirds of whom are communicants. Although some of the more remote islands of the Pacific remain officially under the jurisdiction of the Presiding Bishop, they have usually been under the care of the Bishop of Honolulu. Samoa was assigned in 1904; Guam, Midway, and Wake in 1949; Okinawa in 1951; and Formosa in 1954. When Taiwan (Formosa) was transferred from the Nippon Seikokwai to the Episcopal Church in 1960, a new Missionary District of Taiwan with more than ten million inhabitants was created by the House of Bishops. Its supervision has been assigned to the Bishop of Honolulu as the bishop-in-charge, and since 1961 he has been assisted by Charles P. Gilson, the resident suffragan bishop.

In May, 1952, when Bishop Kennedy visited Okinawa, which had recently been placed under his jurisdiction, he confirmed sixty lepers and the following April confirmed forty more. This almost completely annihilated island suddenly came into prominence during World War II, and the Episcopal Church decided to make it a missionary venture in 1949. Norman B. Godfrey of the Diocese of Albany and William C. Heffner, a recent graduate of Virginia Theological Seminary, were joined by Gordon G. Nakayama, a Canadian priest whose Japanese ancestry made his language facility an invaluable asset in the work on this island. The Japanese government had long maintained a leper colony on Okinawa in which were Anglican converts bound to the church by the service of Aoki-san, a lay reader and himself a leper. Following the bishop's visit, four seminarians from Central Theological Seminary in Tokyo came for a summer to live among the islanders, who were divided between the leper colony and the Episcopalians in the American garrison. The prospect is that this mission, where more than one thousand of the fifteen hundred members are communicants, shall ultimately become a part of the Nippon Seikokwai.

The Philippines, three thousand islands lying about five hundred miles off the China coast and formerly a part of the Spanish empire, were constituted a missionary district of the Episcopal Church by the General Convention meeting in the fall of 1898, the year of the Treaty of Paris, which had also brought Puerto Rico and the Hawaiian Islands under the jurisdiction of the United States. Following the Spanish-American War, two Army chaplains, John F. Bolton and C. C. Pierce, remained in the islands; the latter has been considered the founder of this mission, for, in addition to ministering to the military personnel, he also held services for non-Roman islanders. Some laymen, sponsored by the Brotherhood of St. Andrew, then at the peak of its influence, joined these chaplains in ministering to the seven and a half million inhabitants. The Roman Catholic Church was deeply entrenched in these islands with about eighty per cent of the population in its membership and with over four hundred thousand acres of land in the hands of Catholic orders. During the revolt against Spain the populace turned against the orders, seized their lands, killed some of the monks, and imprisoned or exiled the remainder.

The Episcopal Church made a very happy choice in selecting Charles Henry Brent as the missionary bishop for these islands on October 11, 1901. Trained among the Cowley Fathers, he had more recently ministered in the slums of Boston. He brought the necessary virility as well as a gentle nature steeped in deep spirituality to this work, which required a great variety of skills to provide an adequate ministry to these diverse people. He found that the Filipinos were still almost entirely Roman Catholic, but there were minority groups of three major types: the head-hunting Igorots in northern Luzon, numbering several hundred thousand, were primitive pagans; the three hundred thousand Moros in the southern islands were militant Mohammedans; and the Orientals, mostly Chinese who had come to Manila for business reasons, were also non-Christian. Brent was very successful in collecting and holding his assistants, and by no means the least of these was Hobart E. Studley, a former Dutch Reformed missionary in Amoy, who came to Manila seeking orders in the Episcopal Church shortly after Brent arrived. The bishop immediately set him to work among the Chinese, whose customs and language he understood and among whom he served patiently but effectively for over thirty years. The Methodists turned over their missions to Studley's care, and a catechist, Ben G. Pay, became the first Oriental ordained in the Episcopal Church in the Philippines. St. Stephen's Church became self-supporting by 1912, and a short time later St. Peter's Church was founded for Chinese using the Cantonese dialect.

As a result of an episcopal visit to the northern Luzon province in 1903, Bishop Brent carefully drafted a plan for mission stations and work among the Igorots that is still in process of fulfillment. The first station at All Saints' Mission, Bontoc, was set up in 1903 by Walter C. Clapp who had accompanied the bishop. Here the church established a dispensary, later discontinued when the government set up a hospital in Bontoc, schools for boys and girls, and many outstations, often with small schools in the more remote villages. After Clapp's death in 1915 Edward A. Sibley and W. H. Wolfe successfully continued this work, often with the support of the American Governor John C. Early, an Episcopalian.

One of the most successful even though temporarily ill-fated ventures among the Igorots was the Mission of St. Mary the Virgin, begun at Sagada in 1904 by John A. Staunton, who had been trained as an engineer before his ordination. With a major emphasis on industrial training, this mission soon became a center for a mill and machine shop, and by 1922 an impressive stone church had been completed. Unfortunately many natives became overly enamored of the economic stability provided by employment at the mission, and the director became less and less amenable to his superiors, even refusing submission to his bishop. When the National Council forbade Staunton to do any more independent fund raising, at which he had become very adept, he resigned in January, 1925, and eventually became a Roman Catholic. Two of the Sisters of St. Mary died accidentally from food poisoning, and the mission, which had suffered so many reverses, was sustained only by the care and patience of Missionary Lee L. Rose; in 1931, Clifford E. B. Nobes arrived as an assistant, with authority to begin training a native ministry. Seven years later Wayland Mandell and John R. Ramsey became full-time teachers in the recently established seminary at Sagada. Seeking only the best qualified persons for the native priesthood, this school trained catechists as well as men preparing for orders so that the church destined for its own national independence should be provided with men qualified for this opportunity. The Sagada school was transferred to Manila in 1946 and became St. Andrew's Theological Seminary in recognition of support given to the Philippine mission by the Brotherhood of St. Andrew. Following World War II the new seminary buildings were completed and dedicated on November 30, 1953.

When the Philippine government opened a summer capital at a cooler location at Baguio in northern Luzon, to provide escape from the tropical climate in Manila, Bishop Brent quickly grasped the opportunity and founded the Easter school for gifted Igorot children in 1906 and three years later the school for American and English children, now called the Brent School. Samuel S. Drury directed the first school and later became headmaster of St. Paul's School in Concord, New Hampshire, and Remsen S. Ogilby, father of the present bishop in the Philippines, supervised the Brent School and later became president of Trinity College at Hartford, Connecticut. George C. Bartter, a British-born priest who came to Baguio in 1903, gave over forty years in unostentatious ministry in this mission and lies buried here among the people he loved.

Risking his life, Brent visited the militant Moros, where, in 1905, he dedicated Holy Trinity Mission at Zamboanga on a tip of Mindanao facing Jolo Island. Among the worshipers here were General Leonard Wood and General Tasker H. Bliss, and General John J. Pershing was baptized and confirmed here. By 1914 a hospital had been completed, and a settlement school for women and children was finished the same year. Several agricultural schools soon followed in Brent's practical program. After fifteen fruitful years Brent's missionary service came to an abrupt end in 1917 when he was advised that he must leave the Philippines because of the danger to his health. Although he had earlier refused election in two American dioceses, he now accepted election as Bishop of Western New York in October, 1917.

After a vacancy of more than a year the House of Bishops chose Gouverneur Frank Mosher, who formerly had worked in China, to succeed Brent. With the Philippines moving toward independence the training of a native staff became more important than ever, and Bishop Mosher immediately set about strengthening the catechetical and seminary training programs. However, the expansion program was not neglected, and by 1927 a new mission of St. Francis of Assisi, Upi, was begun by Leo G. McAfee among the Tiruray, a tree-dwelling tribe in one of the wildest sections of Mindanao where at least a dozen outstations soon gave evidence of the successful penetration of the area. To assist Bishop Mosher, after seventeen years of difficult service, the House of Bishops on October 16, 1937, named Robert F. Wilner as his suffragan, with special responsibility in the business administration of the district.

When Bishop Mosher resigned two years later, Norman S. Binsted, formerly the Bishop of Tokohu in Japan until that nation reorganized all religious bodies into a national religious system in 1940, was transferred to this mission; after proving himself completely adaptable in a climate of entirely different churchmanship, he was elected Bishop of the Philippines in 1942. World War II brought reverses for the church and suffering and deprivation for the missionaries and native Christians as the Japanese troops overran the islands. Eventually both bishops and all American priests and mission workers were arrested, and many of them, like Arthur Richardson, former headmaster of the Brent School, spent four years in an infamous concentration camp in Manila. Bishop Binsted was rescued by paratroopers from Los Banos just before he was to have been executed.

Following the war a group of some twenty priests and about a million and a half of the laity who had broken from the Roman Catholic Church in 1920 sought to continue their church as catholic in doctrine and liturgy and appealed to the Episcopal Church for orders. On the recommendation of Bishop Binsted the House of Bishops agreed, and on April 7, 1948, three priests of the Philippine Independent Church were consecrated as bishops by Binsted and two other Episcopal bishops. As its liturgy this church has adopted the Book of Common Prayer in Spanish, and its candidates for the ministry are trained in St. Andrew's Seminary. When full intercommunion with the Episcopal Church was established in 1961, Bishop Isabelo de los Reyes ordered the church bells rung in every parish. On Bishop Binsted's retirement in 1957 Lyman C. Ogilby succeeded to this responsible post, where he is now assisted by two Filipino suffragans.

The war brought almost complete destruction to the church's properties in Japan, including seventy-eight churches and many parish halls, rectories, and schools. Realizing the importance of maintaining a strong Christian influence in the Orient where anti-religious ideologies were winning the continent, Episcopal Church leaders immediately supported the Nippon Seikokwai and its heroic and competent Bishop Michael H. Yashiro in their reconstruction. Within six years of the close of the war forty American missionaries were serving under Japanese bishops and a million and a half dollars had been contributed for rehabilitation. Both in China and Japan the Episcopal Church had been most successful with its educational institutions: in China it had had a part in building Huachung University; and in Japan its St. Luke's Hospital became the famous St. Luke's International Medical Center. St. Paul's College, founded in Tokyo in 1907, with Henry St. George Tucker, later to be the well-loved Presiding Bishop of the church, as its first president, within twenty years was recognized by the Japanese government as a university. In addition to all other contributions to that country, the Episcopal Church presented a nuclear reactor, which was completely installed at St. Paul's University by 1961.

The Episcopal Church is now in communion with the Spanish Reformed Church and the Lusitanian Church in Portugal, which were formed like the Old Catholic Church when they broke away from the Roman Catholic Church after 1870 because they refused to accept the infallibility of the Papacy. The Spanish Reformed Church was organized in 1889 and, to avoid political implication, was assigned by the Archbishop of Canterbury to the jurisdiction of the Primate of the Church of Ireland. Subsequently, as the churches in Spain and Portugal required more frequent visitation, they were reassigned to the American bishop in charge of the American churches in Europe. On April 29, 1956, Bishop Stephen E. Keeler of Minnesota, then in charge of these churches, and Bishop Reginald Mallett of Northern Indiana joined with the Bishop of Meath, Ireland, to consecrate Santos M. Molina for the Spanish Reformed Church. Recently intercommunion was established with those confirmed or ordained by bishops in the Church of South India.

While hardly comparable to the missions in the American West and the Latin American and Oriental areas, the great cities of Europe were not neglected in the expansion of the Episcopal Church. More and more members were living abroad, and each year increasingly large numbers of tourists visited Europe. Before the end of the nineteenth century Episcopal churches were established in important cities like Paris, Rome, Geneva, Florence, Nice, and Dresden, and more recently Munich and Frankfurt. These self-sustaining parishes are not a part of the church's mission program but are bound together in the Convocation of American Churches in Europe, directly under the jurisdiction of the presiding bishop. They have been visited by other bishops to whom the visitation has been delegated from time to time; recently they have come under the care of Bishop Stephen F. Bayne, formerly of the Diocese of Olympia, while he served until 1964 as the executive officer under the Archbishop of Canterbury to coordinate the missionary work of the Anglican churches.

XXI

THE CHURCH
IN THE MODERN ERA

The accelerated pace of social and political change that followed World War I brought to the Episcopal Church a reorganization of its national structure, a revised Prayer Book and Hymnal, an enlarged and strengthened educational program, and far wider outlook and more inclusive spirit in its relations with other churches.

Probably the most significant single administrative act of the General Convention since 1789 was the creation in 1919 of a central administrative organization, The Presiding Bishop and Council, changed three years later to The National Council of the Protestant Episcopal Church in the United States of America. Similar executive improvements had been made by other major Protestant churches and had long been anticipated but slow in developing in the Episcopal Church. The first step in this direction was to make the presiding bishop an elected officer. From the beginning, this office had automatically fallen to the senior bishop in order of consecration; many men were aged before inheriting the position, and all of them lived to advanced years—five died between the ages of seventy-six and eighty-two and the other five between eighty-six and ninety-one.

In 1901 a new canon had provided that the senior bishop having jurisdiction in the United States shall be the presiding bishop, but all other attempts at altering the system had failed. In part this delay was due to a reluctance to change the system during the incumbency of Bishop Daniel Sylvester Tuttle who had held the office for sixteen years. The new canon adopted in 1919 required that the presiding bishop shall be elected by the House of Bishops and confirmed by the House of Deputies and provided that it should not take effect until the end of Tuttle's administration. The presiding bishop died in April, 1923, and before the convention assembled in the fall of 1925, two more bishops had briefly occupied this office. Bishop Alexander C. Garrett of Dallas served ten months, and Bishop Ethelbert Talbot of Bethlehem held the office for almost two years. The first elected presiding bishop, Bishop John Gardner Murray of Maryland, brought genuine administrative skills to the office but died after four years. Bishop Charles P. Anderson of Chicago died after serving less than three months, and at a special meeting in March,

341

1930, Bishop James DeWolf Perry of Rhode Island was elected by the House of Bishops and confirmed at the convention the next year.

The new canon provided that the presiding bishop shall be elected for a term of six years with the possibility of re-election but that he shall retain jurisdiction in his diocese. In the nature of the case the increasing duties of the presiding bishop in a rapidly growing church deprived his diocese of his major attention and meant that a suffragan would be chosen to administer the diocese. When Bishop Perry was not re-elected after his first term and returned to his diocesan duties for another ten years, a new problem arose. The General Convention in 1937 accordingly revised the canon to provide that a presiding bishop shall serve until the age of sixty-eight. For six more years, while the church considered the possibilities of establishing a primatial see in Connecticut or in Washington, D.C., this still left unsolved the problem of the administration of his own diocese. Eventually in 1943 further revisions were made requiring a presiding bishop to resign his see within six months of his election; although he has no diocesan jurisdiction, the presiding bishop now has his official seat in the Cathedral of SS. Peter and Paul in Washington, D.C. In this office Henry St. George Tucker, Missionary Bishop of Japan from 1912 until he became coadjutor in Virginia in 1926, gave a decade of able leadership during the difficult war years until 1947, although he resigned from his jurisdiction in Virginia only in 1944.

In 1947 he was succeeded by Henry Knox Sherrill, former rector of Trinity Church, Boston, and Bishop of Massachusetts during the preceding seventeen years. In addition to directing the central administration of the church during a time of reorganization, Bishop Sherrill, who assumed this office in full-time service, led the Episcopal Church into far wider interdenominational participation in the National Council of Churches of Christ in the United States of America, of which he became the president, and in the World Council of Churches, where he also served in a similar capacity. At the General Convention of 1958 Bishop Arthur Lichtenberger of Missouri became the presiding bishop of the church and directed the National Council in the period of transition from the old national headquarters at 281 Fourth Avenue into the newly erected Episcopal Church Center at 815 Second Avenue, New York. Because of ill health he resigned in 1964.

The reorganization of the structure of the church under the National Council after 1919 brought all its agencies and boards under the direction of this body, consisting of four bishops, four presbyters, and eight laymen to be elected by the General Convention, and eight members to be elected by the provinces. Subsequently four representatives of the women's work of the church were added to the council. Originally the council divided its work into five departments: Missions and Church Extension, Religious Education, Christian Social Service, Finance, and Publicity. These divisions have been altered little save in title except that Missions has been divided into the Overseas Department, under the direction of Bishop John R. Bentley, who will be succeeded in November by Bishop Stephen F. Bayne, and the Home

Department, under Bishop Daniel Corrigan. In 1963 Miss Carman St. John Wolf became the director of the Department of Christian Education when David R. Hunter resigned to become the associate secretary of the National Council of Churches. The Department of Christian Social Service is now the Department of Christian Social Relations, and the Department of Publicity has been renamed Promotion.

Three General Divisions of Laymen's Work, Women's Work, and Research and Field Study have been added, and The Seabury Press and the Office of Administrative Services have been brought under the supervision of the Council. The Domestic and Foreign Missionary Society of the Protestant Episcopal Church in the United States of America retains its corporate structure, and under canonical provision, its functions are performed by the National Council. Among the primary responsibilities of the Council is the preparation of an annual budget to be submitted to the General Convention and an annual report to the church at large and the General Convention. In the latter function the *Episcopal Church Annual* and *The Episcopalian*, a bi-weekly official journal begun in 1960, play an important role. The Episcopal Church, with such central executive administration unique in Anglicanism, has become the most effectively organized church in this communion.

Early in January, 1920, the new National Council held the first of the four quarterly meetings required in each year. For the first time in its history, the Episcopal Church now had a central administrative authority with executive heads in each department, making possible a close supervision of all the church's activities as well as the planning and projecting of new programs. The church naturally reacted positively and negatively to such centralization of authority: one supporter rejoiced that at last the church had its own "curia," while another, probably with tongue in cheek, complained that the government of the church was no longer in the hands of the traditional three orders of bishops, clergy, and laity but of a fourth order of "executive secretaries." Not the least of the benefits of this reorganization was the larger place provided for the services of the laity in the church. Typical of many more laymen who would serve with marked efficiency was Lewis B. Franklin, who gave up a promising financial career when he resigned as a vice-president of a leading New York bank to become the treasurer of the Council, an office in which he served nearly thirty years. Similarly, Franklin J. Clark, who served from the beginning until 1946 as the secretary of the Council, was typical of many other clergy who on full- or part-time have effectively served the church through this agency.

The stimulating effects of war-time efficiency influenced many American churches to undertake programs of survey and advance. Leading the Episcopal Church to similar action, the forward-looking General Convention of 1919 initiated the Nationwide Campaign aiming "to bring the spiritual and material resources of the Church to bear more effectively and adequately upon her whole task as witness to the Master." One of the most discernible of the lasting results of this effort is the annual Every Member Canvass which, when first introduced in this campaign, in one year more than doubled the gifts for general missions to about three million dollars. The increased involvement of the church in social and community problems stimulated the interest and participation of many laymen, who, in turn, translated their concern for the church and its work into increased financial support. There is unquestionably a direct connection between the church's engagement in creative and progressive movements of community and national importance and the sharing of intelligent laymen in the work and program of the church.

While statistics are only a partial index of any life and growth in the church, at least it is significant that while the Episcopal Church had just received its millionth communicant about the time the first guns were fired in World War I, it would more than double that number in the next generation. The church was growing more rapidly than the exploding population, improving its ratio of communicants to the population from one in ninety-eight to one in eighty-six and its baptized membership from one in about seventy to one in fifty-five. Meanwhile the gifts to the church increased proportionately so that, while the church in 1901 gave a total of almost fifteen million dollars for all purposes, by 1961 the United Thank Offering gifts and the budget of the National Council alone approached that sum, while the total giving of the church was well in excess of two hundred million dollars. Missionary zeal was probably never more evident than at the time of the epoch-making General Convention of 1919. The following year sixty-four missionaries were appointed and gifts for missions reached an average of $2.75 per communicant. During the depression of the next two decades this figure dropped to one-third this amount, and only in recent years has it again approached this level.

A wholesome effect of the Nationwide Campaign was the more universal identification of the membership with the life and work of the church. As the laity achieved an increasing role in the operation of the church, which had once received its major financial support from endowments, large individual gifts, and pew rentals or sales, a much wider participation in the support of the church became evident. Pew rentals were slowly abolished and only rarely may now be found, large individual gifts are still occasionally received, but the local, diocesan, and national budgets of the church are now largely met by the voluntary weekly contribution of lay people for whom the church has become identified with their lives.

In the first half of the twentieth century while the church was greatly concerned about righting social injustices, it slowly became conscious of inequalities in the salary scales of its clergy. At the turn to the twentieth century wide gaps often existed, so that in a diocese where a few top salaries reached $4,500 and $5,000 men in rural parishes were receiving $800 or even less. As such inequalities were corrected and wages generally increased in the United States, further inequities appeared. In 1950 the rector of the church whose predecessor had received $4,500 in 1900 and who was now the highest paid priest in his diocese was receiving $6,500. With the loss of the dollar's purchasing value this rector was singularly less affluent than his predecessor.[1] Generally, clergy salaries have improved in the last decade, minimum salary scales are common in most dioceses, fringe benefits, such as group insurance plans, are not unusual, but only rarely have the salaries of men in leading posts and parishes kept abreast of those of comparable status before World War I.

The achievement of the church that has brought the clergy the greatest sense of security was the establishment of the Pension Fund on an actuarial funded basis in 1917. As early as 1853 the General Convention had authorized the incorporation of a fund for the relief of aged, infirm, and disabled clergymen and widows and orphans of the deceased clergy. Little was done for twenty years, and by 1874 the sums paid to twenty-six retired clergy averaged less than one hundred dollars a year. Fifteen years later 178 beneficiaries each received about one hundred and eight dollars, derived largely from publishing royalties and charitable gifts. In a major effort to fund these pensions adequately, in 1907 an attempt was made to raise $5,000,000, but three years' efforts brought in only $118,000. When Bishop William Lawrence of Massachusetts first became concerned about this need of the church in 1910, he discovered that there were about fifty national, state, and diocesan societies providing for clergy relief but with no uniform regulation and in amounts ranging from about fifty to four hundred dollars annually. In that same year Lawrence, who had proved his administrative genius as diocesan since 1893 and had served for fifteen years on the Board of Overseers at Harvard University, sponsored a resolution at the General Convention that resulted in the appointment of a joint commission to study the matter. With the assistance of Monell Sayre, an actuarial specialist, Lawrence prepared a detailed report for the convention in 1913 which was approved. It provided that the Pension Fund should be the only pension system of the whole church, that the annual premiums should be scientifically calculated, and that a sufficient fund should be raised to provide the money needed for the clergy who would retire before the complete system could come into full operation. The premiums were calculated at seven and one-half per cent of the rector's salary; later these rates rose to ten and then to fifteen per cent. These premiums were to be paid annually by the congregation and considered as a deferred salary that would provide an annual retirement income at the age of sixty-eight of about half the clergyman's average salary.

Bishop Lawrence, who would later raise almost $800,000 for the War Commission of the church and more than $10,000,000 in two campaigns for Harvard University, tentatively took leave of his diocese and from his office in New York introduced novel campaigning methods since become common practice in campaigns of professional fund raisers. By March 1, 1917, the necessary $5,000,000 had been oversubscribed, the largest single fund ever raised by a church through voluntary contributions. So well had the campaign succeeded that six months later additional gifts brought the total to $8,750,-

000, an achievement that has made possible the successful continuance of the Pension Fund to the present.

Before his election to succeed Phillips Brooks, Lawrence had successfully applied his administrative gifts as dean of the Episcopal Theological School. Later, as the diocesan, he carefully planned the separation of the Diocese of Western Massachusetts from the Diocese of Massachusetts in 1901. He also established a cathedral, chartered in 1909, in St. Paul's Church, Boston, and founded *The Church Militant*, the only diocesan paper then having a paid subscription list. Few men have achieved highest distinction in so many fields; Bishop Lawrence had few peers as a churchman, administrator, or social leader, and he lived to be ninety-one years of age. One of the indications of his unique stature is the rare honor that came to him as the recipient of two honorary degrees from Harvard: on his election as a bishop he had received the Doctor of Divinity degree, and at the age of eighty-one, having concluded eighteen years as a member of the small controlling corporation, the President and Fellows of Harvard College, he was awarded the degree of Doctor of Laws.[2]

The Episcopal Church has faced the question of church unity and the possibility of uniting with other church bodies in every generation from its beginning. During the last century the relations with the Church of England have also become much closer and more cooperative, and not the least of the reasons has been the decennial Lambeth Conferences of the Anglican Bishops. Prompted by a suggestion from the Synod of the Church of England in Canada in 1865, Archbishop Charles T. Longley invited 144 Anglican bishops to Lambeth Palace in London in September, 1867. Although these meetings lasted less than a week and only seventy-six bishops attended— nineteen of them from the United States—it quickly became apparent that such meetings could have only beneficial effects, both on the life of each church represented and through their wider cooperation. At the second Lambeth Conference eleven years later, Archbishop Archibald C. Tait had prepared a much more extensive program, and the one hundred bishops— again nineteen from the United States—remained almost four weeks. While the topics discussed at the nine Lambeth meetings have ranged over the wide field of theological thought and church problems, these conferences have never become legislative but have remained primarily for the common counsel and advice of bishops. Nevertheless, by virtue of their being the united voice of the bishops of all Anglicanism, their findings have invariably carried great weight in directing the mind of the world-wide Anglican communion. Usually the attitudes of the constituent Anglican churches toward a newly formed church or churches with whom union is being considered is colored by the discussion of these matters before the bishops at Lambeth. So after an earlier strong approval by Lambeth, the General Convention in 1961 voted to approve a concordat with the proposed Church of Lanka, embracing former Anglicans, Baptists, Presbyterians, Methodists, Congregationalists, and members of the United Church of South India. On completion of this union, an agreement similar to the one with the Old Catholics will be arranged to provide full communion between the Church of Lanka and the Episcopal Church.

In the American church in about 1870 William Reed Huntington published *The Church Idea, an Essay towards Unity* in which he set out the centrality of the Anglican position, pointing out that Romanism was an exaggeration, Puritanism a diminution, and Liberalism a distortion of the idea of the church as the Kingdom of God. Realizing that unity could never be achieved by acceptance of any one existing system, he suggested, however, that since Anglicanism stood on four basic principles—The Holy Scriptures, the Primitive Creeds, the two Dominical Sacraments, and the Historic Episcopate—the Protestant Episcopal Church was the best single hope for union among the churches in America, a position never seriously denied.

So serious was the concern for Christian unity at the General Convention in 1886 that it voted "to enter into brotherly conference with all or any Christian bodies, seeking the restoration of the organic unity of the Church, with a view to the earnest study of the conditions under which so priceless a blessing might happily be brought to pass." A Joint Commission on Church Unity circulated the Chicago Quadrilateral among no less than eighteen church bodies during the next six years and received cautious but friendly replies from almost all of them. For approximately eight years negotiations were carried on with the Presbyterian Church with a common sense of agreement except on the fourth point, the episcopate. The Presbyterians were hesitant to accept any definition that distinguished bishops from presbyters and asked that intercommunion precede further negotiations, since this should be possible if all churches are part of the visible Church of Christ regardless of polity. Unable to dissociate the validity from the form of the ministry, Episcopalians could see no further hope of progress, and the Presbyterian General Assembly in 1894 voted to suspend negotiations until "mutual recognition and reciprocity" could be achieved. From the beginning the episcopate has been the chief obstacle in Anglican proposals for unity; although the indispensability of point four is hardly negotiable, modern Anglicans and Episcopalians may be much more favorably inclined to consider the prior question of mutual recognition and intercommunion.

In the brief negotiations with several bodies of Lutherans during these years, it became clear almost from the beginning that the chief impediments were not in polity but doctrine, despite Henry Melchior Muhlenberg's much earlier statement that an affinity of doctrine existed in these churches. One of the Lutheran bodies proposed the Augsburg Confession of 1530 as a basis for discussions in place of the Quadrilateral. When nearly two hundred Anglican bishops gathered at Lambeth in 1897, they must have concluded that a mere willingness to negotiate Christian unity was less than their full obligation, for they resolved that the Anglican churches should not merely make themselves available but should try to arrange conferences and representative meetings for united humility and intercession.

The last quarter of the nineteenth century also brought the Episcopal Church to consider its relations with the Church of Sweden, the Russian Church, and the Old Catholic Church, which was organized after Vatican Council I in 1870 by former Roman Catholics, largely in Germany, Austria, and Switzerland, who refused to accept the dogma of papal infallibility. Although the Episcopal Church had received a number of Swedish Lutheran churches into its communion during the colonial period, it had never come to any specific conclusion about its relation with the Church of Sweden. In 1892 the General Convention appointed a joint commission to study Swedish orders, which in no wise increased good will in Sweden. For the next six years the church studied the question but dropped the matter then indefinitely, leaving the anomalous situation that the Church of Sweden is in communion with the Church of England but not with the Episcopal Church.

When the Russians began to settle along the Pacific coast about 1862, the Commission on Unity approached the Russian Church in the hope of ministering to their people and opening better relations between the churches. Although for many years correspondence was limited to the exchange of official documents, a growing friendship, taking many forms, developed between the Orthodox and Anglican Churches. English and American churchmen visited Orthodox gatherings and received courtesy visits in return, Orthodox students were received in Anglican seminaries for part of their training, and Orthodox bishops advised the people to attend the Anglican churches when they could not attend services of their own church. In 1922 the Patriarch of Constantinople, comparable in his primacy among the Orthodox bishops to the Archbishop of Canterbury among the Anglicans, pronounced Anglican orders valid, and in this judgment he was soon followed by his peers in other Orthodox Churches. That this pronouncement came after almost four centuries of Anglican history was probably due not only to the increased friendly relations of the recent years but also to the willingness of the Orthodox bishops, after careful investigation, to disagree with the Bull *Apostolicae Curae* of Pope Leo XIII, in which on September 13, 1896, he had declared Anglican orders invalid. While the Patriarchal pronouncements did not lead to intercommunion or mean entire agreement in doctrine or polity, they have led to very close and friendly associations on a basis of equality. In many areas where small numbers of Orthodox reside, they have been welcomed into the Episcopal churches, and occasionally organized Orthodox congregations have been using Episcopal churches for their services.[3]

Interestingly, the Old Catholic Church, which had received its orders from the See of Utrecht and held its first synod in 1874, also recognized the validity of Anglican orders at a Congress held in September, 1925. The Joint Commission on Church Unity had been in communication with this church for years, and the Old Catholics now responded with the hope that they might have "more intimate and powerful contact with the Church of England and her daughter churches, on a truly Catholic basis." Representatives of the

Old Catholic Church, the Church of England, and the Episcopal Church met at Bonn in July, 1931, and drafted a basis by which it was mutually agreed that the churches could recognize their mutual catholicity and independence at the same time and enjoy full intercommunion without presupposing doctrinal, devotional, or liturgical agreement. By informally approving this agreement at a special meeting in 1932, the House of Bishops concurred that each church believed the other to hold all the essentials of the Christian faith. At the General Convention two years later, the bishops again approved the Bonn agreement, and in 1940 the House of Deputies concurred in a similar action; since that time the two churches have happily enjoyed intercommunion.

As early as 1893 some Polish Roman Catholics in the United States withdrew from that church and formed the Polish National Catholic Church. Having reecived his consecration from three Old Catholic bishops in 1896, Bishop Anthony Kozlowski proceeded to organize the church which, by the turn of this century, had eighty thousand members served by twenty-six priests and about eighteen thousand children in twenty-five schools. Although several attempts had been made as early as 1901 and 1910, under the administrations of both Bishop Kozlowski and his successor, Bishop Hodur, to establish closer relations with the Episcopal Church, it was not until 1940 that the General Convention approved intercommunion with the Polish National Catholic Church as well as with the Old Catholics. Since the orders of both churches stemmed from the See of Utrecht, it was natural that the Episcopal Church should have extended its action to include the Polish National Catholic Church. Only after six years did agreement come from the leaders of this church, so often spurned by the Episcopal Church; it brought to reality intercommunion with a church that now had about two hundred and fifty thousand communicants in the United States and probably more in Poland. For those concerned about the succession in the American episcopate, some interest will accrue from the fact that Polish National Catholic bishops have participated in several consecrations in this church: on November 6, 1946, Bishop Jasinski assisted at the consecration of Harold E. Sawyer, who became Bishop of Erie, and on October 28 of the following year, Bishop Misiasek assisted when Bishop Horace W. B. Donegan of New York was consecrated. At the consecration of Charles P. Gilson, Suffragan Bishop of Honolulu serving in Taiwan, at the time of the General Convention in Detroit in 1961, Bishop Isabelo de los Reyes of the Philippine Independent Church and Bishop Francis C. Rowinski of the Polish National Catholic Church joined in the apostolic ceremony of laying-on-of-hands.

Less successful were the attempts of the Episcopal Church to affiliate the Uniats, Eastern Rite Christians in communion with Rome, who had come from middle Europe to this country before 1900. When these Christians were about to abandon the Roman Catholic Church in 1920, Rome sent John Torok, a Uniat priest, from Europe on a special mission to this church. In Washington, D.C., he met several members of the Episcopal Church's

Foreign Born Division of the Department of Missions, just then beginning its responsibility for the church's dealings with the Eastern churches, and he looked with favor on their invitation to unite the Uniats with the Episcopal Church. About this time Bishop Gorazd of the Czechoslovakian National Church, formed by the union of most of the churches in that country after World War I, visited the United States and suggested that Torok might serve this cause best by seeking consecration from Orthodox bishops in Europe. There appeared to be no obstacle, but when he returned as Bishop Torok in 1925, he discovered that the General Convention of the Episcopal Church had never acted on the plan and that the men of the Foreign Born Division had really exceeded their authority in encouraging him.

Seven years later, Bishop Frank E. Wilson of Eau Claire proposed that Bishop Torok should become his suffragan and then bring his Uniat followers into union with the Episcopal Church. In order to facilitate this plan Bishop Wilson made the proposal to the General Convention, which resulted in the canon, since called the Canon on Alien Rites, which permitted a congregation to retain its own rite after becoming affiliated with the Episcopal Church. With the approval of Presiding Bishop Perry the title "Assistant to the Bishop of Eau Claire" was given Torok by Bishop Wilson in 1935. But the House of Bishops would not agree; without impugning the validity of his consecration, the bishops refused to accept Torok as a bishop in the Episcopal Church. After a short period in Puerto Rico, Torok served as a priest in the Diocese of Long Island. The Uniats, after separating from Rome in 1942, formed a new Carpatho-Russian Church, which soon had forty priests and its own bishop.[4]

The Canon on Alien Rites, which provides for the possibility of union with churches having the historic episcopate, remains among the canons of the church.[5] The body now responsible for such relations is the Joint Commission on Cooperation with the Eastern and Old Catholic Churches, an agency of the National Council. The American Church Union, sponsoring a threefold program of teaching, defense, and service, for many years has sought to produce greater visible unity within the Episcopal Church as well as to promote mutual understanding and closer unity between the Orthodox, the Roman Catholic, and the Old Catholic Churches. Canon Albert J. duBois is the general secretary and executive director of the Union, which publishes *The American Church News*, a monthly magazine, *The American Church Quarterly*, a theological journal, and *Faith and Unity*, an ecumenical quarterly.

Early in this century there apparently was a serious attempt to try to lead a considerable portion of the Anglo-Catholics from the Episcopal Church to Rome. The movement had its beginnings in Philadelphia, where Henry R. Percival, rector of the Church of the Evangelists, became the leader of an extreme high church group. Among his disciples were William McGarvey, William W. Webb, and Maurice Cowl. When Webb became president of Nashotah, he came to share the strong anti-Roman position of Bishop Charles

C. Grafton of Fond du Lac and may have helped prevent the maturing of the plot. In the spring of 1908 three priests at Nashotah went to Rome, and the following May four more defected in Philadelphia, including McGarvey, whose name is usually attached to this schism. More than twenty years later Joseph G. H. Barry, who had succeeded Webb as president at Nashotah, declared that there had indeed been a conspiracy to lead the entire high church party to Rome. Professor Burton Scott Easton was less certain about the size of the plot, which he felt had grown to illusory proportions in the imagination of Professor Sigourney Fay at Nashotah, but he also admitted that there was a conspiracy to form a schism of respectable size. That no more than twenty-one priests left the church may have been due in part to the impetuosity of its leaders, who triggered it prematurely, but more likely to the stabilizing influence of Bishop Grafton, who must have been relieved by the departure of the radicals. He wrote many articles and delivered many addresses urging loyalty to the church; by his own strong catholicity, surpassed only by his loyalty to the Episcopal Church, Grafton demonstrated not only the propriety but also the value of such churchmanship within the comprehensiveness of Anglicanism. In the years since then, defections to Rome have been very infrequent and invariably as individual choices.[6] On the contrary, the reception of Roman Catholics into the Episcopal Church has been steadily increasing. In a period of twenty-five years after World War I, forty-five Roman Catholic priests were received as priests in the Episcopal Church, and in the last ten years of that period more than twenty-six thousand Roman Catholic laymen became Episcopalians. At the present time almost seven thousand Roman Catholic converts are received into the Episcopal Church each year.

When the Federal Council of Churches, representing about seventeen million members of most of the major churches in the United States, was organized in 1908 to make possible closer cooperation and united action on non-controversial matters, the Episcopal Church was represented by members of the Joint Commission on Unity but did not become a constituent member. For many years this church participated in the work of the Federal Council by sharing in its commissions on Church and Social Service, Church and Race Relations, and International Justice and Good Will. Despite several attempts to achieve fuller cooperation during the next thirty years, the Houses in the General Convention were never in concurrence on this disputed question, which even William Reed Huntington opposed on the ground that federalism was a bad substitute for the church union he desired. Bishop Charles H. Brent so ardently championed the church's full cooperation with the Federal Council that he lost supporters who might have won him the election as presiding bishop in 1925. Finally in 1940 the Episcopal Church became a constituent member of this body, which soon became the National Council of Churches of Christ in the United States of America, a constituent part of the World Council of Churches. Bishop Brent and the Episcopal Church had a large part in the founding of the World Conference on Faith and Order, which held meetings at Lausanne and Edinburgh in 1927 and 1937 before becoming a part of the World Council of Churches. Following approval of Brent's original idea for the Conference, J. Pierpont Morgan supported the work of a joint committee of the convention with a gift of $100,000. When the first conference opened in early August, 1927, four hundred delegates representing ninety autonomous churches came together, not to resolve or legislate, but to discuss and define as clearly as possible mutual agreements as well as variant opinions about such major topics as the nature of the church, the ministry, and the sacraments.

During the last generation the Episcopal Church has made three major attempts at organic union with other churches: with the Congregationalists between 1910 and 1923, with the Presbyterians between 1931 and 1946, and since 1958 with the Presbyterian and Methodist Churches and the United Church of Christ. This last effort is still in its elementary stages and has recently been expanded to include several other American churches in the proposed union. The plan, which resembles the highly regarded constitution of the Church of South India, is based on the so-called Blake-Pike Proposals. It was first presented in 1960 to the National Council of Churches in San Francisco in an address by Eugene Carson Blake, the Stated Clerk of the United Presbyterian Church in the United States of America, who had previously reached agreement with Bishop James A. Pike of California. Regular meetings of the commissioners of these various groups continue, while several of the churches carry on independent negotiations that will probably bring about unilateral church unions within this decade.

While other men wrote about church unity in the early years of this century, no one wrote so effectively as Newman Smyth, a Congregational minister of New Haven who, with uncanny accuracy, predicted in his *Passing Protestantism and Coming Catholicism* that Catholic modernism would permit Rome ultimately to become warmer in its relations with the Protestant churches. Commenting favorably on the Lambeth Quadrilateral, he told Episcopalians that they had both the opportunity and the responsibility to become the mediating church among all the churches to put its principles into operation. The General Convention in 1910 received a communication from the National Council of the Congregational Churches announcing that it had appointed five commissioners, led by Newman Smyth, to confer with the Episcopal Church about unity. When the Episcopalians took no action, the Congregationalists, who had now added Williston Walker, the eminent church historian at Yale, to the commission, appealed to the presiding bishop in 1918 for an immediate response. The House of Bishops, meeting in April that year, received from the committee to which this matter was referred only a cool report, pointing out major differences between these churches.

While a favorable climate was created at the epoch-making General Convention in 1919, little more than preliminary legislation and encouragement for the Joint Commission on Unity was accomplished at that busy session. After working carefully with the Congregational commissioners during the next triennium, the Joint Commission presented to the General Convention in 1922 the Concordat with its vital section on "Proposals for an Approach toward Unity." Realizing that actual union at this time was not feasible, the commissioners proposed a beginning that would make intercommunion possible in particular instances by providing for supplementary orders for some Congregational ministers. The fear of bishops seemed to have vanished, and the generous concessions of the Congregationalists led the bishops and deputies to try to formulate a canon that would permit the acceptance of the treasures of each for the common enrichment of both churches.

The Concordat proposed that Congregational ministers might receive ordination without becoming members of the Episcopal Church and without denying their ministry or ceasing to be pastors of their congregations. When the canon was finally presented for adoption, these provisions had been carefully incorporated with a final clause requiring that the congregation whose minister was to be ordained not only should agree to such ordination but should also declare "its purpose to receive in the future the ministrations and the Sacraments of one, who shall have been ordained to the Priesthood by a Bishop." This point had been broached in 1919 and discussed during the triennium by the commissioners. Congregational commissioners, realizing that it would literally make complying congregations Episcopal parishes, objected to this clause, and the Episcopal commissioners advised the convention against its inclusion. The Committee on Canons in the House of Bishops nevertheless recommended its inclusion, and with this amendment it was approved and sent to the House of Deputies, where it passed by a substantial margin among the lay deputies but by a small majority in the clerical order. Meeting in 1923, the National Council of the Congregational Churches, on the motion of Newman Smyth, supported by the eminent clergyman and author, William E. Barton, voted to lay the Concordat on the table and the issue was closed.[7]

Other stipulations in this canon, which has never been repealed despite several attempts to do so, provide that a minister applying for ordination shall subscribe to the Apostles' and Nicene Creeds and admit to communion only validly baptized persons. He is also to be willing to meet with the bishop for counsel and cooperation and be amenable to him in faith and conduct. If properly licensed, such a minister may officiate in the Episcopal Church "according to the prescribed order of this Church," and he may become a rector of a church if he promises conformity to the doctrine, discipline, and worship of the church. Although at that time the Concordat seemed to have been a complete failure, many of its features have since been considered seriously in ecumenical negotiations. On at least three occasions this canon, then numbered eleven and now thirty-six, has been used in ordinations in the Episcopal Church, and there is some confidence that it may prove to be a useful instrument in future ecumenical ventures of this church.

An ecumenical spirit that has widely prevailed in the Episcopal Church in recent decades was expressed as early as 1912 when Bishop Charles P. Anderson addressed the annual convention of his diocese in Chicago on "The Manifestation of Unity." Having declared that union and unity were not identical nor mutually exclusive he went on to say that men could effect union but unity was a gracious gift of God. He suggested that since men need not choose between them they might even discover unity through union. He asserted that unity is the will of Christ and a fundamental dogma of the Christian religion and "the manifestation of this unity is the duty of Christ's disciples."

By the time the General Convention assembled in 1928, the Episcopal Church had begun to feel a growing ecumenical spirit, generated by the progress toward Christian unity in the Church of South India and such world-wide gatherings as the Missionary Conference in 1910 and the Faith and Order and the Life and Work Conferences of 1927. The pastoral letter from the bishops had dealt with it, and it seemed so right to adopt with enthusiasm Bishop Brent's proposal to the convention for a Joint Commission to confer with the Presbyterians and Methodists on Christian morality, looking toward organic unity. By 1931 the Commission's title had become "Approaches to Unity," and it was authorized to include the Lutherans and to deal specifically with the problem of union. Supported now by the increasingly friendly attitude toward other churches expressed by the Lambeth Conference of 1930, the Episcopal commissioners carried on their responsibility with alacrity. However, the Methodists were engaged in bringing together their own several branches of the church, and the Lutherans had become similarly involved so that only the Presbyterians and the Episcopalians remained to consider union.

Among the many outstanding leaders of various shades of churchmanship who served on the unity commission during these critical years, no one exceeded Bishop Edward L. Parsons in constructive influence. Brought up a Presbyterian, he had imbibed the liberal spirit of Professor Charles A. Briggs at Union Theological Seminary and, when denied ordination by his presbytery, sought orders in the Episcopal Church. Having served as a curate under William Reed Huntington, he very early became a liturgical authority and was a leader in the 1928 revision of the Book of Common Prayer. By 1936 the bishop had prepared a Proposed Concordat, which he circulated among the commissioners; it clearly stated that the two churches purposed organic union and proposed a basis including a mutual recognition of ministries, full intercommunion, and an interchange of ministries after supplemental ordination by a bishop or authorization by a presbytery.

Because of the careful preparations and the congenial climate that had just seen the foundation laid for the future World Council of Churches, it came as no surprise, nevertheless with great delight, when the General Convention in 1937 voted unanimously to invite the Presbyterian Church in the U.S.A. to declare a common purpose to achieve organic union and to take immediate steps toward this end. Charged with such a major responsibility, the Joint Commission was enlarged to fifteen, equally divided between bishops, priests, and laymen, and reflecting varied views of churchmanship. The following May the Presbyterian General Assembly enthusiastically accepted the invitation and appointed a similar commission.

At this point the Presbyterians outran the Episcopalians, who had sharply divided views that apparently had not been fully evident in the meetings of the two commissions. Furthermore, since the Presbyterians had received the Proposed Concordat without clarification of its tentative nature, it was prematurely considered by them as an operating basis, even though some Presbyterian leaders had expressed strong objections to recommissioning of the ministry on the ground that it meant reordination. In 1940 the General Convention voted to admit Presbyterian ministers into Episcopal Church pulpits, but the House of Deputies was not yet ready to concur with the House of Bishops in advising members of the Episcopal Church situated beyond the ministries of their own church to associate themselves with a Presbyterian congregation.

Discarding all previous plans, the commissions, during the next triennium, prepared two documents, *Joint Ordination* and *Basic Principles*, pointing more specifically toward complete organic union with complete unity in government, ministry, and membership. Storms of controversy soon arose in both churches over the latter document, which proposed wide diversity of organization and worship and a double transmission of orders through the episcopate and the presbytery, with an equality of rights and powers among bishops, presbyters, and ruling elders in official gatherings. Churchwide discussions soon became more intense in both bodies; among the Episcopalians, the American Church Union actively opposed the plan, which was in turn supported by the Episcopal Evangelical Fellowship, a body of progressive evangelicals organized to preserve the catholicity of the church in its inclusiveness and its evangelical character in a clear witness for the gospel. For Episcopalians, unfortunately, this hour of opportunity became an occasion for the emergence of high party spirit and differences.

To the General Convention assembled in Cleveland in 1943 the commission, then heavily weighted by men of liberal spirit, brought majority and minority reports that were never presented. Pressed for time by the war crisis, that convention did little but vote to continue the commission with a fairer balance of party representation and to refer the union to Lambeth for consideration. Working covertly, the commission prepared *The Proposed Basis of Union*, which was not published until the early fall of 1946 just before the next meeting of the General Convention in Philadelphia. Its chief issue of controversy proved to be the basis of the mutual recognition and the extension of the authority of the ministry, and the key passage lay in the order for such recognition: "The Ministry of the Word and Sacraments which thou hast already received is hereby recognized: and the grace and authority of Holy Orders as conferred by this Church are now added . . . ." *The Witness* and *The Churchman*, the more evangelical and liberal independent church papers, favored it, while the more conservative, *The Living Church*, editorialized against it. No little confusion had been introduced by a statement of President Henry Sloane Coffin, of Union Theological Seminary, before the Presbyterian General Assembly the preceding May that the report, then not yet published, would indicate a mutual recognition of ministries with no extension of ordination.

The majority and minority reports of the commission were hopelessly dissonant. Because of the late appearance of the *Basis*, there had not been the usual free and full discussion before the convention assembled; this made the floor of the convention an arena of exciting debate. During the convention the Archbishop of Canterbury, Geoffrey Francis Fisher, spoke enthusiastically about the common elements and the historic basis of the unity in the Anglican Communion, which Bishop Parsons later declared helped to determine the outcome. Finally, while the Presbyterians anxiously awaited the decision, the convention voted to instruct its commission to prepare a new statement, in harmony with the Lambeth Quadrilateral, implying that the previous one was not and therefore unsatisfactory, and to refer it to the next Lambeth Conference. Many Episcopal leaders, who counted courtesy almost as important as an Anglican principle, were embarrassed at what was obviously, albeit unintentionally, a shabby treatment of the Presbyterians to whom they had proposed union and made overt concessions and then on acceptance had withdrawn them. Understandably pained, the Presbyterians turned to their own family problems and set about reuniting the Presbyterian Churches in the United States. On reflection the Episcopalians seriously began to consider the wise counsel of Bishop Parsons that the church must first resolve its basic internal differences on these major issues before it proceeds further to involve other communions.

Not dismayed by abject failure, the newly appointed commission drafted a new statement of the Episcopal Church, which was grounded in the Lambeth Quadrilateral and approved by the Lambeth Conference of the Anglican Bishops in 1942. It stated with great clarity that while Anglican formularies "pronounce no judgment on other ministerial successions. . . . They define ministers within this historic stream as 'Ministers of Apostolic Succession' . . . and they make the preservation of this succession a matter of scrupulous discipline." Perhaps only divine purpose will suffice to explain how, after only twelve years, Presbyterians have invited Episcopalians, and even now they sit with others about the ecumenical conference table to consider the developments from the Blake-Pike Proposals.

When the General Convention in 1913 received several petitions for the revision of the Prayer Book, it named a joint commission of seven bishops, seven presbyters, and seven laymen, asking it to prepare "such revision and enrichment of the Prayer Book as will adapt it to present conditions," provided, however, that no changes were proposed in faith and doctrine or in the name of the church. From the commission's first report three years later it became evident that this revision would be much more complete than that in 1892 and that *The Book Annexed*, prepared thirty years earlier by William Reed Huntington and his associates, would prove of invaluable benefit in this effort. This project consumed much of the time of the General Convention for more than a decade until finally the book was approved in 1928. At last the church had a Prayer Book that its best scholars and liturgists could approve and that provided flexibility in its services and an adequate number of prayers for a wide variety of occasions. Much of the enrichment of the Book was distinctly American, for among the eighty-three prayers that appeared for the first time, five were by William Huntington, five by Bishop Charles Slattery, four by Bishop Edward Parsons, and eight by the Rev. John W. Suter, custodian of the Prayer Book for many years. Beyond a new appreciation for the treasure in its liturgy, the Episcopal Church had also achieved new insights into the nature of its worship. In its first report in 1916 the commission, which had been asked to refrain from altering the dogmas of the church, correctly stated that "faith or doctrine is involved in each expression of worship; and every proposal for revision or enrichment does necessarily touch them." Realizing also that no revision could be final since the liturgy was a vital part of the changing life of the church, the convention in 1928 established a permanent Liturgical Commission, which has continued this creative process and recently has published a series of Prayer Book Studies, looking toward still further revisions in the living liturgy of the church.

By a similar process of careful study and revision begun in 1910, the Episcopal Church produced a new hymnal, which was approved in 1916 and appeared two years later for use in the churches. Despite the fact that 126 new hymns had been introduced, this book never proved adequate, and by 1937 the General Convention assigned further revision to a new commission. Second only to the Prayer Book in its significance for the worship of the church, *The Hymnal 1940*, now in common use in the Episcopal churches, has provided lower pitched tunes for the improvement of congregational singing and a larger proportion of German chorale and plain-song tunes.

Both negative and positive actions of some significance were enacted by the General Convention in 1949. Three dioceses and a missionary district had elected a woman as a deputy to the convention, and the House of Deputies in organizing for business that year decided by 321 votes to 242 that women were excluded by the constitution. However, a joint commission was appointed to study the question, and three years later the convention sustained the previous action of the deputies. Women do sit in some diocesan conventions, on local vestries, and on the National Council of the church. Strengthening the marriage canons of the church that year, the convention made it obligatory for persons about to be married to sign a Declaration of Intention, indicating their concurrence with the church's teaching that marriage is for life and their determination to abide by it. This convention also resolved to permit the administration of the Holy Communion by intinction, but an attempt to add such permission in a rubric in the Prayer Book failed three years later. Although the resolution on intinction was motivated primarily by reasons of health, it is interesting that generally it has been opposed by Anglo-Catholics and favored by more liberal churchmen. During this period the church purchased an official residence for the presiding bishop at Greenwich, Connecticut, and a national conference center nearby, which is known as Seabury House. The Episcopal Church now has twelve such national conference and retreat centers in the United States.

Before the close of the nineteenth century the church had inaugurated the perpetual diaconate, but when it became discredited through misuse as a short cut into the priesthood, it was discontinued. By 1952, however, the bishops saw greater use for this office, which, with proper safeguards, was re-established that year, making possible a wider extension of ministerial service. With all of its structural and institutional improvements, the church was not forgetting its increasing responsibility in service at home and abroad. The postwar convention sessions were marked by appeals from the missions for aid in extensive reconstruction. The church responded in 1949 by adopting the National Council's budget of more than five and a half million dollars and pledging to send more than half of it into missionary work; within the last fifteen years these missionary expenditures of the National Council have doubled, and at the same time attempts have been made to reduce administrative costs. For a number of years the Episcopalians have been expending about four times as much for local parish work as for missions and benevolences; many vestries have aimed at reducing this ratio to two to one, and in several responsible parishes the local expenditures are less than funds contributed beyond the parish. Across the church, however, probably no more than three per cent of receipts reach the foreign mission field and perhaps another three per cent is expended for church extension in the United States.

When the United States passed its first peacetime draft law in October, 1940, the General Convention then in session immediately created a new Army and Navy Commission and named as its director Bishop Henry K. Sherrill, who gave it most of his time for the next four years. The response of the Episcopal clergy far exceeded government assigned quotas of 185 chaplains for the Army and thirty-seven for the Navy. Within three years the church had 412 chaplains in service, and before the war ended about ten per cent of the active priests of the church had seen military service. Almost as unparalleled as this record was the fact that the church during these years raised approximately a million and a half dollars over and above its regular budget to provide for the equipment and other needs arising from these services. Although the General Convention in 1949 considered the possibility of asking the House of Bishops to name a suffragan to be in charge of Episcopal chaplains in the armed services, this responsibility was assigned to the Armed Forces Division, a subsidiary of the National Council's Home Department. The war also raised the questions of conscience for the clergy and laity with strong pacifist convictions, many of whom during the past twenty-five years have been associated in the Episcopal Pacifist Fellowship. But there have been no celebrated cases recently like that of Paul Jones, Missionary Bishop of Utah, who during World War I had been so vocal about his pacifist convictions that his loyalty was suspected; eventually the House of Bishops accepted his resignation because of his impaired influence but did so "with full recognition of the right of every member of this House to freedom of speech in political and social matters, subject to the law of the land."

Among the American churches few bodies have shown as great an interest as the Protestant Episcopal Church or contributed so largely in leadership to the cause of racial, economic, and social justice. Despite considerable opposition and with little sympathy or support from without, the church has continued its educational and social work among the American Indians at the same time that it has provided religious guidance for them. During the more recent years of mounting tension, brought on by the delay in granting Negroes their constitutionally guaranteed civil rights, the Episcopal Church has provided sympathetic guidance and direction as well as both moral and material support in the effort to eliminate this injustice. More fully integrated than any other Protestant body, this church has officially shown its concern by assigning the direction of this portion of its responsibility to an associate secretary in the Division of Domestic Missions, the Rev. Tollie L. Caution. Late in 1959 a convention of clergy and laity organized the Episcopal Society for Cultural and Racial Unity, popularly known as ESCRU, to bring about greater implementation of the inclusive nature of the church and the elimination of all barriers in the church based on race, class, or national origin. Individual clergy and laity have participated in prayer pilgrimages, sit-ins, protest marches, and some have served terms in jail to emphasize the urgency of this crisis, which thousands more have supported less demonstrably by preaching and local Christian efforts. At least one southern-born impeccably trained white clergyman, after several years of a promising ministry on the staff of a major northern parish, chose to become the rector of a Negro parish in a large city in the deep South.

With a social interest second only to their theological liberalism, a significant number of churchmen, both Catholic and Protestant in their inclinations, have come to the fore during the last generation. Stimulated by the English authors of *Essays, Catholic and Critical*, which appeared in 1926, American churchmen, including such distinguished scholars as Frank Gavin and Cuthbert A. Simpson of the General Seminary faculty and Frederick C. Grant, then dean at the Seabury-Western Theological Seminary, brought out eight years later a volume *Liberal Catholicism and the Modern World*. The spirit of Liberal Catholicism was succinctly stated by Gavin in its Introduction: "to preserve the best of the past in the light of the best of the present so as to build for the best of the future." He defined the coveted privilege and awful responsibility of Anglicans "to bear witness to a Catholicism that is not imperialistic but free; and to a liberalism that has its living roots in the congenial atmosphere of a vital tradition." At about the same time a similar volume, *Liberal Evangelicalism*, brought from England the witness of the Anglican Evangelical Group Movement with which as many as six hundred English clergy were affiliated. Liberal evangelicals in the American church, many of whom have since been associated in the Episcopal Evangelical Fellowship, were quickly stirred to share in a similar attempt to stress the positive contributions of the Reformation and evangelical Protestantism while preserving a tolerant and non-controversial attitude so indispensable for the cultivation of a liberal climate of religious life and thought. Duly appreciating the catholic emphasis on the corporate life of the church, the liberal evangelicals sought to save the church from deterioration through overemphasis on such externals as mere intellectualism or ritualism. They wished to modernize evangelicalism but also to preserve the religious fervor and depth of conviction often lost in modernism. Fortunate was the Episcopal Church that once sharply divisive party alignments had become almost cooperatively complementary; on many points allegiances were indistinguishable. Both schools beneficially influenced each other, and neither can now be understood without the other.

These times also markedly influenced the personal religious lives of many Episcopalians. In the early 1920's Frank Buchman, a Lutheran clergyman, began a religious movement which has variously been called Buchmanism, the Oxford Group Movement, the First Century Christian Fellowship, and, more recently, Moral Rearmament. He hoped to help individuals achieve an empirical type of self-authenticating religious experience akin to conversion that should become the basis of a clear Christian witness in public testimony and service. The genius of the movement seemed to lie in its ability to bring together upper and middle class groups, usually for long weekends, for prayer and mutual edification through testimony. Because of the personal nature of the appeal and the peculiarly intimate nature of its confession-like testimonies, this unusual religious movement probably influenced a disproportionately large share of Episcopalians. During the last twenty-five years the movement has changed its emphasis to personal evangelism, and in keeping with its new name, it seeks to win key persons in all nations and so to influence world history. Because of the strong emphasis on repentance, conversion, and divine guidance, this movement appeals most to men and women whose religious backgrounds have been objective and formal.

Many of the laity of the Episcopal Church have been helped to develop their own devotional and prayer life by the work of the Forward Movement, instituted by the General Convention in 1934 and since 1940 under the direction of the presiding bishop. Its primary publication, *Forward Day by Day*, a booklet of daily Bible readings and meditations, is issued five times a year, and more than four hundred thousand copies are distributed. The Forward Movement also publishes more than 150 pamphlets on religious subjects and other topics related to personal living.

The Episcopal Church also felt the impact of Christian Science and by it may have been led to give thought to the often neglected relation of religion and health. Beginning about 1906, Elwood Worcester and his assistant Samuel McComb introduced a healing ministry to Emmanuel Church, Boston, where, during the next quarter of a century through the cooperation of several sympathetic psychiatrists and other physicians, they carried on a healing ministry that came to be known as the Emmanuel Movement. Acknowledging the power of mind over body, they based their practice essentially on religion. Grounded on a belief that through faith and prayer man is able to draw on the limitless divine resources, this ministry proved helpful to hundreds of persons who attended the regular meetings or sought individual counselling. The efforts of Dr. Worcester, who had earned a doctorate in psychology in Germany, were most successful in dealing with persons afflicted with functional nervous disorders, although he and the staff did not neglect alcoholic and drug addicts. The physicians examined all patients, detailed records were kept, and individual therapy was usually followed by moral and spiritual re-education in the church where regular meetings with periods of prayer were conducted. The movement was widely copied by Episcopalians and others, making for a proper recognition that such a healing ministry is an integral element in the gospel and normal in the life of the church. In 1928, prayers for the Unction of the Sick were introduced in the Prayer Book, and more recently the International Order of St. Luke the Physician was organized. It is a non-monastic order for those within the church who desire to make the ministry of healing a part of their vocation.

In addition to these specialized ministries, the Episcopal Church from the beginning has been a leader among the American churches in building hospitals and providing medical services and eleemosynary services. Although hospitals and many other similar institutions of the church have been merged with community institutions, the church still maintains throughout the world sixty-eight hospitals and convalescent homes, eleven residences and rest homes, eighty-three institutions and agencies for the care of the aged, and an even larger number for children and youth.

Not unrelated to this special ministry is the similar correlation between religion and social work that claimed the interest of many clergy and was discussed in many summer conferences of the church. With support from the Diocese of Southern Ohio, Dr. William Keller, a physician and an Episcopalian who was actively interested in social work, opened the Cincinnati Summer School in 1923 to provide an opportunity for young men in training for the ministry to have supervised practical experience in institutional and family welfare, health services, rehabilitation, and even penology. By 1936 the program in Cincinnati was expanded into a full year program, and Joseph F. Fletcher came from the church's Division of Industrial Relations, where he had been a research assistant, to become the dean. By 1944 the idea of clinical training for the ministry had become so popular that it was incorporated in many of the seminary programs; Dean Fletcher and the Cincinnati school moved to the Episcopal Theological School in Cambridge, where such training has continued to be a regular part of the curriculum.

A school for the postgraduate training of the younger clergy of the church became possible when Alexander Cochran presented Bishop James E. Freeman of Washington, D.C., with a half-million dollars to erect a building that was completed in the close of the cathedral in 1929 and an additional million dollars for its endowment. Bishop Philip Mercer Rhinelander had just resigned his jurisdiction in Pennsylvania and became the first warden of this College of Preachers; his rich academic background at Harvard and Oxford and his experience as a seminary professor made him a happy choice for the post he held for more than ten years. Usually about twenty-five invitations are sent to priests, who have had from five to fifteen years of parish experience, to spend a week in residence for intensive Bible study, theological lectures, and criticized preaching. Thousands of the Episcopal clergy have been stimulated by this study and fellowship to make ordered study a natural step to improved service to the church. With a similar purpose but primarily for its own area, the Diocese of California conducts the Bishop Block School of the Prophets in the close of Grace Cathedral. American clergy have also occasionally been invited to share in the more extended program of study of the faith, worship, and common life of the Anglican Communion at St. Augustine's College, Canterbury.

With the strong historical orientation of Anglicanism and the large place given to private school, college, and theological education, it appears anomalous that it was not until 1910 that the Church Historical Society was organized and then by a group of laymen led by William Ives Rutter. In 1940 the General Convention finally designated the Society as an official agency of the church. For about fifty years its collections of the sources relating to the history of the Episcopal Church were housed at the Philadelphia Divinity School until their removal to the new library building of the Theological Seminary of the Southwest at Austin, Texas, almost a decade ago. Since 1932 the Society has continuously published *The Historical Magazine of the Protestant Episcopal Church*, a quarterly journal now generally regarded as a major source for a study of Episcopal and American church history. In addition, the Society has published about fifty separate major and minor studies dealing largely with subjects of national and diocesan interest.

Following approval by the National Council in October, 1951, the Seabury Press began its significant service as the official publication agency of the church the next January. The church had long maintained a Division of Publications to produce the educational and publicity materials for the church, but the major works of its scholars were issued by commercial publishers. This church press became a necessity when the new religious education curriculum and the volumes of The Church's Teaching Series were envisioned. More recently, Seabury Press has published Prayer Books and Hymnals of the church and has also ventured into commercial book publication, limiting its titles largely to areas of interest and value to the church. During the last generation the church has produced two series of textbooks for use in the church schools, which have grown from about two hundred thousand teachers, officers, and pupils in 1920 to more than one hundred thousand teachers and officers and almost nine hundred thousand pupils. In the 1920's the Christian Nurture Series was produced under the direction of the Rev.

William E. Gardner, the first general secretary of the General Board of Christian Education from 1910 to 1925, and his able successor, the Rev. John W. Suter, Jr., who later became custodian of the Prayer Book. About twenty years later the Seabury Series was begun under the direction of the Rev. John Heuss, who later became rector of Trinity Church in New York.

After Christian Education became a responsibility of a department of the National Council in 1920, Young People's Fellowships, where older boys and girls met in informal groups with minimal official oversight, spread far beyond Michigan and Massachusetts where they had begun during World War I. The church saw its youth program grow under limited part-time direction until 1940, when the Division of Youth was formed with the result that thousands of young people have come to look upon their church as the normal center for much of their activity. To provide opportunities for healthful and congenial vacations as well as serious pursuit of religious interests, the church now maintains almost two hundred summer camps and conferences for young people and adults.

The church has also expanded its facilities for young people in the colleges and universities, where it discovered by 1928 that Episcopalians were three and a half times more numerous than in the national population. Slowly the Division leaders were able to induce rectors living near college campuses to assume responsibility for religious oversight of college young people near them, and by 1930 more than twenty men and women had been placed in full or part-time positions of religious guidance on campuses. By 1940 a separate Division of College Work was created and soon each diocese had its own department, with a director responsible for assignment of clergy to campuses within its borders. More than a thousand college chaplains, most of them on part time but officially designated, are now serving the college young people of the church. At Columbia University, where chaplains have long been Episcopalians, Stephen F. Bayne had a very successful ministry of five years until his election as Bishop of Olympia in 1947, and James A. Pike gave a dynamic leadership there from 1949 until he became Dean of the Cathedral in New York.

This century has seen marked advances in the training of the clergy of the Episcopal Church. For the first time in 1910 the General Convention appointed a Commission on Theological Education; the church had been training its clergy almost entirely in independent schools, for only the General Theological Seminary in New York was established by and under the direction of the General Convention, while the other nine seminaries had all been incorporated independently. Greater emphasis has been laid in recent years on studies in practical theology, pastoral counseling, Christian education, and the history and methods of missions, and course requirements have been reduced offering larger freedom of election. The General Seminary introduced a tutorial system of instruction in 1926, and a few years later the Episcopal Theological School introduced a senior tutorial system and comprehensive general examinations. The Berkeley Divinity School moved from

Middletown to New Haven, Connecticut, in 1927; the Seabury Divinity School united with the Western Theological Seminary to become the Seabury-Western Theological Seminary in Evanston, Illinois, in 1933; and the Church Divinity School of the Pacific first moved from San Mateo to San Francisco in 1911 and then to Berkeley in 1930.

To provide further facilities for training men on the Pacific coast for the ministry, Bloy House Theological Training School was begun in Los Angeles, and the Episcopal Theological Seminary in Kentucky, originally chartered in 1834, was reactivated at Lexington in 1951. In order to provide theological training for candidates for orders who must support themselves by full-time secular work during their training the School of Theology of the Diocese of Long Island was begun in 1955. Beyond the borders of the United States the church now has four theological seminaries: Cuttington College and Divinity School at Suacoco, Liberia, West Africa; the Episcopal Theological Seminary of the Caribbean at Carolina, Puerto Rico; St. Andrew's Theological Seminary in Manila, the Philippines; and the Theological Seminary at Porto Alegre, Brazil.

In recent years the number of candidates for the ministry in the Episcopal Church has not increased proportionately with the growth of its membership, and little more than half of them have been brought up in the Anglican Communion. Several of the seminaries have been filled to capacity, while others have recorded the rise and fall of applications common to similar institutions in other churches. Generally, the rising trend in applications after World War II has abated, and most theological schools have had a declining number of applications for admission. In 1921 there were 343 candidates for holy orders in the Episcopal Church and by 1934 the number rose to 534, but by 1943 many men were in the armed services and the number declined to 306. Following World War II not only the number but also the quality of candidates improved, and among them was an increasing number of men of mature years willing to leave successful business and professional careers for the church. The church in the United States now has 667 candidates for the ministry and 928 postulants; ordinarily a postulant does not become a candidate until he has successfully completed his early theological studies. The list of postulants reached a record number of almost twelve hundred about a decade ago.

Throughout the church there are now almost ten thousand clergy and more than seventy-seven hundred parishes and organized missions. In addition, there are probably a thousand vacant churches, many of them unable to support a rector. About twenty per cent of the clergy are non-parochial, including many men in retirement and a large number of educators and teachers. Although it is difficult to be precise about the clergy shortage in the Episcopal Church since expert judgments have varied from eight hundred to fifteen hundred, it is probable that one thousand ministers could be absorbed if they were available. During the same period in which the number of postulants and candidates has been declining, the number of lay readers has substantially increased, occasionally by more than a thousand in a year. There are now over fourteen thousand of these men, set apart after training and episcopal appointment, who are authorized to conduct Morning and Evening Prayer and to read approved sermons.

Although several agencies of the church have for more than a century provided financial aid for theological students, no church-wide program of recruiting men for the ministry was undertaken until 1920 when the Department of Religious Education assigned this task to a new Commission on the Ministry. In addition to two theological scholarship agencies in Virginia and Connecticut, founded in 1812 and 1827 respectively, the Society for the Increase of the Ministry, incorporated in 1859, offers aid to postulants and candidates on a church-wide basis, and the Evangelical Education Society, organized in 1862, assists theological students "who are in hearty and practical sympathy with the Evangelical teachings of this Church." As recently as 1961 the National Council created a permanent Division of Christian Ministries under its Home Department.

Never has the Anglican Communion had such a complete sense of unity in life and purpose as in this period following the Anglican Congress in Toronto in August, 1963. Here came representatives of the 348 dioceses and almost forty-four million baptized members from all parts of the globe to reappraise their history and present condition and to have a look at the opportunity and responsibilities before them. Taking a significant part in this congress were the representatives of the almost 3,600,000 baptized members in the 104 dioceses and missionary districts of the Protestant Episcopal Church. Most prominent among these was Bishop Stephen Fielding Bayne who, by virtue of his coordinating position in Anglicanism during the past four years, was responsible for planning the congress. Never before had so many Anglicans come together from so many nations to consider so responsibly the major issues confronting Christianity as a whole and this Communion in particular.

New confidence has arisen from the rediscovery of the long neglected Christian resources among the laity, whose skills, energies, and insights are more widely than ever marshalled in the work of the church. Realizing that the laity, like the clergy, can be sustained in their work and witness only by an adequate sacramental life and worship in the local churches, these leaders resolved to find ways whereby Anglicans everywhere may find in the services of the church not merely a congenial atmosphere but experiences of enrichment and power for Christian service. Determined that the church must listen to the culture in which it lives rather than merely preach to it, these churchmen set about to discover the true purposes for which the church exists. With the genuine Anglican perspective that sought to rediscover in its catholicity the genius of its heritage while in true Protestant spirit it brought a most critical judgment to examine its order, the church determined on the destruction of old isolations and inherited attitudes and a radical change in priorities.

One of the frequently uttered themes of the congress stressed mutual responsibility and interdependence in the body of Christ. There was a full recognition that this meant the death of many old things and a willingness to forego many desirable things, both inescapable and essential experiences necessary to the rebirth of Anglicanism, not for its own sake but only for Christ's sake and the church. Recognizing the unique unity in its political, racial, and cultural diversity, the Anglican Communion has determined to bring this unity and interdependence to a completely new level of expression and corporate Christian obedience. This challenge to Anglicanism was most succinctly phrased in the question whether she is to be a mere survival from the past or whether she will join the human race, to be used by God as a formative influence and an instrument of His will in this new phase of human history. Whether the Episcopal Church proves worthy of its Christian trust and will join other Anglicans to answer this question affirmatively depends upon its development of a degree of responsibility and an intensity of dedication commensurate with the richness of its heritage and the scope of its inclusiveness.

NOTES

(References to *The Historical Magazine of the Protestant Episcopal Church* will be indicated by *HM*.)

I. THE BACKGROUND IN ENGLAND

1. For further reading see Moorman, John R. H., *A History of the Church in England* (New York, 1954).

II. THE CHURCH IN VIRGINIA

1. Poor, John A., *A Vindication of the Claims of Sir Ferdinando Gorges, as the Father of English Colonization in America* (New York, 1862), pp. 134 ff.

2. Edward Lewis Goodwin says the first Holy Communion was held on July 1, 1607, on the Third Sunday after Trinity (*The Colonial Church in Virginia*, p. 20). He quotes Captain Smith's description of the first place of worship and his appraisal of Hunt that he had earnestly sought "to set forth quietness, peace and love" among his parishioners, "not suffering them to be partakers of the Lord's table until he knew them [apparently meaning Smith and Wingfield] to be reconciled. . . . Many were the mischiefs that daily sprung from their ignorant (yet ambitious) spirits, but the good Doctrine and exhortation of our Preacher Mr. Hunt reconciled them, and caused Captain Smith to be admitted to the Council. The next day all received Communion." William Stevens Perry (*The History of the American Episcopal Church*, I, 46) says that the first sacrament was administered on the Third Sunday after Trinity, June 21, 1607 (sic). William W. Manross (*A History of the American Episcopal Church*, p. 7) accepts May 14, the day after landing and so does F. L. Hawks (*Contributions to the Ecclesiastical History of the United States of America*, I, 20). Smith was apparently welcomed into the church on May 13, although many others still remained in jail.

3. Hawks, *op. cit.*, p. 33; Stith's *History of Virginia* (Sabin reprint), 1865, p. 33.

4. Brydon, George MacLaren, *Virginia's Mother Church and the Political Conditions Under Which It Grew*, I, 72.

5. Pennington, E. L., *The Church of England in Colonial Virginia*, pp. 35 f.

6. Henry E. Huntington Library, BR Box 117.

III.   Beyond Virginia in the South

1. Goodwin, Mary F., "Christianizing and Educating the Negro in Colonial Virginia," in *HM*, Vol. I, No. 3 (September, 1932), pp. 143–52.

2. Jones, M. G., *The Charity School*, 1938.

3. SPG MSS (Library of Congress Transcription), B8, 51.

4. Lawson, John (Surveyor General of North Carolina), *A New Voyage to Carolina* and *A Journal of 1000 Miles through several Indian Nations* (London, 1709, 1714), p. 12. Lawson includes the second Charter of Charles II, pp. 239–54 and an abstract of the Constitution of Carolina, pp. 255–58. Dalcho, Frederick, M.D., *Historical Account of the Protestant Episcopal Church in South Carolina*. (Dalcho was also an assistant minister of St. Michael's Church, Charleston.) Hewatt, Alexander, *An Historical Account of the Rise and Progress of the Colonies of South Carolina and Georgia* (London, 1779). (Hewatt was minister of the Scots' Church, Presbyterian, at Charleston before the Revolution; he died in London in 1824.)

5. It is barely possible that from among these Huguenots the Rev. Samuel Maynadier had migrated to serve in the church at Oxford, Talbot County, Maryland, until his death about the middle of the eighteenth century. See Perry, *op. cit.*, I, 317; II, 407–36.

6. Woodmason, Charles, *Carolina Backcountry on the Eve of the Revolution*. Ed. by R. J. Hooker, 1953.

7. See Introduction by L. H. Butterfield in the 1954 *Annual*, Institute of Early American History and Culture (Richmond, Va.: The William Byrd Press, Inc., 1954).

8. Original Letters XII, p. 128; *ibid.*, p. 273.

9. *Ibid.*, XIV, p. 128; Hawkins, Ernest, *Historical Notices of the Missions of the Church of England in the North American Colonies previous to the Independence of the U.S.* (London, 1845), p. 89.

10. *Journal*, I, 39.

11. *Journal*, XIII, 187; XVIII, 479; XIX, 123.

IV.   The Church in Massachusetts

1. *Magnalia Christi Americana*, III, xi.

2. Savage, James, *John Winthrop's History of New England*, 1853, p. 16.

3. Hawkins, Ernest, *op. cit.*, "Governor Dudley's Report," pp. 23 ff.

4. *Review of Dr. Mayhew's Remarks*, 1765, pp. 43 f.

5. *Observations on the Charter and Conduct of the SPG in Foreign Parts with Remarks on the Mistakes of East Apthorp* (Boston, 1763), p. 107.

6. *An Answer to Dr. Mayhew's Observations* . . . (Boston, 1764), p. 68.

7. *A Serious Address* . . . (Boston, 1748), p. 132.

8. *The Religion of Jesus Christ the Only True Religion, or a Short and Easie Method with the Deists*; also the anonymous *Choice Dialogues by a Godly minister and an Honest Countryman concerning Election and Predestination* in which he openly opposed Congregationalism. He also republished in London Leslie's

Short and Easie Method with the Deists, to which he added Ignatius's *Epistle to the Trallians* and a lengthy *Discourse Concerning Episcopacy,* p. 41–127.

9. During the course of his trial, Checkley secretly published *A Modest Proof of the Order and Government Settled by Christ and His Apostles,* first issued by Charles Leslie in 1695, which brought two prompt replies to these classic defenses of episcopacy. Edward Wigglesworth in his lengthy *Sober Remarks on a Book lately Reprinted at Boston entitled A Modest Proof . . .* (Boston, 1724), 78 pp., attacked Checkley and defended Presbyterianism, saying that episcopacy could lead only to Rome. Checkley quickly replied in his *A Defence of a Book lately reprinted at Boston entitled A Modest Proof . . .* (Boston, 1724) in which he reciprocated Wigglesworth's more belligerent spirit and added his *Animadversions upon Two Pamphlets.*

10. *Remarks upon the Postscript to the Defence of a Book Lately printed in Boston entitled A Modest Proof . . .* (Boston, 1724).

11. *Historical Collection of the American Colonial Church,* III, 665. *The Speech of Mr. John Checkley upon His Tryall at Boston in New England* (London, 1730) including "A Discourse Shewing who is the true Pastor of the Church of Christ," "Ignatius to the Trallians," and "A Specimen of a True Dissenting Catechism upon Right True-Blue Dissenting Principles."

V.   Beyond Massachusetts in New England

1. Pennington, Edgar L., *The Church of England in Colonial New Hampshire and the Rev. Arthur Browne* (Hartford, 1937), p. 20.

2. SPG MSS Letters V, 154.

3. Hawkins, Ernest, *op. cit.,* p. 116, 167; Updike, Wilkins, *History of the Episcopal Church in Narragansett, R.I.* Ed. Daniel Goodwin. 2nd edn. (1907), I, 483.

4. MSS Letters XXI, 417; Updike, *op. cit.,* III, 68, 77, 92.

5. Berkeley, George, *Works,* III, 210, 232.

6. Letter of Berkeley to Dr. Martin Benson, April 11, 1729, published May 29, 1946, as a letter presented to the Fellows of Davenport College.

7. Letter of H. Barclay and J. Robinson to the vestry of Trinity Church, New York, quoted in Perry, *op. cit.,* I, 440.

8. Beardsley, E. Edwards, *Life and Correspondence of Samuel Johnson,* pp. 79, 81.

9. *Ibid.,* pp. 154 f, 170.

10. Turell, Ebenezer, *Life and Character of The Rev. Benjamin Coleman,* pp. 59–61.

11. Beardsley, *op. cit.,* pp. 15, 19 f, 31.

12. Beardsley, E. Edwards, *History of the Episcopal Church in Connecticut,* p. 39.

13. Clap, Thomas, *The Annals of History of Yale College to the Year 1766,* p. 32; *Diary of Stephen Sewall, Chief Justice of Massachusetts,* quoted in Perry, *op. cit.,* I, 255.

14. Beardsley, E. E., *History of the Protestant Episcopal Church in Connecticut*, p. 217.

15. Hawkins, *op. cit.*, 185; SPG Original Letters, XL 63.

16. MSS Letters XXI, 465.

17. Thoms, Herbert, *Samuel Seabury, Priest and Physician, Bishop of Connecticut*, 1963.

VI. The Church in New York

1. Brodhead, John R., *History of the State of New York*, 1853 ff., II, 44.

2. *Ibid.*, II, 300.

3. *New York Colonial Documents*, III, 399, 415.

4. Klingberg, Frank J., *Anglican Humanitarianism in Colonial New York*, p. 5.

5. MSS Letters III, L 168; Hawkins, *op. cit.*, p. 281.

6. *Ecclesiastical Records of the State of New York*, 1916, pp. 1303–17; 1333–35; 1579–80.

7. Quoted in Perry, *op. cit.*, I, 325; *Collection of Papers of SPG* (London, 1719).

8. Journal of SPG (Library of Congress Transcriptions) VIII, April 13, 1739.

9. *Twelve Anniversary Sermons Preached before the Society* (London, 1845), p. 36.

10. Secker's Sermon quoted in Klingberg, *op. cit.*, pp. 213 ff.

11. Ogilvie Letter quoted in Perry, *op. cit.*, I, 330.

12. *Sermon on "The Felicity of the Times"* (Cambridge, 1763).

13. SPG Letters, XIX, L 89; Hamilton, Milton W., "Sir William Johnson of Johnson Hall" in *American Heritage*, III, 3 (Spring, 1952), 20–25; Widdemer, Margaret, "Prince in Buckskin" (Joseph Brant), *ibid.*, 26–28.

14. SPG MSS (L. C. Trans.), A2, 124.

15. *Ibid.*, A4, 68.

16. *Ibid.*, A7, 215–18; 204–06. The Department of History of the Carnegie Institution has published a five-volume study of these interrelationships: Catterall, Helen T. and Hayden, James J., *Judicial Cases Concerning American Slavery and the Negro* (Washington, 1926–1937).

17. SPG MSS (L. C. Trans.) B2, 6a; Journal of SPG (L. C. Trans.), XVI, July 20, 1764.

18. Journal of SPG (L. C. Trans.), XX, January 19, 1775.

VII. The Church in Pennsylvania and New Jersey

1. "Some of the many false, scandalous, blasphemous and self-contradictory Assertions of William Davis, faithfully Collected out of his Book, printed anno 1700, entitled, *Jesus the Crucified Man, the Eternal Son of God etc.*, in exact Quotations word for word, without adding or diminishing." Signed by George Keith and Evan Evans (Philadelphia, 1703), 12 pp.

2. However, at this point he was primarily referring to Lutheran pastors in New York; *Journal*, 1944, I, 566.

3. Rightmyer, Nelson W., *The Anglican Church in Delaware*, 1947, p. 97; Johnson, Amandus, *The Swedish Settlements on the Delaware*, 1911, 2 vols.

4. Dorr, Benjamin, *A Historical Account of Christ Church, Philadelphia . . .* , (New York, 1841), p. 54.

5. Hawks, Francis L., *Contributions to the Ecclesiastical History of the United States*, II, 183.

6. Burr, Nelson, *The Anglican Church in New Jersey*, pp. 597 f, 621; Klein, H. M. J., and Diller, William F., *The History of St. James's Church* (Lancaster, 1944). Tired by the travel involved, Craig petitioned the Society for a permanent mission and was assigned in 1753 to Sussex County, Delaware. Richard Locke was supposed to return to Lancaster but found the congregation there so fond of Craig that he went on to serve in Delaware in Craig's stead. This left Craig to his "waste places."

7. Burr, *op. cit.*, pp. 160, 143 f, 622, 636.

8. *Ibid.*, pp. 330, 608, 610 f, 612, 619, 642.

9. William Skinner to Secretary SPG, January 9, 1749.

10. Lydekker, John Wolfe, "Michael Houdin, First Rector of Trenton, N.J.: Intelligence Officer at Quebec and Missionary at New Rochelle, N.Y." HM, V (1936), 312–24.

VIII. THE STRUGGLE FOR THE EPISCOPATE

1. Hawks, Francis L., "The Episcopate before the Revolution" in *The Protestant Episcopal Historical Collection*, 1851, pp. 138 f.

2. Swift, Jonathan, *Works*, XVI, 48.

3. Appendix to *Journal* p. 139, quoted in Hawkins, *op. cit.*, p. 378.

4. SPG Journal, pp. 185–87; Burr, *op. cit.*, pp. 342–48.

5. Hawkins, *op. cit.*, p. 385.

6. Massachusetts Historical Society Collection, Ser. III, Vol. IV, p. 492; Tudor, William, *Life of James Otis of Massachusetts* (Boston, 1823), p. 136.

7. Turell, Ebenezer, *Life and Character of the Rev. Benjamin Coleman* (Boston, 1749), p. 127.

8. Wells, William V., *Life and Public Services of Samuel Adams* (Boston, 1866), p. 157.

9. Mather, Cotton, *Magnalia Christi Americana* (Hartford, 1820), Vol. I, Bk. III, Pt. 1, Sec. VII, p. 219.

10. Porteus, Beilby, "A Review of His Life and Character" prefixed to *The Works of Thomas Secker* (London, 1825), 6 vols.

11. Hawkins, *op. cit.*, p. 393.

12. *Ibid.*, p. 395.

13. Stiles, Ezra, *A Discourse on Christian Union* (1761), pp. 102, 114; see also Bridenbaugh, Carl, *Mitre and Sceptre* (1962), pp. 10–14, 19 ff.

14. *Minutes of the Convention of the Delegates from the Synod of Philadelphia and from the Associations of Connecticut held annually from 1766 to 1775* (Hartford, 1843), p. 68.

15. *Ibid.*, p. 23.

16. Morse, Jedediah, *Annals of the American Revolution* (Hartford, 1824), pp. 197–203.

17. *The Rev. Jonathan Boucher's View of the Causes and Consequences of the American Revolution in Thirteen Discourses* (London, 1797).

18. Mayhew, Jonathan, *Observations on the Charter and Conduct of the SPG.*

19. Caner, Henry, *A Candid Examination of Dr. Mayhew's Observations.*

20. Apthorp, East, *A Review of Dr. Mayhew's Remarks on the Answer* (London, 1765), pp. 55 f.

21. Chandler, T. B., Letter to the SPG, January 15, 1766; SPG (L. C. Trans.), Ser. B., 24, 90.

22. Hawkins, *op. cit.*, pp. 400 f; Ewer, John, *A Sermon preached before the SPG, February 20, 1767* (London, 1768).

23. He suggested eventually that the letter was spurious. Blackburne, Francis, *A Critical Commentary on Archbishop Secker's Letter to the Rt. Hon. Horatio Walpole concerning bishops in America* (Philadelphia, 1771).

24. *A Collection of Tracts from the Late Newspapers*, 1769, II, 195 f; "Timothy Tickle" in Mr. Gaine's *Gazette*, October 3, 1768; "A Whip for the American Whig," XXVI.

25. *A Collection of Tracts from the Late Newspapers* (New York, 1768), 406 pp.

26. Hawkins, *op. cit.*, p. 401; Chandler, T. B., *Life of Samuel Johnson*, p. 207.

IX. THE CHURCH AND THE AMERICAN REVOLUTION

1. Only three were considered disloyal to England. Thomas, R. S., *The Loyalty of the Clergy of the Church of England in Virginia to the Colony in 1776 and their conduct* (Richmond, 1907); *William and Mary Quarterly*, V, 200–03.

2. Gifford, Frank Dean, "The Influence of the Clergy on American Politics from 1763 to 1776" in *HM*, X (1941), 117 ff.

3. Hobart, Noah, *A Serious Address to the Members of the Episcopal Separation in New England* (Boston, 1748), pp. 134 f.

4. Clergy to the Secretary SPG, October 3, 1765.

5. Original Letters, xix, 1, 178; Hawkins, *op. cit.*, p. 301.

6. *A Sermon Preached before the University of Oxford, Dec. 13, 1776, on Psalm 7:9* (Oxford, 1777), pp. 22, 24.

7. *American Archives*, Ser. IV, I, 802.

8. *Ibid.*

9. Inglis, Charles, *Letters of Papinian* (New York, London repr. 1779), pp. 28–38.

10. Leonard Cutting letter to SPG in 1781 in Hawkins, *op. cit.*, p. 310.

11. *The True Interest of America Impartially Stated*, p. 39.

12. Burr, *op. cit.*, pp. 394, 630 f.

13. Original Letters, XVII, 1–233; Hawkins, *op. cit.*, p. 314.

14. SPG Journal (L. C. Trans.), XXI, January 17, 1777; Klingberg, Frank J., *Anglican Humanitarianism in Colonial New York*, pp. 181 ff.

15. Wallace, Paul A. W., *The Muhlenbergs of Pennsylvania* (Philadelphia, 1950).

16. Turner, C. H. B., *Some Records of Sussex County, Delaware* (Philadelphia, 1909), p. 239.

17. *The American Journal of Ambrose Serle, 1776–1778* (San Marino, Calif., 1940), pp. 259 f; Rightmyer, *op. cit.*, pp. 25, 170 f.

X.   THE CONSTITUTIONAL CONVENTION

1. Dr. George Berkeley, eldest son of Bishop Berkeley, in a letter to Dr. John Skinner, Bishop of Aberdeen, March 24, 1783.

2. Stowe, Walter H., "State or Diocesan Conventions" in *HM*, VIII (1939), 231; Lydekker, J. W., *Life and Letters of Charles Inglis*, p. 219, for clergy present; White, William, *Memoirs of the Protestant Episcopal Church*, 1836, pp. 333 ff.

3. *Ibid.*, p. 84 f.

4. Burr, *op. cit.*, p. 584.

5. *Minutes . . . Maryland Convention*, 1784, p. 16.

6. White, *op. cit.*, p. 33.

7. Hook, Walter F., *The Disestablished Church in the Republic of the United States of America* (London, 1869), p. 54.

8. White, *op. cit.*, p. 21.

9. Seabury, Samuel, *Address to the Clergy of Connecticut, August 3, 1785* (New Haven, 1785); Hardy, E. R., "The Significance of Seabury" in *American Church Monthly*, Vol. 37, No. 1 (January, 1935), pp. 26–40.

10. Chorley, E. Clowes, "The General Conventions 1785, 1786, and 1789" in *HM*, IV, 252 f; Manross, W. W., "The Inter-State Meetings and General Conventions 1784, 1785, 1786, and 1789" in *HM*, VIII, 261–70; White, *op. cit.*, pp. 22–25.

11. Salomon, Richard G., Appendix to *The Case of the Episcopal Churches in the United States Considered*, by William White, 1954.

12. Chorley, E. Clowes, *The New American Prayer Book*, p. 49.

13. Nuss-Arnolt, William, *Proceedings of the Church Historical Society*, Part I (Philadelphia, 1915), pp. 25 f; Loveland, Clara O., *The Critical Years*, pp. 185, 194; Hawkins, *op. cit.*, p. 409.

14. White, *op. cit.*, pp. 115 f.

15. Smith, Horace Wemyss, *Life and Correspondence of the Rev. William Smith* (Philadelphia, 1880), 2 vols.

16. Detailed changes may be seen in Chorley, *op. cit.*, or in Parsons, Edward L., and Jones, Bayard J., *The American Prayer Book.*

XI.   THE CRITICAL EARLY YEARS

1. Lowndes, Arthur, *Proceedings of the Church Historical Society*, II (1916), 62 f.

2. Meade, William, *Old Churches, Ministers, and Families of Virginia*, p. 29.

3. *Journal of the Diocese of Maryland* (Baltimore, 1791), pp. 8, 15.

4. *Ibid.*, p. 4.

5. The House of Bishops felt uneasy about the necessity to recognize the resignation of Bishop Provoost, and in consecrating Benjamin Moore, whom the Diocese of New York had clearly elected as bishop and head of the diocese, the House specifically stated that they were consecrating him "as assistant or coadjutor bishop during Bishop Provoost's life . . . to be dependent on such regulations as expediency may dictate to the church in New York, founded on the indisposition of Bishop Provoost and with his concurrence." Quoted in Perry, *op. cit.*, II, 152.

6. Whitehead, Cortlandt, *Early History of the Church in Western Pennsylvania*, in *Proceedings of the Church Historical Society*, I (1915), 30.

7. *Ibid.*, pp. 31 f.

8. *Journal of the Convention of the Clergy and Laity . . . May 18, 1785*, p. 16.

9. Davies, Samuel, *The State of Religion among the Protestant Dissenters in Virginia*, pp. 22 f, 29.

10. *Charge to the Clergy . . . , May 27, 1807*, p. 5.

11. *Sermon in Trinity Church*, New Haven.

12. *A Charge to the Clergy . . . , May 27, 1807*, pp. 5, 26, 28 f.

13. *A Further Reply to the Objections against the Position of a Personal Assurance of the Pardon of Sin by a direct Communication of the Holy Spirit*, pp. 7, 12.

14. Rightmyer, Nelson W., "Joseph Pilmore—Anglican Evangelical" in *HM*, XVI, 181–98; Burr, *op. cit.*, pp. 313 ff.

15. *Minutes of Some Late Conversations between the Rev. John Wesley M.A. and Others* (Dublin, 1789), pp. 10 f.

16. *Minutes of the Methodist Conferences, 1773–1813*, p. 5; Atkinson, John, *Memorials of Methodism in New Jersey*, 2nd edn., p. 54; Raybold, G. A., *Reminiscences of Methodism in West Jersey*, p. 11.

17. *Fac-Similes of Church Documents: Papers issued by the Historical Club of the American Church, 1874–79*, Privately printed; Overton, J. H., *John Wesley*, p. 199; Jackson, T., *Life of Charles Wesley*, 1841, II, 392; Curteis, G. H., *Dissent in its Relation to the Church of England*, 1871, pp. 378 ff.

18. Letter to William White, April 24, 1791.

19. Letter to Samuel Seabury, May 14, 1791.

20. *Minutes of the House of Bishops, General Convention, 1792*, quoted in Perry, *op. cit.*, II, 126.

21. *Ibid.*, II, 142.

Pratt, John J., *How the Bishop Built the College*, p. 19.

Chase, Philander, *Reminiscences*, II, 262.

Pratt, *op. cit.*, p. 23.

Caswall, Henry, *America and the American Church*, 1839 edn., pp. 311,

Chase, Philander, *Defence of Kenyon College* (Columbus, 1831), 72 pp.

Supplement to *The Western Herald and Steubenville Gazette* in the Henry
ntington Library.

Chase, *op. cit.*, p. 64.

Alton (Ill.) Telegraph, July 26, 1845; *Journal*, Diocese of Illinois, 1843–57.

Sangamo Journal, Springfield, Ill., February 13, 1836; *Peoria Register*, De-
22, 1838, and April 6, 1839; *Illinois Advocate*, Edwardsville, Ill., Decem-
, 1835; Pease, Theodore C., *The Frontier State 1818–1848*, 1922, p. 436.

Chase, Philander, *Address before the Convention* . . . , *Springfield, Ill.*,
6, 1845.

Western Citizen, Chicago, April 27, December 14, 1843; October 21,
ber 26, 1844; September 15, October 20, 1846; Pease, *op. cit.*, p. 376.

XIV. THE GREAT MISSIONARY OUTREACH

Greene, Howard, *The Rev. Richard Fish Cadle, a Missionary of the Pro-
Episcopal Church in the Territories of Michigan and Wisconsin in the
Nineteenth Century* (Waukesha, Wisconsin, 1936).

bid., pp. 44 f; Hanson, *The Lost Prince*, chs. 21, 22.

An Appeal to Members of the Protestant Episcopal Church in Behalf of the
h Scholarship Society . . . (Hartford, 1831), 16 pp.

Richmond, William, A *Discourse* . . . *Mission of the Bishop of Connecticut
h the Valley of the Mississippi in 1829–30* (London, 1830).

Third Convention Journal, May 27, 1828.

Noll, Arthur H., *History of the Church in the Diocese of Tennessee* (New
1900), pp. 183 f.

bid., *passim*.

White, Greenough, A *Saint of the Southern Church, A Memoir of the Rt.
Nicholas Hamner Cobbs, First Bishop of Alabama* (New York, 1900),
.

Parks, Joseph H., *Leonidas Polk* (Baton Rouge, 1962).

Colton, Calvin, *Thoughts on the Religious State of the Country; with
ns for Preferring Episcopacy* (New York, 1836), p. 8.

White, Greenough, *An Apostle of the Western Church*, pp. 171 f.

Journals, Diocese of Indiana; Perry, *op. cit.*, II, 256 f.

Greene, *op. cit.*, p. 134.

*Journal of a Tour in the Indian Territory performed by order of the Do-
Committee of the Board of Missions* . . . *in Spring of 1844 by their
ry and agent*. . . .

XII.   NEW GREAT LEADER

1. Stone, J. S., *Memoir of Milnor*, p. 178.

2. Henshaw, J. P. K., *Memoir of the Rt. Rev. Richar*

3. Tyng, C. R., *Record of the Life and Work of th*
Tyng, p. 37.

4. Meade, William, *Old Churches, Ministers, and Fa*

5. Allen, Alexander V. G., *Life and Letters of Phillips*

6. McVickar, John, *The Early Life and Professional*
p. 280.

7. White, William, *Memoirs of the Protestant Epis*
p. 255.

8. Lowndes, A. L., "Church and State . . ." in *Pr*
Historical Society, II (Philadelphia, 1916), 69.

9. *The High Churchman Vindicated*, 1826, p. 6.

10. *The Churchman, A Charge . . .* , 1819, p. 5.

11. *The High Churchman Vindicated*, p. 20; *The*
pp. 15 f.

12. McVickar, *op. cit.*, p. 186.

13. Thomas Sykes of Guisborough in Churton, E., *N*
p. 137.

XIII.   THE FRONTIER CHUR(

1. White, William, *The Integrity of Christian Doctri*

2. *Journal . . . Third Annual Convention . . . Dioces*
1828), pp. 15 ff.

3. Clark, Thomas M., *Reminiscences*, p. 57.

4. Tyng, C. R., *op. cit.*, p. 508.

5. White, William, *An Episcopal Charge on the Sust*
Church . . . (Philadelphia, 1831), 20 pp.

6. White, William, *The Past and the Future*, p. 3.

7. Thomas, Edward, *A Sermon preached before the P*
for the Advancement of Christianity in South Carolin
(Charleston, 1830).

8. *Fifth Annual Report of the Society for Advancem*
pp. 5 f.

9. Kemper's Address in *Church Register*, January 26,
p. 351.

10. Griswold, B. B., "An Unwritten Chapter in the
the West" in *The Churchman*, XVIII (1858), 22.

11. Chase, Philander, *A Sermon before the Right Wo*
(Columbus, 1818), 23 pp.

12. Dix, Morgan, *A History of the Parish of Trinity C*

13. Salomon, Richard G., "Early Days in the Chu*
Life, Vol. LVII, No. 5 (June, 1953).

15. Breck, Charles, *The Life of the Reverend James Lloyd Breck, D.D., chiefly from Letters Written by Himself*, p. 546.

XV. THE OXFORD MOVEMENT AND PARTY SPIRIT

1. Albright, R. W., "Conciliarism in Anglicanism" in *Church History*, Vol. XXXIII, No. 1 (March, 1964), pp. 1–20.

2. Newman's article in the *British Critic*, 1839; *Tracts for the Times* (New York, 1839), p. 4.

3. *Thoughts on the Religious State of the Country* . . . , 1836, pp. 198–200.

4. Henshaw, J. P. K., *Memoir of the Life of Bishop R. C. Moore*, p. 287.

5. *Extract from an Address at Annual Convention* (Hartford, June 8, 1847), 10 pp.

6. McIlvaine, Charles P., *Oxford Divinity, Compared with that of the Roman and Anglican Churches* (London, 1841), p. 538.

7. McIlvaine, Charles P., *The Chief Danger of the Church in These Times* (New York, 1843), 47 pp.

8. Chase, Philander, *A Letter to a Bishop of the Protestant Episcopal Church* (Peoria, 1843), p. 6.

9. Rev. Dr. Rensselaer, a N.J. Presbyterian minister writing in *American Church Review*, October, 1859, pp. 441 f.

10. Hayes, Charles W., *Diocese of Western New York*, pp. 146 f.

11. Whittingham, William R., *The Doctrine of this Church and that alone to be held and taught by the ministry of Christ in the Protestant Episcopal Church USA* (Baltimore, 1849), 43 pp.

12. Whittingham, William R., *The Work of the Ministry in a Day of Rebuke* (Baltimore, 1846), pp. 13 f.

13. Brand, W. F., *Life of William Rollinson Whittingham, Fourth Bishop of Maryland*, II, 319.

14. *Ibid.*, p. 443.

15. *Ibid.*, pp. 447 f.

16. White, Greenough, *A Saint of the Southern Church*, pp. 174, 247.

17. Hopkins, John H., Jr., *The Life of the Late Right Reverend John Henry Hopkins*, p. 216; Hopkins, John H., *The Novelties which Disturb our Peace, Four Letters* (Philadelphia, 1844).

18. White, Greenough, *An Apostle of the Western Church*, pp. 123 f.

19. Howe, M. A. DeWolfe, *Memoirs of the Life and Services of the Rt. Rev. Alonzo Potter, D.D.*, pp. 254 ff.

20. *Trial of the Rev. O. S. Prescott* (Cambridge, 1851).

21. *Sermons*, I, 15.

22. Smith, Hugh, and Anthon, Henry, *The True Issue for the True Churchman. A Statement of the Facts in Relation to the Recent Ordination* (New York, 1843), 54 pp.; Anthon, Henry, *The True Issue Sustained* (New York, 1843), 54 pp.; in Appendix are Jay, John, "The Progress of Puseyism" and "Puseyism and Its Champions."

23. *The Churchman*, July 22, 1843.

24. *Ibid.*, August 26, 1843.

25. *Centennial History of the Diocese of New York*, p. 109.

26. *Proceedings of the Board of Trustees*, II, 419.

27. Breck, *op. cit.*, p. 8.

28. Hopkins, John H., *op. cit.*, Fourth Letter, pp. 64 f.

29. Turner, Samuel H., *Autobiography of the Rev. Samuel H. Turner, D.D.*, pp. 208 f.

30. *General Convention Journal*, 1844, pp. 227–50; *HM*, V (1936), 191–95.

31. DeLancey, William H., *Episcopal Address to the Annual Convention of the Diocese of Western New York* (Utica, 1846), pp. 11 f.

32. *Proceedings and Debates of the General Convention of 1844*, pp. 91–95.

33. *The Proceedings of the Court for the Trial of Bishop Benjamin T. Onderdonk, December 10, 1845* (New York, 1846). On the first ballot twenty-four, a majority but not two-thirds, voted for deposition and seventeen for suspension; subsequently the required number of votes supported suspension.

34. Perry, *op. cit.*, II, 280.

35. Burgess, George, *List of Persons Admitted to the Order of Deacons in PECUSA, 1785–1857* (Boston, 1875), pp. 12–45.

36. Noll, A. H., *History of the Diocese of Alabama*, p. 206.

37. Riley, Theodore M., *A Memorial Biography of the Very Reverend Eugene Augustus Hoffman*, I, 594.

38. Ives, L. S., *Address to the Convention in North Carolina*, 1851.

39. *Journal of the New York Diocese*, 1855, p. 108.

40. Brand, W. F., *Life of William R. Whittingham*, p. 261.

41. Henry E. Huntington Library, BR Box 117 MSS; West, Edward N., "Historical Development of Music in the American Church," in *HM*, Vol. XIV, No. 1 (March, 1945), pp. 15 f.

42. *The Living Church*, LXXI, 463.

43. Croswell, Harry, *A Memoir of the late Rev. William Croswell . . .*, p. 353.

44. Noll, A. H., *History of the Church in Tennessee*, p. 116.

45. *Alabama Diocesan Convention Journal*, 1849.

46. Shanklin, J. A., *Some Objections to the Episcopal Church Considered and Answered* (New York, 1858), p. 36.

47. *The Episcopal Doctrine of Apostolic Succession Examined, Being a Reply to "An Episcopalian's View of a Sermon"* by William S. Potts (St. Louis, c. 1840), 41 pp.; *An Episcopalian's Comment on the Reply*, 24 pp.

48. Jarvis, Samuel F., *A Sermon in St. Thomas's Church, N.Y., June 26, 1836.* 50 pp.

49. *The Western Episcopalian* quoted in *The Episcopal Recorder*, January 28, 1860.

50. Stone, J. S., *Memoir of the Life of James Milnor*, p. 631.

51. *Pastoral Letter*, April 3, 1815, pp. 18 f.

52. *Address to the Convention of the Diocese of N.Y.,* 1822.

53. Tyng, S. H., *Letter to Bishop Horatio Potter,* p. 12.

54. *Episcopal Address to the Annual Convention of New Jersey . . . May 30, 1838* (Burlington, 1838).

XVI.   THE CIVIL WAR AND MISSIONS

1. Wright, John, *Early Prayer Books of America* (St. Paul, Minn., 1896), p. 407; Brydon, G. MacLaren, "The Confederate Prayer Book" in *HM,* XVII, 339 f.

2. Henry E. Huntington Library, BR Box 117 MSS.

3. *Pastoral Letter,* pp. 10 f, in Clebsch, William A., ed., *Journals of the Protestant Episcopal Church in the Confederate States of America* (Austin, Texas, 1962), Part III, p. 226.

4. *An Exposition of the Character and Action of the Late General Convention* (Utica, N.Y., 1865), p. 18.

5. Clebsch, *op. cit.,* Introduction.

6. Benjamin, Marcus, "The Consecration of Bishop Wilmer of Alabama" in *Proceedings of the Church Historical Society,* IV (Philadelphia, 1927).

7. *Letter,* March 2, 1868, BR Box 117, Henry E. Huntington Library.

8. *Address to the Annual Convention of the Diocese of Kansas . . . May 12, 1869,* p. 14.

9. Albright, R. W., *Focus on Infinity,* pp. 122 f.

10. Clark, Thomas M., *Our National Crisis,* pp. 24 ff.

11. Albright, R. W., *Focus on Infinity,* pp. 94, 104 f, 120, 122, 131.

12. *Report of H. Forrester to Board of Missions,* 1877.

13. Kendrick, J. M., *Annual Address of the Bishop of New Mexico and Arizona, October 1, 1890.*

14. *Journal of Primary Convocation . . . in the Missionary Jurisdiction of Northern California, May 6–7, 1875.*

15. *Report of Committee on the Question of the Episcopate of Maryland touching the interests of the District of Columbia.*

16. *Form for making Catechists . . .* printed by the Yankton Agency on their own St. Paul's School Press, 1878; *English and Dakota Service Book, being Parts of the Book of Common Prayer set forth for use in the Missionary Jurisdiction of Niobrara,* 1881.

17. Howe, M. A. DeWolfe, *Life and Labors of Bishop Hare,* p. 399.

18. Johns, John, *A Memoir of the Life of the Rt. Rev. William Meade . . .* pp. 117 f.

19. Muller, James A., *Apostle of China,* 1937.

XVII.   DIVISION AND UNITY

1. Later that year this sermon was expanded into his book, *The Church-Idea, an Essay towards Unity.*

2. Appendix to William H. Cooper, *Reminiscences of Seventy Years,* in Henry E. Huntington Library, pp. 1–10.

3. *The Churchman,* New Series, II, pp. 367 f.

4. *Journal of General Convention,* 1868, Appendix, pp. 423 f.

5. *Protest,* Chicago, Ill., Feb. 18, 1869, in Henry E. Huntington Library.

6. Cooper, William H., *Reminiscences of Seventy Years,* p. 432.

7. Cummins, Alexandrine M., *Memoir of George David Cummins,* p. 233.

8. *Ibid.,* pp. 314 f.

9. Cooper, *op. cit.,* pp. 475–85.

10. *Ibid.,* pp. 495, 548.

11. *Debates of the House of Deputies,* 1871, p. 506.

12. Letter to Elizabeth Mitchell, Nov. 20, 1873, in Albright, R. W., *Focus on Infinity,* p. 159.

13. *Journal of the General Convention,* 1874, pp. 185–88.

14. DeMille, George E., *The Catholic Movement,* rev. edn., p. 125; *Trial of O. S. Prescott . . . on charges of heresy* (Cambridge, 1851), 30 pp.

15. Cooper, William H., *op. cit.,* p. 420.

16. *HM,* II, 205–10.

17. *An Open Letter to the Rev. F. D. Huntington, Bishop of Central New York,* 1883.

18. *Catholicity and its Relationship to Protestantism and Romanism,* 1879, p. 86.

19. Bird, Frederick M., "The Church's Hymnology" in Perry, *op. cit.,* II, 631–50; West, Edward, *op. cit.,* p. 15; Satcher, Herbert B., "Music in the Episcopal Church in Pennsylvania in the Eighteenth Century" in *HM,* XVIII, 372 f.

XVIII.   THE CHURCH AND MODERN THOUGHT

1. For details of revision see Chorley, E. Clowes, *The New American Prayer Book.*

2. Forms and correspondence work of Mary Morris Jones in BR Box 117 in the Henry E. Huntington Library.

3. Albright, R. W., *Focus on Infinity,* pp. 258 f.

4. *John Whopper, The Newsboy* (Boston, 1871).

5. Letter to Elizabeth Mitchell, May 12, 1874, in Albright, *op. cit.,* p. 160.

6. Letter to Arthur Brooks, October 27, 1887, *ibid.,* p. 316.

7. Brown, William Montgomery, *The Blessing of Unjust Criticism* (Cleveland, 1889), pp. 23 f.

8. Brown, W. M., *Communism and Christianity,* pp. 7 f.

XIX.   SOCIAL ACTION AND THE RISE OF THE ORDERS

1. *The Parish Advocate,* Pittsburgh, December, 1893.

2. Scudder, Vida D., *Father Huntington,* pp. 78 f, 113–40.

3. *Religious Communities in the American Episcopal Church and in the Anglican Church in Canada* (West Park, N.Y.); Williams, Thomas J., "The Beginnings of Anglican Sisterhoods" in *HM*, XVI, 350–72.

XX. THE WORLD-WIDE MISSION FIELD

1. *The Associate Mission for the Pacific Coast*. No. 2. September, 1867.

2. *Journal of the Diocese of California, Jan. 23–25, 1900*, with Sermon by Bishop William P. Nichols (San Francisco, 1900), 183 pp.

3. *Journal of Primary Convocation in Northern California* (San Francisco, 1875).

4. Thomas, N. S., *Diary and Letters of J. W. Cook*, 1919, including two letters of John Cornell to Thomas, p. 130.

5. Sherrill, Henry K., *Among Friends*, p. 42.

6. *Ibid.*, p. 57.

XXI. THE CHURCH IN THE MODERN ERA

1. DeMille, George E., *The Episcopal Church Since 1900* (1955), pp. 41 f.

2. Lawrence, William, *Memories of a Happy Life*; Sherrill, H. K., *William Lawrence*.

3. Emhardt, William C., Burgess, Thomas, and Lau, Robert F., *The Eastern Church in the Western World* (Milwaukee, 1928).

4. DeMille, *op. cit.*, pp. 63 f.

5. Wilson, Frank E., *Bishop Torok*, MSS in the General Seminary Library.

6. DeMille, George E., *The Catholic Movement in the American Episcopal Church*, Ch. 9.

7. Smyth, Newman, *A Story of Church Unity* (New Haven, 1923).

BIBLIOGRAPHY

(In this bibliography reference to *The Historical Magazine of the Protestant Episcopal Church* is abbreviated to *HM.*)

Abiding Values of Evangelicalism. Papers and Addresses at the 75th Anniversary of the Evangelical Education Society, Philadelphia, 1938.

Albright, Raymond W. "Conciliarism in Anglicanism," *Church History*, XXXIII, 1, (March, 1964).

———. *Focus on Infinity, A Life of Phillips Brooks.* New York, 1961.

Allen, Alexander V. G. *Life and Letters of Phillips Brooks.* 2 vols. New York, 1900–01.

———. *Phillips Brooks, 1835–1893.* New York, 1907.

Allen, T. G. *Memoir of the Rev. Benjamin Allen.* Philadelphia, 1832.

Anderson, James S. M. *History of the Church of England in the Colonies and Foreign Dependencies.* 3 vols. London, 1845.

Andrews, W. G. "The Parentage of American High Churchmanship" (The Reinicker Lectures for 1898–99), *Protestant Episcopal Review*, January, 1899.

Anglican Liberalism. By Twelve Churchmen. New York and London, 1908.

Anglican Theological Review, The, 1918–   .

Anstice, Henry. *History of St. George's Church, New York.* New York, 1911.

Apthorp, East. *Considerations on the Character and Conduct of the Society for the Propagation of the Gospel.* Boston, 1763.

Aspinwall, Marguerite. *A Hundred Years in His House: The Story of the Church of the Holy Trinity.* Philadelphia, 1956.

Ayering, Benjamin, compiler. *Memoirs of the Reformed Episcopal Church. . . .* New York, 1880.

Ayres, Anne. *The Life and Work of William Augustus Muhlenberg.* New York, 1880.

Banner of the Church. Boston, 1831–32.

Barnes, C. Rankin. *Ethelbert Talbot (1848–1928).* Philadelphia, 1955.

Barry, Joseph G. H. *Impressions and Opinions.* New York, 1931.

Basic principles proposed for the union of the Presbyterian Church and the Protestant Episcopal Church. 1942.

Bate, H. N. (ed.). *Faith and Order, Lausanne, 1927.* New York, 1928.

Beardsley, E. Edwards. *The History of the Episcopal Church in Connecticut.* 2 vols. Boston, 1883.

————. *Life and Correspondence of Samuel Johnson, D.D.* Boston, 1887.

————. *Life and Correspondence of the Rt. Rev. Samuel Seabury, D. D., First Bishop of Connecticut and of the Episcopal Church in the United States of America.* Boston, 1881.

Bedell, Gregory T. *Sermons.* 2 vols. Philadelphia, 1835.

Bell, G. K. A. (ed.). *The Stockholm Conference, 1925.* London, 1926.

Bernardin, Joseph Buchanan. *An Introduction to the Episcopal Church.* New York, 1954.

Berrian, William. *Memoir of the Life of the Right Rev. John Henry Hobart, D.D.* (Vol. I, *The Posthumous Works of the Late Right Reverend John Henry Hobart, D.D.,* 3 vols. New York, 1832–33).

————. *An Historical Sketch of Trinity Church, New York.* New York, 1847.

Boucher, Jonathan. *Reminiscences of an American Loyalist, 1738–1789.* Boston, 1925.

Brand, William Francis. *Life of William Rollinson Whittingham, Fourth Bishop of Maryland.* 2 vols. New York, 1883.

Bray, Thomas. *A General Review of the English Colonies in America with Respect to Religion.* London, 1698.

————. *A Memorial Representing the Present State of Religion on the Continent of North America.* London, 1700.

Breck, Charles. *The Life of the Reverend James Lloyd Breck, D.D., chiefly from Letters Written by Himself.* New York, 1883.

Brewer, Clifton H. *Early Episcopal Sunday Schools.* New York, 1933.

————. *A History of Religious Education in the Episcopal Church to 1835.* New Haven and London, 1924.

————. *Later Episcopal Sunday Schools.* New York, 1939.

Brilioth, Yngve Torgny. *The Anglican Revival: Studies in the Oxford Movement.* London and New York, 1925.

————. *Three Lectures on Evangelicalism and the Oxford Movement.* London, 1934.

Brown, Lawrence L. *The Episcopal Church in Texas.* Austin, 1963.

Brown, W. M. *My Heresy.* New York, 1931.

Brydon, George MacLaren. *The Episcopal Church among the Negroes of Virginia.* Richmond, 1937.

————. *The Established Church in Virginia and the Revolution.* Richmond, 1930.

————. *Virginia's Mother Church and the Political Conditions Under Which It Grew.* 2 vols. Philadelphia, 1952.

Burr, Nelson. *The Anglican Church in New Jersey.* Philadelphia, 1954.

————. *The Story of the Diocese of Connecticut.* Philadelphia, 1962.

Cameron, Kenneth Walter. *Index of the Pamphlet Collection of the Diocese of Connecticut.* Hartford, 1958. 169 pp.

Caner, Henry. *A Candid Examination of Dr. Mayhew's Observations.* Boston, 1763.

Carus, William. *Memorials of the Right Reverend Charles Pettit McIlvaine, D.D., D.C.L., Late Bishop of Ohio in the Protestant Episcopal Church in the United States.* London and New York, 1882.

Caswall, Henry. *America and the American Church*. London, 1839; 2nd edn., London, 1851.

Chandler, Thomas Bradbury. *An Address from the Clergy of New York and New Jersey to the Episcopalians in Virginia*. New York, 1771.

———. *An Appeal to the Public in Behalf of the Church of England in America*. New York, 1767.

———. *The Appeal Defended*. New York, 1769.

———. *The Appeal Farther Defended*. New York, 1771.

———. *A Free Examination of the Critical Commentary on Archbishop Secker's Letter to Mr. Walpole*. New York, 1774.

———. *Life of Samuel Johnson, D.D., First President of King's College, New York*. New York, 1805.

Chase, Philander. *Reminiscences: An Autobiography Comprising a History of the Principal Events in the Author's Life to A.D. 1847*. 2 vols. Boston, 1848.

Chorley, E. Clowes. *The Centennial History of Saint Bartholomew's Church in the City of New York, 1835–1935*. New York, 1935.

———. "Early Preaching in the American Church," *American Church Monthly*, XXIV, 3 (November, 1928), pp. 215–29.

———. *The History of St. Thomas in the City and Diocese of New York, 1823–1945*. New York, 1946.

———. *Men and Movements in the American Episcopal Church*. New York, 1946.

———. *The New American Prayer Book*, New York, 1930.

———. *Quarter of a Millennium: Trinity Church in the City of New York*. Philadelphia, 1947.

Christian Witness, The. Vols. 1–28. Boston, 1835–63. In March, 1841, it became the *Christian Witness and Church Advocate*.

Church, R. W. *The Oxford Movement: Twelve Years, 1833–1845*. London, 1891.

Churchman, The. Hartford, 1804–11; 1813–16; 1821–23; New York, 1825–.

Churchman's Almanac, The. 1830–1922. After four changes in name this year-book was absorbed by the *Living Church Annual* in 1922.

Church Congress of 1874: Papers and Addresses. New York, 1874; *ibid*., 1875 ff.

Church Journal, The. New York, 1853–75.

Church Register, The. Philadelphia, 1823–29.

Church Review, The. New York.

Clark, Thomas March. *Evangelical Principles and Men* (Sermon). Philadelphia, 1890.

———. *Reminiscences*. New York, 1895.

Clarke, C.P.S. *The Oxford Movement and After*. London and Oxford, 1932.

Clebsch, William A. (ed.). *Journals of the Protestant Episcopal Church in the Confederate States of America*. Austin, Texas, 1962.

Coleman, Leighton. *The Church in America*. New York, 1895.

Collections of the Protestant Episcopal Historical Society. New York, 1951.

Congdon, Charles T. "Memoir of the Rev. Ferdinand C. Ewer," F. C. Ewer's *Sanctity and Other Sermons*. New York, 1884. Pp. xxvii–lxxxiii.

Cooper, Miles, and others. *An Address from the Clergy of New York and New Jersey to the Episcopalians of Virginia*. New York, 1771.

Cowley Fathers, The. Cambridge, 1930.

Cox, Sir G. W. *Life of Bishop John William Colenso.* 2 vols. London, 1888.

Crapsey, Algernon Sidney. *The Last of the Heretics.* New York, 1924.

Creeds and Loyalty, Essays on the History, Interpretation and Use of the Creeds. By Seven Members of the Faculty of the Episcopal Theological School, Cambridge, Mass. New York, 1924.

Cross, A. L. *The Anglican Episcopate and the American Colonies.* Cambridge, 1902.

Cross, F. L. *Darwell Stone, Churchman and Counsellor.* Westminster, London, 1943.

Crosse, Gordon. *Charles Gore: A Biographical Sketch.* London, 1932.

Croswell, Harry. *A Memoir of the late Rev. William Croswell, D.D., Rector of the Church of the Advent, Boston.* New York, 1853.

Cummins, A. M. *Memoir of George David Cummins, D.D., First Bishop of the Reformed Episcopal Church.* New York, 1878.

Curtis, W. R. *The Lambeth Conferences.* New York, 1942.

Dalcho, Frederick. *A Historical Account of the Protestant Episcopal Church in South Carolina, from the First Settlement of the Province to the War of the Revolution.* Charleston, 1820.

Dashiell, T. Grayson. *A Digest of the Proceedings of the Conventions and Councils in the Diocese of Virginia.* Richmond, 1883.

Dawley, Powell Mills. *The Episcopal Church and Its Work.* Greenwich, 1955.

DeCosta, B. F. (ed.). *Memoirs of the Protestant Episcopal Church in the United States of America, containing: I. A Narrative of the Organization and of the Early Measures of the Church; II. Additional Statements and Remarks; III. An Appendix of Original Papers.* By the Right Rev. William White, D.D., edited with Notes and a Sketch of the Origin and Progress of the Colonial Church, by the Rev. B. F. DeCosta. New York, 1880.

Dehon, Theodore. *Sermons on the Public Means of Grace; the Fasts and Festivals of the Church; on Scripture Characters, and Various Practical Subjects.* 2 vols. Charleston, 1821.

De Koven, James. *Sermons Preached on Various Occasions, with an Introduction by Morgan Dix, S.T.D., Rector of Trinity Church, New York.* New York, 1880.

DeMille, George E. *The Catholic Movement in the American Episcopal Church.* Philadelphia, 1941; rev. edn., 1950.

———. *A History of the Diocese of Albany, 1704–1923.* Philadelphia, 1946.

Dix, Morgan. *A History of the Parish of Trinity Church in the City of New York,* 6 vols. New York, 1898–1906.

———. *Church Progress in Fifty Years.* New York, 1867.

Doane, George Washington. *A Word for the Church.* Boston, 1832.

Doane, William Croswell. *The Life and Writings of George Washington Doane, D.D., LL.D., for Twenty-Seven Years Bishop of New Jersey, containing his Poetical Works, Sermons, and Miscellaneous Writings.* 4 vols. New York, 1860–61.

Documentary History of the Diocese of Vermont. Claremont, N.H., and New York, 1870.

Dyer, Heman. *Records of an Active Life.* New York, 1886.

Eastburn, Manton. A *Brief View of the Nature of the Holy Communion; and of Certain Erroneous Conceptions of its Character.* Boston, 1843.

Eckenrode, H. J. *The Separation of Church and State in Virginia.* Richmond, 1909.

Egar, John H. *The Eucharistic Controversy and the Episcopate of Wisconsin.* 1874.

Ely, Richard T. *Social Aspects of Christianity and Other Essays.* New York, 1899.

Episcopal Church Annual, The. Formerly *The Living Church Annual.* New York, 1892–.

Episcopal Churchnews. New York, 1951–1960.

Episcopalian, The. Philadelphia, 1960–.

Ewer, Ferdinand C. *Catholicity in its Relationship to Protestantism and Romanism.* New York, 1879.

———. *The Failure of Protestantism.* New York, 1868.

———. *A Grammar of Theology.* 10th edn. New York, 1880.

———. *Sanctity and Other Sermons.* With an Introduction by Bishop George F. Seymour and a biographical sketch by Charles T. Congdon. New York, 1884.

———. *What is the Anglican Church?* and *An Open Letter to the Right Rev. F. D. Huntington, Bishop of Central New York.* New York, 1883.

Foote, H. W. *Annals of King's Chapel.* 2 vols. Boston, 1882–96.

Freeman, G. W. *The Rights and Duties of Slaveholders.* Charleston, 1837.

Gadsden, Christopher E. *An Essay on the Life of the Right Reverend Theodore Dehon, D.D., Late Bishop of the Protestant Episcopal Church in the Diocese of South Carolina.* Charleston, 1833.

Gailor, T. F. *Some Memories.* Kingsport, Tenn., 1937.

Gavin, Frank S. B. (ed.). *Liberal Catholicism and the Modern World.* New York, 1934.

General Conventions of the Protestant Episcopal Church, Journals of, 1785–1835. Edited by W. S. Perry. Claremont, N.H., 1874.

"General Theological Seminary, New York City, History of, 1821–1936," *HM*, V (1936), 145–264.

Gifford, Frank Dean. "The Influence of the Clergy on American Politics 1763–1776," *HM*, Vol. X, No. 2 (June, 1941).

Goodwin, E. L. *The Colonial Church in Virginia with Sketches of the First Six Bishops.* New York, 1927.

Goodwin, William A. R. *History of the Theological Seminary in Virginia and its Historical Background.* 2 vols. Centennial Edn. New York, 1923.

Gore, Charles (ed.). *Lux Mundi.* London, 1889; 2nd edn. New York, 1890.

Grafton, Charles C. *A Journey Godward of a Servant of Jesus Christ.* Milwaukee, 1910.

———. *The Works of Rt. Rev. Charles C. Grafton.* 8 vols. Edited by Talbot Rogers. 1914.

Grammer, Carl E. (ed.). *Abiding Values of Evangelicalism.* Philadelphia, 1938.

Green, William Mercer. *Memoir of the Rt. Rev. James Hervey Otey, D.D., LL.D., the First Bishop of Tennessee.* New York, 1885.

Greene, Howard. *The Reverend Richard Fish Cadle.* Waukesha, Wis., 1936.

Greene, M. L. *The Development of Religious Liberty in Connecticut.* Boston, 1905.

Griswold, Alexander Viets. *Convention Addresses.* Boston, 1818, 1825, and Middlebury, 1827.

———. *Discourses on the Most Important Doctrines and Duties of the Christian Religion.* Philadelphia, 1830.

Gwatkin, Thomas. *A Letter to the Clergy of New York and New Jersey.* Williamsburg, 1772.

Hallock, Donald H. V. "The Story of Nashotah," in *HM*, XI (1942), 3–17.

Hardy, Edward Rochie, Jr. "The Catholic Revival in the American Church, 1722–1933," N. P. Williams' and Charles Harris' *Northern Catholicism*, pp. 75–116. New York, 1933.

Harris, R. V. *Charles Inglis.* Toronto, 1937.

Harrison, Hall. *Life of the Rt. Rev. John Barrett Kerfoot.* 2 vols. New York, 1886.

Hawks, Edward. *William McGarvey and the Open Pulpit: An Intimate History of a Celibate Movement in the Episcopal Church and of its Collapse, 1870–1908.* Philadelphia, 1935.

Hawks, Francis Lister. *Contributions to the Ecclesiastical History of the United States of America,* Vol. I, *Virginia;* Vol. II, *Maryland.* New York, 1836–39.

Hawks, Francis Lister and Perry, William Stevens (eds.). *Documentary History of the Episcopal Church in Connecticut.* 2 vols. New York, 1863.

Hayes, C. W. *The Diocese of Western New York.* Rochester, 1904.

Haywood, Marshall DeLancey. *Lives of the Bishops of North Carolina.* Raleigh, 1910.

Henshaw, J. P. K. *Memoir of the Life of the Rt. Rev. Richard Channing Moore, D.D., Bishop of the Protestant Episcopal Church in the Diocese of Virginia, Accompanied by a Selection from the Sermons of the Late Bishop.* Philadelphia, 1843.

Higgins, John S. *One Faith and Fellowship.* Greenwich, Conn., 1958.

Hills, G. M. *History of the Church in Burlington, New Jersey.* Trenton, 1876.

Historical Magazine of the Protestant Episcopal Church. 1932–.

Hobart, John Henry. *An Apology for Apostolic Order and Its Advocates.* New York, 1807.

———. *The Candidate for Confirmation Instructed.* New York, 1816.

———. *The Christian's Manual of Faith and Devotion: Containing Dialogues and Prayers Suited to the Various Exercises of the Christian Life, and an Exhortation to Ejaculatory Prayer, with Forms of Ejaculatory and Other Prayers.* New York, 1814.

———. *The Churchman: The Principles of the Churchman Stated and Explained, in Distinction from the Corruptions of the Church of Rome, and from the Errors of Certain Protestant Sects.* New York, 1819.

———. *The Church Catechism Enlarged, Explained and Proved from Scripture, in a Catechism drawn up, with alterations and additions, from various approved Catechisms.* New York, 1827. 105 pp.

———. *A Collection of Essays on the Subject of Episcopacy.* New York, 1806.

———. *A Companion for the Altar.* New York, 1804.

———. *A Companion for the Festivals and Fasts.* New York, 1804.

———. *A Companion to the Book of Common Prayer, with an Explanation of the Service.* New York, 1805.

———. *The Corruptions of the Church of Rome Contrasted with Certain Protestant Errors.* New York, 1818.

———. *The Excellence of the Church.* New York, 1810.

———. *The High Churchman Vindicated.* New York, 1826; Boston, 1832.

———. *The Hobart Correspondence, 1798–1806.* Ed. by Arthur Lowndes, in *Archives of the General Convention.* 6 vols. New York, 1911.

———. *The Nature of the Ministry.* New York, 1815.

———. *The Origin, General Character and the Present Position of the Protestant Episcopal Church.* Philadelphia, 1814.

———. *The Posthumous Works of the late Rt. Rev. John Henry Hobart, Bishop of New York.* 3 vols. New York, 1833.

———. *Sermons on the Principal Events and Truths of Redemption.* 2 vols. New York, 1823.

Hodges, George. *Henry Codman Potter, Seventh Bishop of New York.* New York, 1915.

———. *The Heresy of Cain.* New York, 1894.

———. *Three Hundred Years of the Episcopal Church in America.* Philadelphia, 1906.

Hodges, Julia S. *George Hodges.* New York and London, 1926.

Holcombe, J. *An Apostle of the Wilderness.* New York, 1903.

Hopkins, C. H. *The Rise of the Social Gospel in American Protestantism, 1865–1915.* New Haven, 1940.

Hopkins, John Henry. *An Humble but Earnest Address to the Bishops, Clergy and Laity of the Protestant Episcopal Church in the United States of America on Tolerating among our Ministry of the Doctrines of the Church of Rome.* New York, 1846. 23 pp.

———. *The Law of Ritualism, Examined in its Relation to the Word of God, to the Primitive Church, to the Church of England, and to the Protestant Episcopal Church in the United States.* New York, 1866. 98 pp.

———. *The Primitive Church Compared with the Protestant Episcopal Church.* Burlington, Vt., 1836.

———. *A Scriptural, Ecclesiastical and Historical View of Slavery,* New York, 1864.

Hopkins, John Henry, Jr. *The Life of the Late Right Reverend John Henry Hopkins, First Bishop of Vermont and Seventh Presiding Bishop.* New York, 1873.

Hopkins, John Henry, III. "John Henry Hopkins, First Bishop of Vermont," *HM,* VI (1937), 187–206; bibliography, 204–06.

———. "The Rev. John Henry Hopkins, Jr.," *HM,* IV (1935), 267–80.

How, Thomas Y. *Vindication of the Protestant Episcopal Church.* New York, 1816.

Howe, M. A. DeWolfe. *The Life and Labors of Bishop Hare.* New York, 1911.

———. *Memoirs of the Life and Services of the Rt. Rev. Alonzo Potter, D.D., LL.D, Bishop of the Protestant Episcopal Church in the Diocese of Pennsylvania.* Philadelphia, 1871.

Huntington, Arria S. *Memoirs and Letters of Frederic Dan Huntington, First Bishop of Central New York.* Boston and New York, 1906.

Huntington, J. O. S. "Beginnings of the Religious Life for Men in the American Church." *HM*, II (1933), 35–43.

Huntington, Virginia E. *Along the Great River.* New York, 1940.

Huntington, William Reed. *The Church Idea.* Boston, 1870; 5th edn., 1928.

Ives, Levi Silliman. *The Priestly Office: A Pastoral Letter to the Clergy of North Carolina.* New York, 1849.

——. *The Trials of a Mind in its Progress to Catholicism.* Boston, 1854.

Jarratt, Devereux. *The Life of the Rev. Devereux Jarratt, Rector of Bath Parish, Dinwiddie County, Virginia. Written by Himself in a Series of Letters Addressed to the Rev. John Coleman, one of the Ministers of the Protestant Episcopal Church in Maryland.* Baltimore, 1806.

——. *Sermons on Various and Important Subjects in Practical Divinity.* Raleigh, N.C., 1794.

Jarvis, Samuel Farmer. *Christian Unity Necessary for the Conversion of the World.* New York, 1837.

Jay, William. *Caste and Slavery in the American Church.* New York, 1843.

Jenkins, Thomas. *The Man of Alaska, Peter Trimble Rowe.* New York, 1943.

Johns, John. *A Memoir of the Life of the Rt. Rev. William Meade, Bishop of Virginia, With a Memorial Sermon by the Rev. William Sparrow.* Baltimore, 1867.

Johnson, E. M. *The Communion of Saints.* Brooklyn, 1848.

Johnson, Samuel. *Works.* Ed. by H. W. Schneider. 4 vols. New York, 1929.

Keble, John. *The Christian Year.* London, 1827. Edited with notes by Bishop George Washington Doane, New York, 1834.

Kemper, Jackson. *Journal of an Episcopalian Missionary's Tour to Green Bay, 1834* and *Documents Relating to the Episcopal Church and Mission in Green Bay, 1825–1841.* Madison, 1898. (Repr. from *Collections of the Wisconsin State Historical Society,* Vol. XIV.)

Kip, W. I. *The Early Days of My Episcopate.* New York, 1892.

Klein, H. M. J. and Diller, William T. *The History of St. James' Church.* Lancaster, Pa., 1944.

Klingberg, F. J. *Anglican Humanitarianism in Colonial New York.* Philadelphia, 1940.

——. "Anglo-Lutheran Relations," *HM*, XVI (1947), 217–22.

Knox, Wilfred L. *The Catholic Movement in the Church of England.* New York, 1924.

Knox, Wilfred L. and Vidler, Alec R. *The Development of Modern Catholicism.* With Foreword by Frank Gavin. Milwaukee, 1933.

Lambeth Conferences of 1867, 1878, and 1888. Official reports edited by the Rt. Rev. Randall T. Davidson. Rev. edn., London, 1896. Later Lambeth Reports: 1897, 1908, 1920, 1930, 1948, 1958.

Lauer, P. E. *Church and State in New England*. Baltimore, 1892.

Lawrence, William. *Life of Phillips Brooks*. New York, 1930.

———. *Memories of a Happy Life*. Boston, 1926.

———. *Sermon in Memory of the Right Reverend David H. Greer*. New York, 1919.

Lee, Alfred. *In Memoriam: Charles P. McIlvaine, Late Bishop of Ohio*. Cleveland, 1873.

———. *The Proper Functions of the Christian Ministry*. Philadelphia, 1876.

Lewis, William H. *Christian Union and the Protestant Episcopal Church and its Relations to Church Unity.*

Liberal Evangelicalism. An Interpretation by Members of the Church of England. London, 1923.

Living Church, The. Chicago, Milwaukee, and New York, 1878–.

Living Church Annual, The. Milwaukee and New York, 1890–1952; published, 1890–99, as *The Living Church Quarterly*; name changed to *The Episcopal Church Annual*, 1953–.

Loveland, Clara O. *The Critical Years*. Greenwich, 1956.

Lowndes, Arthur (ed.). *Archives of General Convention*. 6 vols. New York, 1911. *The Hobart Correspondence, 1798–1806.*

Lydekker, J. W. *The Life and Letters of Charles Inglis*. London, 1936.

Manross, W. W. *The Episcopal Church in the United States, 1800–1840*. New York, 1938.

———. *A History of the American Episcopal Church*. New York, 1935; 2nd edn., revised and enlarged, 1950.

Mason, John M. *Essays on Episcopacy and the Apology for Apostolic Order and its Advocates Reviewed*. New York, 1844.

Masterman, C. F. G. *Frederick Denison Maurice*. London, 1907.

Maurice, J. Frederick. *Life of Frederick Denison Maurice*. 2 vols. London, 1884.

May, Henry F. *Protestant Churches and Industrial America*. New York, 1949.

Mayhew, Jonathan. *Observations on the Charter and Conduct of the Society for the Propagation of the Gospel*. London, 1763.

McConnell, Samuel D. *American Episcopacy*. New York, 1889.

———. *Essays Practical and Speculative*. 1900.

———. *History of the American Episcopal Church*. 3rd edn. New York, 1891.

McCulloch, Samuel C. (ed.). *British Humanitarianism*. Philadelphia, 1950.

McIlvaine, Charles P. *The Evidences of Christianity*. New York, 1832.

———. *Justification by Faith*. Columbus, Ohio, 1839.

———. *No Priest, No Sacrifice, No Altar but Christ: Or the Doctrine of the Protestant Episcopal Church concerning the Ministry and the Eucharist*. New York, 1850.

———. *Oxford Divinity, Compared with That of the Romish and Anglican Churches*. London, 1841.

———. *Reasons for Refusing to Consecrate a Church Having an Altar Instead of a Communion Table, Or the Doctrine of Scripture and of the Protestant Episcopal Church As To a Sacrifice in the Lord's Supper and a Priesthood in the Christian Ministry*. Mt. Vernon, Ohio, 1846.

————. *Righteousness by Faith, or the Nature and Means of our Justification before God.* Philadelphia, 1862.

McNamara, John. *Three Years on the Kansas Border.* New York, 1856.

McVickar, John. *The Early Life and Professional Years of Bishop Hobart.* Oxford and London, 1838.

Meade, William. *Old Churches, Ministers, and Families of Virginia.* 2 vols. Philadelphia, 1857.

————. *Pastoral Letter on the Duty of Affording Religious Instruction to Those in Bondage.* Richmond, 1853.

Michael, O. S. *The Sunday School in the Development of the American Church.* Milwaukee, 1904.

Miller, John. *A Description of the Province and City of New York, 1695.* London, 1843.

Miller, Spencer, and Fletcher, J. F. *The Church and Industry.* New York, 1930.

Moorman, John R. H. *A History of the Church in England.* New York, 1954.

Morehouse, Frederick Cook. *Some American Churchmen.* Milwaukee, 1892.

Mozley, J. B. *The Theory of Development: A Criticism of Dr. Newman's "Essay on the Development of Christian Doctrine."* New York, 1879.

Muhlenberg, William A. *Evangelical Catholic Papers.* New York, Ser. 1, 1875; Ser. 2, 1877.

————. *An Exposition of the Memorial of Sundry Presbyters.* New York, 1854.

————. *Memorial of Sundry Presbyters of the Protestant Episcopal Church.* 1853.

————. *What the Memorialists Want.* New York, 1856.

Muller, James A. *Apostle of China.* New York, 1937.

————. *The Episcopal Theological School, 1867–1943.* Cambridge, 1943.

————. *The Government of the Episcopal Church.* Cambridge, 1929.

Newman, John Henry. *Apologia Pro Vita Sua.* 1864.

————. *An Essay on the Development of Christian Doctrine.* 1845.

————. *Tracts for the Times.* 3 vols. New York, 1839.

Newton, Richard. *Liberal Views of the Ministry in Harmony with the Bible, the Prayer Book and the Canons.* Philadelphia, 1868.

Newton, R. Heber. *The Morals of Trade.* New York, 1876.

————. *Philistinism: Plain Words Concerning Certain Forms of Modern Scepticism.* New York and London, 1885.

————. *Right and Wrong Uses of the Bible.* New York, 1882.

————. *Social Studies.* New York, 1887.

Newton, William W. *Dr. Muhlenberg.* Boston, 1891.

————. *Yesterday with the Fathers.* New York, 1910.

Norton, J. N. *The Life of Bishop Ravenscroft.* New York, 1859.

Norwood, Percy V. "Jubilee College, Illinois." *HM,* XII (1943), 44–58.

O'Grady, John. *Levi Silliman Ives, Pioneer Leader in Catholic Charities.* New York, 1933.

Onderdonk, Henry U. *An Essay on Regeneration.* Philadelphia, 1835.

Overton, John Henry. *The English Church in the Nineteenth Century, 1800–1833.* London, 1894.

Packard, Joseph. *Recollections of a Long Life.* Edited by Thomas J. Packard. Washington, 1902.

Parks, Leighton. *Intellectual Integrity.* New York, 1923.

——. *What is Modernism.* New York, 1924.

Parsons, Edward L., and Jones, Bayard H. *The American Prayer Book.* New York, 1937.

Pascoe, C. E. *Two Hundred Years of the S.P.G.* London, 1901.

Pastoral Letters from the House of Bishops to Clergy and Members of the Protestant Episcopal Church in the United States of America from 1808–1844. Philadelphia, 1845.

Pastoral Letters of the House of Bishops. 1844 ff.

Pennington, E. L. *Apostle of New Jersey, John Talbot. 1645–1727.* Philadelphia, 1938.

Perry, William Stevens. *The Alleged "Toryism" of the Clergy of the United States.* 1896.

——. *The History of the American Episcopal Church.* 2 vols. Boston, 1885.

—— (ed.). *Historical Collections Relating to the American Colonial Church.* 4 vols. Hartford, 1870–78.

—— (ed.). *Historical Notes Illustrating the Organization of the Protestant Episcopal Church.* Claremont, N. H., 1874.

—— (ed.). *Journals of the General Convention of the Protestant Episcopal Church, 1785–1835.* 2 vols. Claremont, N.H., 1874.

Perry, William Stevens, and Hawks, Francis Lister (eds.). *Documentary History of the Episcopal Church in Connecticut.* 2 vols. New York, 1863.

Pittenger, W. Norman. *The Episcopalian Way of Life.* New York, 1957.

Polk, W. M. *Leonidas Polk, Bishop and General.* 2 vols. New York, 1915.

Pope, William C. *Life of the Rev. James DeKoven, D.D., Sometime Warden of Racine College.* New York, 1899.

Potter, Alonzo (ed.). *Memorial Papers.* Philadelphia, 1857.

Potter, Henry Codman. *The Citizen in His Relation to the Industrial Situation.* New York, 1902.

——. *Reminiscences of Bishops and Archbishops.* New York and London, 1906.

Price, Annie Darling. *A History of the Formation and Growth of the Reformed Episcopal Church, 1873–1902.* Philadelphia, 1902.

Rainsford, William S. *A Preacher's Story of His Work.* New York, 1904 .

——. *The Story of a Varied Life: An Autobiography.* New York, 1922.

Randolph, Edward. *Letters and Official Papers.* 4 vols. Boston, 1899.

Ravenscroft, John Stark. *The Works of the Rt. Rev. John Stark Ravenscroft, D.D., Bishop of North Carolina, Containing His Sermons, Charges, and Controversial Tracts; to which is prefixed A Memoir of His Life.* 2 vols. New York, 1830.

Read, Newbury Frost (ed.). *The Story of St. Mary's, The Society of the Free Church of St. Mary the Virgin, New York City, 1868–1931.* New York, 1931.

Recent Recollections of the Anglo-American Church by an English Layman. 2 vols. London, 1882.

Reed, S. M. *State and Church in Massachusetts, 1691–1740.* Urbana, Ill., 1914.

Reformed Episcopal Church, Journal of the First General Council of the, 1873. New York, 1873.

Richardson, George L. *Arthur C. A. Hall, Third Bishop of Vermont.* Boston and New York, 1932.

Riley, Theodore Myers. *A Memorial Biography of the Very Reverend Eugene Augustus Hoffman, D.D.* (Oxon.), D.C.L., LL.D., *Late Dean of the General Theological Seminary.* 2 vols. Jamaica, N.Y., 1904.

Rising, Franklin S. *Are There Romanizing Germs in the Prayer Book?* 1868.

Ritchie, Arthur. *Sermons from St. Ignatius' Pulpit.* Milwaukee, 1903.

———. *Six Sermons to Men, Preached in St. Ignatius' Church.* New York, 1888.

———. *What Catholics Believe and Do.* Milwaukee, 1891.

Sanford, Louis C. *The Province of the Pacific.* Philadelphia, 1946.

Schroeder, J. F. *Memorial of Bishop Hobart. A Collection of Sermons on the Death of the Rt. Rev. John Henry Hobart, Bishop of New York. With a Memoir of his Life and Writings.* New York, 1831.

Scudder, Vida D. *Father Huntington, Founder of the Order of the Holy Cross.* New York, 1940.

Seabury, Samuel. *Discourses on Several Important Subjects.* 2 vols. Hudson, N.Y., 1793, 1798.

Seabury, Samuel. *American Slavery.* 2nd edn. New York, 1861.

"Seabury Sesqui-Centennial Number" of the *HM*, III (1934), pp. 121–228.

Seabury, William Jones. *Memoir of Bishop Seabury.* New York, 1908.

Selwyn, Edward G. (ed.). *Essays Catholic and Critical by Members of the Anglican Communion.* New York, 1926.

Shepherd, Massey H. *The Oxford American Prayer Book Commentary.* New York, 1950.

Sherrill, Henry Knox. *Among Friends.* Boston, 1962.

———.*William Lawrence: Later Years of a Happy Life.* Cambridge, 1943.

Shinn, G. W. *King's Handbook of Notable Episcopal Churches.* Boston, 1889.

Shiras, Alexander. *Life and Letters of Rev. James May, D.D.* Philadelphia.

Simcox, Carroll E. *An Approach to the Episcopal Church.* New York, 1961.

Simpson, W. J. Sparrow. *The History of the Anglo-Catholic Revival.* London, 1932.

Sketches of Church History in North Carolina. Wilmington, N.C., 1892.

Slafter, E. F. *John Checkley, or the Evolution of Religious Tolerance in Massachusetts Bay.* 2 vols. Boston, 1897.

Slattery, Charles L. *Alexander Viets Griswold Allen, 1841–1908.* New York, 1911.

———. *David Hummell Greer, Eighth Bishop of New York.* New York and London, 1921.

———. (ed.). *The Protestant Episcopal Church in the U.S. Church Congress 1924 on its 50th anniversary.* New York, 1924.

Smith, B. B. *The Church Temperance Society.* New York, 1881.

Smith, H. W. *Life and Correspondence of the Rev. William Smith, D.D.* 2 vols. Philadelphia, 1880.

Smith, John Cotton. *A Plea for Liberty in the Church.* New York, 1865.

———. *The Church's Law of Development.* A Sermon. New York, 1872.

Smith, Laura Chase. *The Life of Philander Chase, First Bishop of Ohio and Illinois, Founder of Kenyon and Jubilee Colleges.* New York, 1903.

Smith, Roland Cotton. *Fifty Years of the Church Congress.* New York, 1924.

Smith, William. *Works.* 2 vols. Philadelphia, 1803.

Smythe, George Franklin. *A History of the Diocese of Ohio until the Year 1918.* Cleveland, 1931.

———. *Kenyon College: Its First Century.* New Haven, 1924.

Southern Churchman. Richmond, 1835–1951; became *Episcopal Churchnews,* 1951–1960.

Spens, Will. *The Present Position of the Catholic Movement in the Church of England.* New York, 1934.

Spirit of Missions, The. (Later *Forth*). New York, 1836–1960.

Sprague, Philo W. *Christian Socialism. What and Why.* New York, 1891.

Sprague, William B. *Annals of the American Pulpit.* Vol. 5. New York, 1859.

Stevens, W. Bertrand. *Editor's Quest: A Memoir of Frederick Cook Morehouse.* New York, 1940.

Stevens, W. B. "The Church in Georgia before the Revolution," *Church Review,* July, 1885.

Stevens, William Bacon. *Past and Present of St. Andrew's Church.* Philadelphia, 1858.

Stewart, Herbert Leslie. *A Century of Anglo-Catholicism.* New York, 1929.

Stone, John S. *Memoir of the Life of James Milnor, D.D., Late Rector of St. George's Church, New York.* New York, 1848.

———. *Memoir of the Life of the Rt. Rev. Alexander Viets Griswold, D.D., Bishop of the Protestant Episcopal Church in the Eastern Diocese.* Philadelphia, 1844.

Stowe, Walter H. "The Doctrine of Development in Theology," *The American Church Monthly,* XLIII (June, 1938), 276–82.

———. *An Encouraging Decade for the Episcopal Church.* Philadelphia, 1946.

———. *The Essence of Anglo-Catholicism.* New York, 1942.

———. *Immigration and the Growth of the Episcopal Church, Joint Commission on Strategy and Policy.* Richmond, 1942.

———. *A Missionary Frontier of the Future: The Foreign White Stock in America.* 1939.

———. *A Short History of the Church in New Jersey.*

Stowe, Walter H., and others. *The Life and Letters of Bishop William White.* New York, 1937.

Sturtevant, Mary Clark. *Thomas March Clark: Fifth Bishop of Rhode Island. A Memoir by his Daughter.* Edited by Latta Griswold. Milwaukee, 1927.

Suter, John W. *The Life and Letters of William Reed Huntington.* New York, 1925.

Sweet, Charles F. *A Champion of the Cross, Being the Life of John Henry Hopkins, including Extracts and Selections from his Writings.* New York, 1894.

Sword's Pocket Almanac. New York, 1816–60.

Talbot, Ethelbert. *My People of the Plains.* New York, 1906.

Temple, S. A. *The Theological Writings of Bishop White.* New York, 1946.

Temple, Frederick (ed.). *Essays and Reviews.* Boston, 1862.

Tiffany, C. C. *History of the Protestant Episcopal Church.* 2nd edn. New York, 1900.

Trevelyan, G. M. *England under Queen Anne.* 3 vols. London, 1931–34.
————. *English Social History.* New York, 1942.
True Catholic, The, Baltimore, 1843–56.
Tucker, Henry St. George. *The History of the Episcopal Church in Japan.* New York, 1938.
Tulloch, John. *Movements of Religious Thought in Britain during the Nineteenth Century.* New York, 1888.
Turner, Samuel H. *Autobiography of the Rev. Samuel H. Turner, D.D., late Professor of Biblical Learning and the Interpretation of Scripture in the General Theological Seminary of the Protestant Episcopal Church in the United States of America.* New York, 1863.
Tuttle, Daniel Sylvester. *Reminiscences of a Missionary Bishop.* New York, 1906.
Tyerman, Luke. *The Life and Times of the Rev. John Wesley, A.M., Founder of the Methodists.* 3 vols. New York, 1872.
Tyler, L. G. (ed.). *Narratives of Early Virginia, 1606–1625.* New York, 1907.
Tyng, Charles Rockland. *Record of the Life and Work of the Rev. Stephen Higginson Tyng, D.D., and History of St. George's Church, New York, to the close of his Rectorship.* New York, 1890.
Tyng, Stephen H. *A Memoir of the Rev. Gregory Townsend Bedell, D.D.* 2nd edn. Philadelphia, 1836.
Tyng, Stephen H., Jr. *The Liberty of Preaching.* Two sermons. New York, 1867.
————. *The Liberty of Preaching: Its Warrant and Relations.* New York, 1867.

Utley, G. B. *The Life and Times of Thomas John Claggett, First Bishop of Maryland and The First Bishop Consecrated in America.* Chicago, 1913.

Vail, Thomas H. *The Comprehensive Church.* Hartford, 1841.
Ver Mehr, J. L. *Checkered Life.* San Francisco, 1877.
Visser't Hooft, W. A. *The Background of the Social Gospel in America.* Haarlem, 1928.

Walker, Cornelius. *The Life and Correspondence of the Rev. William Sparrow, D.D., late Professor of Systematic Divinity in the Episcopal Seminary of Virginia.* Philadelphia, 1876.
————. *Memoir of Rev. C. W. Andrews, D.D.*
Walworth, Clarence E. *The Oxford Movement in America, Or Glimpses of Life in an Anglican Seminary.* New York, 1895.
————. *Reminiscences of Edgar P. Wadhams.* New York, 1893.
Waylen, Edward. *Ecclesiastical Reminiscences of the United States.* New York, 1846.
Webb, Clement C. J. *A Century of Anglican Theology and Other Lectures.* New York, 1924.
Webb, William Walter. *Nashotah House.* Hartford, 1903.
Weeks, S. B. *The Religious Development in the Province of North Carolina.* Baltimore, 1892.
Western Episcopalian, The. Gambier, Ohio, 1843–67.

Wetmore, James. *Vindication of the Professors of the Church of England in Connecticut.* 1747.

Whipple, Henry B. *The Lights and Shadows of a Long Episcopate.* New York, 1899.

White, Edwin Augustine. *Constitution and Canons for the Government of the Protestant Episcopal Church in the United States of America, Adopted in General Conventions, 1789–1922, Annotated, with an Exposition of the Same, and Reports of such Cases as have arisen and been decided thereunder.* Published by Order of the House of Deputies. New York, 1924.

White, Edwin Augustine, and Dykman, Jackson A. *Annotated Constitution and Canons.* Greenwich, 1954.

White, Greenough. *An Apostle of the Western Church: Memoir of the Right Reverend Jackson Kemper, D.D., First Missionary Bishop of the American Church, with Notices of some of his Contemporaries.* New York, 1899.

————. *A Saint of the Southern Church: Memoir of the Right Reverend Nicholas Hamner Cobbs, D.D., First Bishop of Alabama, with Notices of Some of his Contemporaries.* New York, 1897.

White, William. *The Case of the Episcopal Churches in the United States Considered.* Philadelphia, 1783.

————. *Commentaries Suited to Occasions of Ordination.* New York, 1833.

————. *Comparative Views of the Controversy between the Calvinists and the Arminians.* 2 vols. Philadelphia, 1817.

————. *Lectures on the Catechism of the Protestant Episcopal Church.* Philadelphia, 1813.

————. *Memoirs of the Protestant Episcopal Church.* Philadelphia, 1820; New York, 1836, 1880.

————. *The Past and Future, a Charge on Events Connected with the Organization of the Protestant Episcopal Church.* Philadelphia, 1834.

Whittaker's Churchman's Almanac (*The Protestant Episcopal Almanac and Directory*), 1854–1908, absorbed by the *Living Church Annual* in 1909.

Whittingham, William Rollinson. *The Priesthood of the Church.* Baltimore, 1843.

Wilberforce, Samuel. *History of the Protestant Episcopal Church in America.* New York, 1849.

Will, Theodore St. Clair. *The Episcopal Church: Heritage of American Christians.* Milwaukee, 1934.

Williams, N. P., and Harris, Charles. *Northern Catholicism: Centenary Studies in the Oxford and Parallel Movements.* New York, 1933.

Wilmer, William Holland. *The Episcopal Manual, or an Attempt to Explain and Vindicate the Doctrine, Discipline, and Worship of the Protestant Episcopal Church as Taught in her Public Formularies, and Writings of her Approved Divines.* 1815; Baltimore, 1822; Philadelphia, 1841.

Wilson, Bird. *Memoir of the Life of the Right Reverend William White, D.D., Bishop of the Protestant Episcopal Church in the State of Pennsylvania.* Philaphia, 1839.

Wilson, Frank E. *An Outline History of the Episcopal Church.* New York, 1938.

Wilson, James Grant (ed.). *The Centennial History of the Protestant Episcopal Church in the Diocese of New York, 1785–1885.* New York, 1886.

Witness, The. Chicago and New York, 1919–   .

Wolley, Charles. *A Two Year's Journal in New York.* London, 1701. Repr. Cleveland, 1902.

Woods, E. S. *Lausanne, 1927.* New York, 1927.

Worcester, Elwood; McComb, Samuel; and Coriat, I. H. *Religion and Medicine.* New York, 1908

Zabriskie, A. C. (ed.). *Anglican Evangelicalism.* Philadelphia, 1943.

———. *Arthur Selden Lloyd.* New York, 1942.

———. *Bishop Brent.* New York, 1948.

Index